The Science of Sacrifice

The Science of Sacrifice

American Literature and
Modern Social Theory

SUSAN L. MIZRUCHI

Princeton University Press
Princeton, New Jersey

Copyright © 1998 by Princeton University Press
Published by Princeton University Press, 41 William Street,
Princeton, New Jersey 08540
In the United Kingdom: Princeton University Press,
Chichester, West Sussex

Library of Congress Cataloging-in-Publication Data

Mizruchi, Susan L. (Susan Laura)
The science of sacrifice : American literature and modern
social theory / Susan L. Mizruchi.
p.   cm.
Includes bibliographical references (p.) and index.
ISBN 0–691–06892–5 (cloth : alk. paper).
ISBN 0–691–01506–6 (pbk. : alk. paper)
1. American literature—History and criticism. 2. Sacrifice
in literature. 3. Literature and anthropology—United States.
4. Literature and society—United States. 5. Rites and
ceremonies in literature. 6. Human sacrifice in literature.
7. Self-sacrifice in literature. 8. Social problems in literature.
9. Scapegoat in literature. 10. Realism
in literature. I. Title.
PS169.S23M59 1998
810.9′353—dc21   97-44317

This book has been composed in Janson

Princeton University Press books are printed on
acid-free paper and meet the guidelines for permanence
and durability of the Committee on Production
Guidelines for Book Longevity of the
Council on Library Resources

http://pup.princeton.edu

Printed in the United States of America

1 3 5 7 9 10 8 6 4 2

1 3 5 7 9 10 8 6 4 2
(Pbk.)

To Saki and Sascha

Contents

Acknowledgments

It is a pleasure to acknowledge those who have contributed to this book. I was fortunate to have begun my professional career eleven years ago with Jon Klancher as my colleague. I am grateful for his friendship, and for his learning, insight, and enthusiasm for this project, which are evident throughout.

I want to thank the scholars and friends who responded to essays or lectures with encouragement and advice: Sylvia Ary, Nancy Bentley, Eytan Bercovitch, Laurence Buell, Elizabeth B. Clark, Emory Elliott, Michael T. Gilmore, Eugene Goodheart, David Mizruchi, Margaret Reid, Deborah Sills, and Julia Stern.

I am grateful in particular to those who read drafts of individual chapters: Mark Mizruchi for his advice on the first chapter; Daniel Aaron for his spirited and informed response to the Melville chapter; Leland Monk, Kim Townsend, and William Vance for careful and comprehensive readings of the James chapter; and Werner Sollors for his extraordinarily helpful comments on the Du Bois chapter.

I want to acknowledge the contributions of my parents, who created a home in which institutional Judaism, Jewish folk superstition, literature, and social science could achieve a certain harmony. I want to thank my father especially for his encouragement, and for the unlimited supply of books from his sociology library.

The book benefited from the detailed and generous reports of three readers for Princeton University Press, Giles Gunn, Orlando Patterson, and Eric Sundquist. I am indebted to all of them, as well as to Deborah Malmud, my editor at the Press, for her expert advice at every stage of the process. Victoria Wilson-Schwartz was the ideal copyeditor.

The National Endowment for the Humanities, the Boston University Humanities Foundation, and the Huntington Library all funded leaves for research and writing. Special thanks to Dennis Berkey, dean of the College of Arts and Sciences at Boston University, for providing generous financial assistance.

No one contributed more to this book than my son and husband. Alexander Bercovitch sustained me with his fierce and loyal love. Above all, I am grateful for the ongoing emotional and intellectual support of Sacvan Bercovitch. Through his own exemplary scholarship, and through his decency, humor, and courage, he showed me what was possible.

The Science of Sacrifice

Introduction

❧

LITERATURE teaches us how to read the past. That is the large claim of this book. The claim is set out within a correspondingly large narrative: literary, social scientific, and theological voices are brought together to tell their versions of a culture's story. A specific group of literary works has shaped this narrative: a literature with distinctive methods, patterns, and ideas, marked by a preference for social types; by recurrent references to the story of Abraham and Isaac, and to other biblical moments of sparing or purification; and by the concepts of equivalence and exchange. The literature is fiction from the period of American realism and naturalism; the culture is America from the late nineteenth through the early twentieth century, a culture defined increasingly by the emerging disciplines of social science. This is a book about reading, or, rather, an infinite regression or progression of reading. For the process I am describing is not only reciprocal but in a sense unbounded. To understand the past is to learn to read it as literature teaches us to. It is also to understand literary authors as readers of texts and to reach beyond these direct engagements to the texts they imply.

I take seriously William Benjamin Smith's *The Color Line* and Frederick L. Hoffman's *Race Traits and Tendencies of the American Negro* because Du Bois did, despite their flagrant racism. D. F. Strauss's *Life of Jesus* and Arthur Schopenhauer's *Will and Idea* also figure prominently in this analysis because of their interest to Melville. In this respect, my book looks like a traditional source study, which it is, in part. As in source studies, interpretation here has at times the feel of detective work. Many of the books that turn out to have mattered to writers like Melville or Du Bois, to sociologists like Edward Ross, Herbert Spencer, or Emile Durkheim—Winwood Reade's *The Martyrdom of Man* (1872), William Robertson Smith's *Lectures on the Religion of the Semites* (1888–91), Nathaniel Shaler's *The Neighbor* (1904)—are unfamiliar to literary historians, and only slightly more familiar to historians of the disciplines. So there are discoveries here, of unexpected affinities and connections among a variety of writers and books. I am convinced, for instance, that Melville knew *The Martyrdom of Man*, a best-seller in his day. I suspect that Gertrude Stein came across, somewhere, Mauss and Hubert's *Sacrifice: Its Nature and Functions* (1898). Even critical commonplaces—Melville's late preoccupation with Schopenhauer—have afforded some surprises. From the perspective of the issues central to this study, *Will and Idea* provides a new source for the cabin scene in *Billy Budd, Sailor*.

In other respects, however, this book could not be less like a source study. While the object of analysis is sometimes an old and forgotten book, it can also be a postmodern play. This study asks you to imagine a continuum from late-nineteenth-century books of theology and social science that are almost never read today, to books of literature that are still read (mainly in classrooms), to recent popular films, and it asks you to accept this continuum as the key to the meaning of our culture. We understand our cultural present, I argue, only if we understand it, through narrative, as vitally connected to a not-so-distant past. We have inherited this late-nine-teenth–early-twentieth-century culture and its dilemmas; we have to learn from its mistakes, because we are its mistakes. "Race matters" of the kind described by Cornell West; the idea of poverty with its standard type, the welfare mother; efforts to distinguish the relative deprivations of race and class in a "classless" society; the ongoing fascination with social Darwin-ism—all became issues in the century previous to our own. These dilem-mas were fixtures of what I will be defining as a "social scientific culture." My point is twofold: America became a social scientific culture in the late nineteenth century, and our own culture is another, differently compli-cated version of it.

This study began with a modest insight: the techniques and philosophies of American literary realism and naturalism were comparable to those of an altogether different social practice that happened to share the same time frame, the developing disciplines of social science. This was not a new idea. It could be found in the first responses to this literature and in any influen-tial interpretation of it, from Parrington to New Historicist treatments. These later interpretations, and those that have succeeded them in the 1990s, identify the recognition of "disciplinarity"—an exploration of the relationship between realism and naturalism and other prominent social discourses of the era—as one of the pressing tasks for my generation of critics. The challenge is to grasp the un-literary dimensions of literature while preserving a sophisticated appraisal of its literary qualities, to dis-cover the aesthetic or narrative dimensions of the nonliterary, without los-ing sight of its objective status as, say, a legal brief or an ethnographic report. This could mean reading the formal properties of texts as expres-sions of legal or economic developments, or noting that lawyers and an-thropologists tell stories too. The main problem with my first ventures in interdisciplinary interpretation was that they seemed to leave the major issues untouched. I could demonstrate that Melville's preoccupation with the secularization of biblical types led him to anticipate the typological methods of the early social sciences, or that Henry James's realist passion for detailing the characteristics of different social types resembled the psychological discriminations made by his brother. But the question was always, And then what? To begin with the premise of "interdisciplinarity," it seemed, was to consign oneself to going nowhere.

My dissatisfaction with these limits led me to probe further into the connection between American literature and social science. The result was the discovery of a third element, religion. From a common preoccupation during this period with social types and social control or vigilance, I came to recognize a common preoccupation with religion and sacrifice. The perception of this deeper link came after years of work on the project. I had returned to poring over the literary and social scientific texts that had always seemed to hold the most obvious prospects for interdisciplinary inquiry: Melville's *Billy Budd, Sailor*; James's *The Awkward Age*; Du Bois's *The Souls of Black Folk*; Simmel's essays, *On Individuality and Social Forms*; Weber's *Protestant Ethic*; Ross's *Social Control*. As I contemplated the literary texts, I realized that in each work a sacrifice was the main event—Billy Budd was hung as "a Lamb of God"; Nanda Brookenham was a Levitican Goat, exiled at the novel's end; Burghardt Du Bois was relinquished in the manner of Abraham's Isaac. Other American literature, from *Huckleberry Finn* (1884) to *The Marrow of Tradition* (1901), also featured sacrificial scenes and ideas. And there were examples in American literary works from earlier and later periods: *The Scarlet Letter*, *The Armies of the Night*, *The Bluest Eye*. There will be occasion to consider some of these other cases in the pages that follow. I want to make it clear, however, that this is not a thematic study. My subject is a specific cultural-historical period and a specific aesthetic and social scientific tradition. I recognized the significance of sacrifice in these literary works and then, almost simultaneously, in Simmel's definition of value, Weber's notion of a Protestant ethic, and Ross's conception of social control. I soon learned that a contemporary literature devoted to sacrifice (and known by most of the social scientists and literary authors of concern to my study) had been written in this period. I think of Robertson Smith's *Lectures on the Religion of the Semites*, Mauss and Hubert's *Sacrifice*, and James Frazer's *The Golden Bough*, to name just a few. The discovery of sacrifice not only expanded the canon of this inquiry but proved to be of profound interest to writers who were already integral to it—for example, Herbert Spencer, Edward Westermarck, or Suzan-Lori Parks.

As I complete this book, I have become aware of other studies on close or related topics: Debora Kuller Shuger's *The Renaissance Bible. Scholarship, Sacrifice, and Subjectivity* (1994); Orlando Patterson's "The Feast of Blood" (1998); even Daniel Goldhagen's *Hitler's Willing Executioners* (1996), which rarely mentions the word, but implies with every vivid documentary detail that the Holocaust was "the sacrifice" of the Jews. I have begun to wonder if we are not entering upon our own intellectual season of sacrifice. If we were to conceptualize our current interest in sacrifice from the perspective of Robertson Smith, we might see it as expressing the struggle of intellectuals to define a clear sense of purpose, to grasp the link between academic work and a more general welfare. The morally charged criticism of René Girard, the pioneering reinterpreter of sacrifice, is understandable in these terms. Written in the era of poststructuralism, in the aftermath of the sixties, Girard's *Violence and the Sacred* (1972) exemplifies the relationship between a theoretical attraction to sacrifice and anxieties about the marginal status of academic life. Girard was partly drawn to sacrificial violence from disenchantment with what he saw as a poststructuralist abandonment of intellectual authority.[1] There is a lesson here for the return to sacrifice among intellectuals of an earlier era, a story I begin to tell in the chapters that follow.

● ● ●

ONE of the main assumptions of this study is that sacrificial thinking in the late nineteenth century is social scientific thinking.[2] When realist writers and sociologists undertook to conceptualize the basis of collective life, they discovered sacrifice. Some, like Melville, Tylor, and Robertson Smith, sought their answers in the "precivilized" past, plowing through biblical and classical texts to recover the injunctions of "the ancient Semites." Others, like Durkheim, Du Bois, and James, intuited the meaning of sociality from the dynamics of modern life. In Du Bois's case, the situation is even more complex. As a trained sociologist, he was in the unique position of understanding the sacrificial basis of social scientific rationalism, while protesting the routine victimization of his people in the ongoing sacrificial practice of lynching. The concept of sacrifice supplied the logic that allowed these analysts to embrace scientific rationality while retaining their allegiance to religious ideals. This logic was compatible with what Alvin Gouldner termed "the piety of functionalism," which dominated social science at the point of its emergence and institutionalization as an explicitly modern form of expert knowledge. From the perspective of functionalism, value was defined in terms of loss; global resources were believed to be limited or scarce; and society was characterized as a closed system of alternating checks and balances.[3]

So deeply embedded is the concept of sacrifice in modern ways of thinking that it can be barely perceptible. It inheres, for example, in superstitious anxieties aroused by good times, as in the saying, "You pay for everything." It is also evident in perceptions of society's mysterious interconnectedness, which is captured by another commonplace: "Step on a crack, break your mother's back." Such phrases confirm the sense of cruelty and danger lurking in the most homely clichés. In significant ways we remain a culture of oblation. It would not be inaccurate to classify certain postmodern events as forms of sacrificial violence. Consider the "do or die" culture of inner-city youth gangs (about which I will have more to say in chapter 1), and the activities of right-wing White supremacist groups, including those responsible for the 1995 bombing in Oklahoma City, conceived as a wrathful act of vengeance. There is also the 1995 ritual slaying of a woman in Framingham, Massachusetts, by her husband, a John Hancock Insurance executive, who beat her to death, and then methodically carved out her heart and lungs and impaled them on a stake in an altarlike formation.[4] To recognize how the category of sacrifice was transformed by a series of turn-of-the-century novelists and social scientists is not only to recognize habits and beliefs still vital in our own time but to understand the necessity of overcoming them.

A critical aspect of sacrificial thinking at the point of its reformulation as a type of modern rationality was its articulation in terms of kinship. Sacrificial categories tended to oppose (as they had from their inception in ancient times) the interests of "strangers"—immigrants and other sorts of transforming or transformative groups, understood as productive of social instability—to the welfare of "neighbors." These strangers might include groups as formerly familiar as the American working class, whose membership grew increasingly aware in this period of possessing a common identity and concerns that required political organization and redress, and women, whose reform activity was directed toward liberalized divorce laws, abortion, and voting rights. The category "stranger" could also apply to those as relentlessly "alien" as Blacks, a group whose progress—educational, economic, and political—in this period was met by expanded Jim Crow laws and lynchings. It was no accident that sacrificial thinking seemed to coalesce in particular around these groups, which were often perceived as vehicles of modern change.

My interest lies primarily in the question of what meaning sacrifice could have had in a particular context. I concentrate on conceptualizations of sacrifice during the dramatically unsettled turn of the century, when the modernization process was at its height and the modern social sciences were formulating themselves as the preeminent means for mediating it. I identify an integral point of affinity between modern literary and social scientific definitions of "society," ascribing certain views of sociality and conceptions of the sacred as fundamental to a turn-of-the-century intellectual life (primarily American, but also Continental and European) shared by literary authors and social scientists.[5] I account for the role of social change and conflict, much of it defined in terms of a vast spectacle of social heterogeneity, in the formation of a social scientific culture. I submit the following sorts of questions to a series of literary and social scientific works: What seems to be the purpose of the sacrificial rhetoric or action being invoked here? How does it unfold within the context outlined by this group of literary or social scientific works? How is it related to other pieties upheld by the same speakers or agents?

Various aesthetes, scientists, and dilettantes, scholarly as well as popular social analysts, wrote about sacrifice and absorbed sacrificial modes of thinking. They did so while retaining commitments to highly sophisticated disciplinary distinctions. There were, for example, the nervous discriminations of Henry James, who sought to protect his aesthetic domain from encroachment from without (on the part of social scientists like his brother William) and from within (on the part of fellow artists like H. G. Wells, more willing to overlook divisions between science and art). Yet James also wrote learnedly about sacrificial myths, made available in this period by social scientists and classicists (Andrew Lang and Gilbert Murray, for example), whose work he knew.

Because a considerable portion of this book is devoted to literary analysis, and also because I presume less familiarity on the part of many readers with social science, than with literature, I want to spend some time here laying out the groundwork of the sociological ideas that will figure throughout. Let me begin by addressing in general terms the ways in which social scientists have themselves conceived the divide between aesthetic works and their own. Sociologists pursued "rational universals," categories that were sometimes defined by contrast with the unwieldy particulars designated the province of poets. "Only the universal is rational," writes Durkheim in *The Division of Labor* (1893), "the particular and the concrete baffle understanding." Elsewhere, he observes that "in each individual thing reside innumerable properties," and they must be handled "as do the poets and literary people who describe things as they seem to be, without any rational method" (xviii).[6] Consider his oppositions: the universal is what can be limited (to a single genus or species) and grasped in rational terms. The concrete is virtually unlimited, open to an unimaginable variation that is best left to "literary people." The positing of sociology as a form of mediation between a literary ground of limitless particularity and a lost horizon of spiritual transcendence reminds us that social science was at the forefront of debates in this period over the potential for universally shared values. The writings of Durkheim and his protégé Robert Hertz, for example, helped to redirect understanding of events like death, once thought to define the fundamental nature of a common humanity across time and culture and now seen increasingly as an indicator of human variation.

Social science confronted the waning reliability of universal ideals—faith in God, the valuation of human life—by offering its own methods as a replacement. Sociology especially, it was hoped, might serve as an instrument of secular recuperation, supplanting religious redemption. It is no surprise to learn that the subject of religion preoccupied these thinkers, no matter how "religiously unmusical" they believed themselves to be.[7] Almost every important theorist of this era maintained live connections to an influential religious heritage. Durkheim supplies the most obvious example; he seems to have simply transferred his allegiance from the overwhelming Jewish orthodoxy of his youth ("a body of practices," he writes, "governing all the details of life and leaving little room for individual judgment") to the equally cohesive modern symbolic system called "society."[8] There are many more examples, including Weber, whose Protestant affiliations (filtered primarily through the maternal relation) can be read as the building blocks of his sociology; William Graham Sumner and Albion Small, who trained as Episcopal and Baptist ministers, respectively; and F. H. Giddings, who waged an ongoing struggle against the example of his minister father. This tradition extends to one of the foremost American sociologists of the twentieth century, Talcott Parsons, whose father was a Protestant clergyman. Significantly, every prominent American realist author confronted a powerful (if not always empowering) religious legacy. Take, for instance, Melville's legendary "quarrel" with the Calvinist God, Stephen Crane's rebellion against his own minister father, Henry James Jr.'s resistance to Henry Sr.'s Swedenborgianism, and Theodore Dreiser's exchange of Catholicism for Spencerianism. As Albion Small, a leading American sociologist at the time, observed, "From the first to last religions have been men's more or less conscious attempts to give finite life its infinite rating. Science can never be an enemy of religion. . . . The more science we have the more are we awed and lured by the mystery beyond our ken."[9]

Social scientists mourned the decline of universals, but sought to exploit it professionally.[10] Their work became a means of establishing a new order of rational universals: universals that were capable of confronting cultural variation and value relativity in a manner designed to recover what was uniform about them. The lingering particulars, those concrete excrescences that "baffle[d]" social scientists were left to literature. While social science constructs instrumental universals for a new age, the aesthetic inherits the ground of history. Modern social scientific theory thus offers a representative reformulation of the aesthetic as the domain of the concrete and particular. As portrayed by Durkheim, Weber, Simmel, and others, works of literature were valuable repositories of how the social was lived and thought. These sociological accounts differed considerably from the classic Marxist position on aesthetics. That formulation, according to John Guillory, "attributed to the domain of the aesthetic the capacity to produce a critique of the capitalist order analogous to, and not at all superseded by, the critique produced in such a text as *Capital*."[11] Sociologists were committed neither to critique nor to transcendence; they sought instead to capture faithfully the components of a society they understood as more or less immune, like the God of the Hebrews, to their offerings. Classic Marxists claimed for aesthetics a power to probe the logic of contemporary social systems that was equivalent to their own scientific analyses. Sociologists drew a sharper line between their own objectives and those of artists, a contrast that had significant ramifications for their reformulations of the social scientific enterprise itself.

The ideal of descriptive purity they claimed for themselves left literature with a compensatory function in intellectual life. Literature became a historical resource for social science when it needed to draw upon actual examples for support. Yet this still fails to explain the special value of literature, for it seems obvious that historical sources would have provided a more copious supply of "real life" examples. What literary sources offered were not only characters more richly drawn than those in history books but a common storehouse of culturally specific types—both situational and human—whose properties could resonate in a variety of unpredictable ways, depending on the context. Thus, Durkheim turns to Musset and Goethe for illustrations of anomic love in *Suicide* (1895); Weber invokes Tolstoy in "Science as Vocation" (1918), when sociology has reached the limits of its potential to contemplate death; and Franklin Giddings concludes his *Principles of Sociology* (1896) with a quotation from Browning's "Sordello" that helps to convey the reciprocity between individual genius and the mass of humanity.

The glimmering recognition on the part of sociologists that the meaning of the aesthetic lay in the ends of social science supplies the foundation for my own understanding of the relationship between turn-of-the-century realist-naturalist fiction and sociology.[12] Let me begin with the preoccupations I see as common to them. They include: the decline of universal values and the scientific challenge to religion; the problem of social conflict and order; and the relationship between historical reality and human constructions or social forms, which branches into questions about the relationship between aesthetics and science. One significant expression of this affinity was the formal preoccupation with type categories. Typological method, perhaps more than any other technique, captured the recuperative ambitions of the sociological enterprise. Rational types supplied the means by which universals could be linked to particular social developments, while retaining their power to represent normative standards. They are the basis of Franklin Giddings's inductive methods, most fully tested in research by his students, who either applied their mentor's vast typological schemes to particular social settings (Williams's *An American Town* [1906]) or elaborated their own typology-based theories

(John Franklin Crowell's *The Logical Process of Social Development* [1898]). They received their most sophisticated treatment in Weber's notion of ideal types.

Weber's description of ideal types is consistent with Durkheim's distinction between the rational clarity of science and the bewildering particularities of aesthetics. The "type," Weber writes, affords the social scientist a view of "the real action, influenced as it is by all sorts of irrational facts (emotional impulses, errors), as a 'deviation' from what might be expected if those performing it had behaved in a fully rational way."[13] The literary is precisely that region of emotion and error. Weber means ideal, not in the sense of a preferred or improved state, but in the sense of a fully predictable one. The typological methods of social science help us to see acts and events in the uniform and universal frame of reference that is obscured by our experience of them. These methods serve to lift things out of the unfiltered realm of the ordinary into the more rarefied air of scientific understanding. This is not to imply that these sociological methods were necessarily narrowing or blinding. As Franklin Giddings observed in his own discussion of types: "Some sociological categories must be broad enough to include the cannibal and the diner out. . . . Some must be broad enough to include the wise man and the ant."[14] It's important to acknowledge Giddings's overall commitment here (at least methodologically speaking) to variety and inclusiveness. But the politics of Giddings's evolutionary gradient should give us pause. His image of the food chain both reminds us that he remains (intellectually) bound to organicism and confirms the compatibility between modern relativism and social Darwinism. Giddings's image suggests that type categories were understood by social scientists themselves as a critical means for confronting a modern spectacle of heterogeneity. Types provided a social taxonomy, a set of classificatory tools for subordinating historically particular individuals and phenomena to limited universal patterns.

Social scientists *earned* their type categories, drawing them out of an indefinable "infinite" that was resolutely historical. There was an undeniable degree of defensiveness in this: their categories were dikes against what they perceived as ungovernable in their contemporary society. What role could literature play in all this: how did literary writers situate themselves in this era of declining universals, where the rational had in some sense become the universal? There is probably no realist writer better equipped to consider such questions than Henry James, who was in the habit of comparing his own literary aims to the scientific endeavors of his brother William, and who wrote extensive treatises on aesthetics that he appended as prefaces to his major novels. It would not be farfetched to consider these treatises as compendiums of "ideal types," serving to highlight the experiential deviations of the novels they interpret. Among the most "scientific" of these treatises, is the preface to *The Awkward Age*, where James adopts a pseudoscientific language of "measurements," and "symmetries" (9). This is his playful way of emphasizing art's inability to operate within such constraints. Yet James also insists that the artist must make his own formal "sacrifice," in keeping with those made by the characters who inhabit its borders. If the matter of art is less "organic" or "real" than the objects studied by social scientists, this only serves to heighten the artist's apprehension of the relationship between universal and rational forms.

How might one compare a literary category like "common sailor" (Melville) to a sociological category like "delinquent girl" (W. I. Thomas), or a literary definition of habit (Stein's "servant girl nature") to a sociological one (Weber's Protestant ethic)? Writers like Melville use types to enhance uncertainty and ambiguity. They show how the boundary represented by "Common Sailor" cannot possibly contain the burgeoning and variegated American working class, or how a term like "the Awkward Age" does little to untangle the web of social conflicts impinging on reproduction at the turn of the century. According to most of the literature in this study (and there are exceptions to the rule, even within works that mainly fulfill it), types represent a universalizing language of social control that does not begin to encompass all that it attempts to rein in. Literary uses of types therefore tend to be multiple, even parodic. Consider, for example, all the different types heaped on the protagonist of *Billy Budd*, or the way in which Du Bois amplifies and complicates his portrayal of Black American existence from a social scientific typology (*The Philadelphia Negro*) to a more literary one (*The Souls of Black Folk*). As employed by contemporary social scientists, types are most often stabilizing; as employed by a corresponding company of literary writers, they are provisional. Both social scientists and writers extol types, but the writers are more likely to question them.

These distinctions between social scientific and literary uses of types are consistent with their different narrative approaches to sacrifice. The social scientists of my study work primarily at the level of *explanations* and *concepts*, informed by contemporary ethnography, statistics, and historical documents. Sociologists like Durkheim, or Mauss and Hubert, enumerate the details of the sacrificial rite. They tell us how they think these function to sustain social order. Or like Simmel and Weber, they employ a sacrificial rhetoric that lends a special intensity to their arguments, by referring them to a frame of reference that is material and economic, but also solemn, and slightly dangerous. The literary authors of my study *stage* sacrifice. They offer a sacrificial theatre, whose purpose is to question different features of the sacrificial enterprise. This is not a restatement of the subversive hypothesis: the claim that aesthetic form is by definition critical of prevailing social norms. Call it rather the disciplinary hypothesis: the self-evident truth that a work of sociology, or anthropology, is designed to fulfill the expectations of a given disciplinary system of explanation. Whereas literature, if not antidisciplinary, might best be understood as supradisciplinary. Yet here too the sacrificial record is somewhat surprising.

For the sacrificial theatres of this book are not confined to aesthetic narratives. Consider the *Tivah* ceremony featured in Robert Hertz's Durkheimian social study *Death and the Right Hand*, a violent mass exercise that culminates in the death of an alien. Or consider Arthur Stanley's portrayal of Hebrew sacrifice as ritual high drama, with "every gesture . . . a kind of moving picture" (see chapter 2 below). Either of these examples, like their literary counterparts, might serve to reveal the deep structure of sacrificial rites. Still, the literary examples work more consistently as second-order reflections. When Du Bois portrays his book as an offering on behalf of a people much sacrificed—or when he contemplates (in his stirring elegy for his son) the morbid characterizations of American Blacks—he is highlighting the practice of sacrificial surrogacy. His dramatization translates the rhetoric and the rite into explicitly politicized terms. These political aspects are especially pronounced in *The Souls of Black Folk*, because sacrificial designs are so variously present here. The same holds for *Billy Budd, Sailor* and *The Awkward Age*. My arguments about sacrifice will be elaborated through readings of these books in the context of other contemporary works. These texts will be understood as rich historical inscriptions of a rich historical world.

The task of reading historically brings me to questions of methodology, and it seems best to begin by clarifying how I understand the categories of social science, social theory, and sociology. I define social science as a general group of disciplines that developed over the course of two centuries (the eighteenth and nineteenth) and reached their critical emergent point at the turn of the twentieth century, when they were institutionalized in the United States as academic disciplines (among them, sociology, political science, economics, psychology, and anthropology) and codified in the works of major social scientific theorists particular to each field. I define social theory as thought about the nature of social processes. Social theory is concerned with identifying general concepts that can be widely applied to concrete situations. This is different from a philosophy of method whose principle concern is to distinguish the discipline in question from other emergent contemporary disciplines (e.g., Durkheim's *The Rules of Sociological Method*, which aims, in part, to define "sociological facts" against "facts" as conceived by neighboring fields). In this formative period, however, there could be considerable overlap between theory and philosophy of method. We will also have occasion to discuss works that are qualitatively inferior to classic social theory. This is because modern social theory was not always written by major figures but sometimes by very minor ones, including those without any disciplinary credentials. There was then, as now, much popularizing of social scientific ideas, especially sociological ones, because of widespread interest in their potential for solving modern problems.

The guiding social scientific focus of this study is the field of sociology, which can be delimited by a few main characteristics. The first generation of sociologists saw human nature as fundamentally social and thus tended to focus on group behavior and forms of collective interaction. Their politics were defined by the necessity of reconceptualizing liberalism in the face of strong challenges from late-nineteenth-century socialist and conservative movements, and also by their growing recognition of cultural relativity. For the most part, sociologists were convinced that instrumental rationality held the potential for mediating change. They had an interest, therefore, in redirecting their methods from scientific metaphors (whether organic or mechanic) that underplayed human capacities for control to those affording some conception of human agency, especially through collective association. Finally, sociologists distinguished their discipline from other social sciences by its synthetic qualities. Sociology could draw upon and unify the diverse collection of social sciences undergoing institutionalization at this time.[15] It will become apparent over the course of my analysis that these synthetic aims were highly successful. Sociology became a varied and complex discipline, capable of incorporating a great diversity of social and political interests.

Perhaps the most critical feature of the dialogue between literature and social science is the role of what I call the "border text." The border text represents a crucial aspect of interdisciplinary discussions from the late nineteenth century through our own time. I see it as a work that at once defines and bridges divisions among professional disciplines (e.g., sociology, anthropology, psychology), and, in turn, between these disciplines and more popular audiences. Marked by their accessible language and broad appeal, these texts cut across emerging specializations, in ways that accentuate the process of specialization itself. Consider a recent example of a border text: the latest social scientific sensation, *The Bell Curve*, an 845-page best-seller that "links low IQ to race and poverty." Two aspects of the book are especially revealing from the perspective of my own study. First, one of the book's authors, Charles Murray, is not, strictly speaking, trained professionally in the specialized areas the book takes up: psychology, biology, statistics. Second, the book ranges over numerous specializations in its effort to make a complex and controversial social issue accessible to a wide audience. Like Charles Murray himself, who is not identified with any particular profession but appears as a type of maverick amateur and policy whiz, the book is positioned clearly outside disciplinary boundaries. It appears to me to be a direct descendant of the kinds of books that are so critical to the chapters that follow, such as Benjamin Kidd's *Social Evolution* (1894), Nathaniel Shaler's *The Neighbor* (1904), and Frederick L. Hoffman's *Race Traits and Tendencies of the American Negro* (1896).

I found that I was able to grasp dominant social issues most deeply in this textual margin between literature and sociology. The authors were sometimes fringe figures, neither sociologists nor anthropologists nor psychologists, who nonetheless wrote significant and influential works of social theory. They were often known by my literary authors. For example, Du Bois reviewed Hoffman, though few scholars read Hoffman today, in part because his ideas seem pernicious and easily dismissible. But border texts are popular precisely because they expose areas of cultural controversy and grievance. We ignore them at our peril, for what is especially striking from the start of the twentieth century to its end is the resurgence of Hoffman's or Shaler's theories on race in a book like *The Bell Curve*. Border texts testify to the engagement of major literary authors with contemporary social theory. They also reveal the outlines of a genuinely interdisciplinary region, one that might be regarded as a precursor to the postmodern literary critical field of cultural studies. Du Bois's *Souls*, which sold more copies than any of his other books, and was read by Max Weber as well as Henry James, is my study's central border text.

I understand the border text as a peculiarly modern phenomenon: it requires a culture with a developed publishing industry, where the concept of the best-seller is relatively commonplace. It also requires a culture in which the institutionalization of disciplines and fields of research is fairly well established. Finally, the border text is the product of a culture with some defined opposition between an intellectual elite, increasingly housed in universities, and popular audiences—the former imagined as the source of ideas, the latter as their (largely) passive receivers.[16] I'm of course talking about the United States at the turn of the century. My definition of the border text presupposes a society in which there is a great deal of interest in the emerging fields of social science, generated by widespread perceptions of intensive social change. This includes unprecedented rates of economic growth, urbanization, and industrialization and unprecedented levels of labor unrest and immigration.

Interest in social science, especially in sociology, grew out of a generalized sense, partly cultivated by sociologists themselves, that the discipline represented a uniquely modern form of expertise. Sociology was a product of the changes it sought to mediate. The sociologist's aim, according to Albion Small, was to compensate for the "fragmentary knowledge" of "the millions" in a modern democracy.[17] Small's view of the sociologist's synthetic purpose included a methodological imperative that I have already mentioned. But it was also democratic. Sociological methods were practical: they could be used in mundane situations by ordinary people. Indeed, sociologists often saw themselves as providing scientific formulations of a socially common sense. Hence, the function of the border text: to translate sophisticated terminologies into a common language. Works such as *The Neighbor*, at the turn of the century, or *The Bell Curve*, more recently, claim to make general audiences feel more in control of the social changes that are controlling them.[18] What these audiences are being controlled by most immediately are the ideological commitments of Nathaniel Shaler, Richard Herrnstein, and Charles Murray.

The rhetorical style of Edward Ross, who exhorted readers of his popular polemic *Sin and Society* (1907) "not [to] *Be good*, but [to] *Be rational*," was typical of border texts.[19] Introduced by the president of the United States (Theodore Roosevelt), who predicted "that its influence will be widespread," the book's title and subject suggest that it was intended to be both accessible and inflammatory. In keeping with Roosevelt's prophecy, Ross reports in his autobiography that he received responses to the book from university presidents, bankers, and schoolteachers, as well as novelists, rabbis, and temperance reformers. Ross was himself a respected sociologist, whose first book, *Social Control* (1901), was described as "the brainiest piece of work that had come from our side of the water in a long time."[20] I have suggested that the border text was a paradoxical achievement, in that it served at once to define and to defy disciplinary divisions. Its role in relation to popular audiences was similar: it both exaggerated and minimized the perceived distance between professional analysts and the larger public.

The idea of specific texts functioning as boundaries between different social groups and different areas of research raises a Frostian quandary. Historically speaking, what regions does the perspective of this study tend to wall in and wall out? My focus on sacrifice, especially as it is formulated in terms of a context where certain groups are consistently seen as victims, while others nearly always appear as beneficiaries of sacrificial rites, yields a rather depressing portrait of American society. I foreground this point in order to be as direct as possible about my aims and procedures. I will not be emphasizing the political gains made by women in this period, though they are implicit in everything I have to say about the modern crisis over women's reproductive roles in chapter 3. Nor will I be highlighting the impressive achievements of working- and middle-class Blacks in the postemancipation era. Nor (again) will I be dwelling upon the vigor and variety of American working-class culture at the end of the century. All of these developments have been amply described, and warrant further description.[21] But the combination of literary authors and social scientists examined here and the kinds of questions—social, aesthetic, and political—that they collectively raise lead me to gloomier emphases. I find it difficult to read *Billy Budd, Sailor* or *The Red Badge of Courage*, Stein's *3-Lives* or Du Bois's *The Philadelphia Negro*, and emerge greatly encouraged about the state of the nation in their time. My study has been tempered by the works that it focuses on. I want to suggest, however, one way in which all of these works can be read as affording a view of human possibility alternative to their grim plots. It requires attributing to them a certain logic whereby these books generate, through their very grimness, the social alternatives that swarm around them. Though the overall perspective of these works is bleak, a properly dialectical approach needs to account for the developments that they imply, a borderland of imaginative redress and political agency. Du Bois, in his role as a public intellectual, might be taken as exemplary of this possibility. In addition to producing his vast scholarship, he was a journalist (editor of *The Crisis*) and activist (a founder of the NAACP, organizer of Pan-African Congresses, and spokesman for socialist causes). Such activities offset the disillusion and even despair that sometimes crept into his more substantive writings.

For the sake of clarity, let me rehearse a commonplace: however tangible in their own right, research areas are still constructions to a point, which is why it is important to be deliberate about the assumptions and methods that limit them. This is paramount for a study that proposes to shed some light on a particular moment in the history of sociology. The scientific ambitions of the field notwithstanding, questions about its roots have long been a source of controversy. Hard scientists may not feel responsible for their past, but social scientists seem convinced that there are significant stakes in the identification of a collective ancestry. Since the debate over the origins of sociology is not my central concern, I will confine myself to a select group of sociologists who have provided analyses of their professional history. From my perspective, what seems especially noteworthy is how little mention there is, in most cases, of an American sociological past, as if the writings of Small, Giddings, Ross, and others represented a professional nightmare, best left to the discretion of historians. The earliest self-proclaimed attempts to recover a sociological tradition by sociologists themselves came in the 1920s. After Albion Small's 1924 *Origins*, the significant contributions include the '40s histories of Harry Elmer Barnes, Floyd House, and the Bernards, as well as studies from the '60s and '70s by Robert Nisbet, Irving Zeitlin, and the Schwendingers. More recent analyses, by Anthony Giddens, Stefan Collini, and Jeffrey Alexander, display both theoretical sophistication and an awareness of how difficult it is to establish the borders between a "modern" field like sociology and a long prehistory of thought about society, between sociology and other contemporary social sciences, and between scientific investigation and the work of more marginal figures, where sociological ideas may exist in inchoate form.[22] Alert to the political investments couched in predominant clichés about the past, these authors try to understand how current disciplinary controversies shape myths about sociology's origins.

Professional development in these arguments is fluid, inadvertent, and wide-ranging, which is consistent with my sense of how border texts function: to pinpoint a more varied dispersal of classic sociological theories (from the likes of Durkheim, Weber, Giddings, Ross) than has been recognized. I read their work as part of an extended social scientific debate in which they were often joined by amateurs, and also in terms of contemporary aesthetic debates and forms of novelistic representation. My assumption here is that there was a common context of thought about the origins of society. One of its features was its international constituency. Most of the sociologists who played a prominent role in formulating the new discipline were educated abroad (usually in Germany, but occasionally in France or in Britain). Since the discipline was seen as a product of the modern interdependence it sought to analyze, it was inevitable that sociology would be conceived as a worldwide (more exactly, a European and Anglo-American) enterprise. No one working in this emergent field could afford to be provincial. So, for example, Franklin Giddings reviewed Karl Pearson's the *Chances of Death and Other Studies* (1897) for the *American Journal of Sociology* as soon as it appeared; Americans read Durkheim before the turn of the century, and the British Sociological Association organized a special forum on his work in the same period; Benjamin Kidd's *Social Evolution*, a border text published in Britain, greatly influenced the first British as well as American sociologists; Albion Small translated and published Simmel (in the *AJS*) in the 1890s; Weber corresponded with Du Bois, consulting him for a reading list on the race question; and Durkheim drew upon British and American ethnography for his theories about religion. The eagerness on the part of the first generation of sociologists to keep abreast of professional developments in other countries matched their openness to the work of nonprofessionals. In this early moment of professional self-definition, boundaries of all kinds tended to be strict in theory (due to sensitivity about the novelty of these fields) but loose in practice.

The literature on sacrifice is marked by an international lexicon through which national peculiarities are discernible. I have mentioned the reliance of the Durkheimian *Année* scholars on the research of British and American ethnographers. This was especially true of their specific ideas about sacrifice, which were based in the theories of British Bible specialists. Sacrificial rites and themes, as presented in social scientific works of this period, tended to be part of a grand international continuum of writings about sacredness and secularity. They captured a prevailing sense of modern society's extensive interdependencies, of the elaborate checks and balances that, in the view of many, defined not only economics but social life in general. They also expressed a sense of distance from a powerfully imagined spiritual tradition. Most of these sociologists came from middle-class backgrounds, and their politics ranged from mild forms of liberalism to conservatism. They were prepared to accept the idea that social apportionments (of opportunity and wealth) would be variable. For the most part, they considered it inevitable that some groups in society would prosper while others suffered—that some law of social equilibrium demanded this.

It is well known that America at the turn of the century was remarkable for its spectacles of economic imbalance. The proximity of rich and poor in the close atmospheres of New York or Chicago, the discrepancy between debilitating poverty and lavish wealth, became the staple of a national success myth, shaped in part by the novels of Theodore Dreiser. Dreiser's narrators are famous for their rapt contemplation of capitalism's four humors—will, character, luck, and training—which makes some stars, others beggars. Max Weber was aware of the unique laboratory afforded by this modernizing urban landscape. He found much to ponder as well in the rural Ohio and North Carolina communities where he visited his German immigrant relatives during his 1904 trip. Despite his admiration for American habits of voluntarism, which he felt politicized its citizens far more effectively than the authoritarian institutional structures of his native Germany, Weber noted a vast array of social problems in this "model of a new society."[23] Labor troubles, "the terrible immigration," "the Negro question" together formed a "big, black cloud" on the American horizon (16).

Weber's view was widely shared by fellow sociologists, who used the United States as a consistent point of reference. There was nothing new in this: Marx and Engels, among others, recognized America as the ultimate modern-capitalist case. The questions that preoccupied sociologists and guided their theoretical speculations were felt to have direct and immediate expression here. The same holds true for the significance of sacrifice in particular. The American context was unusually susceptible to sacrificial rhetoric and acts, for reasons I have highlighted above: prevailing convictions of its vastly discrepant levels of opportunity and wealth, and the incomparable extent of its social heterogeneity.

My literary examples have a similar international scope. All of the writers with whom I am concerned studied in Europe or on the Continent (James, Norris, Crane, Du Bois) or traveled extensively there (Melville). Some became permanent exiles (James, Stein, Du Bois). This cosmopolitanism is reflected in the settings of my primary works. *Billy Budd* comes into focus somewhere between late-eighteenth-century Europe and late-nineteenth-century America; *The Awkward Age* is concerned with the decay of a British leisure class; and *The Souls of Black Folk* seems more appropriately addressed to the world at large than to Du Bois's benighted American neighbors. Each of these texts, which provide the focus in turn of chapters 2, 3, and 4, opens out into an extraordinary range of methods and issues. The first is typological. *Billy Budd* is preoccupied with the task of "cataloging the creatures of the deep." The novella's cryptic narrator takes an analytical, one might even say "interdisciplinary" (anthropological, biblical, aesthetic, sociological), approach to the problem of social heterogeneity in different modern cultures. James's titular category, "the Awkward Age," anticipates Weberian ideal types. It seeks to capture the process of historical change through the identification of a normative figure equally applicable to individual and social conditions (adolescence as well as societies in transition). Both James and Weber can be seen as sustaining Tonnies's typological framework of modern change (*Gemeinschaft* to *Gesellschaft*), though Weber would have rejected this conceptual straitjacket, and James would probably not have known it. Du Bois recognized as profoundly as Melville and James the perils of rational typologies. This explains his transition, in the space of three years, from the sociological types of *Philadelphia Negro* to the provisional literary types of *Souls*.

The connections between my literary and social scientific subjects goes beyond the mere use of types. All of the authors in my study were absorbed with the problem of social control. Vigilance is a privileged sense in these works, an ideal condition of attention and concern. It involves the erection and maintenance of boundaries, both conceptual (as in a penchant for disciplines and types) and actual (as in a constant awareness of threats to social borders and dramatizations of disorder or its possibility). The privileging of vigilance expresses the view of society as a worldwide web of interrelations that can only be experienced through sharp apprehensions of immediate effects (the shortage of rain for Russia's wheat crop inflating the price of American breakfast cereal). Such ideas served to alleviate social responsibility for acts and events whose causes were readily apparent. Vigilance—intensification of sight coupled with anxiety about what eluded detection—had more to do with horrors that were known and controllable than with those that were not. This complex and ambivalent formulation of social consciousness and agency is basic to the dramatic action of my principal literary examples. *Billy Budd* begins in spectacle: all eyes fixed in fascination upon the figure of a Handsome Sailor, whose ultimate echo is the handcuffed Billy Budd, hung from the ship's yardarm. *The Awkward Age* begins with the sighting of a four-wheeler, which inspires the usual Jamesian flurry of interpretation: Who is it for? Whose social form does it represent? This sighting foreshadows a later image of another (this time, speculative) "post-chaise," which the novel's elderly "priest" may use to shepherd the sacrificial lamb into exile. *The Souls of Black Folk* begins with a paradigmatic (mis)apprehension of Blacks by Whites. The invariable White failure to penetrate the "mystery" of Blackness is resolved in the funeral procession of chapter 11, where Black identity is conflated with the final "mystery" of death.

From the sailor's dogwatch of Melville's sea story to the vigilante lynching committees that hover sinisterly at the margins of Du Bois's Black Belt, an emphasis on vigilance reveals how apprehensions of certain human bodies have changed. *Billy Budd* confronts changes in the administration of working-class male bodies in a modern social order. Here, natural and barbaric constraints give way to the tempered legalism of formal "executions." *The Awkward Age* devotes much attention to the reproductive capacities of White female adolescents. The female adolescent becomes the hope of the middle and upper classes and a metaphor for all forms of production, from the modern nation's capacity for self-regeneration to literary creation itself. *The Souls of Black Folk* at once confirms and challenges constructions of the Black body as a site of decay. Typological method achieves its fullest realization in these different attentions to the fate of the human body. These books help us to see the paradoxical function of types, as means for both forgetting and remembering bodies. Types help us to remember by identifying the body as determinate: the Philadelphia Negro can be none other than this. They help us to forget by eliminating the idea of privacy: the body as physically known to one, despite its mediateness, is evacuated.

The subjects of vigilance and corporeality extend to another concern shared by all of the writers in my study: the problem of demographics. Again this can be grasped through the details of exemplary literary texts. Melville worries about the numbers of immigrants entering the United States at the end of the nineteenth century, a human sea vividly apparent to him through his role as Customs House inspector for the Port of New York until 1885, the year he began writing *Billy Budd*. James imagines the turn-of-the century society of his bourgeois and aristocratic characters as perfectly sterile. Dispossessed of its reproductive capacities, and of its capacity to transfer its values and customs to succeeding generations, it is helpless before the collective demographic power of social "inferiors" at home and abroad—Jews, the poor, primitive populations. Du Bois's early writings are immersed in demographic debates on the survival capacities of Blacks in the twentieth century. Here again, Du Bois provides the most pronounced case of an interest common to all three writers. This is partly because his marginal social position motivated an especially profound questioning of widely recognized "problems" and "solutions." It is also a consequence of his self-imposed marginality vis-à-vis literary and social scientific practice. In the chapters that follow, I show how the demographic preoccupations of each work are elaborated through the reformulation of a universal category: *Billy Budd*, the category of Origins; *The Awkward Age*, the category of Reproduction; and *Souls*, the category of Death. The question addressed to Billy Budd early on, "Do you know anything about your beginning?" (437), circulates aboard the *Bellipotent* like a contagion. No member of this "motley" ship's crew, nor any event that befalls it, escapes the taint of ambiguous cause. This seems appropriate given the novella's larger purpose: to replace a worn-out myth of biblical origins with an alienating myth of social scientific origins. Reproduction in *The Awkward Age* is radically contextualized. Far from a mysterious feminine faculty independent of human control, it is recognized as a politically live attribute, too valuable to be overlooked by dominant social powers. *Souls* exposes turn-of-the-century efforts to refashion death in blackface, as a means of sublimation and displacement. In each instance, a universal is recognized in resolutely particular terms.

These works serve as various confirmations of the modern insight that universals are apprehensible only through the associations they take on in specific contexts. These particularities are not unlimited. The universal category of sexual reproduction, for example, is associated with women; the category of death, with degraded or subordinate groups. These universals in turn afford a limited range of social action in each chapter. Melville's interest in origins results in a narrative about the transformation of social order, now seen as an invention sustained by identifiable authorities. The work's threatening subplot views workers as compliant, even romantic individually, but menacing collectively. James's interest in reproduction generates a plot about the transformation of social welfare; formerly centered in maternity, it is now seen as the province of the liberal state. The novel's subplot portrays the female adolescent as a figure for women in transition, challenging traditional roles, and resisting accommodations essential to the status quo. Du Bois's interest in death leads to a plot about the transformation of sympathy from a universal sentiment to one whose effects are exclusive and even disingenuous (to the extent that it retains the mythology of its former inclusiveness). Du Bois's subplot is the double threat posed by a Black collectivity: whether through its imperceptible penetration of society (intermarriage, "passing") or as an isolated mass, threatening to Whites. Finally, each example confronts a central theoretical issue as historical event: in Melville, the making of a modern working class; in James, the gender basis of the welfare state; in Du Bois, the racial subtext of the sociology of sympathy.

In both fiction and works of sociology, vigilance is the privileged sense, and sacrifice is the privileged act. Sacrifice is necessary to the maintenance of social order, the achievement of a certain level of culture, and the per-

petuation of a certain kind of economy. Sacrifice, according to these authors, is not only necessary to modern Western society, it is basic; it makes
society what it is. Thus, Durkheim's primitives in *Elementary Forms* reach
the height of collective intensity through mourning rites that include sacrificial forms of self-mutilation and revenge. The famous postulate derived
from these rites—"men do not weep for the dead because they fear them;
they fear them because they weep for them"—provides an accurate summary of sacrificial transactions. The social is defined by what is *given up* in
order to reproduce it. None of the thinkers in my study was more aware of
these definitions than Melville, James, and Du Bois. Du Bois's portrait of
sacrifice is the most vivid and categorical. He describes how he has relinquished his own son (in a gesture as literal as Abraham's surrender of Isaac)
and reads his own sacrifice in the context of the sacrifices made by a Black
collectivity as a matter of routine. James takes a moral approach to the rite
of sacrifice, by dramatizing how the civilized satisfactions of a degenerate
modern circle are earned at the expense of its female adolescents. The ideal
form of social welfare—the maternal high ground represented in the novel
as the Moon or the Marble Arch—is sacrificed on behalf of a collective
appetite for sexual liberty and pulp fiction. Melville's writings adhere most
faithfully to the religious pathway that is the source of all this literary and
social scientific interest in sacrifice. Measuring at every turn how far modern man has fallen from the altars of ancient belief, they also reveal him as
all the more caught up in its wrought frame. Melville's historical kaleidoscope in the opening pages of *Billy Budd*, which takes us from the Black
sailor to the Assyrian Bull to the modern worker, is designed to convey the
durability of sacrificial devotions. This is consistent with another formal
continuity confirmed by Melville's text: that sacrifice has been an inducement to narrative from ancient times to modern.[24]

Billy Budd confirms not only a formal but an historical continuity: the
dominance of sacrifice as a social practice. For if there is a single message
in my book, it is the relevance of sacrifice as social thought and social
action, supporting the most entrenched as well as innovative institutions
(from charity to life insurance) and mediating the most complex developments (from the "invention" of homosexuality to the rise of racial segregation). Chapter 1 analyzes social scientific narratives of sacrifice, as parts of
standard works and as the focus of more esoteric studies; it concludes with
an exploration of selected literary texts that helped me to recover this cultural mythology. Chapter 2 examines Melville's treatment of sacrifice.
Typee, Moby-Dick, Clarel, and *Billy Budd* (the chapter's literary center) guide
this inquiry into the subject of origins—biblical versus secular—and corresponding questions of heterogeneity and social control. Chapter 3 explores
turn-of-the-century preoccupations with the scapegoat mechanism—sacrifice in one of its most prominent ancient forms. James's *The Awkward Age*

provides a cultural lens, exposing a range of mythic, social scientific, and theological perspectives on sacrificial powers of purification. Chapter 4 describes Du Bois's early writings as powerful commentaries—at once social scientific and aesthetic—on a set of dilemmas that resonate with peculiar force in our own time: the decline of humanitarian sentiments, the rationalization of death rites, the relationship between Black elite and Black masses. I end with Du Bois because more than any other works addressed in this study, his early writings testify to the salutary and even redemptive possibilities afforded by the intellectual embrace of sacrifice.

ONE

Sacrificial Arts and Sciences

❧

THIS CHAPTER is about a literature that expressed the moral and political conventions of Anglo-American culture in the late nineteenth through the early twentieth century. It was a literature both about democracy and the coherence of a democracy, about the relationship between religion and secularity. All of the writers whose works I examine here (and throughout this book), from sociological theorists (whether American, British, or European), intellectuals, and amateur social observers to literary authors, participated in the creation of an American social scientific culture. This diverse array of thinkers was united by a shared interest in the identification of general principles for a modern, heterogeneous society. The term "society" itself assumed a particular gravity at this historical moment. Many of the writers in this study saw themselves as deliberate architects of a new "science of society."

Attempting to explain the meaning of "society" for their own time they turned to the earliest known attempts to define the nature of social life. Like the late-eighteenth-century framers of the Constitution, who drew upon classical models—the constitutions of the early Greek and Roman republics—in drafting their design for a modern democratic state, these architects of a modern social order sought their models in an ancient tradition. What they found there were narratives of sacrifice. All of these quests for original ideas about social organization, from William Robertson Smith's account of Hebraic traditions (*Lectures on the Religion of the Semites* [1886]) and Sir James Frazer's treatment of Vedic myths (*The Golden Bough* [1890]) to *The Principles of Sociology*, according to Herbert Spencer (1876–96) or Franklin Giddings (1896), from Melville's *Billy Budd, Sailor* (1891) and Crane's *Red Badge of Courage* (1895) to Du Bois's *The Souls of Black Folk* (1903) and Stein's *3-Lives* (1906), led to the discovery of sacrifice as a key social sacrament.

My subject is not the rite of sacrifice per se. It is rather, the dynamic relationship among different forms of social theory—mainly literary and social scientific, but also theological—that shared an interest in sacrifice. Writers like Robertson Smith and Frazer, Spencer and Giddings, Melville and Du Bois came to know sacrifice as a ritually exact event, and as a way of understanding. Their works were classifications of sacrificial acts as well as examples of sacrificial thought. These descriptions of sacrifice were marked by extraordinary care and comprehension. Some even convey religious awe in catalogs that can range from (seemingly) every article ever worn by a victim to every rationale ever given to solemnize a victim's demise. At the same time, sacrifice was a far-reaching, one might even say overworked, metaphor in this period. In social science, in literary realism and naturalism, in a renovated theology, in any analysis that took seriously the idea of society, sacrifice (as form or content) was likely to be invoked. My analysis is a narrative about a narrative, the recovery of a recovery of sacrifice as society's originating mythology.

My claim that a preoccupation with sacrifice was unique to a late-nineteenth century narrative about the nature of society requires some explanation. The idea of a monolithic entity called "society" was not a late-nineteenth century invention. The most persuasive arguments locate the beginnings of the "society" concept in post-Renaissance Europe. Social science, they suggest, emerged as a discrete form of inquiry together with natural science.[1] The Scottish Enlightenment was another point of origin, with its exemplary formulation in Adam Ferguson's "Civil Society." Given the extent of early interest in society as such, I find it especially revealing that sacrifice did not materialize as a prominent feature of prior analyses. What was its attraction for late-nineteenth-century social theory? Most obviously, sacrifice was a religious rite, a form of communication with God. In biblical Hebrew, the root term is *korban*, "to bring near," which implies a conviction of distance between the human and divine. We can understand from this how sacrifice might have suited a late-nineteenth century atmosphere of spiritual crisis: the waning of doctrinal commitment among intellectuals, the challenge posed by science to the social dominance of religion. In short, sacrifice is associated with spiritual loss.

It is also associated with heightened perceptions of threats to social unification and order. Historians of social science have emphasized the extraordinary social pressures that accompanied the institutionalization of the disciplines in America. By recognizing the emergence of social science as an historical event defined partly through narratives of sacrifice, my analysis brings those pressures to the center. For sacrificial rites are identified not only with periods of social instability in general but with the dilemma of social heterogeneity in particular. Sacrifice fortifies social borders—between kin and non-kin; animal and human; man and God—by its very staging of their threatened collapse. Finally, and perhaps most importantly, sacrifice provided the preeminent mythology for an expanding industrial-capitalist society. The simplest link between sacrifice and capitalism is familiar as social scientific cliché: the rebirth of primitive "barter" in a modern exchange economy. More complex continuities between sacrifice and capitalism lie in class distinctions that in turn sanction distinctions of reward and benefit. A capitalist system, like an ancient sacrificial one, tends to justify inequities through structural differences that are made to appear natural. Where a traditional kinship system stresses blood identity, a modern capitalist might stress "merit" or industry. But both factors are meaningful across contexts. Sacrifice provided the requisite mythology, and professional social science provided the scribes, the new priesthood capable of transforming mythology into prophecy. Social scientists, like the authors of the New Testament, sought to encode principles and to indoctrinate potential disciples into their new "religion of humanity," a religion, I am suggesting, built on an ancient foundation of sacrifice.

This chapter analyzes the social scientific literature of sacrifice, which was critical to Anglo-American culture from the late nineteenth century through the turn of the twentieth and beyond. The first part lays out my principal assumptions about sacrifice. The second, third, and fourth parts explore how sacrifice figures in the work of major social scientists (from Edward Ross to Weber). Here I look at sacrifice as a component of theories we have valued for other reasons (e.g., *Social Control, The Protestant Ethic*), and also as the central focus, in its own right, of important social scientific studies (e.g., Hubert and Mauss, *Sacrifice: Its Nature and Functions*). My purpose is to highlight the extent of interest in this configuration, and how it conforms to the basic principles of specific thinkers and schools of thought. All of the works discussed in this chapter will be reexamined with greater specificity—conceptual and contextual—in later chapters of the book. The fifth part turns, briefly, to literary works and disciplinary questions. I hope this will serve to introduce subsequent chapters and to emphasize (once again) that literature is my route to this social mythology.

Some Meanings of Sacrifice

My understanding of sacrifice is historical. But I don't mean to minimize the timeless aspect of a phenomenon whose mythical origins extend to the moment when the first offering was set out for the gods in the hope of ensuring peace among "heathen" neighbors. By acknowledging, however mutedly, the timelessness of sacrifice, I am accepting the possibility of a symbolic continuum between ancient and modern religion. As Peter Berger has noted, the Hebrew God (in contrast, presumably, to more magical gods) already displayed an immunity to the claims of sacrificial exchange.[2] This implies that there was a quality of nostalgia in the earliest sacrificial practices. We can detect wistfulness about the rite's viability and legitimacy in some of the first recorded testimonies. These implications can be taken as warnings that I intend to keep in mind as I proceed, in order to avoid (as much as possible) confusing what appears to be a universal property with what is resolutely particular to modern adaptations of it.

In our rush to be historical critics, we have sometimes missed what may be genuinely universal.

Yet to acknowledge affinities between ancient and modern anxiety about the efficacy of ritual acts, is to record a deeper historical debt than seems at first apparent. The prevalence of sacrificial representation in different times and places is potentially indicative of the rite's own acute sensitivity to historical change. It may be that sacrificial thoughts and rituals become prominent in periods when fears of social instability are especially pronounced. This is not some overriding claim for outcroppings of irrational drives in times of social distress. Nor do I wish to reanimate the old debate about the undercurrent of primitivism in modern society. I want to emphasize the variability of rational behavior from primitive times to our own. Even for Durkheim, who distinguished his views from those of Lévy-Bruhl, primitives were neither more nor less rational than moderns: they were more or less rational depending on the context. Sacrifice was not *made into* a rational science at the turn of the century. Rather, there was a recognition (on the part of authors like Hubert and Mauss, Robertson Smith, Durkheim) of the rational system that sacrifice *had always been*.

In turn-of-the-century America, sacrifice was bound up with modernist conceptions of interdependence, which view society as a (sometimes) bewildering web of relatedness. From such a perspective, the power of knowing, the capacity for clarity, is transferred from the gods to society in general, and to social scientific experts in particular. These views are typical of functionalist thinking, which manifested, especially at this early stage, a strong tinge of spirituality, bordering on superstition. An interdependent world was a dangerous place.[3] According to Thomas Haskell, modern intellectuals became increasingly aware of inhabiting a "global" social network that established interdependencies among "strangers" who would "never encounter each other . . . face to face." This principle seems fundamentally opposed to Weber's critique of rationalization, where the complaint concerns the reductiveness of modern life, the prevailing preoccupation with minutiae. "Our greatest art," Weber writes, "is intimate and not monumental." Yet here too, depersonalization and remoteness are key: the individual or phenomenon is shrunken to its smallest possible dimensions in order to identify its most uniform attributes. These attributes in turn facilitate ease of transmission. Georg Simmel's "non-social imponderables"—small idiosyncrasies of belief and character—have no place in a modern bureaucracy, which, in Weberian terms, aims to know as little as possible about those organized within its framework.[4]

These circumstances, in the minds of many who adhered to functionalist ideas at this time, contributed to a general draining of social vitality. Devitalization was a consequence of declining faith in the potential for causal prediction, the feeling that those things that most affected society were also most immune to human understanding and control.[5] The same functionalist principles could also foster a more positive outlook: a view of society as awesomely integrated and stable. Fredric Jameson has characterized this classic functionalist disposition as "a vested interest in Being." Jameson's choice of phrase is far from arbitrary, given his subject—in this instance, Max Weber's problem of faith.[6] "Vested" interests is suggestive of priestly endeavors, while the main ontological question pertains to God. The holiness of the social whole in functionalist conceptions is consistent with descriptions of the Calvinist-Protestant Deity: all-powerful, far removed from human insight and powers of persuasion, His acts everywhere felt and nowhere apparent. To grasp the role of functionalism as a secular religion is to understand how society could itself have been conceived as an entity that required sacrifices, with its own cast of groups prepared to shoulder this spiritual burden.[7]

My reference to the Protestant God raises an important question about the relationship between the concept of sacrifice and Protestant ascetic ideals of self-denial. While these two paradigms share broad resemblances, I believe that they are ultimately quite distinct. Sacrifice is properly understood as a collective ritual, expressing a sense of group risks and benefits, and addressed to higher powers on the group's behalf. I find it revealing that William James, whose *Varieties of Religious Experience* (1902) generated a great deal of interest at this time, had virtually nothing to say about sacrifice, in marked contrast to many contemporaries. In one brief paragraph toward the end of his book, James admits that the subject of sacrifice is a "most essential" element in "most books on religion," and then goes on to make short work of it. James's indifference to sacrifice has much to do with the overriding focus of his study: his decision to be "individualistic throughout." "Religion," in James's view, occupies "herself with personal destinies."[8]

Sacrifice, in contrast, impels the analyst to ask "institutional" rather than "individual" questions.[9] This is different from ideals of self-denial that focus mainly on what isolated individuals must give up in order to gain spiritual efficacy. There is a definite strain of optimism in asceticism: renunciation is a positive good, strengthening and supporting the self. At the same time, asceticism is an act of disembodiment. The principle of exchange or reciprocity, if present at all, is barely perceptible. The ascetic enterprise is self-sufficient. The beginning, middle, and end of spiritualization is the individual whose body becomes a text for the inscription of trial and bliss. This excruciatingly individualized focus is a diminishment in its own right: the borders drawn so closely around the suffering self are reflected in the strict limits placed on human appetite. Sacrifice is less direct and more unpredictable, in keeping with its wider range of application and benefit. It is also more mutable. One could say that nothing in sacrifice is what it appears to be. Surrendering becomes an occasion for communal celebration; powerlessness becomes a form of control; fear becomes hope; the profane becomes sacred; innocents are killed and the guilty are allowed to live. Victor Turner has even suggested that sacrifice has a "certain generosity" (198).

Yet when we are made to confront the specifics of blood sacrifice, a different order of judgment is introduced. When sacrificial destruction is seen as the expression of a particular politics, in which whole groups are categorized as expendable while others are designated as beneficiaries, the more generous aspects of the rite tend to disappear. No matter how fully camouflaged it is by a bureaucratized role in a modern system of exchange, regardless of the context in which it appears, sacrificial thinking invariably reduces at some point to its fundamental identification with ritual violence. To invoke the word "sacrifice" at the turn of the century in particular was to call up a familiar but disturbing constellation of events, available in textual form through the narrative record of a biblical past and through ethnographic accounts of a primitive present. To invoke the word was to commit oneself to solemnity. In this context, sacrifice implied spirituality bordering on peril.

The play of the word "sacrifice" throughout Georg Simmel's critical analysis of economic exchange (1900) provides an exemplary case of this fused potential. "The detour required to attain certain things," he writes, "is often the occasion, often the cause as well, of perceiving them as values." He continues, "if we observe which human achievements attain to the highest honors and evaluations, we find them always to be those which manifest, or at least appear to manifest, the most depth, the most exertion, the most persistent concentration of the whole being—which is to say the most self-denial, sacrifice of all that is subsidiary, and devotion of the subjective to the objective ideal."[10] Notice, first, Simmel's immediate replacement of "self-denial" with "sacrifice." Simmel not only seems to prefer the sound of the word (which is further indicated by its repetition throughout the essay), but he seems intent on emphasizing that he has selected "sacrifice" over "self-denial." Though they might be understood, conventionally, as synonymous, the fact that he uses one consistently over the other confirms his desire to keep them separate. He appears to want his readers to know that he is talking about reciprocal, murderous losses, rather than those of a more self-sustaining kind. Notice, next, what is happening with the word "detour" in the first sentence, where it stands in, or substitutes, for the word "sacrifice." Here the distance between signifier and signified collapses, as detour performs its literal meaning through the role that it plays in Simmel's argument. A detour can be an "evasion" from what is expected, or a "turn[ing] from the original meaning," in this instance, sacrifice. His rhetoric, in other words, can be seen to enact a crucial feature of the sacrificial process by offering up this self-proclaimed substitution. The effect of this rich encoding is an implicit conjunction of sacrifice and subterfuge. Simmel may be stressing the covert nature of sacrificial destructiveness, as a way of exposing the even more covertly malign effects of a modern exchange system. The poetical quality of Simmel's apprehension raises some critical questions about the relationship between social scientific and literary uses of sacrifice. Despite the variations among different approaches, social scientists tend to use sacrifice in two ways. It can be part of a rhetorical arsenal, as in Simmel's notion of sacrificial exchange or in the idea of "intellectual sacrifice" common to Weber and Durkheim. Or it can be understood as an objective manifestation of a given culture's spiritual functions, as in *Sacrifice* (1898) by Mauss and Hubert, or in *The Elementary Forms of the Religious Life* (1916) by Durkheim. Sacrifice for all of these social scientists is less a point of affliction to be dramatized or questioned than a recognizable phenomenon that evokes a predictable set of associations or inspires rational explanation.

These predictable associations were most often human ones. There was a marked tendency in social theoretical treatments of the time (particularly by Americans) to humanize sacrifice. One example of this type of humanization was the idea of "the costs of social progress." In the words of *AJS* editor Charles Ellwood, "Progress everywhere waits on death—the death of the inferior individual—and nowhere more so than in racial problems."[11] Ellwood's statement was unusually blatant. Few would have cast the sacrificed as so deserving of their fate. More often, those who recognized the implications of their claims assumed an apologetic air. Nathaniel Shaler, for example, professed sadness over the anticipated disappearance of African Americans, though he welcomed the unimpeded advance of human sympathy he predicted in its wake. Edward Ross mourned the sacrifice of the aggressive Aryan spirit, deftly dissociated from the Aryan body, to the necessities of a modern social order. And the economist Simon Patten's list of definitive exclusions and antipathies appears to have been representative of the sacrificial sentiments that pervaded social science in 1895. "Each class or section of the nation," he writes, "is becoming conscious of an opposition between its standards and the activities and tendencies of some less developed class. The South has its negro, the city has its slums. . . . Everyone is beginning to differentiate those with proper qualifications for citizenship from some class or classes which he wishes to restrain or to exclude from society."[12] Patten's observation seems a perfect redaction of the process by which, as René Girard observes, "whole categories of human beings" are "systematically reserved for sacrificial purposes in order to protect other categories."

In terms that serve to gloss Patten's remarks, Girard characterizes sacrifice as controlled or rationalized violence, designed to preclude further violence. This is effected in two ways. By selecting a sacrificial victim who is innocent, society avoids the risk of contamination by violence. And by substituting an innocent victim drawn from groups loosely, if at all, integrated into the social order, society protects itself from the likelihood of vengeance. Girard goes on to describe sacrificial violence in biologically determinist terms that are inconsistent with his circumscribed and brilliantly woven theory of surrogacy. At times his descriptions call to mind romantic characterizations of the sublime. Vengeance is a "raging hunger," or a "violence too long held in check" and threatening to "overflow its bounds." Girard concludes his study with the hope that the "essential violence" that has long enveloped Western society, will finally be "expose[d] to the light of reason."[13] Girard's illuminating theory could profit from some exposure to the light of history: in this case, a turn-of-the-century context in which sacrificial schemes are fundamental to definitions of society. Considered historically, the identities of sacrificial victims appear even less arbitrary and playful than the already suspicious Girard presumes.

From this historical perspective, sacrificial violence looks positively staid and middle class. This is in contrast to the aristocratic stamp Girard gives it. The middle classes were heavily invested in sacrificial rhetoric. But they were not necessarily—in fact, they were rarely—the group actually making the sacrifice, or experiencing any absolute deprivation. Their mission was to *rationalize* sacrifice. The groups consistently identified with sacrifice in turn-of-the-century America were those perceived as politically threatening. Sacrifice, in this particular time and place, was an elaborate spiritual balancing act: favor for one group required the suppression or elimination of another, usually conceived as debilitated or unstable. This is captured in key literary examples. Melville's common sailors (and their diabolical doubles, the immigrants), James's awkward females, and Du Bois's Black folk were groups rife with political tension for the Anglo-American middle classes. The social statuses of these groups can be specified beyond their identification as classically dispossessed *pharmakos* populations. They represent people in process (in Van Gennep's ritualized sense of the term), whose evolving identities provoke crises about social stability and threaten changes resisted by society.[14] The human victims designated by these categories (Billy Budd, Nanda Brookenham, Burghardt Du Bois) are childlike (or children themselves), their innocence magnified by their sacrifice. But the constituencies they represent are demonic and threatening (the working-class hordes, modern women, emancipated Blacks). Middle-class society rationalized a quasi-sacred ideology of sacrifice in an era of abundance by identifying its victims as groups uniquely worthy of sacrificial treatment. When sociologists like James Williams (*An American Town* [1901]) lamented the social decline initiated by the evasion of properly sacrificial behavior, they were deliberately assuming a ministerial posture and, more indirectly, a God-like ability to determine human life chances. Williams confirmed his discipline's spiritual function, by exhorting colleagues to frame "a sociology which ministers can preach, teachers teach, and the people talk about and believe in."[15]

At the point of the discipline's modern prescription and institutionalization, the ties between sociological formulations and the religious belief they were in some sense designed to supplant were pronounced. In time, these ties became more muted, receding into specific (often minor) concentrations within sociology or identified increasingly with other social sciences, such as anthropology, where religion remained a primary research area. Functionalism, which is commonly recognized as a foundational theory for early sociology, can be understood as spiritually—even superstitiously—tinged. Alvin Gouldner, as we have seen, went so far as to label it a "piety." He derived his characterization from the double-edged, near-contradictory aims of sociology as conceived by a Comtean tradition. While sociologists wanted to improve and influence society, they also sought to distance it. Their dilemma, Gouldner believes, was resolved in part by investing society with a sacred aura. Society became the religion of humanity and sociology the priesthood that fostered devotion to the social whole. This is all familiar enough. Its interest, from my perspective, lies in the susceptibility of this utilitarian creed to sacrificial thinking. In his "non-functionalist manifesto," *Central Problems in Social Theory*, Anthony Giddens discovers a far greater pervasion of functionalism than suggested by Gouldner's island of piety. Within the terms of Giddens's broad-based polemic, any theory that identifies a social system with needs, operating independently of the social actors in it, can be categorized as functionalist. The category applies as readily to Marxist models of social reproduction as to Durkheimian conceptions of the social organism. Giddens counters with his own sociological rule: all social action is knowledgeable, while change is inherent in all forms of social reproduction.[16]

Change is the key word. Like sacrifice, functionalism (at least in its non-Marxist versions) is an ideology that exploits change in order to ensure stability and permanence. It posits a hauntingly stilled world, one that can withstand the inevitable transition from enchantment to disenchantment.[17] Weber's elegant formulation is at the center of Fredric Jameson's exploratory treatment of his work. Jameson emphasizes Weber's sense of spiritual diminishment under rationalization and employs psychoanalytic method to situate that sense within the bourgeois family of the late nineteenth century. In contrast to Gouldner, who locates Weber's immunity to functionalist thought in his preoccupation with the listlessness and despair of bureaucratic society, Jameson considers these preoccupations the route to Weber's functionalism. For the Weber of the "Science as Vocation" essay, "the various and unrelated zones and dimensions into which the individual life of a man is shattered in the modern world and which make of the process of living a kind of random sacrificing, now to public, now to private deities of all shapes and conceptions," have the effect of "dividing the realm of *Realpolitik* . . . from the preoccupations of ethics." Such a dilemma is as appropriate to "the great realistic novelists" as to the Weberian sociologist engaged in "the functional study of society."[18] The response to this demand for sacrifice is a condition equivalent to religious faith itself, "a kind of aesthetic vested interest in Being," or an "ontological commitment to the massive density of social being and experience."

This particular formulation of "ontological commitment," however, is from Jameson's challenge to Americanist New Historicism, written twenty years later. Fundamental to the latter critique is the claim that this method marks "a return to immanence," the abandonment of a structuralist method that had facilitated "the enlargement of the object and the possibility of establishing a whole range of new relationships between materials of diverse kinds."[19] Abandoning *structure*, Jameson implies, these New Historicists implicitly embrace *function*. In Jameson's treatment, Americanist New Historicism is made to appear as a species of Weberian functionalism. This seems quite plausible, if we recognize the roots of Americanist New Historicism in a Foucaultian version of sociological functionalism. It is striking how readily one hears echoes of Durkheim on the role of morality while reading Foucault on ideology.[20] Jameson's reading of New Historicism is likewise consistent with his earlier treatment of Weber. Consider Jameson's wonder over a New Historicist economics that sidesteps Marx. The result is "'a montage of historical attractions' . . . in which extreme theoretical energy is captured and deployed, but repressed by a valorization of immanence and nominalism." Then there is New Historicism on the market: an "absent common structure . . . some all-encompassing fatality," which parallels Weber on "rationalization" as "a kind of impending doom."[21] I want to make clear that Jameson's sustained response to Americanist New Historicism displays a respect for its interpretive power, which I share.

If the affinities between these two analyses are as marked as I am suggesting, there may be a strategic reason why Jameson himself stops short of the comparison. For the shared pieties of Weberian functionalism and Americanist New Historicism do yield quite distinct descriptions of modern social reality, a matter having as much to do with tone and attitude as with ultimate premises. Jameson's use of Eisenstein to characterize the

New Historicist sense of context—"montage of historical attractions"—suggests the type of high spirits generated by an amusement park: we should enjoy our historical high while it lasts but refrain from claiming any *permanent* transcendence. Nor should we really want to know too much about what thrills us. Nothing could be further from the gravity of Weber, even if it accords with Jameson's characterization of him as "the intellectual specialist, who knows the *how* so well that he comes to doubt the *why*." But Weber never stops insisting, in the tones of doomsday prophecy, that progress is costly. Indeed, the New Historicist perspective seems more consistent with another turn-of-the-century vision, especially identified with the United States: an optimistic ideal of consumer fulfillment (articulated in works such as Simon Patten's *The Basis for a New Civilization*) that portrayed sacrifice as a dated ideology. Anticipating the attacks on Americanist New Historicism, the critique of this consumptive ideal emphasized how it overlooked the ongoing deprivations and inequities of a consumer society.[22]

Jameson glosses these past and present critiques in what is perhaps the largest point of *Postmodernism*. In a section entitled "Demographies of the Postmodern," Jameson notes an overriding "impression" of "the West . . . that without much warning and unexpectedly it now confronts a range of genuine individual and collective subjects who were not there before." This is precisely, it seems to me, the situation that confronts social analysts at the turn of the century. Though this situation was most pronounced in the United States, we should recall that Weber recognized the American dilemma of social heterogeneity on his 1904 visit in part because it corresponded to parallel, though more muted, spectacles in his native Germany. The unique contribution of sociological method, as represented by the work of Weber, was its blending of demographic apprehensions and functionalist solutions into a form of social spirituality. This is consistent with one of the most suggestive insights that Jameson draws from Weber: the idea that religion's decline as an *end* value actually catalyzed its worldwide extension. "Calvin did not desacralize the world," Jameson writes, paraphrasing Weber, "he turned the *entire* world into a monastery."[23] Weber's classic dialectical formulation suggests that the loss of something contributes to its intensification. It is this principle that lies at the heart of the sacrificial rhetoric of early sociology. The sections that follow will move from milder to more dramatic examples of sacrificial rhetoric and action, leading up to a consideration of classic interpretations of sacrificial rites that began appearing during this period. These final explicit treatments, by Robertson Smith, E. B. Tylor, James Frazer, and Mauss and Hubert, will take us to some literary examples, which will serve to introduce the book's subsequent chapters.

Sacrificial Detours in Simmel and Others

Given the importance of sacrifice for Simmel's central theory of exchange, it's not surprising to find the concept mentioned in nearly all of his writings. Indeed, wherever Simmel's principle of exchange is operating, and there are very few places where it isn't, the concept of sacrifice is bound to figure prominently. I want to consider briefly, in turn, Simmel's reading of fashion as a process of equalization and prostitution as a negation of it; his reading of the miser as social type; and, finally, his understanding of how a modern society constructs poverty as an essential status. Exchange, according to Simmel, is implicit in all human action, including the actions of isolated individuals. The behavior of Robinson Crusoe on his island is no different from that of any participant in an elaborated common market. Exchange is basic to human socialization, and sacrificial thinking is fundamental to it, impressed on our minds like the undulation of ocean waves—"a continuous alternation of profit and loss, an ebbing and flowing of the contents of life."[24] Variation is essential, necessary to the system. The dynamic is permanent, but there must be a constant renewal of objects, statuses, human beings themselves. Simmel's argument unfolds like a shifting body of associations, akin to a succession of ripples made by a stone thrown into a pond. The concept of sacrifice is the stone that activates the pond of exchange. Every ripple in the argument evolves from the idea that sacrifice is "the condition of all value" (49). Were all of life's requirements satisfied, Simmel speculates, "so that at no point was sacrifice involved, men would simply not have *economic* activity, any more than do birds or fish or the denizens of fairyland" (54). There is no image better suited to Simmel's point than fishes and fairies: without sacrifice there would be no society as known.

In his essay on the poor, Simmel claims an unmistakable continuity between the actions of the first Christian whose "sacrifice" in the form of alms signified his salvation and the modern social order that seeks to "mitigate certain extreme manifestations of social differentiation, so that the social structure may continue to be based on this differentiation."[25] The New Testament exchange of alms for salvation, like a modern economy where assistance sustains the status quo, is focused on the giver. According to Simmel, "poverty is a unique sociological" phenomenon, determined, not by some absolute criterion of deprivation, but "by the fact that others—individuals, associations, communities—attempt to correct this condition" (178). Simmel doesn't make the point as forcefully as Du Bois, who argues that society *needs* the poor in order to define positive value and relative success. But the claim is implicit in everything Simmel has to say about poverty. Though we have to resist confining all of Simmel's thought to a single sacrificial solution, it's telling that even fashion fulfills the function of "compensation" and "balance." Fashion, like poverty, is structured by a systemic need for "the uniformity and the change of the contents of life." Women's *lack* of social effect stimulates their appetite for fashion, with its illusory promise of individuation. "Therefore, the emanicipated woman of the present . . . lays particular stress on her indifference to fashion."[26] Simmel regards fashion as a manipulative industry, essential to the qualification of newfound middle-class freedoms. Simmel's language here is nearly identical to his description of exchange, where the "sacrifice" made for any object "forms the limit . . . to which the value of the object being given away can rise." In fashion, "the moment of acquired height marks the beginning of decline" (318). In both cases, what is really being sacrificed is the potential for absolutes.

The same is true of the miser, who might be conceived as the hero of Simmel's essays, a heroism defined by his resistance to the ebb and flow of capitalist equilibrium. The ultimate aesthete, Simmel's miser finds "satisfaction in the complete possession of a potentiality with no thought whatsoever about its realization."[27] And yet, when the miser's tendencies are seen in conjunction with Simmel's analysis of prostitution, they take on a far less heroic cast. Though his methods are the opposite of the prostitute's, the consequences of his actions are exactly the same. If the miser defies exchange by withholding himself from its processes, the prostitute and her customer embrace its logic so fully that its formal structure disappears. The effect of prostitution is the denaturing of exchange: exchange becomes a perversion, or "trick" version of itself. Because the actors in the exchange have themselves become the matter that is exchanged, have assumed, in Simmel's words, "the status of mere means," the *meaning* of exchange is obliterated.[28] There is no one there (whether beneficiary or recipient) to make the requisite sacrifice.

It's revealing that Simmel doesn't go on to read prostitution as a necessary residue of exchange, an essential relief that foregrounds, invaluably, the beneficial sacrifices normally entailed. He may intend this implicitly. Or we may have reached the endpoint of Simmel's logic, where rational analysis meets, and becomes, belief. The basic components of morality and religion are all present in Simmel's theory of sacrificial exchange. I think it is fair to say that Simmel is committed to the value of balances in modern life, not from a sense of loss, but from a sense of plenitude and contentment with modernity. Sacrifice is a loaded term for Simmel, and he uses it carefully, sparingly, not because he fears it, but because he respects it. Simmel emphasizes the rational dynamics of sacrificial exchange: exchange is a voluntary relation whose purpose is the construction of value. What remains distinctive about Simmel's functionalist analyses, especially seen in conjunction with those of his fellow sociologists, is that there is, in fact, so little demoralization. There is none of Weber's fatalism, nor is there much of Durkheim's preoccupation with compulsion and coercion. In the face of these interpretations, Simmel's work seems a beacon of optimism, a testament of faith in human rationality and independence.

Durkheim is ever aware of potential disruptions to the delicate system of checks and balances called "society." It may seem difficult to imagine how a concept that assumes such stature as a source of stability in his argument can be at all precarious. From the beginning of the famous chapter 5 of *Suicide*, which advances Durkheim's theory of anomie, we are made aware of the category's essential equilibrating function. Society is defined as both productive of inequality and as the utmost in constraint. It is in the nature of society to distribute its revenue unequally. The real work of any social logic, Durkheim suggests, is to convince society's members that their lot is just. Traditional society saw "birth as the almost exclusive principle of social classification"; modern society recognizes only "hereditary fortune and merit."[29] As the role of inherited wealth continues to decline, there will be less need for social regulation. Without doubt, however, the rule of collective authority requires "of one or another group of men, usually of all, sacrifices and concessions in the name of the public interest" (251). Durkheim's willingness, however qualified, to concede the inequality of sacrifice is consistent with the larger claim that society's inevitable progressiveness is always balanced against a tendency toward equilibrium. On the one hand there is social vitality; on the other, social death. But one could argue that Durkheim's moral is that both sides lead to the same dead end. "Poverty protects against suicide because it is a restraint in itself," he writes in a famous postulate. "The less limited one feels, the more intolerable all limitation appears" (254). As a protection in itself, poverty checks the potentially infinite and destructive spiral of human desire.

The strongly spiritualized, even superstitious overtones in Durkheim's theory of anomie have not escaped the attention of readers. In what way, strictly speaking, could "poverty" be understood to "protect"? And what might be the source of this protective obligation? Durkheim's image recalls Robertson Smith's Semitic priests arrayed in the sacrificial skins of their victims. In these ceremonies, Smith notes, the skin is believed to possess "the force of a charm." Such observances, he concludes, predominated "at the stage of religious development in which the god, his worshippers, and the victim were all members of one kindred."[30] Durkheim here corroborates religious explanations that stress the moral advantages of poverty and then turns to the subject of spiritual diminishment in modern life. Religion has been replaced, he argues, by "the appetites . . . [now] freed of any limiting authority. By sanctifying them, so to speak, this apotheosis of well-being has placed them above all human law. Their restraint seems like a sort of sacrilege" (255). Appetite, thus sanctified, assumes greater and greater importance in Durkheim's theory, becoming a synonym for anomie, as well as a symbol for the spiritual decline its uncontained rule helps to bring about.

Consider how this is prepared for by the following references: the workman who feels that he has not received "his desserts" (250); the unrestrained "appetites" (in Greece and Rome) that led to "revolt" (251); the majority fueled by the promise of an ever "richer prize" (253). The disembodied figure of Durkheim himself is relevant here: "this face and this body of an ascetic . . . a voice animated by an ardent faith that in this heir of the prophets burned with the desire to forge and temper the conviction of listeners." This spiritualized reading (by his disciples) of Durkheim's physique is echoed in one of the few jokes the austere scholar ever indulged in publicly: his punning allusion to the combined secular and sacred allegiances of the professorial "chaire" (which means an academic office as well as a church pulpit).[31] Durkheim's preoccupation with the category of appetite seems to have been consistently informed by his apprehension of a toppled, but still seductive, religious order in which appetite is carefully ritualized and regulated. Just as every consumptive act in a society ruled by the commensal meal of the ancient Semites refers to this sacrificial rite, appetites and eating patterns for this descendant of orthodox Judaism express a fully elaborated and collectivized spiritual condition. In a modern society where appetite has assumed a (perverse) sanctity of its own, the ideal state is deprivation or hunger. Hence, the Durkheimian maxim: poverty protects.

In keeping with this, oblatory sacrifice (as opposed to Robertson Smith's festive meal) becomes the preferred rite of Durkheim's model community and its successful agents, those most suited to limit and renunciation. Durkheim's anticipation of modern appetite at its most unaccommodated—the culturewide propensity toward suicide—brings him to some surprising conclusions. Consider, for example, his discussion of marriage, or, more specifically, marriage's reversal, divorce. Durkheim's theory was judged remarkable, not least of all for its conclusion that men need marriage and women don't. Marriage, according to Durkheim, is not a dynamic relationship between two differently socialized individuals, but an absolute exchange, one that is always beneficial to men and either neutral or harmful to women. Because women are "naturally limited," he argues, they don't need the conjugal bond (272). Given the terms that have dominated this chapter—appetite, constraint, renunciation—it's hardly surprising that Durkheim comes to reflect explicitly at its end upon sacrifice. It is conventionally assumed, he writes, that marriage requires "a sacrifice made by man of his polygamous instincts," an act through which the beneficiary, the woman, finds security. On the contrary, it is the man who is tormented by the excessive freedoms of the unmarried life, freedoms that dispose him to greater levels of suicide than his married counterparts. It is finally the woman from whom the "sacrifice" required by the exchange is exacted

(275–76). The bad news is that men are dependent on marriage in the abstract and women in the flesh. The good news is that marriage restores women to their traditional sacrificial role, a fact that is confirmed by a decidedly modern variation on marriage: divorce.

No sociological theorist is more convinced than Durkheim of the dangers posed by appetites that exceed a functional equilibrium. Nor is any sociological theorist more unequivocal about the benefits issuing from a monolithic society that imposes a stranglehold upon those appetites. Durkheim himself acknowledged Robertson Smith's influence on his post-1895 writings, and I would argue that we can see the impact of Smith's reading of sacrifice, the importance of the ritual meal in particular, throughout chapter 5 of *Suicide*. But there is little direct evidence that Durkheim absorbed the whole of Smith's theory, in particular, as suggested by the passage on "skins," the idea that sacrificial protections weaken appreciably as society becomes more heterogeneous. It took an American sociologist especially aware of how modern social life threatened kinship to make that connection. In Franklin Giddings's *The Principles of Sociology*, the historical underpinnings of sacrificial protections are brought into the foreground of the analysis.

Giddings, a reader of Durkheim and Robertson Smith, begins his section on "the costs of progress with a classic formulation of the equilibrium principle. "Material and intellectual progress is not an unmixed good," he announces in tones of foreboding; "these costs of progress are for the most part borne vicariously. The beneficiaries of new methods or of new arrangements themselves rarely suffer the distress."[32] A page later, Giddings describes rising suicide and divorce rates as expressions of social vitality, in terms reminiscent of Durkheim and drawn from the same statistics (Morselli on Italy and Dewey on New England). Citing new pressures on the New England farmer, the variations and improvements demanded by modern living—even his clothing must be "in style"—Giddings notes that rising expectations threaten "mental balance" (348–49). Giddings's theories illustrate how widespread the theory of anomie was in the years leading up to the 1897 publication of *Suicide* (Durkheim had himself tested the theory in *The Division of Labor* [1893] and *The Rules of Sociological Method* [1895]). Most prominent in Giddings's analysis is the recognition of the human costs of progress and his consequent willingness to admit qualifications into the principle of laissez-faire. On the one hand, Giddings holds fast to the inevitability, indeed the value, of social and economic inequities. On the other, he argues that the immature and degenerate require assistance—above all, so as not to destroy the delicate balance of the social order. Giddings shares Durkheim's awareness of the fact that religious values and, specifically, notions of appropriate sacrifices have altered considerably in the modern era. The traditional or "ethical" family, he notes,

SACRIFICIAL ARTS AND SCIENCES

"sacrificed the inclinations of individuals"; the modern or "romantic" family "has sacrificed patrimony and tradition," even "children" (352).

Like his European colleagues, Giddings believes that the essential equilibrium of social life requires certain measures of privilege and deprivation, as real on a societal level as the losses and gains that accrue in a family, or in a single human body. We will have occasion to consider Giddings's more direct account of sacrificial rites. What makes this initial analysis especially valuable, I think, is the way it anticipates—largely unconsciously, I believe—a subsequent discussion of more brutal forms of sacrificial action. The same contrast, between more and less explicit invocations of sacrificial rhetoric, appears in the work of another prominent American sociologist, E. A. Ross. In Ross's case, the split falls between two books: his orthodox sociological study, *Social Control* (1901), and the more popular *Sin and Society* (1907). In the first study, Ross's understanding of progress, like Giddings's, is founded in the necessity of sacrifice, the securing of benefits from losses; the natural social equilibrium exacts payment from one part of the system for expenditures in another. At the beginning of his study, Ross highlights approvingly "the sacrificing of one corps of an army to save the rest," and at the end, he worries about the likely decay of the American character, now sacrificed to modernization. As with Giddings, Ross's sense of the volatility of sacrifice is more apparent in other places, where he betrays convictions of its persisting spiritual force.

The sacrificial rhetoric I have been tracing from Simmel through Durkheim and Giddings was, for the most part, indirect. Few contemporary analysts sought or achieved a theoretical perspective on this rhetoric— whether that meant identifying its antecedents or confronting how the category and its assumptions expressed contemporary social tensions and conflict. Simon Patten's commentary on the strangely humanized binomialism of modern capitalist life appears the closest that social scientific rationalism came to apprehending the wider social and political implications of functionalism. There were other occasional glimmers. F. H. Giddings's student John Franklin Crowell, for instance, argued that society was a struggle for survival among different types, an argument that presumed the natural disappearance of entire categories of human beings. But Crowell's compendium of "postulates," "axioms," and "principles" was doggedly abstract, recounting in markedly dispassionate terms the human consequences of "typal conflict . . . conquest, toleration, or extinction."[33] Notice how the gentle term ("toleration") is bracketed (as if for safety) by the two martial alternatives ("conquest" and "extinction").

W.E.B. Du Bois was uniquely sensitive to functionalist reasoning. *The Philadelphia Negro* is filled with examples that confirm White attempts to bring all Negroes into conformity with a pathological (and eminently expendable) type. One of these critiques appeared in a retrospective on the writing of *The Philadelphia Negro*. Here, Du Bois christened functionalism "the mud-sill theory of society," and went on to argue (in keeping with Simmel's "construction of poverty" theory) that the modern West not only needs but invents states of deprivation. This, according to Du Bois, is its perverse ideological condition: the need to set plenitude and success against loss and degradation. Human beings don't have to think this way, but social mindsets of this kind are at least as old as the race philosophies of the late eighteenth century. "Civilization," Du Bois writes, "not only permitted but must have the poor, the diseased, the wretched, the criminal upon which to build its temples of light."[34] This definition comes in the wake of a discussion of Hitlerian fascism, which represents for Du Bois yet another variation on mud-sill rationalism.

In his analysis of Baudelaire's story "Counterfeit Money," Jacques Derrida pauses to specify what he labels subsequently *"the economy of alms."* Derrida's interpretation is helpful for pinpointing the particular claims of Simmel and Du Bois. "The beggar has a regular activity, ordered by codes, rites, sociotopological necessities. . . . The beggar's estate has often been considered—and sometimes designated in a barely metaphoric fashion—as a profession, a status, or a social function. . . . The beggar keeps the outside within and assures an identity by exclusion, the exception made (*fors*) for an interior closure or cleft." The purpose of alms in this account is explicitly sacrificial, which is to say, "regulatory." Derrida distinguishes sacrifice, a form of social control, from the *"phenomenon of gift,"* which he associates with "chance." The exchange is marked as a functional reciprocity or reparation by the protagonist's painstaking preparations: he "carefully separated his change" before leaving the tobacco shop (according to his companion it is "a singularly minute distribution!").[35] Baudelaire's intriguing tale of counterfeit alms is finally closer to Simmel's exchange principle than to Du Bois's critique of it. The depth of that indictment was anticipated by only one other thinker, Friedrich Nietzsche, in *The Genealogy of Morals* (1887).

More than Schopenhauer, his contemporary, or Simmel, his descendant, Nietzsche deserves to be called the philosopher of sacrifice. Though Nietzsche's philosophical bias disposes him toward a universalism that differs considerably from the sociological theories we have been tracing, his largest concern in the *Genealogy* is the endurance of human values: what has changed and what has remained the same. "Wherever on earth solemnity, seriousness, mystery, and gloomy coloring still distinguish the life of man and a people, something of the terror that formerly attended all promises, pledges, and vows on earth is *still effective*: the past, the longest, deepest and sternest past, breathes upon us and rises up in us whenever we become 'serious.' Man could never do without blood, torture, and sacrifices, when he felt the need to create a memory for himself."[36] Nietzsche's claim for the interdependence of pain and memory extends to the principle of economy. Western society, he suggests, foreshadowing Weber on the Protestant ethic of capitalism, has always read debt as guilt. Nietzsche notes that the root of the word for guilt in German is "the very material concept" of debt (62–63). The real issue, he explains, is "equivalence," the idea that every injury, every loss, can be repaired, "even if only through the *pain* of the culprit" (63). Compensation becomes "a title to cruelty," cruelty becomes "pleasure" in part because it is "recompense" (64–65).

This pathological drive, in Nietzsche's view, dominates Western culture. He goes on to enumerate its different forms: the individual members of a community are debtors in relationship to the community as a whole; a worldwide "'advance' can even be measured by the mass of things that had to be sacrificed to it"; the idea of a collective tribal indebtedness to "the sacrifices" of the ancestors (71, 78, 89). This final form of indebtedness is ongoing, since the ancestors "never cease, in their continued existence as powerful spirits." Sometimes "a wholesale sacrifice, something tremendous" is required: "the notorious sacrifice of the first-born," for instance (89). So powerful is this idea that every misfortune is actually greeted with relief, since it "*diminishes* fear" of the ancestral spirits. The notion of man's guilty indebtedness persists beyond the organization of communities on the basis of blood relationship. It culminates in the image of Christ, "the maximum God" who takes unto himself mankind's debt. In Nietzsche's paraphrase, "the creditor sacrifices himself for his debtor, out of *love*" (90, 92). Nietzsche seems beside himself with the paradoxical absurdity of this gesture. But he speculates that the absurdity of this Christian drama may be just what is needed to release mankind, once and for all, from the base principle of exchange.

What is remembered most often about Nietzsche's discussion of sacrifice in the *Genealogy* is the ethnic inflection he gives it. "Priestly vengefulness" is an outgrowth of Jewish life. Jews are "that priestly people" who perfected the "priestly form" of life, a form that is "*essentially dangerous*" but "interesting." Because of the Jews, the human soul acquired "*depth*" and "*evil*" (33). It also acquired the power of contradiction and metamorphosis. It was the Jews who achieved the awesome transvaluation of values: who transformed impotence, wretchedness, and suffering into blessedness and even love. Nietzsche's incontrovertible claim is that we no longer recognize the impact of this morality because "it—has been victorious." Christianity, he argues, bought the "bait" of this Jewish priesthood. For the ultimate act of its "secret black art" is to "deny the real instrument of its revenge . . . and nail it to the cross" (34–35). Nietzsche emphasizes the spiritual point: Jews have triumphed through the imperceptible absorption of their creed by the Christianity that supposedly supplants it. But he sidesteps the historical point: Jews have been paying with their lives ever since the death of Christ. This does not make him an anti-Semite. It does, however, make his work as much a symptom as an analysis of the ethnic rivalries that lay behind a philosophy of sacrifice.

These rivalries were foregrounded dramatically in a contemporary study by Hermann L. Strack, *The Jew and Human Sacrifice* (1891). A German theologian, who subtitled his work "An Historical and Sociological Inquiry" and drew on many of the authors whose studies have special significance for this analysis (including Robertson Smith, Clay Trumbull, and James Frazer), Strack typifies the surprising affinities afforded by the subject of sacrifice. Strack's book is unusual in part because it seeks to defend Jews against precisely the charges leveled by Nietzsche and largely upheld by a vast international range of folk superstition, whose consequences he documents in bloody detail. Contrary to what is commonly believed, and periodically avenged (a parade of historical horrors is his record of vengeance), the Jewish people have never practiced human sacrifice. Strack supports his argument with a careful reading of Jewish law. But the sign that he remains overwhelmed by the controversial status of his claims is the striking disclaimer that prefaces them. "I here affirm that all my ancestors were of pure 'Christian-German' descent," Strack declares, anticipating charges that his conclusions are a product of "what the Rabbis had stuffed him with."[37] The literature on sacrifice never gets more visceral than this.[38]

"Tallow out of Cattle, Money out of Men": Sacrificial Economies in the Protestant Era

The kind of reasoning that required a loss for every gain, that saw every benefit in terms of its sacrificial return, had a biblical correlative that appeared especially captivating to literary authors and social scientists in this period of intense modernization and capitalist-industrial expansion. The story of the fall from static innocence into a world of action and consequence was replayed endlessly in contemporary realist and naturalist literature, which took the punitive themes of the biblical source to new extremes. The sins of Adam and Eve would be repaid by the endless torture (mental and physical) visited upon characters (and, by extension, readers) in these fictions. According to writers like Frank Norris and Gertrude Stein, human beings would exist for time eternal in a Calvinist gloom of debt. These writers seem to derive sadistic pleasure from detailing the predicaments of human beings in distress, which explains the irritation, even outrage they can inspire in readers. These narratives can be classified as pathologized retellings of the fall. All victories, advantages, good times, all pleasures, including sexual ones, are caught in the rounds of a sacrificial economy. In Norris and Stein, Simmel's worst nightmare has become the commonplace.

One could argue that these fictions contain "visions of excess." It is possible to imagine any of their characters cutting off an ear in the manner of Vincent Van Gogh and mailing it to a chimerical love object. Georges Bataille labels such acts "sacrificial mutilation" and believes that their effect is a liberation from "polite society," rather than a confirmation of it. I invoke Bataille's paradigm as a revealing counterpoint, because I find the sacrificial worlds of Norris and Stein ultimately quite contained.[39] They may be best described as disenchanted, in Weber's eloquent sense of the term. *McTeague* opens on a forsaken Sunday—the Lord's Day as an occasion for indulging base appetite. The "gilt cage" of the protagonist's canary (a contrast to Weber's "iron" one) may suggest some susceptibility to material pleasure. But it is no less symbolic of human entrapment in the modern age. Norris or Stein would have appreciated Weber's image for faith, a "ghost" that "prowls about in our lives." And they share a Weberian nostalgia for lost force. According to all three, entropy—the draining of social vitality and passion—is a greater danger than its opposite, violence or apocalypse.

Weber's much studied attitude toward faith has been understood as the sublimated response of a rationalist who has discovered himself to be "religiously unmusical." The complexity of Weber's position becomes more apparent when compared with other contemporary solutions to the trial of spirituality. Among Weber's scientific colleagues, were those who subscribed to Karl Pearson's claim, that religion's "true basis . . . may be the deification of the human mind and of its supremacy over matter." This would make scientists into "high priests," while those who failed to maintain the requisite objectivity would be "ministers in the devil's synagogue."[40] Pearson's bourgeois rationalism depends on oppositions and exclusions. Scientists are "priests" guarding the altar of objectivity from the desecrations of Jewish "devils." For Weber, it is not a matter of incorporation, where scientific rationality absorbs or saves an embattled faith. Weber tends to treat the question of religious belief as a wager or gamble that can never be won. He appears resigned to the impossibility of ever making "the intellectual sacrifice" required by the religious life. Yet he also seems embittered by the cost exacted on either side of the equation, whether the devotion that demands reason's denial or the reason that cannot support faith. Weber's preoccupation with the endurance of the religious perspective, especially as this pertains to the relationship between religion and science, has everything to do with the prominence of sacrificial rhetoric in his major writings. Nor is it accidental that he characterizes the religious struggle in explicitly sacrificial terms. The rite for Weber, as for many others, becomes a means for expressing fears about the fragile potency of belief in his time, and it helps him to articulate the persisting human need for protection in a still mysterious universe.

I noted earlier that Weber looked to the United States as a model for the process of modernization. American religion provided another critical referent for Weber. Gerth and Mills point out in their introduction to Weber's writings that the United States at the turn of the century was a model for the future, in part because Protestantism had its "greatest scope" here (17). The Protestant receptivity to secular ideals, among them voluntarism and materialism, fostered political as well as economic progress. This is the notorious Weberian confederation of Protestant religion and capitalist development. I introduce it in order to confine it from the outset, because the subject of sacrifice is a separate issue, despite some overlap between the two. One difference is that Weber's unification of Protestantism and capitalism presupposes a central role for religious ideals, a centrality that sacrificial rhetoric tends to put in doubt. Weber's sacrificial rhetoric is most accurately understood as a residue of his powerful conceptualization of Protestantism. It retains certain structural resemblances to Protestantism, while lacking its larger foundation.

Weber offers his own invaluable guide to the relationship between Protestantism and sacrifice: the portrait of Benjamin Franklin in *The Protestant Ethic*. Perhaps in recognition of Franklin's own penchant for one-liners, Weber resorts frequently to sound bites in attempting to capture the essence of Franklin's "clever and malicious philosophy." Among the most revealing of them is the maxim adapted from Ferdinand Kurnberger: "They make tallow out of cattle and money out of men."[41] What interests Weber about this creed is that it is a spiritualized "ethos" as well as a functional or practical theory. It is both ideal and material, form and content. The greatest sin for Franklin is the failure to make use of something, to convert an expenditure into an asset. Whatever goes into a system as energy or nourishment must come out as material gain. By the same token, there is no gain without loss or sacrifice. And visibility is its own sin. In a proper system of exchange, there is no "unproductive waste" (52); indeed, there is nothing at all to look at. Horror, by contrast, is spectacle, a noxious feast for the eyes. Weber's emphasis on "Franklin's eyes" is consistent with a key element of sacrificial exchange: the superstition of protective understatement. Weber's image provides another perspective on Durkheim's notion of protective poverty. Self-diminishment is the norm because God won't tolerate any light other than his own. "The assiduous belittlement of one's own deserts," Weber continues, glossing Franklin, is also the means of "gain[ing] general recognition later" (52). One remains muted, so as not to excite either the envy of one's neighbors or the resentment of powerful spirits. Weber cites a passage from Franklin's *Autobiography* that makes the link between this ritualized humility and the rite of sacrifice even more explicit. Advising that it is best to keep oneself "out of sight" while venturing on business enterprises, Franklin promises that "The present little sac-rifice of your vanity will afterwards be amply repaid" (193).

Weber's reading of Franklin foregrounds compatibilities between the most apparently diverse phenomena, including superstitions, cannibal ap-petites, and functionalist ideas of equilibrium. Weber shows how Frank-lin's obsession with conversion (time into money, waste into products) is motivated by a superstitious dread and envy of transcendent authority. Like Durkheim, contemplating the desire that threatens the stability of a modern social order, Weber's Franklin fears the unaccommodated: God's power and his own rankling aspirations to it. Franklin's advice about remaining "out of sight" suggests not only a desire for self-diminishment before malevolent and invisible forces but the attempt to master them through their own tactics. Durkheimian anomie is especially pertinent to Franklin's interest in bodily functions. As Weber puts it, echoing a fa-mous Pauline doctrine: "He who will not work shall not eat" (159). The prospect of nourishment here (as in sacrifice) is bound up in postulates and controls. The preoccupation with appetite on the parts of Weber (*Protestant Ethic*) and Durkheim (*Suicide*) expressed their anxiety about the forces (constitutional or social) that threatened to disrupt the balances of a functional system.

In their minds, human ambition (hubris) is as dangerous as divine mal-ice. Durkheim's approach is the more literal: he sees human aspirations embodied as appetites, whose unchecked expansion promises epidemic rates of suicide, and eventual social chaos. Society's role, therefore, is to impose constraint. Perhaps because Weber's was a limited case study, he could afford to be more open to the potential monstrosity of human ambi-tion. There seems no end to the hubris of "cunning little Benjamin," whose ego is most enlarged when he appears most diminished. Take Franklin on the necessity of concealment while embarking on courageous acts. God is responsible for this standard: the God who remains out of sight, but encourages the observant to recognize "His finger in all the de-tails of life" (124). Like so many other biblical allusions to the divine hand, this one recalls the paradigm of the Egyptian plagues as the sign of "God's Finger" or divine compensation.

The same biblical image is given an obscene twist in Bataille's essay on sacrificial mutilation. The essay begins with an account of an embroidery designer who tears off his finger following an "imperative order" from the sun. Though Bataille tells us that this automutilator is "a painter in his spare time," his primary vocation should give us pause. For this act of self-mutilation appears to be a sacrificial payment, exacted, according to the raving logistics of the designer, for his rivaling of God's own designs. In Bataille's modern setting, the extravagance of sacrificial acts are inversely related to their paltry effects (61). Weber's analysis of Franklin, in contrast, presumes an eighteenth-century spiritual context in which terms like blasphemy and sacrifice carry moral weight. He seems less certain about the carefully calibrated devotions of the Baptist converts he observes during his 1904 trip to America. "The question of religious affiliation," according to Weber, was invariably posed as a matter of "credit." Baptism secures to the individual "the deposits of the whole region and unlimited credit without any competition" (303, 305).

This almost parodic adaptation of Franklinian economics is not confined to the business communities of Pennsylvania and North Carolina. Weber found evidence of such spiritualized bookkeeping everywhere, including the Chicago academic scene, where students sought to avoid their required chapel attendance by accumulating religious "credit" in other ways.[42] But it was not until later in his career, in the famous 1918 lecture "Science as Vocation," that Weber captured the problem of spiritual diminishment in a full way. The central place that religion holds in Weber's thought, and the particular significance of sacrifice within it, is exemplified by the fact that he can't seem to get his mind around the purposes of science without reference to both. Religion itself, as I have noted, is defined as an "intellectual sacrifice" (154).[43] Here again, Weber is anticipated by Durkheim, who invokes the idea, in reference to religion, as early as *Suicide*. "Religions can socialize us only in so far as they refuse us the right of free examination. They no longer have, and probably will never again have, enough authority to wring such a sacrifice from us" (376).[44]

Turning to Weber with Durkheim's concept in mind, what's immediately noticeable is the absence of an evolutionary dimension in Weber, a theorist renowned for the historicity of his concepts and often contrasted to Durkheim on precisely such grounds. "The capacity for the accomplishment of religious virtuosos—'the intellectual sacrifice'—is the decisive characterization of the positively religious man" (154), Weber observes. And in one of the most famous passages in his writings he declared: "We live as did the ancients when their world was not yet disenchanted of its gods and demons, only we live in a different sense. As Hellenic man at times sacrificed to Aphrodite and at other times to Apollo, and above all, as everybody sacrificed to the gods of his city, so do we still nowadays, only the bearing of man has been disenchanted and denuded of its mystical but inwardly genuine plasticity" (148). Though Weber's topic throughout is the process of rationalization and its impact upon spirituality, he seems willing here, perhaps more so than anywhere else, to acknowledge affinities between ancients and moderns. Weber doesn't go so far as Durkheim, who labels the intellectual sacrifice demanded by religion obsolete in a scientific age. His point is, rather, that such sacrifices would be comforting, if we could make them. Weber's bleak alternative is a religious sacrifice of some sort. For he never doubts that the sacrificial impulse, the ideal of spiritual interdependence, the need to make offerings to something on behalf of someone, remains strong.

Weber's insistence, in spite of his claim that moderns are spiritually drained and forever condemned to religious dissatisfaction, can only be understood in the context of his essay's larger topic, "science as a vocation." The subject of vocation recalls the theme that is central to *The Protestant Ethic*. Weber's concern here, as in the earlier study, is devotion: the prospects for principles greater than individuals. But from *Protestant Ethic* to "Vocation," devotion becomes submission. The comic wagers of Franklin, however bleak (or even cynical) at times, are now grimly sacrificial. This is the center of Weber's historical argument, and it is all too familiar. When spiritual investments are no longer vital, and people don't know where to turn for religious satisfaction, the hunger for submission and sacrifice knows no bounds. The problem of science as a vocation is precisely that science can feed the mind but not the spirit. Weber's sense that the waning potential for genuine devotion in the modern era actually intensifies the appetite for sacrifice confirms theories that align the rite with loss and disconnection. Sacrifice is the human cry of loneliness in the universe, the attempt to fill a void through hallowed acts of destruction. While sacrifice can be read in the more balanced terms Weber adopts in *The Protestant Ethic*, this reading is more apocalyptic, in keeping with the historical trajectory Weber's essay anticipates: the rise of German fascism. Weber's critique is aimed at academics who exploit the authority of their offices, and a cultural thralldom to submission, by adopting strong political positions. In this respect his critique anticipates the impending devastation of intellectual objectivity in the sacrificial hysteria of Hitler's Germany.

This seems to be the point of the essay's closing nod to the United States, ironic as always, but envious at the same time. The limitations of the American student provide a safety net of sorts: better frivolous and irreverent than demoralized. His German counterpart is forever in search of a "Weltanschauung." The danger is that he might find it. While Weber evidently read his nation well, he was also of it, and it's obvious that his own obsession with the draining of vitality predisposed him to certain intellectual blind spots. Weber shared the hunger of his fellow Germans for submission, for extravagant modern displays of sacrifice. At his essay's end, Weber stands beside "the demon who holds the fibers" of every human life (156). This stance is typical of the gloom that so often descends in Weber. No reader can forget the "nullity" and "petrification" that concludes *The Protestant Ethic*. To recognize the compatibility of such nightmarish scenarios with some of Hitler's own is not to accuse Weber of fascism. It is only to concede a certain limit to the way in which social experience can be read in any given time and place, a limit that sometimes makes for unexpected resemblances. Weber may have felt that the United States was more immune to the sacrificial seizures that plagued Germany. But this assumption was not shared by fellow social observers in America.

American sociological debates of the time reveal Americans as equally, if not *more* disposed toward sacrificial rhetoric and rites. This rhetoric was not only in place earlier in America than in Europe or England, but it may also have been more pervasive—cutting across elite and popular discourses, running from aesthetic to social scientific representations. I have classified Edward Ross's curious manifesto, *Sin and Society*, as a border text for its tone as well as for its subject. The book, as I have suggested, was more widely read than the usual sociological publication. It also appears to have been perceived as a fulfillment of the preacherly role that remained the subliminal aim of sociologists well into the twentieth century. More revealing than Ross's success in proving "our need of sociology," however, was his apparent conviction that in order to be widely influential, the sociologist had to address matters of immediate historical import. Ross sets out in his book to castigate modern America's various "adulterators, peculators, boodlers, grafters." His primary complaint is that killing is too easy. Contemporary morality is so weak that death has become casual, routinized. The "up-to-date criminal" merely pulls a trigger, and a life is "snuffed out." Ross contrasts this to an ancient custom of "sacrific[ing] . . . human beings to the devil."[45] Ross's claims seem at odds with those of Robertson Smith, who sees sacrifice as an expression of uncertainty about both the value of human life and the clarity of social and universal boundaries.

Ross is advancing what might be called a romance of sacrifice. He argues that moderns no longer kill ritually because they don't care enough about human life to make an offering of it. His ideal is the superstition that inspired the bloody rites of the fifteenth-century Frenchman Marshal de Retz. This was spiritual commitment, and its loss is real (33). Yet Ross's nostalgia contradicts the other half of his argument, which details the monumental fears and rivalries that motivate similarly treacherous acts in modern America. Modern society is filled with "primitive-minded people," who make their presence known through a type of mob behavior that serves as Ross's reference throughout: lynching. In one breath Ross justifies lynching as a response to criminal outrages (his example is the Sam Hose affair) and condemns it as lawlessness (32, 34; see also, 13, 15, 36, 138). Ross can't bring himself to confront just what is at stake in modern sacrificial practices. He apparently thinks his quarry is the bloodlessness of modern crime and the obliviousness of modern justice, but his real complaint is the lack of moral clarity that ensures that moderns will never confront the true sources of endangerment. Ross can't get underneath the sacrificial principle, because his book is a symptom of it. His subject is the social heterogeneity that demands sacrifice but contributes to its displacement. Spiritual entropy, imaged as the "spread-out manner of life" and the mitigation of "competition" by "regulation," is alleviated only by instances where people (of one kindred) band together to assert their sacrificial agency (against outsiders). Ross's book can be read as a defense of sacrifice, but one that misunderstands the rule of sacrificial substitution that it uncovers.

Ross does not lament the lynch mob per se, only the fact that it so often gets the least culpable victim. The lynch mob hoists "the red-handed slayer," rather than "the seller of infected milk," whose offense is more far-reaching; Sam Hose, rather than "the corrupt boss" whose greed kills "twelve-hundred." As Ross notes, "thanks to the space that divides sinner from sinned-against, planetary crimes . . . excite far less horror than do the atrocities of Jack the Ripper" (3, 15–16, 34). Ross observes how sacrifice affirms divisions between categories of people ("sinner from sinned-against"). And he emphasizes the way victims are drawn from marginal groups whose members rarely perpetrate the most socially debilitating crimes. Ross stops short of likely conclusions, however, because he can't confront the implications of what he sees. America's silent majority, he everywhere implies, feels besieged, by "the disappearance of free land" and "the triumph of the big concern over the little" (139). Vigilante acts are the last resort of the overlooked.

Ross ends with the uninspired notion that society is secure when all adhere to "the rules of the game." Under such terms, there is general acceptance of requisite "sacrifices." When the rules are generally believed to have been forfeited, "the harvest is bloodshed, lynching, mobs, and race friction." In other words, when the formal and institutional mechanisms for managing vengeance are gone, sacrificial agency becomes the right of the "public," and there is no protecting certain kinds of people (144, 138, 34). One might call these, in Ross's terms, "literal victims" (Blacks, Jews, Italians), surrogates for those who really threaten society. Ross comes close to embracing his own insights halfway through the book, when he lists the different crusades of the time: against "negroes . . . against 'anarchist' immigrants, against the Mormons" (89–90). All of these, he notes, are mere smokescreens for "the onslaught of internal enemies." But Ross is so caught up in his own craving for intensity that he sometimes mimes the venting that he otherwise criticizes dispassionately. Ross's argument resembles the subsequent literary analysis of René Girard, by providing a brilliant diagnosis of sacrificial designs that falls prey to their seductions.

Simon Patten's *The New Basis of Civilization* (1907), another popularization by a contemporary social scientist, confirms the vitality of the sacrificial principle. Patten's approach, however, is a departure from others, because he has little admiration for sacrifice (frank or covert). One might expect Patten's disdain to result in denial of its universal character. Instead, despite his opening assurance that we no longer need "sacrifice" in our state of "peace and plenty," his book becomes a case for the ritual's resilience. Patten takes the offensive from the start, summoning every term he can think of to substantiate his attack. Sacrifice is "forlorn," "circuitous," "abortive," "a fantastic code made from . . . terrified fancies." It is even unpatriotic: Patten identifies sacrifice with the "immobile misery" of Russian fiction that "sickens the sensitive American."[46] In light of these complaints, Patten's closing reversal, his late attempt to recuperate sacrifice for a modern setting, is rather stunning. He seems aware of the need to explain himself: "Sacrifice is a well-established quality. It is only necessary to turn it in new directions." The reasons for Patten's about-face are more complex than he allows. And they have something to do with the subject that brings him to it: "social control." Like other "sensitive American" analysts writing at this time, Patten recognizes the regulatory advantages of sacrifice. He contrasts "the old sacrifice," which always required some material renunciation, to a new sacrifice that seems vaguer but all-encompassing. "It will create an environment of idealism which will uplift and control a nation" (179–80). Patten's study is a revealing exercise in the incorporation of sacrifice within a prosperity ethic. The inequities and conflicts of a heterogeneous capitalist society made the alliance seem inevitable.

Toward Sacrifice as Act and Event

Thus far I have dealt with rhetorical and metaphorical uses of sacrifice. I want to turn now to portrayals and analyses of sacrificial rites themselves. By including both figurative and documentary approaches in this exploration, I am suggesting a continuity between rhetoric and social action. The rhetoric of sacrifice normalizes and facilitates enactments of the rite. Make no mistake: when these social scientists used the term sacrifice, they had in mind an exact procedure. The extent of interest in sacrifice during this period is confirmed by the development of a classic literature on the subject, much of it written by the same social scientists who assumed its terminologies, all of it known to them.[47]

Of the major sociological theorists, Durkheim was most directly engaged with the rite of sacrifice. The role of Robertson Smith's work (which drew on Fustel De Coulanges's classic, *The Ancient City* [1864]) in the reorientation of Durkheim's own in the midnineties had something to do with this fact. Durkheim was especially attracted to Smith's insistence on the collective nature of religion: that religion had more to do with sustaining community than with saving souls. Central to Smith's interpretation was a view of sacrifice as the mechanism of communal cohesion. Sacrifice, according to Smith, was a "repast," a collective meal, whose "substance" was shared by human beings and gods. Sacrifice, Durkheim wrote, following Smith, fortified both unity with God and among kin. Durkheim highlights the potential contradiction in a practice that allows profane persons to ingest the food of gods but answers his own question with the variety of rituals designed to prepare them—fasting, praying, elaborate self-adornment—for the sacred occasion. He also accepts (with qualifications) Smith's understanding of sacrifice as a sacred meal that completes social communion. He is more skeptical about Smith's related theory which views the totem animal, that symbolic embodiment of the collective kin, as the original consumptive object. Overall, he finds Smith's definition too narrow. Sacrifice is about alimentary communion, but it has as much, if not more, to do with oblation. Durkheim insists (and this is his key contribution, with Mauss and Hubert, to contemporary theory on sacrifice) that the rite has a major renunciatory component. Human collectivities have long been "guilty" of the circular reasoning that disposed them to give back to their gods a little of what they received from them.[48]

Durkheim's own reasoning here betrays some of the inversive circularity that is his trademark. If common wisdom holds that human beings make offerings to their gods because they fear them and owe them, Durkheimian wisdom holds that divine power, divine identity, depends on these very fears and debts. Gods exist, according to Durkheim, through the sacrifices of human beings: "Men make their gods, or, at least, make them live; but at the same time, it is from them that they live themselves. So they are regularly guilty of the circle which, according to Smith, is implied in the very idea of a sacrificial tribute" (383). For Durkheim, this is because "the sacred principle is nothing more nor less than society transfigured and personified" (388). Could human beings submit to powers so utterly dependent on themselves were it otherwise?

The gods not only live in the human mind, they *are* the human mind, in its fundamental, collective sense. This is what Durkheim means when he says, "The things which the worshipper really gives his gods are not the foods which he places upon the altars, nor the blood which he lets flow from his veins: it is his thought" (388). The soul is a sacred collective principle, the source of individual identity, and the object of continuous "sacrifices." The principle of sacrificial exchange, by which human beings and their gods exist, becomes a universalized category of mind. From the beginning of time, the principle has shaped social reality. And this in turn reveals another basic need: the need for others, the varieties and degrees of interdependence that make up human life (390). Sacrificial rites are the ongoing means for revitalizing these mutual associations.

It would seem that death, the other dominant term in this section of *Elementary Forms*, would threaten this sustaining chain of references. But it serves as yet another link in the chain. Just as gods exist because human beings give them things, death is defined by mourning. Like sacrifice, mourning, its close kin, strengthens social bonds. In Durkheim's account, mourning and sacrifice flow into one another. Mourning rites invariably entail sacrificial mutilations and culminate in acts of vengeance against a victim. His analysis is spurred by dissatisfaction with interpretations that attribute the ferocity of mourning to the demand for memorialization. How can the idea that the dead want to be regretted, he asks disparagingly, explain the "cruel sacrifices" exacted in mourning? "What reason has the dead for imposing such torments?" (444). Society, he goes on to argue, demands the torture. It needs ferocious displays to confirm its own endurance of the assault.

Durkheim finds support for his claims in the fact that the victim sacrificed at the structural culmination of mourning rites is always drawn from outside the immediate community of mourners. The victim is always a "stranger," who is not "protected by the sentiments of sympathy inspired by a relative or neighbour" (446). This is consistent with his claim that mourning's "cruellest rites" are reserved for community members with a "smaller social value"; "scapegoats" are more often women than men (447). In time, an explanatory layer accrues. The concept of the soul enters "the mythology of mourning," to rationalize the intense rites performed on behalf of the dead. The concept assists in the transformation of the "relative" into that "enemy" who requires terrible oblations. All aspects of the rite, as Durkheim conceives it—the self-mutilations, the discharge of collective rage upon some alien victim, the discovery of the soul—converge in one of his most famous postulates: "Men do not weep for the dead because they fear them; they fear them because they weep for them" (447). The need for the collectivity to affirm itself through displays of emotional fever is satisfied by a continuous supply of human corpses. Since weddings or births fall within the same category of feverish rites, the difference of death, from Durkheim's perspective, calls for specification. Death is a unique assault upon the possibility of group definition. The ultimate defiance of human interdependence, death threatens society's very prospects for self-preservation. It elicits some of Durkheim's most unguarded images. He wavers, for instance, between organicism and psychologism in noting that "the social sentiment is painfully wounded" (448). Society is a great yelping beast, moaning pathetically, craving blood. Collective violence is demanded in recompense for its "wound." Thus, death serves at once to aggravate and to enlarge the social mind.

Durkheim's classic treatment of religion as the means and ends of collective bonds, his reconciliation of faith and modern science, tells much about social scientific views of sacrifice in this period. Sociology becomes the handmaid to a society whose mystified power derives from its introjection of God.[49] Durkheim's language, as always, is revealing. "Society . . . appears to us as an authority which contains us, fixes limits which resist our infringements, and before which we bow with religious respect; in the latter sense, it is a friendly and protecting power, a nursing mother. . . . In one case, it is like the jealous and fearful god . . . in the other, it is the divinity who cares for us and for whom the believer sacrifices himself with joy."[50] A spiritualized society combines maternal nurture (as in Weber's Protestantism, or James's image of Queen Victoria's reign) with paternal omnipotence. Society and God are collapsed as humanity's source and limit, while science and sacrifice become synonymous forms of agency.

Moderns are believers too. Society is their ultimate sacrificial beneficiary; sociologists are the priests who translate the mysteries of social process and help determine the appropriate offerings. As Durkheim writes in the eloquent conclusion to *Elementary Forms*, "The old gods are growing old or [are] already dead, and others are not yet born. . . . The feasts and ceremonies of the past"—Christians celebrating Christ's life and death; Jews remembering the Exodus from Egypt—"do not excite the same ardour in us." He goes on to discover in science "a more perfect" religion (475–77). While Durkheim concedes that moderns have difficulty "imagining what these feasts and ceremonies of the future could consist in" (475), it is with the assurance that they are latent in the spiritual structures of modern society. Like Comte, he anticipates the fleet of sociological initiates who will be pivotal in the identification of new occasions. Durkheim predicts that the selections themselves will be crucial. His example of one modern ritual occasion that failed also reveals the limited range of his own socialist politics: the "cycle of holidays" established in the aftermath of the French Revolution for the sake of periodically revitalizing its principles. The rituals died out, because the principles could not accommodate religion's complex double purpose: social explanation and spiritual renewal.

Durkheim never strays far from his fundamental aim: to identify the ongoing need for religion in an age of social science. This is not because he believes that irrational needs persist in modern times, but because he respects the profound reasonableness of sacred acts. Speaking of the primitive, he writes, "The rites which he employs to assure the fertility of the soil . . . do not appear more irrational in his eyes than the technical processes of which our agriculturalists make use." His point is that meaning is always defined by the ritual actor. This openness to a variety of ritual forms and willingness to concede the continuity of religious past, present, and future made Durkheim's sociology especially alert to the significance of sacrificial action in the modern era.[51] Durkheim's attempt to locate the reason in primitive ritual is echoed by Max Horkheimer and Theodor

Adorno. "Odyssean cunning," in their reading, typifies the deviousness of sacrificial worship: the subjection of "god" to "the primacy of human ends." The worshipers are in turn subjected to the deceptions of "the disbelieving priests."[52] There seems no end to deception in their asymptotic account, which casts Odysseus (with a cynical optimism reminiscent of Nietzsche on Christ) as "the hero who escapes from sacrifice by sacrificing himself." This act becomes their symbol for a negative or self-negating evolution, whereby historical process compulsively nullifies its own advance. The process as they describe it is collectively informed, but consistently internalized. "The history of civilization is the history of the introversion of sacrifice" (55). Sacrifice is the ultimate dialectical action, simultaneously irrational and rational: its irrationality makes it "transient," yet "it persists by virtue of its rationality" (53).

"The custom of human sacrifice," according to one source they cite, "is scarcely known at all" in "the lowest levels of" culture, but seems to be most consistently associated with progress. Among the Africans, "the more powerful the nation is, the more significant the practice of sacrifice" (51–52). Their claim for the susceptibility of modernity to sacrifice is stamped by a larger conspiratorial claim for the oppressive reach of a barbaric culture industry. Yet there is a valuable lesson in their insistence on the enduring attraction of sacrificial ideas over time. Their analysis helps us to understand what was at stake in the revival of interest in sacrifice on the part of so many theologians and social scientists of the late nineteenth and early twentieth centuries, from Robertson Smith and Frazer to Hubert and Mauss, Durkheim, and Freud. Horkheimer and Adorno see "the institution of sacrifice" as "the occasion of an historic catastrophe," which eventually becomes internalized as the ultimate capitalist subjectivity. Thus, "the subjected repeat upon themselves the injustice that was done them" (51). As they portray it, an attraction to sacrifice expresses a discomfort with civilization. The interpretation of Adorno and Horkheimer is finally most illuminating by contrast. For their characterization of sacrifice as an internalized Western sensibility contradicts an unvarying assumption of late-nineteenth-century discussions: that sacrifice was a fundamentally collective enterprise.

Of all the authors on sacrifice, William Robertson Smith is probably the least familiar to late-twentieth-century readers. An established Old Testament scholar at Aberdeen University before his 1883 appointment to a professorship of Arabic at Cambridge, Robertson Smith was widely known to contemporaries as the editor of the *Encyclopedia Britannica* (1881–88).[53] He was also known for his major work on sacrifice, *Lectures on the Religion of the Semites* (1889, second edition, 1894), delivered at Aberdeen over the course of three years (1888–91). His first (and last) effort in the anthropo-

SACRIFICIAL ARTS AND SCIENCES

logical analysis of religion drew the attention of a wide interdisciplinary audience, which included social scientists as well as theologians. Smith's *Lectures* can be distinguished in a preliminary way by a few main assumptions. Smith, like Tylor and later anthropologists, was an evolutionist. He believed that every society—contemporary and archaic—was in process, progressing toward his own more enlightened one and exercising ever greater intellectual control over this transformation. Smith's evolutionism was consistent with a Judeo-Christian outlook that saw the moral development of a chosen people culminating in the message of Christ. "When we wish thoroughly to study the New Testament doctrine of sacrifice," Smith observed early on in his *Lectures*, "we are carried back step by step till we reach a point where we have to ask what sacrifice meant, not to the old Hebrews alone, but to the whole circle of nations of which they formed a part" (3).

Smith, like his follower Durkheim, emphasized the priority of ritual (practice) over myth (belief). Concrete physical acts, he argued, expressed and perpetuated moral conditions. For Smith, the story of religion was a story of practices and institutions rather than beliefs and ideas. Ancient religions "had for the most part no creed." They were, rather, "a body of fixed traditional practices, to which every member of society conformed as a matter of course."[54] Smith also shared Durkheim's respect for the representations of past and present social actors. Smith noted in an 1870 lecture, "We have no true history where we cannot pierce through the outer shell of tradition into the life of a past age, mirrored in the living record of men who were themselves eyewitnesses and actors in the scenes they describe."[55] Two other prominent aspects of Smith's thought seem especially "sociological": the claim that civilized religious practices could be better grasped through comparative study of simpler ones, and the notion that religion tended toward the rational and ethical rather than the superstitious and demonic.

Robertson Smith opens his *Lectures* with a startling insight about the representation of sacrifice. Every reader of the Old Testament must be struck by the fact that the book's most pivotal rite is never directly described or explained. Sacrifice is "taken for granted" as an essential component of religious observance (3). He notes that this is partly because sacrifice was widely practiced by nations other than the Hebrews in their own and preceding times, so there was little need for elaborate signposts. But we can understand the observation as revelatory in still other ways. For he is also highlighting the tendency of sacrifice to function as an implicit rite, a code or language so deeply embedded in a culture's imaginings that it remains oblique to outside analysts, more so than other rites. These reflections take him immediately into questions of kinship and boundaries:

whose rites were these, exactly? how did they compare to the heathen practices that provided a continuous supply of negative examples for the Judean prophets?

The rite of sacrifice, according to Smith, is inseparable from the problem of nationality. His attempt to delineate sacrifice is part of an effort to sort out differences between the "Semites" and their neighbors. Among his most valuable testimonies is the antique range of certain scholarly recognitions. The linguistic basis of ethnicity, for instance, has long been the starting point of analysts who understood the task of designating "ethnical characters" as largely a matter of language. Language is the closest we come to "a natural classification" (6,7). Religion is the clearest expression of "a *natural* society" (29). And the gods are identified as full social participants; they and their worshipers constitute a family of reciprocal obligations. The ancient Semites, this makes clear, viewed the religious and secular spheres as coextensive. The site of this reciprocity was the sacrificial meal, whose contents, shared by humans and gods, provided a "sacred cement" (313). Smith's rite of consumption *with* the gods supplies a source (some say *the* source) for the later symbolic consumption *of* God in the Mass.[56] In the earliest versions of sacrifice, he maintains, the sacrificial flesh consumed was the totem animal, the semisacred embodiment of the link between human and divine. The consumption of the tribal totem was a periodic ritual whose reenactment served to revitalize a natural bond.

Most who have adapted Smith's work on sacrifice have accepted Durkheim's criticism that he not only exaggerated the importance of the sacrificial meal but mistook its contents as a totem animal.[57] In his own *Encyclopedia Britannica* entry on sacrifice, for instance, Smith highlights "the ancient technical language of the priestly ritual, in which the sacrifices are called [*lechem elohim*]." Smith translates this Hebrew phrase as "food of the deity." Yet the strict translation of *lechem* (which he no doubt knew) is "bread," not the more generic "food." This lexical preference (the use of the narrower term to represent the whole) emphasizes the most benign form of sacrifice, a grain offering, which is consistent with Smith's trademark emphasis on the commensal meal. He concludes, "If all sacrifices are not convivial entertainments, at least the tendency is to give to all feasts, nay to all meals, a sacrificial character by inviting the god to partake of them."[58]

It's fair to say that Smith did minimize oblation to some extent, partly from a will to read the religious life as an expression of human ideals. When he states early on in his *Lectures* that the Semitic religions were framed as "positive" cults, that they derived from the "teachings of great religious innovators" speaking from "divine revelation," he means to distinguish them from the blind compulsions and fears that inspired the devotions of "heathens" (1). He defines religion as "a loving reverence for

known gods who are knit to their worshippers by strong bonds of kinship."
This is distinguished from "the savage's dread of unseen foes" (54–55). But
he was not so much avoiding history (or a significant change in the rite) as
making a particular historical case: for the sophistication of communion as
a sacrificial form. Religion not only strengthens social bonds, but enhances
the connection to a world beyond them, a purpose which grows increasingly essential over time. His recognition of this necessity is the clue to
his own broader apprehension of sacrifice. For he was not nearly so confined to the idea of communion as some have claimed. His view of religion
as a mechanism of kinship, his demonstration of how religious rites were
transformed to accommodate increasing levels of social heterogeneity
and differentiation, is what made it especially important for contemporary
social scientists.

One of Smith's principal concerns was the composition of homogeneous clans that were based on the idea of constitutional affinity among humans and between humans and their gods. Over the course of the book it
becomes clear that he is more interested in the precariousness or impossibility of this ideal than in its objective detailing. His preoccupation with
the breakdown of kinship is evident in the concessions that he introduces
into his description of the sacrificial rite itself. In more ancient times, he
explains, when the rite was intended to provide sacramental flesh, a premium was put on the victim's holiness and perfection. No one would have
conceived a camel or sheep as any less precious than a man. At this point
animals were not substitutes for humans; they were sacrificed as highly
valued beings in themselves. Indeed, "the animal life" was "deemed purer
and more perfect" than the human. One explanation often given when
animals are substituted in sacrifice—that the human life was the more valued—is, therefore, only partly true, for in most ancient traditions, as we
have seen, animals were sacrificed for their "sacred" natures (361).

All this was lost, Smith contends, when humans no longer acknowledged a kinship with animals. It was at this point that the practice of sacrificial substitution began in earnest. Victims were chosen not for their holy
associations but because they were regarded as somehow expendable.
"Wherever we find the doctrine of substitution of animal life for that of
man, we find also examples of actual human sacrifice." Naturally regarded
as "more potent," human sacrifices were reserved for especially solemn
occasions or "seasons of extreme peril" (366). Thus the institutionalization
of sacrificial substitution marked the start of "piacular sacrifices" themselves: rites performed not for the sake of communal bonds but in order to
appease offended spirits. Sacrificial substitution represents a general intensification of the stakes of sacrifice. Sacrifice takes on the character of atonement, a method for dealing with social crises, at precisely the time that
human sacrifice (and the substitutions that accompany it) becomes wide-

spread. For Smith, the acceptance of value distinctions between the lives of animals and human beings represents the beginning of the end, so to speak. Such distinctions eventuate in distinctions between kin and other human kinds. "It had begun to be recognised that human life, or rather the life of a tribesman, was a thing of unique sanctity" (361).

One of the most obvious signs of this development was the idea that "the victim *qua* victim possesses a sacrosanct character" (362). If, formerly, victims were selected for a condition of holiness "natural" to their "kind," now holiness was *acquired* through the rite. Such a change sanctioned the practice of sacrificial substitution and with it one of the most pernicious features of sacrificial ideology: the idea that the most degraded social members were uniquely suited to sacrifice, and even "honored" by their selection. "The older Semites when they had recourse to human sacrifice were more strictly logical" in their insistence that the victim be kin (362). Sacrifice, according to the newer conceptions, might well be a "privilege" reserved for certain social types. Still, there was constant anxiety about the fraudulence of substitution, so that, for example, "the Carthaginians, in a time of trouble, felt that their god was angry because slave boys had been privily substituted for the children of their best families" (363). Other worshipers were extravagant in their selection of victims. The Saracens, for example, nearly always chose "a young and beautiful captive." And the practice of substitution became the norm "all over the world" (362–63). No one imagined that the requirements of deities had really changed (that the victim must be kin persisted in the minds of all ritual performers); people had simply found a way around them. The book includes fascinating accounts of how these nervous believers handled the daring fraudulence of their sacrificial substitutions. In Rome and in Mexico, sacrificial victims were disguised in a ritual "make-believe . . . to which the gods were polite enough to shut their eyes." Such deceptions were necessary to these antiquated cultures, whose members still believed themselves bound to "traditional rules" (364).

The result is a new ideological category of the dispensable: those whose lives, for military or civil reasons (prisoners, criminals, slaves), are understood to be less precious than others. Smith seems less interested in establishing some causal chain of relations than in describing each development as vividly as possible. Subsequent readers were invited to glean the historical narrative embedded in his fantastic web of detail. This story concerns the discovery of difference and atonement as a way of dealing with increased contact among diverse nations, competing for lands, resources, and, above all, spiritual favors. The historical intuitions of Robertson Smith take us right up to Nathaniel Shaler's *The Neighbor*, where two men can be distinguished as victim and beneficiary of the sacrificial rite simply on the basis of the relative permanence of their skins.[59]

"Human sacrifice," Smith concludes, "stamps relatively advanced and especially decadent peoples, among whom the difference between human and animal life is clearly understood." The "re-emergence of the human victim enhanced religion," and even "became an obsession among certain peoples" (631).

The most revealing aspect of *Lectures on the Religion of the Semites* from an historical point of view is its nostalgia. Sacrificial actors from the end of the most ancient times were ever at a loss in comparison to a previous era's sense of plenitude and connection. The gods then were accessible, palpable, even made of the same foodstuffs. Smith's story sounds too close to descriptions of his own present to be coincidental. There is the growing recognition of distinctions between humans and animals, and between different kinds of humans; the expansion of lands, and with it, increased contact among strangers. All of this "progress" impacts on sacrifice, which now expresses ideas of atonement and features the subterranean and treacherous practice of substitution. *Lectures* can be read, like so many social scientific studies of the day, as a variation on Tonnies's *Gemeinschaft* and *Gesellschaft*, now applied to an "antique" past and its sacrificial rites. Once expressive of close "natural" bonds, these rituals gradually receded into complex expressions of social interdependence and rivalry. Smith was primarily known in his own time for one part of his analysis, the reading of sacrifice as a celebration of homogeneous bonds between humans and their gods. But surely the most powerful and sustained aspect of his argument is this account of historical transformation. Contemporaries may have been so eager to embrace his myth of a unified *communitas* that they overlooked the other side of his story: the social development and differentiation that replaced this primal unity. Though they criticized his overly unified view, they were dazzled by it, so much so that they slighted the strong historical narrative embedded there.

René Girard's theories are worth considering again in this context for their related, but finally sharply opposed, conception of religion's function. While *Violence and the Sacred* is ultimately compatible with views of religion as an affirmation of collective bonds, it offers a critical twist along the way. Religion, according to Girard, is a repository for violence. It serves as a mediator and siphon for an inevitable and sometimes overpowering vengefulness. Religion's principal means for managing violence is "the surrogate-victim mechanism," which allows the community to satisfy its demand for justice while avoiding contamination by violence. Society punishes a pure or "innocent" victim in a formal enactment of arbitrary violence designed to stave the flow of vengeance. For Girard, then, sacrifice is a sanctioned, even beneficent act, a form of controlled violence designed to save the community, which threatens to be consumed by a potentially interminable violence. Girard's interpretation is based on a notion of sacrificial deception. In keeping with the discussions of Robertson Smith or Adorno and Horkheimer, substitution here is a manipulation of the gods. An element of chance or play is present in every sacrificial rite; the victim is always a surrogate for the community as a whole. Girard makes much of the necessary attributes of such victims. They must *resemble* others, but differ fundamentally. He quotes Joseph de Maistre's observation that victims were usually "the gentlest, most innocent creatures, whose habits and instincts brought them most closely into harmony with man" (2). Next, victims needed to be loosely integrated into the community, so that their death would not incite demands for vengeance.

Ritual violence, Girard argues, is essential to the restoration of a lost *difference*; hierarchy requires it. Sacrifice, in other words, is about the need for categorization. But this is precisely where the recovery of the historical perspective laid out by Robertson Smith becomes most valuable. For Smith reads the activity of categorization that supports sacrificial substitution as the beginning of some communal end. It is the fall into the habit of distinction. The onset of social classification is a title to history and cruelty, emblematized in the institution of human sacrifice and in the particularly cruel practice of sacrificial substitution. For Girard, in contrast, categorization is an eternal need, at once essential and artificial (an outgrowth of biological drives, an expression of transcendent play), like the violence that supports it. The burden of Girard's analysis is to demonstrate the universality of ritual violence while commending the role of reason in containing it. Thus he dismisses the argument of Frazer, who limits the practice of sacrificial substitution to "races who stand on a low level of social and intellectual culture" (317).

Embracing the "scientific" perspective, Girard calls attention to the rigorous standards upheld by his own methods and terms (315). Yet this scientific ideal remains inconsistent with his attraction to sacrificial violence. Beyond the criteria of science lies the ultimate target of Girard's violent necessity: poststructuralist skepticism itself. Only a spectacle of violence, it seems, has the chance to disturb the complacency of a poststructuralist position that disclaims language's capacity to express truth (316–18). Girard's reading of Freud's *Totem and Taboo* reflects his own bias toward the "reality principle." Freud, Girard notes approvingly, located the origins of ritual violence in a primal scene: a sacrificial murder and consumption of the tyrannical father by his sons. This was a version of the original totem meal at which the community ingested a symbolic representative of its animal ancestor as a means of self-perpetuation. One of Freud's great achievements, then, was the refusal to dissolve sacrificial rites in fantasy or dream structures. According to Girard, official psychoanalysis has been dismissive of *Totem and Taboo* because it undermines the family romance model in favor of "the mechanism of religion."

The role played by sacrifice in *Totem and Taboo* is identical to the role played by cultural prohibitions like incest (219). Blood sacrifice, like the incest taboo, requires that ritual catalysts be selected from outside. Such requirements serve to stabilize and protect a community by extending its external associations in a perfectly controlled way. Community is sustained by the institutionalization of limits on human desire, just as it is sustained by the practice of controlled violence through substitution. Girard's Freud is a version of Durkheim: society cannot exist without religion, because religion provides the safety valve for the release of collective violence. Freud understood the murderous roots of ritual, as well as sexuality's potentially divisive function (212). But his continuing investment in the family model led him to overlook the importance of the victim for his theories. What Freud missed was the crucial role of surrogacy. In this he is not alone, for the subject of surrogacy also poses problems for Girard's own theory. Indeed, throughout Girard's study, the concept of the surrogate victim seems to obscure as much as it illuminates. His claim that the successful management of sacrificial violence depends on difference and "misunderstanding" is familiar. We take him to mean that sacrifice is a magical exchange whereby the designated victim is taken for an acknowledged debtor, who can be the entire community. Equally familiar is his assumption that all ritual participants—actual and implied, human and divine—are aware of the "deception." But Girard introduces some confusing elaborations of these sacrificial commonplaces when he begins to speculate on practices of double substitution. He observes at one point that ritual violence always includes a double substitution: surrogate victim for the collectivity, and then an outsider for the surrogate. Sometimes, he points out, there is no substitute, and a surrogate from inside is sacrificed (269–73).

But it is precisely on the grounds of determining "inside" from out that Girard's argument breaks down. For as highlighted by sacrificial rites in one case after another, there really is no such thing as being wholly inside or wholly outside. No matter how foreign an enemy, there are always terms available for converting him or her into a neighbor, given the will. "He is from a different neighborhood, but he is nevertheless an Italian"; "she is a Hebrew, but she, like me, is a Semite"; "he is definitely strange, but he is a human being." Léon Bing's recent study of Los Angeles youth gangs, composed mainly of African-American males, reveals revenge rituals and presiding definitions of neighbors and strangers consistent with the sacrificial models under discussion. The book's very title, *Do or Die*, appropriates, with its own spin, the sacrificial maxim *do ut des* ("I give so that thou shouldst give"). In the dead-end world of the Crips and Bloods, one sacrifices another ("do") so as not to be sacrificed oneself ("die"). But this is not fully consistent with the logic of sacrifice. What is most revealing about the activities of these gangs is the way they implicate and distort sacrificial logic. It is possible to see postmodern gang life as a local specification of the limits of sacrificial thinking.

The culture represented in *Do or Die* might be read as an adaptation by negation of the sacrificial rite. Given the attention paid to eating in so many treatments of sacrifice we have discussed, it's revealing how often the gang members of this book are represented near food or at meals. But mainly these youth live on air, or perhaps on the (sacrificial) smoke from their guns. In one exemplary scene, a prison repast, the mundane food (low-fat milk, tossed salad, spaghetti dished up by attendants "wearing plastic shower caps and disposable sterile gloves") is so incommensurate with the inmates' raging appetites as to be a parody of them. There seems no possible way for these paltry offerings to accomplish their ostensible aim, the transformation of enemy into brother.[60] In these gang worlds, race ultimately has little to do with who is "homie" and who is "offbrand." These youths fraternize easily with members of rival gangs in jail. But they will, with equal ease, blow the same rival's head off back on the streets, a sign of their notorious devaluation of life in general. But it is also an indication of the ever-shifting, essentially labile nature of categories such as neighbor and stranger in postmodern urban America, where notions of neighborliness and strangeness, inside and out, are utterly context-bound. In fact they can be understood as the grantors of specificity within each context. Thus, at every place in his analysis where Girard writes "violence," I would write "kindred."

The universal constant is not the need or desire to release aggressive impulses, but rather the intent to discover kin, to confirm the likeness (or, if myriad reasons preclude that, the antithetical difference) of the other. But even within this constant, as the historical record shows, there is considerable variation. Take the case of the Bloods and Crips. From the perspective of the dominant culture, there is little to distinguish these rivals. They are nearly always Black, nearly always "disadvantaged," nearly always deficient in "marketable" education and skills. In short, they are as alike as any American youths can be. Yet from their own perspectives, they are marked by differences worth dying for. And the most prized of these differences are defined in terms of kinship or "family."[61] When I suggested earlier that this culture can be understood as a negation of sacrifice, I meant to confirm how it also serves as its intensification. For what's most striking about this gang world is that there is no functioning doctrine of sacrificial substitution. Anyone and everything in "the neighborhood" is considered "fair game"—including a baby blown away because its mother happened to dress it, inadvertently, in red shoelaces, an offense to the sacred totem color of the Bloods (105). The aim of these youth gangs, it seems clear to me, is not simply to promote a culture of terror. It is rather to affirm a certain (sacred?) intensity that is missing from their world. It goes without saying that theirs is the ultimate in ritualized societies. More importantly, this striving for intensity is reflected in the fact that they don't practice sacrificial substitution. For as Robertson Smith argues, substitution from the outset was a forlorn concept, signaling the introduction of mediation into the spiritual process. And one of the principal ideals governing the lives of these gang members is the destruction of such barriers.[62]

Modern Sacrifice

The beginnings of this situation—the obsession with kinship, the craving for intensity—lie in turn-of-the-century America. Of course, the truest origins are located in an ancient biblical domain, and the subsequent adaptations of it, that proved so fascinating to later social scientists. But its fullest elaboration took place in the modern period. Noting how often kinship is defined in terms of food prohibitions, Robertson Smith pinpoints the principal attractions of sacrificial practices in his *Encyclopedia Britannica* entry: "the world-wide prevalence of sacrificial worship points to a time when the kindred group and the group of commensals were identical, and when, conversely, people of different kins did not eat and drink together."[63] Smith's collection of categories—sacrifice, kinship, and appetite—provides a bridge to some of the more explicit treatments of sacrifice I want to turn to next. All of these social scientific authors, E. B. Tylor, who anticipated Robertson Smith's work, Frazer, who knew it, and Mauss and Hubert, are in basic harmony with his focus. Their theories confirm that the ritual of sacrifice expresses a longing for a formerly unified, homogeneous society of kindred, framed within a society now consistently faced with the spectacle of "different kin." The pressure of this longing helps to explain why these studies so often claim the universal legitimacy of their own social scientific models. It is as if the ideal of unity is transferred to something they can themselves control: their own methods.

E. B. Tylor's account of sacrifice in *Primitive Culture* opens with the observation that the "types" of prayer ("a request made to a deity") and sacrifice ("a gift made to a deity") practiced in ancient times, are detectable "unchanged in social life to this day."[64] Above all, Tylor is impressed by continuity—transhistorical and cross-cultural—and sacrifice is his key entry in this regard. "The innate correspondence in the minds of men," he writes, "is enough to produce in distant and independent races so much uniformity of development, that three or four headings will serve to class the chief divisions of sacrificial substitution among mankind." These four divisions include the substitution of part for whole (the part given to God, the bulk to the worshipers); the substitution of mutilations—a finger joint or sometimes even a lock of hair—for human sacrifices; the substitution of a less for a more valued life; the substitution of effigies for real victims (399). Tylor eventually comes to accommodate the obvious variation from primitive to highly evolved religions. But his universalism turns out to be formulaic, a gesture of respect in its own right, paid in all of these contemporary writings on sacrifice. Mauss and Hubert, for example, state at the start of their book *Sacrifice*, that their interest lies in questions of logical as opposed to historical priority. They are concerned to document "natural systems of rites."[65] And Robertson Smith cites the "marked and fundamental similarity between sacrificial worships in all parts of the globe," as support for his claim that the rite derives from a single type.[66]

Another formula first advanced in Tylor's *Primitive Culture*, or at least readily accessible there, is the fascination with linguistic development, especially as it pertains to the subject of sacrifice. His study can be understood as an outline for an idiosyncratic anthropology of linguistic change, which for him invariably registers decline: "Our language displays it in a word, if we do but compare the sense of presentation and acceptance which 'sacrificium' had in a Roman temple, with the sense of mere giving up and loss which 'sacrifice' conveys in an English market." "Throughout the history of sacrifice," he continues laconically, "it has occurred to many nations that cost may be economized without impairing efficiency. The result is seen in ingenious devices to lighten the burden on the worshipper by substituting something less valuable than what he ought to offer, or pretends to" (399). Belief in powerful deities, a sense of moral gravity and hope, seem to give way in Tylor's analysis to the self-interested calculations of the market. Secularized exchange replaces a heightened worship. There is not much that is surprising or revolutionary in Tylor's treatment, unless it is recognized as the work of an anthropologist known for his impatience with a reflexive spirituality.[67]

Tylor seems exceptionally responsive to such attachments here. What explains this uncharacteristic wistfulness? It has something to do with the type of history he provides, which might be classified as sacrificial in its own right. We gain in shrewdness and efficiency what we lose in ethical sensitivity. We acquire in diversity and interest what we concede in communal identity. Historical process has itself become a sacrificial mechanism. As if to reinforce his own testimony for the rite's persistence, Tylor ends with a survey of sacrificial rites up to the late-nineteenth-century present, most of them examples from folklore. He describes the live animals sacrificed still in parts of Bulgaria and Russia and the more benign practice of offering a portion of the porridge to the fire gods in Germany. But the most far-reaching modern example, in its implications for both the ongoing importance of the rite and its transformation over time, is the current controversy between Protestants and Catholics as to "whether sacrifice is or is not a Christian rite" (406–8, 410). There may be little chance for consensus about the source or purpose of sacrifice, but that very fact testifies to its ritual vitality.

Of all the social scientific works from this period that share a preoccupation with sacrifice, Sir James Frazer's exhaustively detailed *Golden Bough* was the most widely criticized and celebrated. The ambition of Frazer's learned and incredibly varied study makes the criticism seem inevitable. But the wonder and tact of his approach to a subject like folk superstition also makes the criticism seem unjust. Frazer shares Tylor's interest in the question of what has become of a rite that was formerly the foundation of every major religion. Frazer was a close friend, some say a "disciple," of Robertson Smith (to whom Frazer dedicated *The Golden Bough* in its first edition). They parted ways, however, over the issue of origins. Stanley Edgar Hyman, for example, believes that Frazer found Smith's practical theory of ritual origins "emotionally upsetting." As Frazer put it, "Every ritual is preceded in the minds of the men who institute it by a definite train of reasoning, even though that train of reasoning may not be definitely formulated in words and promulgated as a dogma."[68] While Frazer conceded the importance of Smith's theories on sacrifice for his own study, he also emphasized how his reading of the sacrament contradicted Smith's. Frazer's theory was more utilitarian; he saw sacrifice as a means of absorbing the qualities of a god or gods. His interpretation was also, like others, more focused on the propitiatory aspects of the rite: sacrifice expressed human fears and aspirations as well as human desires for communion.

Frazer's attraction to vestiges and ruins impels his pursuit of beginnings. What inspired human beings to make offerings to gods in the first place? What led to the eventual sacrifice of humans or substitutes for them? He recounts the tradition of sacrificing kings on the verge of old age, a practice designed to spare society the spectacle and effects of their decline.[69] He dwells momentarily on totems, describing the members of the Crocodile Clan, whose fetishistic regard for animal kin led them to refuse any utensils with a shred of its skin (31). But his main concern is the custom of child sacrifice among royalty. Frazer discovers it to have been extraordinarily widespread—common to Siamese, Semites, Greeks, and Slavs—and enforced, particularly, during national calamities. Offered as a substitute for the king himself, in the name of the people as a whole, the sacrificed son was thought a suitable propitiation for the vengeful gods.

Frazer is especially eager to know whether the practice was original to the ancient Hebrews or borrowed from those they conquered. This concern preoccupies him as fully in the final volume, *The Scapegoat*, as in the third volume, *The Dying God*. He is inclined "to surmise that the chosen people may have brought with them into Palestine the seeds which afterwards sprang up and bore such ghastly fruit. . . . The pious Jewish historian who saw in Israel's exile God's punishment for sin, has suggested no explanation of that mystery in the divine economy which suffered the Sepharites to continue on the same spot the very same abominations (171). Frazer's observation is noteworthy for at least two reasons. First, it portrays sacrifice as inevitable to cultural development. Take any culture, transplant it, and sacrificial practices will "spring up" among them. Second, it suggests through its reference to "divine economy" that there is something deeply modern, or at least deeply familiar about such customs. Frazer knew Tylor's *Primitive Culture*, and his predecessor's idea of a sacrificial economy was probably vivid in his mind. Frazer includes an interpretation of the two primary sacrificial scenes in the Hebrew Bible as further substantiation for his claim that sacrifice is basic to Semitic (and by extension to all) religions. According to Frazer's reading, the Passover story in Exodus and the story of Abraham in Genesis share a common theme: the Hebrew redemption *from* sacrifice. The Hebrews could only be liberated from a custom that was obligatory (179).

Having established the prevalence of child sacrifice in ancient times, Frazer sets out to find some explanations for the practice. He dismisses the claim that child sacrifice expressed an anxiety about the collective food supply, since it was so often confined to the firstborn (who would not have been viewed in nearly so threatening a light as the third or fourth). Moreover, he adds, "savages do not take such thought for the morrow" (187). Frazer is careful to emphasize the rite's variability: no one explanation will serve for every culture. Among the Semites and the Italians, for instance, sacrifice was clearly understood as a necessary tribute, demanded by God or gods. Firstborn sons were sacrificed for their value and their dispensability: a personal sacrifice was required of the king, and he himself could not be spared (188). But Frazer also cites West African and Hindu beliefs that firstborn sons compromised fathers, sapping their "vital energy" or threatening their thrones. In these traditions, firstborn sons were thought to be reincarnations of grandfathers, who might, in the persons of these sons, demand the return of their thrones. "His existence is at the best a menace to yours, and at the worst it may involve your extinction" (188–89). These beliefs were dramatized in some Hindu sects by the funeral rites performed for men during their wives' pregnancies. Frazer observes of child sacrifice in general that "long after the barbarous custom had been dropped by others, it continued to be observed by kings, who remain in many respects the representatives of a vanished world, solitary pinnacles that topple over the rising waste of waters under which the past lies buried" (194). Kings are repositories of remnants, he suggests. Their very existence militates against change. Yet in order to maintain power, a king must provide at least some semblance of progress; he must preside over change even as he resists it. A similar paradox applies to parenting, where offspring symbolize the dual prospect of permanence and extinction. In both cases, success imperils stability.

Frazer's driving purpose in *The Scapegoat* as well as in *The Dying God* is to find a reasonable explanation for sacrifice. He seems to fear that the kings perched so precariously upon the waters of civilization were mirrors for his own contemporary social order. Frazer knows his civilization as the issue of this shifting past. Hence the urgency of his quest for explanations both causal and synthetic. The proximity of Easter, Passover, and the Jewish festival of Purim, as well as structural parallels in their defining rites—crucifixion, sacrificial sparing, hanging—provide support for his argument about sacrifice in *The Scapegoat*. For here, the explicit purpose is to illustrate the pervasiveness of sacrifice, "held all over the ancient world from Italy to Babylon."[70] The necessity of divine sacrifice is a given in his argument. He wants to show how the practice evolved from the earliest sacrifices of declining kings (227–28), to the substitutions of their firstborn sons, to the use of the socially expendable—"someone from the poorer classes," "an ugly or deformed person," "a condemned criminal" (408–9, 253, 255). Frazer records in lyrical detail the barbarisms that extended from Mexico to Greece and Rome, from India to Asia Minor.

All of these examples reveal sacrifice as basic: to kingship, to the society represented by the office, to faith itself. "It is possible that such sacrifices of deified men, performed for the salvation of the world," Frazer writes in the conclusion to *Scapegoat*, which concludes *The Golden Bough* as a whole, "may have helped to beget the notion that the universe or some part of it was originally created out of the bodies of gods offered up in sacrifice" (409–10). The central importance of sacrifice for his study is signaled by the decision to end with an account of it. His specific case: Babylonian and Vedic myths that trace the world's origin to the dismembered bodies of gods. Once they had conceived the idea of a human world, what materials did these gods have to work with, after all, but their own bone and tissue? In his primary example, Frazer describes how the Vedic God orders another (presumably smaller?) god "to cut off his, the Creator's, head, and with the flowing blood mixed with clay he kneaded a paste out of which he molded men and animals" (410). With one gruesome image, Frazer effectively transforms Robertson Smith's sacrificial mechanism from a harmonious dinner, symbolizing alimentary communion, to a divine bloodbath, symbolizing expiation. Gods and men become one, in the minds of the mythic authors who interest Frazer, through a violent rite of self-dismemberment. In these myths, divinities have to take themselves apart to put a world together.

One obvious moral is that world making is no benign activity. Beyond this, is the implied meagreness of universal supplies. For the most insistent point of these myths is that the world has to come from something that already possesses formal shape, something with value. There is no material excess; there are no unused substances lying around, suitable to the task of creation. World making requires the sacrifice of the most treasured beings—the gods themselves. Frazer's conclusion anticipates Simmel on exchange, where value "accrues to the desired object . . . through the measure of the sacrifice demanded in acquiring it." The creation of an entity as miraculous as society demands divine blood. It also foreshadows Weber on Franklin, where neither pleasure nor nourishment is possible without a loss or expenditure. Franklin's calculating finger, that Weberian symbol of hubris recording every waste and gain, prefigures Frazer's Indian God, whose fingers mold a world from his own "blood" and "clay." Frazer notes how this original divine sacrifice is recollected in a daily Brahman rite. In this way, the Brahman believes, the world is continuously reborn in sacrifice.

Let me be clear about what I take all this to mean: sacrifice, according to these writers, is essential to social life. Society's beginnings can be traced to the gods who sacrificed their own bodies on its behalf. Sacrifice in turn became the foundational social act, society's means of spiritual subsistence. The requisite offerings were assumed at first as royal obligations, the revitalizing sacrifice of kings, and subsequently made through various forms of substitution. Early on, these substitutes were themselves sons of kings, savored of the divine. But they were drawn increasingly from the ranks of social aliens, whether definitive outsiders or elements within that could be classified as estranged or expendable. These included social deviants and unfortunates, groups that were always available for this basic purpose, groups whose very criminality or debility grew out of this sacrificial necessity.

In most of these analyses, the transformation I have described is presented as a mystery in need of explanation. Every author takes a stab at it, none with great success. An offhand comment by Frazer takes us partway to a satisfactory rationale: "When a nation becomes civilized, if it does not drop human sacrifice altogether, it at least selects as victims only such wretches as would be put to death at any rate" (227). Frazer stops short of possible historical claims. He seems content with the assurance that these "wretches" are easily identified. But it remains unclear under what circumstances the taking of a life (against the will of the victim) by a collectivity might become inevitable.[71] At some point in human history, presumably the point of "civilization," the role of sacrificial object lost its appeal. It became difficult to persuade victims to accept the eternal rewards implicit in their sanctification through sacrifice. At that point, there developed a concept of individuals and groups uniquely suited to the beneficial transformations of sacrificial rites.

The limits on Frazer's historical insights are self-imposed, as evidenced by the cautious evolutionism that brings his multivolume study to an end. Noting the marvelous paradox of sacrificed gods and spared priests, Frazer concludes, "Well is it, not only for the priest but for mankind, when with the slow progress of civilization and humanity the hard facts of a cruel ritual have thus been softened and diluted into the nebulous abstractions of a mystical theology" (411). There is little hint here of the ties between executions and sacrifices, between individual deaths, "at any rate," and society's need for victims. Sacrifice survives, but it is now rendered completely benign. It is not only "softened" but has also absorbed a quality of intellectualism, as implied in the phrase "nebulous abstractions." Sacrifice has become a mere glimmer, a mental fragment compelling alone for those still capable of submission to a "mystical theology."

The real drama of this muted close is Frazer's avoidance of the one inference his own dramatic account of the dying god could have produced: that society is unequivocally dependent on rites of sacrifice. Without the sacrificial body of some god or gods, it could not exist. And society's appetite for sacrifice has been evolving ever since that initial gift. The rite's symbolic reenactment is a requirement extending from these mythic origins to society as we know it. It may be that Frazer's own distaste for the cruel and irrational caught him in the end. Or perhaps he was insufficiently interested in his social present to become absorbed in the details of its own "divine economy." The best explanation may be a "disciplinary" one: that Frazer, as an anthropologist, was disinclined to pursue the sociological implications of his findings. Such deductions were best left to analysts of a more Durkheimian stripe, Henri Hubert and Marcel Mauss.

The overriding aim of Mauss and Hubert's *Sacrifice* is to suggest a continuum between ancient religious practices and modern conceptions of society. Their methodological purpose, to treat sacrifice in strictly sociological terms, is the means to their claim for its enduring significance in an era of social science. This claim is consistent with unacknowledged elements of previous interpretations. Tylor, as I have suggested, betrays a surprising air of regret in tracing the diminution of sacrificial devotion over time, a regret that implies his dissatisfaction with what has replaced it and receptivity to its continuing impact. More markedly, Robertson Smith highlights again and again the "rationality" of sacrifice. This is most evident in "Sacrifice," his contribution to the *Encyclopedia Britannica.* Intended for a wider audience, the piece is a distillation of his views on sacrifice and offers some of his main theories in an accessible and especially revealing form.

Smith's treatment is designed for generalists; indeed it might be understood as a "sacrificial border text." The rhetoric of modern expertise that he adopts here seems appropriate to his own anthropological habits of mind and to the expectations of an audience seeking both authoritative and encyclopedic information. But his ambition above all, an ambition consistent with the work of Mauss and Hubert, is to confirm the modernity of this most ancient, and by some accounts, most heathen custom. It's not that modern society is still irrational; throughout he implies that sacrifice can be understood as a form of scientific rationality. Thus the behavior of the gods at the ritual feast was only legible to experts specifically equipped to read the deity's responses. And interpretations that hold the persisting totemic significance of certain sacred animals in advanced countries to be merely symbolical, are dismissed as unscientific. Finally, the thinking that changed the wolf god into the wolf slayer becomes "a touch of . . . rationalism" (134-35). Smith can apprehend history as an evolving rational script because he understands religion as the foundation of a rational sociability, and sacrifice as the foundation of religion for all times and places. Sacrifice is "the natural expression of respect and homage . . . a merely conventional way of expressing religious feeling" (133). He concludes, "we must not forget that from the beginning this ritual expressed, however crudely, certain ideas which lie at the very root of true religion, the fellowship of the worshippers with one another in their fellowship with the deity, and the consecration of the bonds of kinship as the type of all right ethical relation between man and man" (138). In all of these measures there are "germs of eternal truths." For Robertson Smith, just as for Mauss and Hubert, sacrifice has a secure place in the modern world.

Mauss and Hubert introduce their account of sacrifice with a claim for the rite's unique openness to ambivalence and contradiction. They sift carefully through previous interpretations, those of Tylor, Smith, Frazer, identifying for each case a single, oversimplified principle. For Tylor, they argue, sacrifice was first gift, then renunciation; for Smith, it was consecration; for Frazer, it was competition and murder. What all these theories overlook, according to Mauss and Hubert, is the basic ambiguity of a rite that is simultaneously communal and expiatory, sacred and profane, nourishing and annihilating. With Mauss and Hubert, we might say, sacrifice absorbs the binomial complexities of structural-functionalism. Their reading is deliberately current. We find little of Frazer's historical layering— from gods, to kings, to wretches. History for Mauss and Hubert is a contemporary tale: the story of the encounter between modern methods and an ancient rite. In their terms, sacrifice has a basic structure (antithesis) and a basic action (transformative), and both are animated by the logical ambivalence of religious faith. The action or plot of sacrifice is the consecration of a (usually) profane, "unfavourable" character (9). Its structure allows for the incorporation of expiatory as well as communal purposes. Sacrifice, as they describe it, is always overdetermined. A sacrificial ritual for the ordination of a priest, for example, includes expiatory (*holah*) as well as communal components. To say that a rite is transformative, that it can turn a profane object into a sacred one, is not to forego a principle of "generic unity" (13). They base their own claims for uniformity in an elaboration of ritual procedure that they hold to be true for all times and places. Sacrifice requires, they insist, a concept of the moral person; a society that lacked the concept could not support the idea of religious consecration essential to the rite. Nor could it imagine a higher order as the ultimate object of exchange. Without the concept "moral person," argue Mauss and Hubert, there would be no basis for faith, nor would there be a basis for society.

The first to consider in detail the actual elements of the sacrificial rite, Mauss and Hubert are also the first to insist that it is always about transformation, that it takes ordinary beings and objects and prepares them for their encounter with the sacred. The scene of sacrifice is another country. One cannot enter here by will, only by fulfilling a set of conditions—obtaining a sacred passport of sorts—akin to that required by any other regional transversal. There must be, they write, "an entry into the sacrifice" (20). For Mauss and Hubert, the stakes of exchanging with gods are high. "Establishing a means of communication between the sacred and the profane worlds" always features a single basic structure: a mediating "victim" that in "the course of the ceremony is destroyed" (97). They describe the sacrificial food offerings—the Hebrew *minha*, an oblation of flour and cakes; or the crushed and baked grains of the Hindu rite (12–13)—that serve as symbolic substitutes for human victims. The worshipers who offer them, according to Mauss and Hubert, behave as though they hold the same value as animal or even human victims. And it is customary during sacrifices of real cows to entreat the animal's relatives "not to avenge the wrong about to be done them in the person of one of their number" (33). The point of these examples is that sacrifice is theatrical; it is a ritual performance, with actors and roles. It can even be called festive. Such an admission is not meant to diminish the gravity of the sacrificial occasion, but it does imply an inverse relationship between celebrational atmosphere and the victim's level of animation and consciousness. The sacrifice of a cow produces more solemn theatre than the sacrifice of a grain cake, and so on up to the sacrifice of the god himself.

Built into the rite of sacrifice, according to Mauss and Hubert, is the hope that the higher spiritual powers care about the human beings who worship them. At the same time, the rite registers fears that this care may go unexpressed. More than any other late-nineteenth-century interpreters, Mauss and Hubert are interested in sacrifice as a reflection of human ambivalence toward gods. These rituals, they point out, were sometimes designed to draw gods closer, but just as often the object was to curb their control over human affairs. Sacrifice could serve at least three distinct purposes: the simple fulfillment of an obligation (to a god or gods), a "prudent" quest for rewards or advantages, or a desire for consecration, some momentary unification of worshipers with powers they neither controlled nor fully comprehended.

The final aim, unification, may be the most revealing, for it speaks to sacrifice's function in heightening the spirituality of the community as a whole. The act of sacrifice ascribes a point in time, a mappable, physical space, where the sacred and the secular meet. The hope that universal and social action might converge, even momentarily, is significant not least of all for its resemblance to the methodological ambitions of the social sciences; in particular, that branch of study that Durkheim, the mentor of Mauss, called, "the science of society." It is precisely the object of sociology to create a dialogue between the rational and the actual: to apply uniform standards or laws to human events, standards that had been framed in response to specific events and actions. Indeed, it seems entirely appropriate that those who were dedicated to formulating this "universal" social description would have been especially interested in a religious rite that represented the ultimate fusion of sacred and secular action. The basic plot of sacrifice, which saw benefits or progress as the inevitable issue of destruction, understandably appealed to this post–Darwinian, pre–World War I generation of sociologists.

I have characterized the theories of Mauss and Hubert as modern. Let me specify that further by suggesting that they reflect the dominant assumptions of modern social science.[72] Theirs is a terminology of ambivalence, contradiction, multiplicity, change. This makes their methods neither more nor less historical than those of Robertson Smith, Tylor, or Frazer. All of them, as I have shown, are intent on understanding sacrifice as an evolving event. What distinguishes the work of Mauss and Hubert is the influence of a historical theory especially associated with their turn-of-the-century present. Their analysis is "historicist" in the sense that it views time as a continuum and sees all perspectives on the past as constructions. In keeping with philosophical historicism, every description, every explanation, is referred to the present.[73] What is its meaning for our own historical stage? One could argue that this imperative is responsible for a quality in their analysis that is missing from previous accounts: moral seriousness. Where Robertson Smith might be described as yearning or nostalgic, and Tylor and Frazer as skeptical, even suspicious, Mauss and Hubert are respectful. They seem to believe that if they are faithful to details, remain open and cautious, they may absorb a touch of awe themselves.

Like the worshipers they describe, Mauss and Hubert draw near to their subject while "remaining at a distance from it," in great part because matters of the spirit are "a fearful thing for the ordinary man" (98). Because they assume so much of the ambivalence they attribute to the worshipers they describe, it is hardly surprising to find Mauss and Hubert at the close of their study discovering a perfectly modern correlative for the traditional divine recipient of sacrifice. The components essential to ritual sacrifice differ little from those things normally demanded and supplied by society. Collective life requires periodic sacrifices to bring individuals into relationship with something greater than themselves. This divine collectivity provides "strength and assurance," in keeping with the contractual benefits of sacrifice. The object of sacrifice in a modern context, in other words, is society itself. Sacrifice is about relationships, sustaining connections of mutuality, which are themselves sources of renewal. In a classic Durkheimian maneuver, Mauss and Hubert have effectively transferred sacrificial benefits from gods to society. This is confirmed by the reverential passage that closes their book. When they suggest admiringly that the image of a god "sacrificing himself for the world" is the limit of ideal worship, even among "the most civilized of peoples," we know that they presume the permanent replacement of holy collectivity for deity. Here is a bit of that ending:

These expiations and general purifications, communions and sacralizations of groups, these creations of the spirits of the cities give—or renew periodically for the community, represented by its gods—that character, good, strong, grave, and terrible, which is one of the essential traits of any social entity. . . . They surround, as if with a protective sanctity, the fields they have ploughed and the houses they have built. At the same time they find in sacrifice the means of redressing equilibriums that have been upset: by expiation they redeem themselves from social obloquy, the consequence of error, and re-enter the community; by the apportionments they make of those things whose use society has reserved for itself, they acquire the right to enjoy them. . . . As society is made up not only of men, but also of things and events, we perceive how sacrifice can follow and at the same time reproduce the rhythms of human life and nature. . . . Moreover we have been able to see, as we have proceeded, how many beliefs and social practices not strictly religious are linked to sacrifice. (102–3)

This conclusion can be read as a manifesto for the ongoing centrality of sacrifice in modern life. Now it is society rather than gods demanding "apportionments" from what it has wrought. Now it is society that confers abundance ("fields" and "houses") and underwrites the sanctity of human contracts ("vows," "oaths," "marriages"). Most importantly, it is society that lets people know whether their allotments are proper and just and concedes "the right to enjoy them." The logic of a spiritualized existence that holds a god or gods responsible for every triumph or mishap, every drought, every death, is now fully invested in what is called the "social entity." Now "cities" breathe with "spirits," and "society," personified as the gods once were with "essential traits" ("good," "strong," "terrible"), craves submission. Sacrifice has proven fully adaptable to modernization. No longer limited to the receding functions of the religious life, though bearing still their powerful imprint, sacrifice informs myriad practices and beliefs ("questions of contract, of redemption, of penalties, of gifts, of abnegation" [103]). Sacrificial thinking has become the basis of a new social morality.

Literary Altars

The great contribution of Mauss and Hubert was their identification of the fundamental ambivalence of sacrifice, its tense intermingling of sacred and profane elements, its collapsing of sentiments like celebration and terror, comfort and rage. None of this is unfamiliar to the literary authors who have helped to inspire this study. Near the beginning of *The Souls of Black Folk*, W.E.B. Du Bois introduces a curious characterization of Black Americans: "Some felt gratitude toward the race thus sacrificed in its swaddling clothes on the altar of national integrity."[74] Blacks can feel safe, he implies, because an altar of "national integrity" is not nearly so threatening as the stone structures that supplied the stage for sacrifices in the time of the ancient Semites. The flimsiness of this altar is obviously a joke at national expense. America has neither the political integrity nor the spiritual gravity essential to sacrifice. Yet it does manage to carry off the murderous proceedings, for the reference to "gratitude" confirms that there *has* been some sort of beneficial exchange.

Du Bois is not the lone witness to the revival of this rite. Contemporaneous American literature is pervaded with sacrificial inference and example. Consider Stephen Crane's foot soldiers in *The Red Badge of Courage*, who are portrayed as offerings to a "blood-swollen god." And what is the novel's titular metaphor if not the amulet of self-mortification (as blood-red as the droplets on Hebrew doorposts in the Passover story) that ensures the protagonist's immunity in battle? Or take the violently sacrificial rhythms of Frank Norris's *McTeague*, where images of gorging and bleeding at highly ritualized feasts suggest that every pleasure requires a recompense to higher powers. There is also the wasted working class of Stein's *3-Lives*, who consult mesmeric "priests" as sources of enchantment in worlds governed by a depleted sacrificial economy. Sacrificial designs, as these examples and many more like them show, resonate throughout the literature of the turn of the century.

I want to suggest that sacrifice is about storytelling; from its beginnings, the rite has occasioned imaginative plots. Consider three novelistic variations on sacrifice, each of them vivid and each advancing a different understanding of its persistence. In Gertrude Stein's *3-Lives*, sacrifice is abstract and circumscribed as a psychic economy. Stein shows how it shapes human thought and speech, from the slightest acts (dressing for a Sunday drive) to the most momentous (consulting the spirits before a major life choice). There is a Darwinian intensity to the society Frank Norris creates in *McTeague*, where the lines between human beings and animals are extraordinarily thin, and survival is just as threatened at the theatre as in the desert. This is a world of cannibalism and communion, of bloodletting rites and festive suppers. Sacrifice in *The Red Badge of Courage* is less excessive, limited to a single deadly form. Crane's novel portrays war as the ultimate sacrificial theatre. Where Stein studies the psychology of sacrifice, and Norris looks at it from the perspective of sociobiology, Crane's approach is more explicitly aestheticized, perhaps because his setting is so unquestionably brutal. Sacrifice in his account is decorum, a container for the chaos of war. I've emphasized differences among these examples. But there is one assumption common to all three: that the working classes (for Norris, immigrant, working class; for Stein, immigrant, female working classes) suffer sacrifice to an incomparable degree, whether as domestic slaves (Stein), doomed brutes (Norris), or mass offerings (Crane).

Like other literary works in this study, Stein's *3-Lives* appropriates sacrificial forms only to distort them. Good Anna, for example, the subject of the first portrait, is a compulsive bargain hunter, who values what isn't given up to get something. The cramped existence of this working-class maid is dominated by a fear of excess. She is at war with any type of inflation. Consider the string of adjectives ("small," "spare," "drawn," "worn") used to describe her. Her young assistant, Molly, is equally "thin," "sallow," and "drab."[75] From the larger perspective of the narrative, the transformation of all these immigrant Annas and Mollies and Lenas from negligent foreigners into domestic functionaries is wearing work. More importantly, some bodies are bound to be wasted in the process of securing for so many the pleasures of a new consumer culture. There is a similar contrast between Stein's authorial persona, who turns out pages of repetitive prose (with the efficiency of a modern machine), and the grimy subjects whose lives she immortalizes. Authorship in *3-Lives* takes many forms. The Baltimore row houses in the book's opening—simple, unvarying, childlike (compared to "dominoes"), yet perfect and necessary in their way—are symbols for Stein's sentences. Then there are the overblown mistresses, the beneficiaries of Stein's sacrificial economy. Miss Mathilda's "joyous, country tramps" recall Stein's own extended walking tours in Tuscany (22). "Life was very easy always for this large and lazy Miss Mathilda with the good Anna to watch and care for her," writes Stein. Invariably plump and helpless (from the perspective of domestic management), these mistresses play Gertrude Stein to their pinched Alice B. Toklas caretakers.

But of all the characters in *3-Lives*, Melanctha's sacrificial proclivities are the most pronounced. They are first hinted at in her attraction to the railroad, which she conceives as a place of "mystery and movement." It acts on her like a spell. Here "smoke . . . comes in rings, and always puffs with fire and blue color," and porters tell tales of "cars and sometimes whole trains [fallen] from the narrow bridges, and always up from the dark places death and all kinds of queer devils looked up and laughed in their faces" (98–99). What stands out particularly in this passage is the racist implications of Stein's "minstrel" imagery. But there are more ultimate and universal terrors pictured here: that the most precious offerings—people by the carload, and possibly trainload—might attract the attention of "devils" rather than gods (worse yet, that the gods might *be* devils? [98–99]). Melanctha has a fatal attraction to sacrificial scenes. The source, we learn one hundred pages later, is a childhood trauma. Following the death of a younger brother, Melanctha overhears her mother wish that "the Lord" had taken Melanctha in his "stead" (213). The maternal imaginary that casts Melanctha as the preferred substitute for her sacrificed brother plagues her until the day she finally succeeds in "getting herself dead." But she dies or "falls" many times before that. The most precise Edenic instance occurs during her affair with Jeff Campbell, which is so fraught with parodic mishap that it seems hard to take seriously in such terms. These elements are downplayed, however, in the account of the affair's decline, which is excruciating precisely because it cannot sustain the story's overall parodic effects. "One day there had been much joy between them, more than they had ever yet had . . . with a green, bright, light-flecked world around them"; then "everything g[o]t all ugly for them" (155). No particular reason is given. Stein hints that the problem could be Jeff's fear of passion, or Melanctha's self-destructiveness, but she never resorts to some perfectly psychological solution. In keeping with the governing philosophy of *3-Lives*, the scene concludes in equilibrium, answering a moment of happiness with an immediate sorrow. Stein neither presses nor questions these exchanges; she merely represents them.

I believe that the form of Stein's religious interests in *3-Lives* place it within the range of literary realism and naturalism. Like Norris and Crane, Stein is convinced of the world's disenchantment; throughout her book, spirituality is portrayed as loss. Consumption in *3-Lives*, as in *The Red Badge of Courage* or *McTeague*, is always somewhat mysterious, though it always reduces in the end to base impulse. Stein keeps close watch on what goes into her characters (whether the fuel is material or emotional) and what comes out. Like these other writers, however, she is less concerned with individual balances than with communal stability as a whole. Her ideal, like theirs, is a division of labor. To this end, she creates rigidly hierarchical worlds in which some squander and others save; some luxuriate while others toil. Stein's class structure is built on moral oppositions that appear as constitutional effects: where mistresses are by nature sensual and indifferent, servants are idealists.

Good Anna radiates moral purpose. She is feared by the Bridgeport tradesmen, not because she is large or mean, but because, like a black cat or an impending natural disaster, she conveys menacing force. Anna is a south German immigrant raised as a strict Catholic. But her habits suggest a different order of spiritual compulsion. Like the typical sacrificial devotee, Anna is filled with doubt. She suspects there are no answers for a "faithful, german soul" (32), that she has only the acts and forms themselves. In one scene, for instance, Anna goes to a fortune teller, a blasphemy, according to Christian convention, inspired by a bout of agnostic uncertainty (Anna is "mixed and bothered in her mind" [58]). Stein's detailed description of this encounter is such a departure from her usual psychological abstractions that it seems almost indicative of religious respect. The switch to present tense suggests that the narrator has entered a trance-like state, or seeks mental parity with the ritual agent. Stein's observation on the point of entry into the medium's workroom is telling: "No medium uses her parlor for her work. It is always in her eating-room that she has her trances" (59).

We are not sitting amidst "the grease of many dinners" and the "all pervading" smell of "meat" because the medium is slovenly; that is, can't bother to distinguish her dining room from her workplace. We are here because her meals *are* her work. In keeping with the strict rules governing entrance into a sacred sphere, the three participants in the rite are conducted through a series of rooms before reaching an inner sanctum. Hindu sacrifice, as described by Mauss and Hubert, has participants moving from the *vihara* to the *vedi*, which corresponds to the altar (26). In the Hebrew and Homeric rites they also catalog, "meat" offerings to the god are consecrated by burning "upon the altar-fire," so that "the consecration accordingly reached him in a pleasant-smelling smoke" (36–37). Now Stein's scene: the "smoked" walls of "her good priest"; her prophecy of trees ("I see—I see—a house with trees around it"), which is fulfilled when Anna goes to her new home to find "trees all round about" (59–61). This may be a spoof, but that doesn't detract from the sacrificial content. Robertson Smith notes how trees, which are associated with "oracles and omens," are believed to impart "a sacred energy."[76] The formulaic quality of the various objects here may likewise reinforce spiritual import. These fortune-teller houses are all the same, just as there are uniform methods for seeking attention from above. In its own dilapidated way, this environment evokes the powerful tie between consulting spirits and consuming meals.

Less significant to me than the question of whether Stein was doing this deliberately (I suspect she was), or whether she had read the literature on sacrifice, is the question of who among her cast she imagined as victims.[77] Throughout *3-Lives*, Stein is clear on one point: some are expended in sacrifice, while others benefit from it. Consider the description of Anna approaching death: "There was never any end to Anna's effort and she grew always more tired, more pale yellow, and in her face more thin and worn and worried. . . . how could Anna eat when she always did the cooking?" (80–81). In Stein, there is no possibility of cooking *and* eating. Refusing to "eat" or "rest," Anna consumes herself. This self-consumption might be viewed as a rare form of extravagance, even misanthropy: she squanders what it is most human and social to keep. Yet her decline is also a perfectly equilibrious act. The same can be said for the life and death of the trilogy's final character, Gentle Lena, whose marriage precipitates a series of relinquishments: to spouse, and then to successive children, until she dies giving birth. Lena is the sacrifice to her husband's dream of maternity; following her death, he carries on as sole "mother" to her surviving children.

3-Lives can be read as the story of three sacrificial victims. Each of Stein's protagonists pays homage to invisible forces as shifting as Melanctha's moods. For Stein, these devotions are a measure of their degradation. Yet Stein also draws repeated contrasts between an emotional spirituality and a dry, institutionalized piety, which suggests that she harbors some appreciation for the style of her characters. *3-Lives* comes as close as anything in the period to capturing the Jamesian "varieties of religious experience." The uncharacteristically concrete quality of the descriptions here confirms Stein's preoccupation with faith's social expression. Consider this brief juxtaposition: Anna arrayed for a Sunday outing and Mauss and Hubert on the costume of sacrificial victims. Anna wears a "brick red, silk waist," "colored ribbons," "bird" atop her head, and "feather boa" (40). In Mauss and Hubert, the "adornments" that "imparted . . . a religious character" to a victim might include "ribbons," "a crown," and elaborate coloration (see *Sacrifice*, 29, 53–54, on the role of birds in sacrifice). Stein could have been thinking of the "red heifer," sacrificed, according to Jewish law, as an atonement (59). We can assume that Stein knew the Jewish traditions that associated the color red with endangerment and protection.[78] A derivation of the biblical Passover, red has retained these miraculous associations. In Yiddish, the language of Jewish folk belief, there is a term, *roite bendyl*, whose nearest translation is "red ribbon." Many Jewish children over time have been decorated with red rags of this kind.

While this particular tradition was probably unfamiliar to Stephen Crane, a history of biblical belief in the spiritual properties of colors clearly informed his extraordinarily sense-driven novel on the Civil War. The "red badge" functions much like the Passover mark. There is a desperation in the protagonist's pursuit of this sign during the apocalyptic campaign of brother against brother. With many Jewish grandmothers, he believes that he must secure a red bendyl or he will surely die. Readers have recognized the color symbolism of Crane's painterly narrative as one means of replicating the immediacy of war. It can also be understood as critical to the elaboration of a key theme: the traumatic guilt of survival. The novel re-enacts sacrifice for a nation still mourning, in order to secure some protection for the living.[79] The circumstances of Crane's protagonist before he gets his red bendyl of courage and launches heroically into battle replicate the position of Crane's readers, who are not expected to have experienced war firsthand. But whom is the novel's intricate system of immunity designed to protect? The concern for relative safety seems inspired by the novel's other large aim: to confer the sensory experience of war. When Crane is distinguishing among classes of soldiers, for instance, he seems committed to protecting his readers. The reader, who can dip in and out of battle at will, is a beneficiary, as opposed to a victim. When there is so much blood spraying around that it is impossible to see the green in a blade of grass, Crane seems intent on drowning all in the carnage—officers, foot soldiers, and reader alike. The novel's first scene offers a reassuring image of clearly marked troops. The colloquial speech of these foot soldiers—their "t'morrah"s and "behint"s and "yeh"s—identifies them as the American working class. Crane reinforces their unrefined idiom through perspective: the narrative is low, close to the ground of the hunched, expectant landscape. We are almost nose-level. Crane sets us up so that we will be able to see and smell every wound on every common, unwashed body. The care with which he describes each ordinary act not only fulfills the purpose of getting his readers into war but suggests that there is something awesome in all the details.

Like all sacrificial objects, these troops are sacred and profane. While sweaty, irritable, and vulgar, they betray certain "virtues," including the thoughtfulness of a Henry Fleming. Crane's distinctive style regularly confuses agent and object. Hills have purposes and feelings, but human beings are denied them. "The cold passed reluctantly from the earth," Crane writes in the opening sentence, "and the retiring fogs revealed an army stretched out on the hills, resting."[80] In comparison to the cold, which feels reluctance, and the fog, which lifts gradually, artfully, the human horde seems distinctly inert. Such reversals seem oddly to mimic the complex hierarchies that structure this territory of death, both within human collectivities and between humans and gods. Foot soldiers are powerless before all: God, nature, officers, the plan and topography of battle. They are mere "buttons" in the war machine, and presumably in the vast beyond where it threatens to send them.[81] Officers are powerless before all but the foot soldiers, because their point of reference includes the civilian authorities their war exploits are supposed to satisfy. The remainder of the frame is a blur; it includes "peaceful" society, gods, the land of the dead, and preoccupies every war participant, most often through the wishful optics of memory. This may sound familiar; no threat to the status quo here. Except that Crane is at pains to claim the difference of war. This is another country, and things are not as familiar as they appear.

One persistent sign of incongruity is how difficult it is for these common soldiers to hold to form. They metamorphosize constantly: one minute they are men, the next minute they are cows or pigs or sheep. It is significant, for example, that Henry Fleming's mother is milking a cow in the scene where her son announces his enlistment. Cows, pigs, sheep are all animals known for their suitability to sacrifice. Crane's point is unmistakable: this is a sacrificial crisis, and the gods are hungry. The common foot soldiers are gifts to "war, the blood-swollen god" (39). For a novel whose reputed aim is to re-create the atmosphere of war, it's striking how much time is spent describing consumption: foot soldiers feeding (43); war gods "gulping" entire brigades (72); soldiers moved (perversely, it seems) by spectacles of death to nostalgic reflections upon meals they have eaten (124, see also 119, 141, 156, 168–69, 178). Henry Fleming wonders at one point, what a certain regiment "had eaten" to inspire its deadly heroism (109). While the energy expended in war may necessitate constant refueling, Crane's interest in food seems tied to his understanding of sacrificial rites. As Robertson Smith would say, sacrifice is the one event in which eating and killing can be equally sacred.

According to Crane's "episode of war," society is itself the blood-swollen god that feeds on human armies. Society is a vast, heaving organism, which requires human sacrifice, though it can sometimes be persuaded to spare a potential victim, if it is properly attired (in red). In the most ritually precise moment of the novel, Crane describes "the dark lines of troops," surrounded by American flags, "the red in the stripes dominating." These flags, Crane continues, "splashed bits of warm color" upon the men in national and also in universal tribute. The forthcoming scene of slaughter, where some will perhaps be spared, is thus sacralized. This is effected by the word "warm," which transforms a mere image into something as palpable as blood. Splashed ceremonially on lines of men, these drops confirm the symbolic significance of sacrifice throughout the novel. Sprinkling blood is of course a standard sacrificial procedure. The act establishes the convenant between God and his servant and provides the pathway for the transfer of spiritual efficacy (and protection) between them. Blood, like food, connects humans and gods.[82] *The Red Badge of Courage* depicts in lavish terms what it means to live and die "under the colors." "Under the colors" is Emile Durkheim's phrase for a military sphere that provides "an eminently fertile soil for suicide" (*Suicide*, 239).

There probably is no more explicit sacrificial analogy contemporary to Crane's *Red Badge* (1895) than Durkheim's *Suicide* (1897). For both Crane and Durkheim, the society of war is an ideal type for modern society. Crane's description of the relentless sociability of war—"a society that probes pitilessly at secrets . . . constantly pricking, discovering, proclaiming those things which are willed to be forever hidden" (106)—reverberates in Durkheim's image of a community that "leaves no one from sight," in which "collective supervision is constant, extending to everything" (221). Durkheim is especially interested in how the common soldiers are motivated to battle of their own accord. How is it that death comes to seem, in this day and age, an individual or group's highest office? Durkheim's explanations include the vigilance that is basic to military life, the amplification of hierarchy and submission there, and the extremity of battle. All of these factors encourage the devaluation of ordinary lives. Durkheim's purpose, in keeping with his larger thesis, is to discriminate the social ends of self-sacrifice. When a Hindu wife performs *sati* (suicide upon her husband's death), when a slave throws himself on the funeral pyre of his master, when a soldier launches into battle, they assume the role of sacrificial offering as a social obligation (220). Were they to evade the expectations of the collectivity, they would be likely to die at its hands. Where anomic suicide in Durkheim's analysis is the result of excessive individuation, altruistic suicide is the result of excessive socialization. These are *learned* tendencies, not inherent peculiarities of individuals. The implication (though Durkheim doesn't say it outright) is that relative valuations of life express socialized differences of class. The common soldier is trained to devalue his life, while the officer's "keener" self-regard makes him "less ready to sacrifice" his own (234). Durkheim's prescription provides an invaluable gloss on Crane's novel. For it is precisely this penchant for the *selective unmaking* of men that defines the inhumanity of the gods and of the war machines that support them.

McTeague is probably the most gruesome work in the American literary canon. Its themes are human bestiality, social Darwinism, miserliness, wife beating, sterility, senility, individual degeneracy, social decline. The "why" of this gruesomeness is inseparable from the "how": *McTeague* derives its astonishing grimness from its dramatization, brutal in detail, of what it feels like to inhabit an anomic universe. The book conveys the emotional atmosphere and physical texture of that world. It is difficult to close out its sights and smells when one is finished reading. Horror inheres in the simple rounds of a sacrificial society, where every human joy demands a sorrow: a child's delight in a birthday toy is immediately compensated by the toy's disappearance in the sea; the pleasure of a birthday picnic is canceled out by the punitive tyranny of a father, and so on. In the most annihilating of these scenes, considered so offensive that Norris was persuaded to remove it from early editions of the novel, a child's theatre treat becomes a ghoulish event when he wets his pants in public and is beaten for it. Nothing else in the book matches this for pain and humiliation.[83] But it is reproduced in more purely symbolic terms: Norris's retelling of the Fall. The moment calls attention to itself as a set piece: "The kitchen was clean as a new whistle; the freshly blackened cook stove glowed like a negro's hide. . . . Trina was in the centre of the room. . . . Never had she looked so pretty. . . . The whole scene . . . gave off, as it were, a note of gayety that was not to be resisted." Then the "deluge," represented through a tidy metaphor that contains it, while also implying its threat: "Suddenly her small hand gripped tightly upon the sponge, so that the water started from it and dripped in a little pattering deluge upon the bricks."[84] In plot terms, the deluge is the letter that strips Trina's husband of professional status and livelihood and initiates the cruel dissolution of their marriage. It looks like "water," but it feels like blood. The scene realizes the sense of foreboding that dominates from the book's opening. What follows is an unraveling of the characters' lives: the fall from the mediation and control of sensual appetites (reconceived as "tastes" and "pleasures") by bourgeois rites of passage (professionalization, courtship, marriage) to the rule of animal instinct.

The novel's desacralized sacred world seems, of all those that will be surveyed in this study, the most authentically sacrificial. It resembles, in certain respects, a social scientific blueprint, though less in the Lombrosian manner usually identified than in the mode of Robertson Smith and Durkheim. Society here is afflicted with anomie. Social bonds have worn thin. Kinship ties—the mother-son bond, cousinship—count for little. Friendship counts for less. Bloodlines transmit debility rather than sustenance. In one four-block radius we find German, Scotch, Irish, Mexican, Black, and Jew. Norris may be trying to ape God by including every possible human kind in his fictional Armageddon. If so, he is a "maximum God" of vengeance, who allows neither exceptions nor substitutes: anyone with the misfortune to wind up in his universe is bound for the sacrifice. In keeping with the air of doom that opens *McTeague*, characters are defined by a range of compulsions and deformities. The protagonist is a beast, introduced like an animal at feeding time. Miss Baker, an agoraphobic old maid, keeps obsessive watch—through the wallpaper—on the activities of her wizened neighbor, Old Grannis, whose days are spent in the equally obsessive task of binding useless magazines. This is a society of hoarders and misfits, all of them consumed with losses and assets, all of them devoted to the miserly prospect of self-containment.[85]

Nothing that happens here, no act nor accident, can escape the glaring, all-encompassing symbolic of sacrifice. Even the commercial lottery that bestows a mythic "fortune" on McTeague's wife, Trina, is rewritten in the sacrificial form of alms. Every winner described by the loquacious lottery agent, who regards myth making as part of his job, is downtrodden: a "poor newsboy," a "bootblack," former "criminals," or hopeless "gamblers," a man "driven to suicide through want" and declared victorious after his death. Each chance event becomes an act of divine recompense. The agent's list reads like the typical selection of the criminal or destitute so often reserved for sacrificial purposes. His claims are consistent with a long biblical tradition linking alms and sacrifice, even if his rhetoric falls short of the exact New Testament reference: "He who doeth alms is offering a sacrifice of praise."[86]

The novel's sacrificial economics extends to the reproductive function. Sexuality, like everything else, is valuable until expended. Though the book is full of misers, and no character escapes the taint of this peculiar malady, it is fair to say that Norris engenders miserliness through his portrait of the twisted Trina McTeague. This is something that seems not to have occurred to Simmel, though Norris's character resembles Simmel's type in other respects. Norris's feminizing of miserliness is consistent with another trait of his women characters: their overwhelming ambition, in particular, their association with modern principles of rationalization and reduction. In descriptions that seem uncannily Weberian, Norris's characters are submitted to womanly processes of miniaturization. Through his wife's efforts, for example, McTeague's gargantuan appetites are refined. Bottled ale replaces boats of steamed beer, a genteel melting-pot snack of hot tamales substitutes for slabs of beef. This echoes the efforts of McTeague's mother, who manages to compress her son's mining trade (in Norris's words, "the caricature of dentistry" [217]), into an expert oral "art."

Why would Norris specify miserliness and reduction as feminine traits? What, in his view, makes this rather inoffensive, even beneficial eagerness for social advancement a polite form of monstrosity? I think it has something to do with Norris's conviction that women harbor what is probably society's most precious commodity. Women in *McTeague* are the reproducers who don't produce, whose bodies shrivel like empty money bags, when they might expand with child. Consider the following indictment by analogy: Trina wailing for her stolen gold, a hypothetical mother mourning her "dead baby's shoe" (198). In *McTeague*, a money sack can support the symbolic weight of scrotum and womb (119, 198), because sexuality has achieved a pure commodity status. More particularly, there is no distinction between female sexuality as an asset a woman possesses and a woman's very identity. As soon as this sexuality is "given out," the woman herself declines in value.[87] As I have suggested, female sexuality in its most obvious commodity form, is reproduction, the means to the working classes' notorious advantage over Anglo-American ruling classes in this era. But the lower classes of *McTeague* are denied this advantage, and with it, the prospect of redemption.

There is no chance for the ritualized type of offering that might end all this vengeance: the sacrifice of the firstborn. It is telling that the novel's protagonist has only one aspiration: he dreams of "a son, whose name would be Daniel." This son would marry and have children, and the whole family would live together in one house: "the dentist saw himself as a venerable patriarch" (109). The novel's lone offspring, the frail "hybrid" of the Jewish Zerkow and Mexican Maria Macapa, dies shortly after birth (135). Why does the initially vigorous Trina McTeague, herself the issue of a healthy family with four children, fail to reproduce? A possible clue lies in Trina's "profession." For Trina has "her own little trade," in addition to her housekeeping chores and lottery investments. She makes toy miniatures of Noah's Ark: chickens, cows, camels, even the ark itself. The only pieces she doesn't make are the manikins—"Noah . . . and all the others"— because she can't compete with "the turning lathe that could throw off whole tribes" far faster than the human hand (76). The implication is that Trina's investment in symbolic sacrifice contributes to her divestment of maternal sacrifice. We might say that Trina is repaid by the novel's sacrificial economy, in typically gruesome fashion, when she sacrifices her fingers to the animals' construction (the poison paint she uses, together with her husband's cruel habit of biting her fingers, results in blood poisoning and amputation).

Trina's inability to make the human figures for her arks seems consistent with the larger social-Darwinist philosophy of literary naturalism. *McTeague* provides an especially malicious form of these ideas by deliberately confusing human and animal behavior. If anything, Norris implies the greater "dignity" of animals. Perhaps they are more worthy of salvation than their human counterparts. Take two successive scenes of combat, one featuring beasts, the other men. First the dogs: "With all the dignity of monarchs they moved away from each other" (123). The subsequent human encounter is as brutal as bloodletting can be, in part because it destroys the pleasures of a seaside picnic.[88] Here is McTeague after Marcus has bitten through his ear: "It was the hideous yelling of a hurt beast, the squealing of a wounded elephant" (133). Nor is there less pain when Norris's characters are "feasting." The McTeagues' postwedding banquet table is an "abandoned battlefield": littered with corpses, "skeleton," "skull," and empty bottles lined up like "dead soldiers . . . a devastation, a pillage" (98). "A dirge, a lamentable, prolonged wail," fills the air, while a departing guest offers "an oracular phrase" (99). Wedding is mourning, eating is sacrifice; for every rite of passage in the novel requires an offering. People do not move from one stage to another without some loss. Still, an offering conveys (however furtively) hope of spiritual return, just as alimentary communion sustains a presumably harmonious kin. And Norris leaves little doubt that his characters are doomed.

Is there a point to all this ritual action? Is the novel's close, a fight to the death for the Scotch-Irish McTeague as well as his archrival, the German Marcus Schouler, to be read as a double offering? Are we to take the sacrifice of this pathological immigrant community as the means to some greater collective salvation? With animals designated the more "perfect" (in Robertson Smith's terms) or highly valued beings, Norris pictures *human* substitutes driven to mutual destruction in the wilderness of Death Valley. Yet it's impossible, in my view, to discover sacrificial "generosity" in a book that offers readers as little as it does characters. The foreclosure of redemptive possibility within Norris's fiction implies its foreclosure without. In *McTeague*, sacrifice is everywhere apparent and nowhere named. Sacrificial rites may feel essential, but they have lost all efficacy. The ending from this perspective is a tableau of foiled sacrifice. No less than three victims are laid before the desert gods: two humans and a canary. But like everything else in this book of stylized excess, the scene ends without spiritual edification, weighed down (rather than lifted) by its sacrificial machinery.

Let me be specific about the resemblances I see between Norris's account and the presentation of sacrifice in studies by Tylor, Robertson Smith, Frazer, Mauss and Hubert. Like these narratives, Norris's text expresses nostalgia toward a rite that its author considers basic to social order. Norris shares the view of sacrifice's persistence in various repressed forms and agrees that it has vanished as a central event of civilized culture. There are no more altars, and the economic variations on sacrifice in the modern context are hopelessly reduced. Norris gives fictional expression to losses more subtly inscribed in social scientific analyses. Moreover, like other literary examples I will be discussing, Norris's effects are often comic, however grimly so. This is never true of my social scientific examples. I am arguing for a continuity of perspective between certain fictions from this period and a classic social scientific literature, both of which display sacrificial nostalgia. At the same time I want to acknowledge the formal, philosophical, and also political differences between the literature and social science I examine.

My purpose here is not to further a "sociology of culture," although I think my analysis encourages a reassessment of the ramifications of such an approach. Rather, it is a plea for greater appreciation of the historical questions evoked by interdisciplinary inquiry. For my exploration of the relationship between literature and sociology at the point when both literary study and social science were being institutionalized in the United States exposes a prevailing ideology of sacrifice that continues to inform (and impair) our culture. This is meant to be recuperative criticism. My implicit argument in each chapter is that we continue to display the symptoms of a prior sacrificial culture (whether the subject is women and welfare, racial equality, or the role of class), and we will continue to do so until we recognize our situation in a historically comprehensive and analytical way. The privileged thinkers in this book see the past in present social forms and anticipate its potential to influence future ones. The subject of historical knowledge raises unavoidable formal distinctions between literary and social scientific narratives of sacrifice. All of them may be, in some sense, constructions or inventions, but we need to distinguish between types of invention. There are distinctions that link endeavors and those that separate them (dividing literature categorically from social science).

Every writer in my study understood the tremendous impact of demographic diversity on modern social development. Many anticipated that a capitalist-industrial society would tend increasingly to promote disparities among its members, disparities that would require rationalization. By highlighting the sacrificial stages set forth in these literary works, I am making a case for their historical insights. I am claiming that literature can reveal things about society that are available in no other cultural form.

I argue for the historical substance of literature from the standpoint of meaningful "allusions" and "sources," but I don't mean to disavow the historical expressiveness of more subtle textual elements. On the contrary. My understanding of what makes literature "historical" calls for some revision in the way we typically imagine the historicity of novelistic form. History is to be found in the accidental and minute, just as much as in the global and thematic. And this is just as true, it is the burden of my study to demonstrate, for a social scientific or theological narrative. A badgering tone, the unfolding of a particular image can be remarkably revealing. An attitude tells as much as a direct reference. Terrible acts register imperceptibly. The sorts of details that I have in mind here might be understood as literature's "numb imperatives," to invoke the idea of a textual body. "Numb imperative" is Pierre Bourdieu's phrase for "social necessity" physically inscribed, "converted into motor schemes and body automatisms." These "schemes" and "automatisms" are what "cause practices . . . to be *sensible*."[89] Bourdieu's image affords a view of literature as sensible inscription. More specifically, we can see literature as an inscription that makes the painful inscriptions of the historical past sensible to present and future readers. For as the chapters that follow demonstrate, sacrifice, more than any other social practice, confirms society's power to impress itself on human bodies and minds.

TWO

The Return to Sacrifice in
Melville and Others

❧

LIKE MANY others who have written on Herman Melville's haunting and powerful novella *Billy Budd, Sailor*, I am drawn to its religious themes. My particular concern is Melville's preoccupation with the narrative's culminating ritual of sacrifice. The meaning of sacrifice was a lifelong pursuit. Explored through the lens of Polynesian religion in *Typee* (1846), the rite is a spur to comparative theologizing. In *Moby-Dick* (1850), sacrifice is a form of spiritual economy, motivating all members—workers and owners alike—of a developing capitalist industry. In *Clarel* (1876), sacrifice is a territorial principle: the ancient means for settling boundary disputes, dividing land, distinguishing aliens from kin. Melville seems to write himself, with growing certainty, into a conviction of the rite's durability. By 1891, the year of *Billy Budd*, sacrifice has become plural and modern, a ritual common to all cultures (Hebrew, Greek, Roman, Christian, Indian, and Chinese), and amenable to economic and juridical evolution (from ancient barter to modern capitalism, from biblical vengeance to modern tort).

The novella's opening image of the black sailor at Liverpool, who fades like a superimposed movie still into "the Handsome Sailor," "the welkin-eyed Billy Budd," establishes the dramatic historical exchange enacted in the story.[1] As a shade from the past at least twice removed, a ghostly reminder of the double casualties of the eighteenth-century slave trade, the black sailor registers the continuities between different sacrificial types.

In Liverpool, now half a century ago, I saw under the shadow of the great dingy street-wall of Prince's Dock (an obstruction long since removed) a common sailor so intensely black that he must needs have been a native African of the unadulterate blood of Ham—a symmetric figure much above the average height. . . . In jovial sallies right and left his white teeth flashing into view, he rollicked along, the center of a company of his shipmates. These were made up of such an assortment of tribes and complexions as would have well fitted them to be marched up by Anacharsis Cloots before the bar of the first French Assembly as Representative of the Human Race. At each spontaneous tribute rendered by the wayfarers to this black pagod of a fellow—the tribute of a pause and stare, and less frequently an exclamation—the motley retinue showed that they took that sort of pride in the evoker of it which the Assyrian priests doubtless showed for their grand sculptured Bull when the faithful prostrated themselves. (430)

With striking brevity, this passage lays out the novella's themes: submission and spirituality, kinship and class, sacrifice and social control. The black sailor is an ideal type and a sacred object, unifying a vast assortment of "tribes and complexions." As a counterpart to this African cynosure, Billy Budd will be a model for the working class. The sailor's first sighting, "under the shadow of the great dingy street-wall," prefigures Billy's "shadow[y]" entrance into the king's service as a victim of impressment. Like most other origins in this narrative, Billy's are mystified. The scene's implicit analogy between sailor impressments and slave auctions, between hidden births both black and white, suggests how slavery lingers, in the ongoing tyrannies of capital over labor and in utilitarian conceptions of bearing as breeding.[2]

The sailor's purity is emphasized. His color is singularly "intense," his blood "unadulterate," his body "symmetric," his teeth genuinely "white": to be sacred, the passage implies, is to be an anomaly. The sailor creates a hiatus, a disruption of conventional routine. He fortifies social order by subverting it. This superlative character is threatening, which is the point of the closing sacrificial image. Sacrifice is a ritual about control, a symbolic stage for the defusion or placation of superhuman powers. But according to this passage, sacrifice has equally to do with the mundane and human. The Black sailor inspires a series of sacrificial recollections, extending back to the early Semites. Sacrifice appears most immediately in the transfer of slavery's mantle from "native Africans" to White sailors. Somewhat further back are the martyred acts featured in any history of the French Revolution. And further back still is the image of sacrificial substitution with animals (Bulls) replacing humans (actual Assyrians) as ritual victims.

Sacrifice is pictured here as a quality of memory. Beyond a ritual event, it is an inducement to interpretation. These two actions—remembering and interpreting—may appear incompatible. Memory is a flow, unsolicited, immune to rational strategies of collection and organization. Interpretation is a skill. Depending on its wielder, it can be smooth or urgent, imperceptible or unbearably charged. What memory and interpretation share is remoteness. Neither is close to the scene of the crime. Remembering and interpreting are compulsive acts. We imagine ourselves subjected to memory; it comes and goes at will. It is difficult to elicit and repress. Nor can those fated to be readers of the signs of experience resist the interpretive impulse. *Billy Budd* is filled with these sorts of absorbed and swollen psyches. In the manner of the sailors he describes in the opening, the presiding consciousness is sometimes "arrested," sidetracked or stopped short. Along with these delays and digressions, qualifications abound ("or then more frequently than now," "occasionally," "in certain instances"). The narrator can be spirited and urgent, piling image upon cliché upon allusion. Elsewhere he stutters, overwhelmed with his task. His way is "obstructed," and he in turn obstructs the way of the reader. This is the narrative pattern throughout. Different contemporary events become occasions for sacrificial reminiscences. Melville's present is made meaningful through its location in a history of sacrifice as long as the memory of human beings.

Billy Budd dramatizes a prevailing habit of Melville's culture: the habit of thinking back to sacrifice. It helps us to understand the urge to recuperate the rite that fired so many theological, social scientific, and literary minds in this period. This opening provides a stage of religious intensity thrice removed. For every vivid image there is an interpretive equivalent. The "bronzed mariners" crowding in on their regal "cynosure" are replicated by the narrator who crowds in on their state of worshipfulness, trying to catch a spark. Memory itself resembles this eager horde, "fitted" to be "Representatives of the Human Race." Memory presses in, a heterogeneous parade of associations. Melville is fascinated by the yield of involuntary expression, what our minds seek to tell us despite ourselves. The world—its human and objective elements—is fragmented. So is religious belief. In bits of rags on the ground we find the key to existence. And when we accidentally stumble on these nondescript truths, our discovery becomes destiny. We can't get there by looking. We are supposed to keep our eyes lowered and wait. Reflections of this kind reveal why sacrifice—presented in *Billy Budd* as both ritual and rhetoric—is hospitable to Melville. Sacrifice is the ultimate religious gesture, because to him it appears independent of belief.

Sacrifice is also basic to Melville's conception of society. Society is interdependent, dominated by rituals of exchange and by ideas of equilibrium, checks and balances, cancellation. This is the social sensibility of the novella's narrator, with his language of equivalence and equivocation. Sacrifice, for Melville, is most authentic in its ancient form, where it expresses profound religious uncertainty (Does God really perceive our smoky oblations?). His sense of the rite is closest to that of the ancient Semites (described in this era by Robertson Smith and Arthur Penrhyn Stanley), who saw belief as a dilemma and worried about the preservation of communal boundaries. This is in contrast to a Christian ideal (described by David Frederich Strauss, Horace Bushnell, and Berdmore Compton), where sacrifice is a divine office and the ultimate testament of faith. Here the question of communal identity is subordinate to an ideal of messianic Christianity. In a reverential departure from both the Hebraic and Christian plots, Melville rewrites the story of the Fall for the modern age. He imagines it as a fall from religious to social types, from neat biblical categories to the rational but ever provisional terminologies of (social) science. Rather than limited and distinct, secure in its significance, sacrifice is omnipresent and never definitive. The "knowers" in this world may be scientists rather than gods, but the sacrificial obligation persists. Melville shares this assumption with various social scientists of his era, from Herbert Spencer, E. B. Tylor, and James Frazer, to Lester Ward, Albion Small, and Edward Ross.

The purpose of this chapter is to elaborate some of these affinities and to examine them in terms of a theological tradition that has long been recognized as foundational to Melville's work. The sacrificial interests of Melville, and contemporary social scientists and theologians, will be viewed as expressions of a common context: a society confronting first Civil War, then the end of slavery, unprecedented levels of immigration, technological and industrial development, capital-labor conflict. Among the most significant of these developments for Melville, as well as for others whose work will figure prominently in this analysis, is the transformation of religion. All of these thinkers were driven to intellectual understanding by personal experiences of religious crisis. For all, sacrifice provided a critical focus. Sacrifice assumed center stage in part as a consequence of widespread interest in comparative religion. It was the one rite identified as common to all cultures. Because sacrifice implicitly sanctioned doubt about God's responsiveness, it was especially attractive to intellectuals caught in their own struggles with faith. The ritual necessity of selecting out victims, identifying those who were both dispensable and sufficiently sacred to warrant sacrificial treatment, also helped to reinforce social boundaries. It afforded a pathway for reflection on the meaning of collective life.

This chapter grows out of a grasp of Melville as a reader. As much as any novelist of his time, Melville's inclinations were scholarly. In addition, his habit of newspaper and periodical reading would have acquainted him with significant developments in various fields. His letters, journals, and writings reveal a particular interest in scientific and social scientific challenges to religious doctrine.[3] In these matters especially, the question of Melville's reading is best approached in a reciprocal fashion. *Billy Budd* can be a guide to Melville's library: we need to read out from the text to sources and back in again. This work, like others, betrays Melville's conversance with the theological disputes of his era: debates on Christ's character (his sweetness versus his duplicity, his transcendent versus his cultural dimensions), on evidence and miracles, on the consequences of Christianity's triumph. Melville's understanding of religion was shaped by a spiritualized sense of social necessity that he shared with many contemporary social scientists. Overlapping patterns of ideas, method, and design between *Billy Budd* and works such as Winwood Reade's *The Martyrdom of Man* (1872) or Robertson Smith's writings on sacrifice (1881–91) suggest first- or second-hand knowledge. In certain cases (Schopenhauer's *Will and Idea*, Stanley's *Sinai and Palestine*) there is an established link between Melville and a work that is critical to my analysis. In others (Reade's *Martyrdom*; Strauss's *Life of Jesus*) the link is more oblique.

My argument does not depend on Melville's direct knowledge of major social scientific arguments of his time, though many were excerpted in journals where he himself published. My premise is a simple one: a novella by a highly intellectual author, written in an era when the emerging social sciences were the subject of much debate in England and America, shares questions and even assumptions in common with major works from these disciplines. Thus, for instance, Melville's fiction continually opposes the rational and the miraculous. But it tends to dramatize such oppositions, oppositions that remain more implicit in the social scientific literature. Moreover, sacrifice in *Billy Budd* appears as a type of "border talk" between traditional religion and modern secularism. To invoke a familiar Melvillian rhetoric of appetite, we might imagine sacrifice as a recipe. "Add three dry ingredients or religious principles: submission, superstition, faith in miracles. Stir over a low (ritual) flame and bring to a boil. Yield: a social scientific chowder of functional interdependence, social equilibrium, and rationalism. Serves a nation." As the greatest theorists in each generation recognized, social science was dependent on religious elements. Because he read Schopenhauer (who was fond of highlighting the antiprogressive features of modern social science) and was aware of Comtean philosophy (as suggested by occasional references), Melville was conversant with these tensions.

My analysis leaves standard views of Melville's own religious trials largely intact. According to critical consensus, Melville neither believed nor disbelieved in God. He believed in faith. His lifelong dilemma was his inability to adhere to any one form of it. In the pages that follow, I amplify Melville's literary and spiritual odyssey by providing some new contexts for understanding it. The first part of this chapter builds a basis for Melville's abiding interest in sacrifice by examining some contemporaneous developments in comparative theology and the higher criticism. This is a vast area of inquiry, and I depend upon secondary sources to make it navigable.

The extensive exploration of other religions in Melville's time and the acceptance of scientific method in biblical commentary provide an important backdrop for Melville's first fictional approach to the problem of faith,

Typee. Melville's account of "heathen worship" exhibits some of the new openness of liberal theology, at the same time that his cross-cultural interpretations betray evidence of new social scientific techniques. Among the discoveries of Melville's alter ego in *Typee* is the modernity of certain primitive practices, including sacrifice. Christianity may have cornered the market on religious enlightenment, Melville suggests, but there is much to learn from native ways. *Typee* exposes the unintentional ironies of theological treatments such as James Freeman Clarke's *Ten Great Religions* or Berdmore Compton's *Catholic Sacrifice*. These works proclaim an openness to other forms of faith, while nervously reappropriating a monolithic Christian dogma. Sacrifice is acknowledged as common to all religions, but is narrowed to its truest divine form in the Crucifixion.

In arguments like these, Christianity serves as a form of liberal social control, eliciting and defusing the threat of spiritual multiplicity. More compatible with Melville's own skepticism, though he disavowed them, were rational approaches to the New and Old Testaments. The application of scientific method to narratives of faith may have irritated Melville, but it struck him so forcefully that it was eventually incorporated into his meditations on religion in *Billy Budd*. The second part of the chapter explores the crisis over religious faith that absorbed so many. This crisis can be viewed as both cause and effect of convictions about religion's multiplicity and of rational reinscriptions of the Bible. In this section, selected literary texts from mid century—*Moby-Dick*, *The Wide, Wide World*, Emerson's *Essays*—guide my approach to different forms of religious reaction. The final section of the chapter analyzes *Billy Budd* from the perspective of the debates previously discussed. The rise of comparative and scientific theology and religious skepticism of various kinds encouraged reflection on sacrificial rites and principles. One of my purposes will be to provide some explanation for this susceptibility, which was especially acute in America. Melville's America was uniquely receptive to sacrifice, and *Billy Budd* can help us to understand why. To this end, *Billy Budd* will be considered as part of a contemporaneous recuperation of sacrifice that engaged sociologists (e.g., Herbert Spencer, Lester Ward, Edward Ross), theologians (e.g., Horace Bushnell, H. Clay Trumbull, Arthur Stanley), and literary authors (e.g., Henry James, Stephen Crane, Frank Norris). The extent and richness of Melville's sacrificial design, can only be apprehended in tandem with these other writings. Sacrifice will be read vertically (from ancient sources to Melville's twin late-eighteenth- and late-nineteenth-century settings) and horizontally (as an interdisciplinary vision of the modern era). Many have recognized the centrality of sacrifice in *Billy Budd*, but we have yet to appreciate the full historical significance of Melville's portrayal. Through a wide-ranging account of sacrificial designs both inside and outside the narrative, I hope to initiate that appreciation.

Rational Testaments
and
Comparative Theologies

Early in the nineteenth century the idea took possession of leading scholars in Europe that the chief scripture given for our instruction in the conduct of life is human experience. . . . It would be possible and instructive to draw a parallel between the vagaries of the social scientists of various names, in trying to get wisdom from human experience, and the different schools of biblical interpretation. — Albion Small, *The Origins of Sociology*[4]

In the wake of late-eighteenth-century political revolutions in France and America, Germany experienced its own revolution, one that was just as influential, though far more muted in form. This was the revolution in approaches to the Bible, known as the "higher criticism." The biblical scholarship of late-eighteenth- and early-nineteenth-century Germany was unique in great part because it was located in universities and therefore relatively liberated from doctrinal control. In the hands of philologists such as Friedrich August Wolf, Johann Gottfried von Herder, Julius Wellhausen, and Ferdinand Christian Baur, the Bible became an organic document, with an original meaning made available by scientific methods of recovery. Like the classics, which these scholars pursued with equal rigor, the Bible could only be fully comprehended through a detailed re-creation of the culture that produced it. They adapted the free and critical spirit of the Jewish philosopher Spinoza, which helped them to see as secular events the divine interventions and miraculous occurrences recorded in the history of the Jews and in the life of Jesus. These historical methods caught on among liberal Christians in America eager to reconcile the claims of science and faith. The dry philology of the higher criticism proved suprisingly seductive, as Emerson said, to "green boys from Connecticut, New Hampshire, and Massachusetts," who devoured "exegetical discourses in the style of Vos, Wolff, and Ruhnken, on the Orphic and Ante-Homeric remains . . . learning [which] instantly took the highest places . . . in our unoccupied American Parnassus."[5] Emerson's observation confirms first, that the American embrace of the higher criticism expressed insecurity about the culture's own theological resources. The American religious imagination was bereft—Emerson's tactful term is "unoccupied"—and therefore uniquely receptive to foreign imports. Second, these German methods accorded enormous power to the interpreter. Reading the Bible became an act of will and mind. Through its rigorous scholarly methods, the higher criticism transformed the Bible into a living enterprise centered in the human consciousness.[6]

95

SCIENTIFIC SCRIPTURE

While the higher criticism attracted enthusiastic adherents, it remained controversial. Edward Everett, for example, complained that by minimizing the claims of an inner divinity, this cold German science threatened a deeper piety. The major bible critics were responsive to reservations of this kind. In his 1815 work *Über Religion und Theologie*, Wilhelm de Wette carefully distinguished problems of knowledge from problems of faith. Historical criticism, he argued, justified faith by providing a secure foundation for it. At the same time, faith was not a matter of rational understanding but of intuition and feeling. The two impulses, toward knowledge on the one hand and belief on the other, provided parallel foundations for modern Christianity. De Wette came closest to his own reconciliation of these two things in his powerful reconsideration of miracles. Miracles were symbolic expressions, which had less to do with empirical possibility than with spiritual self-reliance.[7] The higher-critical demand for historical accuracy paradoxically freed the Bible from doctrinal claims of truth. Liberated by history, the word of God, according to Theodore Parker, could now be submitted to "the oracle God places in the breast."[8] By way of David Friedrich Strauss's *Life of Jesus* and his own fiery transcendentalism, Parker translated de Wette into a more daring historical method, and a more spirited defense of piety. Historical criticism, Parker announced in his revolutionary "South Boston Sermon," exposes the relativity of Christian doctrine. "The heresy of one age is the orthodox belief and 'only infallible rule' of the next." This indeed was Christ's message: a genuine Christianity makes us outgrow any form or any system of doctrines we have devised, and approach still closer to the truth.[9] The authors of the Scriptures were "men who in some measure partook of the darkness and limited notions of their age." Christ was an intellectual innovator like any other. "It seems difficult to conceive any reason," Parker writes, "why moral and religious truths should rest for their support on the personal authority of their revealer, any more than the truths of science."[10] This is quintessential Parker: unqualified dedication to the Bible, expressed as a relentless critique of absolutism. The Bible, he argued, echoing de Wette, verified intuitive faith. And faith evolved. The inspired believer was part of a universal community that extended from ancient times to the present and included early Semites, contemporary "heathens," and the gentle Jesus himself.

Parker's reformist sentiments, his attraction to historical and relativist approaches, his conviction that the existing New England theological establishment needed shaking up, his interest in European cultural imports, all found a more magisterial and centrist expression in Emerson's "Divinity School Address."

Historical Christianity has fallen into the error that corrupts all attempts to communicate religion. It has dwelt, it dwells, with noxious exaggeration about the *person* of Jesus. Men have come to speak of revelation as somewhat long ago given and done, as if God were dead. . . . I look for the hour when that supreme Beauty which ravished the souls of those Eastern men, and chiefly of those Hebrews, and through their lips spoke oracles to all time, shall speak in the West also. The Hebrew and Greek Scriptures contain immortal sentences, that have been bread of life to millions. But they have no epical integrity; are fragmentary; are not shown in their order to the intellect. I look for the new Teacher that shall follow so far those shining laws that he shall see them come full circle.

With this challenge, Emerson launched the century-long agenda of New England liberal theology. Sidney Ahlstrom calls it "a distinctive American phase of a great alternation of mood and mind that affected most of Western Christendom."[11] This shift in "mood" was a spiritual outcome of a larger Enlightenment, as well as a derivation of revolutionary politics in France and America. The story of Emerson's attack on Unitarianism is a familiar one, but worthy of brief review. Christianity had become hardened and monumental, according to Emerson. It had lost the ability and urge to speak. Belief for Emerson was embodied, tangible in a voice or a gesture. This is why he admired an Eastern spirituality, so resonant and material that it could be imagined as a type of nourishment. Emersonian religion was a plane of particularity, like Emerson's cabinet of nature, where small artifacts exuded divine presence. Though it sounded almost pantheistic, Emerson's thought was a novel blend of Kantian idealism, Spinozan ethics, and Swedenborgian mysticism. He was drawn to oriental religions, from the high philosophy of India to the hieroglyphics that figured so prominently in the popular and academic revival of Egyptian antiquities.[12]

Typically, Emerson found room for optimism where the more cautious Melville saw only grounds for irony or lament. For Melville, comparativism destroyed a holistic theology; for Emerson, it liberated the creative spirit. Emerson's poet embraced a human but still monumental obligation: "to reconstruct mythology for himself and his era." Now "as human a document as Newton's *Principia*, the Vedas, and the Koran," the Bible became, "one among many mythical frames of reference."[13] As this suggests, the higher criticism assisted in the reception of comparative theology. If one effect of locating the bible in history was to enhance its aesthetic properties, another was to expose what the sacred texts of the Christians and Hebrews had in common with those of other cultures. To conceive religion as having a history, as having evolved like any other human endeavor or field of inquiry, was to see it as a configuration or arrangement. Recognizing religion's alteration over time revealed its heterogeneity. Interpreters not only described Hebraic observances but asked how they came to be.

Mysterious Jewish rituals were Semitic conventions, beliefs and practices partly acquired from neighboring nations, and Paul was an adaptor of Greek thought.

The history of Bible criticism in the nineteenth century provides a valuable backdrop for Melville's own forays into comparative religious analysis. I will have more to say about Melville's more direct appropriation of these scriptural techniques in a later section on Stanley and Strauss. The new interest in religion as a multicultural design, like the introduction of objective standards into biblical study, can be understood as part of a common effort to reconcile religion with the claims of science. Both represent steps toward the "modernizing" of religious practice, an endeavor of ongoing concern to Melville. Melville's fiction, like the theories of social scientists such as Herbert Spencer, Robertson Smith, and Albion Small, was intimately tied to the rational methodology of these Bible critics. His first novel, *Typee*, written at the height of these doctrinal controversies in Melville's native New England, can be seen as his way of entering into them from a strategic distance. At times, Melville's narrator assumes the stance of a "higher" critic, whose account of primitive religion displays the customary blend of sympathy and detachment. In keeping with the methods of comparativism, he draws constant analogies between primitive and modern spiritual practices. He shares the Transcendentalist view of religion as an organic unity stretching over time and across cultures, limited only by the skeptical soul. Yet his comparisons of savage and civilized worship are most often a means for exposing the hypocrisies of Christianity. The comparative method, as applied by the narrator of *Typee*, amounts to a running catalog of Christian crimes against humanity.

There are at least two reasons why the narrator can only think about Christians while gazing upon primitives. On the simplest level, Melville is rehearsing a cliché. We set out to discover the other and all we find is ourselves. This can inspire hopelessness and melancholia—a chronic complaint of this speaker. Consider the gnawing "melancholy" that fills his ruminations on a "minist[ry]" of birds. "Perched aloft among the immovable boughs of the majestic breadfruit trees . . . purple and azure, crimson and white, black and gold . . . sailing through the air in starry throngs; but alas! the spell of dumbness is upon them all." Their muteness, so unusual for any breed of this species, is a threat. It magnifies his own sense of strangeness, parodying his exclusion from this native world, whose resistance to him is symbolized by this spectacular unresponsiveness. Though indifferent, the birds are at the same time peculiarly vigilant, even demanding. They watch him watching them, as if enumerating his differences, "with steady curious eyes." Theirs is a visual endgame. They don't answer or relieve his mystification; they mime it steadily. He tries to imagine their "commiserat[ion]," but all he can verify is their attention.[14] Nothing about the native inhabitants he describes is certain. He displays, in presumably compensatory fashion, an absorption with his own mental states. If he is sure of anything, it is that he doesn't understand. This perpetual state of knowledge deprivation is never without religious overtones. As he confesses, in what may be his single most important insight: "For my own part, although hardly a day passed while I remained up on the island that I did not witness some religious ceremony or other, it was very much like seeing a parcel of 'Freemasons' making secret signs to each other; I saw everything, but could comprehend nothing" (202). Though the tone is casual, even commonsensical, the content is pure terror. Terror for the narrator is possessing a plenitude of detail, without a shred of faith. Nothing is unavailable to his rational mind. He can see, describe, and list. He can tell us the color of a bird's wing; he can identify the tree upon which it lights. But he cannot grasp the purpose of this airborne ministry, nor what its soundless sermons might mean to an attending human flock.

When it comes to matters of religion, Melville is suggesting, cross-cultural misunderstanding may be doubled or worse. That's one point of this scene, which turns a stranger-native divide into the chasm between man and nature. There is something relentless in the difference of these particular birds of a feather. Any animal is a world apart, but these exotic creatures are residents of an altogether alien somewhere else. Religious matters present similar interpretive dilemmas. Concerning any given religious practice, the worshipers themselves are invariably in the dark. Believers, by definition, deny the content of ritual acts. Religion is memory urging us on for reasons we couldn't grasp if we wanted to. The point is that we don't want to. Having faith is not wanting or needing to know. This is the basic paradox of Melville's narrative. You can't be outside faith to understand it, and if you're in it, you don't understand it, you just do it. The very desire to apprehend religion is itself the sign of a fallen state. To see spirituality in terms of questions is already to be out in the cold. The higher-critical craving for facts and for evidence of miracles, the urge to compare different forms of belief, is for Melville an indication of the general dwindling of faith. In this sense, the narrator's condition is representative of larger intellectual trends that Melville sees as endemic to the nineteenth century. Evidently, the paradoxical nature of scientific approaches to worship seems not to have troubled other analysts. Just prior to his own disavowal of knowledge, the narrator cites the "eminent voyagers . . . Carteret, Byron, Kotzebue, and Vancouver," who remain unfazed by their inability "to obtain anything like a clear insight into the puzzling arcana of their faith" (201). Melville's voyager, in contrast, is obsessed. His obsession is so great that the novel becomes an exploration of the godless psyche—its sense of deprivation, and the eventual sense of purpose derived from this state.

That sense of purpose has everything to do with the subject of sacrifice. It is critical to Melville's conception in *Typee* that the narrator, at the inception of his Polynesian researches, imagines sacrifice as their culmination. "Next week we shape our course to the Marquesas! The Marquesas! What strange visions of outlandish things . . . carved canoes . . . savage woodlands . . . horrible idols—*heathenish rites and human sacrifices*" (17). He is not disappointed. Sacrifice is what he anticipates; sacrifice is what he finds. But this is not because he has "discovered" the Marquesas. Rather, he has discovered himself through his exploration of another culture. For Melville, to discover oneself is to discover one's culture. To discover one's culture in oneself is to understand what it means by religious faith. So when the narrator announces that he sees everything, but comprehends nothing, we may infer that a similar vacuum is the state of belief in nineteenth-century Anglo-American life. Judging from the "frank acknowledgment" of this situation by other interpreters he has just cited, most of the narrator's contemporaries are able to take this in stride. He, on the other hand, is overwhelmed with anxiety. The figure for his anxiety is fear of sacrifice: will he or won't he become a victim of the Typees' reputedly ravenous ritual appetite. To call this anxiety a "figure" is not to deny the possibility the text confirms of the Typees' actual practice of human sacrifice. It is only to say that our apprehension of the rite is confined to one disturbed and disturbing consciousness. Faith for Melville's narrator is a vacuum filled by sacrifice.

More precisely, religion in nineteenth-century America and England is a container filled by thought about sacrifice. As portrayed in *Typee*, sacrifice is a preoccupation of moderns. It is an analytical export applied to primitive civilizations. Melville doesn't seem to care whether there is objective cause for this intellectual attitude, whether this particular set of "heathens" actually practice sacrifice. He is more interested in the fact that Western visitors like his narrator think they do. From the legendary unreliability of *Typee*'s first-person witness, it is not far to the idea that the nineteenth century has "invented" sacrifice. Melville's novel becomes an exploration in its own right of the nineteenth century imagination of sacrifice: what are its motivations, purposes, limits? Significantly, the narrative provides not a trace of evidence for any actual sacrifices. It is all in the narrator's head, and we know what a prison that is. The ship that he abandons is a site of "servitude." He anticipates the search that will follow his "escape," replete with bounty and rifles (34–36). From the moment he flees, however, he is emprisoned by his own psyche. The first indications are subtle: he can't see very well. "I had supposed," he relates early on, that "on gaining the heights we should be enabled to view the large bays of Happar and Typee . . . but here we were disappointed" (55–56). When they do obtain views, they are unrevealing: "the whole landscape seemed one unbroken solitude, the interior of the island having apparently been untenanted since the morning of the creation; and as we advanced through this wilderness, our voices sounded strangely in our ears, as though human accents had never before disturbed the fearful silence of the place" (58–59). What are these men if not ancient Hebrews, wandering in the desert, their faith dwindling with their rations, looking about for something to sacrifice? We don't need more to convince us that the novel is about the obsession with faith. But we have to keep in mind that it's always at least twice removed. These characters are moderns, Anglo-American sailors of the nineteenth century, confronting natives supposedly removed from them in level of cultural evolution. And like the nineteenth-century intellectuals whose foragings into ancient religious practices (whether Semitic, Roman, or Christian) they mirror, it seems impossible to separate what they imagine from what they expose. We can't trust our guide. Nor does he expect us to, because he doesn't trust himself.

The lone account of sacrificial feasting in the narrative is a parade of qualification. "It is a singular fact," the narrator announces at the outset, "that in all our accounts of cannibal tribes we have seldom received the testimony of an eyewitness" (260). He goes on to offer murky detail on "mysterious packages," and a potential victim, "covered with blood dust," compelled to endure "extraordinary suffering and exertion" (261). The narrator relates how he is whisked away at what appears to be the inception of this "hideous rite" (263). He insists that he is able to catch a "slight glimpse" of what is, perhaps, the remains of a "human skeleton." But his mind is so overcharged by this point that the Typee native's disclaimer, "pig, pig," seems more persuasive (265). "Mystery" prevails at the end, when the narrator confesses his ultimate ignorance concerning the fate of his comrade Toby (280). Meanwhile, his closing "escape" from the island reproduces his opening escape from the ship. What the narrator cannot escape, these repetitions suggest, is the equivalence between savage and civilized experience. In passing from Typee to his homeward-bound ship, he merely exchanges one mental prison for another. That prison is the silence of his own faithless narrative.

Lest we underestimate the force of the narrator's spiritual desperation, we need only recall the charges of blasphemy that dominated the novel's reception. Typee's American editor was so unnerved by "ministerial customers" decrying the book's "licentious, un-Christian" content, that he convinced Melville to excise most of the passages on religion (312). Is it any wonder that Christian missionaries and their defenders resented statements like the following: "Among the islands of Polynesia, no sooner are the images overturned, the temples demolished, and the idolaters converted into *nominal* Christians, then disease, vice, and premature death make their appearance. The depopulated land is then recruited from the rapacious hordes of enlightened individuals who settle themselves within its borders, and clamorously announce the progress of the Truth" (221). If such obvious diatribes had been the only casualties of Melville's attempts to placate contemporaries, they would be less revealing from the perspective of New England theological debates. But the other type of observation that was also excised, consistently, concerned the problem of evidence or religious certainty; in particular, the relationship between fact and faith. Consider the following reflections, which oppose virtuous belief to virtuous action. Highlighting the "hospitality," "courage," and "friendships" that prevail among wild Arabs, North American Indians, and Polynesians, respectively, the narrator concludes with a contrast between cultures dominated by statutes and those committed to devout actions. This seems straightforward enough. No Christian would reject a plea for the unification of divine sentiments and deeds. But his point about civilized faith goes further. The dependence of this kind of belief on narrative form— whether "the statute book," "essays on virtue and benevolence," or even "that beautiful prayer breathed first by the lips of the divine and gentle Jesus"—is a sure sign of diminishment. The Fall, as conceived here, is a fall from consensual, spontaneous faith to the interpretive wranglings that govern matters of the spirit ever after. Among the qualities that evoke narrative admiration is the Polynesian "unanimity of feeling." He writes enviously, "I do not conceive that they could support a debating society for a single night" (229).

What are we to make of the inscrutable reference to "the divine and gentle Jesus"? Is Melville merely asserting the ephemerality of prophetic pronouncements? The moment the words are out of his mouth, they become subject to attenuation, misappropriation. Does Melville identify? Is he staking an authorial claim to this prophetic originality? Or is this a subtle critique of the embodied God himself? Does the idiomatic stamp of this hallowed image disable submission to it? One effect is to establish the importance of context in religious interpretation. When the words of Jesus enter the world, they become equivalent, in some sense, to the missionaries who mouthe them. Their status or meaning is determined by their application in different circumstances. Used to fortify brutal actions, Melville suggests, they absorb that brutality. Christian principles are not immune to the actions they inspire. If this were Melville's only point—that Christian precepts can be misapplied—then this passing note on Jesus would be less threatening. Melville leaves room for another possibility: the actual hospitality of Christian precepts to a certain brutality. This is not as subversive as it sounds. Melville's insinuation is no stronger than the usual claims of contemporaneous Bible critics. It amounts to the assumption that Jesus was an historical figure, a product of ancient Semitic culture. Therefore judgments about his "divinity or "gentleness" are naturally limited by the customs of that culture. We are dealing here with *ancient* notions of "divine" or "gentle." And there may be a more immediate affinity between the world of the ancients and the realities of nineteenth-century missionary life than the devout at home are prepared to admit. Readers of Melville's later works might find it difficult to separate the suspicious tone here from the mixed fortunes of Christ figures throughout his fiction. Is Melville's Christ forever compromised? And if so, what might he have in common with another compromised Christ of this era, the notorious Christian God of *The Life of Jesus, Critically Examined*?

The complexity of Melville's perspective in *Typee*, which revolves between extreme skepticism and the despair aroused by belief, has something in common with the religious contortions of a figure Melville apparently disdained himself: David Friedrich Strauss, *The Life*'s author. Strauss, like Melville, was imprisoned in his intellect, which distanced him irrevocably from faith. Both believed themselves bound to the penalty of the Fall, in sharp contrast to the careless inhabitants of prior or primitive cultures. Melville's sense of distance was shaped into an extraordinarily allusive fiction, with special emphasis on theological issues. Strauss's expression of this distance took scholarly form in a theological analysis of incomparable sophistication. Both became religion's self-appointed interpreters. Interpretation in each case bespoke defense. But these aims were often misunderstood.[15] In part because their religious struggles were rather conventional, descriptions of their respective conditions can sound interchangeable. Take the following characterizations: "He no longer could enter the camp of faith and affirm its rites and practices, but neither could he leave it, for he continued to draw spiritual sustenance from it." He had a "romantic pathos for the presence of and participation in the divine, a pathos born in part of the experience of God's absence. He therefore considered himself a defender of religion against its real enemies, the naturalists and atheists who cut the nerve center of divine-human unity by an exclusive veneration of man and the espousal of abstract ideals."[16] He can never be "a true scholar, he is too dependent upon mood and is too preoccupied with himself." The subject of these descriptions is Strauss. But it could easily have been Melville.

What explains the affinities between Melville and this German theologian, often credited with having supplied *the* rational foundation for scientific historicism? Common sources have something to do with it. Both men were immersed in a German intellectual tradition made up of romantic, idealist, and mystical elements. They discovered Schopenhauer late in life and embraced his pessimism as a means to the revitalization of their flagging intellectual spirits.[17] Philosophers like Fichte, Hegel, and Spinoza informed their outlooks on theological questions. Their respective apprehensions of the Bible were tempered by philosophy. Despite their genius, or perhaps because of it, they had notorious reception problems. Strauss and Melville towered over colleagues in theology and literature, but their professional careers presented a crushing series of disappointments. They died in relative obscurity, respected but neglected. In both cases, creative energies seemed protected from dismal dispositions and personal misfortune. This comes through in the romantic optimism each conveyed in their comments on writing. Strauss describes himself in a letter of 1837 as "shedding a skin," adding "but what is to replace the theological skin I do not yet see."[18] Compare this to Melville's famous image of 1851, "Three weeks have scarcely passed, at any time between then and now, that I have not unfolded within myself. But I feel that I am now come to the inmost leaf of the bulb, and that shortly the flower must fall to the mould."[19] Strauss's self-characterization appears to be animal, where Melville's is strictly vegetable. But there is a common sense of the writing self's kinship with a nature whose genius lies, if not exactly in deception, in remarkable feats of translation. I refer to nature's translation of obvious bad news— like decay and death—into the miracle of a lion shedding skin or the passage of a tulip from splendor to mold. From within these commonplaces of creative becoming, Strauss and Melville help us to see the common work of theology, literature, and nature. The purpose of all three is to reconcile the universal blows of human experience. They hush up uncomfortable generalities by shifting our attention to particularities. They help us accept the inevitable—death, above all—by enhancing our sense of the ordinary. So the theologian dwells on the motivations of belief, such as fear. The writer invents an enraged sea captain seeking vengeance on an unusually brutal sperm whale with a name. And nature's conviction about the preeminence of its loss-and-gain design is lodged in the dynamic fur of a lion.

Strauss's *Life of Jesus* (1846) is credited with providing the earliest modern example of "alienated theology." If it is not the first in a train of nineteenth-century beginnings, it is unquestionably one of the century's most infamous examples. Alienated theology was from the start nondenominational; any religion would do. One could be alienated from the symbols and myths of biblical religion, from traditional doctrines and creeds, from a sense of vocation. Strauss's work typified the religious falling-out that at once precipitated and helped to sanction widespread secularization. Though Strauss himself suffered profoundly from these effects—the substitution of knowledge for faith; the growing prestige of rational experts— there is no doubt that his own theological innovations contributed to them. Strauss never shied away from the revolutionary implications of his ideas. Through the tormented believer, another side was always visible: the smasher of idols, the youthful genius who produced the first volume of the *Life* at the age of twenty-seven. The most enduring legacy of *The Life of*

Jesus was its demonstration of a new critical method for the reading of the Gospels. Previous interpreters already mentioned (Wellhausen, Baur, von Herder) had accomplished some of this work. But like any book that turns critical trends into a vision powerful enough to support a name and attract disciples, Strauss's combined concreteness and urgency. One could recognize in *The Life* both the obsessions of previous interpreters and where they missed his magnetic whole. The main point of Strauss's argument on the Gospels was the predominance of its mythical elements. Through close analysis, he showed how little actual history there was in the New Testament. This argument was complemented by his questioning of appeals to history as a justification for faith. Christianity, he suggested, had more to do with mythology than history. According to *The Life*'s modern editors, Strauss's theories set the agenda for all future theological inquiry on the nature of the absolute and the consequences of "relativism." Strauss liberated Christianity from history, denying both Christianity's claims to historical legitimacy and history's relevance to Christian faith. Yet this liberation was based on the most rationalized historical methods ever applied in Bible study. Anyone invoking historical method with the sophistication of Strauss was obviously committed to it. And there had to be some disdain on his part for an object of analysis so radically disassociated from these methods. Strauss's other main points reinforced suspicions about his Christian sympathies. One of the most objectionable, from the perspective of contemporaries, was his dismissal of Christianity's futuristic eschatology. This apocalyptic vision, Strauss believed, inhibited and even precluded the allegiance of forward-thinking moderns. It exemplified for him the dangerous enthusiasm embedded in the gospel. Strauss also rejected the concept of transcendence and in its place advanced a vision of human autonomy. He was not oblivious to the dilemma his conclusion posed for Christian theology. God might or might not be independent of the material universe. But there was no question of Christianity's dependence on this doctrine.

As this example shows, Strauss had a penchant for paradox. There is no formulation that better captures this frame of mind than his fantastic theorem on the "disappearing minimum." Christ's "unity of the divine and the human" is so perfectly vital that it is capable of reducing "to a disappearing minimum all hindrances of this unity."[20] In a profane mix of rationalism and faith, Strauss presses us to accept a miraculous proposition as a scientific postulate. Faith should get us there: our faith in Christ's holiness. And science should satisfy us as to its effects: the energy of this unity will act on "hindrances" (skepticism?) like a chemical solvent. What's especially intriguing about Strauss's "disappearing minimum" is that it reverses his critical method. Strauss's treatment of the Bible relies on science while appealing to faith. The "disappearing minimum," in contrast, relies on faith while appealing to science. What's similar is that in both instances the subject of the appeal is secondary or irrelevant. It's hard to convince most readers of *The Life*—then or now—that Strauss's purpose was to shore up faith. And it seems unlikely, in this later example, that Strauss really expects audiences to accept the scientific properties of miraculous acts.

The effect of *The Life* is to turn biblical testimony into a vehicle of modern skepticism. Strauss's analysis of the seven parables is a case in point. The analysis opens upon an interpretive standstill: Matthew says that Jesus delivered seven parables in succession, but "modern criticism, however, has doubted whether Jesus really uttered so many of these symbolical discourses on one occasion." Everything follows from this initial skeptical claim. The parable becomes "a kind of problem, to be solved by the reflection of the hearer." Gospel truths relayed by a divine messenger are reconceived as simple examples of how "the teacher" tries "to convey real instruction" (345). As an alternative to the dazzled disciple, Neander is introduced, a more measured Greek exegete, who provides new ground rules for assessing the where and when of Christ's prophecies. Neander binds order to outcome: we can presume parables to be consecutive where "they lead to the same result" (345–46). There follow pages of intertextual scrutiny, testing and discarding centuries of interpretation on the intentions behind and validity of Matthew's judgments. The margins of Strauss's text border a near chaos of exegetical controversy. It is a sea of authorities—Hess, Schulz, Olshausen, de Wette, Schneckenburger, Storr, Tholuck, Fritzsche—figures who become inseparable from the sacred parchment they struggle to decipher. Every footnote inscribes a life; each one confirms the intellectual seductiveness of these sacred texts. One scholar after another has dedicated himself to the resolution of a single line, and resigned himself to the inconclusiveness of the task. This is holy work; it is also interpretation. This is what inspires Strauss. Jesus is less important.

It could be argued that the footnotes to Strauss's chapter on the parables contain his essential message. The chapter's first utterance is a footnote. One glance at the note's contents reveals why Strauss deemed it worthy of top billing, and also why he exiled the message to a note. The note displays the compactness and solemnity of a biblical decree: "All that relates to the sufferings, death, and resurrection of Jesus is here excluded" (334). Strauss's text diverts our attention from the prophet and his experiences. It draws its inspiration from, and tries to inspire us with, the controversies he arouses. The mythic Christ—the healer and sufferer who walked the streets of Jerusalem and Nazareth—holds little interest for Strauss. Christ appears to best effect, from Strauss's perspective, in the act of interpretation itself. Describing the debate over the meanings of a psalm, Strauss writes, "Jesus here gives a model of interpretation, in conformity, not with the text, but with the spirit of his time" (359). Jesus comes to life in Strauss's text as an historically determined interpreter, akin to those his discourses inspire. To put Jesus on a par with the fleets of interpreters who crowd Strauss's footnotes is to make him a product of his culture. Like all of them, Jesus provides a version of his thought that reflects the preoccupations of his age. To identify Christ as a model interpreter is, for Strauss, to locate him in history. Judgments on the conventionality of Christ's behavior in choice instances (for which Strauss is famous) follow naturally from this. Contemporary readers found it condescending, if not downright hostile. Here is Strauss on Christ's discourse at the house of the Pharisees: "We grant that Attic urbanity is not to be expected in a Jewish teacher, but even according to the oriental standard, such invectives uttered at table against the host and his guests, would be the grossest dereliction of what is due to hospitality" (362).

Strauss was not alone in his effort to separate the historical from the mythic Christ. *The Life* exemplifies a comprehensive version of the qualifications and challenges that were being formulated in readings of Christ's character throughout the nineteenth century. A particularly empathic complement to Strauss appears in a work owned (and annotated) by Melville, William Alger's *The Solitudes of Nature and of Man* (1867). Alger's aim to reconcile the contradictions of Christ's character—his sincerity and good works on the one hand and his "unapproachable egotism" on the other—appears to be addressed to a stream of prior commentary.[21] Alger's path to the real Jesus is through the paradigm of the unique genius. To be grasped fully, Christ must be seen in a company of prophets, including Moses, Buddha, Mohammed. All of these figures were endowed with divine attributes. All attracted disciples and formulated principles adaptable to symbolic and institutional uses (378). Because Alger is dedicated to the idea of Christ's "transcendent personality" and "inspired originality," his conclusions seem especially striking. Perhaps a consequence of Alger's subject ("solitude"), Christ appears as one who has grown neurotic from too much time spent alone. "His words to Simon, 'Thou gavest me no kiss when I came in,' " reflect the disordered sentiments of an abandoned lover (390, 392). Alger's account of Christ's indignation and invective almost intimates (despite itself) that Christ made a mission of his own victimization.

Alger's special pleading on Christ's behalf was something of a ritual in its own right. Many other theologians of the era seemed convinced of the prophet's need for vindication. In his optimistic, encyclopedic history, *Christianity in the United States* (1889), Daniel Dorchester discovers champions in strange places. A "distinguished living sociologist," Dorchester writes, speaking of Herbert Spencer, "undesignedly bears his testimony to the *rationale* of moral principles inculcated by Jesus Christ. Nor can he resist the acknowledgment that the conclusion he has reached is . . . a verification of Christ's teachings."[22] With this unerring positivist as acolyte, Dorchester moves bravely in the next section, entitled "From Christ Discarded to Christ Honored," to the recovery of some notoriously lost souls. In a remarkable act of excavation, he manages to cull endorsements from seemingly every modern who ever denounced Christianity. From Rousseau we hear, "If Socrates lived and died like a philosopher, Jesus lived and died like a God"; from Fichte, "His followers are nations and generations"; from Strauss, "He is the highest model of religion within the reach of our thought"; and from Renan, "a matchless man, so grand that though all must be judged from a purely scientific point of view, I would not gainsay those who, struck with the exceptional character of his work, call him God" (661). We have to remember that each of these comments is the culmination of a considered attack on Christ's transcendence. Yet Dorchester's procession of renovated skeptics proves his point: the tenacity of Christian faith in the face of the most deliberate challenges. Dorchester's confidence derives from his fierce antimodernism. He truly believes that modern ideas and methods have little chance of improving on traditional religion.

Such was not the case for Max Scheler, an early-twentieth-century German sociologist who responded to the same nineteenth-century debates. In his first book, *Ressentiment* (1912), Scheler advanced his theory on the disease of modernism: the relativistic psychology that characterized individuals who lived for others rather than for themselves. "The mind of *ressentiment* man," Scheler writes, "is filled with envy, the impulse to detract, malice, and secret vindictiveness." In Nietzsche's own prior formulation of the concept, "the idea of Christian love [is] the most delicate flower of *ressentiment*."[23] It should be noted at the outset, that Scheler himself reveres Christ. The defense he offers in *Ressentiment* against Nietzsche and other previous detractors is the work of a believer. But he is not a believer in the sense that seems most consistent with the sentiments of a Strauss or a Melville. From those perspectives, belief is absolute; you don't choose to embrace it or not to. Once you go over the cliff of disbelief, there is no return. For Scheler and other modernists, belief can be assumed, like a nationality. T. S. Eliot, who took up British citizenship and Anglicanism, is an example of this. Scheler concedes that while faith is not an absolute, it is an absolute good. According to Scheler, "there is not a trace of *ressentiment* in all of Christ's teachings." He says it with conviction and intends it as the highest compliment. The problem is that he says it again and again. The flatness of Scheler's echoing disclaimers would give even an insensible reader pause: "Yet all this cannot make me believe in *ressentiment* on his part." "I spoke of Jesus' 'mysterious' affection for the sinners. . . . Is this an element of *ressentiment*?" "In this affection for the sinners we can find no *ressentiment*" (95, 98, 100, 103). Scheler is nervous because he finds *a lot* of resentment in Christ. This even applies to the Christian act of sacrifice. Ressentiment morality dictates a love of the small, poor, and weak that is really just submerged hatred of the large, wealthy, and powerful. It is twisted and consuming. Formal speech expresses the reverse of what is meant; the self smothers on a low flame, as in the case of John Claggart in *Billy Budd*. The biblical parable of Ananias, which is so vividly invoked in Melville's novella, also becomes part of Scheler's arsenal against the rage of ressentiment. For Scheler, Ananias is the ultimate ressentiment figure, opposed to the ideal Christian model of sacrifice. Ananias's is a crime of insincerity as well as robbery. In Scheler's view, this biblical moment registers a continuity of belief from ancient to modern times. In the time of the apostles, he points out, no one believed that "man's moral constitution could in any way be changed by the establishment of new property relations. . . . Christian love and sacrifice *begins* where the demands of 'justice' and the dictates of positive legislation end" (111–12).

What are we to make of Melville's appropriation of the biblical story? The differences are compelling. To begin with, Melville casts his anti-Christ, John Claggart, as Ananias. Moreover, Melville's adaptation denies transcendence. He locates his central sacrificial event within a modern class structure. As "a man on the move," Melville's Ananias is representative of petit bourgeois restlessness. For Melville, sacrifice is an historical event. It has everything to do with "the demands of 'justice' and the dictates of positive legislation." Scheler's *Ressentiment*, on the other hand, attempts to recuperate a fallen Christ from the rational methods of Renan, Strauss, and company.

SPIRITUAL TOURING

I have described the higher criticism and the various historical treatments of Christ that either defined its methods or issued from it. There was at that time another prominent type of theological analysis that also drew upon scientific rationalism and contributed to religion's secularization. I refer to theories on comparative religion and the narratives of exploration and travel that served as their primary mode of expression. Some of the most popular of these narratives were catalogs of holy sites. With scientific precision, nineteenth-century visitors to Palestine pinpointed the geography of miracles and charted the demographic balances and regional divisions that shaped the ancient Semitic territories. Arthur Stanley's *Sinai and Palestine* (1865) combines sacred history and sacred geography in its effort to let the Bible speak again. The book's introduction forges an implicit link between the ambitions of the higher critics and his own geographical inquiry. As the location of "the most important events in the history of mankind," the spur to ongoing religious controversy, the key to various sectarian disputes, the focus of world diplomacy, the Near East represents layers upon layers of historical experience. The historical present "intermingles itself with the scenes of the older events, thus producing a tissue of local associations unrivalled in its length and complexity."[24] Stanley's reading turns the land into a book among books. The territories of Sinai and Palestine become documents, in dialogue with actual biblical texts. Bible study for Stanley is a conversation between the environment and ancient books, twin keepers of the past. Stanley's preferred scripture gives some idea of his loyalties. He admires the Book of Joshua for the "precision" of its "terms" and for its "boundaries carefully laid down." Like the higher critics, Stanley is preoccupied with method. The religion of the Jewish people, "in the highest sense," might have come direct from God. But that doesn't make it any less human. It is a product of "particular times" and impressed by "those 'bounds of habitation,' which God had 'before appointed' and 'determined' for them" (xi, xiii–xiv). For Stanley, the land is a partner in the scientific enterprise. Facts, it is said, are stubborn and geographical facts happily the most stubborn of all." Land is the ideal source, because it is objective, and because it survives (albeit in altered form). There is no pretense in rock or fauna. "If they cannot tell the whole truth, at any rate, so far as they have any voice at all, they tell nothing but the truth" (xviii). Sacred geography, Stanley maintains, can support or annul biblical testimony on miracles.[25] Once the land is brought into consideration, these questions can be decided on more rational grounds. If the holy site is inhospitable to the miracle supposed to have occurred there—for example, the Red Sea passage—then the miracle is apocryphal.

Stanley's preface advances his assumptions and methods and lays claim to the land as his body of evidence. His introduction reveals another facet of the book: here he confronts the complex intonations of kin and alien, of deprivation and plenitude, in the ancient world. Egypt is an appropriate starting point, Stanley suggests, because it defined the inner regions of the Israelite consciousness. Israel had Egypt on the brain, in part because they were kept there, and in part because they were not. The Israelite bodies might have been delivered up from bondage, but the Israelite mentality remained there. "The heart of the people," Stanley writes, "was always 'turning back'" (xxviii). Stanley offers a few explanations for this absorption. Egypt had long been "the land of plenty . . . the Oasis of the primitive world." We see it first through the envious eyes of Abraham, outside, looking in upon the den of splendor: "palace and home . . . long trains of slaves and beasts." Israel submits slavishly to Egyptian designs (an ironic foreshadowing of its ultimate status there). The desired fate of the ambitious young man, as portrayed in the story of Joseph, is incorporation "into the reigning caste."

Stanley's argument, at first, seems simply that Egypt was rich and pros-
perous, and the Israelites were understandably envious. But his claims are
far more subtle and profound. Comparative thinking comes naturally to
human beings and the nations they form. There is something in the mind
that reverts inevitably, he implies, to contrasts: between relative states of
plenitude and deprivation, between my idea of reasonableness versus
yours. The Israelites could neither dream nor create without the spectre of
Egypt before them. "The law in Sinai is a protest, though with occasional
resemblances which set off the greater difference;—against the scenery of
Egypt" (xxviii–xxix). Egypt is "necessary" to Israel, a mode of contrast that
is equally essential to Stanley's narrative. The importance of equalization
or equivalence extends to his closing image of the Egyptian Sphinx: "enormous head . . . its great ears, its open eyes, the red colour still visible on
its cheek." It takes memory, Stanley counsels, to regard the monument
properly. "What must it have been," Stanley asks, "when immediately
under its breast an altar stood from which the smoke went up into the
gigantic nostrils?" (liv). Stanley's sphinx is a giant god of sacrifice. The
"gigantic nostrils of that nose, now vanished from the face" make the
image a casualty of its own sacrificial appetite. Centuries of gorging on
smoke offerings have barred all future consumption. The universal balance
sheet requires recompense even from a sphinx. Stanley's pyramids are a
site of diminishment. A shadow of "what they must have been . . . broken
or choked with sand," the pyramids seem to account for the opening where
Egypt appeared on top of the world. Call this a sacrificial sensibility, the
philosophy of the fearful. Egypt is full; Israel must be empty. The kind of
people who believe this are those who take comfort in the red cheek of the
Sphinx, thinking that it might ward off evil.

Given the prominence of sacrifice in the preface and introduction, it is
not surprising to see the rite listed as a local pastime—along with conquests
and coronations—in the book's opening. Sacrifice is the way of this land.
Stanley's journey is filled with references to its ritual occasions, from the
commonplace (Abraham and Isaac) to the obscure (the sacrifice of the red
heifer beyond the Jerusalem gates) (3, 247–48, 184–86). And it becomes a
fixture of his comparative method: he treats, for example, the shared origins of Christian and Hebraic practices, given the proximity of their ritual
sites, and he examines the formulaic resemblances between Easter and
Passover (247–48, 132–34). In one especially revealing discussion, Stanley
is moved to theoretical reflection on the nature of intellectual sacrifice. His
subject is evidence for miracles, and his test case is that miracle of miracles,
the Red Sea crossing. Stanley weighs his interpretive options (Josephus
versus the Alexandrine troubadours versus the Septuagint) and traverses
with obsessive care every potential route, even discriminating sea depths
and wind velocities to determine natural resistance. All for the sake of the

most likely explanation, which he reaches in his own miraculous display of imitative form. He settles on "the narrower end of the gulf" as the obvious point of passage. How else to explain, he asks through the authority of simple arithmetic, "the passage of 600,000 armed men . . . in the limits of a single night?" Stanley's is a rather Straussian conclusion. Dismissing claims for the crossing of the sea at its broader part as "comparatively modern," he turns to the early Christian and rabbinical sources, which propose a *"circuit,"* rather than an actual *"transit."* According to these interpretations, the Israelites touched lightly on water and then returned to the Egyptian shore, their journey cut by three days. Stanley notes that the case for this ancient reading has been "faithfully" made—maps and all—and implies that its legitimacy is unshakeable. More intriguing is Stanley's final word on the controversy, which he calls "a curious instance of the sacrifice of the whole moral grandeur of a miracle, to which men are often (and in this case necessarily) driven by a mistaken desire of exaggerating its physical magnitude" (36–37). People care too much about miracles, Stanley implies. So they nurse them until they are so ungainly that the only solution is their absolute reduction. Stanley's questions are the inevitable issue of empirical inquiries into sacred texts. Like Strauss, Stanley seems bewildered by the appetites he serves: the clamoring of the devout for truth. The truly devout do not question the length of the river or the number of people passing. These cravings represent a sacrifice twice removed: a belief offering on the altar of intellect.

Stanley's analysis places him securely beyond the borders of the spiritually resonant land he describes. His two-volume *History of the Jewish Church* (1862) further confirms his scientific marginality. Across both books a respect for faith persists. Science not only qualifies or legitimates the claims of scripture, it enhances them. Scientific method disables a "rigid acceptance" of biblical authority. "The advance made in Biblical science" has sustained appreciation of the work's "beauty"; "more careful study of the Bible has brought us back to the original sense." Until we free ourselves from doctrinal truths, we can't know what there is to appreciate in the Bible. Knowing is the path of science; appreciating, the path of aesthetics; believing, another world altogether. Theology, the writings of Stanley and Strauss tell us, hovers uncomfortably on the margins of all three. Yet uncertainty doesn't hamper intellectual work; it empowers it. This is why some of the most sophisticated reflection on "science" (and social science) in the mid- to late-nineteenth century was carried out by theologians.

Stanley's powerful delineation of the Egyptian Exodus in his *History of the Jewish Church* exemplifies the highest type of social scientific theology. In this work, Bible criticism and comparative method provide means for conceptualizing the era's most significant institutions and events, from slavery to Civil War. By comparison, the portrait of Israelites and Egyptians in *Sinai and Palestine* seems preliminary. There is something "peculiar," Stanley warns mysteriously at the outset, "in the story of the Exodus." This was no "mere case of ordinary insurrection of a slave population against their masters." It was rather an instance of "dread, an aversion entertained by the oppressors towards the oppressed as towards an accursed and polluted people." He goes on: "It is not an ordinary river that is turned into blood. . . . It is not an ordinary nation that is struck by the mass of putrefying vermin lying in heaps by the houses, the villages, and the fields. . . . It is the cleanliest of all the ancient nations, clothed in white linen, anticipating in their fastidious delicacy and ceremonial purity, the habits of modern and northern Europe."[26] "The exodus was a crisis in Egyptian as well as in Hebrew history," Stanley observes. The word "ordinary" echoes like a mantra through this description, forging a link across the centuries between this miraculous event and recent events in another exceptional nation, America. This is the scapegoat ritual for all times and places; the rhetoric of crisis is familiar. Ancient Egyptian and Israelite, modern American and African become parts of one historical allegory, where racial discriminations separate sacrificial sufferers from beneficiaries. The "curse" imagined by the white-robed and fastidious Egyptian forebears of the modern West translates readily as the curse of Ham. The plagues in the Hebraic version take the usual path of vengeance by reproducing as monstrosity the formerly contained enemy. They fulfill the aspirations of enslaver and enslaved. As different forms of defilement (lice, vermin, boils) culminating in the human body at its most degraded (death), the plagues justify Egyptian fears. "Behold the true nature of the Israelites writ large in the various pollutions delivered on their behalf." From the Israelite perspective, the wretchedness visited upon the Egyptians is the revenge of the oppressed. Through divine fiat, equilibrium is achieved: the condition of enslavement is transferred to the enslaver.

Parallels between African-American and Israelite slaves were commonplace in nineteenth-century religious and abolitionist tracts, but rarely did interpreters capture Stanley's level of ritual abhorrence. One generic exception was the slave narrative, by African-American authors such as Frederick Douglass and Harriet Jacobs. In these powerful allegories of Black-White conflict, every act of violence, the ordinary to the horrific, conveys superstitious dread. Every sexual exchange, from a whisper to a rape, has symbolic weight. From Douglass's lyrical opposition of white ship sails and earth-colored slave, through Jacobs's nightmare of recalcitrant house servants roasted on spits, and on to W.E.B. Du Bois' Black soul as the walking dead of modern America, African Americans anticipated and confirmed Stanley's allegory. Blacks are the defiled Israelites of the modern age. According to these works, an American slave society is hopelessly permeable. Hence the urge to beat, brand, and kill. Melville produced his own allegories along such lines (in "Benito Cereno" and *Moby-Dick).* And he also recorded his firsthand impressions of the Holy Land. Melville's thoughts on faith, and the overall slant of his preoccupation with antiquity, are made vivid in the book devoted to Palestinian beliefs and rituals in *Clarel* (1876): "Concerning Hebrews."

Throughout this epic poem, Melville, like Stanley, displays an appreciation for the great and the small. He is as attracted to amulets and phylacteries, the different instruments of Hebrew faith, as he is to abstract questions of fact versus belief. Melville seems as familiar with pieces of parchment nailed to Palestinian doorposts (the modern form of Passover protections) as he is with the philosophical idiom of Spinoza, Strauss, and Niebuhr. But it is in "Hebrews," where he traces the evolution of "Judaic doubt," that Melville's handle on the dilemmas peculiar to Jewish belief are especially apparent. This canto is foreshadowed by the introduction of the poem's lone Jewish protagonist, the apostate Margoth, two cantos earlier. Stanley's 1862 account, where the Israelites are identified with pollution, prepares us to read significance into Margoth's first appearance, near "the dung-gate." The threat from this Jew, however, seems more intellectual than physical. He is "an Israelite, say, Hegelized—Convert to science." His geologic hammer signals spiritual destructiveness. He prefers rocks to the "Bare solid texts from Bible old" (193–94). But his natural "cullings" are not those that inspired Stanley. Margoth disdains faith in any form, whether convention or "superstition." And Margoth's apostasy (which seems to be widely shared among his people) makes him repugnant. Against an ideal company of ancient believers ("Aaron, Moses . . . closeted alone with God") Melville sets a fallen parade of moderns ("Jew banker, merchant, statesman"). As with every other proposition in this epic, there is room for qualification here. The equation of Jews with materialism is overturned by a later portrait where they embody the struggle between ancient practice and modern invention. As Derwent comments, "Range, they range—In liberal sciences they roam." Jews come to symbolize a nineteenth-century ideal: "Faith's leaning tower." Derwent is again admiring: "Faith leaned from the beginning; yes, If slant, she holds her steadfastness" (202–3). Doubt is Jewish, according to *Clarel's* different speakers. Some praise this tendency; others damn it. Whether couched in the mystic wisdom of the blind Spinoza or the "visionary" Margoth, Hebrews have embraced skepticism and remained Hebrews.

Melville's attraction to the Hebrew slant on things may reflect his spiritual bleakness, as diagnosed by Hawthorne before Melville's departure for Palestine: "If he were a religious man, he would be one of the most truly religious and reverential."[27] Melville's state is legible in the journal record of his Palestinian tour. In some respects the *Journal,* like others he kept, is disappointing, a mere inventory of sights, companions, and dinners. Yet at times, the Holy Land takes on a raw and pressing desolation. In these passages the vacancy of Palestine becomes powerfully receptive to Melville's own. "No country will more quickly dissipate romantic expectations than Palestine—particularly Jerusalem," Melville writes. "To some the disappointment is heart sickening." Like any privileged place or character, the Holy Land must suffer. "Is the desolation of the land," Melville asks, "the result of the fatal embrace of the Deity? Hapless are the favorites of heaven" (517). The most haunting scene in the Palestine *Journal* is the account of his daily vigil at the Holy Sepulchre. Melville confesses that this site where Christ was tortured and buried became the obsession of his visit. It was visible from his hotel window, and he was drawn to it, as if by a curse. He appears in his daily rite as an ambivalent onlooker, seated in the gallery above the tomb. His focus, however, is not the tomb but those who surround it. As he writes in the *Journal*, "Almost every day I would hang looking down upon the spectacle of the scornful Turks on the divan and the scorned pilgrims kissing the stone of the appointing" (518). Melville's image of himself hanging over the edge suggests some physical impulse to throw his support to one side or the other. Whether the scornful or the scorned, it doesn't seem to matter. Yet the frequency of these visits, his admission that they are "sickening," and that he is "glad to escape" each time, suggests another level to this allegory. For Melville's self-portrait hints at a voyeuristic, even pornographic obsession. These visits become unsavory trysts: the author's daily need to look (for a fee) upon these acts of submission and contempt turns them into a kind of sex show. Like others, he is willing to pay for his desperate satisfactions. But Melville keeps returning, because there is no possibility of satisfaction. Spirituality, now linked to sexuality, is as compulsive as the basest impulse.

SYNTHETIC CHRISTIANITY

All of the authors we have considered in detail so far represent variations on a common theme. Strauss, Stanley, and Melville (in *Clarel* and his Mideast *Journal*) accept that modern science has become the inevitable companion of Scripture and theology. All seem willing, more or less, to grant the qualification of religious value that accompanies the advance of science. Religion here is neither monolithic nor immune to rational inquiry. Even more important to some writers was the idea that an openness to science need not be a spur to religion's fragmentation. In books such as *Ten Great Religions* (1871) and *Catholic Sacrifice* (1875), authors like James Freeman Clarke and Berdmore Compton argued that religion was actually unified by a rational, comparative method. These works exemplify how a certain theological enterprise, quite differently represented in each work, was able to absorb the threat of modern science. Everything about Clarke's *Ten Great Religions* suggests optimism.[28] As he concludes, in a characteristic appropriation of scientific argument: "The opinion of the positivist school, that man passes from a theological stage to one of metaphysics . . . is not in accordance with the facts we have been observing." Science has invigorated theology.[29] Christianity is wasting its time with sectarian disputes over miracles or evidence, over natural versus supernatural explanation. Christianity's sole concern should be the recognition of its mission as "the universal human religion" (492).

For its prophecy of a certain doctrinal pragmatism, Clarke's book is unparalled in this era. Christianity works because of its unique catholicity. It has proven adaptable in part because it is so fully sympathetic to "the nature of man" (14). The ten other "great religions" discussed in his book are "ethnic religions" (30). They serve the provincial purposes of their largely homogeneous populations. But the modern world, really one great international community, requires a religion that can supply "the religious wants of all the races of men" (492). Christianity, in Clarke's reading, is a Hegelian synthesizer. It can enfold and harmonize opposing forces and factions into a spiritual whole suitable to all human kinds. Christianity is the ideal Enlightenment religion, for it "always accepted something and gave something in return" (493). It is the culmination of centuries of religious progress. Clarke's book invests Christianity with a modern purpose. The borders of nations are closing down; enter Christianity, to heal the manifold ethnic divisions bound to arise. Where Melville's missionary glass is half-empty, Clarke's is half-full. According to Clarke, missionaries have succeeded in making Christianity available to the world, and they will accomplish still more in years to come. Among the threads that Clarke finds common to all religion (his specific referent is Brahmanism), "sacrifice is still the act by which one comes into relation with heaven" (101).[30] Sacrifice, in Clarke's reading, appears as a fixture of *ethnic* religions. Here too, Christianity is similar but different. It's not that Christianity lacks a model of sacrifice. But it is precisely Christianity's role to revise it, more or less out of existence. This appears as easily achieved as spoken. Sacrifice becomes atonement, transposed into "at-one-making power" (508). Expiation and crucifixion disappear. *The Life of Jesus* may be Clarke's guide to Christianity, but the story bears his own peculiarly optimistic stamp. The fact or manner of Christ's death goes unmentioned.

If Clarke's book represents Christianity with the sacrificial bite taken out, Berdmore Compton's achievement in *Catholic Sacrifice* is to bring sacrifice back into the center of things without compromising Clarke's gentler message. According to Compton, Christianity is the ultimate religion for the very reason that it offers the most wholesome and enabling vision of sacrifice. As he announces early on, "We are not too timid to be a follower of the most eminent English theologians, as they were of the ancient Fathers, and regard the Holy Eucharist as a *Sacrifice*, in the strict sense of the word."[31] Strict sense means ritual sense, and Compton goes on to discuss every possible detail, from blood sprinkling to stroking the heads of sin-heaped goats.

The point of *Catholic Sacrifice* is to distinguish the Christian notion of sacrifice (largely connected with praise) from the Hebraic (primarily defined as expiation for sin). Along the way, Compton offers an invaluable account of the rite's evolution. In the Old Testament, he observes, sacrifice is a direct consequence of man's fall. It is only "after the Fall" that "we find traces of the existence of sacrifice, and of its approbation, necessarily implying its Divine institution." Sacrifice expresses "that desire of nearer access to God," and thereby testifies to the fact of human banishment (27, 26). Even this early, Compton marvels, there is a distinction between sacrifice as gift offering (for services rendered or anticipated) and sacrifice as redemption from sin. From the first comes the Christian idea of sacrifice as praise and thanksgiving. The eucharistic sacrifices have not a "tincture of controversial bitterness." From the second comes the Hebraic concept of atonement. "If Israel does it badly," Compton writes, "despises His altar or table, someone else shall do it" (34, 40). The distinction between the bloody sacrifice of the Hebrews and the bread offerings of the Christians spawns a whole theology in which good works and faith replace crippling doubt. This is in fulfillment of Compton's opening aim, to liberate Christian sacrifice from "the fatal Jewish mistake of setting the means above the end" (2). The differences between Clarke and Compton are instructive. Clarke is a Transcendentalist of the most liberal kind; in his view, ritual has no place in a universal Christianity. Compton is a defender of traditional Christian doctrine, and *Catholic Sacrifice* is a collection of sermons that ends with a plea for charitable contributions from an assembled congregation.

What all these analyses have in common is the view of Hebrew sacrifice as a barbaric remnant. In both cases, Christianity is framed against the backdrop of a crude and punishing Judaism in which worship is conceived as sacrificial expiation. Both invoke a milder sacrificial ideal, whether Clarke's version of a liberal Christianity, in which sacrifice becomes the unmentionable, or Compton's rewriting of the Eucharist as pure celebration. Matthew Arnold's 1881 study of the Bible, *Literature and Dogma*, takes these arguments one step further. He is at once more radical in his separation of the Old and New Testaments (and consequently, Judaism and Christianity) and more ambitious in his claims for the Bible as literature. The Bible's literary elements, in Arnold's view, have absolute priority. "The language of the Bible," he writes, "is literary, not scientific language." Arnold is no revolutionary; he merely intends that aesthetics receive its spiritual due. This means equality with other dominant systems of explanation. "He who has art and science has also religion," he remarks.[32] Arnold adapts Goethe's theory of "Aberglaube," which he translates as "extra-belief." This poeticized spirituality, which builds on superstition in a positive sense, is not necessarily at odds with science. It contributes to what becomes for Arnold an ideal Christian maxim: "Attend to the feelings and dispositions whence conduct proceeds." This is distinguished from a Hebrew devotion to "outward acts." The Old Testament views religion "as a national and social matter"; the New Testament makes it "personal" (87, 96, 93). Christianity cultivates a sacrificial sensibility, to replace the crudity and violence of sacrificial acts. "Cleanse the inside of the cup," Jesus says, avoid "Corban." Ultimately, for Arnold, a literary apprehension of the Bible replaces a scientific one, just as Christian sacrifice replaces the sacrifices of Jewish law. Arnold appears to concede the trials of his introspective ideal, in referring to the "puzzling" quality of Christ's teaching. Perhaps he senses the pressure of a different kind of violence in the ritual's repressed Christian form. Again, he quotes Jesus: "He that loveth his life shall lose it, and he that hateth his life in this world shall keep it unto life eternal. . . . It *is* so; try it yourself and you will see it is so, by the sense of living, of going right, hitting the mark, succeeding, which you will get" (174–75, 186). Arnold's quotation captures the anxious undercurrent of his interpretation as a whole: what you don't see is sure to get you. The deepest Christian virtue is undetectable. If it's *not* there, we won't know. Loyalty to Christ's teachings eludes the naked eye. Melville's treacherous anti-Christ, John Claggart, fulfills all of Arnold's prescriptions for the proper Christian life, even in his evasion of "hitting the mark" (which recalls the narrator's conviction that he will "never hit" Claggart's true nature [*Billy Budd*, 447]). In his characteristically twisted handling of a spiritual agenda, Melville turns Christian inwardness into waywardness.

Clarke, Compton, and Arnold represent the retreat of Bible study from the frontiers laid open by the higher critics. Comparative theology becomes a confirmation of Christianity's Hegelian destiny as the ultimate synthetic religion. Aesthetic appreciation of the Bible affords the ideal union of inner and outer conduct. Yet there was also in this period a type of theological inquiry that sought to exploit that expansion. Possibly no book of the late nineteenth century better exemplifies this trend than H. Clay Trumbull's extraordinary interdisciplinary exploration, *The Blood Covenant* (1885). Delivered as a series of lectures at the Episcopal Divinity School in Philadelphia and later gathered into a book (like Compton's), Trumbull's researches, in his own words, "indicate that the realm of true Bible theology is as yet by no means thoroughly explored." His preliminary sketch of that territory includes every conceivable intellectual practice and narrative form, from the anthropological travel writings of Livingstone and Stanley, through the theology of Robertson Smith, to the biblical and classical methods of de Wette and Anderson (*Norse Mythology*). He seems familiar with every culture, from the ancient Semites to Anglo-Saxon to African. Trumbull's analysis has none of the usual teleological pressures. There is no Christianity waiting in the wings to declare itself. To grasp the Bible in its profoundest sense, Trumbull tells us, is to recognize how far "outside" its meaning takes us. The Bible's power lies in the elasticity of its borders. Interpreters have long recognized that Bible study is enriched by knowledge of the languages, archaeology, and customs of Bible lands. Trumbull welcomes recent intellectual developments that have inspired more varied, cross-cultural approaches. The tendency has been to view the Bible as an exclusively "Oriental" book. Bible scholars are now "finding profit in the study of primitive myths, and of aboriginal religious rites and ceremonies, all the world over." Trumbull is describing his own book. It is possible to see in his description at least one ancestral line for later anthropological and, more generally, social scientific methods. He proposes to study one rite, the rite of blood covenant, which is at once essential to "many important phases of Bible teaching" and visible, in "historic traces . . . from time immemorial, in every quarter of the globe."[33] Why have biblical commentators missed this universal rite? Trumbull asks, with all the humility of one overtaken by the excitement of his discovery. Perhaps because they have been unduly parochial. Trumbull advocates more heterogeneous theories and practices. While he seems to accept that a comparativism like his own (there is not one contemporary social theorist of importance who is overlooked in his researches) is not for everyone, he remains committed to his demand for a deeper, broader theology.

Trumbull's guiding rite defines the deepest aspiration of human society. The blood covenant, as he portrays it, is about the construction of kinship. It represents an inviolable bond between two human beings of any creed or kind. Trumbull cites Livingstone's description of his own inadvertent covenant with a young woman, the result of blood squirted into his eye during a surgery on her leg (14–15). The very existence of this rite the world over is a sign of the universal yearning for kinship. And scholarship itself, Trumbull implies, undertaken in the proper holistic spirit, has the power to make "all the world akin" (57). Trumbull's brand of Bible study anticipates a type of social scientific mindset that I believe to be uniquely hospitable to Melville. It will therefore prove an important part of the analysis in section 3 below. But to conclude the present phase of the discussion, let me turn to a type of Bible criticism, that might be seen, contra Trumbull, as a backward glance. In such writings as *Sociology for the South* (1854) and "The Relation of Organic Science to Sociology," authors like George Fitzhugh and Joseph Le Conte expressed the exigencies of their antebellum moment, while participating fully in the biblical conversation we have traced from late-eighteenth-century Tübingen.

The value of these works, and the reason why they provide the culminating example here, is their extension of this biblical conversation into explicit reflections on the emerging social sciences. Fitzhugh and Le Conte assume that the status of Christian doctrine cannot be assessed apart from this modern field of inquiry. In this, they were registering one notable outcome of the higher criticism, reflected in all the writings we have discussed so far: the consensus that the Bible was somehow up for grabs. It required reclamation, possibly by a particular form of study, or discipline, as it would be termed by the late nineteenth century. We can read Matthew Arnold's aim to save the Bible for literature as one such attempt. The biblical defense of slavery is another. The fascination of Fitzhugh's *Sociology for the South* is its revaluation of everything that midcentury "moderns" were learning to despise. Slavery from this perspective was the highest ideal, while freedom was a hollow creed. Equally "cold" and "dreary" is the abolitionist doctrine that denies one "property in man." How else is one to fulfill the Christian precept to "love thy neighbor"? Fitzhugh's slave society preaches self-denial over self-development. The same ethic holds for all society's members: "The masters . . . if they perform properly their duties, have more cares and less liberty than the slaves themselves."[34] In *Cannibals All* (1857), a continuation of the earlier book (Fitzhugh called *Sociology* "synthetic" and *Cannibals* "analytic"), Fitzhugh reiterates these claims more aggressively, denouncing what he sees as the dominant principle of political economy: that man "can only be just to himself, by doing wrong to others." He goes on to decry usury in the name of Moses and points out that all of his prophecies were designed to inhibit competition among the Jews and "beget permanent equality." Like previous interpreters, Fitzhugh considers the Bible the highest portrait of human character and need. Here man is "the most social" and "least selfish of animals."[35] Proof of slavery's "necessity," he declares, can "remove the greatest stumbling block to belief in the Bible." This claim issues in an attack on Bible criticism (especially as adapted by abolitionists): "texts, detached and torn from their context . . . the distorted and forced construction of certain passages," reducing "the Bible to a mere allegory, to be interpreted to suit every vicious taste and wicked purpose" (129).

I have suggested that Fitzhugh's arguments typify a certain mid-nineteenth-century antimodernist stance. What's unique about them is Fitzhugh's decision to define his ideal society against what he apparently considers to be the formal, if not disciplinary, practice of "sociology." Fitzhugh and fellow slavery apologist Henry Hughes have been credited with introducing the latter term into the American lexicon. Sociology, according to Fitzhugh, is the master plan of a fallen world. His book helps to codify social and intellectual developments that were well underway in this period. The institutional origins of American sociology lie in the 1865 founding of the American Social Science Association, whose roots can be traced to the creation in 1851 of a Board of Aliens Commission by the State of Massachusetts. The charge of this board was "to superintend the execution of all laws in relation to the introduction of aliens in the Commonwealth." The genesis of American sociology—from this Board of Aliens Commission, to the American Social Science Association, and on to the 1905 founding of the American Sociological Society (now known as the American Sociological Association)—reveals that, from its beginnings, sociology's goal was the mediation of social diversity. The "science of society" may be said to have developed in response to the threat of social difference.[36] Social scientists throughout the period devoted themselves to immigrant causes. While there was a certain optimism in their zealous activity on behalf of the immigrant, the tenor of their attention suggests anxiety. A random sample of papers from the American Social Science Association between the years 1870 and 1890 includes "Pauperism in New York City" (1873), "The Negro Exodus from the Gulf States" (by Frederick Douglass), "The Emigration of Colored Citizens from the Southern States" (1880), "Immigration and Nervous Diseases," and "Immigration and Crime" (1889). An organization whose motto was *Ne Quid Nimis* ("Everything in Moderation") could not have confronted the waves of immigration with complete confidence.[37] Fitzhugh ends *Sociology for the South* with an attack upon methods of human classification that become standardized by sociologists in the late nineteenth century. "We abhor the doctrine of 'The Types of Mankind,'" he writes, "first, because it is at war with scripture, which teaches us that the whole human race is descended from a common parentage; and secondly, because it encourages and incites brutal masters to treat negroes, not as weak, ignorant and dependent brethren, but as wicked beasts, without the pale of humanity" (95). In reality, however, the very rational social engineering methods that Fitzhugh supposedly despises share his purpose: the subordination of the racially different.

Joseph Le Conte's work provides a valuable complement to Fitzhugh's because it embraces both the biblical defense of slavery and sociology. Yet Le Conte's case for sociology is derived from an altogether different lineage. Le Conte anticipates the work of a later generation of southern sociologists, who would mourn the loss of slavery as an incomparable system of socialization. In place of Fitzhugh's political economy, Le Conte invokes an organic sociology based in the laws of evolution. It is a sign of the utter uncertainty of what was meant by "sociology" at the time that two men writing in the same antebellum southern context, drawing upon similar social scientific and theological sources, and endorsing the identical institution of slavery could arrive at such different conceptions of the sociological enterprise. For Le Conte, the existence of slavery had always signaled a civilization's health, and a fair assessment of American slavery required a "comparative" sociological method that could document this. "By the comparison of human governments and organizations, of all kinds and degrees," he wrote, "the institution of slavery, as it exists in the Southern United States, may be placed on a scientific basis that is absolutely invulnerable." In Le Conte's view, southern slavery was neither Edenic nor anachronistic; it was perfectly rational. "The dogmas of universal liberty and equality," he believed, would eventually be exposed by the superior empiricism of comparative method. As "the gradual development of the divine idea in the human reason," social scientific organicism posed no threat to a theology that extolled the design of God's universe.[38]

The sociological treatistes of Fitzhugh and Le Conte can be seen as examples of a new genre, the social scientific romance of slavery, which culminated in the apologia for slavery formulated by Jerome Dowd (and others) in the *American Journal of Sociology*. More rational treatments of the institution took more sentimental forms. In the preface to Harriet Beecher Stowe's *Uncle Tom's Cabin*, for example, the Black is anything but a "member of the family," socialized into an ideal posture of self-sacrifice. He is "an exotic . . . a character so essentially unlike the hard and dominant Anglo-Saxon race, as for many years to have won from it only misunderstanding and contempt."[39] Like the sociological theories being developed in this era, Stowe's novel combines racist ideology with a commitment to empirical description. Within its delineation of the various slave regions and slave economies, it offers a catalog of different forms of social organization, including the Christian humanitarianism of the Shelbys, the utopian idyll of the Quakers; the anomic world of Augustine St. Claire (where social roles are chaotically mobile and independent of the larger southern caste system); and the autocratic regime of Simon Legree (where all power is centralized in a single despotic authority).[40] Part moralism and part social realism, Stowe's narrative combines emotional harangue with objective detail.

Stowe's realism is marked by racial determinism. Her characters adhere to a model that limits both Whites and Blacks. Simon Legree, who has realized an innate brutality despite his mother's "unwearied love, and patient prayers," is the most dramatic example (528). Stowe's biologism also supports a caste system: light-skinned Blacks are superior to dark-skinned ones. The latter are the particular objects of a containing Christianity. Atheistic and educable mulattoes like George Harris foretell a black pride and agency that resists assimilation. Thus, Stowe stresses the need for strict distinctions between Blacks and Whites, at the same time that she locates the highest Black potential in mulattoes—that is, in the Blacks who are

most White. The novel's close predicts freedom, education ("the first desire of the emancipated slave," Stowe writes, "is for *education*" [627]), and
deportation. In his own closing letter, George Harris aggressively embraces separatism, wills himself shades darker, and denounces the efface-
ments of the American melting pot. "You will tell me, our race have equal
rights to mingle in the American public as the Irishman, the German, the
Swede," he proclaims. "Granted they have. . . . But, then, *I do not want it*"
(610). The tension between Harris's light-skinned superiority, which facilitates his radical message, and his Black nationalism mirrors the larger tensions of the novel. In Stowe's world, only the mulatto can articulate the
ideal of difference so essential to any genuinely radical program. Stowe's
dilemma is revisited in the conflicting agendas of Booker T. Washington
and W.E.B. Du Bois. Washington's alter ego enacts the syndrome of self-
hatred in literal terms, by washing away his difference (the narrative
abounds in hygienic rituals), while Du Bois's ironic "final solution" to the
problem of the color line—make Blacks disappear through mass extermi-
nation—presages his own far from ironic emigration to Ghana.[41] Despite
its final prophecy of exile, *Uncle Tom's Cabin* leaves an opening for late-
nineteenth-century parallels between Blacks and immigrants.

Stowe's Uncle Tom and Melville's Billy Budd suggest the psychological
continuities between slaves and lower classes.[42] This is only to confirm the
obvious: slavery did not vanish miraculously from the American consciousness with its formal end in 1863. The institution, and the debates over
social and racial difference that it initiated, persisted in the circumstances—social, economic, and psychological—of Blacks, in the imaginations of later realist writers, and in the writings of sociologists. In the late
nineteenth century, the question of how to assimilate over three million
former slaves into society coincided with the question of how to assimilate
increasing numbers of foreign immigrants, whose presence both resembled and overshadowed the circumstances of Blacks. The influx of external
immigrants heightened awareness of what I have called "internal immigrants."[43] A prominent feature of late-nineteenth-century American society was the rising visibility of panhandlers, hobos, and other populations of
homeless and unemployed. These marginal figures, who haunt the pages
of realist fiction, attest to the limits of assimilation. They represent the
domestic casualties of a late-nineteenth-century capitalist industrial system.[44] These two consecutive historical events—slavery's end and immigration's intensification—point to one large problem: the coherence of a
modern society rapidly losing its grip on traditional sources of control.
The first examples of sociology in America, last-gasp defenses of slavery,
reveal a discipline partly rooted in the charged atmosphere created by
the decline of a slaveocracy and the anxieties about social order and social
difference that accompanied it. Despite its own qualification in this era,

religion retained a critical authority. As Melville wrote in a note to the late poem "Naples in the Time of Bomba," the church "proves of far more efficacy in bringing a semi-insurgent populace to their knees than all the bombs, bayonets, and fusilades of the despot of Naples."[45] In the following pages, I look at examples of religious skepticism from a variety of fields. These were in part the issue, in part the cause, of the developments we have been describing. The significant point is the persisting power of religion, which lingers, forcibly, despite the different challenges to it.

The Varieties of Religious Doubt

The religious domain in the human soul is like the area of the American Indians, which . . . is year by year ever more restricted by their white neighbors.
— Strauss, *The Christ of Faith and the Jesus of History*[46]

In his 1873 book *The Study of Sociology*, Herbert Spencer offers a classic formulation of an emerging sociological perspective. Through the image of a "single meal [where one] may take in bread made from Russian wheat, beef from Scotland, potatoes from the midland countries, sugar from Mauritius, salt from Cheshire, pepper from Jamaica," he captures "the incalculable complexity of the influences under which each individual, and a *fortiori* each society develops, lives, and decays."[47] Spencer's interrelated society, where ties are at once concealed and far-ranging, provides a typical conception of modernization. In their descriptions of the professional sociologist, American founders like F. H. Giddings and Albion Small portrayed a deep, coordinating seer who could unite "the fragmentary knowledge of societary relations" possessed by "the millions."[48] They derided simple empiricism and distinguished the discipline of sociology from the disparate fields of social science by the commitment to "critical methodology" over "humanitarian sentiment."[49] Like the European authors of classic sociological works—Max Weber and Georg Simmel in Germany and Emile Durkheim in France—American sociologists heralded the rise of a "value-free" social science.[50]

The demand for "scientific" credentials preoccupied even ministers. The Reverend Henry Ward Beecher proclaimed in 1872 that "a science of management" was essential knowledge for every minister, and he recommended that the works of Spencer be added to the clerical curriculum.[51] In his book on the rise of the medical profession, Paul Starr traces changing attitudes toward authority and science from the Jacksonian to the Progressive Eras. The common sense ethic of the Jacksonian period, which tended to view scientific knowledge as widely accessible, gave way to an elitism that set scientific knowledge beyond the comprehension of the majority. "The less one could believe 'one's own eyes,'" writes Starr—"and the new world of science continually prompted that feeling—the more receptive one became to seeing the world through the eyes of those who claimed specialized, technical knowledge, validated by communities of their peers."[52]

Professionals had a stake in promoting anxiety about the complexity of social life. More than any other professional, the sociologist based his claim for expertise on his special capacities of sight. Just as illness, from the physician's point of view is "good for business," so is indeterminacy for sociologists. Herbert Spencer's famous parable of the warped iron plate articulates the sociologist's relationship to this indeterminacy. An imaginary dialogue between a social reformer and a neutral observer before a warped iron plate becomes a parable on the ineffectiveness of most social observation and action. "How shall we flatten it? Obviously, you reply, by hitting down on the part that is prominent." But the attempt to flatten the plate by striking the prominent part only produces another warp. "A pretty bungle we have made of it. Instead of curing the original defect, we have produced a second. Had we asked an artizan practised in 'planishing' . . . he would have taught us how to give variously-directed and specially-adjusted blows with a hammer elsewhere: so attacking the evil not by direct but by indirect actions."[53] Spencer's parable has been rightly understood as a sociological endorsement of laissez-faire capitalism. But it also represents a claim for social dominance founded on professional expertise. Like the practiced planisher, the sociologist knows how to penetrate surfaces to apprehend the invisible causes that escape ordinary observation.

These sociological claims could have a far less abstract dimension. Spencer's multicultural supper illustrates his interest in basic and ordinary conditions, such as "the material composition of a man's body," or the way a "squabble between a consult and a king in Abyssinia . . . obliges you to abridge your autumn holiday" (16). Spencer is equally concerned with the alimentary and the parliamentary. But why would a meal be the proper register for the varieties of human interdependence? The image has an extraordinary range. I believe its roots lie in the most ancient form of communion, the sacrificial meal. Through the collective consumption of a sacrifice—usually a sacred totem animal—all became one. Revised by Spencer for the modern age, the rite retains some of its former security. There is something profoundly optimistic in his vision of a worldwide kinship based on a common taste and food supply. Here there is no division between those who bring appetites to the table (consumers) and those who bring merely (their own) flesh and blood (consumed). Another reference (on the same page) to the parasitical institution of American slavery recovers this repressed content. To consult Spencer's subsequent three-volume work, *The Principles of Sociology*, with its evolutionary account of sacrificial acts up to the present, many featuring human victims, is to recognize that this other content was never far from Spencer's mind. Spencer's prophecy in *The Study of Sociology* predicts a global harmony based on the unification of human aspirations. The object of a modern world order is to create a continuum of desire: common taste for a common stock of commodities. Yet it also harks back to other sacrificial practices where determinations of kinship could separate consumer from consumed. Spencer's image is past- and present-minded. The "barbarians" featured in the gloomier ancient record represent both a heritage and an ongoing potential.

RELIGIOUS REMNANTS

Spencer's double-sided meal reveals the complicated religious sensibility that informed the writings of major sociologists. To be sure, faith was not easily accommodated to these rational enterprises. Their attitudes toward religion might best be termed "Hebraic," which is to say that they understood its claims in intellectual terms.[54] Religion was a collective "need," essential to community. Nevertheless, it is not surprising that nearly all of them experienced a crisis of belief. William Graham Sumner's story is representative. Trained as an Episcopal minister, he was diverted by his discovery of Spencer, which led to a professorship in social science at Yale. In Perry Miller's words, Sumner "put his religious beliefs in a drawer and turned the lock. . . . Upon unlocking it, he found the drawer empty." The lives of other sociologists reveal similar shifts from spiritual to empirical loyalties: Franklin Giddings was a minister's son, Lester Ward, a minister's grandson; and Herbert Spencer was educated by a clergyman uncle.[55]

For the first generation of sociologists, rationality did not replace religious faith, it absorbed it. By characterizing the relationship in this way, I do not mean to imply that this response was involuntary or unconscious. Albion Small's example conveys the extent of their awareness. Small trained as a minister at the Newton Theological Institution from 1876 to 1879, and then pursued the social sciences in Germany from 1879 to 1881.[56] Small appears to have felt no particular angst in shifting from one course of study to the other. Throughout his career, he argued for the interdependence of religion and social science. As he wrote late in life, "From the first to last religions have been men's more or less conscious attempt to give finite life its infinite rating. Science can never be an enemy of religion. . . . The more science we have the more are we awed and lured by the mystery beyond our ken."[57] Here science is an anomic yearning in search of a higher principle. But as early as his ambitious position paper on "The Scope of Sociology" (serialized from 1899 to 1902 in the *American Journal of Sociology*), Small was writing about religion in similar terms. "Religion is not a local nor a racial but a human want," Small wrote, "and the want will not be satisfied until it has reached a universal expression.

Every movement of men to satisfy the religious yearning has been a vicarious sacrifice for all humanity, in expressing its want and in experimenting with means for achieving its desire. The transfusion of religious conceptions has been going on since the first human consciousness of awe and fear."[58] Small's observation acknowledges religion's multiplicity at the same time that it denies to any one religion a "universal expression." He quotes Paul's "sociological lectures" in support of his comparativist claim: "we are members one of another."

Yet spiritual life, and by implication, social life in general, according to Small, is a process where some benefit precisely because others give, or are given up. Small devotes a special section of "The Scope of Sociology" to the social principle of "vicariousness," which is defined as a means of social equilibrium. "Vicarious sacrifice" ensures that "the world is not a gift enterprise," that everyone puts in what he gets out (361). The phrase "vicarious sacrifice" may have a specific theological referent: Horace Bushnell's *Vicarious Sacrifice* (1866), a standard theological text that Small would have encountered during his ministerial training. Bushnell himself was a kind of theological maverick, who was converted back to Christianity after a crisis of faith by the writings of Samuel Taylor Coleridge. Bushnell's interest in atonement was enhanced by events surrounding the American Civil War. He was overwhelmed with a sense of mission when his delivery of *Vicarious Sacrifice* to his publisher coincided (to the day) with the martyrdom of Abraham Lincoln. While the war, as Sidney Ahlstrom observes, lent an "existential urgency" to Bushnell's work, "vicarious sacrifice" is no terrible creed.[59] Its benevolent (and rather commonplace) purpose was the transformation of Christian sacrifice into a vision of sympathy and love. Against the somber theology of the Edwardseans, Bushnell set a principle of divine presence. Christ, who is "profoundly identified with us in our fallen state," overflows with sympathy for the human condition. Rather than necessity or penance, sacrifice is a psychic embrace. It is as tangible as maternal love or patriotism. Sacrifice is live and practical (41). Take Bushnell's "love," call it "dependence," and you have Albion Small's idea of a " social fact." In Small's view, *"perpetual vicariousness,"* give and take, is elemental. When it is absent or undeveloped, there is no society as such. When it is "interrupted" or foiled, there is social disturbance. An economy of Christian love, where God's sacrifice brings human beings out of sin and its "penalties," becomes an "economy of reciprocity" (359–60).

Still, there is a crucial difference between the models of Small and Bushnell. Bushnell's sacrificial love pictures a fundamentally weakened self. The Ideal beings who give themselves (as mothers or soldiers) recall the sentimental heroines of Susan Warner or Harriet Beecher Stowe. Warner's *The Wide, Wide World* (1850) provides a tacit critique of sentimental Christianity through the equation it draws between devotion and self-abnegation.

Warner's protagonist, Ellen Montgomery, is a love junky, whose addiction becomes the means to her violation by others. Mothers are missionaries, socializing Christian subjects into ideal sentimental states of abjection. Hence the aggressive typography of the novel's opening, a gravestone cross that encloses (or imprisons) the first letter of the narrative's first word: "Mama." The image serves as prophecy and plea. It prophesies two inseparable fates: the mother's martyrdom and the daughter's punishing psychology of dependence. The plea has to do with an insight built into Warner's text about differences in male and female spiritual prerogatives.[60] Warner draws a contrast between maternal and paternal authority that parallels a characteristic division between the New and Old Testament Gods. Paternal authority fulfills an Hebraic model; it is remote and un-challengeable, arbitrary, even irrational. Maternal authority is Christian; intimate and tender, this deity sets up house in the soul and cultivates submission from within. Christian love, sentimental novels reveal, puts individuals at the mercy of social tyranny—whether the aggressive moral-ism of John Humphreys or the sadism of Simon Legree.

Albion Small's recasting of Christian "vicariousness" as a rational prin-ciple takes these fictions to their logical conclusions. Small perceives the dangerous social imbalances supported by a sentimental Christianity. His vision of social interdependence is not about psychic deprivation or defeat. Rational reciprocity preserves the integrity of self and collectivity. Bushnell's "vicarious sacrifice" serves Small as a negative analogy. He was more receptive to other theological models. Consider, for example, the use he makes of the higher criticism in *The Origins of Sociology* (1924). Small accepts (unambivalently, it seems) a Comtean program of social spiritual-ity. "Early in the nineteenth century the idea took possession of leading scholars in Europe that the chief scripture given for our instruction in the conduct of life is human experience. . . . It would be possible and instruc-tive to draw a parallel between the vagaries of the social scientists of various names, in trying to get wisdom from human experience, and the different schools of biblical interpretation." One point of comparison is the shaping of the Bible (and social facts) to support "incongruous and contradictory counterfeits of wisdom . . . systems of positive or negative faith"(9). The Bible, like the text of society, is a site of interpretation, an inducement to theory. Small shows how certain methods of Bible reading that developed in the nineteenth century paved the way for the now preeminent field of sociology.

Sociology, from this perspective, is heir to an innovative Bible criticism. In a brief chapter on Niehbuhr, Strauss, and Ewald, Small notes how they "focalized tendencies which were related to systematic and historical theology as the larger historical movement was related to social science in general." The higher criticism, he concludes admiringly, "left a permanent impression upon religious thinking in the Western world" (90–91). One of its most important contributions was the liberation of the sacred sense from theological confinement. The higher criticism revealed, writes Small, quoting Ranke, that "in all history God resides and lives and gives Himself to be known . . . Wherefore, whatever happens, our business is to decipher this sacred hieroglyphic. In that way also we serve God. In that way also we are priests and teachers" (93–94). Equipped with its own ritualized method, sociology appears as a type of modern priesthood. The distinctiveness of this lineage cannot be overemphasized. Sociology derives positivist method from an early-nineteenth-century revolution in Bible interpretation. This unlikely source in turn invests a deliberately mundane enterprise with divine purpose.

Small was not without company in making these claims. Throughout the early years of the *American Journal of Sociology*, the sociologist was compared, in the words of one contributor, to "his not remote kinsman, the theologian." The chief difference, according to Victor Branford, was that "sociologists . . . have all had social experience," while only some theologians "have had religious experience."[61] In the same forum another participant declared that "sociology is a essentially a spirtual science . . . the religion of the future." Small himself had felt compelled in a previous issue to distinguish true sociology from the popular variants associated in particular with Graham Taylor's Christian sociology. "Partial in content, but potent in political effect," Taylor's "sociology" was moral activism parading as bona fide science. Small includes in his critique a revealing image of professional legitimacy drawn from T. H. Huxley: "The laboratory is the fore-court of the temple of philosophy; and whoso has not offered sacrifices and undergone purification there, has little chance of admission into the sanctuary."[62] This metaphor conveys much about the fortunes of religion in this era of sociological development. Religious sentiments of the reform type are rejected as soft and sentimental. They are equated with the popular social science that so closely resembled sociology as to threaten its objective credentials. These advocates needed to be excluded, if not in practice (there was no way to bar them from the forums or journals, judging from their consistent representation there), at least in ideal terms. By rejecting these looser sociologies, however, some of them religious at base, sociologists were not closing out religious concerns. Far from it. As Small's borrowed metaphor suggests, religion was a consistent point of reference for an emerging rational orthodoxy. But in identifying their sociological method with religion, American sociologists often reverted in particular to an ancient Hebraic model. There are a few explanations for this. First, Christianity, as I have suggested, was associated with social scientific amateurs like Graham Taylor. Second, there was a special resonance in the dilemmas of the Hebrews, whose stark rites expressed an ingrown, even paranoid disposition. To the largely White and middle-class membership of early American sociology, the trials and solutions of Judea may have seemed surprisingly familiar. Third, there was also a compatibility with Hebraic forms themselves: the emphasis on community and conformity, on the sacredness of law and language, on the remote (as opposed to embodied) nature of authority.

These allegorical attachments have something in common with the religious practices of the first Puritan settlers in America, a parallel confirmed by Dorothy Ross in *The Origins of American Social Science*. Ross attributes to the first generation of sociologists a strongly spiritualized sense of American exceptionalism that recalls Hebraic notions of a "chosen people." The lingering religious claims presupposed by her arguments deserve special emphasis.[63] Albion Small's image of true science betrays this residual investment; a realm where "fore-court[s]" are distinguished from "sanctuar[ies]," and "sacrifices" are offered in hope of "admission." These preparations evoke the rites of passage that are standard for any professionalization process. The modern vocation of sociology revitalizes, as it builds upon, these rites. Strenuous application in the laboratory assumes the gravity of sacrificial procedure and helps to distinguish sociological objectives from the "hasty first thoughts composing the popular sociologies."

Prevailing sociological wisdom regularly distinguished religions most amenable to scientific analysis and even adaptation. Edward Ross, for example, in his influential study *Social Control* (serialized in the *AJS* during the 1890s), proclaimed that "The wise sociologist will show religion a consideration it has rarely met with from the naturalist." He coins the term "social religion" to characterize "a purely religious sense of nearness to or communion with a superior consciousness . . . [that] generate[s] beliefs as to invisible bonds between self and others."[64] Ross is less interested in the uses of vocational rites than in understanding religion's social function. For Ross, a feeling of community is synonymous with a sense of divine presence. Social ties are always slightly mystical, never fully rational. Ross, like Small, imports an ancient analogy to fortify his modern case. He draws on Robertson Smith to claim that: "The original doctrine of kinship recognized no difference of degrees. . . . It is something mysterious and absolute, like the drop of negro blood that shuts one out of white society in the South" (200). In ancient society, as Ross describes it, kinship and faith are of a piece. Worship affirms kinship and delineates aliens. The community is united by collective consumption and divided by judgments of ritual expendability. Modern society is no different, though the prospects for clarity grow more elusive over time. The drop of blood harbored by a human body escapes detection, in sharp contrast to the drop displayed on Hebrew doorposts. Yet both specify a certain relationship to commu-

nity. The blood that conceals strangeness spells the doom of society's effort to distinguish inside from out. The visible blood on lintels symbolizes
the divine preservation of a certain select community.

Ross shares Small's evolutionary awarenesses: he is also familiar with a
nineteenth-century challenge to faith. "Geology, or higher criticism, or
comparative mythology," he writes, "may undermine particular beliefs
with which ethical-religious feeling has associated itself. But the soul of
religion has a marvellous and little-suspected power of escaping into
new forms of belief" (213). *Social Control* conceives order as both an outcome and a fulfillment of traditional religion. Ross's rationalism, like
Small's, seems not to have lessened his interest in a wider mystical principle. Instead of breeding religious contempt, rational method enhances
an appreciation for religious thought. Both Small and Ross tend toward
Hebraism in the following sense: they place greater weight on religion as
a mode of explanation than as a mode of being. Religion for them supplies
an intellectual method that is, ultimately, consistent with their own strategies of reason.

To Lester Ward, nothing could have been further from enlightenment.
Religion appears in his work as the superego that has to be conquered
before a properly scientific sociology can emerge. No part of Ward's work
better illustrates this premise than the absolute contrast between the first
and second books of his multivolume *Glimpses of the Cosmos* (covering the
years 1858–71), a vast compilation of his writings.[65] Most of the essays in
volume 1 appeared originally in Ward's own inflammatory journal, *The
Iconoclast*. All issues of sociological importance are framed with reference
to some theological controversy. "We are to-day, as it were, on the eve of
a religious crisis," Ward announces at the volume's start, "the rationalistic
element has risen high enough to encroach upon the superstitious element—there has been a shock, and the latter power has girded itself anew
for the subjugation of the former" (44–45). Religion is not without scientific interest. The essay "Comparative Theology," for instance, recommends that religion be taught synthetically: "a scientific and historical
study of the many apparently incongruous and discordant religions which
have prevailed in the world, would unfold the most profound and useful
truths respecting human nature" (223). But religion, for Ward, is ultimately at odds with science, which "is ready to sacrifice its most cherished
theories the moment they are found not to square with that one great
standard, truth" (54). Ward cites Lincoln, Jefferson, and Frederick
Douglass as companions in apostasy. And he predicts the "slow and gradual," but irreversible, displacement of theology by science. "The process,"
he writes, "is a dilution rather than a deletion, a purification rather than a
purgation" (160). "Christian practice" is barbaric, Ward hints, in a subsequent description of how the Eucharist sanctions the consumption of

"human flesh" and "human blood" (173). It's telling, in light of his disdain for religion—whether as spiritual prospect or intellectual subject—that Ward makes no distinction between Christian and Hebraic traditions. The rule of kinship codified in Judaism, he suggests, justifies open season upon aliens: "You must not harm a *Jew*, but treat a *gentile* as you please," which in modern America becomes "you must not harm a *white man*, but treat a *negro* as you please" (81). Ward's religious history is a nondenominational tale of conquest, suffering, and death. By the second volume, religion has disappeared entirely, replaced by topics such as plant physiology and comparative anatomy. For the remainder of Ward's career, religion is simply opposed to the "dynamic" interventionist sociology he idealized. Other sociologists continued to ponder the religious legacy and its implications for their field.

Herbert Spencer, for example, was convinced that religion was meaningful to social science. Spencer's *Study of Sociology* (serialized simultaneously in England and America), which introduced the discipline to a wide Anglo-American readership, devotes a chapter to "The Theological Bias." Spencer begins with the familiar assumption that religion and science are mutually exclusive. "Each system of dogmatic theology with the sentiments that gather round it," he writes, "becomes an impediment in the way of Social Science" (294). At the same time, the sociologist is uniquely equipped to see value in "alien beliefs and the fanaticisms which maintain them" (298). He recognizes "great benefit" in the social "unification" religion affords (299). Spencer goes on to pose a continuity between theological and sociological method. "The special theological bias," he notes, "inevitably pre-judges many sociological questions" (301). Theology "has not arisen rationally but empirically." And it does formulate, "with some approach to the truth, the accumulated results of past human experience" (305).

At first it seems that Spencer's recuperation of theology is based on a principle of complementarity or balance. Religion demands faith; reason cultivates consent. Both are necessary. But as Spencer argues elsewhere, rational inquiry may even increase religious appetites. This may sound familiar, and in part it is: science "enlarges the sphere for religious sentiment. From the very beginning the progress of knowledge has been accompanied by an increasing capacity for wonder."[66] Scientific knowledge will always return us to religious meaning. Spencer, like Small and Ross, is impressed with religion's tenacity. In critiquing "the anti-theological bias," he complains that it "under-values religious institutions in the past, thinks they are needless in the present, and expects they will leave no representatives in the future. Hence mistakes in sociological reasonings."[67] This is no simple affirmation of mystery, despite it all. Religion is being refashioned here, I would argue, as a mode of explanation. And in this sense, Spencer, like Small and Ross, implicitly favors an Hebraic model, where the relationship to God is explicitly intellectualized. Humans are forever questioning, rationalizing, explaining. God is a point of inquiry, a mystery in need of explanation. Social science is an explanation in search of mystery. If not exactly parallel, these are reciprocal quests. It was this aspect of Hebrew religion that I believe sociologists like Spencer, and later Small and others, were picking up on. Religion is neither nullified nor abandoned by the rise of science. Social science confirms the formal compatibility of faith and reason.

LITERARY MARTYRS

The enormous impact of Herbert Spencer's writings in England and America has been well documented. A critical aspect of this currency was the dissemination of his ideas by others. Winwood Reade's *The Martyrdom of Man*, for example, published in 1872, "was so widely read that it reached an eighth edition twelve years later, and may be counted as one of the agencies which popularised Spencer."[68] The book's value for my purposes is enhanced by the fact that in some respects it seems more fictional than scientific. Indeed, it seems downright Melvillian. Reade and Melville share a fascination with human types. *The Martyrdom of Man* is filled with the sorts of catalogs and processionals that appear throughout Melville's fiction, whether he is describing the crew of the *Pequod*, the pilgrims of the *Fidèle*, or the Revolutionary delegation of Anacharsis Cloots. Both approach the classification of diversity with a passion that is at once celebrational and anxious. There is a similar cosmic gloom, and a similar preoccupation with cancellation and reversal. They see virtue and vice as interchangeable. "Every virtue has its attendant vice, which is excited by the same stimulants, which is nourished by the same food," Reade wrote. "Martyrs and persecuters resemble one another; their minds are composed of the same materials."[69] Notice Reade's assumption of the limit on universal matter—an assumption that drives his argument—as well as the focus on consumption. Even more significant is the fact that this passage appears in a description of a specific human career.

Reade's dark and inspired life of Christ has powerful implications for Melville's characterizations in *Billy Budd*. Like Melville, Reade notes a potentially devastating chasm between salvation and works. Jesus "did not display the spirit of a persecuter in his deeds; but . . . in his words." Reade's Jesus is filled with ressentiment: "Not only the inoffensive rich were doomed by Jesus to hell fire, but also those who did anything to merit the esteem of their fellow-men. Even those who were happy and enjoyed life— unless it was in his own company—were lost souls." Christ's followers "were not to give alms in public or to pray in public; and when they fasted, they were to pretend to feast; for if it was perceived that they were devout men, and were praised for their devotion, they would lose their reward" (182–83). The devout were caught in a taunting house of mirrors, which could only reflect back a distortion of their souls. If things looked straight, there was a sure sign of doom. Christ, as glossed by Reade, ordained an absolute divide between virtue and visibility. Any sign of secular favor could nullify the eternal value of a deed. Meanwhile, Christ himself is charged with "the wildest extravagance of speech." His failure at Jerusalem, and consequent rage against "successful rivals," drove him into a "bitter abuse" for which he paid with his life (184).

Other features of Reade's version of Christianity are more predictable. Faith and knowledge are mutually exclusive. He can sound bitterly nostalgic, as in his account of how Christianity gradually "lost its democratic character" (199). He continues, "the bishops were all of them ignorant and superstitious men, but they could not all of them think alike. As if to ensure dissent, they proceeded to define that which had never existed, and which, if it had existed, could never be defined. They described the topography of heaven. They dissected the godhead, and expounded the immaculate conception, giving lectures on celestial impregnations and miraculous obstetrics" (201). His politics are also conventional, on the order of enlightened irony. The French Revolution is a mixed affair, with "senseless fanatics" like Marat at the helm. While the slave trade is an unqualified brutality ("never was so much human suffering condensed into so small a space"), suffering is the price of progress (302, 295). This notion of the sacrificial payoff is the heart of his book. On one description: "a savage gentleman is always surrounded by a host of clients, who come every morning to give him the salutation, who chant his praises and devour him alive" (378). Those who nourish you will be sure to make food of you. "Nature has raised us to what we are," Reade observes near the end, "by provisional expedients" (412). All benefits derive from the "Inequality of Conditions"; there are "men who roll in carriages, and men who die in the streets" (417).

Reade is dazzled and depressed by the creed he immortalizes. He despises martyrdom. It is depraved "that mankind should be elevated by misfortune, and that happiness should grow out of misery and pain." His very next pronouncement, however, restores the toppled regency to the throne: "a season of mental anguish is at hand. . . . The soul must be sacrificed; the hope in immortality must die. A sweet and charming illusion must be taken from the human race" (447). The displacement of religion by science represents the final stage of martyrdom. Truth, beauty, hope—all are destined for smoke at the altar of the God of Reason. Compared to Melville, Reade seems a matching glove turned inside out. The content is the same: doubt and ressentiment, primitive nostalgia balanced by learning, elitism tempered by democratic idealism. Yet Reade is trapped by a theoretical controversy that inspires Melville. He remains inordinately attached to martyrdom. His narrative becomes a paradoxical testament to antiprogressivism.

In Melville's view, martyrdom and sacrifice survive, even under the rational cover of science. Because he is never so enamored of the constructs that blur Reade's vision, he never stops recognizing their permutations. Melville knows that science will never evaporate religious dilemmas: he sees how much it is motivated by them. His conscious embrace of the modern struggle between them was perhaps nowhere more dramatically represented than in *Moby-Dick*. Melville set the stage for this contest in his characterization of the novel in a letter to Hawthorne: "I have written a wicked book, and feel spotless as the lamb." Wherein does the wickedness lie? Is it a function of the novel's relentless relativism, its equalization of all religion, Christian, heathen, Hebrew, Hindu? Is it the blasphemy of doubt, which is indulged to a morbid extent, from the opening actions of the suicidal Ishmael (who joins a crew governed by a suicidal captain as his antidote) to his final, inexplicable salvation?

Or is it the spectacle of submission itself? Ishmael turns it into an art form: from his cheery analog between the life of a common sailor and the lot of lower orders ("grasshopper," "slave") to "The Whiteness of the Whale," where all explanation—political, legal, religious—is nullified by instinct. Submission to instinct, in plot terms, is submission to Ahab, the anti-Enlightenment messenger of death. As Thoreau observed in *Walden*: "I believe that men are generally still a little afraid of the dark, though the witches are all hung and Christianity and candles have been introduced" (176). They're afraid of the dark, and just as afraid of the light. Melville's colorless catalog inverts the usual oppositions between rationality and irrationality. Where society submits raw nature (rage, fear) to artificial forms (the ten commandments, the penal code). Melville submits a transhistorical, cross-cultural wealth of white injunctions to a chaotic translucence. His white rites are propertyless, their only content the invisible stares of the human beings who have imagined them over time. Melville's point is that your own injunctions can't be trusted to protect you when you need them. Faced with a similar dilemma, Emerson wrote "Whim" on the doorpost of his house.

Emerson at the threshold is defiant. He is aware that entryways are holy, that God would prefer a different inscription. In substituting "Whim" for "Yahweh" he is violating a commandment and taking a monumental risk. This is no minor rebellion. Emerson is serious about the layers of meaning built into the arches of dwellings. He knows that to write God's name at the door is to claim membership in a kin group and to claim certain protections on the basis of it. Emerson's gesture directly repudiates these declarations of affinity. The specific lines from "Self-Reliance" read: "I would write on the lintels of the door-post, *Whim*. I hope it is somewhat better than whim at last, but we cannot spend the day in explanation. Expect me not to show cause why I seek or why I exclude company."[70] Emerson is shunning universal protections conferred on the basis of group life. He is saying, in effect, "I'm not expecting God to spare me or mine." Some guilty recollection of this defiance may be detectible in the elegiac "Experience," published five years later. But he is evidently shunning most of all the collectivity that sanctions such superstitions.

There seems no end to the radical implications of "Self-Reliance." As Emerson wrote in another renowned part of the essay, "A foolish consistency is the hobgoblin of little minds; adored by little statesmen and philosophers and divines. With consistency a great soul has simply nothing to do. He may as well concern himself with his shadow on the wall" (153). Here again, Emerson is tempting fate, by imperilling an object that is synonymous with protection. Who has never looked upon a wall for comfort and noticed that it projects back terror, because of something there or not there? Blankness, we know from Melville, is scary, as is the face you weren't expecting, your own or someone else's. To Emerson, rational calls for explanation are equivalent to magic or witchery. Those who adhere to them are as afraid of their shadows as those who swear by witches and ghosts. It all comes down to the fall of man, he argues in "Experience." "We have learned that we do not see directly, but mediately, and that we have no means of correcting these colored and distorting lenses which we are, or of computing the amount of their errors. . . . Nature, art, persons, letters, religions, objects, successively tumble in, and God is but one of [our] ideas."[71] God is simply a name on a list. This is what we have come to. Divinity is just another thing that satisfies our craving for variety—the other consequence of the Fall. We need stimulation because we're so aware of what we miss. In "Self-Reliance," human mediate-ness seems answerable to bold declarations. Explanation might be secondary, but fear is real. In "Experience," the diagnosis is clinical. Like a physician who denies pain because he can't conceive someone else's, Emerson keeps his eye on the cure rather than on the affliction. He seems unimpressed with the fact that something out there is causing terror or torment, heaping on grief. This is undeniably a response to enormous pain; the fact that he is in mourning cannot be overlooked. Still, we are confronting an intellectual advance or change. Doubt is no longer staged as a contest between different notions of God or universal meaning. It has become a quality of mind that keeps the world at a distance. The intensity and waywardness of the earlier essay is gone. Jesus has become "the 'providential man'" (in quotation marks)—a "good man" simply because many have agreed that this is so (269).

The world's of *Moby-Dick* and *The Scarlet Letter* remain spiritually charged in ways that the Emerson of "Experience" might have envied. One of the questions raised by Hawthorne's classic has to do with which protagonist, Hester or Dimmesdale, submits most fully to the social and theological decrees of the Puritan community. Both have been seen as defiant in their respective interpretations of how to account for their sin. Dimmesdale's defiance is his concealment and distortion of penance. There is something extreme according to the novel's narrator, in the hybrid zeal of his worship, fortified by "the lore of Rabbis, and monkish erudition" and by "the old, corrupted faith of Rome." The "bloody scourge" he keeps in his "secret closet," the "vigils," and the "constant introspection wherewith he tortured, but could not purify himself" all suggest a punishing extreme at odds with Puritanism.[72] Hawthorne's portrait of Dimmesdale verges at times on parody. There is something unmistakably adolescent in the image of a pale young man locked in a room, struggling to purge his sensual urges. Dimmesdale is the oversexed boy, whose efforts at control partake of the same excessive source. As this implies, Dimmesdale is highly conventional. He worries obsessively about public opinion. He exploits his suffering to professional advantage. Hawthorne stresses the ministerial coinage in his wasted and distracted aspect (161–62, 231). Dimmesdale's suffering for profit is contrasted with Hester's suffering for its own sake. He "had never," Hawthorne writes near the end, "gone through an experience calculated to lead him beyond the scope of generally received laws. . . . As a priest, the framework of his order inevitably hemmed him in . . . safer within the line of virtue, than if he had never sinned at all." Whereas "the tendency of [Hester's] fate and fortunes had been to set her free. The scarlet letter was her passport into regions where other women dared not tread" (217–18). Hawthorne here reverses the gender stereotypes of sentimentality. It is the male character, ambitious, successful, widely admired, who is "hemmed in." Hawthorne's hero is contained, metaphorically at least, by the ultimate domestic convention, the art of the hem or stitch (in contrast to the narrator of the Custom House preface, who denies he is "conversant with such mysteries" [61]). Meanwhile, the heroine wanders on the edge of an "untamed forest."

I am not suggesting that Hawthorne is endorsing this reversal. He registers it, in order to confirm the revolutionary threat of his heroine, a threat that is universal and political. Hester's danger is written into the red letter that defines her. The symbol is so volatile that Hawthorne has us believing it hot to the touch. The letter's color is a sign that it is inflamed and that others should keep away. It signifies a blood protection that encloses the bearer within a circumference where no harm can come. This is especially significant given Pearl's conflation of the letter on Hester's breast with the milk that was inside it. Her mother's overwrought seal of protection is indistinguishable from Pearl's original food source. This is why she is desperate that Hester reclaim it. But who *is* this symbol designed to protect? Hester considers Pearl her penance, even her curse. "Except when the child was asleep, Hester had never felt a moment's safety; not a moment's calm enjoyment of her" (120). The letter may protect Hester *from* Pearl, but it hardly seems a protection *of* her. It is relevant in this regard that Jewish law strictly forbids the mixing or confusion of elements brought together in Hester's symbol. Mother's milk must not be crossed with any cooked or edible portion of the blood and flesh it sustains.

The letter represents a dangerous mix of milk and blood, nurture and punishment, restraint and desire, innocence and sin. Hence the emphasis on thresholds in the novel's first chapter: the margins between the natural and the man-made, social and natural law, the crowd and the individual, conformity and deviance. All of these things must be kept distinct, or there is the risk of anarchy. Hester embodies that threat, just as her tendentious letter contains her own. Her inscription tempts fate every bit as much as Emerson's inscription on his doorpost. This explains her repeated thoughts of suicide: at least she can choose the moment of annihilation. "She was patient,—a martyr, indeed,—but she forebore to pray for her enemies; lest, in spite of her forgiving aspirations, the words of the blessing should stubbornly twist themselves into a curse."

Hawthorne's own nineteenth-century reading of Jesus highlights the continuities between cursing and praise. Hester's twisted prophecies anticipate the deformed speech of *Billy Budd*'s anti-Christ, John Claggart. Like Melville, Hawthorne offers two rather than a definitive one. For Dimmesdale is the ultimate Christ, as illustrated by the dramatic pietà at the close of the novel. His sin "revealed" at last, Dimmesdale "stood with a flush of triumph in his face, as one who, in the crisis of acutest pain, had won a victory. Then, down he sank upon the scaffold! Hester partly raised him, and supported his head against her bosom" (268). In Hester's case, deception prevails. Her body expresses penance because her prayers are unreliable. Precisely because her penance is physically inscribed, her thoughts are free to wander. Hawthorne might have written Melville's letter about the "wicked book" himself. For Hester's heresy strikes at the heart of Christianity. Hawthorne emphasizes the pathology of his "martyr" (109). Her "heart had lost its regular and healthy throb. . . . At times, a fearful doubt strove to possess her soul, whether it were not better to send Pearl at once to heaven, and go herself to such futurity as Eternal Justice should provide" (184). Infanticide and suicide: the rhetoric is Protestant, but the impluse is satanic. Hawthorne may be staging a melodrama that is distanced from his own perspective—the woman is becoming hysterical or he may be highlighting a danger that any society must anticipate. It is this blend of awe and anxiety that makes Hawthorne's fictional account of deviance a key forerunner to Emile Durkheim's work on social ritual.

Moby-Dick is part of the same intellectual universe. All of these writers see a continuum from the impulse of nurture and nourishment that underwrites social order to the consumption and parasitism that enlarge it, in a potentially annihilating way. The most "wicked" reading of Melville's epilogue suggests that the sharks sport padlocks and the seahawks "sheathed beaks" to limit the competition for a cannibalistic deity (470). The divine appetite has little tolerance for other groping mouths. The cannibal instinct is preeminent here. Melville's doubt has to do with the nature of God's own predatory leanings. The novel includes many passages where a superficial harmony conceals a more profound parasitism. There is no better example than the portrait of nursing whales in the chapter entitled "The Grand Armada." The scene discloses layers upon layers of protection: "a serene valley lake" set in the center of the harpooners "commotion." Further in still, "at the centre of the lake," are "cows and calves; the women and children of this routed host." And finally, "beneath this wondrous world . . . floated the forms of the nursing mothers of the whales." None of these layers, including the sacred maternal center, is preserved from the harpooners' lances. "If I am here recording this scene for you," Ishmael implies, "then they are already unsafe." He is the empathic naturalist with the parasitical relationship to violence. But perhaps his bitter cataloging of the sacrifice will prove instructive. The heart of the violence is captured by the novel's Christian, Starbuck. He notes how "long coils of the umbilical cord" become a "natural line," entrapping the offspring for slaughter. Then comes Ishmael: "when by chance these precious parts in a nursing whale are cut by the hunter's lance, the mother's pouring milk and blood rivallingly discolor the sea for rods." As if to underscore the violation, he adds, "the milk is very sweet and rich; it has been tasted by man" (325–26). The image anticipates another midcentury narrative where laced mother's milk symbolizes more far-ranging violations. In Harriet Jacobs's *Incidents in the Life of a Slave Girl*, a little girl is sent a cup of sweetened milk by a master whose predatory intentions are exposed by the presence of an openly predatory snake.[73]

What these incidents have in common, is the perception of how parasitical norms—humans feeding on whales, or White southerners feeding on Black slaves—nullify natural protections. No mother can protect her young in a society that sanctions the cannibalizing of weaker or simpler creatures by stronger or craftier ones. Nor is the analogy between slave mother and whale mother arbitrary. Melville's analogy between the Black slave and the sperm whale is a mainstay of the novel's historical allegory. "Far above all other hunted whales," his is "an unwritten life," according to

Ishmael (118). Some of the most terrible moments of parasitism are also quite comical, in their billing as forms of gentility. In "Stubb's Supper," the guests at the second mate's whale banquet are swarms ("thousands upon thousands") of sharks. The skill of these sharks, at "goug[ing] out such symmetrical mouthfuls" of whale flesh remains, for Ishmael, "a part of the universal problem of all things." In contemplating the sharks, "quarrelsomely carving away under the table at the dead meat," Ishmael is reminded that they can be seen shadowing "slave ships crossing the Atlantic, systematically trotting alongside, to be handy in case a parcel is to be carried anywhere, or a dead slave to be decently buried" (249–50). The passage is classic Ishmaelese: the diabolism of the social and universal order enfolded in comic irony. There is a price to be paid by a consciousness that sees evil beneath the surface of every human occasion. By the passage's end, Ishmael is nearly blubbering, about "the propriety of devil-worship and the expediency of conciliating the devil." Like the narrative that circles round to deposit Ishmael carefully within the limits of the society he abandons in the opening, these incidents circle round to Melville. Critics have devoted considerable attention to the question of where his sympathies lie. Some find it obvious: the book runs on Ahab's energy; or it's clearly Ishmael's, since he is the one who is saved.

Recent critics have been more comfortable with the idea of an indeterminate book, or a book that insists on both sides of its split narrative.[74] Ishmael the compromiser needs Ahab the flagrant consumer of men. Ishmael's liberalism is cold; Ahab's animism is warm. Ishmael's dialogistic concessions depend on Ahab's monologic force. This message of interdependence is written into the title: *Moby-Dick; or, The Whale*. The first book is Ahab's; the second is Ishmael's. In the version called *Moby-Dick*, the whale is personalized, and the novel becomes a revenge tragedy. In the version called *The Whale*, any leviathan will do. It needn't be *the whale who took my leg*. The book becomes a materialist catalog, an attempt to know the whale by way of its anatomical variety. It would be tempting to call the first version full of meaning and the second devoid of it; the first emotional and defiant, the second rational. But Melville's spiritual perspective cannot be so neatly sorted out. He is both skeptic and believer, just like his two alter egos.

The link between them is sacrifice. It's not incidental that the *Pequod* sets sail at Christmas. Ishmael meets Ahab at the point of this ritual form. In Ishmael, we have the constant pressure of his faith—part Christian, part democratic—that "the universal thump is passed around." Whether the terms are "physical or metaphysical," eventually all accounts are paid. The conviction extends to the deus-ex-machina ending, where Ishmael, who has paid, and who (we are assured) will continue to pay, is saved alone. Ahab's philosophy is more bitterly biblical: You disabled me, I strike back with every force at my command. These are the ravings of conventional revenge. Ahab's means can also be seen as a fulfillment of sacrificial worship. Like the ancient Hebrews, he searches desperately for a sign from God. And he does it all to get a response from Him. Yet Ahab is self-consuming. He is burning inside—a sacrifice on his own inner altar. Melville describes how "these spiritual throes in him heaved his being up from its base, and a chasm seemed opening in him, from which forked flames and lightnings shot up." Waking, "with his own bloody nails in his palms," Ahab is himself an inflamed offering (174). As supplicant, oblation, and Godhead, all rolled into one, he is pure violation. It's difficult to imagine that Melville could ever get more grim than this. The depiction of sacrifice in *Billy Budd*, however, a depiction that is in every way more deliberate and formal, is for these very reasons grimmer still.

Melville and the Science of Sacrifice

The laboratory is the fore-court of the temple of philosophy; and whoso has not offered sacrifices and undergone purification there, has little chance of admission into the sanctuary. — T. H. Huxley, quoted by Albion Small, *American Journal of Sociology*, first issue (1895)

> *Though the virgins of Salem lament,*
> *Be the judge and the hero unbent!*
> *I have won the great battle for thee*
> *And my Father and Country are free!*
>
> *When this blood of thy giving hath gush'd*
> *When the voice that thou lovest is hush'd*
> *Let my memory still be thy pride,*
> *And forget not I smiled as I died!*
> — Byron, "Jephthah's Daughter,"
> *Hebrew Melodies*[75]

My purpose in this section is to retell the story of sacrifice in *Billy Budd* as an historical tale. I want to set the story's portrait of sacrifice in context, to identify the local, international, biblical, philosophical, and social scientific grounds for Melville's own staging of the rite.[76] I have suggested that Melville's portrayal of sacrifice in *Billy Budd* is overdetermined. Sacrifice is an economic rhetoric as well as a sacred dictate. Offerings are made to Old Testament Gods and by New Testament Gods. Sacrifice is a ritual of war and a proper rite of peace. It is ancient and modern, evolving from the early Semites to a modern beyond. The narrative is rich in sacrificial occasions: highly formal procedures that draw on multiple intellectual frameworks. In the following pages, I plan to highlight three in particular. The first is the double sacrifice at Trafalgar of Admiral Nelson and his formerly mutinous crew. The second is extratextual but, I believe integral: a description from Melville's copy of *Will and Idea* of a white squirrel who sacrifices himself to a predatory and mesmerizing serpent. The third is the account of the preparations for Billy's sacrifice. Each of these scenes, I will show, testifies to the range and depth of the sacrificial design of *Billy Budd*.

CULTURE OF VIGILANCE

The sense of urgency that informs the treatment of sacrifice in *Billy Budd*, and by extension, all the late-nineteenth-century meditations on sacrifice discussed here, derives from the particulars of its multiple historical contexts. Set on the nervous British seas of the late eighteenth century, in the aftermath of the mutinies at Nore and Spithead and their historical shadows, British Jacobinism and Revolutionary France, the story becomes a test case for the problem of social control. Political anxiety in *Billy Budd* is double-edged. The novella is equally rich in its evocation of nineteenth-century characters and scenes, from the national crises of slavery and Civil War to the pressures of immigration, social heterogeneity, and class conflict.[77] All of these developments help to explain the general preoccupation with vigilance. Aboard the novella's fogbound ship, the ability to control what is seen, and by whom, is a measure as well as a source of power. The sailor's dogwatch, the most common rite of the ship society, and the first level of a highly formalized hierarchy of sight, is strictly supervised by the officers. At the next level, John Claggart, the master-at-arms, otherwise known as the "chief of police," operates surreptitiously, his surveillance methods invisible to all, including the captain. Captain Vere has the greatest stake in controlling perceptions, and he is at once the character most troubled by the complications of seeing aboard the *Bellipotent* and the primary agent of obscurity. Vere acts in a variety of ways to limit the sight and understanding of his crew: consciously (Vere "so contrived it that [his steward] should not catch sight of the prone one" [477]); unconsciously ("Vere advanced to meet him, thus unconsciously intercepting his view" [478]); and finally, as a matter of "policy" (engineering "the maintenance of secrecy, the confining of all knowledge" aboard ship [480]). All the concerns over watching and being watched derive from a prevailing fear of social disorder.

Like its companion rite, sacrifice, vigilance is a cross-disciplinary enterprise in this period. It is, to begin with, a point of controversy in contemporary Bible interpretation. Matthew Arnold's *Literature and Dogma*, for example, articulates a traditional Christian distrust of the visible: outward acts offer little proof of inner conscience. Yet watching is also credited with a higher purpose in certain biblical texts. Arthur Stanley quotes a passage that describes the prophets as watchmen: their predictions delivered "from those lofty watch-towers of Divine speculation."[78] This residue of spiritual power carries over into a contemporary sociological literature, which accords its own high purpose to watchfulness. An early *American Journal of Sociology* essay, "The World's First Sociological Laboratory," describes a watchtower at the social scientific institute of Scottish sociologist Patrick Geddes. The "Outlook Tower" is the instrumental equivalent of Edinburgh intellectualism, which specializes in the survey method. Edinburgh University, for instance, is the academic home of Robertson Smith's *Encyclopedia Britannica*. The Outlook Tower affords the sociologist a view of "both near and distant things." From his height, the sociologist sees "every variety of modern life, from the worst of Scottish slums" to "the monuments of modern arts and sciences." Voyeurism acquires an elevated, scientific purpose here. As a variation on the survey method, watching becomes another objective means of accumulating knowledge. "If one can learn to observe accurately in watching these shifting scenes, he should be equipped with a method by which he may study the geography of the world, and, through that, social institutions."[79]

The idea that sociological method was founded in some sense on watchfulness is already familiar from the arguments of Albion Small, F. H. Giddings, and Herbert Spencer. To understand how vigilance came to be viewed as a means of accounting for society's different components, or as a means of limited participation in social processes ("participant observation"), we need to know something more about the embattled scene of disciplinary origins. I refer here to both the late eighteenth century, when "the prophets of Paris" wrote their major works, and the late nineteenth century, when sociology took hold in the United States (and, less markedly, in England). In *The Prophets of Paris*, Frank Manuel explains why "the sorely tried Judeans" provide his model for a sociological "priesthood." Saint-Simon, Comte, Turgot, and Condorcet were "great moral teachers," who approached the problems of French social life as spiritual diseases and offered "sacred remedies." These men demanded a cultish commitment from their disciples: the followers of Saint-Simon considered him a latter-day Jesus, while those of Comte considered him a latter-day Saint Paul. The object of sociological analysis was religion and social organization rather than politics and government. Their failure to find grounds for their utopian projections in a political world seems an inevitable response to revolutionary violence. According to Comte, Saint-Simon, and even Condorcet, who was sympathetic to radicalism, "revolutions distorted and confused the basic social, moral, and religious issues."[80] While the prophets advocated respect for the common man, they had little faith in his political judgment. They were elitist in their conceptions of legislative process and scientific method. Sociology was based in common sense, but this did not make it susceptible to mass appropriation.

Melville's Captain Vere has much in common with these observers of revolution. Vere too is described as biased toward books which "in the spirit of common sense philosophize upon realities" (446). He is neither reactionary, like other aristocrats of the era, nor carried away by democratic fervor. He opposes revolutionary politics because they seemed "at war with the peace of the world and the true welfare of mankind" (447). Yet Billy's transfer from the *Rights-of-Man* to the *Bellipotent* is clearly a move from a liberal democracy to a military state (434). One could even argue that Vere needs an atmosphere of crisis to sanction an authority structure natural to his own upper-class station. This is not to deny that there are genuinely threatening circumstances aboard the *Bellipotent*. It is only to say that these threats are entirely class-inflected. There is probably no single image in the story that more neatly captures these anxieties than the picture of the officers during battle standing "with drawn swords behind the men working the guns" (444). The same supple relationship between inside and out is confirmed by the naval-chronicle adaptation of the novel's events. Here Billy becomes a strange assassin, while the stranger Claggart becomes a patriot. All the while it gets things wrong, the chronicle moralizes: These are straitened times, and it is possible that enemies of the nation will find their way inside. What we learn from this is the great resistance on the part of rulers to the idea that natural kinship might be out of sympathy with the national interest. Equally unimaginable is the possibility that political acts might have ambiguous motivations or consequences, blurring established hierarchies.

In his Civil War poem on the New York draft riots, "The House-Top" (1863), Melville's subject once again is an instance of inside turned out. The poem describes the rioting of White laborers in reaction to a provision that allowed the wealthy to buy their way out of the Civil War Draft. The price tag on immunity was three-hundred dollars. The Conscription Act ensured the usual pattern of sacrificial exchange. While the wealthy offered substitutes, the poor could only offer themselves. The rioting lasted for three days and was only stopped by the arrival of Union troops, who were forced to turn their guns on their own prospective comrades. "The considerate historian" instinctively suppresses such ugly events. The poem anticipates some of the analogies drawn in *Billy Budd* between ill-used White sailors and their ill-used human cargo (Black slaves). For one outcome of the Anglo-French War was the British navy takeover of the triangular trade, which included the slave trade. In strictly formal terms, Melville believed, there was a parity between the fortunes of slaves and the fortunes of White laborers under capitalism.[81]

But Melville's poetic account dwells on the deeper irony of the relation. They may be partners in sacrifice, but the two groups are pitted resolutely against one other. Although the poem's perspective betrays little sympathy for either side, its harshest sentiments are reserved for the White workers, described throughout as "ship-rats." The rioters are so many "rats—ship-rats/And rats of the wharves." Melville recalls with frank nostalgia the "civil charms" and "priestly charms" now gone and implies that a new bestiality has risen in its wake, man regressed "whole aeons back in nature." He reads this uncivil protest, as "a grimy slur" on democratic faith, and wonders at the wisdom of a polity that views man as "naturally good . . . never to be scourged."[82] Melville's elevated view from the "House-Top" resembles the remote vigilance afforded by the Scottish Outlook Tower. "Priestly spells," possibly even social scientific ones of the prophetic Parisian sort, are preferable to the rule of these "ship-rats." Melville's note to the poem highlights a convergence among the actions and fates of French Revolutionary agitators, American laborers, and (former) Black slaves. He quotes Froissard's response to "the remarkable sedition in France": "I dare not write the horrible and inconceivable atrocities committed." Melville's comment: "The like may be hinted of some proceedings of the draft-rioters." Their incendiary response to a provision that created, Melville concedes in quoting their rallying cry, "a rich man's war and a poor man's fight" recalls the worst atrocities of the French Revolution (367). Though unsympathetic to their violence, Melville understood the basis of the rioters' complaint. But he couldn't help noting the terrible irony of its expression. Melville's opening image of "the roofy desert . . . Vacant as Libya" calls attention to the greatest casualties of the riots. Melville lights upon Libya—a preferred colonial site for the deportation of ex-slaves—to emphasize the group that bore the brunt of this working-class violence. During the rioting, Blacks were tortured and lynched, and a Black orphanage was burnt to the ground. "The House-Top" may be the angriest poem Melville ever wrote. The incident makes him see red: the "red Arson" that reminds his readers of the riots' most helpless victims, Black orphans.

"The House-Top" is invaluable for its layers of historical awareness: the French Revolution, the draft riots, the victimization of newly freed Blacks, the decline of religious belief, and the nostalgia for the former rule of fear (based in superstition and violence) all come into play here. It helps to reveal the kinds of connections that Melville was making in the era leading up to the writing of *Billy Budd*. Three years after writing the poem, Melville took a job as a custom house inspector at the Port of New York. From 1866 to 1885, he was able to observe his fellow humans from the more grounded perspective afforded by a firsthand experience of immigration. Melville's correspondence from this nineteen-year period yields few direct impressions of his daily activities as an inspector, and his biographers have generally regarded it as a degrading interruption of his literary vocation, an unfortunate excursion into the fallen world of political spoils and trade economy.[83] Apart from a record of impressions, what might Melville have witnessed as an inspector for the New York customhouse in this era? By 1884, the average number of steamer ships entering the port of New York was forty a week; the job of the customs inspector was to examine the baggage of passengers, native and immigrant, assess the validity of their customs declarations, and collect duties on imported goods. "Inspectors, through long practice, become involuntary disciples of Lavater, and such expert critics of human nature that they almost intuitively detect attempted fraud." Among the passengers inspected, the immigrants were invariably "a motley crowd . . . representatives of forty-four different nationalities." By "1883 the number of immigrants recorded was 405,352. . . . [but] immigrants being poorer now than formerly, only $9360 were collected in duties." The work of the customhouse inspector was an exercise in vigilance, demanding "watching, exposure, and fatigue." And the customhouse itself was "the most scientifically organized and economically administered of American national institutions."[84] It is essential to an understanding of *Billy Budd*, that for nineteen years prior to its writing, Melville worked in an institution that was based on a certain empirical and categorical expertise and was dedicated to the enrichment of the national government.[85]

In its themes, characterizations, and narrative structure, *Billy Budd* confronts the rationalization of social life that absorbed other intellectuals of the period. The novella's world, rigorously ordered yet menacingly heterogeneous, is full of the sorts of responses we have described: it pictures characters trying to locate the visual perimeters of a fogbound world and claiming the superiority of their own insights and classificatory schemes. *Billy Budd* addresses many of the issues that are raised by the theories and methods of sociologists like Albion Small and Herbert Spencer: the exploitation of innocence; professionalization and the social inequalities it underwrites; the controlling aims of social typologies and the forces that resist them. The story's society features a proliferation of types as well as characters who elude classification altogether. Characters continually name one another—even more than is usual in Melville's works. The fact that characters' names fluctuate and the accuracy of given labels is contemplated and questioned contributes to a prevailing sense of indeterminacy. By extension, to have authority is to establish control over the act of naming. Captain Vere assumes the power to name things, to label and to interpret, as crucial to his rule. But Vere's systematic typing efforts are quite distinct from the sailors' naming. When members of the crew name each other—"Board-Her-in-the-Smoke" for Dansker or "Jemmy Legs" for Claggart—they are recording an individual characteristic. The names do not enforce any particular form of behavior, though they can serve as a warning. When a character is typed, however, he is set on an expected and predictable course of behavior. Sailors' nicknames are insiders' jokes, familiar mainly to the seafaring commonalty. Types, by contrast, are immediately recognizable and universal; they serve to emblazon and predetermine character. And they are binding precisely because they are affixed by an authority.

Social types remind individuals of their sacrificial obligations to the collectivity. They are Captain Vere's means of establishing social regularity. Vere anticipates Edward Ross's admiration for a method that induces a citizen to "martyrize . . . himself for the ideal we have sedulously impressed upon him."[86] Types are also the aesthetic analog to the brutal underpinnings of his ship's regime. Thus it is appropriate that Vere's famous testimony to the power of social forms appears at the close of the execution chapter, in which he has realized the martyred destiny of his authorized type. "With mankind," he would say, "forms, measured forms, are everything; and that is the import couched in the story of Orpheus with his lyre spellbinding the wild denizens of the wood" (501). Vere's belief in social regularity is explicitly aestheticized. Both successful social orders and successful art are "spellbinding"; they function to absorb and contain the wild elements in human nature. Rulers and artists subdue through mystification, by imposing an authority so all-encompassing and mesmerizing that it can be wholly internalized. Vere's authority is osmotic: so subtle and surreptitious that it makes deliberate effects appear inevitable. On the other hand, Vere recognizes that a ship society craves pageantry and decorum. It is an ideal setting for the mingling of sacred and profane elements. Aboard the *Bellipotent*, ship decks speak. One's location at a given moment can express ambition or urgency (470, 475). Being out of place can have terrible consequences (451). Decisions on the setting of scenes can predetermine their outcome (481). A position in a room can compromise or reinforce authority (482).

Though the instinctive innocence of the common sailors is stressed, this innocence turns out to be a product of careful engineering, instated precisely because they are so savvy. Sailors, the narrator remarks at one point, are "like villagers, taking microscopic note of every outward movement or non-movement" (491). From the cautious removal of his interview with Claggart to closed quarters, to the "unostentatious vigilance" that circumscribes Claggart's burial (492), elaborate care must be taken to control their sight. Vere exaggerates the uncertainty of others while denying his own. This allows him to label freely, without competition. As the lone comprehending member of the ship's company, Vere can make his own forms look disinterested. This is reinforced by his demeanor. "Any landsman, observing this gentleman not conspicuous by his stature and wearing no pronounced insignia . . . noting the silent deference of the officers retiring to leeward, might have taken him for the King's guest, a civilian aboard the King's ship" (445). Yet the hidden brutality of Vere's "policy" is hinted at with its comparison to that of "Peter the Barbarian" (480).

There is something "alien" in Vere, to those unfamiliar with ancient wisdom. Melville takes these implications even further. Vere's nostalgia is likened curiously, even contradictorily, to a "migratory fowl" with no sense of place. Melville's apparent aim is to distinguish an alienation that is intellectual and domestic (a "queer" bird at home), from a bona fide difference (a truly strange bird). Vere may have odd ideas, but he is no foreign national (Claggart). Vere's ideal, "forms, measured forms," expresses his allegiance to an older era of class stability and resistance to new ideas, especially those from "across the Channel." Yet the same ideal also signifies another intellectual plane for his sympathies: the philosophy of an empirical social science and the cataloging language of social-functional types that accompanies it. Vere's anxieties and methods are akin to those of a new social scientific generation for whom irrational terror of a world seeming to elude traditional forms of belief combined with a commitment to empirical detail. Vere's transitions from a state of uncontrollable anxiety about social chaos to a method of rational and systematic typecasting are evident in the collection of scenes that follow Claggart's accusation against Billy. Claggart's testimony throws Vere into a state of "perplexity," which "proceeded less from aught touching the man informed against . . . than from considerations how best to act in regard to the informer" (474). Vere may be seen at this point as the aristocrat, threatened by the unreadable aspect of Claggart.

Claggart is a man on the move, the quintessential outsider, compared to "the uncataloged creatures of the deep." All details of character confirm this alien status. His complexion is "*singularly* contrasting with the red or deeply bronzed visages of the sailors" (my emphasis). Some "sea gossips" speculate that he is a "*chevalier.*" We are told that "nothing was known of his former life," but despite this attempt at self-erasure, "there lurked a bit of accent in his speech suggesting that possibly he was not [English] by birth, but through naturalization in early childhood." Claggart is the immigrant on his way up: "upon his entrance into the navy . . . assigned to the least honorable section of a man-of-war's crew, embracing the drudgery, he did not long remain there"; his "superior capacity . . . ingratiating deference to superiors . . . [and] austere patriotism" combine to ensure his rise (448–50). Yet it is precisely the intensity of his commitment to assimilate that marks his difference. Every note of his demeanor conveys exaggeration and struggle; every gesture is *acquired* rather than *native* . Not surprisingly, it is the "naturalness" of Billy's virtue that most arouses Claggart's envy and antipathy.

Billy, in contrast to Claggart, conveys spontaneity and ease, and among all the characters, he is the most readily typed. The ideal "primitive man," he is Rousseau's savage, Caspar Hauser, and Adam all in one. And more still. Billy Budd may be the most overdetermined character in American fiction. He is the sculptured Bull, the nautical Murat, Aldebaran, Bucephalus (430–31); a Catholic priest (433); Apollo (434); Hercules (436); David (459); Joseph (474); and Isaac (490). And these are only the direct allusions. Billy's ties to Christ, subtle and ongoing, are complicated by the fact that Billy's nemesis, John Claggart, actually bears the Saviour's initials. The ease of typing Billy is not lost on Vere who casts Billy as martyr—"fated boy"—following his blow to Claggart. Billy is pastoral: at one with nature, his characterization implies an eternal order of upper and lower classes. Claggart is history: his characterization implies indeterminate, uncontrollable forces, among these the threat of ambitious immigrants moving into the mercurial middle classes. Claggart disrupts Vere's "settled convictions," described as a "dike against those invading waters of novel opinion social, political, and otherwise" (446).

Despite their differences, however, there are significant affinities between Billy and Claggart. Billy is an immigrant too (though, as a victim of impressment, an unwilling one, closer to a slave than to the aggressively mobile Claggart), and he is at times also alien and mystifying to authorities. The first lieutenant, for example, misconceives Billy's farewell salute to the *Rights-of-Man* as a "sly slur at impressment" (435). Likewise, where Claggart's speech is accented, Billy suffers at times from a common immigrant handicap, the inability to speak at all, which parallels his illiteracy, his inability to read the signs of his experience. Billy and Claggart suggest a distinction between internal and external immigrants; where Billy has wholly internalized the requirements of the social order, Claggart maintains a distance from those requirements, which he exploits for his own ends. Where Billy is acquiescent and easily typed, Claggart is threatening and foils it. This brings us to the gravest danger posed by Claggart's character, that far from being uniquely alien, he pinpoints the condition of alienation that is endemic to the rational world of the *Bellipotent*. Only Claggart and Vere are apprised of the radical separation between being and understanding: "One person excepted [i.e., Vere], the master-at-arms was perhaps the only man in the ship intellectually capable of adequately appreciating the moral phenomenon presented in Billy Budd" (459). Vere cannot fully exploit the tools of alienation until their human emblem, who also recognizes their uses, is dead.

With Claggart out of the way, Vere is free to implement his rational-functionalist methods. First, Vere types Billy's blow, "the Divine judgment on Ananias," thus setting the event within a providential order of retribution: "an eye for an eye, a tooth for a tooth" (478). Then he moves to the objective language of martial law and classifies Billy's deed as a "capital crime," to be dealt with categorically by the legal sanctions designed for such offenses at sea. Vere's unstable blend of fatalism and empiricism reveals the inseparability of objectifying language and the chaotic social world it seeks to regulate. Vere not only uses types, but in classic social scientific form, he collapses claims about intention into the necessities of the system. At Billy's trial, he stresses the jurors' functional obligations, rejecting any agency that is not predetermined by them. As social functionaries, the jurors are mere witnesses to the system: "however pitilessly that law may operate in any instance, we nevertheless adhere to it and administer it" (486–87).

Vere emphasizes social interdependence, uniformity of consciousness, and typicality, all rhetorical forms of containment that point toward an inevitable outcome: Billy's hanging. This is not to deny Vere's own tortured sense of indeterminacy but to suggest that in addition to the fog that blinds all of society's members, there are mysteries strategically implemented by social authorities. Vere's uses of indeterminacy are most pronounced at the trial scene, where he coerces defendant and jurors into his own viewpoint by magnifying their uncertainties. At one point, for example, Vere interrupts the court's deliberations to note their "troubled hesitancy" (485), prescribing the court's irresolution in order to impose his own judgment. The court is not so much without its own opinions as incapable of voicing a view contrary to the captain's (488). The marine soldier's request to hear witnesses "who might shed lateral light" on the proceedings suggests the court's allowance of only a single authoritative point of view (484). I think Melville means to emphasize the overwhelming complexity of Vere's position, a complexity that can be taken as an ironic commentary on the polarized state of *Billy Budd* criticism.[87]

Melville goes out of his way to make the issue of motivation increasingly ambiguous. Vere is in a tough place in a world he can't control, for all he tries. The question is, why act so forcibly and unequivocally, given those limits? Benthamite logic, with which Melville was familiar, argues against capital punishment on the grounds of its irreversibility. "The punishment of death is not remissible," Bentham writes in *The Rationale of Punishment* (1830). E. A. Westermarck completes his point: "In every other case of judicial error compensation can be made, death alone admits of no compensation."[88] The execution of Billy Budd is not only at odds with liberal social theory; it violates the principles of traditional moral philosophy. Such perspectives provide an opening for a political reading of Vere's actions. For Vere is not simply denying obscurity; he is actively fomenting it. His own authority rests on the perceived chasm between his own expertise, the uncertainty of his officers, and the ignorance of the ordinary sailors. Through both gestures and argument at the trial, in his "closeted interview" with Billy, in his manipulations of the crew before, during, and after the climactic cabin scene, Vere struggles to impose a uniform vision upon the ship's company. Each member of the ship inhabits a particular level of sight within the ship's social structure, which also exists within a dominant network of sight. Vere's role is to manage that network in the manner of the professional sociologist, to coordinate the various parts of a vast, specialized society into a limited unity of consciousness. This brings us to the character who is most resistant to Vere's typologies: Claggart.

UNCATALOGUED CREATURES OF THE DEEP

At the moment of his direct accusation of Billy, all are transfixed by Claggart's eyes. Claggart's centrality here evokes the scene of his private testimony to Vere, which leaves Vere more anxious about the informer than the potential mutineer. In both instances, Claggart is the repressed catalyst. Even the story's title seems a displacement of its own action: it foregrounds the still point of its character triangle and suppresses its real agent. The same is true of the story's double deaths. While Claggart's murder and corpse are concealed, Billy is formally executed, his hanging body the sign of Vere's power. The extent of that power is mental as well as physical, and it may be even richer than we have suggested. Vere's staging of a confrontation between Claggart and Billy in his cabin reads like a page out of Lavater's *Essays on Physiognomy*: "Bring guilt and innocence face to face, and examine them; in your presence," Lavater writes. "Remark their walk when they enter, and when they leave the judgment-hall. Let the light fall upon their countenances; be yourself in the shade. Physiognomy will render the torture unnecessary, will deliver innocence, will make the most obdurate vice turn pale, will teach us how we may act upon the most hardened." Now consider these scenes from *Billy Budd*: "Something exceptional in the moral quality of Captain Vere made him, in earnest encounter with a fellow man, a veritable touchstone of that man's essential nature. . . . 'Now, Master-at-arms, tell this man to his face what you told of him to me,' and [Vere] stood prepared to scrutinize the mutually confronting visages" (474–76). The alterations from Lavater to Melville are telling. The supposed innocent, Billy, is the one who turns pale, and Vere learns little about respective states of guilt and innocence from looks alone. More significantly, Vere's expectations in bringing accused and accuser together are catastrophically foiled. He loses control of his experiment, as the two objects of scrutiny become dangerously animated. If Lavater is behind this, then Melville is exposing, above all, the gulf between theory and practice.[89]

What makes Claggart unpresentable is the fact that he is unrepresentable. As he approaches Billy in the cabin, the description moves into past progressive tense: Claggart's eyes, "those lights of human intelligence, losing human expression were gelidly protruding like the alien eyes of certain uncatalogued creatures of the deep. The first mesmeristic glance was one of serpent fascination; the last was as the paralyzing lurch of the torpedo fish" (476). Heaping simile upon metaphor upon simile, the sentences struggle to type a figure who seems fundamentally immune to typing. The crucial phrase, "uncatalogued creatures of the deep," stamps Claggart as the unknowable outsider. When authorized as an epistemological truth, indeterminacy facilitates strategy making; it underwrites linguistic and political "play" or manipulation. When it appears in a person or in a collection of persons, it thwarts artful or dictatorial control. Moreover, the phrase establishes an opposition between "creatures" who are not cataloged and human beings who presumably are. The image of creature populations beneath the sea who resist cataloging is meaningful by analogy, that is, in contrast to human populations on land, who can be statistically known. To be known, as this passage defines it, is to be cataloged, perhaps even according to the latest demographic techniques. Interest in the assessment and control of population can be traced back at least as far as the first American census in 1790.[90] But it was not until the Civil War that such categorical thinking became codified and institutionalized.[91] The task of tracking and counting human beings acquired a particular urgency during this traumatic national encounter with mass death. Population analysis developed further in response to the pressures of mass immigration. The threat of mercurial hordes of creatures beneath the sea in *Billy Budd* figures the threat of mercurial hordes of immigrants riding the seas en route to Melville's America.

Claggart's story resembles a type of fantasy about immigration that captivated Americans in the 1880s, especially those of Vere's class: on their own, aristocrat and commonalty (represented by Vere and Billy) exist in Edenic harmony; the arrival of the alien serpent portends disruption and possibly chaos. As John Higham observes, following the Haymarket bombing of 1886 (after which six immigrants were executed as supposed provocateurs), "the dread of imported anarchy haunted the American consciousness. No nativist image prevailed more widely than that of the immigrant as a lawless creature, given over to violence and disorder."[92] The critical word here is "creature," which echoes the description of Claggart, as well as much of the newspaper rhetoric of the time, rhetoric that cast immigrants as "venomous reptiles," "the very scum and offal of Europe," "snakes," and "inhuman rubbish."[93] As "creatures," they are faceless and swarming; they may be seen but not discerned. And this is precisely the effect of Claggart: in a society where indeterminacy is a key to dominance, spontaneous obscurity threatens authority.

The most elaborate speculations on the powers of indeterminacy in *Billy Budd* center on a description of Claggart's "nature":

"Natural Depravity: a depravity according to nature," a definition which, though savoring of Calvinism, by no means involves Calvin's dogma as to total mankind. Evidently, its intent makes it applicable but to individuals. Not many are the examples of this depravity which the gallows and jail supply. . . . It folds itself in the mantle of respectability. It has its certain negative virtues serving as silent auxiliaries. It never allows wine to get within its guard. It is not going too far to say that it is without vices or small sins. There is a phenomenal pride in it that excludes them. It is never mercenary or avaricious. In short, the depravity here meant partakes nothing of the sordid or sensual. (457)

This passage describes a type that is immune to social description. Characterized by invisible nouns and adjectives—"negative virtues," "silent auxiliaries," "without vices," "nothing . . . sordid or sensual"—depravity is faceless and unchallengeable. While it is exceptional (an attribute of rare individuals not of "total mankind"), it is imperceptible. Indeed, it seems incompatible with the human condition itself. Natural depravity is an escape from classification, an evasion of social controls ("the gallows and jail"). Like insanity, it seems fundamentally resistant to interpretation. The surgeon ponders, "To draw the exact line of demarcation [between sanity and insanity] few will undertake, though for a fee becoming considerate some professional experts will" (479). Here, as in so many instances, indeterminacy is susceptible to exploitation by "experts." Through such speculations, the story moves beyond anxieties about social indeterminacy to consider these assumptions within a political dynamic, as strategies of identifiable agents.

Ostensibly the most self-sacrificing character in the ship's society, Claggart applies the ideal of sacrifice to his own mutable ends. He neither opposes nor criticizes Vere's rule; he bleeds it. Inevitably rather than consciously antagonistic, Claggart threatens Vere's order precisely because he is so identified with it. The alien outsider and lowest ranking officer, he is the brute force behind Vere's authority. And, paradoxically, as the brutal fact of Vere's power, the invisible Claggart renders visible what Vere would prefer to conceal. He reminds Vere that his power rests upon an external force that he can neither identify nor control. But Claggart's role as the ship's "chief of police" also suggests the self-scrutinizing propensities of the immigrant, who internalizes social anxiety toward his threatening difference. Claggart's character points to the double function of the immigrant in American society as an unpredictable catalyst between capital and labor: on the one hand, reinforcing the status quo as a cheap workforce in pursuit of assimilation; on the other hand, representing all the qualities of the alien that threaten social stability. In a single encounter, Vere's perceptions of Claggart can range from a sense of his "tact in his function" to a sense of his "patriotic zeal . . . supersensible and strained" (472). Among the implications of this passage is the idea of an absolute separation between sacred and secular understanding. Claggart's depravity presents a quagmire that is amenable to spiritual diagnosis alone. Scientific methods of detection must bow before "Holy Writ." They recall similar sentiments from *Clarel*: "Nearer the core than man can go / or Science get."[94]

As the "scorpion" for whom "the Creator alone is responsible" (459–60), Claggart's character raises a subject that has long absorbed critics of *Billy Budd*, its retelling of the Edenic myth. In the words of Milton Stern, the novella is "a reworking of the Adam-Christ story, placing prelapsarian Adam and the Christ on a man-of-war, and demonstrating the inevitability of the Fall and the necessity of the Crucifixion."[95] It is appropriate that Stern finds not one but two general typologies—a sign, as I have suggested, that the narrative destabilizes type categories, and also that it teaches as well as represents the activity of typing. The Edenic myth held a particular fascination for Americans in the late nineteenth century; the tale of the "fall" into technology, and modernism generally, was told and retold by classic and popular writers, social scientists, and even scientists. When Henry James, for example, writing of Hawthorne, proclaimed the succession of America's great provincial romancer by America's great cosmopolitan novelist, it was precisely in terms of a new national consciousness that had "eaten of the tree of knowledge."[96]

My reading of *Billy Budd* in the context of contemporaneous developments in social science complements and extends traditional emphases on its biblical dimensions. Both the biblical analogy, which casts Billy as a prelapsarian Adam, and the sociological analogy, which casts him as the man of nature in the hands of a professional elite, view innocence as a deadly liability. By fastening on the experiences of innocence in modern society, the novella reveals the ideological continuities between certain views of providence and certain views of technology. Descriptions of late-nineteenth-century industrialization tend to inspire nostalgia for a more integrated social Eden.[97] Any narrative of the Fall is a narrative of loss: to represent the end of innocence is to be barred from its timeless space as an inhabitant of history. All of these fatalistic schemes suppress a critical historical dimension of the opposition between innocence and knowledge as dramatized in *Billy Budd*: that the plot has very specific political and class contours. Billy's deathblow to Claggart is as self-regulatory as his blessing of Captain Vere just prior to his execution; for Claggart alone can activate Billy's potentially subversive energies. As a satanic force, Claggart can effect the fall into knowledge that would destabilize Vere's providential/paternal power over Billy. Claggart does only half the job: Billy's murder of Claggart kills the potential for opposition in himself and ensures his own containment by Vere's Edenic order.

Melville thus complicates the Edenic myth, casting Adam as the agent of his own containment, an Adam who *resists* Satan and history. Since the classic Fall is also a fall into language or plotting, we might say that Billy, in striking Claggart dead, disables the story.[98] Vere's strategies leading up to Billy's death effect a draining of the very possibility for story. From the cabin scene on, details are left increasingly to the reader's imagination: from Vere's solitary ruminations, which "everyone must determine for himself by such light as this narrative may afford" (480), to Billy as Moses in "closeted" interview with God (489). At the same time, however, the narrative continues to oppose the rapidity of Vere's plot: "Of a series of incidents within a brief term rapidly following each other, the adequate narration may take up a term less brief, especially if explanation and comment here and there seem requisite to the better understanding of such incidents" (490). The opposition between Vere and Claggart is transferred to Vere and the narrator, who finally kills him off with a cannon blow from the Athée, a profane vessel designed, it seems, to deny Vere's neat biblical categories.

The narrator is the observer apprised of the limits of observation, who watches the clash of submissive force (Billy) and unconscious agency (Claggart) through the spectacle of Vere's power. In contrast to Vere, who merely uses history to his own ends, and Billy and Claggart, who represent, respectively, a mythical exemption from history and an untheoretical absorption in it, the narrator is a careful historian. While defiant of generic constraints, he nevertheless sanctions the search for social clarity. To avoid types in a world where eluding definition is a source of power—herein lies the tie that binds the characters and narrative consciousness. In a description of "the Great Mutiny," which "national pride along with views of policy would fain shade . . . off into the historical background" (440), the narrator calls attention to the political agency of narration. "Such events cannot be ignored," he continues, "but there is a considerate way of historically treating them. If a well-constituted individual refrains from blazoning aught amiss or calamitous in his family, a nation in the like circumstance may without reproach be equally discreet" (440). As a member of the family, the historian's subversive potential is defused. This places the "historian" of *Billy Budd* in a trap of definitions: to write critical history is to risk being typed as either alien or insane. Yet he has "inside" knowledge that contradicts the naval-chronicle version of events. The narrator must tell a critical tale without being stamped by the telling. He aims at a *conscious* exploitation of invisibility, which is best pursued, he says, "by indirection." This has little to do with the classic neutrality of omniscient narration. By conceding his own vulnerability to labels, which he struggles to avoid, the narrator opposes the conventions of realist fiction. The narrative can be seen as a critique of realism that incorporates its methods and undoes them. Reflecting upon the political motivations and ramifications of character typing, the narrative *studies* rather than *exemplifies* it. Thus, the narrator observes at one point that Billy is somewhat reminiscent of Hercules, but adds that this "was subtly modified by another and pervasive quality" (436). Or he compares Billy to Adam, but so equivocally as to undo the comparison: "Billy *in many respects* was little more than *a sort of* upright barbarian, *much such perhaps* as Adam *presumably might have been* " (438, my emphasis).[99]

Marked by qualification, evasion, inversion, and digression, the narrative method is itself a challenge to the politics of indeterminacy and the stringent controls that are its issue. In answer to Captain Vere's crisp functionalist categories, the narrator highlights the plot's ragged edges. Where Vere wages war on his uncertainties, the narrator makes uncertainty the basis of his aesthetic method. His narrative is a monument to indecision; he accepts and builds upon what Vere flees. The narrator dismisses military and generic rules at the same time that his digressive and fragmentary narrative formally counters them. "In this matter of writing," he observes, "resolve as one may to keep to the main road, some bypaths have an enticement not readily to be withstood. I am going to err into such a bypath. . . . At the least, we can promise ourselves that pleasure which is wickedly said to be in sinning, for a literary sin the divergence will be" (441). A disingenuous apology for literary extravagance becomes a claim for the critical potential of literary form. The narrator has eluded the limits of history writing by labeling his own enterprise fiction. Because of the respect accorded his work, the historian must omit and suppress. The comparative indifference to fiction makes it a richer historical source. Where history breeds a discretion bordering on censorship, the presumed innocuousness of fiction liberates its access to impulsive truths.

The designation of the narrative as "inside" sets it in opposition to the objective forms of social (and aesthetic) theory that it also represents. The narrator mediates among different systems of knowledge, all represented as impartial approaches to social facts. Consider the elegy at the close of the execution chapter. "And now it was full day. The fleece of low-hanging vapor had vanished, licked up by the sun that late had so glorified it. And the circumambient air in the clearness of its serenity was like smooth white marble in the polished block not yet removed from the marble-dealer's yard" (501). With the sun reduced from its former glory to the figure of a greedy pet and the air contained in an image of blank marble, the passage defuses the horror of Billy's execution. Glory is shrunken to greed, and air commodified to marble—marketplace metaphors that foreshadow Billy's final self-image as a "pendant pearl" dangling "from the yardarm-end" (504).

All of these boundary makers—executioner, marble dealer, writer—are equivalent (whether disciplinary, capitalist, or literary). Most resonant here, however, is the narrator's frank admission of the writer's complicity with these other agents of civilization. Billy's execution is normalized by a series of aesthetic figures. The passage affirms the connections between lyricism and barbarism, between civilization and the savage impulses it denies but underwrites. In the act of criticizing the brutalities of social forms, the narrator locates the sources of his own narration. Fiction reveals the inseparability of social and literary effect. What the social disciplinarian sacrifices to confirm his power, the writer sacrifices for coherent aesthetic form. Sacrifice, *Billy Budd* reveals, is the common thread uniting late-nineteenth century narratives of literature, theology, and sociology.

SOCIOLOGICAL AND THEOLOGICAL RETURNS

In *Adam Smith and Modern Sociology* (1907), Albion Small displays his usual sensitivity to the pulse of his field. What is noteworthy in Smith, according to Small, is his subtle recognition of what might be called the sacrificial side of economics. Smith's original formulation of laissez-faire was far different from the ethic eventually codified by his disciples. As summarized by Smith's first biographer, Dugald Stewart, this ethic holds that "the growth of national wealth implies a sacrifice of the character of the people." Small's Smith (like Stewart's) never abandons an ideal of genuine social equity—"the natural equilibration of the claims of all the members of society" (125). Still, Smith's persistent emphasis on the moral over the material dimensions of his theory does not mitigate the fact that "his analysis of moral phenomena would not now satisfy anyone." Small concludes, "The humor of the situation was in the fact that the very people who most zealously fed the altar-fires of this superstition [laissez-faire] had first taken elaborate precautions to build up around their own interests the most rigid system of legal safeguards that had ever surrounded vested right."[100] Small's terms recall the sacrificial thinking that informs his own "Scope of Sociology" series, where Defoe's Crusoe and Friday ("Each not only needs the other, but each may so act as to sacrifice the other's welfare entirely") provide the paradigm for human association.[101] Sacrifice may be banished from the realm of rational possibility, but it remains a critical category of social thought. A central tradition of sociology, stretching from Spencer through Ward, Ross, and Giddings, confirms this.

In his *Study of Sociology*, Spencer observes that sacrifice "continues as an ecclesiastical usage long after having died out in the ordinary life of a society" (106–7). He then goes on to document the extent of its persistence, both as a model for social action and as an intellectual construct. The book abounds in references to the rite: from vivid historical images (the sacrificial excesses of the French Revolution, the "enormous armies . . . sacrificed in inexcusable wars") to symbolic allusions (the Crucifixion is omnipresent) (136–37, 155). Spencer's idea here is the incitement of working-class appetites for compensatory blood exchanges. The Napoleonic era is marked by sacrifice. One notorious example features Napoleon's "cold-blooded sacrifice of his own soldiers . . . merely that his mistress might witness an engagement" (157). Spencer compares this to the wanton British naval expenditure of sailor lives. Is there any wonder about the mutiny at Spithead? (162–63). Spencer seems to favor a single explanation for sacrifice's persistence: the transitional state of his society makes it uniquely susceptible to this ancient form. "We who live midway in the course of civilization," he writes, "have two religions." One is the religion of "self-sacrifice"—the ideal message of Scripture. The other is the practical religion of "blood revenge." "He notes that the same men are priests of both religions" (178–79). He goes on to identify self-sacrifice as a futile creed, for victims and beneficiaries alike. Though this altruism remains a social ideal, it is a religion of enmity or blood revenge that serves a more valuable social function, according to Spencer. It is at once more successful and more economic in the "killing-off of inferior races and inferior individuals" (199). Spencer's complaint is the hypocrisy of a people that preaches unqualified altruism—"makes self-sacrifice a cardinal principle"—while urging "the sacrifice of others . . . when they trespass against us" (201). Significantly, however, Spencer never questions the inevitability nor the mutual reciprocity of these two codes. Indeed, he seems to accept that the powerful interdependence of these religions ensures their eternal equilibrium.

In his *Principles Of Sociology* (1876–96), a standard work that served as a model for other sociologists, Spencer devotes a whole section to sacrifice. Like other analysts we have discussed, Spencer associates sacrifice with a certain level of cultural development. Sacrifice has little conceptual power, he notes, without an accompanying theory of the afterlife. The rite originates in practices of ancestor worship. God's image was vested in the dead; hence the setting of sacrificial ceremonies at grave sites. Spencer traces sacrifice from Palestine, Greece, and Africa to New Zealand, China, and Wales. No culture, according to his appendix, is exempt from it (1: 186–89, 191–94, 782–811). Sacrifice, he points out, in an argument that would echo throughout a subsequent sociological literature, has always been a principal means of affirming social bonds. Sacrifice was a celebration of community, and groups would come to "offer sacrifices at each other's festivals." And Spencer recognizes the tie between sacrifice and nurture. He quotes a Chinese saying to this effect: "Whatever is good for food is good for sacrifice" (2:213). The prospect of nourishment has its own familiar Darwinian twist: some die, so others can eat.

What remains implicit in Spencer's argument is the idea that sacrifice as a collective, even "festive," act, is inseparable from the idea of sacrifice as a loss that either compensates or anticipates some equivalent gain. Sacrifice is built into the hierarchical structure of society (3: 95–106). It is the means by which authorities display power and exact payment from their subjects. In outlining the genesis of ecclesiastical institutions, Spencer points out that the priest who officiated at sacrifices was always the highest political authority. He argues that many of the most notorious wars in history were motivated by priests seeking offerings for their gods: "Did not men's pre-possessions render them impervious to evidence, even their Bible readings might raise doubts; and wider readings would prove that among mankind at large, priests have displayed and cultivated not the higher but rather the lower passions of humanity" (3:107). In ancient Rome, "the priestly func-tion of the Roman commander was such that in some cases he paid more attention to sacrificing than to fighting" (3:111). And among the primitive Germans, priests actually engaged in battle (3: 112–13). Spencer's conclu-sion seems only partly ironic: "Now-a-days people have become unaccus-tomed to these connexions, and forget that they ever existed. The military duties of priests among ourselves have dwindled down to the consecration of flags, the utterances by army-chaplains . . . to the God of love to bless aggressions, provoked or unprovoked" (3:115). If Spencer's irony is unde-veloped, Melville taps more readily into his for the portrait of *Billy Budd*'s army chaplain, which recalls the image of Billy as a "priest" or "fighting peacemaker." Melville seems ever aware that "the God of love" and those who serve him are suspiciously amenable to war. Spencer's history of the ecclesiastical professions allows us to read the martial affinities of priests as an outgrowth of God's own intimate ties to death.

As a whole, Spencer's remarkably varied account of sacrifice illuminates the question of its interest for contemporary intellectuals. His surprising receptivity to spiritual problems, together with a frank evolutionism, made his work an ideal source for a new synthesis of religion and science. Sacri-fice provided one critical bridge between religious faith and scientific posi-tivism. The rite was not only central to all religions but integral to Darwin-ian theory—at least as understood by social Darwinists like Spencer.[102] What was the doctrine of the survival of the fittest, if not sacrificial: the expulsion of the weak so that society as a whole could progress? Asa Gray, amateur theologian and botanist, found the different creeds compatible for precisely these reasons. The Creation could be viewed as the initial stage of an evolutionary process, whose mechanism was sacrifice. This was cor-roborated by theologians such as John Fiske and Lymon Abbot (*The Des-tiny of Man* [1872] and *The Evolution of Christianity* [1892]), who advanced a new brand of scientific theology.[103] Such reconciliations were the rule rather than the exception. Historians have long recognized the attempt to harmonize Darwinian and theological principles as a critical task for Anglo-American social science. This is one of the main points of Richard Hofstader's *Social Darwinism in American Thought*.[104]

Spencer's sociology, like others of the time, brings the rite of sacrifice to the center of this familiar story. Social Darwinism caught on among theologians in part because it accorded with this major religious practice and philosophy. Sacrifice revealed a key continuity between standard theological and scientific ideas. And this reciprocity also proved the durability of Hebraic and Christian doctrine. Evidence of these assumptions in other major sociological works confirms their currency. In *Social Control* (1901), Edward Ross, like Spencer, seems at first doubtful about the efficacy of ritual in the modern age. Sacrifice is a remnant. We no longer attach any gravity, he observes, to "eating an impure animal," "letting die the sacred fire," or "failing to offer the proper sacrifice." Yet we soon learn that these sentiments and practices have not disappeared; they are simply transferred to the social order. Ross uses the theories of Robertson Smith to make his case (65–66). Religion's universal purpose, Ross notes, was to express fears and beliefs about the "Unseen," through acts of prayer and sacrifice. In a modern *"social religion"* we find similar means and ends (197). But here the aim is "to generate beliefs as to invisible bonds between self and others" (207). The object of traditional religion is God; the object of social religion is community. In both cases, sacrificial rites are prominent. The "readiness to self-sacrifice," Ross proclaims, "has been of vast ethical benefit to European civilization." It is *"natural* to us" (314, 316). For Ross, just as for Winwood Reade, martyrdom is the ideal social condition. Yet Ross's theory has none of Reade's crushing ambivalence. In a characteristic display of conspiratorial optimism, Ross celebrates the benefits of martyrdom, a form of "bind[ing] from within." There must be "the illusion of self-direction even at the very moment he martyrizes himself." Ross concludes, "The secret of order is not to be bawled from every housetop," nor is control a "gospel to be preached abroad" (244, 441). Given the dominant categories of Ross's sociology—force, social control, sin, mystery, and secrecy—his own attraction to sacrifice seems inevitable. Lester Ward's sociology is another matter altogether, which makes its hospitality to the rite that much more compelling.

Ward's account of sacrifice in *Dynamic Sociology* (1883) is especially dramatic because it is based on an actual historical event, which he reproduces (along with reactions to it) in his own narrative. The event is "the Great Burmah Massacre," and Ward's source is the *New York Tribune* for April 13, 1880: "The seven hundred men, boys, girls, priests, and foreigners sacrificed at Mandalay for the restoration of the king's health, were buried alive—not 'burned,' as previously stated—under the towers of the city walls. The deed was done to appease the evil spirits." This is followed by an editorial from the *United States Economist* declaring the incident "a blot on the civilization of the nineteenth century," adding "Had such a wholesale massacre occurred in the most remote and inaccessible regions of Africa, there might be an excuse alleged for non-interference on the part of civilized governments, but no such reason can be given in this instance. Burmah is one of the important kingdoms of the far East."[105] This is an odd (though increasingly common) instance of a sociological bias reflected back upon itself by journalism: (we might have thought sacrifice a distant enterprise, but it is closer to home than we think. As if to prepare for the extremity of his ultimate example, Ward first treats sacrifice (and companion superstitions) with surprising respect. He cites firsthand accounts of the rite drawn from Darwin, Tylor, and Spencer (among others) and joins the chorus confirming its extension to "considerably high grades of social and political life." He looks at asceticism and self-torture as parts of the same ritual whole. Ward concludes that sacrifice is a "code" of modern social life. "Not alone by the national code, but also by the moral and conventional codes, we are all *required* to make constant sacrifices and sustain many important losses." Sacrifice is fundamental to citizenship ("national"), ethics ("moral"), and even common sense ("conventional") (608).

Ward's interest in the Burma case may betray anxiety about the place of sacrifice in his own society. Given its infiltration of our own civilization, he implies, it's helpful to see it staged upon occasion, in extremis. This is supported by his introduction of the massacre. "Lest it should be supposed that the era of sacrifices is over, and all concern about them uncalled for, I append the following telegram from the *New York Tribune*." And Ward seems especially drawn to the question of victim identities. His chapter includes other itemized lists comparable to the catalog of those "offered up" in Burma: "men, boys, girls, priests, and foreigners." What's striking about these inventories is the transition they betray, from rather obvious (i.e., traditional) assortments of victims (slaves and wives) to assortments admitting no selectivity whatsoever (289, 290, 291). The horror of the horror at Burma is that sacrifice appears to have lost its exclusion clause: no one is safe. Sacrifice is neither a priestly ritual nor a predictable fate. It is simply an arbitrary way of expressing power, available to any "monster-king" with enough arrogance to use it. Sacrifice has become a whim of distant monarchs eager to make an impact on an international stage.

Hence the moral of Ward's Burma: it's open season on sacrifice. Late-nineteenth-century theologians were coming to similar realizations. This may be why their works display such detailed attention to ancient, and sometimes contemporary, sacrificial procedure. No nineteenth-century analyst described the ritual with more drama and insight than Arthur Stanley in his *History of the Jewish Church* (1862). Written over a decade before the major sociological works of Spencer and Ward and the theology of Robertson Smith and Clay Trumbull, Stanley's study can be seen as a critical precursor to these later accounts. Stanley begins with the obvious: sacrifice is a basic spiritual impulse, common to all known religions. One of the "purest feelings . . . is the craving to please, or to propitiate, or to communicate with the Powers above us by surrendering some object near and dear to ourselves. This is the source of all Sacrifice." This is qualified by another distinctly "moral instinct" that "the Creator of the world" is only moved by "a pure life and good deeds." The implication is that sacrifice appeals to a sensual deity, as greedy as the humans who worship him. Stanley distinguishes Hebrew from Christian sacrifice. Abraham's offering of Isaac represents an acceptance of God's will, but a rejection of sacrifice. The Old Testament record reveals a decline in the practice over time (1: 51–52). This is why the sacrifice of Jephthah's Daughter is such an anomaly; Stanley sees Jephthah as one who "sank below his age" (1:394). The biblical narrative, he notes, "trembles with the mixed feeling of the action" (1:395). Stanley chides other interpreters for trying to sanction the event. The text's "original sense," which "more careful study of the Bible" has helped restore, reveals "deep pathos": a father and daughter gripped by one of the most "fierce superstitions" in human history.

Yet Stanley sees a difference between the sacrifice of Jephthah's daughter and the more conventional slaughter of unwilling victims—the Greeks or Gauls buried alive in the Roman forum. Jephthah's daughter is "the willing offering of a devoted heart, to free, as she supposed, her father and her country from a terrible obligation." Her act expresses the "pure obedience and love, which is the distinguishing mark of all true Sacrifice" (1:397–98). Notice what has changed. Sacrifice is no longer degrading but ennobling. Hebrew and Christian sacrifice become complementary. Sacrifice assumes the mingled sense of gift and wedding, with God the designated beneficiary of both. This Christian sense explains why Stanley is so impatient with interpretations that insist that Jephthah's daughter was devoted as a nun, rather than sacrificed. What higher end than an immediate ecstatic union with her Maker? It took until the nineteenth century for Jephthah's daughter to receive her due, in the poetic treatments of Byron and Tennyson. The moral of "Jephthah's daughter," as Stanley reads it, is the purification of sacrifice: from a bloody remnant, embarrassing to civilization, it is transformed into an ideal of high culture. Blood gushes in Byron's poem, but the more memorable image is the fount of sentiment— love of family and nation. What sort of love makes someone "smile" at death? A love of the highest sacrificial type. Under advanced systems, according to authoritative sources, the victim goes willingly.

Modern sacrifice, in other words, is an expression of national loyalty. Rather than a ritual necessity performed at the expense of subordinates or aliens, sacrifice is redefined as a model dedication to norms. Sacrifice has become internalized as social conduct. This sounds very close to Edward

Ross, and Stanley's anticipation of an emergent social scientific literature is evident in his own terminology: his reference, for instance, to "a sacrificial system" (2: 248). Stanley applies this term, I want to emphasize, to the earliest heathen practices. Even the hypothetical victims dragged screaming to the altars in Canaan were falling short of an exalted potential. This is consistent with the rite's near magical investment in transformation, where the most violated enemy becomes a divine medium. Sacrifice is about compliance. An ideal victim understands the necessary equivalence between collective and individual propitiation. It is in the nature of sacrificial decorum to believe in a union of personal and communal need. Recognizing the smiles of a sacrificial victim as the fulfillment of ritual convention provides another context for the execution scene of *Billy Budd*. From this perspective, Billy Budd's blessing, on the point of death, of the sacrificial beneficiary, Captain Vere, expresses neither acceptance nor irony. It merely confirms sacrificial procedure.

Stanley's emphasis on internalization in high sacrifice, his attention to the evolution of sacrificial morality, appears to qualify his original sense of the rite. We have to take him at his word when he asserts, following a description of the Sermon on the Mount, that sacrifice was never again about "the blood of bulls and goats," but about "the perfect surrender of a perfect Will and Life" (1:499). But this can be read in two ways. It may be hagiography, or complaint—in the spirit of Edward Ross. Stanley does seem finally most intent on recapturing the visceral power of the rite. While he may, in theory, prefer moral sacrifice, his narrative confirms the persisting attraction of the ceremonial kind. Altars and "gloomy superstitions" still compel, though the better neighborhoods discourage them. Take Saul, who is prevented from sacrificing Jonathan. "What was tolerated in the time of Jephthah," Stanley comments, "was no longer tolerated. . . . It was the dawn of a better day" (2:19). Stanley's harsh but ambiguous handling of Saul is suggestive on a number of grounds, perhaps most of all for its resonance with Melville's depiction of Captain Vere. Saul's "religious zeal was always breaking out in wrong channels, on irregular occasions, in his own way," Stanley writes, "the unhingement of his mind, which is perhaps first apparent in the wild vow or fixed idea which doomed his son to death, gradually becomes more and more evident. He is not wholly insane. The lucid intervals are long, the dark hours are few" (2:26). Vere, even before Claggart's murder, is pedantic and detached from the common sense. Following the cabin scene, however, Vere becomes dangerously emotional, inspiring troubled speculations from his officers. Vere's exclamations dooming Billy to death are "convulsive," "vehement." It takes several minutes for him to resume his "wonted manner." One officer wonders whether Vere is "unhinged." Another ponders the basis of his "aberration" (478–80).

Stanley's portrayal culminates in a description of the Jewish priesthood as a sacrificial institution. He seems drawn to its plainly barbaric content. The Temple's arrangements, he writes, were "not those of a cathedral or a church, but of a vast slaughter-house. . . . There was the huge altar, towering above the people. . . . Underneath was the drain to carry off the streams of blood." He explains, "The intrinsic meaning of ancient sacrifice lay in its opening an approach to God by a gift of the offerer, a gift valuable in proportion as it represented the entire dedication of the life. Hence the prominence of the warm flowing blood in the ancient world." Blood is the primitive equivalent for the smiling face of Jephthah's daughter. It is the mark of complete submission to God: the willingness to offer up vital fluids. As Stanley portrays it, the ancient world had a material and sensual register for the relationship between God and his worshipers. Priests were chosen for skill and brawn alone: "the robust frame . . . the quick eye and ready arm which could strike the fatal blow." While "Butcher and Priest are now the two extremes of the social scale . . . they were once almost identical" (2:254–56). Though we might be tempted to recoil in disgust from the barbaric nature of Jewish religion, their standard of civilization, Stanley reminds us, was high in comparison to contemporaries. His conclusion depicts Hebrew sacrifice as ritual high drama. "Every gesture, every color, every ornament, was a kind of moving picture, in which the Israelite was reminded of the Invisible Ruler; in which the Invisible Ruler was (if one may say so) to be reminded of His earthly and distant subjects. . . . When the warm blood of the slaughtered ram left its red stain on the ears, and thumbs, and toes of the priestly family; when their hands were filled with the smoking entrails of the victims and with the cakes of consecrated bread, it was the intimation that the self-sacrifice of the whole nation was acted in their persons" (2:458–59). Blood sprays with abandon here, staining everyone in the vicinity. Sacrifice, as described by Stanley, was a domestic festival. We are asked to imagine all the members of a 'Cohanim' clan—priest, wife, children, extended family—dipping their hands in "entrails" and grabbing greedily at "consecrated bread." The claims of animal appetite seem preeminent. The ritual is about hunger and its appeasement. But Stanley is also careful to stress the meaning of the event from the perspective of participants. He tells us what these ritual actors see, how they interpret their actions, what they are feeling. This is the sensual dimension of his argument. The nation watches, but as ritual beholders of this sacrificial theatre, their presence completes it. This may look revolting to us. To the Israelites, "the Invisible Ruler" was implied in every blood drop, in every thread of ram gut. Stanley seems to anticipate the discomfort of his Victorian audience. They preferred softer dramas, with smiling daughters yielding up their bodies to seal pacts between the nation and God.

Stanley's account of the Jewish priesthood accords ultimately with the conclusions of social scientific interpreters: neither form of sacrifice—hard or soft—was obsolete. To this end, Stanley concludes, in his appendix, with another powerfully graphic treatment of sacrifice: "the one only Jewish Sacrifice lingering in the world." His description of this 1854 Samaritan ritual is based on eyewitness reports. As if to discount skepticism, Stanley is even more precise than usual, including a map of Mount Gerizim, the sacrificial site. All the proper forms are in place: a group of men in sacred (all-white) costume, gathering on a mountaintop to recall Abraham and Isaac and to recite prayers. Enter a small flock of sheep, and a mounting sense of urgency. The prayers reach a "furious" pitch as the sun descends. Suddenly, the men brandish swords, and the sheep are slaughtered within minutes. They dip their fingers in the streaming blood and mark "the foreheads and noses of the children." Stanley describes the "vast column of smoke and steam" that fills "the moonlit sky" during the roasting of the sheep. He highlights "the rigid exclusiveness" of the rite, which allows foreign spectators but forbids them to "eat thereof." And finally, he depicts the ravenous consumption of blackened flesh. Stanley closes his account with a personal confession: the ritual ends on what is for him the morning of Palm Sunday. He notes how strange it feels to know that the "simple" Christian rite, so peacefully observed, is derived from "the wild, pastoral, barbarian, yet still instructive, commemoration" (1:559–65). Stanley seems uncertain about the place of sacrifice in a modern context. His sense that it might be "instructive" seems a lame rejoinder to his spectacular portrait. The key to Stanley's extensive depictions of sacrifice may be the three-word phrase that introduces them: "the Sacrificial System." What could be meant by this? Stanley seems to find in the rite an articulation of the aims and purposes of all worship, the rational groundwork of faith. Blood flows; God sees. God resides in the visible gestures of the butcher-priest. Stanley might not admire the sacrificial system, but he can't help envying it.

Like Stanley's *History of the Jewish Church* and Robertson Smith's *Lectures on the Religion of Early Semites*, H. Clay Trumbull's *The Blood Covenant* confirmed the very different project that traditional theology had become by the later nineteenth century. His research illustrates that as the religious domain grew ever more embattled, the field of theology grew ever more inventive in its approach to method. Trumbull, as I have suggested, is eager to prove affinities among different forms of worship. Sacrifice, from this optimistic perspective, is about breaking down barriers: among human kinds, between man and God. The blood of the sacrifice provided "common life"; the flesh, "common nourishment." He argues that "in all religions the longing, whether grossly or spiritually apprehended, to enter into the closest possible union with the adored being, is fundamental."

Trumbull is an enthusiast. Every religious impulse is legitimate, even admirable. Hence his reading of cannibalism as "a religious sentiment, and not a mere animal craving" (182–84). He is careful to point out that his interpretation is widely shared. By partaking of sacred food, offered up in the form of a human being, worshipers believed that they became one with their God. Trumbull betrays none of the detachment or ambivalence that is so prominent in Spencer, Ward, or Stanley. Like an explorer he seems too overcome by his fascination to fear. The inspiration behind Trumbull's analysis is most evident in his treatment of familiar themes and events. For example, there is his handling of the "sacrifice" of Isaac. Trumbull places Abraham's act in context, stressing the special attitude of the "Oriental" father toward his son, a life he prizes "far more than . . . his own." "To die without a son is a terrible thought. . . . His future is blank." Trumbull believes that "the Western mind" has had difficulty grasping the full gravity of an Oriental father yielding up a being he regards as his own more vital self. Trumbull's earnest theology is incompatible with the subsequent Freudianism of James Frazer, who stresses the competition between father and son. Trumbull cites the stream of imitations spawned by Abraham's example, from the sacrifice of Siralen in India to the story of Amys and Amylion in Great Britain (224–28). The Hebrew Exodus from Egypt is for Trumbull a further twist on the same blood covenant. This time the Israelites call upon God to fulfill his end of a pact sealed with Abraham. Where Abraham had given of his blood in the original covenant, God now gives his own, in the form of the sacrificial lamb. The lamb's blood would mark the doorposts in a token of divine protection, and its flesh would be consumed to confirm the intercommunion of human and divine. Trumbull, like Stanley, traces the Passover covenant down to the Samaritan sacrifice on Mount Gerizim. But in Trumbull's version, the blood is placed on the foreheads of the children, a mark "between thine eyes." Trumbull sees this as a version of the phylactery, the sacred amulet worn by Jews in daily prayer. This "permanent ceremonial" is yet another expression of the blood friendship between God and man. Some rabbis even find support, according to Trumbull, for the idea that God is himself at times arrayed in the phylactery. Another derivation of the same rite is the symbolic significance of red cloth or thread, which is substituted for the phylactery in times of persecution. Red functions as a substitution for an act of faith that imperils the worshiper (233–37).[106]

Trumbull is drawn to sacrifice for its intensity and for what it represents about the universality of worship. Sacrifice in his view is not a thing of the past. It is a live interdisciplinary event. In the manner of the most powerful social observers of his era, Trumbull combines the instincts of the antiquarian with the idealism of the social scientist searching for new ways of formulating universal problems of social order, communal bonds, the relationship between humans and Gods. But Trumbull adds a dimension that is only present in the most charged examples: the drama of a believer in the know, struggling in the most intellectualized terms with the dilemma of faith. The stakes of this struggle were thoroughly familiar to the philosopher and writer at the center of the analysis that concludes this chapter: Schopenhauer and Melville.

Melville's critics have long been aware of Schopenhauer's significance to *Billy Budd*. Records confirm that in the years before his death in 1891 Melville borrowed Schopenhauer's works from libraries and bought translated volumes as they appeared. We know that Melville was drawn to Schopenhauer for a pessimistic philosophy common to both. Yet the details of their shared dispositions and intellects remain, for the most part, relatively obscure. I believe that an important aspect of their intellectual affinity is their shared ties to a contemporary context of theological and social scientific writings on sacrifice. Schopenhauer was preoccupied with the subject. Sacrifice was, in his view, one of the fully convincing postulates produced by religion. What's striking is Schopenhauer's sense of the varied institutional forms taken by the rite in the modern era. In *Will and Idea*, he defines sacrifice as "resignation generally," adding that "the rest of nature must look for its salvation to man who is at once the priest and the sacrifice." In *Counsels and Maxims*, life insurance is characterized as "a public sacrifice made on the altar of anxiety. Therefore take out your policy of insurance!" In *Studies in Pessimism*, prostitution among the female poor in London is "a dreadful fate: they are human sacrifices offered up on the altar of monogamy."[107] The first example presents sacrifice as a state of exhaustion. The universe has come to the end of its rope. Something must be done to restore a functional equilibrium. "Man" is the ritual actor who can be counted on to pay the price of continuity and order. Schopenhauer's terms here are high philosophy, with a social and political edge. "Man" is not quite as universal as it sounds. Clearly, some will be priests, others victims. In the second example, Schopenhauer recognizes life insurance as a modern form of ancient sacrifice. Every type of human being over time has been moved by the fragility of existence to make payments to some imagined force or order. The impulses behind the stone edifices with their offerings to God are reborn in the insurance industry: if I can offer something up, or make *sacrifices* here and there, perhaps I can control my fate, or that of those I care about. The derivation of this idea helps to explain why people seem to believe, against all apparent logic, that death comes more readily to those who are unprepared. In the third example, monogamy becomes an ideal comparable to divinity. We hope it's there; we want to believe it is; but we're often fairly certain that it's not. Human sexuality, Schopenhauer notes, is polarized. We need to believe ourselves better than we are. Certain women are the sacrifice to this deception.

Everywhere he looks Schopenhauer sees sacrifice, because he considers it essential. A religion, he writes of Hinduism, that "demands the greatest sacrifices and which has yet remained so long in practice in a nation that embraces so many millions of persons, cannot be an arbitrarily invented superstition, but must have its foundation in the nature of man." The same conviction inspires Schopenhauer's uncharacteristic receptivity to the Old Testament, whose doctrine of the Fall provides the best "explanation of our existence." And his description of Christian sacrifice is the most dramatic of all: writing of Bruno and Vanini, he observes that they were "sacrificed to that God for whose honour incomparably more human sacrifices have bled than on the altars of all heathen gods of both hemispheres together." Schopenhauer joins previous analysts of world religions in declaring sacrifice common to all of them. "Many millions, united into nations, strive for the common good," he writes, "each individual on account of his own; but many thousands fall as a sacrifice for it."[108] Most of these statements appear in *The World as Will and Idea*. More specifically, most of them appear in a section of the book entitled, "Characterisation of the Will to Live." They bracket what may be the most grave and haunting moment in all of Schopenhauer's pessimistic philosophy: where the White Squirrel leaps voluntarily into the jaws of the predatory serpent.

Schopenhauer's anecdote was powerful enough to become a preoccupation of Max Scheler's, who integrated it into his theory of sympathy. For Scheler, the Squirrel's behavior represented a sympathetic identification so complete that its only possible end was self-annihilation. The anecdote held attractions of its own for Melville, who would have encountered it, like Scheler, in Schopenhauer. The scene appears to have provided the inspiration for the cabin scene in *Billy Budd*. Why has no one recognized the significance for Melville of this passage in Schopenhauer? Perhaps because Melville didn't mark it, or because the scene is in French. Yet the pages preceding and following it are marked. (Melville's highlighting of another French passage confirms his reading knowledge of the language.)[109] The most likely explanation, in my view, is that Melville absorbed the scene somewhat unconsciously. I find it revealing, for example, that *Billy Budd* shares the anecdote's summer setting. The passage, I believe, made a strong impression on him, although he may not have immediately registered its significance.

Schopenhauer's anecdote, drawn from a French newspaper, extends over a two-page footnote, and it focuses on a white-headed squirrel, agile, strong, distinguished by a rare grace and charm. This spontaneous creature flits fearlessly from bough to bough in the uppermost reaches of a jungle tree, itself of an unusual type, the "kijatile." An explorer hovers nearby, armed with a gun, watching, as the squirrel is bewitched by a cobra, which lies in wait below. The serpent is all eyes: their yellow glare provides his sole means of attack. There is not a shred of physical force, only an animal magnetism bordering on genius. The explorer, who relates the details of the encounter confesses that he might have intervened. He could have released the squirrel with a single spray of bullets. But he also is caught—in the snare, he implies, of science. He lets curiosity—an eagerness to follow the confrontation through to its natural denouement—triumph over pity. Yet he too is a victim of instinct. This drama of animal sacrifice makes its human participant helpless. The explorer is paralyzed, because he is equally identified with the one who desires food and the one who provides it.

The emotional intensity of Schopenhauer's conclusion draws attention to the incident. The introduction is relatively understated. "In the Siècle, 10th April 1859, there appears, very beautifully written, the story of a squirrel that was magically drawn by a serpent into its very jaws." The conclusion conveys a feeling of raw panic. Schopenhauer begins with pedagogical restraint. "In this example we see what spirit animates nature, for it reveals itself in it, and how very true is the saying of Aristotle quoted above—*Natura doemonia est, non divina.*" Schopenhauer can be read as predatory in his own right, seizing upon this scene in professional eagerness, as "an argument for pessimism." The stops are out in the very next sentence, however. "That an animal is surprised and attacked by another is bad," he writes, "but that such a poor innocent squirrel sitting beside its nest with its young is compelled, step by step, reluctantly, battling with itself and lamenting, to approach the wide, open jaws of the serpent and consciously throw itself into them is revolting and atrocious. What monstrous kind of nature is this to which we belong!"[110] To call the squirrel's response a "lament," to invest its torment with the quality of contradiction, is to make it human. The squirrel is emotionally overwhelmed by its fate, just like Schopenhauer. The squirrel, as he presents it, is more saddened than terrified. It's not enraged; it doesn't rebel. It's wounded. Still, it goes voluntarily.

This is a large part of the atrocity for Schopenhauer. The squirrel's acceptance of its doom, its active assistance of its antagonist, brings him near to revulsion. It all comes down to the question of nature. The squirrel's response to the snake is a realization of the squirrel's essential goodness. The good tend to acquiesce, spontaneously, to whatever comes their way. They are content in life, because they are compliant with death. Goodness is balanced by evil, embodied in the torpid snake, that can only tolerate other versions of itself. The two states, good and evil, exist in tense equilibrium. Melville marks a passage later in the same volume of *Will and Idea* where Schopenhauer quotes Leibnitz approvingly: "the lame excuse for the evil of the world [is] that the bad sometimes brings about the good" (395). Why is this "lame"? Isn't this the ultimate idea of the white squirrel anecdote? Not from Melville's perspective (nor even from Schopenhauer's). It is precisely the point of *Billy Budd* that divisions of this kind don't hold in real life. Good and evil are never concentrated in individuals, only in myths. The mythic perspective belongs to the explorer of the squirrel anecdote. Recall that the incident is recounted from his point of view, a view that alternates between empathy and clinical absorption. Schopenhauer is drawn to both sides: to the squirrel, eaten alive, and the serpent, who rests afterward in a state of complete satisfaction. This is the condition to which every beast (human and animal) aspires: the calm that follows replenishment.

The contest between eater and eaten, beneficiary and sacrifice, becomes an opposition between good and evil because of a need to explain their different fates. We want to know why one survives and one perishes. We have to feel that this dispensation is inevitable and justified. Melville suggests an alternative: that the serpent represents an inherent, universal type of antipathy. Evil and innocence are present in everyone. That's why we can't identify fully with either. In keeping with this, the anecdote reveals a profound human intolerance for uncompromised good. Edgar Allan Poe called this instinct "the Imp of the Perverse," an instinct so pronounced it puts the agent of innocence at war with himself. Melville shares this conviction. Against those who mourn the inability of goodness to triumph over evil, he pictures the inability of the good to triumph over their own inner capacity for evil. This is one reason why innocence, represented in Billy Budd and the white squirrel, is complicit in its own destruction. Those possessed of a high degree of virtue are bound to possess an equally strong penchant for vice. The same held true, in the minds of some high critics, for Christ himself. A common reading of the Crucifixion as the world's intolerance of virtue is balanced by the idea of virtue's inevitable attraction to vice. In the face of this, actors murder (the snake); intellectuals doubt (the explorer). The cabin scene in *Billy Budd*, where the unsuspecting Billy walks straight into the trap set by Claggart, complicates such claims even further.

Claggart deliberately advanced within short range of Billy and, mesmerically looking him in the eye, briefly recapitulated the accusation.
Not at first did Billy take it in. When he did, the rose-tan of his cheek looked struck by white leprosy. He stood like one impaled and gagged. Meanwhile, the accuser's eyes, removing not as yet from the blue dilated ones, underwent a

phenomenal change, their wonted rich violet color blurring into a muddy purple. Those lights of human intelligence, losing human expression were gelidly protruding like the alien eyes of certain uncatalogued creatures of the deep. The first mesmeristic glance was one of serpent fascination; the last was as the paralyzing lurch of the torpedo fish. (476)

If Claggart is clearly identified here as the destructive "serpent," the *Bellipotent* is no Eden. And Claggart's reptilian associations are also, as I have suggested, richly contemporaneous. Claggart is the alien "offal" immigrating in plaguelike numbers to America at the end of the nineteenth century. The mention of a lurching "torpedo fish" may further specify his difference, by recalling a cold rabbi from *Clarel*, who is described in the same terms. Claggart's glare, like that of Schopenhauer's snake, is stunning. Both serpents are all eyes, their eyes pure activity. There is no trace of physical intervention: no hand is lifted, no net comes down. The white subject is caught by a single glance. Single, not simple; for the lair is psychic. The white squirrel and the blanched Billy are internally twisted and torn. The quickest, surest solution is the explorer's route: binomial oppositions. Self-division becomes a form of agency; the victims become agents of their own destruction. In Billy's case, this means kill and be contrite; strike and be good. Billy in this scene embraces fully his reputation as "the fighting peacemaker." In the most classic American sense, Billy attempts to redeem himself through violence. This is also the classic sacrificial sense.

The cabin scene is foreshadowed by an early description of Billy's role aboard the *Rights-of-Man*, where he functions, "like a Catholic priest striking peace in an Irish shindy." At first, his power is all aspect. His virtue radiates, "sugaring the sour ones." One roughneck alone resists, an envious precursor to Claggart, named Red Whiskers. The significance of this figure, who calls Billy a "sweet and pleasant fellow," lies in his former life as a butcher. One day he provokes Billy by poking him, as if he were "a sirloin steak." Billy, "quick as lightning let fly his arm," in an assault as instinctive and immediate as his blow to Claggart. But here, fate checks Billy's violence, and the resolution is peaceful. Everyone, including Red Whiskers, loves Billy (even more now, since affection is intensified by fear). The sailors wash his clothes and darn his socks, and "the carpenter" builds him a special chest. The scene is full of spiritual markers. Billy is a "priest." In Arthur Stanley's Hebraic sense, he is a butcher of the butcher. The "fire-red whiskers" of the real butcher symbolize the sacrificial flames of aggression and protection (433–34). Their shade may explain why he is spared the ultimate effects of Billy's violence. But the strongest content here is Christian.

Billy is a type of Christ—an historicized type. As the "fighting peacemaker," who is dubbed snidely "a 'sweet and pleasant fellow,'" Billy is

171

Strauss's Christ, and Reade's, and even partly Alger's. He is the suspect Christ, who shares initials with the bighearted Jack Chase of the dedication, as well as the serpent John Claggart, who more than opposes every virtue represented by the savior. Like the butcher, Red Whiskers, Claggart is also mired in biblical doubt. He is the one who questions the reliability of Billy's sweet talk. Claggart and Red Whiskers raise enough doubt to make Billy's violence seem the fulfillment of an inner propensity. But civilization, Melville reminds us, never fully condemns violence. Even a high spiritual form like Christianity sees violence as a route to love. Melville wants us to remember that there are many sides to Christ. This is why Claggart can recall "the man of sorrows" and speak in a voice as "sweet" as Billy's (454). The compound Christ that is formed through a blend of Claggart and Billy applies equally to Billy alone. The issue of Christ's "personality" is just as complicated when it is confined to one character as when it is dispersed among several. It's not necessary to rehearse all the traits Billy shares with Christ. He is a "lamb of God," whose yard-end gallows becomes a collector's item—"a piece of the Cross"—to his disciples (497, 503). Billy also unites within himself a series of oppositions: he is pure and mixed, common and noble, perfect and flawed, gentle and violent. To complicate matters further, Melville invests his legendary innocent with the knowledge of potential mutiny, which Billy fails to disclose out of loyalty to his fellow sailors (465). At the same time, Melville protects his Christ from critique, through frequent hints that doubt of Billy's virtue is itself the sign of a fallen state (e.g., 469). But as with all such claims in this narrative, the reader is led to wonder whether the very opposite is not closer to the truth.

The Red Whiskers scene does more than foreshadow the events in Vere's cabin; it establishes their symbolic centrality. For both incidents capture the intricacy of the story's response to the nineteenth-century controversy over Christ's character. Billy's tautological butchery of the butcher in the story's opening prepares for his butchery of Claggart in the cabin, where Claggart's body is "raised . . . from the loins up," like a side of meat (477). This is the work of the double-edged Christ, whose words can soothe and wound, whose powerful arm is designed for the doubled ritual office of butcher and priest. He can be both sacrificer, and sacrifice for humanity's sake. Melville is ever alert to the potential and inherent hypocrisies of a ritual meal where some eat and others are eaten. Throughout *Billy Budd*, characters are imaged as food, both animal and vegetable. Some look desperate for a good meal; others like the edible contents of one. Crucial confrontations occur at mess halls, over bowls of spilled soup. Claggart is especially identified with food. This seems odd given his ascetic, even monastic aspect. If he eats, it has no effect. Like an engine at permanent high throttle, Claggart is always in need of fuel. Claggart's envy, described as "the greediness of hate for pabulum" (461), is compared to the legendary Othello's jealousy—"the green-ey'd monster, which doth mock / the meat it feeds on."[111] Claggart devours Billy, with malice as his condiment. But Claggart is equally self-consuming. Perhaps out of sympathy with the narrative's deepest implications, his taste for Billy is apt "to recoil upon itself" (458–59). Like his creator, Claggart sometimes has difficulty distinguishing himself from Billy—hence his "reactionary bite" (459).

An important feature of their doubling is the sacrificial flame kept burning, presumably in the most reverential sense, in both. Claggart's inner flame signals a defect or deficiency, while Billy's signals spiritual and emotional plenitude. Claggart's fire, "lit . . . from within," is undetectable. "The bonfire in [Billy's] heart," makes his whole body "luminous" (458). Billy simmers gently, while Claggart stews on such a high flame that he seems destined for ashes before he can be eaten. In any case he holds small promise as a ritual meal. Claggart's ritual dissonance is confirmed by the lack of ceremony that attends his conversion from man to corpse. There is something distasteful in the preparation of his body for burial. It seems appropriately handled by "certain petty officers of his mess" (492). But there are no traces of priestly effect, and the corpse seems distinctly unappetizing. In *Billy Budd*, only prime human specimens achieve the status of person food. Consider the ceremonial splendor that surrounds Billy's death. His sacred character makes for his delectability. His prone body is enhanced, lit by the "oil" of war contractors "whose gains are seen as a portion of the harvest of death" (493). When he is committed to the sea, the fowl circle round, displaying "an animal greed for prey." Following his symbolic ascension, Billy is a "lamb of God," whose fleece is "licked up by the sun" (500–501).

Everyone, it seems, feeds on Billy: humans (war contractors), animals (sea fowl), planets (sun). This suggests, in the bleakest Darwinian terms, Billy's place at the bottom of the food chain. But it also confirms the tie between eating and believing, food and faith. Sometimes, it is an honor to be eaten. Does the same honor apply to Schopenhauer's squirrel? Is this what propels him into the jaws of that mesmerizing snake? What else would provoke an animal or human to such a self-destructive act? In *Billy Budd*, people and creatures eat not only to sustain themselves but to get closer to one another and even to God. This is why some can even be persuaded to offer themselves up as food. Such a logic might underlie the mesmerized actions of the squirrel: it could be attempting to connect with a deity. In this light, the reference in the passage to the squirrel's nest takes on momentous significance. For the squirrel (whether male or female the report doesn't say) may be engaged in an exemplary act of self-sacrifice on behalf of its young.

Billy, who is entirely sufficient unto himself, has no nest to worry about. Yet his own desperate action may also represent an attempt to communicate with a Providential power. Billy's blow to Claggart can be read as a displaced plea. A murder happens because someone is unable to speak. In a "convulsed tongue-tie," Billy is "prompted [to] yet more violent efforts at utterance" by Vere's encouragement. Then, "quick as the flame from a discharged cannon at night, his right arm shot out, and Claggart dropped to the deck" (477). Billy's inadvertent violence is invested nevertheless with great spiritual portent. He may lack the deliberateness of an empowered ritual actor. But he does fit the demeanor of a victim. Melville has already compared him, strangely, to "a condemned vestal priestess . . . being buried alive" (476). And then, as in the rather different case of the squirrel, Billy is prepared to give himself in order to save himself (or others). Far from unusual, this is, we know, the utmost in sacrificial convention. Killing, including suicide, is an elevated act. This is the way an alienated humanity communicates with a remote God. By offering God something, the worshiper secures his attention. In time, he hopes to get more: good will, bounty, or protection. For the most sacred rites, reserved for the most serious requests, the offer of a human victim is thought to underscore the gravity of the plea.

What an ancient Hebrew or modern Christian calls ritual necessity or faith a nineteenth-century social Darwinist calls instinct. Built into the beings of squirrel and snake is an urge to destruction or sacrifice. There is a need to snuff out a life for the sake of something neither can fathom. They're incapable of understanding their plight. But it's not just because they're animals, for the explorer also resists the depth of the drama played out before his eyes. This naturalistic call and response requires many levels of interpretation. First, there is the "neutral" eyewitness account, preserved by the newspaper. The scientist-explorer doesn't act morally; his job is to watch and wait. His objective record supplies a documentary base for universal truths. The next narrative frame belongs to the pessimistic philosopher, who reads the scene as an allegory of the Fall, an evocation of "man's fate." At the furthest remove from the explorer are the literary deliberations of Melville in *Billy Budd*. The urge here is to enrich and complicate: an elemental drama becomes a map of social, political, and theological intrigue. The purity of science and philosophy is sacrificed on the altar of aesthetic "truth uncompromisingly told" (501). Melville's concrete tale transforms naturalist philosophy into thick literary description.

Melville seems caught in the grips of his own pressing sacrificial interests, which is reflected in his apparent eagerness to introduce every conceivable type of the rite. He is not only interested in sacrifice's function as a form of alimentary communion but also in how it articulates faith—how it reaches out to God. And like every other author discussed in this study, from Stephen Crane to Gertrude Stein, Melville also sees sacrifice as expressing the human need for protection, considered as both a universal and a political concern. Probably the most vivid hint of this is the narrative preoccupation with blood. Blood in *Billy Budd* is about inheritances and legacies, about inspiration, warning, and safety, and about ceremonial give and take. The black sailor in the opening possesses "the unadulterate blood of Ham" (430); Billy's "noble descent" is "as evident in him as in a blood horse" (437); Billy's skin color is normally "rose" (436, 458). Nelson's name is described as "a trumpet to the blood" of his men, which is qualified by the "insolent . . . Red Flag" raised in mutiny at Nore and Spithead (442, 440). Claggart's "defective . . . blood" is realized in the "ill-blood," overwhelming and insurmountable, he feels toward Billy (448, 460). In contrast, Billy's perilously unsuspicious nature is reflected in his "warm blood" (462). The story's dramaturgical second string, the host of seafaring oddities, features its own scarlet symbol system, including the bloody butcher Red Whiskers and the "brick-colored" Red Pepper. And Claggart's eyes sometimes throw off "a red light" of their own (468). Claggart emphasizes the role of red as warning: "a mantrap may be under the ruddy-tipped daisies" (473). And he himself is described as holding "the blood-dyed coat of young Joseph," in the manner of "the envious children of Jacob" (474). Melville tells us in as many ways as possible, in the sequence of events leading up to the cabin scene, that there is danger in the air. Someone is bound to die. And it is telling that the rose is entirely sucked out of Billy's cheek at the moment of Claggart's accusation (476). At peace with himself, just before his execution, the rose returns (493), only to be transferred to the dawn after his death (497).

The color red is not an incidental detail in this novella. It is a power, a value. This is how it appears in the passage on Admiral Nelson, where the "Red Flag" is capitalized to specify it and to underline its potency. The flag is an emblem of political terror, a "red meteor of unbridled and unbounded revolt" (440). Revolutionary fervor here is "contagious": "blown across the Channel" via "live cinders." This is furthered by the metaphor of nations as individuals who are either defective or "well-constituted." A healthy state, Melville implies, can withstand conflagrations of any sort. He is clear about the source of terror here. The Red Flag is hoisted within the British navy: this is internal uprising. Red, in this example, does not protect against threats from outside; it confirms that outside has become inside. The tars have lost their dedication to protecting England from the threatening embers of an enflamed France. Patriotism is "converted" to class warfare, "for a time." Eventually, the rebellion is defused, and the strains of the patriotic Dibdin resume their function: a martial air that keeps the din down. But the Red Flag that "wiped out" the British colors remains a threatening totem symbol of revolt. The replacement of a national symbol by a form of ritual primitivism or superstition—the washing-out of political definitude in a universal sea of red—implies that folk forms are not always at the service of dominant designs. Melville, as always, is politically shrewd rather than predictable. He notes that rebellion, like sacrifice, is a functional act. Mutiny helps to channel steam, and ultimately to reaffirm national loyalty.

Yet things are not so harmless as they appear. First, there is a reason for all this official circuitry (the rhetoric of contagions blown across channels). If things were so neat and harmonious, a compensatory sacrifice would be unnecessary. Melville affirms that the terrible loss of men following Nelson's victorious death is intentional. The surviving officers deliberately "overruled" Nelson's "sagacious dying injunctions . . . to anchor" imme-diately (442). Mutiny is only barely contained by words like "distemper . . . irruption . . . fever," conditions readily limited to a body. The underside of this polite language is the conversion of the Red Flag of mutiny into a sacrificial image. The flag, in this sense, prophesies the bloodbath at Trafalgar—the "plenary absolution," where the former mutineers are sac-rificed by the thousands. This is mass death as a form of oblation. The common sailors repay the balance on their dissent account with the one thing they have to exchange: their lives (441).

Melville's view of collective sacrifice differs from that of contemporary social scientists and theologians. Lester Ward's discussion of "the Burmah Massacre," for example, claims that anyone is fair game: men, women, chil-dren, priests, and foreigners. A contemporary theologian like Horace Bushnell would insist on the potential glory available to all through sacrifi-cial devotion. He recognizes no differences between elite and working-class contributions to the Civil War effort. Melville has no illusions on this point, as is evident in his bitter poem on the New York draft riots. While he is no defender of the "river-rats" who vent their rage on helpless Blacks, he highlights the disparities built into oblatory rites. The national continuum of sacrifice—from disenfranchised Blacks, to poor Whites, to wealthy elites buying their way out of battle—is an ascending differential of cost and benefit. A similar reasoning prevails in *Billy Budd*. As I will be arguing in conclusion, Melville sees all three of his central protagonists in sacrificial terms. Each combines extraordinary force with a special quality of intelligence or emotion. Yet each is slightly marred. Vere is a "queer" aristocrat (447). Claggart is a mysterious, even "abnormal" petty officer (448). Billy Budd has a determining vocal defect. Each combines elements of the sacred and the profane. The narrator's assessment of Billy applies to all three: "Billy was a striking instance that the arch interferer, the envious marplot of Eden, still has more or less to do with every human consignment" (439).

Melville links mass sacrifice to the lower classes. He believes that the social group with least to give always gives most. Melville does not sentimentalize the common sailors, but he is sensitive to the pecking order of his society. The most striking implication in Melville's portrayal of Nelson's glorious sacrifice is that his voluntary death is somehow causally related to "the deplorable loss of life by shipwreck" that succeeds it. Nelson's self-sacrifice for the sake of military fame appears to be balanced by the involuntary sacrifice of sailors, who are consigned to everlasting anonymity. Nelson is further compromised by the label "priest." He draws up his own "will and testament" and officiates as victim and beneficiary at his own "sacrifice" (442–43). Obviously, there can be no such deliberateness on the part of the sailor masses. Melville implies an interdependence between the two events in pointing out that the sailors, many of them from the crews of Nore and Spithead, helped Nelson win his "naval crown of crowns" (441). But the point of the exchange remains unclear. Does the loss of Nelson *require* the loss of an entire crew? Is there an equivalence here: the death of a great man and the death of many common ones? What is the relationship between an individual's voluntary sacrifice for honor and a collectivity's involuntary sacrifice for nothing at all?

The passage raises the question without answering it, but the reference to his "naval crown of crowns" may take us closer to Melville's view of Nelson. A subsequent passage highlighting the possible "foolhardiness and vanity" of Nelson's "ornate publication of his person" may also recall certain characterizations of Christ. In the same passage, Melville hints that the death of so many sailors might have been prevented had Nelson avoided his glorious "challenge to death" (442). Is he suggesting by way of Nelson that the price of Christ's loving submission was mass submission? Like a priest, Nelson arrays himself in sacramental clothing, "the jewelled voucher of his shining deeds." Like a god, he is immortalized by his acts. The image of Billy as "a pendant pearl" in the final ballad encourages a comparison beween his sacrifice and Nelson's. Contrasts make the strongest impression. Nelson's jewels distinguish him as an extraordinary soldier; they help to mark his ultimate heroism; they enclose him in a godlike aura. Billy doesn't *wear* precious articles, he *is* one. He is precious, but he is also criminal, offered up in vindication of a capital offense. In Billy's case, sacrifice is both inevitable and accidental. Social deviation is itself inevitable: some man has to fall, according to the story's logic. But it need not be Billy. In Nelson's case, sacrifice is a form of self-mastery. The rite ensures the immortality of an already idealized military figure. Nelson's end arouses envy; "the spot where the Great Sailor fell" becomes a shrine (442). Captain Vere would have favored such a death for himself (502). Billy's fall is a reminder of collective victimization. The sailors preserve chips from the spar at which Billy is hung (503), to honor a "man as incapable of mutiny as of wilful murder" (504). Billy may be innocent, but his commonness or expendability makes him liable to the forfeit of his life. And this is where the full significance of the Nelson sequence comes into focus. For while Nelson is not criminal, the common sailors who fall in the aftermath of his glory are. Their lives are given unwillingly as payment for their betrayal.

I have suggested that Billy and Claggart function as doubles. In their scenes together, they merge and diverge. Confronting one another in Vere's cabin, for example, both are transformed from states of "calm" or credulity to traumatic "paralysis" (476–77). And they also continuously balance each other. We are to believe that Claggart's "spontaneous antipathy" is *caused* by Billy's harmlessness. But Billy only appears harmless in relation to the menacing Claggart: the narrative goes on to show that he is anything but harmless. Claggart proves fatally unsuspecting on this point. But isn't this reminiscent of Billy? To call the pair opposites is only to confirm their interdependence and reversibility. Claggart and Billy appear alike in their oppositeness, because they are two parts of one sacrificial exchange. Claggart's expertise is deviance. He is the designated understrapper who smokes out dissent, the hangman whose presence aboard ship may function as his own criminal penance. Billy appears a model innocent, but his capacity for violence is underscored early on, and the narrative makes much of his imperfection. Doesn't Billy, in certain respects, also recall "the transgressor of the Middle Ages harboring himself under the shadow of the altar"? (449). Good and evil cancel one another out, within individuals and across society as a whole. "An undiminished eternity is always open for the return of any event or work that was nipped in the bud. In this world of phenomena true loss is just as little possible as true gain": Melville's highlighting of this passage from Schopenhauer's *Will and Idea* can be read as endorsement. It may have inspired his development of the sailor protagonist who is "nipped in the bud."

Melville never doubted that the universal habit of equivocation was the living drapery of death. In *Moby-Dick*, he called it "whiteness." When innocence and guilt look so much alike that they can be exchanged without bothering anyone's sense of logic, then ethics become meaningless. These are not the aftershocks of the events in Vere's cabin. That fatal confrontation is only possible because the void exists in the first place. "In the jugglery of circumstances preceding and attending the event on board the *Bellipotent*, and in the light of that martial code whereby it was formally to be judged, innocence and guilt personified in Claggart and Budd in effect changed places. In a legal view the apparent victim of the tragedy was he who had sought to victimize a man blameless; and the indisputable deed of the latter, navally regarded, constituted the most heinous of military crimes" (480). This explanation seems itself "indisputable": the exchange of guilt and innocence precedes any *actual* circumstances. There is no such thing as loss and gain; innocence and guilt are so unstable that they are indistinguishable. I am not suggesting that Melville thinks it fair that his protagonist is "nipped in the bud." My point is that he so utterly complicates the motivations and consequences of human acts as to make responsible judgment impossible. Nor is Melville endorsing Vere's actions with these implications. In this light, Vere's delirium following Billy's murder of Claggart, his urge to prosecute and refusal to commute the sentence, can be read as a desperate search for clarity.

Vere's execution of Billy is sacrificial in the classic sense. Vere wants to purify a world grown dangerously impure. An ideal human specimen with a glaring imperfection, Billy Budd embodies Vere's elusive purity. The smoky atmosphere of the narrative is indicative of the sacrificial fires kept perpetually burning on behalf of greater moral and spiritual focus. It is hardly accidental that the novel's prophet, Dansker, is "an *Agamemnon* man," whose nickname is "Board-Her-in-the-Smoke" (452). The narrator explains, mysteriously, that his name is derived from his "blue-peppered complexion" and from the scar that cuts across his "dark visage" like "a streak of dawn's light." Added to these sacrificial intonations are references to his "ancient wrinkles" and "primitive" wisdom. He is an oracle, "a salt seer," with "a smoky idea" (452, 453, 455). The image of Agamemnon, who offered his daughter in sacrifice; the scar earned in battle (led by the self-sacrificing Nelson), representing sacrificial mutilation; his general association with fires and burns; the attribution of ancient and primitive characteristics—all represent a kind of sacrificial overkill. They do more than establish his sacrificial credentials. They suggest that the act's ritual implications have become so overdetermined that they are mainly ornamental. Needless to say, Dansker is no redeemer. He takes cynical pleasure in the suffering he notices and anticipates. His one pure insight, for the story's world, is that pleasantries or good inevitably produces ill-will or evil.

Dansker understands, in keeping with the story's deepest intelligences, that good motivates, even requires, evil. A man has got to fall. The gods are hungry, and a prime specimen had better be offered up. The inevitable obscurity of moral problems, the elusiveness of spiritual purpose, increases the likelihood that certain people will be put at risk. This is the argument of the passage where Vere's fatal urgency is unfolded: "The greater the fog, the more it imperils the steamer, and speed is put on though at the hazard of running somebody down. Little ween the snug card players in the cabin of the responsibilities of the sleepless man on the bridge" (489). This passage highlights a collective morality that presumes clarity and order to be dependent on sacrifice. The more chaotic things appear, the greater the need for a ritual killing. The passage appears to specify a certain type of victim. It is the little man, whose protection from the natural elements symbolizes his extreme susceptibility to social forces. Still, things are so smoky in this passage that it's difficult to tell who's being sacrificed and for what purpose. But two highly ritualized set pieces immediately following it offer signposts: the first is the "closeted" interview between Vere and Billy; the second features the preparations for execution. Here is that first "Old Testament" scene: "the austere devotee of military duty, letting himself melt back into what remains primeval in our formalized humanity, may in end have caught Billy to his heart, even as Abraham may have caught young Isaac on the brink of resolutely offering him up in obedience to the exacting behest." We are given a glimpse and then closed out, as the passage ends in the form of a caveat. "But there is no telling the sacrament. . . . There is privacy at the time, inviolable to the survivor; and holy oblivion, the sequel to each diviner magnanimity, providentially covers all at last" (490).

The greatest reservations in this scene are at the expense of Captain Vere. For it is he who aspires to the image of an Old Testament patriarch, whose experience his own actions directly violate. Horace Bushnell offers a concise appraisal of the common knowledge on this point in the year 1876. "Human sacrifices have been offered by every people of the known world except the Jews. . . . For the very point of the command upon Abraham to sacrifice his son, is to show him, in the end, that no such sacrifice is wanted—that obeying God is the deepest reality of sacrifice."[112] God tests Abraham, then liberates him once his faith is confirmed. Vere's demand for sacrifice is at once grandiose and inaccurate. He is a poor Bible scribe, and possibly faithless as well. For would there be a need for human sacrifice at all if faith were sufficiently strong? These qualifications effectively sever the link between Melville's appropriation of Abraham's text and these theological sources. A stronger backdrop for Melville's irony is supplied by contemporary anthropology. James Frazer, for example, would understand Vere's desire to get certain unsettling challengers permanently out of commission. Claggart is the most immediate threat; Billy (exchanging places once again with Claggart) does Vere's dirty work for him. Now the avenger must go, before he starts requesting favors. Whatever irony we might detect here, however, is gone by the succeeding chapter, which pictures the preparations for execution. Here, detail by detail, we see how a man is transformed into a sacred object.

In Melville's portrayal, a ship provides a uniquely solemn stage for this transformation. Where else but on the high seas can an ordinary man become a channel to God? Indeed, so naturally suited is the *Bellipotent* to the requirements of sacrifice that this ritual office seems sinisterly destined. The "upper gun deck" is "in general . . . free," as if perpetually poised to meet its sacred office (492). "The bays formed by the regular spacing of the guns" are singularly suited to the containment of a body (493). The "customary" black paint on the guns provide the proper shade for setting off the "white . . . shroud[ed]" victim (493). The usual array of "battle lanterns" are doubly sacrificial. They are "fed with the oil" of the war contractors, "whose gains, honest or otherwise, are in every land an anticipated portion of the harvest of death" (493). Their deadly glow is "dirty . . . pollut[ing] the pale moonshine" (493). And yet all together these parasitical lanterns, symbols for the parasitism of the war industry, are reminiscent of "confessionals or side-chapels in a cathedral." No other single image in the novella approaches the sacrificial power of these murderous emblems, carving a sacred path to peace. It makes sense, given the inspiration of this setting, that Billy should begin his own unprompted act of self-consumption. The growing visibility of skeleton beneath his skin results from the "secret fire" beginning to "devour" his "tissue." Billy recalls a "child," in a now serious recollection of Isaac's (potential) fate. Unlike a child, however, Billy anticipates his end. In fact, Billy is more "barbarian" than child. He responds to the chaplain's overtures like a "superior *savage*." Evangelical Christianity is "a gift placed in the palm of an outreached hand upon which the fingers do not close" (494–95). This image goes beyond the minor point that Christianity has little appeal for backward peoples— which Melville knows was not the case.

This is a major resistance to belief conveyed as a polite dissonance. Billy discreetly refuses the pressure of Christianity by refusing to participate in an exchange. But Melville makes clear his resistance is groundless. Billy's defiance is foiled from the start, because he is already part of the exchange. His martyrdom is not simply a fact of war but a fact of life. That's why this "regular priest . . . lifted not a finger to avert the doom of such a martyr to military discipline" (495). Rather than powerless to avert Billy's death, the chaplain is committed to it. What could be more appropriate to Christianity than the death of an "essential innocen[t]?" Nor is Billy himself precluded from this common sense. Martyrdom is a universal language. Whatever the "savage" religion to which he subscribes, it can be counted on to include its own version of sacrifice. The chapter's continuous coupling of profanity and spirituality, war and peace, gentleness and predation, confirms its recognition of sacrifice as a modern form of social necessity. Melville doesn't endorse this; he records it. Billy, however, has fully absorbed it. His final words must be read in this light.

Yet the narrative seems so ambivalent in its presentation of Billy's words as to be directly responsible for the critical controversy they have aroused. Billy's blessing of Captain Vere is, first, "so unanticipated coming from one with the ignominious hemp about his neck." Next, it is termed "a conventional felon's benediction directed aft towards the quarters of honor." Finally, it is "the clear melody of a singing bird" (497). Billy's words are at once surprising and prescribed, a sign of generosity and the fulfillment of a criminal's last rite. Moreover, it's particularly important that the tone recalls the voice of a bird, if Billy's melody is recognized as Hebraic. I have already suggested that Byron's *Hebrew Melodies* appears to have had some impact on Melville's thinking in *Billy Budd*. Billy is characterized as a David (459), and his melodious voice may invoke the "loftiness and purity" of David's hymns, as described by Byron at the start of his poetic cycle: "How many hearts have they softened, of how many wretched beings have they been the secret consolation!"[113]

The melody with most pertinence to *Billy Budd* features the story of Jephthah's daughter, whose voice narrates Byron's poem. She remains nameless throughout, known only by her willing sacrifice on behalf of family and country, father and God. All of these beneficiaries are conflated in the poem, which opens with "Since our Country, our God—Oh my Sire! / Demand that the Daughter expire." The poem's conclusion stages the glories of submission to sacrifice. "I have won the great battle for thee / And my Father and Country are free! / When this blood of thy giving hath gush'd / When the voice that thou lovest is hush'd / Let my memory still be thy pride / And forget not I smiled as I died!" Jephthah's daughter achieves an ideal selflessness with her act. Indeed, she is grateful for a higher martyred destiny than that afforded the ordinary "virgins of Salem." She is only too happy to provide her life's blood for the sake of father and country. This martyr is banking on immortality: the voice will live on in memory, along with the valiant smile at death. Jephthah's daughter is the Christ who welcomes blows and wounds because he knows they will ensure the highest seat in heaven. Billy Budd may partake of the same tradition. Duty can be awful, enabling, and rewarding at once. The "vocal current electric" that resonates through the ship's company, is a sign that he, like Christ and Jephthah's daughter, has gauged the circumstances correctly (497). The name of the beneficiary is erased; Billy alone endures. The point here is no longer suffering as a key to salvation. Billy's vow, like the smile of Jephthah's daughter, concerns a certain relationship to death. In the course of being offered up, these two smiled at their fates and went down in history because of it. But these are not, of course, ordinary instances. These are sacrifices; death here is purified, normative, which is to say that it has become a form of willed behavior. The comparable dramas of Jephthah's daughter and Billy Budd provide another way of considering sacrifice in the nineteenth century—as choice rather than fate. Billy is a hero to the common sailors on the *Bellipotent* and beyond it, not because he falls, but because he chooses to die in a particular way. He chooses death as a willing sacrificial victim. To the "wedged mass of upturned faces," Billy represents control in the face of death, which is an understandable fantasy for any group so accustomed to dying in great numbers (497). This is his significance for the sailor collectivity that echoes his closing injunction. His significance for Melville is altogether different. For I think that Melville is distinguishing individual from mass experiences of sacrifice. Any individual, the story presumes, given the right personal attributes and collection of circumstances, can fall victim to sacrifice. The prophetic chariot that opens the execution chapter could be read as an attempt to link Billy's martyred destiny to Nelson's. The crew that falls in the aftermath of Nelson's heroic death may be radically distinguished from him, but the highest specimen of common sailor is not.

To fall victim to sacrifice is, in *Billy Budd*, an honor that one must be sufficiently odd or defective to merit. The gods must be paid off, with an adequately exceptional being. But that being has to be a bit off to attract their attention. In fact, it seems at first difficult to ascertain who exactly *is* sacrificed in the novel. Reading allegorically, it could be the worker (Billy Budd), the ambitious immigrant (John Claggart), or the bachelor (Captain Vere). It could be sacrifice as communion or sacrifice as expiation. It could be about the fall of gods, a God, men, or a man. The mutability and openness of Melville's sacrificial portrait is consistent with inherent properties of the rite, as presented, for example, by Mauss and Hubert in their 1898 *Essay on Sacrifice*. They describe the shifting notions of criminality evident in different ritual enactments. They even suggest that sacrifice was itself in some instances "a crime, a kind of sacrilege": "the death of the animal was lamented. . . . Its pardon was asked before it was struck down. . . . Under the influence of these same ideas the instigator of the slaughter might be punished by beating or exile. . . . The purifications which the *sacrificer* had to undergo after the sacrifice resembled moreover the expiation of a criminal" (my emphasis). More obviously, the victim was also sometimes identified with criminality, so that "there is punishment and sacrifice at one and the same time."[114]

Guilt in *Billy Budd* is similarly unbounded. Following the cabin scene, it attaches freely, logically, to all three principals. Vere is tortured, wracked with guilt. Like a priest, standing before an innocent animal with the knife upraised, Vere begs forgiveness from his gentle victim. So convincing is the presentation of Claggart's criminality that his murder seems a fair penalty. Finally, Billy is a criminal in the most basic military terms. According to Robertson Smith, in the ancient sources criminality and impiety merge. "These coincidences between the ritual of sacrifice and of executioner are not accidental," he writes, "the man who has killed his kinsman or his covenant ally, whether of design or by chance, is impious." Execution becomes a moral as well as religious imperative. Smith introduces a distinction between murder (the killing of kin) and manslaughter (the killing of a stranger). He goes on to show how a greater intermixing of different kin led to the application of blood revenge to manslaughter, so that all members of a kin group were viewed as accomplices to a murder committed by one of them. The death of any member could serve as expiation. The mortal sin of an individual thus affected the entire community. So when a tribesman was executed for spilling tribal blood, his death restored harmonious relations between the collectivity and its God. But the purposes of intertribal sacrifices were never so clear. In either event, the community's aim was "to narrow the responsibility for the crime and free itself of the contagious taint by fixing the guilt." Smith confesses at one point that these "natural" explanations never became "formal dogma, for ancient religion had no official dogmas, but contented itself with continuing to practise antique rites, and letting everyone interpret them as he would." Smith's conclusions have special relevance to *Billy Budd*, where sacrifice happens in a thicket of moral irresolution. As time wore on, he suggests, "the moral value" of such scenes "was probably not very great; and where an actual human victim was offered, so that the sacrifice practically became an execution, and was interpreted as a punishment laid on the community by its god, the ceremony was so wholly deficient in distributive justice that it was calculated to perplex, rather than to educate, the growing sense of morality."[115] Smith's observations highlight a paradox: the moral sensibility developed in keeping with the increasing complexity and elusiveness of moral solutions.

The moments leading up to and following the execution of Billy Budd, represent a crisis of sacrificial interpretation every bit as precise as the evolutionary development described by Robertson Smith. Vere struggles to find the proper sacrificial container for these double deaths. Claggart's is "the divine judgment on Ananias," with Billy cast as an "angel of God" (478). Billy's is the offering of an "innocent" on behalf of "naval usage and tradition" (486, 488). The most questionable sacrificial typology applied in these closing pages is also the most ancient: Abraham and Isaac (490). Melville's point is clear: all of these forms apply, because none fits securely. It's not because sacrifice is anachronistic but because it was always a shady enterprise. Like Robertson Smith, Melville understands sacrifice as a rite that achieves special prominence when "lines of distinction"—among human kinds or between morality and sin—become aggravated or altogether indistinct.

Melville, like Robertson Smith, recognizes a fundamental resonance between his own society and the ancient societies that were especially beholden to sacrifice. Robertson Smith's exhaustive record of the different sacrificial types might be seen as the objective version of Melville's novella. For if Robertson Smith is bent on the antiquarian campaign of recuperating sacrifice in all its variety, Melville's purpose is to dramatize the meaning of that variety. Melville alone understands the variousness of sacrificial practices through the ages as one continuous expression of moral uncertainty. As far back as it can be seen, sacrifice, according to Melville, represents a search for moral coherence. It is an attempt to exonerate an impure world through the imposition of typological purity. In this respect, *Billy Budd* has something in common with another American realist fiction, Twain's *Huckleberry Finn* (1884). Twain's novel abounds in sacrificial scenes: scapegoat rituals, the victimization of animal substitutes, melodramas of self-sacrifice. This propensity for sacrificial theatre is a main component of the novel's renowned burlesque. There may be no scene that more powerfully evokes this theatre than the depiction of a pack of pigs lolling in contented squalor until they are set upon by vicious dogs. The child narrator describes the human "loafers" who initiate this small tragedy: "There couldn't anything wake them up all over, and make them happy all over, like a dog-fight—unless it might be putting turpentine on a stray dog and setting fire to him." The flaming dog has an obvious reference point for Twain's post-Reconstruction South: the lynchings of Blacks. In the hazy world of *Huckleberry Finn*, where moral discriminations are as obscure as the "dull line" of the sky at sunrise (chapter 19), ritual murder is possibly the only thing that makes people feel alive.[116]

By introducing the categories of ritual purity, I mean to stress motivations for Vere's urgency that go beyond military or disciplinary considerations. I am referring, of course, to the story's homoerotic themes.[117] I want to specify the historical bearings of these themes, reexamining them, briefly, in terms made available by my larger focus on sacrifice. Historians have charted the links between legal persecutions of homosexuality and perceptions of social instability in general. It seems hardly surprising that sanctions against social deviance would intensify in times of extreme distress. The anxieties over social order that dominated the eighteenth-century setting of *Billy Budd* lent a special ferocity to the persecution of sexual deviants. One sign that this type of persecution has special resonance for Melville's narrative is the fact that one of the most notorious cases in this period features the name of the novella's chief authority. In July of 1810 (and it may be mere coincidence that the case shares the July setting of *Billy Budd* and Schopenhauer's white squirrel anecdote), British constables raided a London club long identified as a site of homosexual prostitution. The club was located on Vere Street, and the incident became widely known by the name given the individuals it targeted, "the Vere Street Coterie." One reason for the high profile of the raid was the social stature of the group arrested (which included naval officers). Only nine of the twenty-three men were ultimately arraigned. The pillory and jail were reserved, predictably, for the least distinguished members of the "coterie." But the publicity was generated by the presumed respectability of the many who got away.

In 1813, a lawyer named Robert Holloway published a pamphlet on the affair, entitled *The Phoenix Of Sodom, Or the Vere Street Coterie*. The pamphlet was intended as a defense of the Vere Street landlord, James Cook, a humble innocent in Holloway's account, who became the fall guy in the case. Holloway was outraged that a nonculprit, or "substitute," as he called him, bore the brunt of legal and public abuse. The implication of his attack on the official handling of the incident was that Cook suffered because the authorities lacked the courage to prosecute the truly guilty. "[Cook and his wife] are sacrificed," Holloway writes in conclusion, that *"the crime of others shall not be atoned for!"* The bulk of Holloway's "treatise" is a salacious detailing of the events at James Cook's: the bevy of male prostitutes with their "feigned names . . . Kitty Cambric . . . a Coal Merchant; Miss Selina, a Runner at a Police office," another called "Miss Sweet Lips." He notes how the usual conventions of prostitution prevail: *"these ladies . . .* have their favorite men," who are themselves "more exalted in life." Holloway describes an especially bawdy club scene: a group of customers, masquerading, with toy dolls, as nursing mothers in a maternity hospital. Along the way, he offers his own theory on the vice of homosexuality: "the natural consequence of transactions which can only be produced by a temporary insanity."[118] The Vere Street incident features some suggestive resemblances to the narrative of *Billy Budd*. Consider the following (in addition to the Vere connection): repeated references to Billy's "sweet" voice or look; the initials common to Claggart and the innkeeper; the summer setting; the characterization of the *Bellipotent*'s crew as a "collection of highborn dames" and the "ambiguous smile" provoked in some of them by Billy's beauty; the attribution of a sudden "aberration" to Vere following Claggart's murder (436, 480). Another sign that Melville was well read in British history of the time is an 1807 court martial aboard the H.M.S. *Bellona* (a model for the H.M.A. *Bellipotent*?), where two sailors were prosecuted on charges of sodomy and sentenced to one thousand lashes each.

As the official who executes, Vere seems unsuited to the category of sacrificial victim. Yet he "falls" as far as anyone else in the novel. There is the gossip and incrimination, attributed by his cousin to "professional jealousy" (480), that follow his handling of the case. And his own immediate downfall on the heels of the execution can be seen as its consequence. Vere never recovers from the anxiety aroused by the narrative's events: his fear of social disorder without, and of his own disordered nature. He follows his role model, Admiral Nelson, to the grave in his own minidrama of self-sacrifice. But his end has none of the sacred glory. "Cut off too early for the Nile and Trafalgar . . . [he] never attained to the fulness of fame" (502). The reference to Nelson here, and the suggestion that Vere was burning with a like "ambition," confirms the losses of this queer and pedantic captain. Like other officers of his time, Vere is consumed with envy of Nelson.[119]

Envy in *Billy Budd* can be understood as a key component of the sacrificial condition—a way of eating oneself up from within. But there is one character, we know, who takes envy beyond the bounds of ritual and professionalism, to the level of psychosis. The term "envy" does not even begin to capture the emotional state of John Claggart, the final member of the novel's sacrificial trilogy. His characterization provides a textbook case for the condition of ressentiment. We are familiar with its clinical features, as described by Max Scheler. Ressentiment is "a self-poisoning of the mind." The condition is typical in societies where "equal rights (political or otherwise) or formal social equality, publicly recognized, go hand in hand with wide factual differences in power, property, and education." Scheler continues, "The origin of *ressentiment* is connected with a tendency to make comparisons between others and oneself . . . and even an ideal like the 'imitation of Christ' is full of such a comparison." Claggart is the ultimate relational self. He is a walking wound, whose misery defines a modern society that runs on the logic of compensatory losses and gains. Claggart's envy "was no vulgar form of the passion" (459). It has ridges and depths. "Assuming various secret forms within him," this emotion occupies every space of his being (459). According to Scheler, the individual gripped by ressentiment does not want to possess the envied object; he needs to *be* him. "I can forgive everything, but not that you *are*—that you are what you are—that I am not what you are."[120] Claggart is *made* to understand Billy, to *burn* with the deprivation of not being him. The only option appears to be an unendurable self-hatred. So the ressentiment figure locates a border being, one who exists between himself and the object of envy.

In Melville's novella, that self-between is the suspect Billy Budd, the potentially mutinous culprit whom Claggart presents to Vere. This figure combines Billy's charisma with elements of the ressentiment personality: vindictiveness, instability, aggression. Claggart invents a Billy Budd to accommodate his own ressentiment. What's striking is the way the real Billy Budd complies with Claggart's phantom version. Billy's murder of Claggart is an eerie fulfillment of Claggart's purposes. Claggart's death represents the ultimate in sacrificial equilibrium. He loses and gains at once. In bringing down the envied object, he gives his life. Billy and Claggart remain evenly matched in the afterlife. Though Vere (somewhat), the ship's jury (to a greater degree), and the common sailors are convinced of Billy's innocence, the naval chronicle, where a sailor's grade is all, champions Claggart's. Like Vere, Claggart is sacrifice and beneficiary at once. He is trapped "inside" his own sacrificial action. What is the significance, in these terms, of the sacrifice of Billy? To some extent, it mirrors Claggart's.

Billy's striking out against another results in his own death. Like all sacrificial actors, neither Billy nor Claggart completely controls the consequences of the rite. Billy's act, however, unlike Claggart's, is direct. Where Claggart is deliberate in his undeliberateness, full of wiles and machinations, Billy's ritual blow expresses a helplessness that seems more consonant with the human relationship to God as Melville sees it.

Billy's action may also be more pure, in the sense that it expresses a certain tribal loyalty. Despite the many hints of his natural superiority or noble descent, Billy is a commoner. Melville makes a particular point of the fact that he never betrays the mutinous sailors who approach him. Billy's membership in the working class makes him a social outsider. This is because tribal affiliations in *Billy Budd* tend to be defined by class rather than ethnicity. The grievances surrounding the Nore mutiny, for example, are aroused by practices ("shoddy clothes" and rations) peculiar to the contractor "tribe everywhere" (443). The average seamen, from this perspective, are aliens, members of an altogether different tribe. This is why Claggart, the serpent with the accent, can double the Anglo-Saxon with the blond curls. In themselves, they come from different "tribes," but together, they represent the threatening shifts and changes that are also implicit in Vere's sexual uncertainty.

Billy Budd, Sailor: An Inside Narrative ushers in sacrifice as a critical means of mediating change in modern society. Sacrifice has a place, Melville claims, in the looming world of the twentieth century, where spirituality and communal bonds diminish, while different human kinds grow ever more prominent. When mass sacrifices are called for, the dispossessed, the laboring poor, those without kin to avenge them, are bound to go down. Melville's reverberating account of the events at Trafalgar leave little doubt on this score. What the novella fails to confirm is the rule or reason of sacrifice in the individual case. By making all three of its protagonists suitable victims, Melville's "foggy . . . tale" precludes the satisfactions of moral advocacy. It may be possible to plead the cause of each separately, but every plea is incomplete on its own. Sacrifice, according to Melville, is not about finding a place from which to speak. It is about speaking and waiting to see what happens. As represented by Billy's blow to Claggart, sacrifice goes out into the world, and there's no telling where it might land.

THREE

Rites of Passage in an "Awkward Age"

❧

AT THE AGE of thirteen, Henry James attended a National Gallery exhibit of works by Pre-Raphaelite painters, and encountered an image of initiation and exile that would remain vivid to the end of his life. James recalled in *A Small Boy and Others*, "The very word Pre-Raphaelite wore for us that intensity of meaning, not less than of mystery, that thrills us in its perfection but for one season, the prime hour of first initiations." Through a haze of recollection and invention, James commemorated the most potent of all these works. Henry Holman Hunt's *The Scapegoat* was "so charged with the awful that I was glad I saw it in company—*it* in company and I the same: I believed, or tried to believe, I should have feared to face it all alone in a room."[1] James's response is not an overstatement. So powerfully conceived is this goat that it diminishes the considerable drama of its surrounding Dead Sea setting. So cloying is the animal's vulnerability that contemplating it for more than a few minutes seems physically impossible. It is easy to see what a sensitive adolescent might have feared. From the flattened horns done up in a ribbon that binds rather than adorns to the strong limbs that sustain an awkward paralysis instead of a natural and confident mobility, everything about it suggests an emerging vigor stopped dead in its tracks, gentleness overwhelmed by implicit violence. The goat is curiously feminized, with its reddish-gold fur and dangling curls, its bestiality tempered by delicacy. Its sorrowful look both appeals and repels. Another version of *The Scapegoat*, begun earlier and finished after the 1856 exhibition, features a darker, bolder animal, with pointed horns. This goat's aggressive, wall-eyed stare is even slightly menacing. The softened, flat-horned version of the exhibition, in contrast, flounders in the helplessness of the sacrificial position.

The theme of James's anecdote is "initiation"; most obviously, into the "mystery"—both thrilling and terrifying—of art.[2] Aesthetic initiation has an explicit physical register: mental awakening is matched by the transformation of the body that confines it. Both have entered upon an unparalleled "season" of growth. The complexity of James's perspective here, the charged response of an adolescent recalled in the monumental tones of a seventy-year-old, enhances his appreciation of the painting's own layered meanings. As James reads it, *The Scapegoat* is not simply about individual

process, how transitions of mind and body are experienced by sensitive souls (human or beast). The painting is also about society, specifically about the protections it affords some of its members and denies others. For the goat is a sin-laden offering, driven into the wilderness on behalf of the community. In this instance, the miraculous red ribbon—destined, the Talmud predicted, to whiten "if the propitiation were accepted"—denotes collective rather than individual sparing.[3] James is ambiguous about what has disturbed his adolescent perceiver most. Is it scarier to be "alone" or "in company"? According to one contemporary reviewer, *The Scapegoat* pictures "a perfect type of innocence and helplessness, sent to die for the superstition, the senseless selfishness, the ignorance and cruelty of the people—a sacrifice of any day and any place."[4] It is as if Henry James wrote the review himself, or read it and let it frame his memory of Hunt's painting. The brief anecdote in *A Small Boy* confirms the tie between adolescent initiation and sacrificial exile, between individual isolation and the dangers of sociability. It highlights the special significance of social protections for those in liminal or vulnerable positions and raises the question of what happens when these protections fail, when rites of passage, the shepherding of society's members from one status to the next, get foiled in some way. What happens when certain rites clash with others, when symbolic acts necessary to one group impair or nullify symbolic acts essential to another?

James's legendary encounter with *The Scapegoat* occurred years before the launching of his own artistic career. Yet the painting appears to have had an enduring impact, reaching literary expression (perhaps more than once) before his 1913 memoir. I refer to *The Awkward Age*, James's own terrible portrait of a feminized innocence done in by a people's "senseless selfishness." There are striking resemblances between James's adolescent reaction to Hunt and the themes of his 1899 novel: initiation, innocence, shelter and exposure. The affinities run deeper. The novel's two female adolescents, Aggie and Nanda, are introduced as photographed images, framed, respectively, by "something that looked like crimson fur" and by "glazed white wood." "Innocent lambs," they are generic kin to Hunt's goat, with its own semblance of crimson fur.[5] A later composite image of the pair amplifies the Hunt parallel. Here, Aggie and Nanda are "lambs . . . one with its neck in a pink ribbon had no consciousness but that of being fed from the hand with the small sweet biscuit of unobjectionable knowledge, the other struggled with instincts and forebodings, with the suspicion of its doom and the far-borne scent, in the flowery fields, of blood" (181). While one beast has been taught nothing, the other has been taught to know its doom in terms that are explicitly biblical. Recall that observances for the Day of Atonement featured two goats; the pure offering was sacrificed in the Temple, while the other (which seems to have caught the imaginations of Hunt and James) was defiled and exiled. The faint, red-tinged ribbon of the ignorant animal is an amulet or, in scientific terms, an immunization against "objectionable knowledge." The "sweet biscuit" is the communion wafer that absolves sin (Aggie has the look of one "prepared . . . by a cluster of doting nuns" [87]). It is also a euphemism for communal good will: we preserve your innocence, celebrate it, then offer you up as a prime specimen. The unfettered neck of the other beast symbolizes a damning knowledge. Thus James reenvisions the banished Levitican goat as a turn-of-the-century female adolescent, with "all the iniquities of the children of Israel" upon her head.[6]

The terror of adolescence for James is in great part a product of the emotions it arouses in others. James's novel, he writes retrospectively in the preface (1908), centers on the threat that this period "of tension and apprehension" poses for society as a whole (11). One of the principal concerns of *The Awkward Age* is the problem of generational conflict. In the scene of the two lambs, James's point of view is closest to that of his fifty-six-year-old reflector.[7] Yet perhaps more than in any other work, James's sympathies are richly multiplied. He employs his unusual technique (*The Golden Bowl* is another example) of designating a dominant character for each of the novel's ten books: Lady Julia, Little Aggie, Mr. Longdon, and so on. James identifies successively with his aging spectator, Mr. Longdon; with the adolescent girls; with Mitchy, the community's virtuous parvenu; with Vanderbank, the repressed homosexual. Rites of passage in *The Awkward Age* are always particular. The novel confirms, for example, that adolescence often accompanies the maternal transition into middle age. As defined by a medical textbook of 1899, menopause signals the end of a process begun at puberty. Hence, the adolescent daughter and her mother represent a pair of human borders—origin and end—for a single biological process.[8] According to anthropological accounts from the period, moderns and "primitives" shared a belief in the scarcity of female reproductive capacities. The onset of barrenness in a mother was the price paid for the fertility of a daughter. Emergent vitality in one human quarter required its diminishment in another. Assumptions of this kind provide a context for understanding why a mother might have regarded the debut of a daughter with "terror."[9] The initiation theme extends to the author himself. Following the catastrophe of his theatre debut James, according to one biographer, settled into his "late period" in the guise of an "aging moralist" ("There is nothing," he quipped, "so dead as a dead play").[10] As England lumbers into the modern era, rites of passage for nations, families, and artists are tested and found wanting.

The novel's titular type stands for historical as well as biological transition. Female adolescence becomes a valuably concentrated model of change. James magnifies this event and shows how it affects and illuminates all social experience. It would seem to have little, if anything, to do with the novel's opening, a description (uncharacteristic in James) of weather conditions.

Save when it happened to rain Vanderbank always walked home, but he usually took a hansom when the rain was moderate and adopted the preference of the philosopher when it was heavy. On this occasion he therefore recognized, as the servant opened the door, a congruity between the weather and the "four-wheeler" that, in the empty street, under the glazed radiance, waited and trickled and blackly glittered. (27)

Vanderbank's recognition of a "congruity" between his hansom and the rain suggests how he has revised an inevitable causal sequence. He has converted his routine response to nature into a natural effect itself. Nature's fluctuations (the rain) and Vanderbank's mode of transport (the vehicle) become equivalent parts of a scene. Imaged as a series of mystified contingencies—time, death, reproduction—nature in this novel (like the female adolescents who are identified with its processes) is alternately manipulated and revered.

The ritual keynote of this opening is purification. James depicts watery rites, the symbolic cleansing designed to rid a community of pollution. The novel's first word, "Save," the image of a vehicle intended, perhaps, for the removal of collective sin, and the emphasis on the character's own ritualized action invite us to read rain symbolically. This was a familiar task for turn-of-the-century social scientists and theologians, anxious about the condition of modern values and beliefs and eager to exploit possible means for their revitalization. The association of rain and water with moral redemption was a commonplace in books by James Frazer, Jane Harrison, and Edward Westermarck.[11] Westermarck noted an ancient tradition linking such rites to acts of charity: "As water will quench a flaming fire, so alms maketh an atonement for sins."[12] The significance of Westermarck's history for James's novel will become apparent in the pages that follow. For now, let me simply emphasize that washing rituals have a special pertinence to initiation ceremonies, which often culminate in a symbolic purification. Salvation in this scene is not an accomplished fact; it is wishful thinking. James begins in prescription, offering an antidote for a social "disease" that has yet to be detailed.

One of my purposes in this chapter is to reanimate some of the preoccupations shared by literary authors, theologians, and social scientists during the time of Anglo-American social scientific development. I want to explore the relationship between debates surrounding the social sciences, especially sociology, and a widespread imagination of decline: declining universals and moral principles.[13] The tensions or antitheses described by

Anglo-American social scientists—nature versus culture, determinism versus instrumentalism, laissez-faire capitalism versus socialism—were very often couched in spiritual terminologies. A survey of works that figured prominently in turn-of-the-century discussions on the state of the nation confirms that morals had become a matter of political as well as literary and scientific concern. These works include Arthur Balfour's *The Foundations of Belief*, Karl Pearson's *The Chances of Death*, Edward Westermarck's *The Origin and Development of the Moral Ideas*, Thomas Huxley's *Evolution and Ethics*, and Herbert Spencer's notorious attack, "The Sins of Legislators." As an avid moral spectator himself, Henry James might have noticed some family resemblance among these areas of interest. For the James family itself embodied the intersection of theological, scientific, and literary inquiry.

Critics have usually minimized the impact of Henry James Sr.'s theology on the fiction of his more famous son.[14] Yet the elder James was at the forefront of early efforts to discover a role for religious devotion in the modern era. He was preoccupied with two subjects that were of special concern to novelists and social scientists—the problem of individualism and the position of women—and his writings reflect an ongoing interest in the subjects of kinship and sympathy. Obviously, there were avenues for the intellectual compatibility of father and son. Exploration of the parallels between Henry James Jr. and his brother William has been more consistent.[15] James was familiar with his brother's philosophical and social scientific ideas, and he often provided an audience for the fierce disputes between William and Henry Sr. on questions of human autonomy. An apparently careful reader of both their writings, Henry's knowledge of prevailing theological and social scientific controversies would have equaled that of any serious intellectual. There is substance, however, in the claim that the younger James was alienated from the professions of his father and brother. Whether the cause was arrogance, rivalry, insecurity, or simple craving for intellectual space, Henry Jr. habitually opposed his own vocational endeavors to theirs.[16]

What seems critical about the *Scapegoat* episode, as captured in *A Small Boy and Others*, is that the fourteen-year-old William, a fledgling painter at the time, was present. The narrative "we" includes him, but his response is omitted. Is this the likely oversight of a vitalized, even traumatized subjectivity? Henry is alive to the meaning of sacrifice. This singular susceptibility to the plight of the goat suggests an intuition of his own emergent sexuality. Heaped with sin and exiled, this feminized beast may represent Henry's glimmering recognition of his complicated sexuality.[17] Henry concedes later in the autobiography (*The Middle Years*) an acute sensitivity to the "material pressure of things." This "pleasure in materiality and embeddedness," in one critic's view, was a "way of resisting his father's ascetic abstractions."[18] But "pleasure," as *A Small Boy* makes clear, is not the only issue of this Jamesian sensibility. In the memorable encounter with Hunt, Henry is overwhelmed by his own openness to a tragically embodied suffering. We have to fill in William where we can, as "company" and, possibly, as a compassion that resists speech. It may be relevant that traumatic illness in the father and brothers took antithetical mental and physical forms. William, who was plagued by a fear of idiocy, had nervous breakdowns resembling his father's Swedenborgian "vastations," while Henry's legendary "hurt" appears to have been physical.[19]

The hypothetical distance between Henry's and William's reactions to sacrificial exile would be of less moment were it not replayed in their work. Like his father, who renounced sacrifice as a backward custom (associated with barbaric races like the Jews), William simply dismissed its relevance to modern civilization. Given the emphatic nature of these positions, Henry James's choice to make renunciation the obligatory gesture of his heroes and heroines and communal sacrifice the basic dramatic event in their lives seems a deliberate departure from paternal and fraternal prescriptions. Rejecting the "fundamental truths of science and religion" extolled by his father, Henry James built a fictional empire from the uncontrollable and ineffable matter of social life. Like so many other intellectuals of his time, James chose a circuitous path, recasting Henry Sr.'s positivistic religion in the ancient, mysterious, and resoundingly metaspiritual tones of sacrifice.

Sacrifice is a convention in James's fiction.[20] It comes naturally to his characters; it drives his plots; it defines social relations. It can be a quality of memory ("The Jolly Corner"); the condition of sociality (*The Sacred Fount*); a political practice, at once ordinary and essential (*The Bostonians*); the source of ritual and belief ("The Altar of the Dead," *The Wings of the Dove*).[21] In the work of the major phase, inclination becomes preoccupation. *The Awkward Age* can be read as initiatory in its own right. The novel provides a preliminary mapping of James's sacrificial imagination. Here sacrifice is transformed from a thematic or dramaturgical effect to a theoretical problem. It is no surprise to learn that James was familiar with an enormous variety of contemporary social scientific works that included prominent treatments of sacrifice. He owned, and apparently read, many of them and knew some of their authors. There is a context, made up of different engagements, some solitary (as in reading), some social (as in friendships and conversations), to help us account for the intellectual overlap between James's novel and these social scientific studies. In keeping with the analyses of Edward Tylor, James Frazer, Gilbert Murray, and William Robertson Smith, *The Awkward Age* portrays sacrifice as a religious rite with significant social and political implications. The novel views sacrifice as essential in times of acute transition. It can help to assuage the insecurity of a weakened nation confronting more resourceful or progressive neighbors. It is critical to the reconciliation of intergenerational conflict. The perverse, upside down world of James's novel features numerous barbarisms. Hatred is the dominant maternal emotion and celibacy the ideal sexual stance (with nymphomania its degraded alternative). Women are tigers and men "carnivorous." Natural processes of succession are distorted, and danger is literalized (rather than ritualized), so that natural terrors—of growth, displacement, and decay—are laid bare.

Society in *The Awkward Age* is beset with a "cosmic paranoia."[22] James's modern England depends on sacrifice. Characters repeatedly voice feelings of disorientation and disconnection from tradition and spiritual meaning. Much is made of religious occasions and forms, as if these might be reinvigorated through sheer force of words. The plot begins with preparations for Easter, and many key scenes are set on Sundays, holy days acknowledged by all and respected by few. The novel is especially concerned with the subject of maternal sacrifice. It explores the new reluctance of women to accept the exclusive roles of reproduction and childrearing in terms of changing cultural assumptions about caretaking and social "welfare." Such concerns provided the dominant themes for contemporary social scientific debate. The laissez-faire position was formulated by Herbert Spencer and Benjamin Kidd, who repudiated governmental attempts to regulate a natural, progressive struggle for existence. This was countered by the ethnic socialism of Karl Pearson and the Webbs (Beatrice and Sidney), who urged state control over opportunities and rewards in order to keep England internationally competitive. The conclusions of Leonard Hobhouse, Edward Westermarck, and Thomas Huxley, which fall somewhere in between these positions, are closest to the prevailing perspective of *The Awkward Age*. They can be briefly summarized. There is continuity between traditional and modern morals, between the decline of the family as a factor in socialization and the increasing role of the state in administering to social needs. All of these writers confirm a shift in conceptions of human welfare: from a local obligation of families and citizens to a bureaucratic function of civil service and private corporations. It is precisely at the point when capitalism's intensification—through heightened industrialization and technological development, spurred by new colonial resources and markets—has begun to realize the prospects for expanded social wealth that the question of collective responsibility for the unfortunate becomes a matter of pressing political significance.

My claim is that modern welfare, as it was conceived at the turn of the century, was a derivation of ancient sacrificial practices. Every now and then this emergent ideology became intelligible to a contemporary observer in these historical terms. Westermarck's *Origin and Development of the Moral Ideas* (1906) and James's *The Awkward Age* are two exemplary records of this understanding. They see public assistance as the culmination of a moral tradition linking alms and sacrifice. Modern welfare was a form of charity, a means by which the rich secured their positions in this life, and perhaps in the life to come. Some of the underlying assumptions of an emerging welfare state that will be brought out in this chapter ranged beyond the insights of any one artist or thinker. But I believe James's novel absorbs many of them as a common consciousness, subject to constant challenge and revision. For the characters of *The Awkward Age*, "tit for tat" (modern London's variation on "do ut des") is not only the basis for all sound economy, it is the way of the world. This chapter examines James's 1899 novel as an enormously subtle, yet comprehensive and informed, account of transition: individual, collective, and national. My object in part is to revalue a relatively neglected work in James's canon. What makes a novel valuable in this reading is the range of its cultural apprehensions, its ability to make aesthetic form resonate with the specific plights of a culture. No work of James's speaks to the pressures and solutions of his time like *The Awkward Age*. *The Awkward Age* is the privileged text in this analysis, and it is also a text among many texts. It is privileged because it reveals sacrifice as a preeminent category of thought. It is a text among many because it speaks, in its own rare way, a common language of sacrifice.

Sacrifice, I argue, is the medium for paranoia in James's fictional society. The general obsession with the rite confirms a prevailing sense of powerlessness before the forces that control human lives. It provides a rhetoric for the revaluation of a waning maternal function. It supplies an ancient sanction for a modern welfare system. Contemporary analysts traced the idea of sacrificial alms from the Talmud, through Roman statutory law, to Christian notions of charity. A portion of all wealth, these various cultures enjoin, belongs by rights to the poor. When modern governments compensated the destitute, they were acting in fulfillment of a long tradition: the rich purchased their salvation by sacrificing part of it to those in need, who thus became instruments of salvation. The wealthy purge themselves of some of their wealth (at the same time spreading it around a bit), to ensure spiritual favor and social stability.[23] Sacrifice is a rite of purification, designed to concentrate (by embodiment) and expel group sin. Finally, sacrifice is conceived as a means for the ritualization of uncontrolled appetite: consumption becomes a way of feeding God or a key aspect of initiation ceremonies (where initiates are alternately starved and feasted). In the first part of this chapter, I focus on questions of a specifically religious nature: the various symbolic rites invoked and violated by the novel's society; the problem of salvation; the characters' rhetorical preoccupation with sacrifice. In the second part, I focus on questions of sexuality; different conceptions of the maternal body; the discourse of homosexuality; the treatment of female reproduction and menopause; the bodily acts of consumption and waste, purity and pollution, that govern rites of passage. In the third part, I focus on conditions of state. The challenge posed by Benjamin Jowett's remark, "If religion is to be saved at all it must be through the laity and statesmen," is assessed through an exploration of how sacrificial ideas mediated the divide between secular and spiritual realms in this era. The principle of sacrificial exchange that animates every human relationship in the novel extends to a larger social policy of sacrificial alms or collective welfare. None of these parts is separable from any other. Their common element is the rite of force and connection that expressed at once spiritual diminishment, the possibility of cultural purification, and a vital economic mode.

Spiritual Conditions

If one were to try to pinpoint the cerebral quality of James's writing, the late work in particular, it would not be inappropriate to say that it approaches at times the tones of theology. One might draw support from James's own frequent references to "the temple of art" or the christening of his literary vocation "a religion of doing." There is obvious irony in James's rhetoric (some of it probably at the expense of his father). But in *The Awkward Age*, he takes spiritual matters seriously in a way that differs from his previous works. He asks us to imagine a society obsessed with its fallen state, a society so secular that every religious gesture seems false and empty. The chasm between the collective will to believe and the complete inability to do so supplies its share of comic occasions, but never without a tragic edge. Beneath every comic deflation of spiritual anxiety lies the threat of real violence. It is as if James's habit of mock reverence had been brought to bear upon a scene of genuine religious desperation and clashed with it. One result is that the observances of the local inhabitants look both barren and excessive. Religious stakes in the novel are high, but they exist in a vacuum. Religious import is everywhere: priests, temples, sacred groves, goddesses, and pagans. People contemplate with great seriousness whether they are, individually or collectively, lost or saved. Some seek institutional blessings, while others take comfort in superstition. The majority of these references are specific to sacrifice: altars, lambs for slaughter, acts of martyrdom and betrayal, cups of sorrow, feasts and oblations. Mrs. Brookenham's Sunday teas, for instance, feature "platters" passed round with "nice little round" offerings (34, 63). It seems hardly coincidental that the novel opens on preparations for Easter, and the characters remind one another continually of its approach. The typical Jamesian atmosphere of conspiracy is brought to a new level of intensity.

This atmospheric pressure is made palpable by the actual air in which many of these encounters take place. The novel's settings are extraordinarily smoky. So many characters smoke, and so much is made of this fact, that a pervasive "mal aria" seems a small price to pay (194). Graver dangers are implied by the imaging of one character as an "extinguisher of fire" (192). As a visitor, on his third cigarette, exclaims: "I never, at home, smoke so much!" (38). It's not simply that the characters make one another nervous, though they do. All this smokiness seems to have a decided religious import.[24] Smoke, we know, is essential to sacrifice. The gods consume it; it is part of what they get from the rite. Smoke purifies and consecrates the ritual ground.[25]

The prominence of sacrifice in the novel proper is confirmed by the preface. The stage is set by a novelistic germ fostered in a "tropic air . . . a deep warm jungle" (10). The entry of the female adolescent into the decadent world of parlor conversation is "a crisis" or "mild revolution" (8). Then comes the plot: freedom of conversation must necessarily "be sacrificed. . . . Some sacrifice in some quarter would have to be made . . . the nature and degree of the 'sacrifice' left very much to one's appreciation" (11). There is little irony in the observation that "these were ugly matters" (11). Sacrifice as presented here may be largely aesthetic and discursive. But such forms are continuous with more blatant acts. Relinquishments staged by artists in the safety of their studies or by conversationalists in the comfort of their drawing rooms are not to be treated with indifference or "levity."

From this perspective, James's confession of dependence on the "light and ironical" Gyp for his own dialogistic experiments seems all the more puzzling (14). Has he borrowed a formal lightness to alleviate his excessively solemn themes? Yet consider another prefatory contrast, between the neglect of his own novel and the extravagant popularity of Gyp. James's image for the indiscriminate audience is "a children's school-feast." The greedy "smack of lips," the clamour for "bread and jam," becomes a metaphor for mass appetite. "The general gullet" inhales the most "savourless dilution" or "boneless dispersion" and bypasses "good solid slices of fiction" (14). This passage seems as light and ironic as anything in Gyp. And the gesture is familiar: James snorting contemptuously at popular taste. But the deeper significance of this passage may be its bizarre inversion of sacrificial convention. These innocent bread and jam eaters summon a horrific (if hypothetical) prehistory of helpless innocents consumed by fire and gods.

The transformation of children, through the perverse inverse logic of this passage, from consumers to things consumed renders them equivalent to James's fictions. Consider the parallel between the monstrosity of *The Awkward Age* (and James's other overgrown offspring) and Mrs. Brookenham's mothering. What might monstrous texts and monstrous mothers have to do with sacrificed children? They represent two ends of the sacrificial enterprise. On one end there are books, James's doomed novels, whose only value is their ritual expendability. James recalls the "complete disrespect" that greeted his monstrous text, which is especially painful in view of the commercial "genius of Gyp" (22). The other end is the monstrous mother who sacrifices her child to win benefits of a more spiritual kind. Sir James Frazer's descriptions of child sacrifice in Polynesia rival the drama of James's own: "Before the introduction of Christianity there was not a single mother" whose hands were not dyed "in the blood of her offspring."[26] Frazer's image reinforces the richness and horror of James's Gyp anecdote. For there is considerable aggression on James's own part: a benighted theatre-going public is repaid with infantilization and sacrifice. James turns from this passage to nurse his grievances in an intimate description of craft. Sacrifice is now a matter of aesthetic transcendence: addressed to the "form lover," a discriminating god who can apprehend all that is given up on his behalf (18).

James's preface provides theory after the fact, the fact being a novel where sacrifice is not only the dominant social practice but the talk of the town. The first dialogue, fast-paced (for James) and informative, between a mature and respectable visitor (Longdon) and a young, sophisticated Londoner (Vanderbank), is termed "an occasion for sacrifices" (44). The idea of Mrs. Brookenham's distortion of the rite, in sacrificing her children instead of herself, is a fixture of her characterization from the start. Mrs. Brookenham is legendary in favoring a barbaric custom of child sacrifice over the maternal self-sacrifice that is sanctioned in modern times. Mitchy makes sacrifices for his love of Vanderbank (85); Lady Fanny is bereft—a condition defined by her lack of "grounds . . . for revenge" (98). Alliances and pacts are sealed through gestures of sacrifice (145). Ancestor worship, with its oblatory requirements, is a central part of the novel's kinship system. Indiscriminateness prevails: these people sacrifice children as readily as preferences. Mrs. Brookenham seems well justified in her perception that the community is "smothered" in "sacrifices" (211).

The novel's careful orchestration of the sacrifice theme is evident in the relationship between its opening and closing scenes: together they symbolize the ritual promise and completion of a single sacrificial event. The salvation prefigured in the rain is fulfilled by the late exile of the adolescent scapegoat. Poised beneath a "glazed" halo of light, suggesting movement, Vanderbank's four-wheeler is nothing less than a sacred conveyance for carrying off collective sin. Sin, like error, as understood by William Blake, can be "cast off" if it can be "given a body." The embodiment of sin or pollution, according to Victor Turner, is the goal of scapegoat rituals. In this classic form of apotropaic sacrifice, the scapegoat becomes a living image for all that is weak, forlorn, excessive, impossible, and offensive.[27] It is the image for everything that needs to be washed away. Rain and the coalescence of sin provide a symphonic beginning and end. And Vanderbank continues to be identified with ceremonials of this kind. For instance, he must first perform obligatory "ablutions and renewals" before joining a group at his home (112). Water is never simply water in this novel. It is always particular: "a cold spring rain," "a favouring rain," a "rain . . . different somehow from other rain" (51, 253, 254).

Yet sacrifice, as the novel portrays it, is a profoundly ambivalent enterprise. As a vehicle of communal redemption, the center of a sacred rite, the scapegoat is also sanctified. It becomes the embodiment of the inevitably double-sided coin of spirituality—at once sacred and profane, divine and secular. This signification, uniform but always mixed, explains why the designation of sacrificial victims can seem so complicated and contradictory. The *Awkward Age* community as a whole is unquestionably impure. This is despite the Duchess's testimony about "*periodical* public washings of dirty linen" (my emphasis), which also conveniently limits pollution by feminizing it. Her reference to the "sport[ing]" of "the articles purified" confirms that only the depraved make a point of their purity (94). Harold Brookenham's defense of his sister's virtue is addressed to a company he knows to be well versed in the Duchess's hard-nosed principles. Yet there is a larger wisdom here that speaks to the complications of sacrificial symbolism. For Nanda *is* pure, in the quality of her insight. She is a "fresh" perceiver, whose insights help to ventilate the noxious atmosphere sustained in part by the Duchess's gloomy realism. Nanda is naturally good, but unprotected. Her adolescent counterpart, the Duchess's ward, Aggie, is sealed off from the world with a primitive stringency. She is like the pubescent girls on the African Gold Coast, confined in cages until their initiation through marriage can begin. Yet the speed of Aggie's coming out betrays some inner defilement that has escaped the notice of her keepers at the nunnery. Natural virtue, many speculate, would have supported a more graceful entry into the social fold (305–6).

Whether doomed by nature or through the effects of socialization, neither female adolescent is spared. Aggie is immolated, then thrown to the ravenous Petherton. The costly pearls she wears, gifts from her "rich" and "hideous" husband, are recompense for the suffering this new status will entail (64, 308). Marriage, as the Duchess says, is "the smoke . . . the soot!—of the fire" (188). Appropriately, Aggie and Mitchy spend their honeymoon in the Greek and Roman regions of sacrifice, with Petherton in tow, preying on Mitchy's fortune and his wife. Nanda's exile might seem preferable to Aggie's fate. And yet the tone of this ending is as dark as anything in the book. Longdon stands ceremoniously before the female lamb, with "raised . . . hands." Nanda proclaims herself "a horrible impossible," and breaks down in utter submission to fate. The narrative calls it "her fall" and compares her "queer quaver" to "the flurry of a wild thing . . . uncaged." There is a marked reciprocity between the priest and the sin-heaped animal. Nanda's suffering, characterized as "their trouble," is shared with Longdon. In the classic sacrificial sense, their roles "both conjoined and divided them" (379–82). The union of Nanda and Longdon accomplishes the mingling of sacred and profane elements, defined by Mauss and Hubert as basic to the rite. "In Semitic ritual," they observe, "the laying on of hands" serves an equilibrating function. Through it, "the two personalities [sacrifier and victim] are fused together" (32). An inevitable result of this mutuality is the metamorphosis of both participants. This is the notorious magic of the sacrificial moment. James's despised goat assumes a divine cast: Nanda is "enthroned in high justice" (382). And Longdon is reminded of his own frailty, in keeping with Mauss and Hubert on "the religiosity" of the priest, which "diminishes progressively from the inception of the ceremony" (55).

Things are not quite so loose, however, as all this implies. Indeed, there are marked continuities between the positions of Nanda and Longdon in their first encounter and at the end. Theirs is a structured, ritual relation, without a lot of room for movement. Longdon's initial reaction to Nanda elicits an intuitive sense of danger. "What will he do to me?" she asks. "Anything dreadful?" Spectators at the scene anticipate the tragic nature of their relation (119). Here too there is a feeling of inevitable mutuality. She is "grim," "sad," "her honesty almost violent" (122–23, 126); he is "kind," "bewildered," needing to be "spared" (124, 126). The scene culminates with the pair together in tears (127). Nanda appears to be the sacrificial agent here, toying with the gods. James writes that "she alternately drew him on and warned him off" (127). Yet both meetings are arranged at Longdon's behest: in the first, Nanda is summoned to meet him; in the last, she responds to an overture on his part. By the end, his control is complete. He exudes an "air" of "final indoctrination," while she acts "with a certain compunction" (382). The preparations for exile are played out with the precision of a minuet.

But there is another scene in *The Awkward Age* that seems especially productive of this end. I refer to Nanda's lone private encounter with her mother. The mother-daughter relation is defined here by the subject of clothes. Far from trivializing their bond, however, this focus has the effect of solemnizing it. Nanda appears in her mother's drawing room in the wake of tea: "charming, feathered and ribboned, dressed in thin, fresh fabrics and faint colours" (231). Though she is a breath of fresh air, this seems only to depress and antagonize Mrs. Brookenham (231). The charming cut of Nanda's clothes reminds the mother of unpaid bills and inspires an image of additional expenses bound to accrue in the high-stakes game of courtship and marriage. Clothes are dangerous. They inspire deception: dressmakers prevaricate, and customers return the favor. One should dress, Mrs. Brookenham recommends, with one's enemies in mind. "It's best," she comments, "if it's a person one's afraid of" (232). Clothes and furniture always have symbolic weight in James's novels.[28] But the task of dressing the female adolescent has a unique gravity in *The Awkward Age*.[29] Nanda's encounter with her mother is foreshadowed by a scene where Longdon and Vanderbank outfit Nanda in period costume. The tenor of their activity is intellectual, even antiquarian, but it's hard to resist a comparison to children playing with dolls. Every detail is worthy of attention, down to the shape of the bonnet and lacing of sandals (121). Obliged to replace their pliable manikin with the real thing, their disappointment is pronounced. All this talk of Nanda's clothes has to do with a subliminal awareness on the part of the community as a whole. This is the collective anticipation of her status as a sacrificial victim, whose dress requires great care.

Are the sacrificial innuendos and allusions, the talk of pollution and purity, anything more than grimly comic reminders of spiritual dislocation? Is there a place for sacrifice in the modern age? Gilbert Murray, a contemporary scholar of Greek literature and religion, whose writings James knew, didn't think so.

The extraordinary security of our modern life in times of peace makes it hard for us to realize, except by a definite effort of the imagination, the constant precariousness, the frightful proximity of death, that was usual in these weak ancient communities. They were in fear of wild beasts; they were helpless against floods, helpless against pestilences. . . . And all the while they knew almost nothing of the real causes that made crops succeed or fail. They only felt sure it was somehow a matter of pollution, of unexpiated defilement. It is this state of things that explains the curious cruelty of early agricultural doings, the human sacrifices, the scapegoats, the tearing in pieces of living animals, and perhaps of living men, the steeping of the fields in blood. Like most cruelty it has its roots in terror, terror of the breach of Tabu—the Forbidden Thing."[30]

The resonance between Murray's image and James's lambs, in their own "fields of blood," suggests a shared world of meaning. Both invoke the idea of agricultural oblations: "the periodical sacrifices" performed by farmers "to procure a shred of flesh for [their] fields," so that they might flourish.[31] Murray confidently projects distance from barbarisms such as these.

Though he was drawn to sacrifice, like so many other theologians and social scientists of his time, Murray had no apparent interest in exploring the basis of his attraction. James makes this attraction the starting point of his narrative. Every feature of Murray's Hellenistic world is anticipated by the one James creates. His characters fear everything: "wild beasts," "defilement," "death." Modern society, as James portrays it, is "frighten [ing]," "morbid" (49, 78). "Perils" are everywhere, and "precautions" are required. "Carnivores" prey on the weak or abject; a sense of apocalypse prevails (76, 184). Characters speak of their world as "fallen" or "past saving" (34, 39, 49). They envision the nouveaux riches as grasshoppers, visitors as swarms of locusts. Together they anticipate "the end of everything": some natural apocalypse seems imminent. There is even a Murray prototype: James's Mitchy, the millionaire "son of a shoemaker," with a golden heart and fortune, is Murray's "good man," resigned to "pessimism." In Murray's words, having lost "self-confidence . . . hope in this life," and "faith in normal human effort," he has developed an "indifference to the welfare of the state" (103). Martyrdom is his only option. What seems especially compelling about the resemblances between Murray's "ancient communities" and James's modern one is that Murray's analytical perspective seems integral to James's text. James seeks to dramatize the continuities between the barbarian past and the present. But he is equally interested in, and eager to explain, the ongoing fascination with sacrifice. Edward Westermarck, whose work concerned the evolution of moral ideas, met James halfway in locating sacrifice in the "past history" of "every so-called Aryan race." He went on to observe that far from a "savage" custom, sacrifice was more prevalent "among barbarians and semi-civilized peoples." His conclusion (borrowed from Winwood Reade) was even more significant: "the more powerful the nation the grander the sacrifice" (1: 434, 436–37).

Sacrifice is always partly about the restoration of boundaries and definitions. According to Victor Turner, "sacrifices express discontinuities and thus create structure." He notes that Latin sacrifice in particular, where ritual action is bound by "written rubrics" and dictated by a "hierarchy of deities," is "linked with the demarcation of frameworks in space and time." The disorder articulated by sacrifice is very often associated with kinship: concerns about the difficulty of preserving ethnic identities, or marking off one communal boundary from another. This is why the practice of sacrifice is so common among besieged or exiled peoples. To sacrifice is to recover a sense of "holiness," whose basis is completeness: the assurance that "different classes of things shall not be confused."[32] Characters in *The Awkward Age* think about things like the place of their civilization in some general universal scheme. They note changes in constellations and planetary movement and use these as points of reference for their own fluctuating alliances. They lie awake at night imagining meteors swallowing up the sky, or the moon falling to earth and crushing it. Beset with the "cosmic paranoia" attributed to "Hellenistic man, who sees danger and threat everywhere . . . the old structure of the *polis* was broken down and man was understood to be a *cosmopolitan*, a citizen of the entire cosmos, and this was too big." This leads to planetary reversals of the kind described by Plato's statesman, where " 'God relinquishes control over the revolution of the cosmos,' and then Fate and innate desire reversed the motion of the world."[33]

A geoplanetary sixth sense is part of the general consciousness in James's novel. Mrs. Brookenham's management of her circle is analogized to the moon's governance of tidal ebbs and flows. Characters are alternately fixed stars and flashing meteors (357–58). Most of their talk is cynical and bleak. They have little control over the forces they imagine close at hand. It seems natural that in such a world "the fortunes of men [would] seem to bear practically no relation to their merits and efforts."[34] Action in *The Awkward Age* is stymied, Hamlet-like. The novel's opening paragraph, for example, offers the spectacle of a man regarding his own habits as objective parts of a scene. Sentence constructions emphasize events over actors— characters are portrayed as *objects* of action. The first interactions described are similarly qualified. Vanderbank, seated in the carriage with Longdon, "became conscious of having proposed his own rooms as a wind-up to their drive." And Longdon refers dreamily to "this queer view of the doom of coming back" (27–28). Like sleepwalkers, they blurt out invitations they are conscious of only retrospectively, submit to actions whose consequences they barely perceive.[35] Characters are taunted with predetermined outcomes presented to them as options to accept or disregard. Such false stagings of choice plague the younger characters in particular—the best and brightest, most likely to harbor expectations. Vanderbank's decision to marry Nanda is nullified by an inexorable "law of kind," presumably, homosexuality. Nanda's decision to accompany her "pistol"-bearing "priest" into exile is voided by the fact that she has nowhere else to go. Falsification in Nanda's case is especially heightened, in keeping with the peculiar injunction imposed on the sacrificial victim by "advanced systems": she (or he or it) "must go willingly."[36]

The exceptional pressures on human agency in James's novel, and in the works of historical theology and social science whose concerns it shares, were codified in the emergent discipline these authors were helping to shape. *The Awkward Age* dramatizes a transformation in social thought. The gradual unfolding of the novel's first paragraph, the scene of "radiant" rain, from an instinctive habitual action, to speculation about action, to a reconceptualization of natural determinations, provides a miraculously compressed allegory of this transformation. A modern worldview that conceives action instrumentally replaces a traditional worldview in which action is founded on received rules of conduct. Social life is reinscribed in a new gospel text, whose dogma is scientific laws of prediction and control.[37] Human action acquires the causal potency of natural determinations, which has a curious double effect. On the one hand human beings appear as powerful agents, capable of altering their world in parity with nature. On the other hand, they are caught like any natural object, in the web of action and consequence that is seen to comprise the social and natural world.

Thus, the novel's characters exhibit contradictory tendencies toward deliberateness and paralysis. Longdon is a ghost from an earlier era, an outsider at the mercy of the conniving London circle whose codes he only partly understands. Yet he is also the source of the novel's plot, the character whose wealth and emotional needs drive the dramatic action. Vanderbank seems incurably passive, subject to the whims of Mrs. Brookenham, and to a vague nostalgic sense of sexual propriety. Yet he is also the man with everything, irresistible to women and men, Deputy Chairman of the General Audit with a "head" for figures in an era that prizes statistics as the source of intelligent social action. Both believe in human abilities to shape social life and recognize the necessity for doing so, yet they are anxious about the prospect, about how far such effects could and should go. Longdon and Vanderbank epitomize the dilemma of Anglo-American intellectuals in the late nineteenth century. They see human actors as more capable of controlling their world but at the same time as more subject to its self-perpetuating processes. James's keen awareness of his era's growing pains makes him intellectually responsive to other periods of pronounced social transition.

The State of the Body

The demoralized social order of *The Awkward Age* informs every type of body featured in the text. The unnatural state of physical affairs is not an outcome of spiritual torment. It is rather another manifestation of physical dis-ease. The idea of aristocratic regression, for instance, was neither original nor unique to the late nineteenth century. The ruling classes had long been vulnerable to charges of degeneracy and decadence. With the rise of social scientific methods of classification, however, the aristocracy began to appear on charts beside other groups perceived as unstable or even as close to extinction.[38] *The Awkward Age*'s Lord Petherton is an upper-class case in point. He is "dangerous," identified with "brutality" and "aggression." To call him "supercivilized" is to imply that any sign of gentility is compensatory: not only hard-won, but also mainly decorative (76). Recall Petherton's relationship to Mitchy, which is frankly parasitic. And Petherton is always threatening to sink his "carnivorous teeth" into Aggie. His appetite for the little round offerings handed out at Mrs. Brookenham's is equally prodigious. But there is no spiritual accent here. Petherton's indiscriminate hunger is the sign of a degradation common to all but identified in particular with women. Lady Fanny, for example, combines the serenity of the domestic pet with the pent-up hostility of the zoo animal, capable of killing a keeper to prove that the wild remains an ongoing danger. She inspires various metaphors: "tame tigress," "great glorious pagan," "some great natural poetic thing—an Alpine sunrise or a big high tide" (96, 134). These images pit a human ideal of cultivation and predictability against some premise of absolute freedom. As a "pagan" dominated by "instinct," Lady Fanny appears immune to mediation. As "natural" poetry—a "high tide," an "Alpine sunrise"—she betrays an enviable (and inhuman) regularity.

Lady Fanny embodies a distinction between nature as an anarchic force and nature as design. Nature's most threatening aspects, as well as their successful containment, reside in one monumentally restless personality. Her naturalization has a curious double effect. Implying a precivilized disorder, it justifies controlling her. Implying poetic order, it signifies the means for her reinscription into the culture. All the novel's women are fixed in "the awkward age," prey to an adolescence they've never overcome. They fulfill the diagnosis made by James's contemporary, the psychologist G. Stanley Hall, that "woman at her best never outgrows adolescence." Hall's maturity index was applied to whole cultures, as exemplified by the claim that "primitive people's represented the childhood and adolescence of the race." In Hall's theories, Anglo-Saxon women of the middle and upper classes are, simultaneously, vessels of racial purity and kin to the "primitive" populations at home and abroad who threaten it.[39] Like the groups whose situations they both reflect and oppose, women are key objects of a culture of vigilance. And yet, in James's depiction, women are accomplices as well as victims. Educators and social typologists, they are society's main boundary makers. Women in *The Awkward Age* represent a sociological ideal: a threatening social group that assists in its own regulation.[40]

Perhaps the most striking thing about James's community of women is its barrenness. Mrs. Brookenham is the only woman who mothers natural children. And in this sense especially, *The Awkward Age* articulates a typical feature of prevailing social opinion. In "Socialism and Natural Selection" (1894), Karl Pearson coined his own tigress image to illustrate a "maternal instinct" gone awry. His controversial *Fortnightly Review* piece makes a case for an intelligent socialism that alleviates certain disparities without eliminating the benefits of international competition. As a nationalist inclined to value Darwinian struggle, Pearson believed that public policy might be split between internal and external prerogatives. He argued that lessening intragroup competition could increase social efficiency without compromising natural selection or national strength. With fellow scientist Francis Galton, Pearson supported a program of eugenics, the systematic recuperation of the elite's reproductive losses. Understood in terms of his essay's overall purpose—a plea for state control over reproduction—Pearson's tiger taunts us with damning analogies. "The evolution of the maternal instinct in the tigress," he writes, is "just as much a product of the cosmic process" as human altruism. We can trust that a mother tiger with "a thoughtful turn of mind" will be "capable of balancing physiological discomfort, maternal gratification, and the pangs of conscience against the pleasures of one hearty meal." If only we could project with such confidence the likely choices of the likeliest human mothers. Maternal reason in a tiger, Pearson implies, may be a safer bet than maternal instinct in women.[41] It is a short step from Pearson's logic to the state of maternity in James's novel, possibly the most unnatural condition of all.

MATERNITY

In the haunting story "The Mother of Monsters," Guy de Maupassant offered his own fictionalization of contemporary resistance to maternity. The story's title refers to an unwed peasant who conceals the shame of pregnancy with a corset of wood and ropes. This "terrible machine" so constricts her growing body that she produces a monster. Discovering that there is money in her "demon," which she is able to sell to a circus, she becomes a "monster-factory," deliberately producing deformed offspring "so that she would have a fixed income like the upper classes." The narrator is "reminded of this horrible story" while regarding a "young, elegant, and charming girl loved and respected by all" at "a watering place much frequented by the wealthy." His view sets off a chain of associations, from this girl, to the peasant woman, to another charming young woman of the upper class, "the most skillful of coquettes," who has two "monsters" of her own because she insists on keeping her "figure graceful right up to the last day." De Maupassant's peasant and upper-class women represent the evil feminine poles of the late-nineteenth-century demographic imagination: on one end is the peasant whose fertility becomes an ominous asset; on the other, the lady who won't sacrifice an inch of flesh. De Maupassant's conflation of biological reproduction and industrial manufacture suggests an implicit solution to the modern epidemic of denatured mothers: the substitution of scientific method for a feminine instinct grown unreliable.[42]

As an avid reader of de Maupassant, James would have known this story. Indeed, it gives one pause to hear him in the preface to *The Awkward Age* characterize the novel, and all of his overgrown works, as "monsters." Yet James is a benevolent creator. His monsters are the fruits of maternal indulgence rather than constraint, as the author nurtures their "endearing" yet "unforeseen principle of growth" (7). The generous maternal author in the preface seems a corrective to the mother in the text, who is distinguished as much by her own "monstrousness" (61, 210, 217, 230, 325, 332) as by her reproduction of monsters. There is no doubt that her children are tainted, but James centers the category of monstrosity in the mother who won't make sacrifices for her young. James seems to have devoted considerable thought to the problem of maternity and its relationship to national decline in this turn-of-the-century period. He responds to the death of Queen Victoria, for instance, in the inconsolable tones of an abandoned offspring: "One had ended by taking her for a kind of nursing mother of the land and of the empire, and by attaching to her duration an extraordinary idea of beneficence. This idea was just and her duration is over. It's a new era—and we don't know what it is."[43] Here, individual and national identity merge and blur: the loss of the motherly queen is a loss of definition on both counts. The withdrawal of the royal breast symbolizes a general decline of maternal feeling that weakens the empire.

This infantile expression of abandonment is linked to another image from the period: James witnessing a medical inspection of undernourished conscripts for the Boer War, a contemporary scene that often aroused denunciations of English mothering.[44] So pronounced was anxiety of this kind that Havelock Ellis declared that "the most vital problem before our civilisation today is the problem of motherhood, the question of creating human beings best suited for modern life."[45] James had long been engaged with these issues. In 1868, he evaluated a group of *Saturday Review* essays on contemporary women, with titles such as "The British Mother Takes Alarm" and "The Modern Revolt" ("the strange reaction against the maternal instinct," this essay reported, "so marked a social feature in America, is spreading rapidly here"). James could not disguise his irritation: the demand that women return to "the ancient fold" was "sensationalism" of the worst sort.[46] As an intellectual modernist, he partly sympathized with this "revolt." He even described literary production as a form of voluntary procreation that might relieve the suffocating expectations upon natural mothers. He was prepared to see in the waning of a certain mode of cultural transmission (associated with motherhood, biological inheritance, generational continuity) new opportunities for social authority and expertise.

James's portrait of Mrs. Brookenham (also known as "Mrs. Brook") in *The Awkward Age* absorbs all the complexity of this perspective. She is undeniably bitter, cold, even mean-spirited. Yet she is also remarkably sympathetic in her quest for the domination and control of her children and herself. She displays, in her first appearance, such a feat of maternal detachment as to suggest a complete reversal of custom. Some surprises are simply physical. The son, Harold, sounds like "a man of forty," while the mother is "silly," and "quavering" with a "light of youth" (52). Others are emotional and extreme. Mrs. Brook is disappointed to discover that her son has not disappeared as hoped but has lingered at home. This is no fleeting irritation: her children, she says, alternately "terrify," "appall," and "kill" her (53, 54). Like the ancient Greeks who confront the gods with fear and deprecation and practice sacrifice to keep them away, Mrs. Brook experiences "a kind of terror" in the presence of her children (51). How can one's children arouse such emotions? Adrienne Rich provides one answer: the age-old "dread of giving birth to monsters." She attributes this to guilt, deriving from women's sense of their sexuality as a source of defilement.[47]

But there are other reasons why women might imagine their children as monstrosities. Children, after all, are aliens temporarily housed within. A woman may feel fear no less than wonder in watching what has been part of her emerge as a different being. Mothering combines the experience of ultimate power (to create like a god) and utter lack of control. Like all things related to childbirth in particular, this doubleness has a physical as well as an intellectual dimension. An essential, though overlooked, aspect of childbirth derives from the proximity of the two reproductive orifices: one yielding life; the other, waste. The yield from the final, pushing stage of natural childbirth is an infant from one orifice and feces from another. The maternal body thus conjoins and divides invention and decomposition. In the ultimate act of creation, the body articulates the inevitability of death. We can understand these twin products of childbirth as the material foundation of maternal ambivalence. They reveal what is most excruciating, "appalling" (52), about becoming a mother: in the triumphant act of bringing forth a life, one's lack of control over one's body is complete. It is perhaps because of this profound contradiction that the symbolic implications of maternity seem so endless. Our thoughts and words struggle to overcome the traumatic duplicity of the maternal body. Following childbirth, as we have suggested, the mother is considered polluted, and most cultures prescribe elaborate cleansing ceremonies (beyond beneficial health measures) for both mother and child. In the majority of these cultures, the mother never completely escapes her taint. This assumption explains the initiation rites designed to sunder the mother-child bond as the initiate is drawn into full community membership.[48] Children must be formally separated from the maternal wasteland if their true social value is to be realized.

But children are also in some sense permanently defiled, at least in the deepest recesses of the maternal imagination, because of their intimate association with her feces. Like waste, children represent bodily processes the woman struggles to control, sometimes successfully, sometimes not. According to Georges Bataille, "the terror that so often accompanies involuntary defecation" is no ordinary matter. He classifies it, along with other conceptions of the foreign body within, as a potentially ecstatic notion that permits an analogy between the human and the divine. We fear what we can't control in our own bodies, because it reminds us of more sacred terrors.[49] Bataille's insistence on the double nature of foreign bodies within helps us to understand Mrs. Brook's abhorrence of her children as an acknowledgment of their sacred character. Children, like the mothers who carry them, are society's most valued and degraded goods, alternately cherished and violated. It is clear then that Mrs. Brook's compulsion to drive her children into various country outposts confirms a conviction of her own monstrosity. She is protecting them by keeping them "in other places," as Harold puts it (54). Yet it is equally obvious that her children are projections of what she most despises in herself, including the simple but terrible prospect of growth.

Mothers fear children because of their initial identification with feelings of physical helplessness. But children also signal maternal vulnerability in another form: the wasting and waning of maternal existence. Children are products of the self destined to outlast it, in the natural course of things. Though all women in her culture fear aging, Mrs. Brook, who has always banked on her youthfulness and gaiety, approaches middle age with acute desperation. Before she is even introduced, we learn that she habitually lies about age (her children's and, by implication, her own [37–38, 57]). And Nanda establishes her loyalty to her mother, once and for all, by celebrating her youth (356). Mrs. Brook's denial of aging, her aspiration to live without paying a biological price, is evidently at odds with the dominant sacrificial wisdom that governs her circle. Mrs. Brook is known among her friends for her refusal to make essential maternal sacrifices. Rather than compromise her decadent and self-indulgent ways, she imperils her offspring by exposing their innocence to the seductive amorality of her circle. The result is the sacrifice of her son's heart (Harold is a cynical gigolo) and her daughter's reputation (Nanda is notoriously "knowledgeable"). Mrs. Brook's maternal lapses are the subject of constant analysis, and she participates fully in her own objectification (61, 81).

Mrs. Brook is the architect of her own sacrificial crisis, which becomes, in effect, a crisis of interpretation. For what is most striking about her relationship to sacrifice is the tension between a general consensus that she has defied it and her own deep conviction that she has not. Mrs. Brook envisions herself as constantly forfeiting and spending, giving up and giving in. Her most obvious sacrifices are monetary. As her son Harold reminds her (after he has stolen five pounds from her drawer): "If I so far oblige you, I must at least be paid for it" (53). Her relationship to the Duchess is founded on the assumption of her loss or sacrifice: Mrs. Brook's "three or four comparatively good" pieces set against the Duchess's "three or four comparatively bad" (56). As a mother, her relationship to consumption, the feeding of others in particular, is a matter of some consequence. James is not known for lavish depictions of food. He tends toward more cerebral forms of consumption such as human parasitism. Mrs. Brook's habits of entertainment are predictably barren, but revealing. She presses the Duchess with her platter of "nice little round" edibles, though she directly limits her intake (63). Her drawing room is the preferred site of circle teas, and she has enough dinner parties to make the different guest lists a blur in her mind (72). She seems a perpetual hostess (the novel opens at the end of a Brookenham dinner), despite the fact that the Brookenhams are somewhat down on their luck. In contrast, Mrs. Brook's manner of feeding her own children seems exceedingly sparse. Her apparent willingness to nurture society at large stands in stark contrast to her treatment of her children. She can hardly wait to get Harold out of the house; there is little chance she will pause to offer him a cup of water, though tea is imminent. Following his departure, she promptly orders service for the eager Duchess (56). Her first statement to Nanda, when she happens to enter her mother's drawing room at the customary hour is a brusque, "Tea's gone" (231). Nanda's quick response is that she has anticipated the small Brookenham reserves by consuming "lots" prior to her return. So much is being spent on her clothes, her mother implies, she can hardly expect food on top of it. In an exceptional reference to a child feeding at home, we hear that Nanda's tea consists of one cup, "very weak, with a piece of bread-and-butter in the saucer" (113). Rather than being nurtured, Mrs. Brook's children are consumed.

In other words, Mrs. Brook feeds her society through her children, who are offered as food in explicitly sacrificial gestures. This is made plain by a dinner at Tishy Grendon's where the assembly appears unusually restless. Vanderbank is the first to arrive, with the look of a man "waiting for dinner" (279). Nanda is described as a "crust" offering to the "poor," what Tishy Grendon has "to live on" (295). Mrs. Brook characterizes her son as "a slighter creature," who attracts "great calm women." The Duchess completes her metaphor: Harold is one of "the little fishes" periodically "swallow[ed]" by "the great calm whales." Mrs. Brook responds by offering him to the nearest. "Harold can be tasted," she tells the Duchess, "if you like" (297). The scene can be understood as illustrating two sides of the same public policy coin. As a crust for those in need, Nanda outlines a milder socialism, the distribution of alms among the wretched to benefit the general welfare. As a little fish sent out to sink or swim, Harold suggests a Darwinian "survival of the fittest" model. Mrs. Brook's children are two different types of offering, representing opposite but complementary initiatives of the modern state.

There is no doubt about the sacrificial implications of the Brookenhams' method of childrearing through "foster-care." Yet there is ambiguity in the gesture. "[My husband and] I work it out between us to show off as tender parents and yet to get from you everything you'll give," Mrs. Brook announces to Longdon. "We deck ourselves in the glory of our sacrifice without forfeiting the 'keep' of our daughter" (300–301). The Brookenhams give so as not to lose, in defiance (not in fulfillment) of sacrifice. This is the claim, not necessarily the reality. And it's not clear whether their motivation is false pride, indifference, or aggression. As poor relatives—all wonder "what they live on" (31–32)—they lack the resources to purchase surrogates. Do the Brookenhams sacrifice their young as kin, because they consider them dear, or as strangers, because they consider them expendable or dangerous? The sign of their expendability is the fact that Mrs. Brook obviously prefers clearing them out, to cleaning up her parlor conversation. Like a Welsh King, Mrs. Brook decides that while her "intellectual habits" are irreplaceable, her child is not (192). (There are, after all, two younger siblings besides Nanda and Harold.) At the same time, the Brookenhams are reminiscent of the impoverished families in ancient times, who might give up one child in order to secure a bare subsistence for the family as a whole.[50] Still, Harold is not exactly sacrificed. Mrs. Brook is quick to point out that "he can't . . . be eaten" (298). All are in agreement, however, that the Brookenhams *have* sacrificed their adolescent daughter. Why is she selected out? What makes Nanda a suitable victim?

According to the novel, an elite's ability to control an emergent female sexuality, and with it their reproductive capacities, is a sign of its ability to control cultural transmission in general. Adolescent females in *The Awkward Age* require society's most elaborate forms of vigilance. As members of a group whose social purpose is both essential and unstable, they project contradiction. James describes female adolescence in the preface as a time of innocence and warns that the social entry of young women demands some purification of cultural habits. In the novel proper, however, the female adolescent is herself a threat to social mores. Every attempt to preserve the innocence of a young woman fails, and every failure is attributed to feminine nature rather than to social effects. Female adolescents are thought to embody a principle of difference. They, and by implication all the novel's women, symbolize society's most threatening yet potentially exploitable aspects. The preface is filled with metaphors of reproduction, and ends with a marked scientific rhetoric that is partly but never fully repudiated (24). This tension between scientific scrutiny and sympathetic insight permeates the novel, which holds a perspective on the circumstances of modern women that can be described as dialectical. *The Awkward Age* contributes to a contemporary ideology that reads women as agents of social decline. Yet it also takes a theoretical approach to that ideology and seeks to bring to light the destructive impact of socialization rituals for women. The novel approaches theory in drawing attention to the social forms impressed upon female adolescents. By showing how little of what is construed as female failure can be attributed to femininity, the novel exposes the fallacy of overidentifying any social group with nature.

This identification was potentially decisive, in part because the question of what could be considered "natural" and what could not was under such close scrutiny at this time. Anglo-American social scientists tended to divide according to their advocacy of laissez-faire versus instrumentalist policies. The premises of social Darwinism were in question and with them, the legitimacy of organic principles as bases for social order. This is why the association of certain groups—women, "natives," the working classes—with nature had such far-reaching effects. It justified their special subjection to social engineering. The fields of "social science" rested upon a paradox, legible in the term itself. Could there be a *scientific, objective* discipline where the (human) subjects to be analyzed were indistinguishable from the investigators themselves? At the point of institutionalization, this paradox was partly solved by the careful selection of groups to be studied—often social aliens or marginals. Their classifications enhanced and formalized already existing distinctions (whether of class, ethnicity, race, or gender).

As I have suggested with reference to G. Stanley Hall's research on adolescence, there was an inclination in this era to feminize social instability. The political crisis of late-nineteenth-century Anglo-American elites was remarkable for the forms it took and the resolutions it inspired. Because this crisis was tied to certain demographic facts—declining elite and bourgeois birth rates, rising lower-class birth rates, mass enfranchisement—it was obsessively figured in feminine terms. The crisis was reconciled in part through an alignment with the social sciences, which displayed an ongoing interest in the question of women's status. This was especially true of debates surrounding the emergence of sociology in the United States and England, where women's roles were a point of extreme controversy. It is from this perspective that we should understand letters like the following, addressed to the English Sociological Society's Forum on Eugenics. The new discipline's "most urgent task," declared Lady Welby, was "the training of all girls for the resumption of a lost power of race-motherhood, which shall make for their own happiness and well-being, in using these for the benefit of humanity." Sociology, she concluded, must help "to prepare the minds of women to take a truer view of their dominant natural impulse towards service and self-sacrifice."[51] Lady Welby's plea comes down to us as a confused cry in the wilderness of early sociology. But it should stand as a reminder of the attention paid in these debates to the changing status of women from all social classes. Bourgeois and upper-class women helped to ensure that women's losses and triumphs—questions of socialization and education; the transformation of maternity in a modern era; legal reforms, including impending women's suffrage and liberalized divorce and abortion laws, their participation in public welfare schemes—would be aired in discussions on this critical new form of social instrumentalism.

Sociologists responded uncertainly to these challenges. Predictably, they encouraged those who, like Lady Welby, reaffirmed traditional roles. But they recognized that the very presence of women's issues (and women themselves) in sociological debates confirmed irreversible changes. It is not surprising that in the work of major theorists, Lester Ward and G. Stanley Hall in the United States and Leonard Hobhouse and Karl Pearson in England, femininity becomes a figure for social disorder. This is all of paramount concern in *The Awkward Age*, whose ambiguous titular term seems designed to draw attention to the inseparability of different states of change—from the individual and particular to the collective and universal. James's drama of female adolescence and the rites of passage designed to mediate it provide an entry into what is perhaps the single most important question for early sociology: how does society mediate change?

ADOLESCENCE

One way, as the novel shows, is by ritual. Change (and those who are identified with it) is often associated with pollution. James implies this in the preface with a series of classifications: adolescence is "revolution" and "crisis" (8, 10, 11); adolescents are "merciless" and these "matters" overall are "ugly" (11). In these ways and more, James explains, a natural instance of growth becomes an "awkwardness" requiring reparatory "sacrifices" (12). James is not unsympathetic to such adjustments, for they make a good story. A writer can trust a teeming social order like London "never [to] leave . . . its true lover and believer long unprovided" (10). A basic property of dirt, ritually regarded, and this is true of modern urban grime, is that its removal requires its concentration. To be eradicated it must be embodied. What better form than the young women who have aroused all the anxiety about social pollution in the first place? This is one of the novel's key points: the female adolescent on whose behalf all the "public washing" (94) is begun is found to be its chief pollutant. Edward Westermarck's observation that sin in many cultures is considered "contagious matter," is enlightening in this respect. Sin, he notes, may be "transmitted from parents to children, or be communicated by contact": culpability can travel from the guilty to the innocent.[52]

Where categories of guilt and innocence are concerned, boundaries are notoriously indistinct. Hence innocents suffer, while sinners go free. Is it any wonder that the prospect of joining such a society seems perilous? Take the metaphor for beauty, "the red flag in front of the steam-roller" (43), and the fate of the female adolescent without it, "social bankruptcy." While the providential protections of the biblical red seem nullified by this image, the terrors of initiation are not. Like any new commodity, the adolescent depends on packaging: "staring, glaring, obvious." As a surplus item, she must create her own market, by cultivating an aura of novelty and, if possible, rarity. Popular taste is unforgiving if there is any hint of exhaustion.

Sources of potential ruination abound. Literary refuse, for example, on the order of the dialogistic "social studies" of Gyp is readily available. James confesses in the preface to having invoked "the Gyp taint " for "protection," suggesting that her influence has functioned like an immunization—innoculating him against her type by infecting him with its properties (14, 15, 21). These unsavory "offerings" are kept under lock and key, away from the young. But by the novel's end, both Harold and Nanda have read the "French novel" at issue, and Aggie engages in "hand-to-hand struggle" to get at it herself (283, 310, 305). In this society, James implies, an appetite for pulp fiction is as inevitable as breathing. These "abject" items neither edify nor satisfy (78). Where appetite rules the cultural marketplace, feeding only stimulates hunger. The collective taste for pulp fiction complicates the pervasive awareness that books are critical vehicles of cultural transmission.[53]

The characters obsess about matters of taste and offer contesting theories on how to promote certain values and outlaw others. Nanda has her own revealing metaphor—as sharp as it is spare—for the female adolescent's relationship to cultural deposits. She is "a sort of little drainpipe with everything flowing through" (260). What's immediately striking about Nanda's image is the way it recalls but mangles the opening properties of cleansing rain. While it might seem at most an innocent container, the more the drainpipe is contemplated, the more degraded it appears. A drainpipe channels extraneous flow or refuse, the very opposite of the precious rain showered like a gift from the sky. A drainpipe is an awkward contraption, associated neither with modern efficiency nor with artful craftsmanship. As a drainpipe, the female adolescent is simply exposed, to "everything" wasteful. The question of whether there is any alternative is the main focus of discussions between the novel's two maternal leads: Mrs. Brook and the Duchess. Their charges, Nanda and Aggie, are the product of opposite educational systems. The Duchess appears to have read her Westermarck, for she treats Aggie like an unimmunized infant in a sea of viruses. Aggie's first appearance suggests that this vigilance has paid off. She is "as slight and white, as delicately lovely, as a gathered garden lily," "shy," "submissive," "rare," and "virgin." Her whole being warns that she must be handled, if at all, "with precautionary finger-tips" (87). The miracle of Aggie moves Mrs. Brook to dramaturgical display: she affects the "shy little girl," all "wonder-struck" and "innocent eye[d]." This perverse parody of Aggie's innocence seems designed to shake or question it. But Mrs. Brook's playacting is no momentary inspiration. It is the keynote of her relations with her own daughter. Rather than "mount guard" in the authoritarian (and oddly sexualized) manner of the Duchess (88, 184), Mrs. Brook's preferred method of education is sympathetic identification. She seeks parity with female adolescents; her aim is to inhabit their perspective. This explains Mrs. Brook's baby talk in her first dialogue with Aggie: she's trying to get it exactly right, and she may have regressed too far ("Why, you dear, good strange 'ickle' thing"). Her perspective is inevitably a false sympathy or consciousness. It is either deflating, as in the imitation of Aggie, or punishing, as in the refusal to protect her daughter in any constructive maternal way. Mrs. Brook's struggle for equivalence is also, obviously, consistent with her anxiety about her own advancing middle age.

A part of her sincerely wishes to be an adolescent, to have this moment, however terrible in its own right, back again. She is always imagining how she might have dealt with Longdon in her daughter's place ("I would have gone in for little delicacies and odd things she has never thought of" [321]). And her own childhood is very much alive in her mind. In the presence of her daughter, what seems "remarkably established," in addition to the lack of any "vulgarity" between them, is the air of friendship (232). They communicate in the manner of intimates who are so deeply alike that silent exchange is the richest source of understanding. Together they mull things over, questioning, clarifying, occasionally changing places, as do friends with a sense of equality sufficient to support role reversals (133). Their competitiveness, unspoken and contained, seems also consistent with close friendships. It is only when Mrs. Brook lets out the stops on this score that the true inequities of their relation, and of the mother-daughter bond itself (the mother's eternal priority and ultimate power of creation), become articulate. "Mrs. Brook spoke as with a small sharpness—just softened indeed in time—produced by the sight of a freedom on her daughter's part that suddenly loomed larger than any freedom of her own" (240). This is none other than the limits of aging set against the freedom of youth. Mrs. Brook's dilemma (and this is the main reason she wants Nanda out of the house) is that her daughter is the sign of her own increasing constraint. Biology serves as the practical measure of this entrapment. Mrs. Brook is struggling to offset a commonplace of mother-daughter relations: the daughter's flowering usually accompanies the mother's decline. If a woman bears children at the traditional and most biologically fruitful age, the daughter is likely to reach full-blown adolescence just prior to the inception of maternal menopause.[54]

James's narrative confirms that Mrs. Brook is experiencing a crisis every bit as perilous as her daughter's. While the daughter's future promises all the glories that prospective thinking can devise, from love and marriage to motherhood, the mother's foreshadows aging and diminishment. The inevitability of Mrs. Brook's course is suggested by her consistent identifica-

tion with planetary movements. Compared at one point to the Marble
Arch as well as to the moon, she partakes of both political and lunar powers. But only the planetary metaphor sticks. She's a "fixed star," and Vanderbank appears as a "flashing meteor" in her "constellation" (357). Moreover, it is because she is aging that her youthfulness is so striking. This is,
of course, a fixture of her own consciousness: "*I'm* not a hundred!" she
shrieks early on, and she doesn't let up on this point (57, 317). But others
seem similarly preoccupied. Everyone cares about Mrs. Brook's state, because she functions as the circle's "anthro-planetary" totem. She is the
source of collective unity or "flow," governing them all, in Mitchy's words,
"as the tides are governed by the moon" (107). Her downfall, in a rush of
maternal violence, spells the end of her dialogistic community. Significantly, where the circle's men, who liken her "performance" to "Sam-
son pull[ing] down the temple," read artifice and intent, she reads growth
and fate. "We've fallen to pieces," she says, "my part was what it has always
been—to accept the inevitable" (313, 312). One could argue that Mrs.
Brook is simply excusing herself. But she may also be asserting, in some
more collective sense, a female vision of destiny against a male myth of
agency. Whether or not this female line can possibly function in some
larger feminist sense seems beside the point here. It's critical that Mrs.
Brook reads the female lot as the accommodation of fate—whether this
office serves one body in particular or the social body in general. The
object of education, in her view, can only be the reconciliation of the female adolescent with a grim social necessity. Mrs. Brook's methods may
look more liberal than the Duchess's, but their ultimate purpose, it seems,
could not be more constraining. Is Mrs. Brook's liberality an expression of
indifference? Is she cultivating a helplessness that appears modern and
open, when it is in fact more "tragic" than anything going (52)? The Duchess seems optimistic in comparison, at least to the extent that her manipulations signal a faith in control.

But how pessimistic, in reality, is Mrs. Brook's perspective? A deeper
confrontation of her position requires another look at her methods of education. Nanda, in keeping with her mother's laissez-faire attitudes, knows
everything, including the plan of her own upbringing. Her mother, she
observes, is "throwing me into the world" (118), a point repeated to a
group of prospective suitors: "I didn't come in the carriage, nor in a cab or
an omnibus. . . . I walked. . . . Mother wants me to do everything" (111).
Nanda has been let in on the theory that guides her socialization. What
would be the point of apprising an adolescent of the process by which she
"learns to become a woman"?[55] Critics have condemned Mrs. Brook's policy and the selfish immorality that brings her to so expose her daughter.
Though Mrs. Brook's name, Fernanda (i.e., to bear Nanda?), would seem
properly sacrificial, she does much to belie it. Her undermining of Nanda's

social possibilities appears deliberate, and even inexplicable, save in the most damning terms of maternal jealousy. She is blatantly disturbed by the challenge to her own sexual prominence posed by the debut of an attractive daughter. Yet there is also a tension between Mrs. Brook's apparent desire to destroy her daughter and another dim desire to liberate her from ultimately debilitating social forms. James refuses to simplify (by condemning as "unnatural") the motivations of his maternal center. As one of a line of resistant mothers in James's fiction (consider, for example, the dissembling Madame Merle from *The Portrait of a Lady*, the demonic Mrs. Farange from *What Maisie Knew*, the hopeless Mrs. Condrip from *The Wings of the Dove*), Mrs. Brook is James's most caustic, yet also, oddly, his most sympathetic, rendering of a maternal figure.

Like James himself, she stages her daughter's education, foregrounding the method and purpose of what Nanda is taught in order to reveal the culture's ritualized constraint of women. And in this way, Mrs. Brook wages war on her own passivity, and on the "fate" of women in general. Mrs. Brook, however, is no revolutionary. Hers is a newly sanctioned maternal image, which she passes on to her daughter. Though indifferent to her own offspring, she is compulsively maternal to society at large. Like Hester Prynne at the end of *The Scarlet Letter*, Mrs. Brook is a consoler of women in a society that institutionalizes feminine grief and consolation, just as it institutionalizes feminine wantonness and constraint. To become a wife in the novel's society is to enter upon a cycle of discontent, debauchery, and regulation. A psychiatric counselor of sorts, Mrs. Brook runs a clinic for the novel's parade of betrayed and dissatisfied wives. The terminology is precise: Mrs. Brook, who "has set up a little office for consultations," who "listens ... strokes her chin and prescribes," is an early advocate of the "talk[ing]" cure (95, 125). As one husband observes, Mrs. Brook's circle is an "institution ... resting on a deep human need," and Mrs. Brook is "wonderful for wives." As long as feminine sorrows persist, there will be a place for Mrs. Brook, who "has helped so many before, and will help so many still to come" (368, 367). Her social service has a primitive corollary in the elaborate kinship networks that returned runaway wives to husbands so that family debts might continue to be absolved.[56]

Mrs. Brook's consolation skills, we have seen, function on behalf of social cohesion, and she manages to transmit them successfully. Nanda has her own circle, where people "clutch" and "cling" to her (236). She performs the sympathetic tasks of solace and repair—"taking a pound of tea ... to her old nurse" or "going to read to the old women at the workhouse"—that occupy middle- and upper-class women in an emerging welfare state (152). "The modern" is her own "note," and Mrs. Brook fashions Nanda as a new feminine type for the twentieth century (133). Together they exemplify the extension of traditional women's activities, as women direct their maternal energies beyond the home in a bid for professional identity and political influence. Mrs. Brook's "training" of Nanda fulfills the resolution of Beatrice Webb (whose choice of a career in social science supplanted maternity) that "the special force of womanhood—motherly feeling—might be forced into public work." Nanda is a test case for a maternal ideal freed from the constraints of marriage and family. Mrs. Brook remains convinced of modern women's losses. The Madonna image with which she herself is associated, however ironically (82), represents a power that her daughter—who is devoid of shadow, humor, and tact—lacks.

James's point is not, I think, that there was more freedom in a mystified femininity. But as a "dialectical ironist" in the modern sense, he recognizes that ideas and events often yield the opposite of their intent.[57] He sees in women's supposed liberation from reproductive roles different opportunities for exploitation. Mrs. Brook's fierce antinaturalism, which is expressed in her denial of her daughter's maternal potential, repeats rather than challenges the restrictive norms of her culture. Nanda's type, "the modern daughter," replicates her mother's highly compromised position. By the novel's end, Mrs. Brook is a target of collective reproach, viewed (in the novel's deepest terms, erroneously) as the cause of her daughter's "sacrifice."

The stress on the mother-daughter relation is only one manifestation of a society in a crisis of generational succession. This is confirmed by the novel's close, where Nanda is guided into exile by Longdon; her jaded brother Harold appears committed to a life of bachelorhood; the childless marriages of the Grendons, the Cashmores, and the Donners remain impaired; and the newly debauched Aggie revels in adulterous union with Petherton. The novel's final word, "tomorrow," rings false in a society without hope for self-propagation. James understands the transfer of energies from parents to offspring as a portentous process, requiring rules of a stringency more characteristic of primitive cultures. His profound grasp of contrasting cultural mores, and of social relations in general, helps him to intuit much social scientific wisdom on the subject. It is significant that Nanda and Harold are introduced as the "older girl" and "older boy." Neither one is prior in a critical anthropological sense. Each status—firstborn daughter and firstborn son—entails its own traditional obligations. The clean split of gender roles in most societies is dictated by a ritual division of labor. Thus, from the beginning of time, firstborn sons have been the object of the most grisly spiritual compulsions. This is only to hint at the extent to which they have been treasured.

Though there are as many explanations for the custom of sacrificing the firstborn son as there are cultures who practice it, James Frazer points convincingly to rivalry as a thread common to almost all of them. It was widely believed, he points out, that the first son absorbed the "spiritual essence or vital energy" of the father. So pronounced were such fears among the Hindu, that certain sects performed mock funeral ceremonies for the prospective father during the wife's pregnancy. A decade before Freud, Frazer offers an "oedipal" gloss on the paternal mindset of ancient times. "His existence is at the best a menace to yours, and at the worst it may involve your extinction. . . . Parental affection urges you to die that he may live. Self-love whispers, 'live and let him die.'" In Polynesia and India, for example, the king's son was thought to be a reincarnation of his father. The old king's return in the body of the son was a call for the restoration of his throne. This was resolved in some instances by a ritual abdication, following the birth of all sons. In other examples, the filial rival was put to death shortly after birth.[58]

The Awkward Age resolves the age-old conflict of father and son, in part, by evacuating it. Fathers are almost entirely eclipsed by mothers. Mr. Brookenham, whose disempowerment is imaged in his consignment to a "peg" in his wife's drawing room (192), plays no significant role in the plot. He is never given a dialogue with his wayward son Harold, though all agree that patriarchal displays of this kind are in order. The social structure might even be called matriarchal. Self-characterized as "an old boy who remembers the mothers" (33), Longdon's point of reference is a maternal lineage. The only relation that fulfills the principle of hereditary transmission is female: a grandmother-granddaughter bond. The circle is "governed" by Mrs. Brook (107), and there is evidence of polyandry. Men are shared by mothers and daughters: Vanderbank is besieged by Nanda and Mrs. Brook; Petherton serves the Duchess and her "adopted" daughter, Aggie (36). The community's most prominent rite is the worship of a maternal ancestor: the miraculous Lady Julia.[59] Longdon's "sentiment for the living," the Duchess observes, "is the charming fruit of [his] sentiment for the dead" (190). His love for Nanda is "a sacrifice to Lady Julia's memory."

According to ancient custom, the dead require a constant supply of oblations.[60] People have children in order to have grandchildren, a human continuity that ensures a proper flow of rites on their behalf. The grandparent-grandchild bond is harmonious, because their interests are thought to be coextensive, even identical. This belief, as we have seen, is sometimes literalized in the idea that the grandchild reincarnates the grandparent. By reviving the grandparent, the grandchild also revives the grandparental claim on the parents' resources. These are the sorts of threats posed by Nanda. There is satisfaction for Mrs. Brook, but also danger, in her daughter's "absolute revival" of her grandmother (120). For the effect of Nanda's resemblance to her grandmother is her mother's erasure. In Longdon's words, "She's *all* Lady Julia. There isn't a touch of her mother" (120).

Because Longdon adopts Nanda on account of her resemblance to her grandmother, Mrs. Brook's loss of her daughter is doubly determined. She loses her by fate (in a hereditary sense) and also by practical arrangement.

Above all, Mrs. Brook is haunted by the threat her eldest daughter poses to her own vitality. Mrs. Brook seems aware that the rise of Nanda's reproductive potential signals the decline of her own. There is no one more prepared than she to read the novel's social order in terms of compensatory gains and losses. She appears committed to a belief that anthropologists have attributed to modern Londoners as well as to primitives. Take the following as a fair summary of her position: there is "a strictly limited fund, of male vitality and female fecundity, which is partly physical but largely metaphysical . . . which must be transmitted to the filial generation to ensure the proper continuity of the family and thus of society but which can only be transmitted at the cost of the parental generation." Parents have "no alternative . . . but to sacrifice themselves for their children." The practice of sacrificing the firstborn can be read in this light as a gesture of "defense," even defiance.[61] It amounts to the parental transmission of the sacrificial *obligation*, rather than the transmission of the sacrificial *protection*. Just how natural *are* all these rivalrous intergenerational sentiments in James's view? He seems to see a certain amount of conflict as inevitable. Things only get distorted and excessive, he suggests, when predictable tensions are not channeled through the proper ritual forms. When a mother allows her own torment to overshadow hope for her daughter, things become twisted. Likewise, when a benefactor's interest in his charge becomes obsessional, reparative rituals, sometimes of an extreme and barbaric kind, are necessary. James's novel takes its relentless course toward sterility and division. This narrative urgency, one could argue, expresses the hidden and not-so-hidden wishes of the novel's partriarchal agent and matriarchal center.

HOMOSEXUALITY

Though few social observers at this time doubted that there was a crisis of generational succession, few approached the dramatic apprehension of James. One exception was Frazer, whose lyrical description of the priest at Nemi in *The Golden Bough* provides as vivid a portrait as any in literature.

In the sacred grove there grew a certain tree round which at any time of the day, and probably far into the night, a grim figure might be seen to prowl. In his hand he carried a drawn sword, and he kept peering warily about him as if at every instant he expected to be set upon by an enemy. He was a priest and a murderer; and the man for whom he looked was sooner or later to murder him and hold the priesthood in his stead. Such was the rule of the sanctuary. . . . It is a sombre picture—set to melancholy music—the background of the forest showing black and jagged against a lowering and stormy sky, the sighing of the wind in the branches, the rustle of withered leaves underfoot, the lapping of the cold water on the shore, and in twilight and now in gloom, a dark figure with a glitter of steel at the shoulder whenever the pale moon, riding clear of the cloud-rack, peers down at him through the matted boughs.[62]

The melodramatic design of this passage makes it hard to believe that Frazer intended an audience of anthropological colleagues. He seems more interested in setting a mood—down to the detail of "melancholy music"—than in establishing facts or theories. The speculative "might be seen," the "jagged" forest, "lowering" sky, and "lapping" water, approach cliché without impairing faith. This is a moment for any time or culture—hence the universal assurance of the passage. Everyone knows the feeling of rivalry. The "rule of the sanctuary" is the law of the land. The scene is about belief, belief that there can be an event for which so deep a consensus exists. According to Frazer, the promotion of order through violence is precisely this type of inescapable event.

Frazer's description conveys the confidence of fundamentals: the terrors of initiation, the growing pains of a new world, the sense of scarcity that so often dominates these myths (there is only one priestly office; there can be only one priest). Frazer's setting is also known as a sacred site for women, Diana's Grove. A statue of Diana had been erected here by Orestes, and pregnant women came to pray and offer sacrifices in hope of early childbirth. One of Frazer's original sources for the scene was a fourth-century scholium on the sixth book of the *Aeneid*. Widely recognized as a story of initiation, this book concerns the rites of succession as they prevailed within an "ancient Italian priesthood."[63] In his analysis of Frazer's text, Jonathan Z. Smith reproduces the parallel moment from the Virgilian commentary. "In the shady tree the gold [branch] lays hidden. . . . After the rite of the sacrifice had been changed, there was a certain tree in this temple from which it was forbidden to break off a branch. However a power was granted to fugitives so that if anyone were able to carry away a branch from that place, he would contend with the fugitive-priest in a duel—for there was a fugitive-priest there before the image of the ancient flight. The office of fighting was given, however, as a sort of substitution of the ancient sacrifice. Now therefore, it took from here this shade of meaning, and it was inevitable that the branch would be the cause of the death of someone."[64]

Virgil and his Victorian successor may be equally present in the priestly implications of James's novel. *The Awkward Age* features superstitious Roman heirs, with their own private "priest" and "pagan" observances (179, 183). The Duchess's venerable "Calabrian sonorities" are "acquired," but this makes her especially aware of their value (58). James was well versed in the classics, and Virgil was a special favorite.[65] When Longdon quizzes Mitchy on "the Virgilian associations of the Bay of Naples," following his return from a Greco-Roman tour, James's own pressing interest can be heard (338). The Duchess's special alertness to the power of sacred groves and the necessity of sacrifice is confirmed by the fact that the portion of the novel narrated from her perspective is filled with echoes of Virgil, and possibly even Frazer. Book 5 opens upon a different atmosphere: we are "in the depths of the forest" (160). This scene of "stone" and "shade" "trees" and "woods," relieves the stifling interiority of the previous segments, all set in urban drawing rooms (157). The interiors that we do see project a pleasing ripeness. Other details seem deliberately antiquated: references to "the twilight of time," anticipations of "the feast all spread," descriptions of houses as "Temples of peace" (168, 169, 171). Depth here is historical, but also spiritual, as suggested by the image of an "old grey church," and references to Sunday services and Christmas gifts (158, 159, 161). And there is gold. Longdon gazes out upon "a golden distance," and "the long golden glow" of social intercourse becomes the "caw" of "rooks . . . at once sociable and sad" (168, 178). Aggie's hard-won "ignorance" is "positively golden" (182), and the Duchess terms Longdon's connection to the Brookenhams a golden link (189). It would be another five years before James would publish his own *Golden Bowl*. But probably he was already familiar with Frazer's multivolume sensation.[66]

While Frazer appears confident that he has identified in his drama of initiation an unavoidable primal scene, James's novel is premised upon a more complex and disturbing possibility: what happens when expected rites of passage are foiled? James's novel confronts a question about the transfer of generational energies overlooked by Virgil and Frazer. What happens when the potential successor evades his ritual obligation? Longdon's preferred successor is Vanderbank, an obvious choice in many respects. He is, in his own words, "the most envied man I know" (30). And there is the matter of his looks, a handsomeness so extreme that it is dubbed "the sacred terror" (227). Described as "beastly good-looking," "infernally well turned out," Vanderbank "dazzles" his lovers to the point of sickness (84, 124, 190). If one were to chart the erotic energy fields of *The Awkward Age*, all positive force would point to Vanderbank. Nanda and Mitchy are united in their willingness to make "almost any sacrifice" on his behalf (85). Longdon's affection for him is also strong, as is Mrs. Brook's (107–8, 191). (There are exceptions: the Duchess and Aggie favor the unrefined attractions of Petherton.) As if to compensate for all the libido channeled in his direction, Vanderbank is distinguished by his own utter lack of it; he seems devoid of passion in any form. There are no easy solutions to the mystery of Vanderbank's passivity, though theories abound. And Vanderbank himself appears as confused as everyone else. He is clinically preoccupied with his condition and invites the collective scrutiny. For him desire is wholly theoretical, a matter of "high intellectual detachment" (225).

The imperceptibility of Vanderbank's preferences provides another entry into the contorted logic of the novel's opening. Why should a character's habitual response to rain be worthy of note? The significant phrase here is "preference of the philosopher," which locates Vanderbank's chronic detachment in a Platonic tradition. Like Plato's philosopher, "who has fallen among wild beasts," Vanderbank neither embraces a climate of evil nor quite escapes its taint.[67] Like everyone else, he is caught, as Mrs. Brook says, "in their . . . native mud" (77). Vanderbank's ideal of mental purity is compromised by his inevitable complicity.[68]

But there are additional sexual innuendos here, issuing from a body of thought known in James's time as Victorian Hellenism. Following Oscar Wilde's trials for "sodomic indecency" in the spring of 1895, as Linda Dowling observes, "it would be difficult to pronounce the word 'Hellenism' without an insinuating leer." Greece was invoked by homosexual apologists in this period, she contends, in order to cast "a veil of respectability over even a hitherto unmentionable vice or crime." The gap in the official vocabulary of the era did not prevent the conviction and jailing of Oscar Wilde for allegedly sodomous activities.[69] Victorian Hellenism represented a new brand of nationalism, one that combined Platonic *paiderastia* with an intellectual imperialism of ideas.[70] The famed Oxford tutor, Benjamin Jowett, who once remarked that he "should like to govern the world through my pupils," typifies the union of Platonic idealism and colonial ambition. His efforts were remarkably successful (a list of former pupils includes no fewer than four colonial administrators, Cecil Rhodes among them).[71] James was undoubtedly aware of these famed tutorials. His descriptions of the "Socratic" Mrs. Brook at her dialogistic teas seem directly inspired by descriptions of Jowett (303), who according to John Addington Symonds, deliberately cultivated a "Socratic" manner ("Now I will give you some tea, O my good friend").[72] Symonds articulated the tension experienced by many who took Oxford Hellenism to heart, the tension between the Platonic idealism tutors preached and the eroticism liberated by their curriculum.[73] In Symonds's words, Jowett "placed the most electrical literature of the world in his hands, pregnant with the stuff that damns him."[74]

The poignancy of Symonds's position was not lost on James, who nevertheless carefully distanced himself from a problem he labeled, "morbid and hysterical." In reply to a friend's urgings that he write a retrospective on Symonds, James dismissed the undertaking as a "Problem—a problem beyond me."[75] James's need to distance himself from a dilemma that was all too familiar no doubt informed his characterization of Vanderbank in *The Awkward Age*. Vanderbank's passivity, his resistance to desire, becomes a

means of articulating James's ambivalence toward a contemporary homoerotic culture in general and his own sexuality in particular.[76] It may
seem overly literal, given the extraordinary complexity of desire in James,
to put too fine a point on Vanderbank's sexuality. Besides, James leaves
an out for every definitive possibility. The ideal of intellectual purity set
forth in the opening offers one means of filling the gap created by Vanderbank's "preference." Vanderbank's allergy to Nanda's "modern slang"
provides another (163–64). There is also the hint of Vanderbank's adulterous passion for Mrs. Brook. Yet from the perspective of a specifically
Hellenistic "slang," the attribution of "prejudice" to Vanderbank presents
a chasm that may be undeniable (259–60). For those interested in representations of homoeroticism, however, this "out" or "blank" would be
precisely the point.[77] Symonds was one among many to invoke Jeremy
Bentham, in describing the experience of "2 favourite prejudices that
are apt cruelly to jar," the one in "disfavour" of Greek love, the other in
favor of "ancient Greece."[78] Early in the novel, Vanderbank is dubbed an
Apollo, and he later declares himself, however ironically, a Greek (108,
199). James appears to appropriate, throughout his characterization, a contemporary Hellenistic idiom of homoerotic narcissism. According to
Plato's *Phaedrus*, the male lover in these terms becomes "a mirror in which
he beholds himself."[79]

This too can be explained in "compulsory heterosexual" terms: might
not anyone so accustomed to being admired look often in the mirror?
Still there is an inordinate emphasis on Vanderbank's relationship to his
own image. In one scene Vanderbank recognizes himself first through
his name inscribed on a book and then as reflected in a chimney glass
(275–76). In another, multiple mirrors create an effect that is near carni-
valesque. Vanderbank's self-reflections are always doubled. He appears in
the "polished glass" of a framed image, and then in "the glass that reflects
the whole scene" (346–47). Vanderbank seems to have an almost compulsive need for self-reflection. This is supported by his willingness to be a
subject of general reflection within the circle at large. Vanderbank's
characterization in this respect may anticipate (without endorsing) the
famed narcissism that figures so prominently in Freud's pathological
definition of homosexuality. The legend of Narcissus portrays excessive
self-admiration as a threat to survival. In Vanderbank's example, the same
paradoxical relationship between self-reflection and self-destruction is at
issue, but with a slightly different twist. Vanderbank's susceptibility to mirrors, and to the mirroring eyes of admirers, does indicate an extreme sense
of vulnerability. This is not only because he can't embrace or admit his
"true" identity. It's also because that identity was a trial—in a very real
sense it was on trial in this era.

Imputations of criminality become explicit in the dramatic encounter where Longdon announces that he has himself "conceived a desire" for Vanderbank's future. Vanderbank, in his usual undesirous state, is enveloped, even emprisoned by Longdon's own profuse desire. As Longdon's plan unfolds, an imaginary trial ensues. The air of detection and judgment is partly an effect of the setting: a room with a raised platform of sorts, so that Vanderbank is "perched aloft," while Longdon revolves edgily around him. This gives Vanderbank the appearance of "some prepossessing criminal who, in court, should have changed places with the judge" (195). A few pages later we learn that Longdon "had mounted to the high bench and sat there as if the judge were now in his proper place" (200). Longdon assumes this position of legal authority just at the point of informing Vanderbank of his desire. Vanderbank's failed compliance is simultaneously anticipated and explained through this hint of transgression. Vanderbank, in his own words, is "a mass of corruption," a term widely invoked in contemporary descriptions of heretical (homo)sexuality (204). In *De Profundis* (1895), Oscar Wilde redirects the term at betrayal itself, that of the lover whose "corruption" proved to be Wilde's, but more importantly his own, undoing. The echoes of Wilde's damnation in this metaphorical account of Vanderbank's trial are unmistakable. Longdon's rejoinder to Vanderbank, who notes "how awfully" Longdon wants him to marry Nanda—"How awfully *you* don't"—is condemnatory indeed (205). The judge has leveled his charge: the absence of a conventional desire signals the presence of an illicit one.

These legalistic proceedings recall a long history, which would have been familiar to James, associating homosexuality with heresy. The liberal theology of Henry James Sr. (grim, at least on these grounds) supplied the ancient link between homosexual practices and spiritual crimes. As interpreted by Edward Westermarck, homosexuality was from the earliest times "intimately associated with the gravest of all sins: unbelief, idolatry, or heresy" (2:486). He dismisses Havelock Ellis's claim that the first sanctions against homosexuality by the Hebrews were spurred by anxiety about their dwindling numbers. As Westermarck notes in his chapter on "homosexual love," Hebrew persecutions of such practices were never simply about "wasting seed." Their judgments of moral or spiritual transgressions were always motivated by anxieties about kinship. Their "abhorrence of sodomy was largely due to their hatred of a foreign cult" (2:487). From the Hebrews to the Mohammedans to the Christians, sodomy "remained a religious offence of the first order" (2:489). Westermarck's historical summary ends with the greater leniency of the most recent views afforded by medical science. As moderns have gradually freed themselves from a punishing theology, "no scrutinising judge can fail to take into account the pressure which a powerful non-volitional desire exercises upon an agent's will" (2:489). Despite their evolutionary optimism, these phrases imply pathological discriminations. An outraged morality has given way to a clinical legalism. Westermarck's overall trajectory is not inconsistent with historical arguments that link increased prosecutions of homosexuals to a sense of imminent social catastrophe."[80] Nor is it necessarily incompatible with the demographic worries that Westermarck insists on divorcing from moral concerns. In the minds of those who inhabit *The Awkward Age*, these problems are of a piece. Society is running out of moral steam; sexual norms are in chaos. It could stand an infusion of absolute values. But some Anglo-Saxon blood from a few young men and women of good standing wouldn't hurt either.

Consider now the homoerotic dimensions of Vanderbank's characterization. There is the early admission of indifference to women, in Vanderbank's comment that Longdon can do "with them . . . every bit *I* do" (37). There is Mrs. Brookenham's own consistent assurance of Vanderbank's preference and the view the reader is so often given of Vanderbank's turned back. In this light, the novel's opening holds yet another significance. In the pervading sexual vernacular, a post chaise symbolizes potential adulterous unions (men carrying off wives in a rush [141, 369]). There is ironic comfort in the opening identification of the post chaise with the pure philosopher who will never use it in that offensive slangy way (164). Vanderbank's conversations with Nanda are filled with attempts to own up to his "kind." In two exemplary instances, Vanderbank brandishes the word like a sword. The first time is in response to her confession that she fears him. "Kindness is kindness," he replies, confirming why she should not (163). "You needn't fear me," he seems to suggest. "I'm the kind of man who prefers my own kind." The second time, he invokes the word in self-protection: kindness here is a hard brilliance that fills the room "to the exclusion of everything else" (347). In this final dialogue, Vanderbank's conviction of kind is like armor. This is so that he might save himself, once and for all, from the fatal leap that would please everyone but himself. But there is no pleasing himself.

Vanderbank's dilemma, and this is where his career so resembles that of Symonds, is that his genuine respect for tradition and displeasure over the degraded state of group morals put him at war with his inclinations. In this sense, he and Nanda are very much alike. Both abhor nothing more than their own impossibility. Yet Nanda's fate is to love the person to whom she's "precisely obnoxious" (260), while Vanderbank neither renounces nor is renounced by a love. His fate is the renunciation of desire itself. Longdon loves Lady Julia (45); Mrs. Brook loves Vanderbank (191); Mitchy loves Nanda (186); Nanda loves Vanderbank (341); and Vanderbank, in the spare phrase of Mrs. Brook, is "a blank" (218). To be without desire is a fate worse than exile, worse than death. If we accept this as the narrative's premise, then we can recognize Vanderbank as another sacrifice on behalf of the novel's community. But it is not the only premise in this novel or beyond it. For when it comes to love, Vanderbank seems hardly a character at all. He is rather a walking set of conditions on homosexual desire. Condition as triumph, since there is no higher Jamesian office than the sacrifice of desire. Vanderbank represents one contemporary solution to the trial of homosexuality: the recasting of renunciation as art.

Vanderbank's dramatic decision—will he or won't he marry the heart-sick Nanda, who has been attractively dowered by Longdon?—is essentially a sacrificial wager. He must sacrifice his "prejudice," or "kind," and marry Nanda, or sacrifice a fortune and refuse her (260, 347). Situations like this would naturally incline an individual to paralysis. Yet he is not exactly paralyzed. Nor is he exactly sacrificed. Vanderbank represents the promise of sacrifice. The most tactile sign of this is his constant smoking: he is a slow-burning ritual conflagration. Vanderbank smokes more than any other character. But he doesn't just smoke; he calls attention to it. His smoking is stylized. He blows smoke rings; he holds his smoke and uses it to stabilize himself in conversation (194, 244–46, 264–69). Consider the following chain of images: "Vanderbank was casting about for cigarettes. 'Be quiet and smoke'" (119); "Vanderbank's smoke-puffs were profuse and his pauses frequent" (246); "Vanderbank smoked with his face turned to the dusky garden and the dim stars" (265); "Vanderbank, with the aid of his cigarette, thoughtfully pieced it out" (269). Smoking is his prop: it expresses his enthusiasm and his despair. Vanderbank is the sort of smoker who prompts others to smoke (29, 38). It seems appropriate that the one gift he offers Nanda, in a narrative which takes account of the flowers, books, and candy she receives from others, is a cigarette case (347–49). This is despite the fact that he clearly disapproves of her smoking and of her search for a case like his that "holds twenty" (160–61).

In a novel that gives so much spiritual meaning to smoke, the actions of a character who smokes as much as Vanderbank ask to be read symbolically. Indeed, according to Jacques Derrida, "Tobacco symbolizes the symbolic: It seems to consist at once in a consumption (ingestion) and a purely sumptuary expenditure of which nothing natural remains. But the fact that nothing natural remains does not mean, on the contrary, that nothing symbolic remains. The annihilation of the remainder, as ashes can sometimes testify, recalls a pact and performs the role of memory. One is never sure that this annihilation does not partake of offering and of sacrifice."[81] Vanderbank, whose situation is so intimately bound up with Nanda's, serves as continual reminder of the sacrificial prospect she will fulfill. His chain-smoking is a warning: someone at some point will be going up in smoke. There is a physical dimension to this prophecy, given the medical evidence, available even in James's time, that smoking leads to physical disease.[82] Mitchy's characterization of Vanderbank as "positively wasted" can be read in more than one way (107). Smoking, like the rite it portends, is both ominous and sublime. Smoking makes Vanderbank jumpy, but it also calms him.

Oscar Wilde offers the most obvious contemporary register for the link between homosexuality and sacrifice. His biographer comments, "For a man who condemned sacrifice, his plays are full of it."[83] Officially, as we have seen, Wilde appears to have conceded the term to his hypocritical lover, Lord Alfred Douglas. In the spring of 1895, Douglas wrote to a London newspaper that the Wilde case had been submitted to "the hand of 'Judge Lynch'" and "the shrieks of the mob" before being properly "tried by a jury."[84] Given Douglas's own trial testimony against Wilde, the false consciousness of this display seems incredible. Despite the fact that contemporaries and scholars ever since have read him as the goat of the century's end, Wilde himself dramatically disavowed sacrifice. "Religion does not help me," he wrote, "my Gods dwell in temples made with hands . . . where on an altar, on which no taper burned, a priest in whose heart peace had no dwelling, might celebrate with unblessed bread and a chalice empty of wine."[85] Wilde's eloquent negations serve more than any assertion to sustain these scholarly claims. Sacrifice retains a spiritual hold by providing a language of religious denial. To deny the sacrificial altar, he knows, is only to claim another minute for the voice (and body) that will eventually serve to kindle the sacred flame.

It seems appropriate in light of this image that critics have recently read the Wilde case in terms of more recent anxieties about the "extinction" of homosexuals. The historical conjunction of Wilde's fall and the first clinical attempts to categorize homoeroticism seems politically meaningful, to say the least.[86] The self-consuming life of James's Vanderbank can be taken as a dramatic enactment of prevailing attitudes toward homosexuality. Vanderbank's sexuality is repressed, closeted, not only in implicit testimony of its pathologizing, but in demonstration of the very process of categorization. As Vanderbank's fate suggests, an excessive degree of self-punishment and moral indictment precedes the production of a status like homosexuality. These excesses expose the strain in a culture, a strain whose result will be the label itself. Vanderbank's self-sacrifice is as much a product of "the Awkward Age" as the "homosexuality" that his offering helps to usher in. The war of categories implied by James's portrait of Vanderbank is ongoing. It endures in an era of AIDS, where anxieties about homosexual difference and survival have become literalized.[87]

Vanderbank's sexual status and the questions it raises are balanced by a certain compensatory and essential status for women. Vanderbank is entirely dependent on Mrs. Brook. He needs her because she is interested in him, understands him, and is able to reflect back to him a sense of himself that feels accurate. Though he ends up resenting her at the novel's end because he is unfulfilled sexually, emotionally, and intellectually, he never stops needing her. To say that this sounds a bit like a son's relationship to his mother is to state the obvious. The analogy works, however, only if it is recognized in some sense as an appropriate paradigm for gender relations in the novel as a whole. All women are mothers in their relations with men. More importantly, authority and control are imagined as somehow originally held by women (whether Lady Julia or her daughter, Mrs. Brook) and, somehow, necessarily wrested from them (by Longdon or Vanderbank) if social order is to prevail. Women's payoff for their relinquishment of power is a place at the symbolic center of men's lives. Things are not quite so simple, however. For this evolutionary script (favored by pessimistic feminists from Virginia Woolf to Adrienne Rich) seems irreconcilable with the novel's powerful homosexual themes.

What is the relationship between homoeroticism and the idealization of maternity? John Symonds's somber speculations at the end of another privately circulated manuscript, *A Problem in Greek Ethics*, suggest one possible connection. Recounting the gradual decline of *paiderastia*, which thrived in Greece and waned in Rome, he observes that one would hardly expect "so peculiar" a custom to "flourish on Latin soil." The term "peculiar" does not have its usual connotation, since Symonds sees a regression from Greek "love" to Roman "lust." Rather, it is Symonds's embrace of homoeroticism's displacement by the Christian cult of Mary that sounds peculiar here. Christian faith brought humanity from a state of "despair" to a full appreciation of woman as "the mediating and ennobling element . . . the spiritual basis of our domestic and civil life" (72–73). In Symonds's account, the containment of homosexuality over time is accompanied (neither cause nor result is implied) by the growing social centrality of women. This centrality is not, of course, without its own barbed wire. Homosexuality had its golden moment: its subsequent destiny was to be the sacrifice to evolutionary development. We find traces of Westermarck and Ellis here—in the reading of homosexuality as a religious violation, in the conviction that orderly social growth requires "productive love." Modern civilization, according to Symonds, is founded on the suppression of homosexuality, which becomes increasingly (and inevitably) unhealthy over time. Its eventual replacement by a Christian maternal cult ensures socially sustaining development and nurture. As the center of a Greek world, homosexuality could be moderated; it could itself function as a critical means of cultural transmission.[68] Its fate ever after was to be marginalized, even pathologized. Woman's revenge, as it were, for her Greek invisibility was a central place in the Christian worldview. Symonds offered a corrective to these developments, with his ideal of a male chivalry that would augment and possibly even supplant this feminine ideal. But his conclusions about homosexuality's decline, and maternity's emergence in its wake, as the submerged centerpiece of a new "patriarchy," is consonant with *The Awkward Age*'s own dark evolutionary reading of gender.

Vanderbank's homosexuality complicates his repudiation of courtship and marriage. According to the novel's community he is defiant, a defiance that prevents individual happiness and limits social prospects in general. This is to emphasize once again the theme of succession: Vanderbank's refusal to pursue Longdon's priestly office, to bear the patriarchal standard on behalf of civilization's advance. In this sense, his passivity contributes to a larger atmosphere of degradation; the novel's society is dangerously reminiscent of the hypothetical matriarchies that preceded the Greco-Roman era.[89] Yet *The Awkward Age* also offers a reassuring progressivism. The subtle counter to the novel's more obvious narrative of decline is the inevitable shift from matriarchy to patriarchy. A Hellenistic Golden Age is nowhere in the novel's historical scheme. Greece, like homosexuality, is a persistent stream of urges or echoes, doomed to incoherence. In the novel's closing scene, Mrs. Brook's circle has "fallen to pieces" (312). Vanderbank withholds himself from mother and daughter alike. At once a lady-killer and a confirmed bachelor, a traditionalist and an expert statistician, Vanderbank has been the vehicle for a form of cultural control that both elicits and disallows feminine desire. His master plan gone awry, Longdon appears as the savior, prepared to adopt the female sacrifice to the social principle of exogamy. Yet what is most pronounced in this final scene is the force of Longdon's own desire. In the patriarchal stage, where proprietary marriage is introduced, Longdon is triumphantly united with the woman of his dreams. Poised with "the post-chaise and the pistols" to carry Nanda off after her "grand public adhesion," Longdon enacts the ceremonial form of wife capture that, according to Veblen, still persists in modern society, in order to recall its primitive roots and to project a more civilized future (369).[90]

This is the other ritual form that Vanderbank resists. He will not reinforce the controls essential to the replacement of a primitive female license, nor will he help to establish a society based on orderly laws of reproduction. Vanderbank's resistance, according to the novel's Galtonian engineer, is a betrayal of his own nature. In the words of the Duchess, Nanda and Vanderbank are "just the people to have . . . a fine old English family" (189). Her prediction, a group of "half a dozen"—two parents, four children—is statistically precise, since four was the calculated minimum number of offspring (cited by demographic analysts) necessary to the maintenance of a stock. The evaporation of these hopes calls for the intervention of the novel's key partriarchal agent or priest, Longdon. He enacts a symbolic sacrifice, by ushering the society's adolescent scapegoat into exile. Longdon's ancient methods of social renewal are enabled, paradoxically, by his conviction of an absolute historical break or disjunction: "everything's different from what it used to be" (382). For Longdon's line includes women of the future as well as the past, and he recognizes in the redirection of modern women one of the major challenges of the age.

Conditions of State

Longdon's application of traditional spiritual and moral codes to questions of sexuality is indicative of a wider tendency in this era that, effectively, detached the maternal principle from its biological location (the female body) and relocated it (as social engineering) in the social body. His prescriptions reveal how elite anxiety was formalized in a preoccupation with ancient means of regeneration and renewal. Sometimes consciously, sometimes not, social theorists and political leaders located the prospects for national growth in laws of kinship and initiation that were associated with less advanced peoples (whether biblical Hebrews or Kafirs of the Hindu-Kush). Dangerous transitions required stringent principles, and it was dimly perceived (and sometimes openly admitted) that "ancients" and "primitives" had an advantage over "moderns" in this regard. Moreover, many recognized these principles as the antecedents of modern legal forms and social mores. Such were the assumptions behind numerous evolutionary studies, from Spencer's *Illustrations of Universal Progress* (1870) to Hobhouse's *Morals in Evolution* (1906). This late-Victorian era can be distinguished from previous turning points in the history of modernism (beginning with the English Renaissance) by the hyperconsciousness of change among intellectuals, artists, and politicians. Other periods had fostered high levels of such consciousness, but none so high as this one did.[91]

EVOLUTIONARY TALES

While James admits in the preface to *The Awkward Age* that "Every age lives, in an 'epoch of transition,'" there is reason to claim a "notorious" instability for his own late-Victorian/Edwardian period (12). England (like America) confronted transformations in women's status, mass enfranchisement and the accompanying threats of socialism and anarchism, rising immigration rates (sufficient to inspire the restrictive 1905 Immigration Act), unfavorable trade balances, the Boer War, impending world war, and among the elite, in particular, an overall spirit of decline. These changes generated a great deal of anxiety about prevailing methods of socialization and cultural transmission, anxiety that figured in the development of the social scientific disciplines.[92] Never before was a generation so convinced of its difference from all that had preceded it. Progress in the modern era depended more and more on the *conscious* direction of evolution. And social science (sociology in particular) supplied a form for this new self-consciousness.[93] For views of a civilization severed from the past, sociologists substituted a tale of progressive development. They forecast the gradual emergence of a society based on "laws of thought." From here, Leonard Hobhouse went on to claim that "reason is itself an instinct."[94] But in fact the faculty was widely understood to be deliberately cultivated.

These social scientists saw no contradiction between organic evolutionism and social engineering. Nor did they see a contradiction between their rational principles and their idealization of feminine instinct. In the evolutionary tales that sociologists told, women appeared at history's climactic end, as reified channels of human reproduction. These narratives seemed directly responsive to the agendas of social reform organizations, so many of them expressing anxieties about female sexuality and reproduction. The National Vigilance Association, for example, founded in 1885, attributed the decline of morals to widespread use of birth control, women's greater access to "corrupt literature, and political challenges to traditional abortion and divorce laws (prohibiting divorce except in cases of the wife's adultery). The organization railed in particular against foreign dramatists (e.g., Ibsen) who portrayed "dissatisfied married women in a chronic state of rebellion ... against all the duties and obligations of mothers and wives."[95] Upper- and middle-class resistance to reproduction was viewed as a cause of dangerous population imbalances between the elite and lower classes. It was also thought to be a contributing factor in the overall decline of social efficiency (as captured in best-sellers such as *Made in Germany* [1896] and *The American Invaders* [1901]).[96] In brief, then, the concerns that motivated social reformers—heredity and population, social degeneracy, the liberalization of women's status—reflected a tendency in this era to feminize and naturalize social decline. The fact that many of these reformers were themselves women made for predictable contradictions and surprising alliances.

From the 1870s through the opening decade of the twentieth century, reports of the lower classes "multiply[ing] like rabbits" dominated the popular press and elite journals. "The poorer they are," commented W. R. Greg, writing for *Fraser's* magazine, "the faster do they multiply." Herbert Spencer corroborated these fears. For Spencer, reproductive rates were inversely proportionate to development: higher evolutionary stages featured lower population growth. Francis Galton's "new religion," eugenics, confronted the obvious question raised by Spencer's theories.[97] How could a social Darwinist vision of species progress be reconciled with the shrinking birth rate of the better classes? Galton's answer was that it couldn't be. Hence, his theory of species decline, founded on the reproductive losses of modern elites. In practice, Galton advocated state monitoring of reproduction rates: identifying "a select class x of young men and women . . . encouraging their intermarriage, and promoting the early marriages of girls of that high class."[98] Eugenics proved as troubling to sociological liberalism as it had to social Darwinism. Was it even possible, let alone conscionable, for a modern society to modify the reproduction rates of different citizens?

Thomas Huxley, a leading scientist and liberal intellectual who played a role in the development of social science (and wrote, not incidentally, about the sacrificial practices of the ancient Hebrews), confronted the question head-on. He labeled the rise in population "the political problem of problems." Its sources were "internal by generation" (that of lower-class "wage earners") and "external by immigration." Overpopulation and the poverty to which it gave rise, could only be eliminated by restricting both.[99] Huxley's observations inspire a Swiftian insight, that worries about population growth always express class anxieties about maintaining power. In this period, whether the complaint was underpopulation or overpopulation the fear was the same: preferred social elements were being overtaken by undesirable ones. "Unless the decline of the birthrate is averted," warned Sidney Webb, "the nation will fall to the Irish and the Jews." From America, G. Stanley Hall concurred that Anglo-Saxons were committing "race suicide."[100] The naming of genetics and population as a "political problem" highlights one of the deepest threats posed by reproductive issues in this era. Elite concern about population—in fact and in theory— was a reaction to the looming reality of mass enfranchisement. Unchecked lower class reproduction meant unlimited lower-class ballots, and eventual social upheaval.

The problem of population remained a key referent of liberal social science throughout this period. The strongest evidence of this fact are the ominous indices of natural and political decline in the notes and appendices of evolutionary studies by Benjamin Kidd, Herbert Spencer, Thomas Huxley, Leonard Hobhouse, and Thorstein Veblen. A potent (though graphic) return of the repressed, these marginalized details threaten to unravel their whole progressive enterprise. Kidd appends to his *Social Evolution* a chart comparing the reproductive rates of different races and classes, while Huxley's references feature the ominous hordes of "Chinamen" and "Hindoostan" ignored by radical land-sharing schemes (i.e., those of Henry George). The notes to Hobhouse's *Mind in Evolution* (1901) catalog the contrasting "fertility" rates of "civilised" and "uncivilised" man.[101] Veblen cites "low birthrate" as a characteristic of his leisure class. "Conspicuous consumption, and the consequent increased expense, required in the reputable maintenance of a child," he writes, "acts as a powerful deterrent." Veblen refers in particular to the "paucity or absence of children" among leisure-class members devoted to "scholarly pursuits." He attributes this to the discrepancy between their status and their earnings.[102] Reviewing Karl Pearson's *The Chances of Death and Other Studies in Evolution*, the American sociologist Franklin Giddings praises Pearson's triumphant account of patriarchy's emergence from matriarchal forms of social organization (described in a chapter entitled "Woman as Witch") while qualifying his sobering record of the low reproduction rates of "cultivated" (as opposed to "poor" and "criminal") elements (described in a different chapter, "Socialism and Natural Selection").[103]

This intellectual borderland represents the impetus for "the structural transformation of the public sphere." In his book of this title, Jurgen Habermas describes the historical moment when public opinion came to be perceived as a "tyranny." Liberal intellectuals turned against the idea of a public conscience and advocated that "political questions be decided not by a direct or indirect appeal to the insight or the will of an uninformed multitude, but only by appeal to views, formed after due consideration, of a relatively small number of persons specially educated for this task." From the ranks of this small elite of experts came the recruits for a new category of social expertise: the disciplines of social science.[104] Middle- and upper-class women, social scientists believed, had their own expert role to fill in the modern era.

The changing status of women, as reflected in surveys of courtship and marriage rites from primitive to modern times, was one key to the rise of a rational civilization. What held constant through various evolutionary stages, according to these analysts, was the view of women's central role as breeders. Moreover, feminine sexuality and reproductive powers were the possession of fathers and husbands, to be exchanged in primitive societies and more subtly regulated in modern ones. Whether understood as the utilitarian means of species preservation or as a "sacred" calling, women's reproduction was cultural capital too precious to be controlled by women themselves.[105] In works such as Hobhouse's *Morals in Evolution*, maternity is a guiding normative ideal. The identification of the maternal instinct with order, an order that builds incrementally from primitive to modern times, has decided contemporary implications. "Very few men have any natural aptitude with babies," Hobhouse writes. Nevertheless, "it is almost a physical difficulty to refrain from picking up a small child who holds out its arms to one, and when he has caught it up a man is inclined to sway with it and dandle it, as women used to do before they had theories."[106] Spencer's concerns, as expressed in *Principles of Sociology*, are similar. "Any extensive change in the education of women," he writes, "fitting them for businesses and professions, would be mischievous. If women comprehended all that is contained in the domestic sphere, they would ask no other" (1:757). Spencer goes on to list the consequences of feminine instincts at work in public affairs, among them the promotion of generosity over justice and individual welfare over common interests (1:757–58).[107]

The evolutionary surveys of Spencer and Hobhouse serve to justify a new traditionalism. Thus, Hobhouse describes the experiences of women as "property" in primitive societies, where they are offered to guests "as a matter of courtesy," and insists that their position even under "mother-right" was "as low as the greatest misogynist could desire." He goes on to detail the fortunes of women who treat their sexuality as their own. In some instances they are mutilated; in others, caged. Or they might be "chased by the women to the sea, covered with dirt and ducked" (159–60, 173–74). With equal ominousness, Spencer introduces a section on "the status of women" with the observation that "the only limit to the brutality women are subjected to by men of the lowest races, is their inability to live and propagate under greater" (1:713). In societies ruled by "the traffic in women," he writes, "the will and welfare of a daughter are as much disregarded by the father who sells her as by the husband who buys her" (1:716). These descriptions of women's degradation in primitive societies have an obvious moral: You never had it so good. Spencer ends with a celebration of industrializing nations that relieve women from taxing labor, thus enabling their propagation of "more and better offspring" (1:731). The euphemistic emphasis on the sacredness of maternity and the hostility toward the extension of women's roles suggest that "the traffic in women" had found a critical new purpose in the era of Spencer and Hobhouse.

Social scientific models of this kind did not go unchallenged. To begin with, these models were themselves partly inspired by the political gains of women reformers (in England as well as in the United States). As I have pointed out, English women of the bourgeois and elite classes (like their American counterparts) had succeeded in liberalizing divorce and abortion laws and were well on their way to achieving universal suffrage (by 1920). More important was the burgeoning of women's reform activity in both countries, as exemplified by the careers of Beatrice Webb and Florence Kelley. Their style of politics, at once feminist and mainstream, has been called "maternalist." Women reformers in this period sought to reformulate skills and ideals acquired in a domestic sphere, in order to apply them in more public forums.

Henry James's perspective was always internationally informed, even though his particular focus in *The Awkward Age* is the status of women in modern England.[108] His summary account in the preface is typically comparative: James sets up a tri-cultural kaleidoscope, a look at female socialization in England, France, and the United States (12–13). James's reading of his novel can be taken as an encouragement to cross-cultural interpretation. Of particular relevance here is an impressive body of scholarship that explores continuities between maternalist reform movements and welfare state development in four Western cultures at the turn of the century.[109] Theda Skocpol's *Protecting Soldiers and Mothers*, for example, centers upon the United States but is concerned with developments in other countries as well, especially England. Skocpol offers a general distinction between "paternalist" and "maternalist" welfare policies: the former, designed by male bureaucrats to benefit male workers and their dependents; the latter, initiated by female reformers to answer the specific plights of women. Paternalism, she argues, which was a response to class struggle, prevailed in England, while maternalism, which was more attentive to the politics of gender, predominated in the United States.[110] From the perspective of social welfare alone, Skocpol argues, England was a success story. Tightly contested elections around the turn of the century compelled English elites from conservative as well as liberal parties to court working-class votes through welfare programs. Political necessity was reinforced by a newly reformed civil service; in effect, a centralized bureaucracy provided an institutional setting for helping to articulate a unified national policy. Welfare administration became a viable avenue for the political advancement of middle- and upper-class men. All of these factors contributed to the creation of "a comprehensive welfare state centered on workingmen during the very period when Americans were failing to do so." The very successes of a British welfare system seemed to ensure the marginalization of women reformers. British women, whose educational opportunities lagged behind those of American women, were treated as "helpers" in reform settlements dominated by men "sporting Oxford and Cambridge degrees." Consequently, women's agendas were lost in the shuffle of more extensive reforms (249, 348).

What's finally most revealing about Skocpol's study is that despite her desire to tell an exceptionalist tale of American triumph, her conclusions ultimately support more pessimistic, even ironic historical accounts. According to Seth Koven and Sonya Michel, maternalist reformers in various countries, whether weak or strong, had difficulty foregrounding women's political interests and sometimes, inadvertently, abetted their neglect. The indifference or hostility toward women reformers often expressed deeper reservations about a "nurturing" state. But the most revealing explanation for the decline of maternalist politics was its resemblance to the evolutionary narratives of contemporary social science. Like these cultural mythologies, maternalist politics set women's skills and interests against a newly dominant social scientific expertise. Whether defined by women or by men, maternalist policies were always attached to some reproductive purpose, ranging from greater availability of abortion to material rewards for mothers of large families (where the mother had a "desirable" class and racial identity: "worthy" as opposed to "unworthy" poor, "citizen" as opposed to "alien"). Tellingly, maternalism was judged "unsystematic and unscientific" by a post–World War I generation of feminists and eventually abandoned (1107–8). But women reformers at the turn of the century and beyond it clung to maternal models for an obvious reason: because they continued to be pivotal in shaping their political and social status.[111] Throughout the industrializing West, policy makers in the era of welfare's emergence were unable to separate reproductive issues from nationalist agendas.

KIN AND NATION

Thus social scientific interest in primitive rites designed to usher women into marriage was part of a more general effort to locate the transhistorical and transcultural foundations of male control over female sexuality and reproduction. The conviction of many social scientists appears to have been fairly widespread: contemplating the bald methods of a primitive social order could be affirmational as well as educational. In keeping with this, there is something exaggerated about the primitive affinities proclaimed by members of Mrs. Brook's circle in *The Awkward Age*. One could say that the tribal ideal that prevails there acquires a quasi-religious intensity, with "all outside the family religion being regarded as aliens or enemies."[112] As intimate as any Gemeinschaft horde, community members read each other's minds and communicate without audible utterances or visible signs. They refer continually to their circle as an extended family or kinship structure. The Duchess emphasizes her *"cousinage"* with the Brookenhams; Longdon is the *"oncle d'Amérique"*; and Mrs. Brook and Vanderbank speculate on their potential siblinghood (187, 143, 146). Mrs. Brook is especially committed to this metaphor: the "we" that designates the circle is never distinguishable from the "we" that designates her family.

Hence the recurrence of the word "kind," almost always connoting generic or species likeness. A representative instance comes in the final encounter between Vanderbank and Nanda. "Vanderbank," comments the narrator, "had not been in the room ten seconds before he showed that he had arrived to be kind. Kindness therefore becomes for us, by a quick turn of the glass that reflects the whole scene, the high pitch of the concert—a kindness that almost immediately filled the place, to the exclusion of everything else" (346–47). Kindness is more important for what it suppresses than for what it signifies. Doubled by the mirror that "reflects the whole scene," Vanderbank's kindness projects a deceptive sense of magnitude. What could be meant by a kindness that excludes? What sort of kindness functions as a boundary? As we have seen, kindness can be a term for same-sex desire, the desire for "kind" that in James leads to the exclusion or "sacrifice" of desire. But kindness is also a rule of kinship. This scene, which dramatizes Vanderbank's final failure to propose to Nanda, suggests that his failure may be an expression of kinship rules. To Vanderbank, Nanda is taboo. In this sense, Vanderbank's celibacy is overdetermined: by his homosexuality, to be sure, but also by social law. Let us recall, for a moment, an earlier conversation between Mitchy, the circle's nouveau-riche "son of a shoemaker," and Nanda, on the topic of hereditary prejudice. "[My knowledge] doesn't shock in you a single hereditary prejudice," Nanda observes. "There's a kind of delicacy you haven't got," she continues, "some other kinds, certainly. But not *the* kind" (259–60). Mitchy's lack of hereditary prejudice, according to Nanda, is the sign of his marginality. This is consistent with a definition that James once gave of prejudice as a "fatal obliquity of vision [that] inheres not wholly in any individual but is some indefinable property in the social atmosphere." The product of "birth, education, association," prejudice is a quality that defines a community's boundaries: insiders feel it, outsiders don't.[113] Though Mitchy describes himself in the very same dialogue as part of the circle "by my contacts, my associations, my indifferences" (262), his lack of hereditary prejudice stamps him irrevocably as an outsider.

John F. McLennan's *Primitive Marriage* (1886) identifies among the clans who inhabited the Scottish Highlands a prohibition against "marriages between members of the same primitive stock." He then goes on to speculate that "originally a man was not allowed to marry a woman of his own clan, and that, subsequent to the interfusion of the clans, the ancient prejudice remained; the rule for enforcing it—the question of degrees of affinity apart—would just be the rule of Manu."[114] McLennan's discussion of Scottish tribal rites has an uncanny appropriateness for a social circle made up of Brookenhams, Vanderbanks, Grendons, and Cashmores, who summer in the Scottish Highlands and hunger for social ritual.[115] Vanderbank's reluctance to marry Nanda may imply an "ancient prejudice" that lingers long after the demise of the original stock. As Nanda explains to Longdon in the novel's closing scene, "[Vanderbank] did his best. But he couldn't. And he's so right—for himself" (382). Like organic art, Vanderbank is true to "the law of [his] kind" (18).

And that "kind" is embattled: besieged, according to its own lights, by Jewish moneylenders, nouveau-riche Americans, and other varieties of disreputable "immigrants." Yet the Brookenham circle is also, as I have suggested, withering away from within, a collective emblem of "degeneration." While Mrs. Brook has the requisite four children to ensure the perpetuation of upper-class stock, her own children promise none. The spiritual consequences are troubling: there may be no grandchildren to fulfill the obligatory rites of ancestor worship. Worries of this kind spurred the nationalist agendas of socialists like Karl Pearson. His *Chances of Death* (1897), which displayed his conversance with the latest statistical methods and social scientific ideas, also reflected his ongoing interest in kinship, folk belief, and comparative religion. All of these subjects informed Pearson's politics, itself a peculiar blend of ethnocentrism, eugenicism, imperialism, and public assistance. "No thoughtful socialist," Pearson wrote, "would object to cultivate Uganda *at the expense of its present occupiers* if Lancashire were starving." There should not be so much "play . . . to intragroup competition," he concluded, that "we should be crushed in the extra-group struggle for existence." Pearson predicted the rampant nationalism of late-nineteenth-century Europe would steer the West toward socialism. Ever in search of ethnic continuities, he found sanction for his theories in the semisocialistic town life of medieval Germany, a socialism that had evolved from perpetual warfare with neighboring states. No weapon in a national arsenal, from superstition to benefits for large families of good stock, should be overlooked in shoring up a people against external threats.[116] Religious beliefs, both conventional and not, were valued as sources of social unity.[117] As I have pointed out, Pearson's positions were articulated against the spiritually weighted social Darwinism of Benjamin Kidd. Pearson sympathized with sociologists like Hobhouse, who resented Kidd's translations of their principles into a popularly digestible form more influential than their own writings.[118] For Pearson, however, the greatest drawback of Kidd's analysis was his advocacy of religion on the basis of its "ultra-rationalism."

Kidd begins his best-selling *Social Evolution* with a claim for the fundamental compatibility of science and religion. Religion can be fully justified on scientific grounds, he believes, though no social scientist has yet taken up that challenge (21–22).[119] He goes on to argue that evolution has always opposed individual interest and collective welfare: the cost of progress is mass casualties. "The evolutionist may be convinced that what is called the exploitation of the masses, is but the present-day form of the rivalry of life which he has watched from the beginning, and that the sacrifice of some in the cause of the future interests of the whole social organism is a necessary feature of our progress." "But this is no real argument addressed to those who most naturally object to be exploited and sacrificed." Progress, Kidd points out, can have no "rational sanction" for most of mankind. Mass reason points inevitably to socialism (69–70). Having acknowledged socialism's rational basis, Kidd introduces, in a pair of chapters entitled "The Central Feature of Human History" and "The Function of Religious Beliefs in the Evolution of Society," a perspective "from another planet." This hypothetical visitor has noticed in every town vast edifices devoted to strange practices, which are dismissed by his scientific guide as products of a residual "instinct peculiar to the childhood of the race." These edifices supply a stage for what Kidd, in a powerful revision of social Darwinism, calls the central struggle of history: between individual reason (progress) and collective feeling (religion) (82–84). The struggle is inevitable; religion and rationalism collide and diverge in one evolutionary *Liebestod*.

As these statements imply, the concept of sacrifice is essential to Kidd's theory. The sacrifice of will is the fundamental individual act; the sacrifice of the masses is fundamental to social welfare. Society depends on religion, and religion depends on sacrifice. "As we understand how an ultra-rational sanction for the sacrifice of the interests of the individual to those of the social organism has been a feature common to all religions we see, also, why the conception of sacrifice has occupied such a central place in nearly all beliefs." It has always been the tendency of religions "to surround this principle with the most impressive and stupendous of sanctions."[116] Kidd is not simply talking here about an impulse of self-denial. He is describing an essential social practice. His attention to the status of the sacrificed majority, as well as to the role of oblatory rites over time, confirms his overriding commitment (despite the charges of Pearson and Hobhouse) to sociological questions.[120]

Kidd's claims for the centrality of religion in modern society found support in Arthur Balfour's *The Foundations of Belief* (1895).[121] Balfour, who was a Tory politician and future prime minister, realized the religious possibility imagined by Benjamin Jowett ("If religion is to be saved at all it must be through the laity and statesmen, & c. not through the clergy").[122] Balfour's antagonism toward an unqualified "rationalism" also recalls Kidd. Balfour's book confirms the extent to which belief had become a matter of scientific and political interest. Theology, he notes at the start, "has enlarged its borders" to include competencies traditional theologians never dreamed of. "For, in truth, the decisive battles of Theology are fought beyond its frontiers" (1–2). A former student as well as brother-in-law of the theologian Henry Sidgwick and a friend of Frederick Myers, a reknowned psychic researcher, Balfour had experimented with the ultra-rational or extrasensory dimension firsthand. Balfour's own attempts to contact the dead were used as evidence against a conventional empiricism. Rationalism, he wrote, can obscure universal truths, "pervert[ing] the judgment of the most distinguished observers . . . making it impossible for those affected to draw the simplest inference, even from the most conclusive experiments."[123] Balfour applauds a certain resistance to explanation as the ultimate type of empiricism. His privileged example is the church's disavowal of periodic efforts to verify the Trinity, inspired, in turn, by Gnostic, Neoplatonic, and rationalist creeds. The church preserved the idea of revelation, he observes admiringly, "in all its inexplicable fulness." Their consistency on this point ensured that no later era would be bound by any particular notion of "truth." Had the church incorporated, for example, an Arian logic, "so alien and impossible to modern modes of thought," they would have inhibited future adherence to a doctrine that still moves "millions of pious souls" (287). Balfour's vision seems more conciliatory than Kidd's, since it claims a scientific, evidentiary warrant for the highest spiritual idealism. But the claim is based on a very idiosyncratic notion of evidence. Balfour's preferred region is "the dim twilight where religion and science are indistinguishable" (294). Science brings us to the summit of faith, and faith keeps us afloat up there. In his scheme, scientific authority is not quite fixed, nor is religious faith groundless.

Karl Pearson offers a harsh indictment of Balfour's dim theology, which he sees as the expression of a "decadent" traditionalism, ill-equipped to accommodate the methods and insights of modern science. Pearson compares Balfour to "a child," who mocks science because its ability to explain "motion, the phases, the shapes and even the physical and chemical surface conditions of the heavenly bodies" stops short of the ability to "bring the moon into the nursery, cut it open and show its actual contents."[124] Any of these charges might be justifiably leveled at the members of Mrs. Brook's circle. Self-consciously decadent, they are also "contrary," willfully benighted (225). For all their high intellectual talk, they seem collectively resigned to a state of resentful bewilderment. James's characters recall Balfour rather than Kidd, and in doing so reveal an important distinction between their respective appropriations of religion. For Kidd, the relationship between religion and science is one of reciprocity. The rational and ultrarational are mutually stimulating; in balance, they afford greater social clarity. Balfour, however, reconciles the antagonism of religion and science by collapsing both in mystery. He celebrates doubt by making it the unavoidable premise of the most powerful theological and scientific systems to date.

The inspiration behind Balfour's views is hinted at by Pearson. As the leading light of an elite in the twilight of its reign, Balfour cannot see (as even Kidd can) that religion has an explicit *social function* in the modern era. From his political and philosophical height, Balfour neither understands modern social processes nor grasps the valuably rational uses of religion. A more practical appreciation of these interdependencies was available in works by L. T. Hobhouse, E. A. Westermarck, Robertson Smith, and Andrew Lang. Aspirations toward higher spiritual value, toward universally sanctioned kinship ties, they believed, were fully implicit in modern social forms. Where analysts like Kidd and Balfour classified religion as irrational and stressed its residual appeal in the modern era, social scientists like Hobhouse and Westermarck emphasized the reasonableness and ongoing vitality of religious ideas. Powerful concepts and beliefs, they believed, didn't linger in some dilapidated state, awaiting recuperation or extinction. They were ceaselessly reinvigorated by adaptation to new methods and institutions. Works such as Robertson Smith's *Lectures on the Religion of the Semites* or Westermarck's *Origin of the Moral Ideas* reveal how subjects supposedly inimical to rational inquiry supplied the basic matter for a modern science of society.

It is mistaken, in my view, to read the moral considerations of these works as quaint and antiquarian, and therefore as out of step with the central preoccupations of modern sociology.[125] I have been arguing that questions of a religious and moral nature were fundamental to the shaping of the modern social science disciplines at the turn of the century, particularly sociology. One key to these concerns is the rite of sacrifice, and accordingly, I have explored the representation of sacrifice through a particular field of issues, defined by a primary literary text, in this case *The Awkward Age*. I have also in each case identified a certain biographical component, some "personal" explanation for the author's interest in the subject and for the shape that these preoccupations took.

James's life offers many points of entry for the social scientific perspective. An obvious source is his career-long interest in the fiction of "social botanists" like Balzac.[126] There is also the influence of personal friends or acquaintances with direct ties to social scientific developments, including Andrew Lang, H. G. Wells, and Thomas Huxley. Among the most compelling of the objective sources is James's library, with its impressive array of social theory. The evidence, from marginalia, letters, etcetera, that James read many of them suggests that his engagement was deep.[127] Without question, however, James's strongest link to social science was familial: the influence of his father, the social scientific theologian and his brother, sometime theologian, more often philosopher and psychologist. Henry James Sr.'s Swedenborgian allegiances brought his interests into line with many of the issues that concerned contemporary social scientists. His religious principles were shaped with the challenges of "science" before him. As one scholar has noted, "science" for such as James and company always meant, "'social' science."[128] The main beliefs of the elder James—his view of the self as realized *in* society, his idea of collective life as an expression of divinity—are compatible with the fundamentals of social science,[129] and his writings on kinship and ritual, which sometimes unleashed a rabid anti-Semitism, have special relevance for other late-nineteenth-century social scientific accounts under consideration here. In fact, some passages from works by Henry James Sr. seem close enough to dialogues in *The Awkward Age* to suggest a direct link.

In *The Secret of Swedenborg* (1869), Henry Sr. identifies a "hereditary consciousness" that "separate[s] us from other men" and precludes our recognition that we are all "of one identical moral substance." As a corrective to these "hereditary prejudices," he poses an ideal of "*kindness*," a "sentiment which makes us feel the fellowship or equality of our *kind*."[130] James's sympathetic liberalism would seem inconsistent with another thread of his argument, anti-Semitism, were it not that James holds "the chosen people" responsible for an exclusivist creed incongruent with his ideal society. Christ is made a Jew, according to James, in order to provide a properly base starting point for his future glorification. In an antithetical sense, Christ is begun low so that he may rise to the highest spiritual standard. His humane nature made him "a stranger in his own home, a self-driven outcast."[131] To James, Jews are anathema, identified with a damning "pride of morality." As James went on to observe, this moralism is "the parent of all sensual and degrading ideas of God, the parent of all cruel and unclean and abominable worship . . . [which] prompts the crucifixion of those affections as especially well-pleasing to Him, and bids me therefore offer my child to the flames."[132] Henry James Sr. comes almost as close as Schopenhauer to justifying anti-Semitism on the grounds that the Jews crucified Christ in fulfillment of their ongoing addiction to sacrificial practices. "What other nation ever lived on earth," he asks in *The Nature of Evil*, "capable *en masse* of such superstition?"[133] James's ideal church prohibits heathen ritual: "no priesthood . . . nor any instituted rites or ordinances . . . no hell." Is it possible to detect echoes of this description in a summary written ten years later by his son Henry? Here is Henry James Jr.'s account, from his biography of Hawthorne, of what is "absent from the texture of American life": "No sovereign, no court, no personal loyalty, no aristocracy, no church, no clergy . . . nor parsonages . . . nor ivied ruins; no cathedrals, nor abbeys, nor little Norman churches."[134] The immediate source is Hawthorne's own despairing preface to *The Marble Faun*: can romance be written "where there is no shadow, no antiquity, no mystery?"[135] Yet James's father may also have inspired his reflections, a possibility supported by the abundance of spiritually toned omissions. Whether read ironically or taken straight, Henry Jr.'s list seems at odds with the paternal source. His larger subject is Hawthorne's scant aesthetic resources, but his target may well be Henry Sr.'s spiritual vacancy. In contrast to his father's triumphant repudiation of intermediaries between man and God, Henry James Jr. laments the loss of religious edifices and ritual sites. It's not only that they enhance the landscape; they may also, in Henry Jr.'s mind, furnish the aesthetic spirit.

The many occasions for philosophical speculation in *The Awkward Age* appear similarly resonant. As the subject of a dialogue between Mitchy and Nanda, "hereditary prejudice" seems pejorative. After all, Mitchy lacks it, and he is the novel's "good man." But we also know that James defended the principle in several places. Remember that he called it "a fatal obliquity of vision," a privilege reserved for social insiders. Mitchy may be regarded as, in some sense, a sacrifice to the concept: Nanda calls him a "martyr" (116). But this only enhances the value of the prejudice he offends. The novelist of discriminating differences embraces what his father's smiling Swedenborgianism rejects. James's preoccupation with the strict kinship rules preserved by ancient and primitive societies is consistent, as I have been suggesting, with any number of social scientific analyses of his day. The father's world was one of theological and philosophical necessity, the son's of ordinary social behavior and the rites essential to its proper mediation. Henry Jr. would have felt more sympathy for what his father called the "carnality" of the Jews, their incredible insistence that "God cares what he eats," "this Jewish typicality, this extraordinary Divine interference with seasons and days, with fasts and festivals, with meats and drinks, with houses and furniture, with dress and decoration."[136] I am less interested in whether Henry Jr. shared his father's anti-Semitic sentiments—he probably did, to some extent—than in the obvious ties between the "sensual" and ritualized way of life his father considered "Jewish" and those recreated in his novels.

While Henry Sr.'s social writings represented a body of thought at once too intolerant and too broadly optimistic, William James's philosophical and social scientific vocation seems to have aroused gender anxieties in his "younger, vainer brother." These anxieties were not without an intellectual payoff. Henry Jr. appears to have cultivated, presumably in response to his brother's work, an alertness to what might be called social science's feminine shadow. In the theories of various social scientists of the era, the subject of women reveals a persisting dependence on disavowed biological categories. From William James's *Principles of Psychology* to Leonard Hobhouse's *Mind in Evolution*, social science displayed an obsession with the essential quality of female traits.[137] Henry James's attention to female development, and to the construction of "femininity" in particular, was part of the same intellectual climate that produced countless evolutionary readings of women's status from primitive to modern times.

Henry James's approach to modern women can be considered a form of social scientific inquiry in its own right, a view of women's clinical interest, given their various conditions of mind, passion, and disease. Like some contemporary social scientists (G. Stanley Hall, for example), James distinguishes his own "feminine" attributes from his "masculine" ones, revering female powers of procreation while aspiring to a male cultural authority that might displace them. Both the Jamesian novel and a developing social science were ideological expressions of an intellectual scene where gender played a central role in mediating social change. They reconcile gender issues in complexly parallel, often contrary ways. In the Jamesian novel, the feminine is central but distrusted, while a masculine scientific ideal remains marginalized yet powerful. In contemporary social scientific writings, a dominant rational ideal is gendered as masculine, while feminine principles are muted but ever potent. It is a matter of perspective and degree: social science disguises its pivotal feminine identifications; the Jamesian novel denies its scientific aspirations.

H. G. Wells was especially sensitive to what he saw as Henry James's envy of positivism. He accused James and his followers of trying to turn professional letters into a science. "Whenever criticism of any art becomes specialised and professional," Wells wrote, "whenever a class of adjudicators is brought into existence, those adjudicators are apt to become as a class distrustful of their immediate impressions. . . . They begin to emulate the classifications and exact measurements of a science, and to set up ideals and rules as data for such classification and measurement."[138] William James shared Wells's suspicions. He had strong ideas about what made good literary criticism and fiction, and he sometimes criticized the scrutinizing habits of the characters in his brother's novels. In a famous letter, he cited "the tendency of [Henry's] personages to reflect on themselves and give an acute critical scientific introspective classification of their own natures and states of mind."[139] His remark would seem to suggest that his brother specialized in representing social scientific thought itself. And indeed Henry James may be said to have helped introduce its generalizing methods: typing, idealizing, categorization by groups. Yet he persistently questioned his affinity for these abstractions, a questioning articulated both overtly, as in his debates with Wells, and more powerfully (if obliquely) in the ambivalence his novels convey toward these categories as devices of social control.

James's fiction knowingly incorporates the social discourses with which it is in dialogue. It is no mere coincidence that social science and literary studies, which James's fiction and criticism helped to inaugurate, were institutionalized at the same historical moment.[140] Nor were social scientists themselves unresponsive to the possible overlap between their own fledgling endeavors and the professionalization of what had formerly been called aesthetic sensibility. There was a surprising willingness on the part of some social scientists to concede a dependence on literary techniques. By the third edition of *The Golden Bough*, for example, Frazer appears eager to promote the ambiguity of his enterprise. His powerful description of the priest at Nemi "had become a question of style and literary tactics." He continues: "By discarding the austere form, without, I hope, sacrificing the solid substance of a scientific treatise, I thought to cast my materials into a more artistic mould and so perhaps to attract readers. . . . Thus I put the mysterious priest of Nemi, so to say, in the forefront of the picture."[141] He wants to have his cake and eat it too. His aims—"haunting," "tragic," "gloom"—seem patently melodramatic. But he makes no concessions on scientific grounds.

The source of Frazer's practicality is his belief in the functional test of truths. Truth may be various, but "conduct" tells. "Superstition" may be "a wrong motive," he noted elsewhere, but it has prompted "multitudes" to "right action." He concludes: "Once the harbour lights are passed and the ship is in port, it matters little whether the pilot steered by a Jack-o'-lantern or by the stars."[142] "Right action" is an unending plot, covering centuries of human history. The methods we use in pursuing the remote and alien are less important than the morals we draw from the encounter. There is no harm in resorting to literary jack-o'-lanterns now and then—that is, if their ultimate end is consensual truth. Exotic terrain—ancient or primitive societies—is unquestionably plain. Frazer assumes that, however it appears, it will yield recognizable meaning.

This was the attraction of "the primitive" for many observers of modern life. In the work of classical theorists like Spencer and Durkheim, progressivists who favored the modern stage of development, descriptions of primitive forms as ideal research objects betray a certain nostalgia. In primitive religion, Durkheim writes, theories and practices "are shown in all their nudity and offer themselves to an examination, it requiring only the slightest effort to lay them open. That which is accessory or secondary, the development of luxury, has not yet come to hide the principal elements."[143] Defined as more simple and even as more real, primitive forms project an invaluable visibility. The romancing of the primitive in an increasingly heterogeneous and conflicted society was an effort by analogy to render that society transparent. Despite their conviction of its essential instability and their faith in modern rationality, social scientists, more than any other group, contributed to the vogue of primitivism that prevailed at the turn of the century. The extension of Western colonial empires, the obsession with origins inspired by Darwinian evolutionary ideas, and the search for fundamental values in an increasingly complex modern society all fueled a fascination with primitive life. *The Awkward Age* testifies to this fascination.

James's characters have become primitives in their desperate "period . . . of tension and apprehension" as they try to accommodate new and alarming liberties. More precisely, James's fictional community is metaprimitive, in that its relationship to primitivism is voluntary, experimental. There is a prevailing belief that an invigorated system of social taboos can alleviate a state of "crisis" (11). In *Totem and Taboo*, Freud specifies a certain "civilized" relationship to primitive methods. He follows up an account of the stringent taboos governing Batta life with the comment of a Dutch missionary, "from what he knows of the Battas he believes the maintenance of most of these rules to be very necessary." James's characters, we might say, reflect like missionaries on their own Batta practices. Social prohibitions, they believe, are "very necessary"; hence their conscious production of kinship rules. Yet they insist that these rules are natural, in order to ensure their mystical power. Like Freud, who describes himself in the note to the Hebrew translation of his book as "completely estranged" from Judaism and "nationalist ideals," yet Jewish in his "essential nature"—a concept, he adds, that will "someday . . . become accessible to the scientific mind"—James's characters maintain an alienated conviction of the binding powers of ancient belief.[144]

James is like and unlike the members of his fictional community. His novel is a comedy of manners, after all, and his characters' self-generated primitivism is treated with a good deal of irony. Yet the comic is never fully James's note, and the book offers a serious, even morbid appraisal of these matters. James recognized the need for powerful, even brutal forms of cultural repair. Like a missionary confronting a Batta rite, James sees sacrifice as essential to the society of *The Awkward Age*. Unlike the missionary, however, who assumes the benightedness of his subjects, James invests his characters with sacrificial consciousness. The novel opens upon a "London life" driven by "tit for tat" (39). People live in states of relative deprivation and plenitude, consumed by envy or bloated with a sense of privilege. Vanderbank's plum of a job, the General Audit, is "A thing a good many fellows would give a pound of their flesh for" (29–30). Objectified in a system of exchange, as an expenditure or a quick source of cash, human flesh is readily prostituted. Yet falling rains and priestly characters confirm the higher purpose of these sensual transactions. Flesh destined for gods is always sacred. To be given is to be saved. One of the most awesome religious customs has been enfolded in present-day marketplace economics.

CHARITY

In James's novel ancient sacrifice is implied in every act of exchange. Economy and spirituality are mutually sustaining. Modern society is based on a rational economics that is fundamentally sacrificial. But it also depends on periodic enactments—whether annihilation or exile—that are generically religious. James's richly doubled sense of sacrifice infuses his every example. In the opening dialogue between Longdon and Vanderbank, states of credit and debit are ever shifting; the continuous talk of loss and gain serves as implicit commentary on it. They deliberately deny each other explanations just as they subject each other to excessive hanging on replies. Thus, Vanderbank is inspired by the "promise of pleasant things" in his new friend Longdon to consider paying for his cab (30). But this very perception (of Longdon's vast wealth) stops him. Given their inequality, Vanderbank cannot and need not tax his limited resources. Instead, he plies Longdon with cigarettes and gossip. In a similar vein, Little Aggie is introduced as the Duchess's compensation: she takes "the place of a daughter early lost" (36). Vanderbank's apparent guilt over the death of a younger brother is filtered through the brother's characterization as an object of special attentions: his mother vacationing at the sea, "for his benefit" (40). As Vanderbank observes, in trying to summarize through Longdon the essential meaning of modern society, "It strikes you that, right and left, probably, we keep giving each other away" (39). People are identified by what is given up on their behalf. The paradox of Miles Vanderbank's pathetically abbreviated life is that he himself becomes the price of the special attentions his survival requires. His situation anticipates the fates of the novel's two female adolescents. In a world where a human life is given over with as much thought as a dinner invitation, it is more than a little ominous that Nanda strikes Longdon from the beginning as "much more like the dead than like the living" (42).

This is all figurative to a degree. These are constructions after the fact. The Duchess's own daughter is "lost"; she sees Aggie as her replacement. Vanderbank's brother is dead; the family struggles to convince itself that everything was done to prevent it. Yet people do suffer extravagantly in this society. They also suffer differentially: some are crushed, while others prevail. When people are offered up rather than things, we are in the highest reaches of solemnity. There is very little disagreement in the literature on this point. Recall Mauss and Hubert on the Hindus, who believed in "the identity" of their gifts (whether grains, bulls, or humans) but nevertheless distinguished between "*objective sacrifices*" of things "real or ideal" and "*personal sacrifices*," more directly affecting the sacrifier. Robertson Smith likewise confirms that human victims were reserved for occasions of "extreme peril." In his discussion of human sacrifice in Greece, Andrew Lang refines Smith's theory, to distinguish a form of sacrifice that is "a survival of cannibalism," where "the human victim is a captive or other foreigner," from "expiatory or piacular" sacrifice, where "the victim is a fellow tribesman."[145]

The degrees of sacrificial action described in these accounts are consistent with the basic script of James's novel. The talk in the opening scene prepares for a novelistic plot centered upon human sacrifice. As I have suggested, the novel's sacrificial economy reproduces and also reinforces its dominant religious practice. Where one is signified, the other is implied. The balancing of ledgers in the preliminary dialogue is constant. Take, for instance, the encounters between Nanda and Vanderbank. Vanderbank obsesses about the various trifles he has failed to give Nanda ("I ought to have sent you some flowers. . . . I haven't even brought a box of sweets" [349]), which are of course mere decoys for his failure to give himself. That failure confirms Nanda's impossibility and ensures that she herself will be given up as the novel's goat. Mrs. Brook is bitterly resentful that the Duchess has "never had to pay" for her excesses (233), but reminds Nanda that every debit will be compensated—eventually. Of Mrs. Brook's children, Harold seems to have taken her counsel most to heart. He not only makes a case for the gravity of the familial sacrifice ("The dear man's taking her quite over. . . . I think we ought to *get* something" [282]), he has also compiled by the novel's end an apparently unlimited string of debts himself. His mother's label for him, a "fish" in a sea of "whales," implies that his payment may be of the highest. As the novel's virtuous oracle, Mitchy, remarks, "Everything's gain that isn't loss" (269). Sacrifice in *The Awkward Age* is tautology: a communal life and death sentence in one. Sacrifice infuses every utterance; it defines every exchange; it determines every act.

The Brookenhams, who "give" their daughter, are by their own lights great sacrificers (298–99). They are poor relations, destined to forfeit where others profit. Mr. Brookenham is a second brother, who inherits the inferior property (32). His public "place . . . Rivers and Lakes," recalls the resentful toad in one of Andrew Lang's favorite myths. Enraged at being denied a taste of honey by a taunting woodpecker, the toad takes revenge by swallowing up "all the water of the rivers and lakes." He becomes so excited by the success of his drought that he begins to dance, causing the stolen waters to gush once again. Lang omits the toad's reaction to his renewed impotence (1:43–44). But one could argue that James dramatizes it, not in Mr. Brookenham, the actual administrator of Rivers and Lakes, but in the person of his wife. Like the mythic toad, Mrs. Brook is infuriated by her inability to control a prevailing dynamic of loss and gain. She too feels that she is denied the taste of honey so accessible to others. The Brookenhams are Judaeans in arid land, surrounded by richer and more resourceful neighbors. As described in a contemporary study of religion, "Judaea was an isolated valley with enough resources to create a national life, yet not large enough to resist invasion." A "steady increase in . . . drought" led to "famine and destitution. . . . The breach between God and man was made broader and more formidable than ever . . . sacrifice was extolled as the cardinal virtue, and hardship as the only road to morality and character. This is the philosophy of defecit expanded and augmented."[146]

Mrs. Brook's special obsession with Jews, especially in their role as moneylenders, is relevant here. She worries that her profligate son Harold has borrowed from them (71) and envisions society overrun by Jews (239). Her nightmare, the "gigantically rich . . . Baron Schack or Schmack," is invested with a peculiar but definitive impairment. This "Jew man," she notes, has an "awful stammer," supposedly because there is "no roof to his mouth" (239). This amounts to an intriguing inversion of the usual Jewish stereotype, where verbal facility enables diabolical schemes.[147] But the handicap imagined by Mrs. Brook justifies the Baron's irrevocable exclusion from the place of meaningful social exchange, the humming salon. He can hire a quick-witted English boy "to do his conversation for him," but this only confirms his permanent estrangement. The image is compelling because it's extreme, an extremity inspired evidently by Mrs. Brook's fear of affinity. Like the legendary Judaeans, the Brookenhams are always in the red. "One doesn't quite know what they live on," Vanderbank comments (31–32). Parental efforts to maintain a stiff upper lip are undercut by the preternatural awareness of their children. Harold wrings every possible quid out of his strapped parents and adds insult to injury with jeering queries ("Do we live beyond our means?" [54]). There is undoubtedly some vengeance in Mrs. Brook's image of this terrible son as a fish offering to maternal whales—better mothers than she, perhaps, but also more dangerous (297–98).

The Duchess's entrance, hard upon the interview of mother and son, provides a complementary account of how the Brookenhams fare against more favored kin. Despite her appearance ("massive," "passionless forehead," "long lip"), a disadvantage beside the light and lovely Mrs. Brook, credit is all on the Duchess's side (58). "Rich with the spoils of Italy," she can indulge "her passions," which include a habitual demand for early tea and the complete sequestration of her daughter (56). Because she has means, she can carry on an affair with the slimy Petherton without compromising her religious respectability. High standards can be bought as well as earned. In the hands of the Duchess, the two are indistinguishable. Good standing is a result of divine intervention; the ability to give more and better offerings ensures continued rewards. Where the Duchess radiates plenitude, Mrs. Brook's lot is scarcity. Her declaration to a group of guests that Nanda has gone off to visit "the workhouse" serves to classify relief work as familial routine (152). Mrs. Brook is also a regular counselor for the needy in her circle. Mrs. Brook's "social work" among kin might be understood as her way of compensating their generosity to her family. She can't repay them in kind, but she can offer what she has—including her daughter. Mrs. Brook's charity work, both among the actual poor outside her circle and the emotionally impoverished within, is a kind of repetition compulsion. She describes her own family as enveloped in "a perpetual mental mourning" and calls them, "a case for that investigating Society" (209). The Brookenhams' status as the central charity case of *The Awkward Age* is one of the more pressing reasons why their children are driven into the sacrificial smoke.

We have considered at length the various motivations of the novel's maternal center and its celibate but eminently eligible bachelor. The motivations of the "ancient" "priest"—the source, I have suggested, of the novel's plot—remain somewhat obscure. Longdon's qualities of reticence, detachment, and seriousness reinforce his spiritual status. Yet the priestly connection is somewhat qualified ("almost . . . a priest"), probably due in part to the controversial status of the priesthood in James's time (27–28). Fredric Jameson manages to concoct, from a postmodern vantage point, a relatively benign image. The role of the priest in late antiquity, he observes, was to release the world from magic, thus creating "the basis for our modern science and technology, and for capitalism."[148] But Robertson Smith outlines a more menacing image of priestly routine, featuring "especially sacrifices."[149] Both accounts inform the mysterious contradictions of Longdon's character. He appears caught between moral absolutism, which is softened by a near childlike capacity for wonder, and authoritarian efficiency. This is a man who, for all his ambivalence and depth, makes his wishes known and gets things done. The office of priest is not only associated with power but, in James's time particularly, with corruption and bad faith. Arthur Dimmesdale is only one portrait in a vast nineteenth-century gallery of dubious clerics. There is also the ending to *The Golden Bough*, which pictures the priest as the greedy consumer of the sacrifice, who would never (like the great dying god) sacrifice himself. Speaking here of Brahmanic tradition, Frazer comments, "Happily this grander theory of sacrifice does not oblige the priest to imitate his glorious prototype by dismembering his own body and shedding his blood on the altar."[150] Priests are in it for what they can get.

Like the priests described by contemporary social scientists, Longdon feeds on the sacrifices of others. The opening scene, where Longdon and Vanderbank exchange personal histories in their efforts to place one another in a larger kinship scheme, provides a revealing abbreviation of Longdon's story. Presumably heartsick over the loss of Lady Julia, Longdon builds a reclusive life from a series of accidents or calamities. The death of Longdon's father confers the customary property inheritance; the death of his sister's husband and son yields him her companionship. Her extraordinary need—"greater than any trouble of mine"—helps to put his own life in perspective. Clearly it helps to sustain him. It may be perverse to read this history in any but the most flattering light. Longdon inherits his father's holdings, like any only son, invests intelligently (the "little place in Suffolk" expands to his Beccles estate), and takes in a careworn sister (45). Still, the image of Longdon as one who profits from misfortune sticks, because it accords with the role he assumes subsequently, upon his return to London. In this sense, he is like Mrs. Brook. As analysts and resident caretakers of the fallen, damaged, and unhappy, they might even be considered rivals—though there hardly appears to be any dearth of business. Given the deterioration of modern London and of its inhabitants, *would* Longdon stay were he not in some way attracted to trouble, or used to exploiting it?

Longdon (like Mrs. Brook) responds to the bereftness of others from a sense of deprivation. If, according to her own lights, Mrs. Brook has less money and luck than almost everyone else, Longdon has neither the savoir faire of most men nor the love that is often its issue. Who in his position would not be seduced by pronouncements like the following: "You're delightful, you're wonderful. . . . we're lost. . . . you find us" (49). However much convinced he is of his own lack ("I'm no judge. . . . I'm no critic; I'm no talker" [49]), his stock in the novel's society runs high from the outset. This has to do, first of all, with his enormous wealth. He is, from Mrs. Brook's avaricious perspective, "the *oncle d'Amérique*, the eccentric benefactor, the fairy godmother" (143). He exudes prestige, recalling "the Primate or the French Ambassador" (213). To others he is a walking tributary or line of "credit": "Is he . . . so rich?" Mitchy inquires; "see, judge, guess, feel!" Vanderbank replies (264). Longdon's wealth carries sacred overtones. He is described as "blessed" (216), in anticipation of the bounty he is expected to bestow upon the community at large. Yet none of these forms of "good press" succeeds in fully disguising a habitual gloom, and possibly more. Nanda as usual is prescient. There is no humor or irony in her question: "What will he do to me? Anything dreadful?" (119). The fact that she both draws him in and warns him off, while "trembling" visibly (127), is an indication that she suspects more than geniality in his preferred protections. She divines that, for Longdon, women are commodities: "You feel as if my grandmother were quite *your* property" (126).

Through Nanda, Longdon accomplishes the ultimate feat of social engineering: bringing the dead back to life. Nanda is a Lady Julia he might possess and control once and for all. This is not to deny the attractiveness of his gifts. What sensitive adolescent would not respond to the loving scrutiny, and presents, of a wealthy man? Every attention, however, is surrounded by steel. His gorgeous house, which Nanda is encouraged to navigate with the air of "a partner . . . in the concern" has the look of a fortress. "The pink and purple surface" of the old brick wall, for instance, is "the fruit of the mild ages" (243). The implication that this old worn "color" is somehow related to the wall's "protective function" is furthered by another image of the house: "red roofed, well assured of its right to the place it took up in the world" (245). Could there be a link between the color red and this assurance of place? Inside, there is, a "look of possession," derived in part from "the tone of old red surfaces" (245). As Mitchy observes of these interior spoils, they appear to have "dropped straight from heaven" (253).

The female "dead" lining the walls, and the fact of Nanda's own sequestration (no matter how willingly), may suggest a deeper set of spiritual obligations. Edward Westermarck refers to a Scotch legend about Saint Columba's first attempt to build a cathedral. "The walls fell down as they were erected; he then received supernatural information that they would never stand unless a human victim was buried alive." Westermarck traces the practice of commemorating buildings and homes with "human . . . blood" from the Druids to mid-nineteenth century Halle, from the Kayans of Borneo to the latter-day Russian peasantry. "A new house or dwelling-place is commonly regarded as dangerous," he explains; "a wall or a tower is liable to fall down and cause destruction of life." It is only "natural, then, that attempts should be made to avert the danger." What "could be more effective than the offering up of a human victim"? One object of these "foundation-sacrifices," according to Mauss and Hubert, was to "create the [structure's] spirit or the protective divinity."[151] Power, in certain instances, might be defined as having the wherewithal to fortify oneself.

Longdon's guard is never down, which is reflected in the fact that for all his wealth he gives very little. The moments of extravagance are sufficiently rare to be noteworthy: the attending cab at Vanderbank's (30), his presents to Nanda (351). His expenditures contrast markedly with those of the novel's other rich man, Mitchy, who gives constantly (71, 79, 85). Longdon has mastered a skill particular to power rather than to wealth. One gives as little as possible, in order to demonstrate that one has nothing to gain in return. The wisdom of Longdon's course is proven by Mitchy's example. Because of his unlimited generosity, Mitchy retains an "immense indebtedness" (82). Dismissed as "bribery," his gifts confirm his irremediable difference (85).

Mr. Longdon's logic is more compatible with that of the Brookenhams. He understands gift giving as a highly ritualized form, designed to preserve status, not to change it. Longdon's gifts are of the sort that preserve structure. They might even be considered a type of potlatch, though hardly the "monstrous" and wasteful version later identified by Marcel Mauss. "Pot-latch," which means literally "to feed" or "to consume," was a form of gift giving (intratribal or intertribal) used by the rich and powerful to establish social dominance. In some contexts, its purpose was humiliation: giving to those who couldn't reciprocate, thus creating insurmountable debt and perpetual subservience.[152] It is telling that Longdon is singled out from the beginning as paying "tribute" (120). James would have known the Latin derivations of the word, which include the idea of a stream contributing its flow to a larger stream. Longdon's "tribute" to Nanda preserves both a synchronic continuity—society as is—and a diachronic continuity, since it celebrates Nanda's resemblance to an ancestor, the revered Lady Julia (120). It affirms both the miracle of genetic reproduction and the promise of pure kinship lines. These things, in Longdon's view, are matters of divine decree. One pays tribute in order to ensure status as well as salvation. This is consistent with Longdon's identification as a churchgoer (253). His piety is rivaled only by the Duchess and Aggie. But in their case, sexual appetite overtakes virtuous intent (despite the constant counsel of their

personal priest). Longdon alone remains uncompromised. Mrs. Brookenham envisions his exalted destiny as a "mysterious box under his bed." Her
instincts all alive, she watches it "grow while he sits there" (142).

What does it mean that Longdon's sole expense is Nanda? She is the
only concern in which he is willing to invest, even to the point of dowering
her. Longdon's decision has to do with what he perceives as the sacred
nature of her cause. She too has a brilliant destiny, caught by another geo-
metric figure: a "bright circle" (200–202). In his ambitious survey, *Morals
in Evolution*, Leonard Hobhouse notes that it was considered a privilege in
ancient Greece to "dower the orphan [or poor] girl." He ties this to a prior
tradition of obligatory almsgiving, which he traces from the ancient
Semitic and Vedic religions to the nineteenth-century Poor Law. In all
these cases, Hobhouse points out, "almsgiving" is "an act of merit." The
remarkably high stakes of the Sanskrit texts can be taken as representative:
"the prosperity of the liberal man never decays. . . . Success attends that
man in the sacrifice, and he secures for himself a friend in the future. He
who keeps his food to himself has his sin to himself" (344). According to
the Koran, "God . . . shall make almsgiving profitable" (346). Under
Christianity, care of the poor was among the duties specific to the priest.
Throughout this long history, what remained constant was the view of the
poor as the means to the salvation of the rich. In the words of Chrysostom,
"they are the healers of your wounds" (349). For Hobhouse, the seven-
teenth century stands as a critical turning point. "It is something to have
recognized," he writes, "that to have the poor always with us is not a blessing and that the duty of the rich is not exhausted by the most liberal giving
of alms" (352). From this point on, approaches to poverty become increasingly rationalized. The poor have "rights" to a "civilized existence" ensured by "independent labour." Hobhouse concludes that modern states—
and he cites broad continuities among Britain, France, Sweden, Denmark,
and the United States—have only begun to articulate this ideal (351).

In a liberal society, charity is a right of the poor because the status is
itself viewed as contingent and temporary. From a more traditional perspective, relative states of wealth and poverty express divine intent. A law
of compensation prevails: poverty and wealth are interdependent; prosperity requires a sacrificial return. There is no interest in the character or
potential of the poor, because their condition serves a higher end. Poverty
is essential to society. The poor don't have needs; the only necessity is that
they exist. The link between sacrifice and almsgiving was confirmed by an
influential standard: the *Encyclopedia Britannica* (1890) entry on Sacrifice.
In an extension of Robertson Smith's discussion of ancient rites, a second
author provides a follow-up account of the Christian liturgy. This author
focuses on a material dimension that is foregrounded in the Eucharist.
Since God was traditionally identified with the poor and recognized as

their protector, gifts to God might be offered in turn to the needy. "Consequently," he concludes, "alms have the virtue of a sacrifice."[153] This is consistent with some of the rite's earliest forms, which held that God imbibed its spiritual emanations, feeding on a sort of cerebral smoke, while its products were given to the poor. In many of these ancient cases, the poor have a distinctive role in sacrifice. If they are not themselves sacrificial objects, they become secondary sacrificial consumers.

Hobhouse's analysis offers a valuable instance of liberal social science confronting an "ancient" mode of reasoning it needs to transcend. To his credit, Hobhouse gives these assumptions a good deal of play in his analysis. He finds a genealogy for modern ideas about social protection in Gospel constructions of charity. But he believes in the gradual and irrevocable development of a rationality that regards poverty as a structural position and relief as a right. In the long run, he believes, poverty will be ancient history, as governments recognize their power and responsibility to eradicate it. In his own study of morals in evolution, Edward Westermarck is less willing to relegate poverty and its handling to the past, in part because he is more convinced of the ongoing vitality of ancient principles. Where Hobhouse sees triumphant breakthrough, Westermarck sees more sobering continuities. His analysis reveals how the practice of sacrificial alms is institutionalized at the turn of the twentieth century in the philosophic assumptions behind social welfare. Many of Westermarck's sources and quotations are familiar from Hobhouse. There is Leo the Great declaring "the food of the needy . . . the purchase-money of the kingdom of heaven." We encounter St. Chrysostom again: "As long as the market lasts, let us buy alms, or rather let us purchase salvation through alms." We hear charity labeled "a safe investment of money at good interest with God in heaven." We find similes from Ecclesiastes: "As water will quench a flaming fire, so alms maketh an atonement for sins" (1:555, 552). But these sources are put to different ends. In Westermarck, charity recovers its own genealogy. Originally, he believes, sacrifice, alms, and fasting were intertwined in a trinity of salvational obligations. At one time, fasting served as a *preparation* for sacrifice. Later, it became a *substitute* for it: the desire for food was *sacrificed* to the deity. As sacrifice declined among the Jews, for example, fasting surged. The fate of almsgiving was similar. As part of the sacrificial procedure, charity was given prior to a sacrifice, or a portion of the sacrifice was given as charity at the rite's conclusion. Gradually, almsgiving, like fasting, took the place of sacrifice (2:316–17). The "three cardinal disciplines which the synagogue transmitted to both the Christian Church and the Muhammedan mosque"—almsgiving, prayer, and fasting—all had their roots in sacrifice.

Westermarck is explicit on this point. Charity is an obligation in the higher religions because of its original tie to sacrifice. "Virtue," he writes, "lies in the self-abnegation of the donor, and its efficacy is measured by the 'sacrifice' which it costs him" (1:553, 565). In contrast to Hobhouse, Westermarck believes the notion of sacrificial alms becomes more prevalent over time, "extend[ing] to wider and wider circles of men." While primitive culture defines the community of kin as charity's limit, higher civilizations broaden this border. The Talmud dictates that alms be dispensed without regard for kinship or religious affiliation. Westermarck sees this legacy realized in modern society wherever concern about "welfare" transcends "the barriers of nationality" (1: 555–58). Westermarck's largest claim, then, is that modern beliefs about charity, including those informing international political questions, are derived from ancient practices. Implicit in his larger argument is a vitally important assumption— call it "methodological"—that Westermarck never quite brings out. This is the idea that any charitable act requires some calculation about kinship. Thus, a primitive may decide *not to give* because the potential recipient is a stranger. Or a Jew may decide *not to refrain from giving* on the same basis. As dictated by religious principles, charity invites judgments about relative conditions of familiarity and strangeness.

The implications of Westermarck's arguments are far-reaching. Most significant, is the way they illuminate a contemporary sphere of public debate on welfare. Let me offer a few propositions, inspired by Westermarck, but not confined to his claims. In any developed civilization, charity is based on an absolute differentiation between the donor and the recipient. Differentiation inheres in the type of exchange that charity is: charity almost always features someone perceived as wealthy giving to someone perceived as poor.[154] Differentiation lies in properties particular to each participant that are understood as *independent* of the exchange. In their book on the history of the Poor Law, Sidney and Beatrice Webb describe poverty as contagion—a characterization that is consistent with the arguments I have described. The poor, they write, "persisted in living at the lower level down to which they were pressed, and by their mere existence in disease and squalor, vice, mendicancy and crime, infecting and contaminating the rest of the community."[155] To practice charity is in some sense to cross or mediate a divide, effectively on behalf of its heightening and perpetuation. Charity has as much to do with the maintenance of borders and categories as its ritual source, sacrifice. I invoke this ritual source in order to amplify the perceived border between rich and poor. It extends, inevitably, to include the border between kin and stranger, pure and impure, God and man, sacred and profane. Charity, like sacrifice, is designed to sustain an equilibrium of difference. The key term here is equilibrium. For the question is, what do I need to give up in order to maintain things as they are against all odds? Modern charity, like ancient sacrifice, is a wager against the unpredictable.

Is it any wonder that Westermarck, in one of his most memorable images, likens sacrifice to modern life insurance? "When men offer the lives of their fellow-men in sacrifice to their gods," he writes, "they do so as a rule in the hopes of thereby saving their own. Human sacrifice is essentially a method of life-insurance" (1:466). Westermarck's genealogy gets underneath the logic of life insurance in a way that we have not seen before. Understood as an act of sacrificial protection, expressing fears of the unknown, life insurance becomes an ancient charm in a modern institutional setting. It is a rational innovation on a community's traditional way of arming itself against fate. If the proper forces are animated, a community can be protected against, and, more importantly, even avert, disaster. Westermarck never confronts the question of which "fellow-men" take the fall and which enjoy the benefits of the policy. Other contemporary social scientific analyses of poverty betray a greater sensitivity to these matters. Social scientists like W.E.B. Du Bois and Georg Simmel share Westermarck's conviction of the profound continuities between ancient and modern practices. At the same time, however, they are more alert to the particularity of poverty's function in modern society. They rise above a certain fatalism in Westermarck's narrative, where continuity implies inevitability. The basis of their theoretical alertness is the recognition that almsgiving has everything to do with matters of kinship and social status.

In *The Souls of Black Folk*, Du Bois recalls his surprise and embarrassment upon learning that all the beneficiaries of a White public relief fund were Black. He had just refused to contribute, he confesses, on the presumption that it would discriminate against his people. In light of his argument as a whole, however, Du Bois's surprise seems unmindful of his own deepest claims, or possibly disingenuous. From that perspective, the Black indigent have a far easier time securing public recognition than the Black middle classes. The Black poor are the ready object of a social conscience that gives (*do*) to social aliens, so that they may be kept away (*abeas*). To be needy, to require alms, is to occupy a defined social place. Or, to recall Georg Simmel's argument, poverty originates in attempts to amend it. Were there no alms, there would be no poverty. The construction of poverty enables the regulation of those whose differing life conditions might be productive of divergent and potentially destabilizing social norms. Poverty, as Simmel understands it, is a purely sociological condition, perhaps the purest there is. This is because it is a status constructed solely within social relations. "Sociologically speaking," Simmel writes, "the poor person" is one "who receives assistance." He is defined by what is done on his behalf.[156] Note that what has disappeared from the analyses of Du Bois and Simmel is any hint of a connection between poverty and nature. They deny that poverty is somehow constitutive of individuals or societies. Few other contemporaries were able to distinguish so clearly in their thinking about charity what was new and old, invention and fate. Most theorists remained entangled in these oppositions.

Simmel and Du Bois allow us to recognize some effects of a more recent "War on Poverty" as the reverse of its design. Like other wars in modern memory, this one has been more successful in defining antagonisms than in muting or eradicating them. Neither Simmel nor Du Bois advocated the abolition of government assistance to those in need. From Du Bois's perspective especially, poverty was the product of a complex set of past and present conditions, hardly susceptible to simple or rhetorical remedies. He implied that a welfare system constructed poverty so as to mitigate the need for more fundamental redistribution or reorganization.

PROTECTION

At the base of many modern notions about charity is a belief, whether acknowledged or submerged, in an economics of scarcity. From these perspectives, society in general and its individual members in particular revolve between the promise of plenitude and the fear of disaster. The poor are regarded as the inevitable casualties of such a system, to be protected because they are kin, or kept away because they are not. A significant portion of contemporary debate about social welfare was centered on this opposition. Was social assistance a matter of *protecting* one's own with the hope of strengthening the collectivity, in the tribal sense? Or was social assistance a means of caring for others as a way of mollifying and controlling them, in the modern colonial sense? Perhaps the most striking aspect of the debates on welfare was how much fundamental agreement there was about its necessity. Though they saw eye to eye on little else, socialists like Karl Pearson and conservatives like Arthur Balfour concurred that in an era of universal suffrage, the endurance of a certain type of civilization required certain compensations.

The reasoning in both cases was consistent with the logic of sacrifice. For Pearson, the maintenance of British imperial strength, a larger readiness to compete against other national powers, required a relaxation of the competitive struggle at home. Aliens or outsiders might be sacrificed (the residents of Uganda, for example), but an English proletariat deserved protection. Charity, in this instance, was defined as a means of sheltering kin for the sake of empowering the national tribe. For Balfour, there was little distinction to be made between the clamoring masses at home or abroad. Social welfare was not a sacred office, facilitating the preservation of *mine* against *them*. Charity was a simple matter of control. "Social legislation," Balfour wrote in a position paper of 1895, "is not merely to be distinguished from Socialist legislation but it is its most direct opposite and its most effective antidote."[157] Lord Salisbury, "the leader of those 'who toil not neither do they spin,'" lent his support to housing reform for similar reasons.[158] The clamoring masses that haunted the era's elites with their threat of socialism and anarchism were to be pacified with alms. A modern social system required payoffs, sacrifices on the part of the haves to the have-nots (at least, when the have-nots were not themselves being sacrificed). Had society grown kinder and gentler? Or had it suddenly recognized the political practicality of values characteristically identified with women and the domestic realm? D. G. Ritchie, who wrote on issues central to social science, distinguished between natural inheritance and inheritance in a "sociological sense," which turns on the socializing agency of mothers. "Religious leaders," he commented, "have understood that their success must depend on their mothers winning the race. When will political leaders come to recognise the same?"[159]

I have already referred to a turn-of-the-century discourse of maternalism, one that "exalted women's capacity to mother and extended to society as a whole the values of care, nurturance, and morality." By suggesting that social scientists detected a continuity between their developing interest in public welfare and women's roles as domestic caretakers, I do not mean to imply that they were deliberately appropriating the maternal principle. Here again, it took a woman speaking before the English Sociological Society to make this assumption explicit. "The woman, more obviously than the man, lives not for herself alone but for others," declared Sybella Graham, "and considers herself as part of a larger whole. The modern and womanly spirit of sympathy and oneness, influencing men as well as women . . . drives us to grapple with the social problems of poverty and disorganisation."[160] Taken together, the remarks of Lady Welby and Sybella Graham bracket the transformation of women's status during the years of social science's development. Implicitly, they trace, in keeping with the concerns of *The Awkward Age*, the reproduction of women at the turn of the century from natural maternal icons to professional consolers, critical functionaries of a welfare state. Responses to this transformation tended toward two distinct but not incompatible forms: on the one hand, an ongoing opposition between feminine instinct and scientific objectivity; on the other, an identification (on the part of many intellectuals) with a legendary female dynamism. The trajectory of Francis Walker's scholarly interests is exemplary, evolving as they did from sustained reflection on the discrepant reproduction rates of American elites and immigrants to a rigorous theoretical distancing of social science from femininity. Advocating a "stern and practical inquiry into the workings of government" and "the facts of society," he warned that "we must regard liberty no longer as a female, but as a fact." Walker's rhetoric fulfills Dorothy Ross's view of "the

aggressively masculine language . . . used to describe science and its purpose of control, [which] suggest that gender fears were among the anxieties
loosed by historical change that scientism could allay."[161]

Yet another outcome of these fears—the opposite of such distancing
tactics—was preoccupation. G. Stanley Hall's supposed reconciliation of
avowed feminine identifications with the masculine authority of science in
a moment of intellectual "crisis" led, he claimed, to a period of "productiveness and creation." In this spirit of synthesis, he christened his new
psychological movement "the woman's science."[162] Hall's personal renaissance suggests a key development in modern social science: its idealized
pursuit of a feminized productivity. Benefiting from what they saw as
women's abdication of their own procreative and nurturing capacities,
some social scientists sought to exploit these powers themselves. Henry
Adams provides another classic instance of this tendency. His unsuccessful
attempts to cure his wife's infertility (he owned *Clinical Notes on Uterine
Surgery with Special Reference to the Management of Sterile Conditions*) led to
a compensatory obsession with the dynamic of sterility and fertility. He
characterized one volume of his *History* as "a part of myself, a kind of intellectual brat or segment," and of the project as a whole he wrote, "I have
only one offspring, and am almost forty-four while it is nothing but an
embryo." Like Hall, Adams prostrated himself alternately before a primitive / matriarchal and a masculine / scientific altar.[163]

For reasons I have discussed, women reformers in England never
achieved a voice in welfare policy equivalent to that of their counterparts
in the United States. There are, nevertheless, significant continuities between these two national developments. British women may have been less
equipped (from an educational as well as institutional standpoint) to define
the reform movement in their own terms. But they were successful in creating a new class of "independent women," whose domain was the public
sphere.[164] Their discourse of maternalism allowed them to confirm a
private ethic of domesticity, while helping to institutionalize voluntary organizations that were "extraordinarily broad-based and influential."[165] In
so doing, they challenged traditional divisions between public and private
spheres. Attempts to reassess, and in some instances to reinvent, longstanding notions of private and public domains were inevitably tied to the
reconfiguration of gender roles themselves. The unprecedented participation of women in the shaping of public policy incited a complex array of
responses, as we have seen. These ranged from lamentations on the order
of Spencer and Ellis to socialist celebrations of women's newfound freedoms by Karl Pearson and the Webbs. Women's traditional associations
with protecting the vulnerable made their participation in the creation of
welfare states seem natural. But the apparent loosening of divisions between public and private spheres could run both ways. That is, women

were helping to define how the state should meet its citizens' needs at the same time that tasks formerly considered private—conception and reproduction, socialization and education of the young—were becoming increasingly rationalized.[166] There was a great deal of attention paid in this period to methods of maternal protection and socialization. My point is an obvious one: these changes had a variety of unanticipated effects. *The Awkward Age*, the work of a profoundly sympathetic, intelligent, but pessimistic spectator of Anglo-American life, offers a man's version of the story from a woman's point of view.

It is significant, in light of these historical controversies, that nearly all the members of Mrs. Brook's circle believe that she has failed to protect her children. It is also significant that nearly everyone, from Mr. Cashmore, the circle's parliamentarian, to Vanderbank, the civil servant, to Mitchy, the millionaire, to the Duchess, who follows a traditional model of childrearing, advises Mrs. Brook on her maternal affairs. Most revealing of all is the identification I have already mentioned: the Brookenhams' designation as the community's "needy" family. Quotation marks here are essential. The "poverty" of the Brookenhams is hardly the condition addressed by modern welfare measures. Yet the Brookenhams do imagine their position in the novel's community in these terms. Their relative circumstances in the society of *The Awkward Age* are pertinent to relative states of poverty and wealth in a larger social context. If the Brookenhams are not really poor in the strict sense, they are bound up in the contemporary welfare terminology that mediated the condition. To begin with, they solicit and accept a variety of charitable contributions, ranging from loans (71–72), "bribery" (85), and free houses (252) to Mr. Longdon's "adoption" of Nanda (289). The Brookenham's relationship to charity is neither casual nor unconscious. They are the self-imagined kin who require intratribal protections. Mrs. Brook proclaims, "in a flicker of austerity": "Your father and I have most to think about, always, at this time, as you perfectly know—when we have to turn things round and manage somehow or other to get out of town, have to provide and pinch, to meet all the necessities, with money, money, money, at every turn, running away like water. . . . I assure you I don't know where to turn—which doesn't, however, in the least prevent everyone coming to me with their own selfish troubles." The narrator comments, "It was as if Mrs. Brook had found the cup of her secret sorrows suddenly jostled" (239–40). She is a martyr, a martyrdom of economic deprivation set against a spectacle of plenty (the "American girl with millions," the "gigantically rich" Baron). Her suffering is intensified by her fixation on injustice and scarcity. Hers is a world where the haves accumulate without effort, while the have-nots scrounge bitterly for every possible advantage. Financial troubles, as Mrs. Brook conceives them, are private, a "secret" source of sorrow. Yet they become inevitably a matter of public adjudication, and therefore of personal shame. Mrs. Brook likens her losses to a deluge ("running away like water"), which conveys her sense of helplessness. Her image raises questions of ritual purpose that have been resonant from the novel's opening. Is there a spiritual rationale for her suffering, a reason why she is poor and these (alien) others rich? Control over her destitution must inevitably run to other hands. It's telling that the terms of reparation she invokes are specifically familial. "Charity," she tells her daughter, "begins at home. . . . *giving*" needn't "go . . . far" (241). Mrs. Brook imagines aliens as the cause of her impoverished state and kin as its source of relief.

This may explain why nearly every time Mrs. Brook "cries poor," an image of the Scottish homeland is sure to follow (239, 252). Scotland is the code word for ethnic affinity in the novel's society. It is a psychic reserve (however seldom they *go* there) that the Baron Schmacks will never penetrate, no matter how many millions they manage to accumulate. Within the fortifications of "kin," relative states of poverty and wealth are minimized, finessed. Blood ties enjoin an obligation of disseminating wealth. This is not merely Mrs. Brook's fantasy; the prescription is widely observed. Nanda echoes her mother's kinship claims. "With everyone helping us, all round, aren't we a lovely family? . . . all living more or less on other people, all immensely 'beholden'" (252). Their own dependence does not prevent Nanda and her mother from functioning in their own right as charitable agents on behalf of more alien poor. James's fictional society distinguishes among types of poverty. The money troubles of kin are accidental, arbitrary. The afflictions of aliens (whether foreigners or the lower classes) are constitutional and definitive. When Nanda and her mother visit the workhouse or behave generously to a maid, they are reinforcing an absolute boundary. Their social-work activity is double-edged. It is a way of relieving or shifting the onus of their own destitution. Mrs. Brook's kindness to her maid helps to mitigate her indecent exposure, her sacrifice, of Nanda (233). They are also performing a valuable service on behalf of their own class. Their relief work contributes to social stability in general. All this is in addition to the counseling they dispense freely to members of their own circle. Their social work—both domestic and public—is a way of distancing need through its rationalization. But this professional advantage does not prevent their own desperation. It rather expresses and enhances it. For the Brookenhams are in the end the only ones who suffer sacrificial losses in *The Awkward Age*. As the curtain descends, Nanda pleads her mother's case before Vanderbank and Mitchy. But it seems likely that Mrs. Brook will be dropped, abandoned, by her two closest male confidants, a likelihood she herself has anticipated (229). And we know the fate of Nanda.

James's portrait of need, charity, and sacrifice raises questions about the relationship between women's prominent social role as protectors *of* a modern welfare state and their evident need for protection *within* it. Significantly, no character remains entirely immune from the novel's sacrificial vocabulary. Vanderbank has his trial; Mitchy is a martyr; even Longdon becomes a bull, darkly cognizant of its doom on the point of a dramatic audience with the Duchess (178–79). Longdon's link to sacrifice may be even more developed than this. Andrew Lang's *Myth, Ritual, and Religion* offers a possible context for the concern of all those in the novel who wonder whether Longdon will be "spared" (124, 155, 292–94). Lang's extraordinary spectacle from ancient Greece holds haunting implications for *The Awkward Age*. "An elderly and most respectable citizen strolling [toward the town-hall]. The citizen is so lost in thought that apparently he does not notice where he is going. Behind him comes a crowd of excited but silent people, who watch him with intense interest. The citizen reaches the steps of the town-hall, while the excitement of his friends behind increases visibly. Without thinking, the elderly person enters the building." Then, "with a wild and un-Aryan howl . . . the good Greeks of Alos" apprehend him, and he is "solemnly sacrificed on the altar." The event is customary, "whenever a descendant of the house of Athamas entered the Prytaneion" (1:258–59). Certain features of this rich and complicated scene bear directly upon James's novel. The author's obvious desire to distance himself from this Barbarian Greek rite ("un-Aryan howl") is consistent with James's comedic touches at the expense of his own Graeco-Roman savages. The image of an elderly citizen, "respectable" but distracted, suggests aspects of Longdon's own self-characterization (31, 49). One can imagine Longdon, at least as pictured in the first scene nervously fiddling with his monocle, marching unwittingly to his doom. Also suggestive is the role of intratribal rivalries in Lang's sense. So fiercely drawn are these minor differences of kinship, the resentment of Greek against Greek ("Alos" against "Athamas") that an individual's chance mistake—he wanders into the wrong neighborhood—can eventuate in his immediate sacrifice. Lang's anecdote is reminiscent of nothing so much as the deadly disputes among youth of the same ethnicity (sometimes direct kin) within postmodern gang cultures.

It is possible to draw at least two conclusions from Lang's portrait that are of special relevance to *The Awkward Age*. One point is clarifying: rivalries within the boundaries of kinship can be as destructive as those without. Lang's understanding of "the wilder element in Greek ritual" as "native" in origin is instructive here. There is no denying the *"local"* *"village"* roots of the most brutal practices, which makes them, in his view, "purely national" (1:254–55). The other point is puzzling: why does James choose to nullify, and perhaps even invert, the play of endangerment in his narrative? Did James have this scene at the back of his mind when he drew up his own portrait of an elderly and respectable citizen entering a Greek "house" that is at once familiar and uncanny? Why would James makes his aging stranger an agent-beneficiary of sacrifice, rather than its victim-object? In James's version, female kin are the only sacrificial victims. And their sacrifice is no stray or incidental matter. Both mother and daughter, in the community's terms, have committed offenses.

The type of sacrifice featured in *The Awkward Age* comes closest generically to "*piacular* sacrifices" as defined by Lang, where the worshiper "fines himself in a child, an ox, or something else that he treasures." It is most common "in cases of crime done or suspected within the circle of kindred" (1:262). At least three of Lang's conditions apply to Nanda's exile: the offer of a treasured offspring, the suspicion of guilt (on the part of parents and child); and the limited imputation of criminality (to the "circle of kindred"). Here again we are faced with James's peculiar insistence on feminizing sacrifice. He displaces the peril of the elderly gentleman, so that he becomes a source or cause of sacrificial danger rather than its object or remedy. He localizes the idea of criminality in the mother-daughter relation. Both are guilty of offenses against the collective sensibility. The mother's "criminality" appears deliberate: she actively repudiates her maternal obligations. The daughter's, in contrast, is inadvertent: helplessly tainted, she soaks up knowledge, as she puts it, through her "pores" (248). James would seem to be offering two different explanations for the failure of women's social protection. By the novel's end, however, these two explanations have collapsed into one. What appears most striking from this enlarged perspective is how much their situations have in common. The good looks of both are considered unusual: derived as much from deep intelligence as from physical characteristics. Both have been extraordinarily alert from childhood. Both betray a quality of coldness or self-protectiveness, developed in both cases, it seems, because they haven't been properly shielded from the world. In mother and daughter, an air of practical realism disguises real vulnerability. If Nanda is innocent, according to the novel's deepest lights, Mrs. Brook is equally so. Thus, there is no legitimate, "penal" justification for sacrifice in either case.

There has to be another reason why women are specifically designated as sacrificial victims. Among the Hindus and Semites, according to Mauss and Hubert, women, along with strangers and slaves, were traditionally excluded from the sacrifice, particularly from its consumption. Robertson Smith traces this to an ancient Semitic custom where the men took wives from strange kin and did not adopt them into their own kinship group. Husbands and wives didn't eat together, because their different tribal affiliations bound them to different taboos on consumption. In keeping with this, he points to cultures where males alone were considered appropriate victims of sacrifice.[167] It's hard to take this idea seriously, in light of Greek heroines like Iphigenia. Yet it appears to be a commonplace among late Victorian interpreters, from Smith to Frazer, that women were largely excluded as beneficiaries of the sacrificial rite and also less likely to serve as its victims. Why then does James feminize sacrifice? Why does he choose to invert Longdon's potential status as elderly victim and make him an agent-beneficiary? Why does James's sacrificial scheme issue in the scapegoating of women who are basically innocent (if complexly and vexedly so)? While Lady Fanny is clearly a buffoon, her typing by the novel's community remains illuminating. Mrs. Brook's admirably compact phrase for the experience of knowing her—"a flash of insight into history"—is as philosophical as it is theatrical. As a "pagan," Mrs. Brook suggests, Fanny affords a glimpse (momentary but palpable) of a sense we might have lost without her (134). The description can also be taken as indicative of a larger, collective status. Women in general are acutely historical, a window to a world of the concrete.

Imagine the relationship between males and females in *The Awkward Age* as a series of oppositions. Where males, typified by Longdon and Vanderbank, are detached, discriminating, idealistic, and superior, females, typified by Mrs. Brook and Nanda, are compromised, knowledgeable, and practical. No social transaction, neither adultery nor divorce, is beneath them. James wants us to recognize their deliberate complicity. The sacrificial stage dictated by their traits is necessarily contextual. Why link women and sacrifice? In part because women, ideally, are agents of the most prominent oblatory form in James's era: maternal self-sacrifice. While this paradigm proved the limit of sacrificial theory for most of his contemporaries, including his brother William, James doesn't stop there. He reaches beyond the mystified envelope of maternal sacrifice to its ramifications—sexual, economic, political, psychological. James's approach to Mrs. Brook shows how Darwinian conceptions of women as preeminently sacrificial (in the biological sense) actually obscure what is most profoundly sacrificial about women's experience.

The Awkward Age's main concern becomes the unique susceptibility of women's social roles to sacrificial speech, gestures, and acts. James attributes this susceptibility to a set of historical coincidences. Most prominent among them is the relationship between changing conceptions of social protection and radical challenges to women's public roles. Women are no longer protecting or being protected in familiar, traditional ways. James's novel dramatizes the crisis that is its consequence. He imports from the "primitive" reaches of adolescence the feminized beast with the red cloth brow, to tell his story about the failure of social protections in the modern age. No one is really responsible, as James presents it, for the crisis at hand.

James and his maternal center are agreed on this point: it is "inevitable" (312). For various reasons beyond their control, women simply can't care for kin as they have in the past. This is despite all theory about the ongoing vitality of the maternal "instinct." Nor can *they* be shielded from the world. Women are in a different place now: as Nanda says, "we're in it all so much" (382). The response of their male companions is to invoke sacrifice. Vanderbank answers Mrs. Brookenham's fatalistic plea with a familiar image of "fire" and "ashes" (315). Meanwhile, Longdon "shepherds" Nanda into exile. Neither response—not the rhetoric of smoke nor the deliberate expulsion of this feminine pollutant—is conceived as a *solution* to the crisis. They merely confirm the fact of it. Women have become vague, disordered, threatening; they symbolize the necessity for new social categories.

Perhaps because it betrays evidence of James's own immersion in contemporary social theory, and also because there is something unusually direct about its subjects—initiation, reproduction, marriage—and their treatment, *The Awkward Age* reads as James's most important cultural study. What makes for this importance, in addition, is the incomparable pressure and intensity that informs James's view of women here. Women in the novel embody the sacrificial rhythms of loss and gain that are endemic to modern society. As live emblems, literal reproducers as it were, of the social whole, women are sacred and abject, makers and waste makers, controlling and controlled, protectors utterly in need of protection themselves. Probably as well as anyone at the time, James recognized how women's identification with acts of protection tied their destiny to the modern state's novel preoccupation with protecting its citizens. He also saw how women's fate rose or fell in keeping with overriding attitudes toward that obligation. Following *The Awkward Age*, according to James, never again would there be anything natural about the task of human protection.

FOUR

Du Bois's Gospel of Sacrifice

IN THE climactic mourning chapter of *The Souls of Black Folk* (1903), W.E.B. Du Bois describes the Atlanta funeral procession for his eighteen-month-old son.

Blithe was the morning of his burial, with bird and song and sweet-smelling flowers. The trees whispered to the grass, but the children sat with hushed faces. And yet it seemed a ghostly unreal day,—the wraith of Life. We seemed to rumble down an unknown street behind a little white bundle of posies, with the shadow of a song in our ears. The busy city dinned about us; they did not say much, those pale-faced hurrying men and women; they did not say much,—they only glanced and said, "Niggers!"

We could not lay him in the ground there in Georgia, for the earth there is strangely red; so we bore him away to the northward, with his flowers and his little folded hands. In vain, in vain!—for where, O God! beneath thy broad blue sky shall my dark baby rest in peace,—where Reverence dwells, and Goodness, and a Freedom that is free?[1]

The scene records a stunning lapse of fellow feeling, an inability to see beyond the Black type to acknowledge a universal grammar of suffering. Du Bois's reproof here is muted and indirect: the abrupt cropping of the paragraph expresses typographically what cannot be conveyed by ordinary language. The moment is isolated, set apart; one must turn away from a human action that replicates the inhumanity of death. This figurative recoiling is confirmed by the immediate details of the parents' departure "northward," to bury their son. Du Bois maintains a "hushed" tone throughout, not because he is too numb to feel this slight keenly, but in order to avoid responding emotionally to a display that has denigrated sentiment itself. For what is being represented by this scene is not just a lack of identification with Black pain but the possibility that sympathetic actions have themselves become the pathway of estrangement. Where we expect to find instinctive recognition of another's feeling, we now find race hatred. It is not simply that sympathy is absent; it is that sympathy is supposed to be there. The encounter derives its dramatic force from the highly structured nature of funeral rites. In all cultures strict rules of etiquette govern expressions of grief and their reception. This denial of sympathy is a violation of custom, obvious to everyone. The air of suppressed violence arises from the expectation of sympathy, on the part of Black

---

FOUR

Du Bois's Gospel of Sacrifice

IN THE climactic mourning chapter of *The Souls of Black Folk* (1903), W.E.B. Du Bois describes the Atlanta funeral procession for his eighteen-month-old son.

Blithe was the morning of his burial, with bird and song and sweet-smelling flowers. The trees whispered to the grass, but the children sat with hushed faces. And yet it seemed a ghostly unreal day,—the wraith of Life. We seemed to rumble down an unknown street behind a little white bundle of posies, with the shadow of a song in our ears. The busy city dinned about us; they did not say much, those pale-faced hurrying men and women; they did not say much,—they only glanced and said, "Niggers!"

We could not lay him in the ground there in Georgia, for the earth there is strangely red; so we bore him away to the northward, with his flowers and his little folded hands. In vain, in vain!—for where, O God! beneath thy broad blue sky shall my dark baby rest in peace,—where Reverence dwells, and Goodness, and a Freedom that is free?[1]

The scene records a stunning lapse of fellow feeling, an inability to see beyond the Black type to acknowledge a universal grammar of suffering. Du Bois's reproof here is muted and indirect: the abrupt cropping of the paragraph expresses typographically what cannot be conveyed by ordinary language. The moment is isolated, set apart; one must turn away from a human action that replicates the inhumanity of death. This figurative recoiling is confirmed by the immediate details of the parents' departure "northward," to bury their son. Du Bois maintains a "hushed" tone throughout, not because he is too numb to feel this slight keenly, but in order to avoid responding emotionally to a display that has denigrated sentiment itself. For what is being represented by this scene is not just a lack of identification with Black pain but the possibility that sympathetic actions have themselves become the pathway of estrangement. Where we expect to find instinctive recognition of another's feeling, we now find race hatred. It is not simply that sympathy is absent; it is that sympathy is supposed to be there. The encounter derives its dramatic force from the highly structured nature of funeral rites. In all cultures strict rules of etiquette govern expressions of grief and their reception. This denial of sympathy is a violation of custom, obvious to everyone. The air of suppressed violence arises from the expectation of sympathy, on the part of Black

269

mourners and White bypassers alike. At the moment when they are invited to provide the most human of responses the Whites "discover" bigotry. There is no sympathetic affinity *in* suffering. There is only sympathy among some who suffer. Sympathy here has less to do with identifying what is universally human about a particular individual than with universalizing a certain set of human particulars.

When Whites look at these mourners and mutter, "Niggers," they are placing Blacks, through their exclusion from sympathy, beyond the borders of community. This is consistent with the passage's color symbolism. The first three colors mentioned are "red earth," "white posies," and "niggers"—a term that thwarts the prospects of a red, white, and blue design. Blue is introduced at the passage's end in the form of a hope or plea ("where, O God! beneath thy broad blue sky shall my dark baby rest in peace?"), to remind us of a national promise unfulfilled. The note of dissonance, however, does not come from the Blacks who embody this execration. While the white posies and red earth are labeled as objective parts of the scene, the color black is enclosed in quotes, an idiom that degrades its speaker.

To accept the possibility that we are being asked to read the social exclusion of Blacks in terms of a foiled national symbol (the American flag) is to accept that the passage has implications for the relationship between sentimental bonds and nationality. The black hole in the flag (where the blue should be) signifies a potential gap between the impulse of sympathy and the rites of an American democracy, a gap that is overlooked in a contemporaneous analysis of race prejudice by the sociologist W. I. Thomas. Thomas suggests that the "dependence of cultural groups on signs of solidarity is seen in the enthusiasm aroused by the display of the flag of our country."[2] The key term here is culture, for "America" is not a single "cultural group" but a plurality of cultures. As Thomas assumes, sympathy is concrete and possessive; it expresses immediate attachments—to family, religion, ethnicity. In the United States, sentimental attachments have always existed in tension with the rational principles ("e pluribus unum," "inalienable rights") that are the foundation of national unity.

Du Bois's scene reminds us that in a heterogeneous country with open borders, sympathy can threaten the citizenry. From this perspective, the scene stages the dilemma of social bonds in a pluralist democracy. It introduces two of the most obvious sources of human commonality, death and mourning, and the sympathetic response to it, and shows how both function to differentiate and exclude. Indeed, one could argue that the red, white, and black scheme of this passage also invokes (in more universal terms) the three elemental body products, but subordinates them to a more dramatically represented politics of color. White is the life source, the color of semen and mother's milk; red is menstrual blood or blood shed in war or hunting; black is feces, the sign of waste, and sometimes darkness.[3] It is no coincidence that convictions of the particularity of death (variations in mortuary practices both within and across cultures) and of the limits of sympathy's harmonizing effects are both especially heightened in this period. Du Bois's consistent declarations of distrust in the sentiments and his attraction to social science are explained in part by his awareness that appeals to the emotions (of the kind on display in nationalist celebrations like parades and fireworks demonstrations, as well as in universal practices like mourning) have so often been vehicles of intolerance.

There is a special poignancy in Du Bois's decision to locate his insights about sympathy in the funeral of his own son. Du Bois, like Emerson, demonstrates an ability to make personal tragedy resonate with collective and, in this case, political meaning. The scene implies that the act of sympathy may require not only the exclusion but the disappearance of certain groups. While we are meant to read the blood in Du Bois's red earth, the color is also intended as a racial property of the bodies buried there. Du Bois's image recalls a detail from an earlier moment of *Souls*: that the territory around Atlanta was "the ancient land of the Cherokees" (286). Describing the battles before the Indian retreat, Du Bois's conclusion confirms the theme of sucession: "Small wonder the wood is red. Then came the black slaves. Day after day the clank of chained feet" (293). This is the history behind the theory of social Darwinism. Arguments for the natural decline of nations, with superior replacing inferior in seasonal progression, are countered by a narrative of force and violence. If the red earth fails to jog our memories, we have the colloquial "pale-faced" to convince us of the parallel. "Observe the fate of the American Indian," Du Bois suggests, "and you will understand current speculation on the destiny of their Black counterparts."

For what is most peculiar about this later moment is the implication that death and "niggers" have become synonymous in White minds. The incident has a disturbing literalness if one takes into account contemporary child mortality statistics for Blacks: 56 percent higher, according to demographers, than comparable statistics for Whites in the urban North and South.[4] In light of these claims, Du Bois's image of the Georgia soil as an unmarked mass grave for Blacks and Indians expands to include the unrealized histories of the Black infant thousands. But the scene's metaphorical implications are equally disturbing: for Whites, Blacks cannot possess a ritualized relationship to death, because they are identified with death.

Du Bois's meditations on survival and sympathy serve to highlight what may be the most far-reaching example in this study: the imagining of Black American culture in terms of death and sacrifice at the turn of the century. One might expect that such associations would be limited to an immediate postbellum context, but they assumed a greater range and intensity at the end of the nineteenth century and even beyond it. These assumptions provided a critical impetus for Du Bois's early writings. And they may, subsequently, have effected major shifts in his life and work, from the decision to abandon a social scientific vocation in the 1920s to his African expatriation late in life. At the very least, they were a preoccupation in this formative stage of Du Bois's highly visible career as a Black scholar and statesman. Du Bois's review of William Benjamin Smith's pernicious study *The Color Line* (1905) explains why. He characterizes the book as a "naked, unashamed shriek for the survival of the white race by means of the annihilation of all other races." It could "easily be passed over in silence," he concedes, did it not reflect "the active belief of millions of our fellow countrymen. . . . This is the new barbarism of the twentieth century, against which all the forces of civilization must contend."[5]

The historic debates that provided the grounds for Du Bois's prophecy were centered in the disciplines of social science. My purpose in this chapter is to reanimate those debates, on behalf of a greater understanding of Du Bois's early thought and a more considered (because historicized) appraisal of our own unreconciled race dilemmas. Americans at the turn of the century seriously debated the possible extinction of Black culture, in discussions carried out mainly in social scientific journals and books, but extending as well to other aesthetic, juridical, and religious arenas. Such speculations, I argue, only become meaningful, in all their historical peculiarity, against the backdrop of two emerging forms of inquiry: social scientific accounts of sympathy as fundamental to sociality and social scientific readings of sacrifice as intrinsic to culture. Growing interest in the function of sympathy as a means of differentiation and exclusion accompanies growing emphasis on the sacrificial destiny of "alien" social groups (e.g., Blacks and Indians). The "dialogue of death" I explore first was remarkable for its variety of participants and occasions. At conferences and in published forums, leading Black academics like Kelly Miller confronted amateurs like Philip Bruce, and prominent sociologists like Franklin Giddings and Edward Ross echoed comparative dilettantes like Nathaniel Shaler. The breadth of these discussions had something to do with the openness of social scientific research at this time (a circumstance described at length in chapter 1), but possibly even more with the specifics of race questions. For the urge to draw ever tighter boundaries *between* Blacks and Whites gave rise, in an oddly compensatory fashion, to an utter disregard for boundaries in efforts to rationalize them.

The dialogue of death bespoke a new "competitive" stage of race relations.[6] People crunched numbers and wrote tracts in defense of a race mythology that cast Black Americans as the casualty of national advance. While some predicted the disappearance of Blacks through a process of assimilation that would revitalize the dominant White race, others agonized over the dangers of "passing," concerned that declining Black population rates reflected the imperceptible infiltration of the White gene pool by mulatto elements. Still others expressed assurance and anxiety at once: they were sure that Black extinction was inevitable in some distant future, but anxious about Blacks as a morbid and threatening factor in present-day society. Mortality arguments blended readily with segregation arguments: while they were still here, Blacks should be carefully quarantined. The racial numbers game was hardly self-consistent; the same data might be used in support of opposite claims, even by the same writer. This is not to imply that there was any uncertainty about the sentiments behind these claims. As Du Bois recognized, the motivations were all too clear. The mythology of Black morbidity was both the means to the containment of a Black labor force and a critical psychic measure, designed to feed the sacrificial appetites of an American capitalist culture. The dialogue of death was specific to an era. But these associations can be traced to late-twentieth-century literary, social scientific, and popular media. One reason for this persistence was the extent of their institutionalization at the turn of the century, in social industries like life insurance, which provides the culminating example of my discussion.

The second part of this chapter, "the evolution of sympathy," explores the changes in moral outlook that were contemporaneous with the dialogue of death. I try to come to terms with a curious feature of the race debates: why, in the most virulent writings, the concept of sympathy was invoked with such regularity. This seems especially strange in light of Ralph Ellison's historical account of the matter. Despite heightened regard for "the moral nature of the Negro problem" in the antebellum era, "with the passing of the Reconstruction the moral aspect was forced out of consciousness."[7] I argue that the play of sympathy helped to express and to shape these changes. Sympathy figures in the race debates throughout the nineteenth century as a measure of progress (did Blacks have a requisite capacity for sympathetic identification and attachment?). It was also a means for predicting a people's susceptibility to assimilation (did Blacks inspire sympathetic identification on the part of Whites?). The reconceptualization of sympathy was made possible by assumptions that were implicit in the first eighteenth-century attempts to define the moral sentiments as the basis of community and social integration. Liberal conceptions of sympathy, I suggest, had always invited the identification of affinities and exclusions. Sympathetic states described by writers like Adam Smith were really states of possession or contagion, where an individual was overtaken by another's point of view. The ascription of a porousness to mental life was part of the general tendency of these theories to conflate emotional and physical experience. For the ease with which another's experience could be internalized was directly related to the other's physical qualities of familiarity or resemblance. These eighteenth-century theorists appear to have been unreflectively motivated by new global tensions arising from interracial, interethnic, and international contact. And turn-of-the-century sociologists in America, such as Franklin Giddings, Albion Small, and Robert Park, drew on these early treatments because they were relevant to their own social dilemmas—race conflict and related tensions between "natives" and "immigrants," the problem of defining kinship and social obligations in a modern context.

These preoccupations will be traced through the work of the nineteenth century's most powerful social analysts, including Charles Darwin and Herbert Spencer, who both wrote major tracts on the social function of morals and emotions. Emotions, according to Darwin and Spencer, were embodied like any other trait. They could be transmitted as part of a genetic inheritance. And they evolved, exhibiting different stages of social advance. I show how such theories were adapted in the racist tracts of Fredrick L. Hoffman and Nathaniel Shaler (who cite Darwin and Spencer and are even, in the case of Shaler, cited by them). My exploration of "the evolution of sympathy" concludes with a look at contemporary critiques of these arguments. I refer to Du Bois's *Souls* and to *The Nature of Sympathy* (1913) by the German sociologist Max Scheler. When sympathy was based in the body, Du Bois and Scheler agreed, it could not give ethical definition to the social mind.

The third part of this chapter explores the debate on Black survival traced in the first part and the "sympathetic" normalization of Black exclusion analyzed in the second, but in the context of a larger symbolic of "sacrifice." In racist ethnography from this period, the ceremonial demise of Black people was presented as the route to national cohesion and renewal. To be sure, authors like William Benjamin Smith assumed that this fate was inevitable. But the dramatic urgency of their rhetoric—hyperbolic references to blood and altars, purification rites and divine appetites—confirms the ghastly events sanctioned by these studies. As Orlando Patterson reminds us, "White Americans were the last western people to practice the grim ancient ritual of human sacrifice, and black Americans, like slaves and ex-slaves in numerous cultures before them, were the slaughtered sacrificial objects."[8] Many Americans at the turn of the century believed in a sacrificial role for Blacks, and some acted on it. In addition to their crusades against lynching—Ida B. Wells and James Weldon Johnson were key figures—Black Americans created a rich literary stage for the politics of sacrifice. With a near ritual repetitiveness of their own—examples here will include Du Bois's *The Philadelphia Negro* (1899) and *The Souls of Black Folk* (1903), Charles Chesnutt's *The Marrow of Tradition* (1901), Ralph Ellison's *Invisible Man* (1952), Toni Morrison's *The Bluest Eye* (1970), and Suzan-Lori Parks's *The America Play* (1993)—Black writers filled the vacant horrors of history with symbolic meaning. The staging of sacrifice as an ordinary and extraordinary aspect of Black American experience was an attempt to come to terms with a dominant cultural legacy. But these stagings can also be understood as ways of recuperating what was culturally indigenous about the sacrificial enterprise. I have in mind, for example, African traditions of vengeance (described by Du Bois and realized by Denmark Vesey and Nat Turner), with their obvious relevance for a postemancipation context, as well as the frank spirituality suggested by the placement of offerings at crossroads. There is yet another form of renunciation, which had special meaning for Du Bois: the self-sacrifice of the elite. Du Bois's "Gospel of Sacrifice" was by definition a common enterprise. This has not been sufficiently understood, in part because Du Bois's pronouncements about the sacrificial demands upon Black elite and Black masses, especially at the start of his career, make little sense without reference to his social scientific allegiances. Elitism was an occupational hazard, given the methodological split between sociological investigators and their human subjects. But some sociologists (Du Bois and his mentor, Max Weber, were exemplary) acknowledged this split in everything they wrote. Du Bois knew that his professional activities were mediated by his Blackness. He had no illusions about the profession's overriding view of his people, and how it affected the reception of his work. It's possible to identify optimism in the sheer size of the Atlanta Studies or in the practical spirit of *The Philadelphia Negro*; yet that optimism, as I will show in readings of these works, was always qualified. However "rational" its methods, however vigorous its aims, sociology, Du Bois believed, was a social fatalism deadly to Black folk.

The Dialogue of Death

The debate that I revive in the following pages is brutal, even genocidal; but, above all, it is familiar. This is because postmodern America—the problems that it faces, the solutions that it imagines—remains, in some fundamental sense, a product of the late nineteenth century. It is also because national thinking on race, in particular, has been narrow and circular. This was what Du Bois seems to have had in mind when he declared it a "serious disgrace to American science that with the tremendous opportunity that it has had before it for the study of race differences and race development, race intermingling and contact among the most diverse of human kinds right here at its doors, almost nothing has been done."[9] Du Bois's comment anticipates Ralph Ellison's image for the Black subject of social scientific research: "a phantom that the white mind seeks unceasingly, by means both crude and subtle, to lay." Du Bois appears to welcome true science, while Ellison predicts the failure of any approach to racial questions, "subtle" or "crude," but their speculations converge on the mysteries of intent.[10] Did race problems elude scientific treatment because of the emotional investments on all sides (North and South, Black and White)? Did this explain the preference for foreigners as lead investigators on race projects, from the German F. L. Hoffman's *Race Traits and Tendencies of the American Negro* (1896), commissioned by the Prudential Insurance Company, to the Swede Gunnar Myrdal's *The American Dilemma* (1946), commissioned by the Carnegie Foundation?

Du Bois's reference to "science" is pointed. For he means to distinguish serious empirical research from a specific group of writings: the pseudo-sociology that set the tone of the era's race debates. Written mainly by amateurs, books like Smith's *The Color Line* and Joseph Tillinghast's *The Negro in Africa and America* (1902) feel safely distant. Their blatant racism relegates them to idiosyncratic period pieces. Yet, as Du Bois suspects, the refrain of these works—Where have all the Negroes gone?—may have expressed the hopes of many contemporaries, who either lacked the brutality to state it outright or the intellectual innocence to believe it wholeheartedly. This combination of brutality and innocence is what gives them historical value. For they provide detailed maps of the besieged White mentality (with an honest image of a Black filtered in here and there). My purpose is to focus in some depth on a group of analysts whose works seem to me especially rich in their evocation of a theme that was extraordinarily widespread. I want to emphasize the extent of this bias. It could be found in works by southern amateurs like George Stetson, who in 1877 predicted that the Black race was "probably a diminishing factor" in American life (his evidence was the aversion among Black women to reproduction). Support came also from northern sociologists like Charles Ellwood, who wrote regularly on race topics for the *American Journal of Sociology* and proclaimed there in 1905 that "progress everywhere waits on death—the death of the inferior individual—and nowhere more so than in racial problems."[11]

SURVIVAL

The Color Line: A Brief in Behalf of the Unborn, by William Benjamin Smith is among the most bleak and eloquent of these tracts. The work of a mathematician, who calls it "an ethnological inquiry," the book is a classic in the authoritative amateur vein. "The writer has had to guard himself especially," Smith warns in the preface, "against the emotion of sympathy, of pity for the unfortunate race, 'the man of yesterday,' which the unfeeling process of Nature demands in sacrifice on the altar of the evolution of Humanity."[12] The preface is a sign of things to come; a florid rhetoric of sacrifice and sympathy will be Smith's route to scientific fact. As one might expect, he never gets there. Smith's ethnological label for his book is appropriate only if one disregards the author's ambitions and takes the book as a ritual object in its own right. From this perspective, the drama of the book becomes the tension between Smith's scientific aims and the punitive Christianity to which he subscribes. Smith seems most confident when he is legitimating southern prejudice by way of a long and ancient history. Here he is, for instance, on the unreliability of the census: "the prejudice against 'numbering the people' has been strong since the days of David and of Judas of Galilee, and the Negro flees from the census taker" (214). Elsewhere, highlighting another stage of spiritual evolution, Smith extols the democratic comforts of the Christian time sense: "The outlook is not hopeless to him who has a sense of the world to come, who lives in his race, who feels the solidarity of its present with its future" (xv).

Yet the extent of Smith's scientific ambitions can be measured by his bibliographic reach. He quotes Hoffman and Walter Willcox (professor of economics at Cornell) on Black morbidity; Lapouge, Darwin, and Bryce on amalgamation; Du Bois and Eugene Harris on Black "habits" (60–65, 194, 225, 243–45, 246). He detects an "infinite melancholy" in *The Souls of Black Folk* and cites Nathaniel Shaler on the life prospects of the mulatto (177, 52–53). The range of Smith's sources shows how these race debates functioned: as heated exchanges among an identifiable group of intellectuals. These debates were, in the main, political dead ends. If anything, they merely confirmed the irreconcilability of the different positions. For example, Smith finds in *Souls*—"the finest product of the Mulatto mind"— only confirmation of his own dire predictions (177). Could there be stronger evidence for the limits of reading as a moral exercise? Can we expect more from a writer who calls Georgia "the watermelon paradise of the Black folk" (208)? Smith is immovable. But his fortification is interesting: a malevolent blend of scientific evolutionism and Christianity. The idea of "social racial equality," he announces early on, is "abhorrent," because "it runs counter to the methods of the mind of God." "All are weak and beggarly," he adds, "against the almightiness of heredity, the omnipresence of the transmitted germ-plasma" (13). Smith has located a perfect balance of divine and rational purpose: hereditary transmission assumes the potency of divine absolutes, while God displays a preference for particular "methods." Smith writes, "the recession, the evanescence, of the Negro before the Caucasion is only one example among millions of the processes of nature" (187). He continues, "the vision, then, of a race vanishing before its superior is not at all dispiriting, but inspiring rather" (187). Humanitarianism becomes faulty religion, the wrong kind of oblation. "All forms of humanitarianism that tend to give the organically inferior an equal chance . . . would sacrifice the race" (191). Science provides the troubling script (race struggle and human demise); religion gives it moral color (it's really uplifting). The final image joins them in a message that equates and dismisses charity on the one hand and social engineering on the other. Sacrifice is organic necessity and also spiritual destiny meted out by God. Science and Christianity are not only dynamically intertwined, they are monumentalized: twin towers with one awesome theme.

The foundations of this alliance, however, are not as secure as Smith would like. This is why he is so obsessed with absolute divisions. Boundaries and markers, it turns out, are not only his rhetorical specialty; they are a religion in themselves. "Wherever borderlines have been closely drawn and distinctly recognized," he observes calmly, "there have been found at least comparative quiet." With the next line, however, we are into Gnosticism and prophecies of the world's end. The Gnostic Balisades, he notes, projects the ideal "restoration of all things," where "every element would seek its own place and there abide forever, and not as if fishes were trying to pasture with sheep upon the mountains" (172–73). Other boundary images are politically charged. Consider the demand that his postulates be inscribed "in letters of gold on the walls of the Public Library in Boston and over the pulpit of Plymouth Church in Brooklyn, on the lintels of the White House, and on the title-page of all future editions of *The Independent* and *The Nation*" (185–86). In his most potent image, Smith glorifies the sacred boundary which he believes to be the source of all things. The color line is the "immediate jewel" of the southern "soul," which she "watches with such a dragon eye, that she guards with more than vestal vigilance, with a circle of perpetual fire" (9). Each of these images contains its own unique theological content. The image of fishes (without loaves and water) appeals to a benevolent Christianity where all creatures, great and small, aspire instinctively to the dictates of the color line. Blacks here are the fishes (a page earlier they are frogs), who can't be trusted to choose survival over self-aggrandizement (whether as "a small frog in a big puddle" or as fish in self-destructive pursuit of sheep on mountains). Smith's metaphor is not limited to a Christian frame, for these fishes and frogs are also Hebraic (unmistakable reminders of the Egyptian plagues). Among you, Smith suggests, Blacks are a pestilence, whether as frogs in apocryphal numbers or as fish out of water, festering on hillsides. Whites in this narrative are sheep, naturally inclined toward self-sacrifice. Above all, these lines have a Levitican rigor. Smith's injunction against boundary transgressions is as ritually precise as any Bible dictate. This is clearly his intention. The book's opening epigraph reads: "Let not man join together / What God hath put asunder" (3). The images of southern decrees stamped in gold on various symbolic doorways in the North is more ambiguous, since it's unclear who these markers are designed to protect. Are these Passover signs some postemancipation version of the fugitive-slave laws, designed to confirm regional interdependence? Is the tone conciliatory (we are only protected if you are) or aggressive (you need these prohibitions as much as we do)? More obvious is Smith's claim that the race struggle has penetrated every branch of northern life, from intellectual (Boston Public Library) to clerical (Plymouth Church) to governmental (White House) to journalistic (*The Nation*).

Smith regionalizes the color line early on (the "jewel" of the southern "soul"), it seems, in order to take credit for what he regards as a national solution. Smith makes no apologies for imperfect agendas in an imperfect world. The color line is invested with every available southern myth: the "dragon eye" suggests nostalgia for antebellum chivalry; the "vestal vigilance," the spiritual underwriting of cultural racism; the "circle of perpetual fire," the ultimate sacrificial threat of the lynch mob (9). Read against images like these, evolutionism seems a pale competitor in Smith's ethical universe. Nor is it possible, with the image of "perpetual fire" in one's brain, to put much faith in the gradualist couplet by Tennyson that heads Smith's penultimate chapter, "A Dip into the Future": "And the individual withers / And the world is more and more" (158). Thomas Nelson Page sounds similar themes in *The Negro: The Southerner's Problem* (1904), but with greater ambivalence. He is prone to mournful reflection on the past rather than hostile contemplation of the present. As a novelist known for sentimental romances of the antebellum South, Page expectedly sings the praises of "the old-time Negro" and characterizes Blacks as "a race of God's creatures to whom I give my sympathy and my good-will."[13] He is capable of admiration for the North, which "may with justice pride itself: that in the end, there was awakened in it a general sentiment for emancipation" (236). At the same time, he highlights the strength of northern sentiment against abolition and includes a section on Lincoln's own highly compromised position (16–19, 237–38).

The balance and liberality of Page's account is the means to his largest claim: Blacks are brief sojourners on the American scene. He begins with an image of Blacks as "Banquo's ghost," and ends with an assured prediction: "the Negro race in America will eventually disappear, not in a generation or a century—it may take several centuries. The means will be natural" (4, 282). The most striking thing about Page's gloomy news is the trouble he has holding onto it. Thus the claim that "the ratio of the death-rate of the race is already much larger than that of the white" (283) is countered in the next chapter by the observation that "The Negro race has already doubled three times in the United States" (288). This second claim seems to overtake the first, as Page warns in conclusion, "We have the Negro here among us to the number of ten millions and increasing at a rate of about twenty-five per cent. every ten years" (298). Page is clearly running scared, as he begins to admit more about the circumstances of race politics into his account. Page gives us a fuller picture of the social terrain that motivates Smith's arguments, which is to say that he helps us to see more ambiguously. In contrast to Smith, whose narrative is crammed with biblical analogies and quotations, Page is a minimalist. Without spiritual support, Malthusianism and Darwinism look more embattled. If growth is inevitable, its direction is not. The same fatalism resonates here, but with far less confidence about the end result. In Page, White lynchers and Black ravishers are part of a common "pestilence," just as both sides of the race debate share a common ship of state.

The stigma of mortality that attached to Blacks as a group in this era helps to explain why the difference of their attitudes toward death became a special preoccupation. Contemporary studies tend to presume a Black relationship to death that is uniquely intimate. Philip Bruce's 1889 book, *The Plantation Negro as a Free Man*, is especially revealing in this respect. Like other southerners writing on "the Negro problem," Bruce does not simply tell us that Blacks are different; he shows us, from his own standpoint, *how*. He believes that Black culture is peculiarly death-tinged: "The thought of death is not absent for a great length of time from their minds." They look upon death with a clinical fascination, lingering over "a dying companion far more curious of the stages of dissolution than keenly aware of the great loss that is soon to fall on them."[14] And in his chapter "Blacks and Whites," where he describes "the social dead-line" between the races, funeral rites provide a key example (45). One might expect, Bruce observes, that the universal solemnity of death would result in fairly uniform responses. Black mourning, however, "is as distinct a custom of the blacks" as any of their social activities. He continues, "this divergence between the social life of the one race and that of the other in those scenes where it would be supposed a common humanity and similar material interests would bring the members of both together, leaves a strong impression upon the observer. . . . the sphere in which the negroes move socially is as wide apart from that in which the social existence of the whites is passed, as if the two races inhabited different countries" (47–48). To see the sensibilities of Blacks and Whites as so divergent that a national (not simply a cultural) divide suggests itself seems at once enlightened and intolerant. It seems enlightened because it implies an equivalence between White and Black ritual. To think in terms of nations is to legitimate practices one might have expected Bruce to discount altogether. What seems intolerant is the claim that national divisions are themselves so complete that "the social life" of Blacks could be unrecognizable to Whites. The tension between these two possibilities indicates how enormous Bruce's task is: the transformation of familiar neighbors (many of them blood kin) into representative strangers.

Bruce's account is especially suggestive as an explanation for why death rites were so essential to the construction of estrangement in this context.

The recognition of Blacks as strangers and the recognition of the living as dead are parallel processes. In both cases, one must accept a being who has been accessible and sympathetic as alien and remote. Du Bois acknowledges the challenge of this alteration in a passage from *Souls* that describes the figures who will "ever stand to typify" the two races in the postemancipation era. The White is "a gray-haired gentleman" "blighted . . . with hate"; the Black is "dark and mother-like" (232). Du Bois's images are personal; they gloss patriarchy, maternity, and the complicated rage that informed, and continues to inform, these twisted relations. Bruce pictures a similar transformation: from mother to other. His scene of death assumes initial familiarity: a White approaches the funeral of a Black friend. In the process of paying his "respects," he discovers the difference of the Black living and dead. It is a primal scene for the recognition of estrangement. The sight of Blacks confronting the alienating spectre of death appears here as a dramatic redoubling: the social dead looking upon their natural dead.

In his Durkheimian study *The Collective Representation of Death* (1907), Robert Hertz notes that in most cultures the death of a stranger or slave will "occasion no ritual," for "their death merely consecrates an exclusion from society which has in fact already been completed."[15] Du Bois's funeral scene reminds us that all cultures define the borders between acceptable and unacceptable peoples by manipulating their associations with death: an association that was increasingly in this era thought to be an arbitrary one. Death was in flux, as suggested by a distinction that had become current between death as a universal versus death as a social particular. As a universal event that "happens" to everyone, it was the great democratizer; as a social event, it expressed prevailing hierarchies and forms of estrangement. W. I. Thomas cites testimony from a range of explorers (including Marco Polo, Charles Darwin, and David Livingstone) on cultures where death's symbolic hue is white. Thomas's catalog, drawn from places as diverse as Africa, India, and Australia, reflects a growing understanding of death as an event whose interpretation varies from one culture to another, with as great or greater consequences for the people left behind as for the deceased person.[16] Through elaborate discrimination of cultural practices and beliefs, typological classification of funeral rites, and philosophical speculation on the reception of death, social scientific analysts sought to submit this fundamentally incoherent event to rational method.

Perceptions of differences in the ritual reception of death were increasingly used to distinguish relative states of kinship and strangeness. While this was especially evident in characterizations of Blacks, it was also used in classifying others, including Jews and Irish, with their curious preferences for shivas and wakes.[17] For those studying groups other than Blacks, the redoubling of alienation afforded by the sight of strangers engaged in mortuary rites had a certain compulsive attraction. This is no doubt why death practices formed such a central part of contemporary ethnography. According to Yarrow, who oversaw the American Bureau of Ethnology's research into the burial mounds of North America, "no particular part of ethnographic research has claimed more attention." Conducted over twenty-five years, this research provides an especially interesting example because of the location of the excavation site (America) and the questions it was equipped to address (the very identity of the first inhabitants). The reports of Yarrow (1881) and Cyrus Thomas (1894) can be understood as halfway between the remote field work on alien tribes that provided the hard data for Durkheim's theories on death and mourning and the type of domestic investigations written up in works by Joseph Tillinghast and Philip Bruce.[18] The most immediate difference between the burial mound reports and the studies I have mentioned is tonal: these reports betray neither condescension nor overt racism. A tone of receptive wonder is possible here, because the subjects have themselves reached the status of remnants. The makers of these mounds were not threatening in any objective sense, nor was there assurance about their identity, though it is obvious from Thomas's narrative that he harbored a preferred reading of it. There was pressure to "discover" an Indian ancestry for these cities of the dead, primarily because Indian land claims were considered more or less settled. While eighteenth-century Americans speculated freely about who was responsible for these grave mounds, by the late nineteenth century few were willing to consider the possible claims of yet another people. The legendary quality of this debate is illustrated by the fact that questions about the scientific testimony contained in these burial mounds continue to conflict with their spiritual portent to this day.[19]

In studies like Bruce's, Black-White difference is regionalized in universal terms: the two groups are divided by a border as absolute as that which divides the living from the dead. Joseph Tillinghast's *The Negro in Africa and America* represents another kind of contemporary racist tract that was more alert to geographical boundaries. In contrast to the studies of Smith and Bruce, which were published by mainstream trade presses (McClure's and Putnam's), Tillinghast's book had the backing of the American Economic Association and included a preface by the respected economist Walter Willcox. Despite these professional endorsements, Tillinghast, like Smith and Bruce, lacked academic credentials in the fields covered by his study, from anthropology and religion to sociology and economics. Tillinghast was simply a southerner, with a pressing interest in what he called "the black peril"(1). Tillinghast, who Willcox notes had access to a great northern "anti-slavery collection" (ii), relies on standard African ethnography (Livingstone, Ellis, Kingsley), eyewitness accounts of the antebellum era (Kemble, Martineau, Olmstead), and social studies from the postemancipation era (Du Bois, Hoffman, Bruce). Tillinghast aims to examine the details of Black life in three contexts, from African beginnings, through American slavery, to freedom. The book is a callous attempt to excuse atrocities against Blacks in America by identifying similar (or worse) practices as indigenously African. But it is also more.

Tillinghast's main argument is a standard in writings on race: the Black is unsuited to modern civilization. The Black appears by chance on American shores, to the detriment of all those eventually affected by his "ironical destiny." The following might be taken as Tillinghast's thesis statement: "In his motherland the Negro received a very poor heritage of industrial knowledge and habit. . . . Yet it was this indolent child of the tropics, of all people in the world, whom an ironical destiny cast into the midst of a great industrial society" (137). The implication that the Black presence in America represents some sort of sport for the gods is designed to minimize the White role in the slave trade. Tillinghast's version of the middle passage, therefore, is remarkably free of White players, while the agency of Africans is dramatically heightened (106). A combination of African greed and fate initiates a chain of events with one inevitable outcome: social disruption for White Americans and certain doom for Blacks. Tillinghast's account of Blacks in the postemancipation era is a fulfillment of this prior scene. The downward trend in Black labor (from skilled occupations to menial ones) realizes an African legacy. "They are forever in search of some easier job," Tillinghast observes; they willingly exchange "the shoeshine" for "the barber's chair," "the hod" for "the bricklayer's trowel," "the hand-spike" for "the carpenter's saw" (186). Tillinghast includes explanations from Du Bois (who blames White prejudice [188–90]) as well as Booker T. Washington (who blames the unions [187]), but privileges, finally, Philip Bruce's fatalism (190). "Surveyed broadly, the outlook for the American negro is not bright," Tillinghast concludes, "it is the hard fate of the transplanted Negro to compete, not with a people of about his own degree of development, but with a race that leads the world in efficiency. This efficiency was reached only through the struggle and sacrifice prescribed by evolutionary law" (227–28).

Tillinghast's "transplanted Negro," in contrast to the analytical still point portrayed by Smith, Page, and Bruce, is a dynamic, even elusive figure. Multiple contexts are necessary, because Blacks are so hard to pin down. Tillinghast's study is also distinctive, for an evolutionary and sacrificial content devoid of religious overtones. This is straight survival talk. Destiny becomes efficency; divine will, scientific intent. Religion is confined to the Black subject, evidence for the limitations on his advance. Meanwhile, Tillinghast, the modern race analyst, cultivates the scientific point of view. He is neither motivated by religion nor dependent on it as source or referent. Religion remains a potent factor in Tillinghast, I believe, but only as a facet of scientific method. Frederick L. Hoffman's *The Race Traits and Tendencies of the American Negro* takes us even closer to "authentic science," though even Hoffman's book could inspire typological responses more appropriate to the antiquarian racism of Smith. Consider the biblical chords struck by Kelly Miller in his review of *Race Traits* for "The American Negro Academy." "The Jews in Egypt labored under circumstances remarkably similar to those of the American Negro," Miller wrote. "Luckily for the Hebrews, there were no statisticians in those days."[20] Miller's immediate point is the distinction between a morally rigorous biblical heritage and the "ugly facts" of "the sociologists." By invoking the analogy, however, Miller encourages speculation on what these two frames might have in common. There may be more spiritual yearning in Hoffman than immediately apparent.

Hoffman's book was probably the most widely cited of all contemporary studies on race. Designed to assess the relative "insurability" of Black lives, the book's metamorphosis (through a series of articles) into a study of Black nature, social conditions, and race prejudice drew the respectful attention of sociologists. This was despite the fact that Hoffman, a Prudential statistician, had no social scientific training. He was an intellectual maverick, as indicated by his varied publication record. In addition to *Race Traits*, Hoffman came out with *History of the Prudential Life Insurance Company* (1900) and a book on pauper burials in large cities (1917).[21] All these writings reflected his interest in survival, from the competing claims of nations to the social relations that grew out of belief in the natural inequality of human kinds. *Race Traits*, for instance, contains a long section on "pauper burials," which Hoffman claims occur with marked frequency among Blacks (his figures for Washington, D.C., from 1888 to 1894, for example, estimate 84.36 percent of pauper burials to be Black, although Blacks made up only 32.89 percent of the total population). Exaggerated statistics of this sort appear throughout the book. Less characteristic is the oddly lyrical and gloomy description that accompanies this data. "Whoever has witnessed the pauper funeral of a negro," he writes, "the bare pine box and the common cart, the absence of all that makes less sorrowful the last rites over the dead, has seen a phase of negro life and manners more disheartening perhaps than anything else in the whole range of human misery. Perhaps only the dreary aspect of the negroes' 'potter's field,' the low sand hills, row after row, partly washed away by the falling rains, unrelieved by a single mark of human kindness, without a flower and without a cross, only the pauper lot itself, may be more sad and gruesome than the display of almost inhuman apathy at the funeral."[22] This scene fulfills an expectation introduced on the book's first page. Here Hoffman says that his controversial contribution to the race debate will explain the notable lack of the "the natural bond of sympathy" that might be expected to exist "between people of the same country, no matter how widely separated by language and nationality."

Race Traits is an eccentric blend of social psychology, liberal philosophy, reformism, statistical analysis, ethnographic description, and racist dogma. Du Bois knew the book and refuted it more than once in sociological writings that appeared between 1896 and the 1903 publication of *Souls*. Du Bois may even have had Hoffman's passage in mind while drafting his own funeral scene. The scenes are curiously compatible; that is, if we consider Du Bois's as the mirror image of Hoffman's. One consequence of opening a dialogue between them is the exposure of the potent and meaningful sentimentality of Du Bois's scene. The "blithe" morning, the "bird and song," the "sweet-smelling flowers" take on an air of aggression when set against Hoffman's drama of nullification: "falling rains" and "bare pine box," "unrelieved by a single mark of human kindness," not even a flower.[23] Hoffman's thesis that Blacks can't mourn properly—they lack appropriate ritual modes and objects; loss with them does not translate into grief—is answered by Du Bois's record of White actions that deliberately destroy the ritual content of Black burials.

The burden of *Race Traits* is the definitive association of Black culture with death, an association that supports Hoffman's developing rationale for their social, political, and psychological isolation in every possible context, from rural Black Belt to urban ghetto. Hoffman disputes arguments that attribute high Black mortality to environmental factors and cites statistics from army and prison records showing that among White and Black recruits given identical food, clothing, and shelter, a disproportionately high Black mortality rate persists. He finds Black mortality to be highest among the younger generation—those at greatest remove from the sustaining framework of slavery. He also introduces a new theme, which might be termed a "sacrificial regionalism": places that are densely populated by Blacks are impaired developmentally, since there is considerable "economic loss involved [for the population at large] in so high a mortality" (60). We can assume that one statistic behind Hoffman's punishing geography is the civic expense of all those pauper funerals.

Hoffman's willingness to concede the double determination of Black doom is reflected in his book's split subtitle, where "race traits" connote the inherent basis of inferiority and "tendencies" the stylistic and cultural practices that nourish these genetic predispositions. Taken as a whole, *Race Traits* more than fulfills its actuarial ambitions, with pages of tables on diseases (consumption, yellow fever, malaria, smallpox) to which Blacks were thought immune but to which they have succumbed, as the century progressed, in great numbers. While Hoffman does admit evidence that certain social pathologies (alcoholism, insanity, and suicide) are rare among Blacks, he either discredits it or interprets it in an unflattering manner. The data on alcoholism, he tells us, is based on inadequate research, while suicide flourishes mainly in "advanced" cultures (143). Needless to say, Hoffman is strictly opposed to race amalgamation. He confesses at the start of his chapter on the subject that he has used the terms "negro" and "colored" "indiscriminately," because "the race is so hopelessly mixed" (177). This circumstance is, according to him, one of slavery's most debilitating legacies, which is confirmed by statistics on the inferiority of mulattoes. There is no necessary contradiction in Hoffman's approving reference to Norwegians, Germans, Irish, and Italians, who all "melt like sugar in a cup of tea." But Hoffman is clearly being inconsistent when he endorses the claim that Blacks display "practically no admixture" (195).

If Hoffman is to be taken at his word when he says early on that Blacks will not survive social isolation (they cannot advance without "constant contact with the White race" [20]), then his final recommendations can only be understood as a form of euthanasia. In what may be the first attack on American affirmative action policies, Hoffman cites special aid to Black medical schools, subsidized medical attention, the frequent selection of Blacks as class orators, as examples of a preferential treatment equally harmful to "weak" and "superior" races. Hoffman's penultimate chapter features an epigraph from Benjamin Kidd's *Social Evolution*: "Man, since we first encounter him, has made ceaseless progress upwards, and this progress continues before our eyes. But it has never been, nor is it now, an equal advance of the whole of the race. Looking back we see that the road by which he has come is strewn with the wrecks of nations, races, and civilizations that have fallen by the way, pushed aside by the operations of laws which it takes no eye of faith to distinguish at work amongst us at the present time as surely and as effectively as at any past period" (209). Like Tillinghast, Kidd and Hoffman declare the absolute independence of scientific "laws" from "faith." As Hoffman writes in his own conclusion, "In the plain language of the facts brought together the colored race is shown to be on the downward grade, tending toward ... gradual extinction" (312). Here too, "plain language" nullifies faith and sentiment. Scientific fact, in these treatments, is rhetorically sufficient.

Hoffman's pseudoscience bridges antiquarian racism and legitimate sociological inquiry. But it's obvious to most readers that there could be no better proof of the elusiveness of "value-free" social science. *Race Traits* represents Hoffman's first articulation of an Aryan nationalism that would eventuate in German fascism. This theme becomes even more pronounced in subsequent work. Hoffman's *History of Prudential*, for instance, specifies reverence for the dead as "an inherent trait of Anglo-Saxon" people, a trait that is institutionalized in the insurance industry itself. His 1917 book on *Pauper Burials* is no less ambitious on ethnic grounds, citing the burial customs of German Anglo-Saxons—the section heading is "Dignity, Simplicity, and Funereal Economy"—as naturally superior. Yet Hoffman's faith in Anglo-Saxon vitality was not supported by all participants in the interracial numbers game. In an *American Journal of Sociology* essay, "Western Civilization and the Birth-Rate," Edward Ross advanced a form of neo-Malthusianism that drew troubling comparisons between Anglo-Saxon self-limitation and immigrant recklessness in breeding. While "nature's grim agencies for adjusting numbers"—"war," "famine," "misery"—persisted, they were increasingly qualified by a modern humanitarianism unanticipated by Malthus's "dismal science." As a respondent to Ross's paper observed, it was a grim fact that "the big families live in little houses and all the little families live in big houses."[24] A different type of race analysis provided even greater qualification of Hoffman's conclusions. Newbell Niles Puckett's *Folk Beliefs of the Southern Negro* (1926) came later than the works I have discussed. But it offers a valuable extension of their arguments.

ASSIMILATION AND MOBILITY

What makes Puckett's book especially revealing is its direct reversal of Hoffman on ethnic themes. As the first sociologist to undertake a systematic study of "Negro folk beliefs," Puckett confronts a possibility that is more compatible with the race theories of Edward Ross and W. I. Thomas. A revision of his Ph.D. dissertation at Yale University, Puckett's book was published in a series entitled "Criminology, Law Enforcement, and Social Problems," which gives some idea of prevailing social scientific attitudes toward Blacks. To glance down the list of other titles—*Penal Philosophy, American Prisons, A Study of Women Delinquents in New York State*—is to recognize that in many sociological minds, Black culture was inherently deviant. Puckett's research seems driven by a particular urgency, most obviously, the need to sort out the continuities and differences between Black and Anglo-Saxon rites. Puckett tells us that he aims both to edify and to save. He wants to make the Negro more accessible, while recording a fast disappearing culture. Despite this antiquarian intent, Puckett's findings take him closer to postmodern social theory. Setting out to appraise "weird, archaic, Negro doctrine," Puckett discovers Anglo-Saxon culture. Begun as an exploration and recovery of difference, Puckett's book becomes a study of acculturation. His conclusions confirm how fully Blacks have assimilated. They also reveal something more disturbing: that this assimilation is facilitated by a White indebtedness to Black folkways.

Puckett's richly idiomatic language makes his own narrative exemplary of this dependence. He establishes the value of folk culture through the image of the Black as a collector of White castoffs. Because he venerates relics, "the Negro" has "become the custodian of . . . the Old South." One now commonly finds Whites "scrambling beneath the dust of many a humble smokehouse and barn" in search of "a four-poster support for a veneered genealogy." The Black is also a storehouse of "mental heirlooms," transmitted from Whites to house servants to "the rural sections—the very woodshed of Negro life." Puckett's study reveals the lower classes in general as a repository of forgotten lore.[25] As Puckett's quotations confirm, it is sometimes difficult to tell who is studying whom. Puckett's interest in African survivals is an extension of his preoccupation with death. "In general," Puckett announces portentously at the start, "the West African does not believe in natural death" (79). Puckett takes up residual African customs early on, it seems, in order to set them aside. But they turn out to supply the bedrock for every southern spiritual belief. These include the idea of a "Dead-land" or "shadow-world" that replicates the world of the living, as well as the peripatetic (and potentially vengeful) soul that obliges survivors to propitiate it by "abstinences of all kinds" (Puckett provides examples of havoc wreaked by the unpropitiated). To this end, gravesites serve as virtual catalogs of individual appetite, while lavish funerals are held at "great personal sacrifice"(91). Puckett finds it impossible, in his effort to assess the distinctiveness of southern Black culture, to rid his analysis of African elements. This presents a real theoretical dilemma: the dependence of Anglo-Saxon culture on authentic African folkways. Puckett knows that his findings are radical, which is why he includes caveats like the following: "most of the ghosts described here . . . are to be found in Africa as well as in America, but one is by no means to suppose that they are necessarily of African origin" (132).

Like the inflammatory tracts they both echo and transcend, turn-of-the-century sociological writings on race were consistently framed in terms of absolute survival. Thus, there is basic continuity with real differences. The most significant difference is that the racist tracts tend toward the monologic and compulsive; their obsession with Blacks is mediated by faith in their impending extinction. The sociology in contrast displays a more sophisticated grasp of racism as a social dynamic. These arguments allow for limited White-Black interaction, including the potential consequences of assimilation. Yet if the circumstances of Blacks seemed to inspire broader humanitarianism among sociologists, this may simply have been because of their greater ability to keep it within rational bounds. The cliché of southern engagement versus northern dispassion was a holdover from the antebellum contrast between southerners (whose relationships to Blacks were notoriously familiar) and northerners (who could tolerate Blacks only in theory—a "race trait" embodied by Stowe's Aunt Ophelia). Though he was not a social scientist, only a northerner renowned for his promotion of Black causes, Thomas Wentworth Higginson, provides an illustration of how remote certain interracial intimacies could be.

What follows is an anecdote from his military diary, covering his time with a Black regiment. The incident is told in the possessive tense of on-going memory: "I have returned from some lonely ride by the swift river ... and, entering the camp, have silently approached some glimmering fire, round which the dusky figures moved in the rhythmical barbaric dance the negroes call a 'shout,' chanting ... some monstrous refrain. Writing down in the darkness as best I could,—perhaps with my hand in the safe covert of my pocket,—the words of the song, I have afterwards carried it to my tent, like some captured bird or insect, and then, after examination, put it by."[26] Higginson's ruminations waver between fear of the alien and wonder, even affection, when the alien is brought near. Black body and song merge and blur, as if we are to imagine by the end a Black singer shrunken (like a "bird or insect") to pocket size. Higginson is drawn to the scene as a social antidote for his own isolation. Yet he is full of judgments and disparaging oppositions: his ride by the river reflects a resolve lacking in this "barbaric" scene. His desire to "capture" a remnant of the culture conveys doubt about its potential incorporation. Whether "naturalist" (like his friend Louis Agassiz), or a "social scientist" (like his friend Frank Sanborn), Higginson is a "silent" figure, regarding his prey at a remove. This private moment with a liberal "sympathizer" holds little hope for the future of American Blacks. Nor is it easy to feel sanguine contemplating Lester Ward's "final great united world-race [which] will be comparable to a composite photograph in which certain strong faces dominate the group, but in which may also be detected the softening influence of faces characterized by those refining moral qualities which reflect the soul rather than the intellect." Ward's 1903 photographic projection, which is based on his anticipation of widespread race amalgamation in the twentieth century, is remarkably free of non-Caucasian attributes. The Black inability to withstand a more powerful White genetic endowment is here presumed.[27] Ward traces this inevitable competition to the cannibalistic origins that he understands as "common" to "every race of men." Men were "the mutual game of one another, and man literally preyed upon man." This gradually evolved into what moderns recognize as "the struggle of races" (728).

Ward strikes a balance between assimilation and extinction. He appears as an independent, even prophetic participant in these race debates. For Ward denies the coherence of race as a concept, given the "completely mixed" condition of all races. "Under this view the term 'race' loses all that definiteness with which it was formerly, and still falsely, clothed, and comes to stand for any group of men who have, from whatever cause, acquired a certain community of characteristics" (729, 731). Ward predicts, with the help of an ethnologist, the ultimate disappearance of race, as "the combined result of miscegenation and the blotting out of the weaker branches. The world will be filled to overflowing with a generalized race in which the dominating blood will be that of the race that today has the strongest claim physically and intellectually" (735). Ward comes back round to a formula of race dominance, with the "strongest" race eventually controlling "every available foot of land on the globe." Still, Ward's is a visionary company, and it's surprising that he carried so few fellow sociologists along with him. But it may be because he had so little, finally, to contribute to the problem of race in America. In his *American Journal of Sociology* essay "The Negro Race and European Civilization," Paul Reinsch adopts a similarly enlightened globalism, proposing to study Blacks in a variety of settings. While he dismisses extinction claims in any comprehensive international sense, he draws a blank on Blacks in America. This is despite his assertion that every national case is essential for a complete picture. Other *AJS* pieces from the period follow suit. Repeatedly, the American Black fades into the background of his own portrait, a bundle of negations: "neither grasping, nor malicious, nor vindictive. . . . For him the future is not."[28] The final phrase is suggestively ambiguous. Does it mean, "He has no sense of the future," or "He has no future here"?

In his classic essay on race prejudice, W. I. Thomas provides an example of the deadly logic built into sociological optimism on race. Here, hope is charged with the leveling mechanisms of a competitive meritocracy. The dominant factor in the liberal marketplace, according to Thomas, is the ability to "get results" (611). Other attributes—distinctions of class, race, even gender—are inconsequential by comparison. As it happens, however, Anglo-Saxon traits tend naturally toward productivity. Thus, Thomas ends up confirming the recession of Black traits over time. The differences between antiquarian racism and sociology, then, lie in practice rather than in theory. In the stark accounts of the Smiths, Bruces, and Tillinghasts, Whites are spectators of an isolated selection process, reflected in a disproportionate Black death rate. From the perspective of sociologists, the race drama looks more provisional: there would be interraction, some assimilation, and then the probable disappearance of the weaker group. The most optimistic among them foresaw a gradual, harmonious resolution to race conflict. They expected Anglo-Saxon attributes and habits to prevail over those of other groups. Proponents of this view could even accept the possibility that "the crossing of races is the essential lever of all progress."[29] While these different readings of Black destiny implied different political positions—stricter and looser forms of race segregation, respectively— both predicted a future America free of Blacks as presently known.

The race was simply incapable, according to these analysts, of surviving on its own in a rapidly modernizing America. Arguments of this sort rarely failed to acknowledge that the Negro problem was inseparable from the social problems generated by modernization. Walter Willcox, for example, used his study of "negro criminality" as the forum for a lament on the impoverishment of modern social forms. Whites, in his opinion, were resting on rapidly eroding "virtues" (familial, religious, civil) that Blacks had never acquired. Blacks were uniquely imperiled, in this view, by the rise of a technological society. Every phase of work and economy was "increasingly diversified" and called for "a constantly increasing amount of industry, energy, and intelligence." Willcox's claims anticipate the thesis of a postmodern study, *The Bell Curve*, whose authors find Blacks similarly unsuited (for constitutional as well as cultural reasons) to the demands of a specialized industrial nation. This backwardness takes expression, according to Willcox, in their continual migration to cities. Though he admits that some Blacks migrate with a sense of purpose, in search of greater opportunities to exploit, most of these migrants are "negro driftwood . . . the potentially criminal class" menacing urban life.

Blacks appear in Willcox's arguments as a type of human refuse in an anxious teleology of modernization.[30] The bleak prospects of twentieth-century democratic society, particularly in regard to matters of race, are attributable to its helpless dependence on public opinion. Willcox's representative case is the arrest and lynching of the Black Georgian, Sam Hose, which demonstrates how a society split by a color line will inevitably generate two public opinions. One unanticipated consequence of these racial divisions is a flowering of "race unity and race pride" (15). Within their separate sphere, Blacks form judgments independent of Whites, and even beyond White comprehension. And the image of an articulate, alternative Black public opinion is even more threatening than the image of a Black criminal underclass. Willcox wonders whether there can ever be a "common public opinion" for both races (25). He concludes that Blacks will probably never be reconciled to American democratic institutions. Worries of this kind motivated Nathaniel Shaler's call for the application of scientific method to the "African Problem." While Shaler clearly prefers outmoded stereotypes (Black simplicity, emotionality, rhythm), he concedes that the race's actual diversity demands the most advanced techniques.[31]

Shaler's ambivalence highlights a paradox that runs throughout these analyses. Blacks represent simultaneously the near and the far: they are the lone indigenous American social problem—"peculiarly our own"—and they are increasingly independent of dominant social values (37). In cities and towns they appear too close for comfort, yet their isolation is a constant worry. Shaler's observation that the internal complexity of Black populations eluded slaveholders despite constant contact suggests the blindnesses afforded by a police state. A looser social organization requires methodologies that are sophisticated as well as far-reaching. For "the Negro problem in the United States is a type of what has to be faced the world about."[32] As the remarks of Willcox and Shaler suggest, the conviction that Blacks eluded stereotypes, that race questions had become the province of science, were steps toward acknowledging that Black political identity had international range. This might enhance impressions of the group's incongruity in an American context. But it also encouraged the reconstruction of race relations on terms consistent with the international basis of American institutions themselves.

Was the situation of American Blacks inseparable from the problem of race contact everywhere? This was the subject of a 1908 debate published in the *American Journal of Sociology*, "Is Race Friction between Blacks and Whites in the United States Growing and Inevitable?" Alfred Holt Stone, the author of the title essay, opens with an account of an 1855 Boston forum on race known as "the Nell Meeting," where the imminent "dying out" of prejudice was anticipated.[33] Holt's objective is to assess the status of this hope in his own era, and he is candid about his suspicion. Race prejudice is inherent and incontrovertible. Natural tendencies become aggravated by the unique pressures of democracy, Holt suggests, advancing what had become a sociological commonplace. "Without other fixed or established distinctions in our social order, we seem instinctively to take refuge in that of color, as an enduring line of separation between ourselves and another class" (690). The term "color" seems somewhat unstable here, finally taking "refuge" itself in the more substantial "class." But Holt wants to claim race as the dominant classification in a liberal meritocracy. The action of his sentence may belie it, but distinctions of rank and creed are mutable, while those of race defy challenge. Yet Holt also recognizes that American race relations have long surpassed a merely domestic frame of reference.

Holt credits Adam Smith with the discovery of a global "interdependence," whose very definition marks the advent of worldwide ethnic strife. Since the time of this eighteenth-century philosopher, contact among different human kinds has increased, but there has been no comparable increase in understanding. Slavery, according to Holt, who draws on Nathaniel Shaler for this point, is a local structure designed to mediate "the normal operation of elementary racial antipathy" (685). Holt goes on to confirm de Tocqueville's prophecy that "emancipation would be but the beginning of America's racial problems" (690). The increased proximity of different races, a growing uniformity of aspirations stimulating competition for limited resources, fears over disparities in population ("natives" losing ground to "aliens") have enlarged the sphere of racism. At the same time, a greater international awareness prevails. Holt perceives the dawning of Black American "solidarity" as part of a "general awakening of the darker races of the earth" (695). Americans may have managed to subdue fears about Black population statistics at home; they have yet to address similar developments abroad. Holt pictures a parade of dark challenges:

the gains of Black farmers across the South, competition from Black workers in northern cities, the recent Japanese victory over the Russians.

As part of an international struggle, American race friction begins to look like a territorial dispute, whose resolution lies in the division of lands and securing of boundaries. Thus Smith's color line is revitalized: from an antiquated instrument of local terror, it becomes a rational method in an international age. If extinction has turned out to be a White fantasy of sorts, Black disappearance can be ensured by other means. There is finally very little give and take in Holt's "debate." Walter Willcox, the first respondent, seems relatively optimistic about the chances of keeping "race friction" within bounds. He bases his hopes in what he perceives to be decreased opposition from Blacks and Whites toward a caste system that institutionalizes Black subordination (822). U. G. Weatherly highlights the effects of increased Black migration northward. The negative outcome is greater unrest among southern Blacks, stimulated by the promise of a northern outlet. The positive outcome is the greater likelihood of a unified national policy on race, given the intensification of northern race conflict (824–25). According to J. W. Garner, race conflict is inevitable given the instability of Black status (828).

That instability takes divergent but invariably threating forms, from the upward mobility of Black landowners and professionals to the unpredictable mobility of Black deviants. In this context, it's worth recalling the example of Pap Singleton, who articulated, famously, throughout the post-emancipation era, the dream of Black mobility. Dubbed "the Moses of the Colored Exodus," for having masterminded migration from the south to Kansas, Singleton (who was active in the 1870s and 1880s) was featured in another *American Journal of Sociology* essay in 1909. Politically shrewd, with an extraordinary gift of the gab, Singleton's craving for media attention (he even testified before the United States Senate) was matched by his success in getting it. Singleton couched a radical politics consistent with Du Bois's own in a rhetoric closer to Booker T. Washington's. He was an expert cultivator of White interests, while aggressively defending Black ones. There could be "no transmogrification of the races," he declared, not because Whites despised the idea, but because he preferred Black sovereignty.[34] Above all, Singleton understood the threat of unlimited Black mobility, and he articulated this threat in his own rich streams of talk. "The colored race," he commented irritably, "is ignorant and altogether too simple, and invests too much confidence in Professor Tom Cat, or some of the imported slippery chaps from Washington, Oberlin, Chicago, or scores of places whence are sent intriguing reverends, deputy doorkeepers, military darkeys, or teachers, to go often around the corrals and see that not an appearance of a hole exists through which the captives can escape, or even see through" (66). Like Washington, Singleton emphasizes Black self-help and favors a practical message over the top-heavy proposals of intellectuals and politicians. But his own highly idiomatic language is anything but direct. For example, Singleton's references to "Professor Tom Cat" and to a "hole" or "escape" hatch help to illuminate a critical moment in Washington's *Up from Slavery* (1901). Near the beginning of his book, Washington describes the "cat-hole" carved into the floor of every "mansion or cabin in Virginia . . . for the purpose of letting the cat pass in and out." The "contrivance" is curious, because the typical slave cabin is full of holes that could readily have "accommodated the cats." What interests Washington especially is the contrivance of decorum. The cat-hole represents the striving for respectability that persists even under the most degraded conditions. More important to Singleton is the idea of a system that affords cats liberties it denies human beings. While Singleton, ever the good republican, idealizes a Black community virtuously and profitably tied to the soil, he deplores concessions designed to keep Blacks forever grounded.

Singleton's main point can be put concisely. American Blacks are in motion: whether up (success) or down (decline); in (migration) or out (emigration). The consensus among participants in the Holt debate is, keep them in their place. One voice alone is raised in protest. As the final respondent, and lone Black participant, Du Bois's task is to confirm the inevitability of the changes acknowledged by his White colleagues, while minimizing their revolutionary implications. At the same time, he must confirm the futility of efforts to perpetuate Black social death through geographical measures. Du Bois stresses the significance of Black political agency in the modern era, which he illustrates by returning to Holt's opening example, the Boston Nell Meeting. Du Bois notes that Holt has overlooked the tremendous change in Black circumstances: no longer, as in 1855, the enslaved beneficiaries of "white friends," they are now, in 1908, public actors on their own behalf. Du Bois describes the democratic ideals common to a spectrum of Black lives, reminding his audience that these "colored" hopes within America are continuous with worldwide struggles. "Not only the Negroes of America, but those of Africa and the West Indies—not only Negroes, but Indians, Malays, Chinese, and Japanese" are determined to contest Teutonic claims of superiority (835). "The world is shrinking together," he writes, "it is finding itself neighbor to itself in strange, almost magic degree." One manifestation of this strange magic is the unlikelihood that "the darker two thirds" of the globe will disappear or recede as a decorative element in some future composite of world races. Rather, they will be prime contenders in the creation of a "new commerce" and a "new humanity." Du Bois's choice of phrase betrays uncharacteristic faith in economics (prompting Americans to solve the race problem and "gain an advantage over the rest of the world" [837–38]). Du Bois is more often impressed with how "race friction" motivates the pursuit of economically *disadvantageous* ends. The source of his economic optimism is unclear, but it is undoubtedly related to his aggressive handling of the term "neighbor" throughout his discussion. Du Bois echoes Nathaniel Shaler's 1904 book (*The Neighbor*) to refute its claims. The magical extension of neighborliness in the modern era brings new obligations (to "be neighborly to the rest of the world") and new ways to betray them ("lynching" and "insult[ing] . . . helpless neighbors"). Du Bois's conclusion, "God save us from such social philosophy!" (838) finds eerie support in one southerner's explanation for why lynchers were impossible to catch: "We're all neighbors and neighbors' neighbors!"[35] It was obviously safer to rely on greed and demographics. Hence Du Bois's redefinition of survival as a biracial term. The hard logic of numbers, he suggests, is bound to favor the world's darker peoples. Segregation is the strategy of desperate Whites, a predictable outcome of unreliable mortality statistics. The story of this transition—the road from mortality statistics to segregation in turn-of-the-century America—provides the plot for the major sociological studies of Du Bois's early career.

THE ATLANTA CHALLENGE

When the editor of the *New York Evening Post* announced in 1905 that the Atlanta University Publications were the "only scientific studies of the Negro question being made today," he was acknowledging the tide of pseudosociology that had preceded their publication.[36] The Atlanta volumes were composed with a view of the social scientific frontier on race as both wide open, with vast territories of knowledge still to be charted, and closed, littered with theories and statistics, many of them inaccurate or extremist. In describing the general plan for these monographs, Du Bois says "the starting point was the large death-rate of the Negroes."[37] Like Kelly Miller assessing Hoffman's *Race Traits*, Du Bois is committed to a full appraisal of the survival question.

It is hard to exaggerate the fascination, of the first volume in the series, *Mortality among Negroes in Cities* (1896), as local ethnography, full of documentary detail and wide-ranging debate. Doctors, college presidents, mothers, and temperance reformers come together to offer their explanations for high Black mortality in a varied chorus of armchair moralism and social criticism. Three arguments, all of them new, dominate. First, Black mortality is a "human problem" of pressing national interest. The future of a modern American nation depends on the state of its urban life, which turns on the fate of its Black inhabitants.[38] Second, intervention is not a possibility but a demand; social science has been redefined as social renovation. Third, the case for inherence is labeled prejudicial. For the first time

295

in a social scientific publication, a *Black* doctor assesses the group's susceptibility to disease, the quality of their health facilities, and the high rate of Black stillbirths. Dr. Butler paints a grim picture of his people as lone laborers in a festering urban underworld. This Dantesque hell of undesirable work features men sweeping streets, digging sewers, and collecting garbage, while pregnant women haul coal and dirty laundry (21). He discounts claims of Black parental neglect and cites instances of Blacks turned away by White doctors worried about their ability to pay. "In the face of all these disadvantages," Dr. Butler asks, "do you not think we are doing well to stay here as long as we do?" (24–25).

Despite its billing as a continuation, "written exclusively by colored men and women," the second Atlanta volume, *Social and Physical Conditions of Negroes in Cities* (1897), replaces criticalness with defensiveness. High mortality becomes the burden of Blacks; there is little mention of their deprivation. In a paper on syphilis, for example, a Fisk University professor claims that the disease has grown to "epidemic" proportions among urban Blacks. Professor Harris, who draws on F. L. Hoffman for support, seems driven by a hygienic self-recrimination that is typical here. He strikes a melodramatic note, picturing the "infants in their graves [who] will rise up in judgment against this evil and adulterous generation and condemn it."[39] It's possible to see in all this self-reflection a deeper kind of social criticism. There is, for instance, a notable lack of consensus about mortality rates (some authors report a decreased Black death rate, while others warn that it is "enormous" and rising).[40] The most revealing contribution opens with a quote from an Atlanta undertaker: "you have no idea . . . how many people are dying from the lack of sympathy."

Reverend Proctor's paper manages to touch upon many subjects that were absorbing Du Bois at the time: the idea of death as a *defining* category for Blacks at the turn of the century; the new prominence of the undertaker as a community figure; the ties between mortality, declining sympathy, and segregation; and finally, the identification of an internal correlative (the distance of the Black bourgeoisie from the Black poor) to an external dilemma (the exclusion of Blacks by the dominant culture). Proctor concludes with a message for the Black elite: "You cannot elevate society by lifting from the top, you must put the jackscrews under the mudsills of society."[41] Du Bois began his editorship of the Atlanta Studies with the third volume, *The Negro in Business* (1899), and the next sixteen volumes continue to assess the mortality question.[42] But they also represent a subtle shift in emphasis. In general, we find fewer death tables and more data on segregation. One significant consequence of segregation, for instance, is the development of undertaking into an exceptionally lucrative Black profession.[43] The irony of the undertaker's success does not escape Du Bois, who seems to have the two previous volumes on Black mortality in mind when he comments that certain businesses owe their subsistence to "the peculiar environment of the Negro in this land." He continues, "Segregated as a social group there are many semi-social functions in which the prevailing prejudice makes it pleasanter that he should serve himself if possible. Undertakers, for instance, must come in close and sympathetic relations with the family. This has led to Negroes taking up this branch of business, and in no line have they had greater success." Du Bois also notes the proliferation of Black cemetery companies, another profitable death industry resulting from "the color line in burial" (14).

There is no mistaking Du Bois's point. Undertaking is profitable because it's an *exclusive* concern (Blacks alone can bury their dead), not because there are higher percentages of Black deaths. Moreover, conventional belief in the group's affinity for death ensures a limited but steady trade in White burials.[44] There is a long history to this "peculiar" state of affairs. In the contemporaneous *Philadelphia Negro*, and later in *The Negro Church* (1903), Du Bois describes the commendation (in 1794) of two Black ministers, Absalom Jones and Richard Allen, who remained behind during the 1792 Philadelphia epidemic to bury the dead, "spending some of their own funds" in the process. Du Bois notes how the piety and fortitude that led to these acclaimed acts had not prevented the pair's ejection from church worship in 1787, when the Methodists decided on segregated services. Allen's autobiographical account of the incident in *The Life, Experience, and Gospel Labors of the Right Reverend Richard Allen* (1833) betrays tempered resentment. "We all went out of the church in a body," Allen writes, "and they were no more plagued by us." Allen's choice of phrase may register the ironic discrepancy between his own poor treatment and his later work burying "bod[ies]" during the "plague." A prior inhumanity did not prevent his own humanitarianism.[45]

The significance of undertaking is not confined to its place among the most profitable of Black businesses. For Du Bois, the success of the Black undertaker has symbolic weight. In contrast to traditional Enlightenment values, which assign the work of death and mourning to "humanity," Du Bois recognizes them as tasks of the ethnically familiar.[46] The death industry provides a commercial answer to Reverend Proctor's spiritual plea. For a major insight of *The Negro in Business* is the real compensations afforded by segregation.[47] In *The Negro in Business*, Black enterprises figure as morbid offshoots of the larger economy, representing what Du Bois terms "the advantage of the disadvantage." Here Blacks themselves profit from "the needs" created by "a hostile environment." Du Bois's arguments anticipate (by a century) those of another sociologist, Douglas Massey, who notes (from Du Bois's time on) the increasing success of businesses dependent on Black enclosure. After 1910, he comments, "professionals and trades-people who catered to white clients and aspired to full membership in American society were supplanted by a class of politicians and entre-peneurs . . . [with] a self-interested stake in the ghetto."[48]

In later volumes of the Atlanta Studies, the mortality question is recon-ceived. Inaugurating "the second cycle" of the Atlanta Studies, *The Health and Physique of the American Negro* was the most significant statement to date on the relationship between population figures and the rise of the color line. The book opens with a stunning photographic procession of "typical Negro-Americans," ranging from the darkest Black to White, a wordless narrative, articulating in the strongest possible terms the doom of racial separation. The paradoxical foundation of this display is familiar to students of race theory: the attempt to catalog racial difference, the very rise of ethnology as a field of interest, discovers only the hopelessly mixed character of all races. Over the course of the nineteenth century, ever more sophisticated techniques for measuring and classifying human kinds were set against the realities of assimilation. The fact was that America was ab-sorbing its different populations, whose own internal variety mirrored the racial variousness of "native" Americans themselves. The same historical events—immigration, colonization, capitalist-industrial expansion—which had given rise to ethnology were rapidly eroding its analytical base.[49]

Racial ambiguity, as these developments imply, ran in all directions. As Du Bois points out, "very few pure Negroes exist." He quotes Livingstone: "the hideous Negro type, which the fancy of observers once saw all over Africa . . . is really to be seen only as a sign in front of tobacco-shops" (16). And he cites "eminent anthropologists," who confirm "that the entire white race has a very high percentage of the African in its composition" (38). Even more alarming is Du Bois's insinuation that Black population statistics are somehow dependent on this indeterminacy. In the commen-tary that follows his silent parade of "Negro" types, Du Bois observes, "the Octoroons . . . pass so easily back and forth between the races that it is difficult to estimate their real numbers. . . . The census of 1890 reported 69,936 Octoroons. . . . there may be as many as 150,000 in all" (35–36).[50] Du Bois's largest claim is the iconic suppleness of the "American Negro," which is reinforced by a different kind of threat. He includes in the same volume parts of the Atlanta University commencement address in which Franz Boas declares ancient Africa the source of all known cultures (19–21). *Health and Physique* thus makes short work of three dominant theories: that Black and White races have become increasingly distinct; that African culture is limited to its American and African variants; that Black culture is regressive. With Africa reinscribed as the first productive culture of the ancient world, Black mortality statistics in modern America become an obvious outcome of social conditions. Place any other group in similar circumstances, and the results will be identical. Du Bois's comparisons range from Russia, England, and Sweden to the Chicago stockyards, where White death rates surpass Black (39).[51]

Du Bois's substantive challenge to the category of Black mortality is qualified by fears that it had assumed a life of its own. In a subsequent Atlanta volume, a correspondent from the Anti-Tuberculosis League of Georgia articulates a common concern when he observes that high Black mortality (whether real or imagined) now "amounted to an actual stigma on the race."[52] Strictly defined as "a mark made upon the skin by burning . . . (rarely, by cutting or pricking) as a token of infamy or subjection," "stigma" always has a potential religious connotation, as in Christ's "stigmata."[53] While the secular sense of the term stresses mental wounding, a label that causes shame or sadness, the religious sense is more overtly physical. Religious meaning also restores historical content: not only the history of Christianity, but the history of Black bodies, marked and tortured in slavery and in freedom. To remember bodies is to acknowledge limitation. If something can be particularized physically, it must also in time be subject to diminishment. The individual slave or criminal will die; this patch of skin will heal. A modern emphasis on the conceptual hurt minimizes this quality of limitation. The loss of physicality, in this instance, actually assists permanence.

The identification of high Black mortality as a "stigma" is significant, because it registers the miraculous independence of stereotypes from social facts. Stereotypes linger beyond the bodies and statistics they describe. This may explain why allusions to the mortality issue in the Atlanta volumes tend to be muted, as if Black analysts want to avoid feeding its flames. But it is also because these studies challenge prevailing race theory through data rather than disputation. These are works of practical sociology: confronting mortality statistics in terms of socioeconomic cause and outcome: addressing every serious qualification, from the segregationism that belies Black disappearance to the "passing" that defiantly stages it. The Atlanta volumes were designed to expose Black existence to the light of empirical method. And most contemporary reviewers, including editors of the *American Journal of Sociology*, recognized them as original documentations of Black American life.[54] This explains their magnitude: endless tables on Black businesses, hospitals, and medical schools; extended photographic series (on the evolution of the Negro body and home); protracted "correspondence" to close each volume. Only detail could fill the vacuum of hearsay and grim mythology, could transform Black Americans from the "phantoms" of sociological analysis to the "bone and flesh" collectivity ushered in by Du Bois at the start of *Souls*.

INSTITUTIONAL RACISM

I have implied an openness to capitalism and assimilation on Du Bois's part in the Atlanta Studies, exemplified by the flattering statistics on Black enterprise and the ironic attention to the extent of Black passing. In other contemporary analyses, such as *The Negroes of Farmville*, Du Bois also charted the gains of Black landholders and businessmen. Here, however, every gain appears as an improbability achieved against terrific odds. Black failure is likely, not only because Whites expect it, but because its likelihood is deliberately institutionalized. Throughout writings of this period, Du Bois outlines what he calls "the economic core" of Black subordination.[55] According to Du Bois, economic relations are *productive* of other differences. Racial distinctions are *less natural* than the class distinctions they so often overshadow. Take, for instance, his description of the color line from *Souls*.

The winding and intricacy of the geographical color line varies, of course, in different communities. I know some towns where a straight line drawn through the middle of the main street separates nine-tenths of the whites from nine-tenths of the blacks. In other towns the older settlement of whites has been encircled by a broad band of blacks; in still other cases little settlements or nuclei of blacks have sprung up amid surrounding whites. Usually in cities each street has its distinctive color, and only now and then do the colors meet in close proximity. Even in the country something of this segregation is manifest in the smaller areas, and of course in the larger phenomena of the Black Belt.

All this segregation by color is largely independent of that natural clustering of social grades common to all communities. (322)

Notice the stress on spatial growth: from "line" to "band" to "nuclei." While the images evolve naturally—the "drawn" line ends in population clusters "sprung up" like weeds—Du Bois sees human intent where another might see accident. The normal logic of racialism is further confounded by the designation of "natural . . . *social* grades." Are we to accept race as mere icing on the cake of class?

Du Bois's description dramatizes the making of a race mythology. Someone, presumably White, has "drawn" the initial "line," which, in final form ("sprung up"), appears inevitable. This explains how local practice can assign "each street . . . [a] distinctive color." Cause and effect have changed places, with social policy physically manifest, actually coloring streets. If this is a transgression, the passage's concluding image pictures a violation of a different order: "a white slum planted in the heart of a respectable Negro district." The oscillating color line not only confuses cause and effect but also precludes casual contact between Whites and Blacks from similar classes. The color line, Du Bois argues, is a fluctuating boundary, like the human relations it affords and obstructs. Du Bois here anticipates Bourdieu's attempt to make descriptive classifications accountable to the fluctuations of social life. "The boundaries between theoretical classes which scientific investigation allows us to construct on the basis of a plurality of criteria," writes Bourdieu, are analogous to "a flame whose edges are in constant movement, oscillating around a line or surface."[56] Classifications, Bourdieu suggests, are pivots for the *potential* identity of group interests and actions. Du Bois's shifting geometry of race ("line," "circle," "nuclei") acknowledges political indeterminacy, but reinforces magnitude. The (standard) capitalization of "Black Belt" conveys both familiarity and danger. A sign of the inversive potential in any policy, segregation helps to shape a resistant Black constituency. Yet the same inversive potential may have an opposite outcome. For Du Bois's mutable symbol also confirms segregation's inability to keep Blacks neatly enclosed.

Du Bois's "The Economics of Negro Emancipation" (1911) admits no ambiguity about the relationship between a certain type of economy and prejudice. Capitalism is cause; racial oppression is outcome. Jim Crow and lynch law are pretexts for deeper designs: "Under the flame of this outward noise went the more subtle and dangerous work," the systematic subordination of Black labor. Disenfranchisement, imprisonment for debt and for breaking a work contract, the neglect of Black education, all contributed to "a backward step in the organization of labour such as no modern nation would dare to take in the broad daylight of present economic thought" (310–11) Du Bois claims the compatibility of modern capitalism and a near medieval caste system of wage slavery. Given the extent of northern investments in the South, their complicity with outrages there is inevitable. Add to this the profoundly fatalistic attitudes "toward the possibility of real advance on the part of the darker nations." The economic complexity of America's race problem, Du Bois concludes, "is but a local phase" of a vaster dilemma. "How far is the world composed of an aristocracy of races, unalterable and unmoveable, by which certain peoples have a right to rule and exploit all others" (312–13).

Du Bois was aware of the role social science played in rationalizing this exploitation. His insight was shared by later Black intellectuals, Ralph Ellison among them. In his 1946 review of Myrdal's *American Dilemma*, Ellison detected, "beneath [sociology's] illusionary non-concern with values," the attempt "to reconcile the practical morality of American capitalism with the ideal morality of the American Creed."[57] Du Bois and Ellison are bleak about Black prospects under capitalism. There were even bleaker projections by Black Americans writing later in the century. It's startling to find, for example, the sociologist E. Franklin Frazier observing as late as 1962, "It may be that in the distant future Negroes will disappear physically from American society. If this is our fate, let us disappear with dignity."[58]

Without the context we have been tracing, from Bruce and Smith through Shaler and Ward, this remark seems idiosyncratic. From within that context, it appears a haunting echo, an antiquarian remnant, confirming the remarkable tenacity of the dialogue of death. Black literary authors such as Ellison and Wright, who picture protagonists literally buried alive in crypts of light (*Invisible Man*) or drawn to death as a vocation (*The Long Dream*), have recognized the Black stigma of mortality as a consistent pattern of thought in twentieth-century America. Their conversance with developments in the field of sociology (Ellison as a respected reviewer and Wright as an advocate, notably of *Black Metropolis* [1945], by Drake and Cayton) grew out of their commitment to challenging racial stereotypes. They knew the idea of Black morbidity as social scientific mythology. From Daniel Moynihan's notorious 1965 report on the moribund Black family to Andrew Hacker's *Two Nations* (1991) the myth endures. American journalism reflects and perpetuates it, for example, by referring to young Black males as an "endangered species." Blacks themselves have even played the death hand, most often with parodic intent. Consider the label "Death Row Records," featuring Rap artists like Snoop Doggy Dog, which regionalizes the creativity of Black youth as a ghostly limbo, somewhere between deviance and a (possibly compensatory?) land of the dead. And there is the "do or die" rhetoric of Black youth gangs, with their violent negation of dominant cultural values (e.g., life). As one gang member put it, "You see enough dyin', then you be ready to die yourself, just so you don't have to see no more of death."[59]

These are emblems in a postmodern context that has also realized an altogether different possibility for Black Americans. Still, the fact that they persist in a time when Black Americans have achieved so much in the way of affluence and influence, signals the continuing power of the dialogue to express and shape American experience. What explains this durability? A strong institutional foundation at the turn of the century has much to do with it. Some of these institutional forms are familiar and have already been alluded to. They include restrictive covenants in the housing industry, Jim Crow laws, the rise of ghetto enterprises. From the turn of the century, recent analysts have argued, segregation was implemented with increasing efficiency, culminating in the residential divide of our own time, a divide so extreme that it merits, in some views, the label "American apartheid." According to Stanley Lieberson, there was an actual "deterioration in the position of blacks over time," a decline that is "hardly to be expected" were it attributable to slavery's aftereffects. My claim is that we have in Du Bois's America, partly in response to the post-emancipation gains and challenges of Blacks, an attempt to reinvent their "social death" under slavery in a new, more intensely metaphorical form.[60]

One of the most far-reaching of these "death industries" was the turn-of-the-century expansion of life insurance, which was introduced in America during the 1850s.

The insurance industry provides an appropriate conclusion to this section, because it reflects, as institutional policy, many of the changes that we have been tracing. In Du Bois's funeral scene, death is a problem of reception: a series of effects and affects, muting trees, silencing children, dimming song, spreading a ghastly unreality over all. From a social scientific perspective, the telling action is compression, the single word that transforms a family mourning the loss of its only child into a statistic, the prejudicial magic that turns a group of individuals for whom death is trauma into a collectivity for whom death is customary. The Whites play the role of serpent in an Edenic idyll of proper mourning. They represent the fall into a certain social scientific knowledge of humanity as universally insignificant and socially estranged. Death here is at once shrunken and enlarged: it is shrunken from a universal to a contemporary plane of explanation and meaning; it is enlarged as a society-centered rather than personal event. In one sense there is nothing particular to racial politics in the idea that death is routinized when it is viewed as something that is happening to a social group rather than to an individual.

Such a difference is the basis for the rise of the life insurance industry, whose redefinition of death, in collective and statistical terms, was, according to F. L. Hoffman, its means of investing it with predictability and control. "What comes so near to certainty, as to the wasting away of the mass," wrote Elizur White, the Insurance Commissioner of Massachusetts, "falls largely, if not wholly, within the dominion of what we call chance, as to the individual."[61] This view prepared the way for the commodification of death, which now possessed a value that could be determined by the laws of probability. In this way and more, death proved beneficial to the living: every death contributed to social progress and fostered the integration of the community. The act of mourning, according to contemporary analysts like Nathaniel Shaler, inspired "a firmer bond between men than any other basis of fellowship can afford," an idea that inevitably implied the reverse—that it exposed differences between them.[62] Death and mourning confirm difference: this was the basis of modern life insurance.[63] Industry analysts like Hoffman claimed a statistical ability to distinguish the varying life chances of racial and ethnic groups. This was consistent with his belief that respect for the dead was an "Anglo-Saxon . . . race trait." Belief turned prophecy when the industry introduced coverage restrictions on other groups. The reluctance on the part of company agents to insure ethnic "others" was neither chance nor whim; it was articulate policy. Hoffman reproduces a circular sent to all Prudential insurance men, establishing "a restrictive course" on "colored risks." Hoffman presents the strategy as a product of "careful investigations," into the group's "excessive mortality" (reinforced by data from his own *Race Traits*).

The obvious outcome then of Hoffman's Anglo-Saxon lineage for "the first-class companies" was the segregation of insurance. Barred from reputable institutions, Black business either fell into the hands of charlatans or gravitated to exclusively Black concerns. Du Bois devotes a section of *The Philadelphia Negro* to a survey of what befalls Black customers, from outright fraud (agents selling policies on behalf of non-existent companies) to policy loopholes (that allow companies to avoid fulfilling legitimate claims). Du Bois sees Black insurance societies functioning reparatively, to offset the blows from "the pernicious white petty insurance societies." As usual, Du Bois and Booker T. Washington are at odds. While "a few years ago no coloured man could get insurance in the large first-class insurance companies," Washington writes in *The Future of the Negro* (1899), "now there are few of these companies which do not seek the insurance of educated coloured men."[64] Insurance now featured a moral exclusion clause. No longer seen as a generalized benevolence, the industry had become discriminating; it offered aid to the "deserving." Prudential Life Insurance had assumed Providential power. Hoffman's *History* reveals the deliberateness of it all. To President Dryden, Frederick Hoffman, and anyone else they could convince, life insurance was a sacred business. A spokesman called it "God's noblest work" (110). Through buying into the Prudential fold one achieved both communion and respectability. It could prove an individual's making and unmaking. "We believe the Prudential has been an inestimable blessing to the workingmen of England, and that the companies engaged in the same line of business here will prove of like advantage to our people," Dryden wrote (140), confirming its democratic and redemptive office. Life insurance was bound to exert a great influence upon the masses. Teaching them industry and thrift, it would enhance their moral and economic condition.

The different elements brought together in Hoffman's book—economy, prudence, spiritual grace—provide a striking endorsement of the Weber thesis. Insurance sales represented a closed circuit of holiness, from agent to policyholder and back again. According to an editorial quoted by Hoffman, no profession benefits more from "the great work that life-insurance agents are constantly doing" than "the ministry." "God will care for those they [the ministers] love, because in His Providence He has led men to organize this great interest of life insurance for their protection" (263). Hoffman, and the Prudential Company as a whole, were expert managers of public opinion. The link they drew between insurance agents and ministers ranged far beyond Hoffman's *History* and company policy statements. The *London Spectator*, for example, commends Prudential "for liberally treating its agents and employees, and for religiously studying their interests" (156). Newark's *Insurance Times* follows suit, declaring that "Giving doth not impoverish," for insurance will ensure "the elevation of the man" (113). This editorial also endorses specific policy: "*the prime object should be the diffusion of its blessings among the masses. . . . Will it pay? . . . Just as low in the scale of society as the effort can be made self-sustaining, should the insurance manager be willing to go*" (111). Insurance was sacred work, but it was also sound economy. In this light, the *Newark Evening Courier* is not guilty of a contradiction when it remarks that insurance was "*calculated to accomplish a work of great beneficence*" (76).

This is a constant of Hoffman's *History*: insurance rests on "*a scientific basis*, a basis which has been ascertained and approved by the highest actuarial ability in this country and in England" (76). Objections to industry policy were classified as "sentimental," which is the term applied to the discrimination charges leveled by a Black member of the Massachusetts State Legislature in 1884. "Such sentimental considerations have very materially influenced legislators at all times and on all subjects," Hoffman comments. "Fortunately, the companies can not be compelled to solicit this class of risks" (153). Hoffman's *History* can be understood as the product of one extraordinarily invested actuarial imagination. But many of the same assumptions are anticipated, by over twenty years, in a paper on life insurance delivered at the American Social Science Association meetings (October 1868). Like Hoffman, Sheppard Homans associates the rise of insurance with "social advance."[65] As one would expect, given Homans's forum, he bases his argument "upon the sure foundation of science" (162). He also sounds the democratic theme: "a company of the people for the people" (167). There is, however, no spiritual inflection; insurance by this account is without otherworldly ends. And the racial theme is muted. It's there, implicitly; but an assertion like "the larger proportion of the insured in The Prudential are native-born" (Hoffman [302]) would seem misplaced. What Homans does corroborate is the idea that insurance identifies a community of values and interests. He also pictures the insurance industry as the product of a certain climate, marked by anxiety about social transformation and heterogeneity.

All this is far more developed in Hoffman's vast *History*, where life insurance is one means by which a modern society constructs kinship. The creation of a national family from the materials afforded by the American scene was hard work. The insurance industry supplied the requisite language, spiritually grave in its own right, and new communal rituals. Insurance was a lifestyle. Company affairs reflect this comprehensive approach. An affair at the home office for company agents is "in the nature of a house-warming."[66] President Dryden augments this domestic emphasis with his picture of the weekly visit by the Prudential agent, which suffuses every house "in an atmosphere of insurance." This is familial work of the highest order. The agent becomes so intimate with each home that he gets to know the "neighbors." Insurance, Dryden's conclusion shows, builds on pre-existing mythologies. An industry for the "masses," it helps to identify those among them destined to hold "power in society." It is prepared to "deal liberally and equitably with its policy-holders to the extent of its ability in an hour of emergency or need" (193–96). Here we confront the relatively new idea of institutional heart: the modern corporation is designed to accommodate "need."

The significance of this principle is confirmed by Hoffman's decision to end his *History* with a more direct formulation of it: Dryden's image of Prudential "taking its root in human affection" (318). Life insurance, in the minds of Hoffman and Dryden, is about protection. This is the message of the famous company logo: an inscribed shield ("A Strong Shield For The Widow And The Fatherless") and rock ("The Prudential has the strength of Gibraltar").[67] All stone and metal, without a groove or nook, the image is absolutely forbidding. Is this the business of protection or proscription? "Don't come near," the logo seems to say, "if you are too weak or too poor." The logo reflects the industry's split purpose: inspiring those it protects and intimidating those it protects against. The same tension is plain in the ambiguity over the industry's dominant category itself. Industry literature reveals a constant slippage between the British term, "assurance," and the American, "insurance." Both Homans and Hoffman tend to invoke them interchangeably. Homans refers, for example, to "assurance premiums" (166), and Hoffman, to "Assurance Associations" (5). Strictly speaking, however, the terms are not equivalent. The word "insurance" puts greater weight on "loss" or "harm." It designates contractual relations, referring to property or persons in an objective sense. The word "assure" is more provisional. It concerns "promises" or "declarations," having less to do with persons as objects of an exchange than with persons as subjects, who have doubts, even feelings.

I'm less interested in this lexical curiosity for its own sake than for what it may indicate about the ambitions of the American insurance industry at this time. For it seems to me that industry analysts like Hoffman wanted all the different registers I have named. They believed that life insurance was a model social organization because it was scientific *and* spiritual; because it appealed to individual initiative *and* to community values; and, finally, because it could be tough on the morbid and degenerate *and* generous to virtuous citizens in need. Life insurance exemplifies the genius of modern institutionalism: an industry that made fatal calculations look like exercises in benevolence and turned discriminatory policies into defenses of public welfare. This was not magic but, rather, the fulfillment of history. The roots of this sympathetic institutionalism lie in changing nineteenth-century conceptions of emotions and their social function.

The Evolution of Sympathy

For historians interested in how ideas change, there are few subjects more compelling than the chain of "recognitions" that led to the long-delayed abolition of slavery in nineteenth-century America. What conditions—moral, economic, political—contributed to this "astounding reversal of fortunes"?[68] In the past decade, scholars have interpreted these developments as part of a larger socioemotional pattern, centered on the social practice of sympathy. Thomas Haskell, for example, has identified as one outcome of capitalism a fundamental progress in Anglo-American conceptions of moral obligation. Few would want to refute Haskell's powerful qualification of Foucault: "to put a thief in jail is more humane than to burn him, hang him, maim him, or dismember him."[69] Like these historians, Du Bois noted broad changes in the moral sentiments throughout what he called in *Souls* "the first century of human sympathy" (356). From Du Bois's perspective, however, sympathy was occasional rather than evolutional: a ritual event with specific social applications. If sympathy contributed to the liberation of Blacks during the war, it contributed to their lynching after it. Du Bois's insight took him beyond Ralph Ellison, who declared that "the moral aspect" had been "forced out of consciousness" in the postemancipation period. Du Bois saw "the moral aspect" everywhere he looked, especially in racist slights and outrages. Sympathy, according to Du Bois, had not disappeared; it had become the medium for inhumane acts.[70] As I have pointed out, a heightened sensitivity to racial and ethnic difference is evident in the earliest attempts to define the moral sentiments as the basis for community and social integration. Mid-nineteenth-century social observers, and especially sociologists writing at the century's turn, increasingly conceived sympathy as a circumscribed, intratribal faculty. Sympathy was limited in application (only felt on behalf of kin) and limited in scope (restricted as an attribute to certain peoples). When turn-of-the-century sociologists advanced these claims, they often invoked a previous literature on the social function of the emotions, whose authors ranged from Hume to Darwin. My purpose in this section is to explore some of the theories about the moral sentiments formulated in the era that has preoccupied historians of sympathy.

EMOTIONAL SELECTION

One of the more peculiar features of racist antiquarian writings such as *The Color Line* or *The Negro in Africa and America* is their recurrent allusion to sympathy. At the most (seemingly) inappropriate times, on the heels of asserting the innate criminality of Blacks, or the benefits of fire for preserving the color line, a writer might suddenly lament the lack of sympathetic ties between Blacks and Whites. William Benjamin Smith calls these impulses involuntary and maintains that he has to "guard himself especially against the emotion of sympathy, of pity for the unfortunate race" (x). Smith's "helpless" stream of reference has something to do with memory. This is his nostalgia speaking, on behalf of a slave system that afforded such emotional patronage. Smith's image of a bygone empathy echoes passages in *Souls*. Du Bois reflects, for instance, on "that finer sympathy . . . between some masters and house servants which the radical and more uncompromising drawing of the color line in recent years has caused almost completely to disappear" (334). Where Du Bois highlights the social and institutional changes that have led to this blockade of feeling, analysts like Smith resort to universals. Through the usual prejudicial wizardry, an alteration in custom with vast social and economic implications becomes a simple race trait. In Smith, cause and effect recede into Blackness. Sympathy between the races is now an impossibility because of inherent Black callousness. Tillinghast cites a source in which a gruesome account of African cannibalism is summarized by the observation that they lack "abstract affection for humanity at large" (67). This extends to intratribal feeling in a later passage: "we are prepared to believe that the African has almost no sensibility to suffering in others, nor compassion for them. Such refinements of the social spirit have never been developed among these peoples" (71).

It is not surprising to hear Philip Bruce sounding the same theme; he links the modern "indifference to the suffering of others" to past plantation behavior, pictured as elaborate "schemes of vengeance" realized through "trick doctors." But it does give one pause to hear it echoed by *American Journal of Sociology* authors like Paul Reinsch, who asserts that "the negroes are always ready for a savage onset, even upon men of very nearly their own flesh and blood."[71] In fact, these are standard adaptations of social Darwinism, which even identifies sympathy, at times, with specific body parts (e.g., the maternal womb [W. I. Thomas]; or the padded underside of fingertips [Nathaniel Shaler]). Du Bois appears to have had more conventional Darwinian notions in mind when he credited their originator, in a 1909 conference paper, "The Evolution of the Race Problem," with responsibility for a "moral change in social philosophy" that supported convictions of "the inevitable and known inferiority of certain classes and races."[72] But Darwin's *The Expression of the Emotions in Man and Animals* (1872) would have served Du Bois's purposes. Du Bois is clearly being ironic here, charging that Darwin's readers have missed the complexity of his arguments. Darwin's "splendid scientific work" has been assumed—it was "the age of Darwin"—rather than understood (150). *The Expression of Emotions* is a challenge to those who think they know Darwin. It's full of concrete, even homely examples (the family pet is a constant referent) and surprising interpretations.

Two themes predominate: one familiar, the other somewhat strange. The first is the theory of evolution, formulated as the transmission and development of feeling. Emotions evolve, like other organs, through "mutation and selection."[73] The second is a principle of universalism. In "The Conservation of Races," Du Bois offers an apt paraphrase of Darwin: "great as is the physical unlikeness of the various races of men their likenesses are greater."[74] To see the emotions in an evolutionary light, Darwin writes in his introduction, is to see the whole subject of expression in a "new and interesting light" (12). This "light," at least by Darwin's own, appears to be distinctly liberal. Darwin includes the questionnaire that served as the basis for his fact gathering. He relates the details of its distribution, among a variety of analysts—scientists, missionaries, explorers—with the aim of reaching peoples who had "had little communication with Europeans" (16). This is all in the name of Darwin's driving hypothesis: "the same state of mind is expressed throughout the world with remarkable uniformity." This is made possible, he writes, by a "close similarity in bodily structure and mental disposition of all the races of mankind" (17). Darwin points out that his sources overall supported his confidence in the universality principle, with one exception. His information has been scant "with respect to the negroes, though Mr. Winwood Reade aided me as far as lay in his power." Darwin's qualification is telling, not because it contradicts his principle (it's intact through the book's end), but because it reveals his method. Darwin specifically rejects data on Blacks in America, which is tainted because they have "long associated" with Whites (21). Darwin is not interested in emotions as social facts. He seeks rather to consider them in isolation as pure biological properties of different peoples.

He aims to test a series of propositions about the emotional life and understand how far it can be applied to species in general. The first is a principle of dependence: certain states of mind yield certain physical movements, a tendency acquired "through the force of habit and association" (28). Over time, we have learned to *express* our feelings by certain movements. Originally, Darwin believes, these physical movements counted as the feelings themselves. There was a much closer, or even absolute, tie between physical movements and feelings. His example is "snarling," which developed from "actual biting . . . a means of aggression, [which] has practically disappeared in the human species" (xii). The second is a principle of physical complementarity or continuity. The physical expression is a fulfillment of the emotion, so that opposite sensations or emotions produce opposite movements. Darwin's example here is the range of emotions exhibited by the family dog when its expectations are heightened, then deflated. He describes the remarkable discrepancy between the animal's aspect, poised for a walk, versus the look it takes on when the walk is curtailed by a trip to Darwin's "hot-house." So pronounced is the animal's transformation, from a physically complete jubilation to utter despair, that Darwin's family even coined a term for it: *"hot-house face"* (57–60). Darwin's third principle is the direct action of the excited nervous system on the body: impulsive actions that are largely independent of the will (83–84, passim). The snake's rattle supplies his key example, as a protective device for making cobras and even more benign snakes terrible to their enemies. He highlights his disagreement with Nathaniel Shaler, who argues that the rattle has evolved as a means of deceiving, attracting, and then paralyzing prey. Darwin prefers the involuntary to the strategic interpretation: the rattle is a reflex action. Making sense of evolution requires consistency; if the rattle were other than defensive, would the snake always use it when "angered or disturbed"? Darwin goes on to list the many creatures that prey on cobras, from pigs and hedgehogs to herpestes (106–8).

Against Shaler's scheme of absolute vulnerability versus absolute power, Darwin posits a more subtle sense of reciprocal danger. Every kind is at once prey and predator, and the process of natural selection ensures a perpetual doubleness of condition. Darwin's resistance to Shaler's naturalist morality play prefigures the ultimate incompatibility between his ideas and Shaler's racialist account of the emotions. All animals need protection, Darwin argues, just as all human beings feel and express emotions in uniform ways. Bodies, across the world, speak a "common" language (185). "To say that a person is 'down in the mouth' is synonymous with saying that he is out of spirits," and this "has been observed with men belonging to various races" (192). He likewise confirms that "with all the races of man the expression of good spirit appears to be the same, and is easily recognized" (211). "Shrugging the shoulders," he notes elsewhere, "is a gesture natural to mankind" (268–69), while the wide-open eyes and mouth is "universally recognized as one of surprise or astonishment" (279). The posture holds for Shakespearian heroes and for Winwood Reade's Guinea Negroes (279). Darwin concludes with a triumphant summary of all these hypotheses: "the young and the old of widely different races . . . express the same state of mind by the same movements" (351).

When Darwin's range is limited to the function of single bodies, universality claims come readily to hand. This is evident in his first mention of sympathy, which he sees as involuntary movement, typified by the tendency of the jaws of "persons cutting anything" to move "simultaneously with the blades of the scissors" (34–35). Darwin intends little more than the idea that the body inevitably parrots the mind. Like grief, where "the head hangs," and there is, as the "Australian aborigines" say, "a chop-fallen appearance," we don't just *feel* sympathy, we *wear* it (177). However, there is internal sympathy of a body for its own mind, and there is the other kind of sympathy (call it "social"), which is a different situation altogether. Darwin even implies that it defies analysis (214). At the very least, "it is a separate and distinct emotion," whether given or received (215). Darwin seems to distrust social sympathy as primarily self-deceptive or inauthentic. The evidence of Darwin's distrust is his suggestion that sympathy excites bodily expressions incommensurate with actual feeling. We are more apt to express our feelings for another's suffering (rather than our own), simply because those feelings are moderate. We indulge the sentiment of sympathy, because we know that we are in control. Darwin's cold point is that we can sympathize with others, not because we feel for them, but because we don't.

As a feeling outside the self calling for a response from within, sympathy complicates Darwin's model, and it's fair to say that he discounts it. Emotions, so far as he is concerned, are less about purposes than about habits and reflexes. He is not interested in what we can feel but in how what we do feel makes us look. His study is a celebration of the sacred (and universal) scripture coauthored by human emotions and bodies. Darwin marvels at the capacity of the body to picture feeling. He imagines artists as poor rivals to nature, who can only portray strong emotions by "the aid of accessories . . . vague and fanciful expressions" terms like "green-eyed jealousy" and "black envy" (79). Poets become painters in their vain efforts to capture emotions through color. In Darwin's mind, these poetic colorings highlight the inaccessibility of the emotions to all but physical representation. Artificial images pale beside the body's *natural* inscriptions: the hunched shoulders or the half-moon mouth that accompany dejection, for example. Darwin's other point seems to be that we can't appreciate what we can't describe in our own terms. All this color coding becomes a sign for what can't be known about another's feelings. Du Bois implies something similar with the curious color symbolism of *The Souls of Black Folk*. Throughout the book, he envisions emotions in color: *awe* over his son's birth is "yellow"; *hope* in the prospects of American Blacks is "blue"; *guilt* is "red." The intensity, and probable futility, of Du Bois's effort is confirmed by the book's dominant color symbol.

The color line is simultaneously colorful and colorless, like the feeling that it walls in and walls out. Within racial bounds, emotions overflow; beyond them, they evaporate. In keeping with Du Bois's "advantage of the disadvantage," the internal fount might be seen to compensate for an external aridity. In Darwin's view, bodies communicate effortlessly, fully, a form of expression that artists imitate in vain, with the help of colors. The presence of color means the distance of nature. In Du Bois, there is nothing natural about emotional expression. The color scheme of *Souls* is a symbolic revelation of the race relations that mediate feeling and its form. One could say that Darwin reads the coloring of emotions as a loss of nature, while Du Bois reads it as a loss of humanity. In his own evolutionary account of the emotions, Herbert Spencer takes a more defined and defiant stance against the type of case that Du Bois is making. While there is much overlap between Spencer and Darwin on the emotions (and the resemblances seem to have bothered both, for each made clear claims for the independence of their discoveries), Spencer's analysis helps us to recognize Darwin's tact. Darwin avoids both predictable associations of lower races and children, and the opposition of savage and civilized. Spencer is more explicit in connecting his research to the question of survival and applying it on behalf of a racialist hierarchy. It makes sense that Spencer would be more of a social Darwinist than Darwin. In Spencer, there is no hint of universalism. He is interested in what emotions reveal about the relative civilization of a people. He presumes emotional differences between "the lower and the higher races," and understands "feelings which are common to both" as "simpler." The process of evolution is a gradual refinement of these basic emotions and the generation of more complex ones.[75]

Emotions, in Spencer's view, express social context. So, for example, he notes the "improvidence" of "savages," and their preference for "giving pain rather than pleasure." He contrasts this with the organized philanthropy of advanced societies, which "establishes numerous institutions" and dictates "countless private benefactions" (313). None of these points contradicts Darwin, but Darwin is less interested in the relevance of his theories to the facts of human history. What Darwin and Spencer share, in addition to a view of sympathy as a measure of social advance, is an interest in how emotions appear. For both, the Shakespearian dictum (quoted by Darwin [279])—"there was speech in the dumbness, language in their very gesture"—is full of meaning. Spencer's alertness to the social function of the emotions seems spurred by his view of physical expression as a form of control. Emotions range in Spencer's analysis: they are socially purposive. Emotions, as he reads them, are often excessive, in search of an outlet. The body acts as a giant receptacle to cushion their impact. In "The Physiology of Laughter," he writes: "the existing quantity of liberated nerve-force" that produces "feeling . . . *must* generate an equivalent manifestation of force somewhere" (198). Hence, "bodily activity deadens emotion." Emotions become harmful when they are inaccessible to physical expression; they may "accumulat[e] and intensif[y]," menacing the self and society (198–99).

The centerpiece of Spencer's writings on the emotion is "The Origin and Function of Music." Here again, Spencer's concern is "proportion" and "intensity"; the relationship between emotions and bodies is a story about the relief afforded by physical "demonstrations" (211). In contrast to Darwin, who gets most of his lyrical moments from quotes, Spencer is a felicitous writer. His essay is filled with vivid catalogs of such demonstrations. Spencer is preoccupied with the interaction of feeling and physique, which is always a difficult balance and rarely the simple proposition Darwin makes it. This is because feeling, for Spencer, is the basis of social connection. He refers to a law of nature, "a law conformed to throughout the whole economy, not of man only, but of every sensitive creature. . . . when the like sound is made by another, we ascribe the like feeling to him; and by a further consequence we . . . have a certain degree of it aroused in ourselves. . . . these various modifications of voice become not only a language through which we understand the emotions of others, but also the means of exciting our sympathy" (220). The highest form this language takes is the arts, in particular, dance, poetry, and, above all, music. The function of music is to translate the "dead words in which the intellect utters its ideas" into live emotions. In this way, ideas become sociable or sympathetic. Music allows the listener "not only to *understand* the state of mind they accompany, but to partake of [it]" (235). We have only to "consider how much both our general welfare and our immediate pleasures depend upon sympathy" to "recognise the importance of whatever makes this sympathy greater" (236). From his thesis, that civilization builds on the continuous enhancement of sympathetic acts and occasions, Spencer goes on to anticipate increasing social progress in this area. Eventually, human beings will be able "to impress on each other all the emotions which they experience from moment to moment" (237).

How remote is this possibility? Not very, according to Spencer. In the essay "Bain on the Emotions and the Will," Spencer elaborates this prospect by negative comparison with primitives. We know how far we have come by how far behind us they remain. They lack the type of aesthetic emotions that are produced in a civilized culture by music; they have little sense of mercy; they cannot be impressed with the importance of "remote contingencies." These are so many ways of suggesting their immunity to sympathetic action, whether as benefactors or as recipients. Civilized emotionality, for Spencer, is a discipline. The gradual development of the proper faculties are to be expected, "under the discipline of social life" (313). To say that savages are behind civilized nations is not to answer the question Spencer poses for himself in the essay: "How are new emotions generated?" (312–13). Through habit and the perpetuation of similar conditions, he ventures, in a close approximation of Darwin.

A look at Spencer's main example, however, suggests that there is more at stake for him. His account of the changing responses of birds to man in "newly-discovered lands," is framed in terms of "national characteristics, of civilization in its moral aspects . . . of emotion in its origin and ultimate nature" (315). Where humans are rare, "birds are so devoid of fear as to allow themselves to be knocked over with sticks. . . . In the course of generations, they acquire such a dread of man as to fly on his approach" (315). It's possible to read this as the outcome of selection—the elimination, over time, of the innocent and the brave. But Spencer prefers to see it as a manifestation of sympathy's evolution. "In each bird that escapes with injuries inflicted by man, or is alarmed by the outcries of other members of the flock (gregarious creatures . . . being necessarily more or less sympathetic), there is established," Spencer speculates, "an association of ideas between the human aspect and the pains." He goes on to surmise "that such ideal reproduction becomes more vivid and more massive as the painful experiences, direct or sympathetic, increase." He concludes that emotion, at least in this early stage, is "nothing else than an aggregation of the revived pains before experienced," a prior physical state "recollected in dismay." This revival becomes modified into a "reflex action": flight at man's approach (315–16).

Spencer makes great claims for his case, which he believes to be applicable throughout the animal kingdom, and beyond it, to the "different nations" of humanity. Sympathy teaches us to flee: the sympathetic recollection of ourselves in a perilous state and, later, sympathy for the general peril of our kind. To imagine the condition of a group that has not developed along this normative pathway, that has not attained the requisite sympathetic impulse, is to understand how Spencer conceives different representative "savages." For Spencer draws an implicit contrast between the bird's evolving sympathy and the emotional limitations of the uncivilized. The birds become his guide to "those higher emotions by which civilized are distinguished from savage." As Spencer insists in his ultimate assessment of Bain's work, emotions have little scientific value as "isolated facts." They achieve significance when examined in "relation" to "national circumstances" (316–17). The shift in perspective from Darwinian biology to Spencerian sociology takes us from a wide-ranging universalism, set within evolving animal and human bodies, to a more discriminating racialism, that sees evolution as a series of dynamic exchanges—between animals and humans, and then between different "national" kinds. This is why sympathy comes in only on the borders of Darwin's discussion but plays such a prominent role in Spencer's.

THE SOCIOLOGY OF SYMPATHY

It's possible to read these works by Darwin and Spencer as odd evolutionary appropriations of the emotions rather than as genuine contributions to an ongoing theoretical conversation about sympathy. This is Max Scheler's view. Scheler's complaint is their confusion of animal behavior—"herd consciousness"—and "fellow feeling." Sympathetic responsiveness is always effortless and mainly positive in their accounts. It is effortless because it is based in species likeness, positive because it is a celebration of commonality. Sympathy becomes a basis of social connection from which non-kin are naturally excluded. Though he makes no reference to nationality or race, nor to any other theorists of sympathy, Scheler's brief account of Spencer and Darwin is notably revealing of continuities between their ideas and those of late-eighteenth-century theorists. In other words, Scheler does locate a central place for Spencer and Darwin in prior and subsequent discussions of sympathy. As I have suggested, eighteenth-century theorists of fellow feeling provided a valuable resource for turn-of-the-century sociologists, who believed their theories were adaptable to an American context. Albion Small, who wrote a book on Adam Smith, and Robert Park, who developed Hume's theories on moral behavior, saw these Enlightenment philosophers as sociologists in the making. In *Adam Smith And Modern Sociology* (1907), Small claims Smith as a key progenitor. Smith's theories, "enlarged and specialized," provide "the methodology for which the modern sociologists are contending."[76] Small summarizes Smith on moral relations as follows: all of our moral judgments depend on a perception of conduct as right or wrong, and on a perception of the virtue or immorality of the agent. Our apprehension of other minds depends on our own experiences. Fellow-feeling, then, is the penetration of other minds. It is agreeable to both sides, spectator and recipient.[77] The spectator approves of the other's feeling only if he can feel himself affected in the same way (37–38). As a whole, despite his respect for Smith's ambitions, Small finds Smith's philosophy "naive" and "speculative." Smith was trying to find "a way of classifying actions in the objective world by finding an order of authority in our affections," trying "to appraise social substance in terms of forms of individual appreciation" (48). Smith, in Small's view, never approached a theory of "moral" (for Small, substitute "social") relations.

Small's skepticism includes modern social theory, which has yet to free itself from "the individualistic and subjectivistic psychology which Smith inherited" (51). Small's critique of Smith resembles Scheler's impatience with Darwin. In both instances, a social theory is judged inadequate to sociological method, whether it models emotional exchange on animal behavior (Scheler/Darwin) or understands sympathy's social function in narrow psychologistic terms (Small/Smith). Robert Park (*The Crowd and the Public* [1904]) appears to have had few misgivings on methodological grounds in appropriating the theories of Hume and Butler. Like other sociologists, Park sees sympathy as a "natural social instinct," rooted in Enlightenment efforts to locate the origins of moral behavior. Major Enlightenment thinkers like Locke and Hobbes, he points out, believed that moral sanctions lay "outside human nature," that they rested "in authority."[78] Park credits Butler and Hume with the earliest recognitions of "a deeper and more inclusive" theory, which held morality to be formed, at least in part, as an inner response to "the feelings of others." People learned to be moral by reading and anticipating the sentiments and expectations of others. Park notes that such an idea was implicit in Bacon's concept of "sympathetic imitation" or "transmission of spirits," and also in Butler's term "the reflection of affects" (32). But Hume took things one step further: for him, sympathetic responsiveness was constitutive. Hume's idea of sympathy, according to Park, was "a resonance between people's feelings, made possible by their identical constitutions," an identification that was as critical to its expression as to its experience.

Sympathy was an involuntary imitation of another's feelings, experienced as if those feelings were one's own. It was thought both to require and to enhance some absolute affinity between individuals. Sympathy assumed a community of likeminded members that it in turn helped to perpetuate. Park accepted the logical outcome of Hume's premises: the denial of universal validity to moral values. For Park, this was a benefit rather than a loss. Hume's denial allowed his "philosophy of ethics" to become "a sociology" (32). For Max Scheler, however, Hume's denial signals a confusion of physical and moral certainty. Scheler's illustration is Hume's naive wonder "that men have waged wars simply on the basis of different skin color." Scheler comments, "The Americans do not hate the negroes because they are black—there being no evidence as yet, that they also dislike the blackness of clothes or materials; they scent the negro under the blackness of his skin."[79]

Scheler's suspicion, that Hume's interpretation of race was a luxury that even an eighteenth-century philosopher could not afford, is echoed in F. H. Giddings's reading of Adam Smith's *Theory of Moral Sentiments*. Giddings attributes the origins of his own famous category "the consciousness of kind" to Smith's "sympathy" or "fellow feeling," but faults Smith for overlooking the ways in which experience restrains feeling. In Giddings's view, sympathetic responsiveness unfolds within a given social reality,[80] and is invariably restricted to members of one's "kind." His definition of sympathy is built on an identity principle: "a sympathetic consciousness of *resemblance* between the self and the not-self." Sympathy also inhibits miscegenation, "rigorously fix[ing] the permissible degree" of difference in marriage (xii–xiii). Giddings's conception of sympathy as a device of exclusion is familiar. The more unusual claim is that sympathy confounds an otherwise "theoretically perfect" social system driven by self-interest. Giddings's conclusions and examples leave little doubt about his own sympathies, though he does have moments of humanitarianism. He notes that the "highly composite" nature of the Black race suggests a potential for progress and observes that true progress for society as a whole would entail an "expansion" in the consciousness of kind. We can assume that Giddings means "extension" here: from family to horde, to tribe, to folk, and on to a "universal brotherhood," whose closest approximation is a Christian philanthropy (238, 359–60). These claims appear irreconcilable: on the one hand, the natural resistance to White-Black amalgamation and the view of an exclusionary sympathy ("consciousness of kind") as the index of civility; on the other, the recognition of Black diversity and the belief that sympathy's extension (beyond the point of recognition) will mark a higher stage of sociality.

For most major sociological theorists, the category of sympathy was a meaningful one. In light of the revisionary Darwinism that marks most of his work, it's not surprising to find Lester Ward falling into line with previous evolutionary accounts of sympathy, which he calls "a class of feelings . . . developed by social progress."[81] Ward sees sympathy as a psychological as well as physiological process that reveals the evolutionary conditions of different social groups. As he puts it, "the recognition of suffering in others is attended, to different degrees in different individuals, and in very close proportion to the grade of physical and mental organization." The power of sympathy increases with the "advancement of the race." Don't look to "savages" for these sentiments, only to "the highest types of manhood." Ward has no particular quarrel with sympathy, until he confronts it in a modern setting. In the highest civilized forms, he suggests, sympathetic feelings become intolerable, relieved only by "benevolent and philanthropic actions." In these societies, "a *luxury of altruism*" becomes a personality trait of individuals who are only content in the neighborhood of suffering. Such types covet "praise for their disinterestedness and their so-called sacrifices, when they are really pursuing the only course that yields them any pleasure" (369–70). It is not a great leap from this critique to Ward's (potentially contradictory) distinction between the sympathies and the intellect. "The most sympathetic persons are those of rather inferior reasoning powers" (371). Ward is the first to articulate a principle that becomes somewhat standard in sociological accounts of sympathy, from W. I. Thomas to Nathaniel Shaler: sympathy is a "soft" or sensitive attribute, confined to mothers and / or primitives. In these accounts, sympathy marks debility rather than civility. Groups are excluded because they *embody* sympathy, not because they *lack* it.

It's worth specifying what has changed here and what has remained the same. Sympathy has lost its privileged status; it has become not only inauthentic but also, potentially, degenerate. Still, it has remained a story of bodies rather than souls. In the earlier version, told by Darwin and Spencer, and anticipated by Hume and Smith, sympathy is a sign of advancement; it's simply unavailable at lower stages of existence. In this later version, sympathy has become a property of the weakest social bodies, defined against a modern ideal of rationality. E. A. Ross offers yet another reformulation of the sympathy story. Like many, he feminizes sympathy, linking it to the reproductive function. While women have been the special cultivators of sympathy, "social selection" has also "put a premium on the more amiable type of man." Yet it is not at all clear that those peoples "most successful as social architects are the most sympathetic."[82] Ross concludes with a vision of sympathy's evolutionary impossibility. In modern society, he suggests, sympathy is not inevitable, but differentiation is. Our society "produces and consecrates stupendous inequalities in condition" (12), which sympathy, a "soft fibre," cannot modify. "Sympathy," Ross warns, "breaks down at just the point where we are increasingly in need of security" (13). Significantly, Ross is most disturbed where Giddings is most comforted. "The farther apart are men in respect to color, race, speech, status," he writes anxiously, "the harder is it for the electric spark to leap across the space between them" (25). This is no doubt a consequence of their respective emphases: Giddings's devotion to "kind" versus Ross's commitment to "social control." Though this is not the overriding thesis of his tough-minded *Principles*, Giddings's reading of sympathy depends on some eventual utopian resolution of social interests and sentiments, a society in which differences have dissolved, whether through extinction or assimilation. Ross's reading of sympathy is part of a larger argument that confronts the need for new mechanisms of control in a modern heterogeneous society.

Throughout the *American Journal of Sociology* in this period, we find analysts seeking to renovate the moral framework of modern life. In the 1906 forum "Social Consciousness," for example, Charles Cooley declares the need "to feel and to effectuate new kinds of right—kinds involving a sense of remoter results."[83] Cooley's essay advances, in a simpler and less embattled form, the concerns of his 1902 book *Human Nature and the Social Order*. While Cooley's object is to establish sympathy as the basis of a modern social order, he ends up demonstrating the category's fragility. The book was widely known in its own time and beyond for the concept of the "looking-glass self." As Cooley presents it, individuals know themselves by their appearance to others. The individual's vacillations between "pride or mortification" are entirely dependent on that external, perceiving mind. Yet Cooley's mirror is strangely permeable. The self sees through to another discriminating self with its own vulnerability to discrimination. Thus, the self, in its befogged and uneasy dependence, is engaged in ongoing assessments "of that other in whose mind" it presumes to see.[84] One could argue that Cooley's looking glass reflects nothing other than an ideal self, which keeps watch on its mundane counterpart. But Cooley intends something more than this, and it derives from his definition of sympathy.

Sympathy, for Cooley, is a "primary communication or *communion*," the sharing of a communicable mental state. Cooley calls it "emotionally colorless"; it appears to be ethically colorless as well. Sympathy is not about "pity" or "compassion" (102–3). It is about "power." An individual who "understands" those around him is "effective" (107). Cooley continues, "a person of definite character and purpose, who comprehends our way of thought is sure to exert power over us" (108). This "sympathetic influence enters into our system of thought . . . and affects our conduct." Sympathy is the image in Cooley's looking glass, the superior but generous other that represents, not our best self, but rather a collective ideal. The sympathetic individual "is large enough to live the life of the race," to "feel the impulses of each class as his own" (109). Up to this point, we are in a fairly broad region, with sympathy extending as far as a liberal humanitarianism can take it. But Cooley's language eventually betrays the tensions of what it is forced to repress. "A man's sympathies," Cooley goes on to suggest, "reflect the social order in which he lives." "Every group of which he is really a member, in which he has any vital share, must live in his sympathy. . . . his mind is a microcosm of so much of society as he truly belongs to" (111). The Emersonian echoes here are unmistakable. (In fact, one of Cooley's contributions is the link he establishes between classical sociology and an Emersonian tradition.) As in Emersonian self-reliance, Cooley's stance also comes down to a question of kinship. Sympathy may express social wealth, but some narrowing of the sentiments is inevitable. "Universal sympathy is impracticable; what we need is better control and selection, avoiding both the narrowness of our class and the dissipation of promiscuous impressions" (113). He writes at another point, "Sympathy must be selective, but the less it is controlled by conventional and external circumstances . . . the better" (114). Finally, sympathy is about "mixing like and unlike; continuity and change. . . . the likeness in the communicating persons is necessary for comprehension, the difference for interest" (120).

Each of these observations pictures sympathy as the means for reconciling social interests: the need for innovation against the requirements of order; the urge for change against the prospects of continuity; the attraction to difference against faith in the known. Sympathy is identified with social effect and broad mindedness, but it also ensures the protection of common goals. The wisely sympathetic individual acknowledges the faculty's limits; he understands where the lines must be drawn. Sympathy widens in Cooley's analysis to include its antithesis, hostility. Cooley coins a term for it, "hostile sympathy." Entering another consciousness, in this case, reveals an "uncongenial" or "injurious" being (234). Cooley is describing the elements of affinity essential to deep antipathy. He glosses Thoreau on this point: "you cannot receive a shock without an electric affinity for that which shocks you" (235). But he is also elaborating a larger principle of the reciprocity between social antagonism and social development. Cooley invokes Simon Patten's idea, set forth in *Theory of Social Forces*, that "civic instincts" are generated by "the feeling of antipathy against the objects or persons who violate them" (244). While Patten goes on to make this "antagonism" the basis of "national honor," Cooley offers a more modest claim, that antagonism, like sympathy, is invaluable to community. He goes on to highlight how various technological media—"cheap printing and rapid communication"—have enhanced "moral sentiment regarding international relations, alien races and social and industrial classes other than our own" (361). But this is all in the context of another Emersonian proposition: "there is always a circle of persons, more or less extended, whom we really imagine, and who thus work upon our impulses and our conscience; while people outside of this have not a truly personal existence for us" (360).

Throughout his book, Cooley confirms the limits of liberalism through the medium of sympathy. Thus, he admires Riis's *How the Other Half Lives*, but reminds us that "our sense of right ignores those whom we do not, through sympathy, feel as part of ourselves" (361). More important, in every age Cooley finds unavoidable, even essential antagonisms. He goes on to list a series of historical occasions, from the Normans and the Saxons to the Europeans and Chinese (362). The modern era is ever more productive of these conflicts, as suggested by the multiplication of alien examples near the book's end. "Negroes," for instance, suddenly appear as representatives of a sacrificial (loss and gain) pattern. Every step toward citizenship (Black enfranchisement) brings "some degeneracy . . . an increase of insanity among them" (403–4). Cooley's book, almost despite itself, provides more evidence for sympathy's demise as a harmonizing social force. Du Bois was well aware of these limits, as confirmed by the regularity with which the term comes up in his writings from the period.

THE DECLINE OF SYMPATHY

Du Bois's account of sympathy in *The Souls of Black Folk* points beyond the experiential and mythic bounds of Black mortality, to the disappearance of certain ideals framed on the group's behalf. The chapter on education features a striking passage describing a burial site. In a rare moment of self-reflection, Du Bois looks out his study window at Atlanta University and records the following:

A boulder of New England granite, covering a grave, which graduates of Atlanta University have placed there—"GRATEFUL MEMORY OF THEIR FORMER TEACHER AND FRIEND AND OF THE UNSELFISH LIFE HE LIVED, AND THE NOBLE WORK HE WROUGHT; THAT THEY, THEIR CHILDREN, AND THEIR CHILDREN'S CHILDREN MIGHT BE BLESSED." This was the gift of New England to the freed Negro: not alms, but a friend; not cash, but character. It was not and is not money these seething millions want, but love and sympathy, the pulse of hearts beating with red blood;—a gift which to-day only their own kindred and race can bring to the masses. . . . the best of the sons of the freedmen came in close and sympathetic touch with the best traditions of New England. (278–79)

There is no moment in all his writings that more starkly evokes the transience of sympathy. Black-White contact has dwindled to hostility and indifference: the book's answer is the ghetto graveyard pictured in the subsequent Black Belt chapter. Du Bois's commemoration of New England's "gift" to "the best sons of the freedmen" recognizes these traditions as accomplished facts within the Black community. A redemptive reciprocity is implied: the decline of interracial sympathy is balanced by a growth of intraracial pride. The wordy tombstone conveys the concise prophecy of segregation. Blacks must seek among "their own kindred and race" the "sympathetic touch" denied them by a wider humanity. To discover a new form of Black agency in the scene is not to deny its pathos. This choice of commemoration—imagine the monumental alternatives to tombs—is itself oddly corporeal. The image attaches sympathy to a particular folk— New Englanders of the 1860s—whose time has passed, which is a way of confirming the transience of society's commitment to this ideal. Liberal sympathy, it seems, has absorbed the mortal stigma of its beneficiaries.

Du Bois was not the only social observer in this period to proclaim the death of sympathy. Nathaniel Shaler regards Negroes as a source of a "sympathy-conveying power [which] has been lost by the civilizing process."[85] Max Scheler classifies sympathy as one of the "essential capacities," which has "atrophied" over time but is still to be found among "primitive peoples, children, dreamers, neurotics . . . and in the exercise of the maternal instinct" (31). Shaler envisions a sympathetic responsiveness that depends on the disappearance of those who literally embody it. Scheler affiliates it with certain groups, effectively rationalizing society's "need" of them.[86] Most contemporary analysts of sympathy seemed convinced of its decline, at least in its properly universal form. As Paul Reinsch wrote in the *American Journal of Sociology*, "the absolute unity of human life in all parts of the globe, as well as the idea of the practical equality of human individuals . . . has been quite generally abandoned." This assumption was shared by commentators directly interested in America's race problem. These include Reverend Proctor, who pleaded for the revival of a wide-ranging sympathy; Professor John Hope, who referred to a spirit of White "race sympathy . . . [that] refuses to hire

Negroes"; and Philip Bruce, who claimed that those "sympathies that have held the whites and blacks together" were receding—the starting point of Hoffman's *Race Traits*.[87]

Was sympathy's decline a direct outcome of the transition from Gemeinschaft to Gesellschaft? Had a warm traditionalism simply given way to the cold interdependencies of industrial society? Max Scheler's definition of sympathy as "the capacity for a specialized identification" betrays a sense of the category's newly circumscribed, even rational role. According to Scheler's definition, sympathy was becoming localized, which was another way of highlighting its unprecedented use as a vehicle of intolerance. One measure of this new restrictive sense was the attempt by some analysts to identify a place on the body where sympathy happened.[88] Attention to the physiology of sympathy, from its association with impaired groups to its categorization as a reflex, suggests increasing awareness of how the sentiments were affected by a daily spectacle of difference. While Nathaniel Shaler had no social scientific training (he was a geologist, who taught Du Bois at Harvard), the prominence of his work in these race debates confirms their openness. He is seldom remembered now, but in his own time Shaler had the attention of Darwinists (*The Individual* [1900] was even cited by Darwin) as well as sociologists (who drew mainly on *The Neighbor* [1904] and related essays).

Like most social Darwinists, Shaler believed that progress was costly, and that the required social sacrifices could never be distributed evenly. Such ideas lay behind his "modulus of alienity," which classified different races and classes by their perceived distance from a middle-class, Anglo-Saxon norm, a distance that, in turn, determined their relative propensities for giving up or giving in. In keeping with his other methodological innovations, the "modulus of alienity" is based on his understanding of how human minds work. Shaler's faith in common sense, may explain his willingness to embrace contradiction. It also explains the striking breadth of his subjects: death and futurity in *The Individual*, social difference and social bonds in *The Neighbor*. Shaler's theories are representative of a certain Anglo-American social scientific approach to sympathy: sensorium-based and sentimental, they identify prejudice and inequities as inevitabilities registered by the body. While an expanded humanitarianism is prized as the highest evolutionary form, this expansion is believed to require a dramatic reduction in the number of social strangers. Shaler's utopian scheme, therefore, includes immigration restrictions, the rapid assimilation of "valuable aliens" (Irish, German, Jew), prohibitions on interracial marriage, limitations on Black suffrage, and the confinement of Black labor "to fields which do not tempt white people" (*Neighbor*, 336).

There are several paradoxes here. Shaler appears dedicated to the application of sympathy beyond kinship bounds but proposes legal, diplomatic, and economic measures designed to limit that application. He expresses misgivings about sociology, but his writings are steeped in its terminologies. A strange blend of Christian humanitarianism and modern science, the tension of Shaler's perspective is caught by a typical conjunction:—the "mathematical" nature of "moral truths" (*Neighbor*, 277). *The Individual*, in contrast, seems a work of straight naturalism. Yet there are clear continuities with Shaler's articles on race and with *The Neighbor*. The writing of mankind's destiny in *The Individual* prepares for the fatalistic treatment of race relations in *The Neighbor*. In keeping with *The Individual*'s organic script, Shaler reads sympathy here as "personally unprofitable," a gift to one's race. This sympathetic race feeling informs modern attitudes toward death, where "the note of despair, the cry as of the victim before the altar" is now rarely heard (*Individual*, 137, 144). Every modern is a potential Jephthah's daughter, voluntarily embracing death as a sacrifice for the good of the community. These are tribal acts, and Shaler is clear about the limited application of this bounty. Individuals relinquish life on behalf of a restricted collectivity. He concedes that this restrictiveness is somewhat contrived. That is, individuals have to keep watch on their sympathy reserves, for in reality, the capacity for sympathetic responsiveness may be endless. The student of faces, Shaler writes, recalling his mentor Darwin, is helplessly drawn to the claims of a common humanity. With some ethnic groups, however, this responsiveness may be more controllable. Shaler characterizes the Jewish face as "a hostile flag tending to arouse prejudices against them" (*Neighbor*, 117). Others, Blacks, for instance, are dangerously inscrutable, and "pains" must be "taken . . . to search behind the sympathetic mask" (*Neighbor*, 121). Both types represent the challenges of a modern urban setting. Confronted by spectacles of this kind, the viewer naturally abandons that "ancient and admirable custom of recognising each of the bipeds as . . . entitled to some measure of sympathetic attention." His only "self-defence" is "to regard them as mere moving things" (165). The assumption that "the neighbor is ourselves in another body," Shaler writes, anticipating his companion study, was "nearer to the truth" in "the lower stages of life" (*Individual*, 172).

Over the book's course, natural principle and social necessity merge and blur. "All sympathetic intercourse," Shaler writes, "evidently depends upon the existence of discoverable identities" (*Individual*, 261). And his preoccupation with narrowing ethnic affinities eventually subsumes God himself: "a mighty kinsman of man is at work behind it all" (*Individual*, 313). Everything that is implicit in *The Individual* takes center stage in *The Neighbor*, whose starting point is the identification of sympathy with "essential" kinship. In the beginning, at least, of this "natural history of human contacts," Shaler's approach appears practical and evolutionary. Sympathy grows out of a long education in "hatred," a residual legacy man never completely overcomes (*Neighbor*, 23). Sympathy is a higher, though consistently selective, impulse. Limited at first to love of offspring, sympathy comes to embrace members of the tribe, known kinsmen, remote kindred, all fellow beings. All races of men, Shaler believes, have reached this tribal stage, which he sees as a "rational" substructure for a spiritual order based on "protection from tribal gods" (26). The concept of intratribal sympathy thus derives from the ancient human relationship to gods, which demanded distinctions between kin (sacrificial beneficiaries) and non-kin (sacrificial victims).

Intratribal sympathy suits an age of sacrifice. According to Shaler, modern sympathies have not evolved beyond it. Shaler's America is no exception. Most human beings, he claims, have a psychic resistance to "aliens," (which includes, in his account, Blacks, Jews, the wounded, and the dead). Shaler finds his classic illustration, appropriately, in a remote and obscure setting: an apparition encountered on a foggy morning walk in Tuscany is "an unclassifiable creature which looked like a cow walking on its hind legs," a sight that inspires "dread" until the subject is revealed as "a man clad in a cow's hide . . . a fellow of our species," and the "sympathies" are activated. Shaler's apparition provokes a contrast between skins that are removable and skins that are not, between differences that can be dismissed as optical illusions and differences that are magnified by a reduction of physical distance (30–31). The man in the cow costume recalls the ancient Semites described by Robertson Smith in his study of kinship and sacrifice, who draped themselves in the skins of sacrificial victims as a means of securing "divine protection." This custom, in which Smith locates the origins of the "robe of righteousness," gives way to a practice of offering sacrificial substitutions—sometimes animals, sometimes social strangers—for members of the community. In keeping with this, one could say that a strange skin that is removable identifies a beneficiary of the sacrificial rite, while a strange skin that is not identifies a victim.[89]

Shaler's thoughts on proximity and strangeness invite comparison with Du Bois's funeral scene, a comparison illuminated by Orlando Patterson's understanding of slavery as "institutionalized marginality," a system designed to answer the contradictory charge of housing aliens within. Patterson cites, among expressions of this contradiction, the Cherokee description of slave identity: they possessed "the shape of human beings, but had no human essence whatever."[90] Shaler's man in the cow costume represents the opposite conundrum: a human being in essence despite his shape, whose reconciliation as human is signaled by his arousal of sympathy. Du Bois's Black mourners pose a far greater dilemma for the spectators of his scene. They are neither human shapes without human essence nor human essences without human shape. To assume their conformity with the structural position of the slave would imply an intimacy and connection that is clearly missing here. This accords with Shaler's conviction that the tragedy of modernity is its terrible capacity to bring strangeness ever closer, without the formal means of keeping it within bounds. Whites can only voice their alienation weakly, through "such terms as Jew, 'nigger' and the like," which are themselves "barriers to sympathetic advance" (196–97). Shaler's inability to separate such categories from their subjects leads him to conclude, in a chapter entitled "The Way Out," that a sympathetic humanitarianism will not reach its highest form until the disappearance of those who fail to inspire it (327–30). Shaler's argument marks Blacks with the quality of an antique or remnant; they are the collective sacrifice to the development of a broad-based sympathy. He implies that these tribal affections are irreplaceable, and beyond this, that the need of them may actually intensify as the field of social difference widens. He admires, for instance, the powerful "ethnic motive" of the Jews, which has helped them to withstand centuries of abuse, and he laments the impossibility of any such motive among "Americans."

Shaler aims to justify an outmoded intratribal sympathy that is nourished by modern social variety but incapable of relieving it. He declares "we are now in danger of underestimating the importance of those differences between groups of men on which the tribal system rested." Overlooking the persistent force of the ethnic motive is like trying to change "the color of men's hides by a process of flaying with a view to implanting a new skin" (49–50). This is one of the astonishing reversals for which racist antiquarianism is justly famous. The potential (and often real) violence to which human beings with the wrong-colored skin are subject, is here imagined as a violence against the category itself. Shaler's metaphor recalls his previous image of the man in the cowhide; it reinforces the same opposition of reconcilable and irreconcilable differences. While some hides are removable without risk, most are not. And prejudice, Shaler insists, is the most stubborn hide of all. As if to prove his point, Shaler's own prejudices are obvious throughout, especially in the chapter on Blacks. Prejudice is a form of sympathy, and both are, by definition, variable. "Sympathy is indeed not one thing, it is a host of diverse impulses. . . . [some] breed the mob . . . others . . . self-sacrifice" (259). Shaler echoes Cooley in labeling hatred "reversed sympathy . . . sympathy to unite the kind, hatred to keep it whole" (257–58).

I want to allow for Shaler's complexity, but not at the expense of what remains monolithic. Shaler is a social Darwinist who believes that emotions are inherent not learned. Sympathy evolves like any other body part. Small adjustments might be made here and there, but man at best is a careful beholder. Looking with care—this is Shaler's sentimental ideal. Near the end of his book, he warns that the neighbor "cannot be captured in a fly net and fixed with a pin in a favorable attitude for study, as some sociologists essay to do. [He] must be caught in the net of sympathy" (316). Shaler's preferred stance has something in common with that of the explorer in Schopenhauer's scene of predation (i.e., white squirrel and snake; see chapter 1 above). He feels for the helpless victim, but his impulses are bound by the call of progress. Both explorer and author are also bound by personal allegiances deeper than science. Born in Kentucky, Shaler retained his southern sympathies while fighting for the Union, just as he played the role of disaffected southerner while studying and teaching at Harvard. Shaler, in his autobiography, reflects on his own tribal motive. He admits to an acute sensitivity to the New England "climate" to "the way people look at or greet you or pass you on the street with no sense of your existence." He confesses that "primitive-minded folk are as blindly sensitive as are dogs and other animals to the manners of folk about them."[91] While one might sympathize with the isolation of this southern "dog" in frigid Cambridge, one can only wonder about Shaler's relationship to the "contagion of motive" that spur the lynch mob at home (299–301). To be sure, Shaler regularly condemned lynching, but he was clearly held by the sentiments driving it.

Shaler comes close to defining sympathy as situation specific, but pulls up short. He remains loyal to his naturalism. Yet his attempt in *The Neighbor* to shape a Darwinian approach to the emotions into a theory of social relations, is consistent with what might be called an American "sociology of sympathy." The work of Max Scheler offers an altogether different sociology, which specifically rejects a natural basis for social affections. Sympathy for Scheler is a deliberate and highly effective social instrument. The obvious sign of Scheler's departure from these previous theorists is that most of his attention to biology involves analysis of biological premise rather than biological process. Scheler's sociology was an eclectic blend of critical sociology (anticipating that of Karl Mannheim), religious idealism (he idolized Saint Francis), and socialist politics (a convention among German sociologists at the time). Scheler himself called it "the philosophy of the open hand."[92] But Scheler was no relativist; he remained throughout his life a defender of moral absolutes. As one commentator paraphrased his main premises: "We ought to sacrifice our physical enjoyment to our duties as citizens of the state; we ought to sacrifice our social well-being to the claims of culture . . . and even those august values should be sacrificed, if the need arises, on the altar of sanctity . . . the altar of God."[93] Scheler's famous adaptation of Nietzschian thought, *Ressentiment* (1912), portrays relativism as a modern pathology. The ressentiment personality is a parody of modern interdependence; he is wholly defined by others obliged to contemplate his own losses in relation to their imagined plenitude. He predominates in a society defined by the promise of mobility and technological change.

Ressentiment has its own method (dialectical reasoning, and all other forms of philosophizing by negation) and its own battery of types (the mother-in-law, the priest, the flagrant criminal). It can include any form of conceptual indirection: "convictions . . . not arrived at by direct contact with the world and the objects themselves" (67). Envy and vindictiveness are its inevitable products, "the falsification of the value tablets" its ultimate form (73). Scheler's 1913 study, *The Nature of Sympathy*, provides another variation on a common theme: the damaged terms of relatedness in Western capitalist society. The paradigm for sympathetic identification here is familial, "two parents stand beside the dead body of a beloved child. They feel in common the 'same' sorrow, the 'same' anguish. . . . they feel it together, in the sense that they feel and experience in common, not only the self-same value-situation, but also the same keenness of emotion in regard to it." For their "friend . . . who joins them and commiserates," such sorrow can only be "an 'external' matter" (12–13). What is critical about this moment for Scheler, and what makes it acutely representative of the status of sympathy in the modern world, is its self-enclosure. The scene is instructive for what it can't reveal about other potential sympathetic circumstances, for how it doesn't pertain, and in this sense it is best understood as an antiexample. In the complementary scene from *Souls*, the force of kinship is also at issue: the failure of White passersby to identify with the grief of a mother and father. Scheler's scene, like Du Bois's, implies that kinship is the final boundary of sympathy: both authors use mourning (a ritual designed to master the separation of the living from the dead, sometimes by denial, as in the idea of ghosts or visitations) to show how the sympathetic response—usually associated with harmony and inclusion, embracing another's experience and extending one's own—functions increasingly in the modern era to distinguish aliens from neighbors. Both scenes picture a series of impediments to feeling: the inability of friend (in Scheler) or stranger (in Du Bois) to empathize with one's pain replicates the distance felt by both sets of parents from their dead offspring. Du Bois's scene dramatizes a double betrayal: their betrayal by fate (which forges an insuperable border between themselves and their child) is seconded by the passing Whites (who express their separation from the community). It is telling in this regard that the Black parents turn away from their son at the moment of death (351), a fulfillment of a folk decree that anticipates the actions of the Whites.

The question of race remains implicit in Scheler, who offers his own familial tableau, I believe, to illustrate the reliance of sympathy, in theory and in practice, on notions of similarity and difference. For Scheler, emotional connection to another human being is facilitated by the recognition of difference: authentic sympathy respects distance and is rewarded by *imaginative* access to others' experiences. The modern world is bereft of "communities of feeling"; it provides little potential for genuine sympathy, not because of its increasing heterogeneity (culturally, ethnically), but because the inability to confront, either in intellectual or in moral terms, the changing configurations of social relations results in the denial of what is profoundly common in emotional life. This universal prospect becomes increasingly remote from Scheler's elusive (and unparalleled) community of parental suffering. He means it to be. The very *idea* of sympathy is a problem for Scheler: his effort to chart the concept's history, to explore its sociological basis, is inspired by his belief that the need to construct a theory about sympathy signals its demise as a harmonizing social force. This is not to call Scheler's theories essentialist—far from it. In his view, as I have suggested, eighteenth-century moral philosophers like Smith and Hume overrate the value of resemblances. Other theorists do worse. Scheler's disenchantments explain why the book has been read as "largely negative."[94] *Nature of Sympathy* seems a virtual catalog of the faculty's false forms. Scheler's first target is the germ theory of the emotions, developed by "the great British psychologists" (xlvi). Potential contagions are everywhere: in objects, other people, conditions (a serene landscape, a rainy day). Scheler's complaint is the disregard of consciousness *and* conscience. This theory "does *not* presuppose any sort of *knowledge*" of feeling (15). Scheler goes on to cite a series of inadequate sympathies, from emotional identification to Schopenhauer's metaphysics. In idiopathic behavior (e.g., ancestor worship), the sympathizer absorbs the other. Under heteropathic conditions (Schopenhauer's squirrel and snake), *the sympathizer* is hypnotically enslaved.

Schopenhauer's theories are a constant referent. Scheler accepts Schopenhauer's account of sympathy's "intentional character" and the idea that it "reveals the *unity of being*" (51). He objects, however, to Schopenhauer's tendency to luxuriate in pity: sympathy, and the suffering it serves, become obsessions instead of moral obligations. There is, Scheler notes, an element of "sadistic *glee* in the affliction of others" (53). The counterpart to Schopenhauer's sadist is the "type who hungers after pity," pleased with the spectacle of others grieving on his behalf (137). The implied ideal here is self-dissolution in "a common stockpot of misery" (55). Schopenhauer's cult of suffering overlooks two things: how little suffering has to do with equalizing pain, and how much it reinforces social inequities already in place. It is as if, from Scheler's perspective, any preoccupation with suffering and sympathy ensures deception. Science is a valuable corrective to flaccid theory and feeling. This contrast is introduced early on, in Scheler's discussion of Fabre's *Souvenirs Entomologiques*, a "storehouse of precise descriptions." Anyone regarding Fabre's example of the wasp, Scheler observes, would admire its miraculous ability to paralyse (without killing) spiders, beetles, and caterpillars, in order to lay eggs upon them. "A surgeon with a scientific knowledge of the caterpillar's nervous system could do no better," Scheler writes in wonder. We can speculate about the wasp's "primary 'knowledge'" of the caterpillar, and leave it at that. Not so with theorists like Henri Bergson, who must read the wasp's apparent delicacy as sympathetic. Scheler is adamant in reproof: this is a case of "hostile action," for the exclusive benefit of "one's *own* species" (28–29).

Scheler's resistance to explanations like Bergson's is part of his overall aim to sever moral from instinctive behavior. His other purpose is to distinguish sympathy from narcissistic projection. Sympathy is neither involuntary expression, nor inhabitation of another being. Most classifications, he observes, foreground the state of the sympathizer. Suffering in these accounts is understood as highly labile: its mere scent can stimulate reproduction. Such a view presumes suffering to be nonspecific, accessible via any number of grief-worn pathways. All of these sympathetic phases turn on a violation of boundaries: the assumption of another's state as one's own. The continuities between *Sympathy* and *Ressentiment* are particularly strong on this point. Here again, Scheler exposes a self unable to abide the discreteness of the other. Physical correspondence overrides any other consideration, as if every human connection entailed some complementary exchange of body fluid. According to "the epistemological conclusions" of *Sympathy*, "the capacity for understanding between minds" is built on the "primitive givenness of 'the other'" (31). He continues, "man must elevate himself 'heroically' above the body and all its concerns, while becoming *at the same time* 'forgetful' or at least unmindful, of his spiritual individuality" (35). Real sympathy is not about "revival" but about "revelation" (49).

Invoking an opposition that is as pressing in current intellectual life as it was in Scheler's time, he declares, "according to the theories we are rejecting, we are supposed, firstly, to be necessarily confined in the prison of our own casual experiences, in all their individual, racial and historical heterogeneity, so that the objects of our understanding and sympathy would represent merely a *selection* from such experience as *we* have actually had." Such theories nullify the potential *"moral unity of mankind,"* as well as the hope that sympathy might ever exert any *"real effective* influence" on experience (49). Scheler illustrates this lost expansive potential through the metaphor of colors. "The variety of emotional tones within the compass of a species such as man, is no less *finite* however large it may be, than the limited number of basic colours he is able to perceive. . . . it is quite wrong to suppose that these basic colours must necessarily be encountered in actual perception and sensation, before they can be 'visualized' at all." Emotions, like colors, don't have to be perceived to be believed. True sympathy is "a genuine *outreaching*" (46–47). Jesus' despair at Gethsemane, for example, "can be understood and shared regardless of our historical, racial, and even human limitations" (48). Sympathy is "a light . . . suddenly shone, or a window opened in a darkened room." Like poetry, it "*extend*[s] the scope of our *possible* self-awareness" (49–50). If Scheler's poetic analogy is conventional, his elaboration of it is not. For his poet becomes the merchant of an ethically ideal sympathy. "An emotion," writes Scheler, "which everyone can now perceive in himself, must once have been wrested by some 'poet' from the fearful inarticulacy of our inner life for this clear perception of it to be possible: just as in commerce things (such as tea, coffee, pepper, salt, etc.) which were once luxuries, are nowadays articles of everyday use in general supply" (253). Scheler's reduction (poetic insights are unique, then become ordinary) captures something fundamental in his view of sympathy. Like the miraculous articles of empire he cites, sympathy is finally a domestic item. If it is to have social value, it has to be as inevitable as salt on the table.

This is Scheler's case for the necessity of boundaries between human beings. But there are deeper continuities, he believes, disguised by sympathy's many illusory forms. While physical states are inaccessible from one individual to another, a community of mind can be variously experienced and expressed. Scheler compares this to the range of a single mind over time: the ability of an individual to "revive" a particular grief at different moments of his life is equivalent to the ability of different individuals to experience a similar grief (differently) together. Is there redemption in Scheler's critique, some means of recuperating sympathy, of setting it on a more fully humanitarian track? "A fully-developed theory of the grades of sympathy," Scheler writes, as if in response, could "yield philosophical enlightenment on everything" (232). Scheler's preoccupation with the inauthenticity of modern emotions implies a recuperative typology of sympathetic states, as if description might itself alleviate the disrepair of modern man. It would even be possible to classify the era's writers on sympathy along a continuum. I would range these theories from confrontations with the vexed and complicated circumstances of sympathy to a symptomatic registration of these circumstances. Near the symptomatic end of the spectrum, we find the heirs of Darwin and Spencer: Shaler, together with sociologists Ward, Ross, and Giddings. Edging toward the critical end, we find Cooley, Park, and Small. The critical end itself includes Scheler, whose antagonism toward the category of sympathy becomes more explicable in light of these other sentimentalizations, and Du Bois. Perhaps sympathy's most powerful modern analysts, both Du Bois and Scheler judge the faculty to be in crisis.

Du Bois's sense of sympathy's negative function in the modern era was set within a larger understanding of the need for different categories. Du Bois dates sympathy as a nineteenth-century faculty (*Souls* [356]) to suggest that it is historically bound—real, not ideal. He concurs with sociologists who portray Adam Smith's sympathetic ethics as an attractive but finally

flawed proposition. At the same time, Du Bois shares Max Scheler's awareness of sympathy's susceptibility to certain modern pathologies. Far from
a "universal" lament over a White failure to sympathize with Black mourning, we might better understand Du Bois's funeral scene as a striking dramatization of a category's decline. For Du Bois and Scheler, sympathy was a
sentimental remnant in a modern world, a world whose fate depended on
unforeseen circumstances and unimagined forms. Social observers in the
first decade of the twentieth century had only a glimmer of what such
circumstances and forms might be.

The Symbolics of Sacrifice

Du Bois's description of his son's funeral procession contains an odd musical detail. "We seemed to rumble down an unknown street . . . with the
shadow of a song in our ears." Whether funeral dirge or some inappropriate tune, clarified suddenly, perversely, from the surrounding din, Du Bois
does not say. What appears inadvertent, however, soon becomes meaningful. For the shadow song in the ears of the parents is completed two chapters later by the whistle in the ears of Black John just before his lynching
(377). This is more than a dialogue between two snatches of song; it is a
symbolic heightening. A natural, if not inevitable, death is completed by a
promise of ritual murder, a sacrificial lynching borne on the wings of "Lo-
hengrin's swan" (368). At the same time, a morbid historical convention or
cliché, Black infant mortality, is reenacted as the ultimate collective
agency. In this section, Du Bois's exchange becomes a model for a dominant pattern of Black imaging at the turn of the century. The mythic status
of Blacks as a group whose sacrifice represents a condition of progress
defied their practical status as a group whose changing circumstances
threatened Whites. Despite the confident projections of social Darwinists,
many were convinced that Black populations required aggressive containment. Through methods of vigilance and vigilante acts, Whites sought to
limit the aspirations and achievements of Blacks from all classes. The sacrificial reading of Black culture provided the continuum between law (Jim
Crow) and violence (lynching). As I have shown, one form this sacrificial
reading took was the preoccupation with mortality statistics, which were
exaggerated to support a collective image of Blacks as an offering on the
altar of progress. Another link to sacrifice was their identification as representative aliens, whose exclusion from intratribal sympathy was balanced
by their incitement of it as victims of ritual revenge.

The sacrificial status of Blacks was widely documented at the turn of the
century: in antiquarian racism, in social science, and in Du Bois's own
works. Yet few grasped the full symbolic portent of this status, or named it
as such. The intensification of Du Bois's musical symbolism—from a natu-

ral death to a ritual slaughter—suggests that he was an exception in this respect. *The Philadelphia Negro* and *The Souls of Black Folk* provide particularly rich records of this deeper content. So did the fiction of later African-American writers. From Du Bois and Charles Chesnutt to Richard Wright, Ralph Ellison, Toni Morrison, and Suzan-Lori Parks, African-American authors stage sacrificial action and sacrificial thought. They recognize sacrifice as a dominant American tradition, at once Christian and social scientific. And they confirm the unique suitability of this Christian science to the purposes of an expanding capitalist nation. At the same time, as I will show, they seek to recover the rite as an indigenous and self-actualized African-American form.

Among contemporary analysts of Black destiny, none makes the case for sacrifice more explicit than Paul Barringer, in his 1900 address to the conference on race in Montgomery, Alabama. His title, "The Sacrifice of a Race," forecasts the degree of this explicitness. Barringer was not an amateur, nor were his views especially extreme. A respected physician, researcher, and chairman of the faculty at the University of Virginia, Barringer was attracted to "sociological problems," which he believed to be "in most cases biological problems."[95] In the Montgomery address, Barringer characterizes southerners after the war as "gathered around their broken hearthstones and desolate altars, trying to keep alive and restore to flame the embers of a civilization." As yet, he adds, "they looked beyond the negro as the source of their then present evils."[96] Could Barringer be unaware of the role that Blacks were playing at the time in reigniting these flames? His awareness comes in masquerade: an image of Black Africans as "trader[s] in human flesh—two women for a 'plug' hat, a man for a handkerchief" (12). Barringer adds cannibalism to the list of African practices, apparently in anticipation of the ritual cruelties imposed on Black Americans in the postwar period. In a universal scheme, he implies, all human acts are eventually compensated. Flesh traders in one land become flesh traded in the next. Sacrifice, in Barringer, is social scientific, a story about the "survival of the fittest" and "the death of the unfit" (16). Still, "destiny," according to Barringer, is a strange thing: sometimes it's controllable, sometimes it's not. The southern slaveholder remains pure, having "made a man of the savage," while northern altruism "loosed him for the sacrifice" (15). Southern slavery represents a state of full credit. Having provided under this system "self-sacrificing care," the former slaveowner can afford to rest on his "gifts" until the race is gone.

Barringer's opening sets the stage for ritual sacrifice: southerners huddled around their cold altars aching for something to burn. But he shortchanges the dramatic potential of his script. A serious tragedy of race relations is reduced to racist farce. Reduction is a standard procedure in these analyses, especially when the subject is sacrifice. This extends from the most blatant examples (Barringer) to the most subtle (Tillinghast). Joseph Tillinghast's discussion in *The Negro in Africa and America* seems subtle because he not only describes sacrificial practices but recognizes how sacrifice functions as cultural theory. It is, first of all, the basis of West African religion, where watering ancestral graves with "the blood of many human victims" is a custom of kings (51). Whenever the assistance of gods is desired "for ordinary affairs," we find animal sacrifices. When there is "urgency . . . the need of protection," we find higher forms, ascending to the "most costly sacrifice of all, that of a human life" (52). Sacrifice is omnipresent, according to Tillinghast, because West Africans have no conception of chance or accident. They see menacing intent everywhere they look. Imagine a people committed to finding a culprit or evil spirit behind every misfortune, and you will know why the rivers stream blood. The African Negro as Tillinghast draws him, by way of travelogues, ethnographies, and hearsay, is a compulsive sacrificer. Through Miss Kingsley's eyes, we witness the "slow roasting alive" of victims, or their "mutilation by degrees before the throat is mercifully cut" (56–57). From Ellis, we learn of offerings made upon news of pregnancy, at initiation rites, during funerals (75–77). Tillinghast includes an image (from Ellis again) of "fresh bleeding heads at the entrance gates to the palace," which "impress all with the power of the king" (83). "Native-born slaves" and captives from "hostile tribes" ensure a continuous supply of victims. This final detail is critical: sacrifice reinforces communal bonds (88).

Tillinghast begins part 2, on the Negro under American slavery, with a recapitulation of all this barbarism, apparently to emphasize "the stupendous task" faced by American slaveholders (102). "West Africa still lived in them," he suggests, in what becomes the refrain of parts 2 and 3 ("American Slavery" and "American Freedom"). Tillinghast offers a version of Barringer's compensatory logic: White outrages against Blacks represent a form of universal justice. The difference is that Tillinghast embraces the logic in its full theoretical import. In a chapter called "Selection," Tillinghast portrays the Darwinian cruelties of the slave trade as an extension of the ritual cruelties of sacrifice. If African rituals provided haphazard population controls, the slave trade introduces a more discriminating demographic science. During the middle passage, Tillinghast writes, "all weakness or disease that had eluded the vigilance of the buyers in Africa, was sure to be eliminated" (108). This is compared to West Africa, where "deathdealing agencies [were] of a harsh and wasteful nature: ceaseless warfare, famines, pestilence, religious sacrifices" (111). Tillinghast's bias is progressive to a point: he claims that even Blacks benefited from scientific method. In time, self-destructive African habits disappear: "the whole sacrificial economy of the former religion was effectively destroyed" (153). While Tillinghast makes a direct analogy between African sacrifice and the

Anglo-American slave trade, he overlooks the potential resemblances between an African "sacrificial economy" and sacrifice's more modern forms. Like Barringer, Tillinghast remains silent about the extent to which his own countrymen have girded themselves in flame against African-American citizens. Yet he seems to have American civilization in mind when he observes, in conclusion, that "Time, struggle and sacrifice have always hitherto been required to create a great race" (228). This is forecast by the book's opening image of the "black peril" threatening "the homogeneity of our national society" (1). There may even be a bit of envy on Tillinghast's part, of all those African customs that so dramatically fortified cultural unity.[97] Were things only so clear in a modern setting.

Other contemporary observers were more aggressive in appropriating barbaric strategies. Thomas Nelson Page openly acknowledges lynching as a form of vengeance, designed to identify the blameworthy. "The rage of a mob . . . would not be satisfied with any other sacrifice than the death of the real criminal" (109). William Benjamin Smith declares no sacrifice too costly for the preservation of the "Caucasian Race." Recall his image of the South guarding that "jewel" of racial purity "with a circle of perpetual fire" (9). Smith's focus on purification highlights a critical spiritual dimension of lynching, which most contemporary analysts of the rite were quick to note. As James Weldon Johnson observed, "lynching in the United States has resolved itself into a problem of saving black America's body and white America's soul." Johnson's spiritual contest is seconded by the secular outrage of William Graham Sumner: "It is unseemly that any one should be burned at the stake in a modern civilized state."[98] Those who considered themselves within the jurisdiction of that "state" probably found this convincing. The problem was that many did not. Winwood Reade recognized this in *The Martyrdom of Man*, where he noted that southerners "did not consider themselves as belonging to a nation, but a league; they inherited the sentiments of aversion and distrust with which their fathers had entered the Union."[99] Descriptions of "a homogeneous people of the same blood and lineage, and possessing common artifacts, customs, and institutions," longing for "political existence," make plain what southerners like Tillinghast could have secretly envied in African tribalism.

LYNCHING

Charges of barbarism and primitive insensibility were another matter. They were invoked, it seems obvious, to excuse atrocities against Blacks. Were White antagonists caught in some perverse state of sympathetic identification that made them helplessly susceptible to the atavisms of their Black victims? There was more to it than this. As Lewis Browne has observed (*This Believing World*), "Men have slaughtered and ravished in

Jerusalem because they had—religion. Men have gouged eyes and ripped bellies because they—believed. . . . Strange potency, this thing, we call religion." Walter White is more particular: "It is exceedingly doubtful if lynching could possibly exist under any other religion than Christianity." The group that did most to substantiate such charges was the Ku Klux Klan, which had its beginnings in this period. From the 1870s through its rebirth after the turn of the century, the Klan sustained "a mystical religious tone." This seemed inevitable, given the number of ministers in its ranks. According to White, throughout the postemancipation era, the White South, "held fast in the grip" of its ministry illustrated "the soundness of the ancient Hebrew proverb, 'As the people, so the priests.'" He adds that one might even "have witnessed ministers of Jesus Christ leading lynching mobs."[100] William Simmons, the Klansman who officiated at the group's "resurrection" in 1915 was a Methodist circuit rider. His specific doctrinal allegiances aside, Simmons knew the value of sacrament. On Thanksgiving night, atop a mountain east of Atlanta, Simmons and his followers "gathered stones . . . to make an altar, on which they placed an American flag, an unsheathed sword, a canteen of initiation water, and a Bible open to the book of Romans, chapter 12."[101]

The Klan modeled itself on ancient Scottish tribal ideas of the "band." Meeting at "dreary, desolate and uncanny" places, Klan members courted the occult. The traditional all-white Klan costume evoked purity and magnitude. The towering hood ensured the magical enlargement of the most diminutive Klan members. The collective self-image, "Invisible Empire," projected the same Alice-in-Wonderland effect. According to one report, "devices were multiplied to deceive people in regard to their numbers and to play upon the fears of the superstitious."[102] The Klan, like other ritual bonding associations of the time (the Boy Scouts, the Rough Riders), cultivated a myth of Anglo-Saxon unity and masculine force in response to threats of their attenuation. Klan symbols conveyed both oedipal anxiety and homoeroticism. In fact, the dilemma for a group like the Klan was how to focus its violent energies. Because sexual crimes ensured heated reaction, they were invaluable in rousing lynch mobs and in rationalizing them after the fact. In a list of common causes for lynching, sexual charges were the most frequent. They range from ridiculous ("paying attention to white girl") to extreme (rape and murder) (167). The idea of sexual retribution was a container for various concerns. It expressed the White preoccupation with Black virility; it fit southern anxiety about the fading power of kinship in a modern interdependent society; and it captured southern fears about demographics. The continuum among all these issues was the stigma of mortality, which now appeared motivated, in great part, by the very opposite concern. The suspicion that Black population growth was in fact quite vigorous, was expressed in reactions to the prospect of Black suffrage, which, in Du Bois's words, "ended a civil war by beginning a race feud" (*Souls*, 238).

Lynching was a monstrous inversion of the mortality issue, the proof that, far from fated, the elimination of Blacks required aggressive action, extending (in the most horrific instances) to the mutilation of their reproductive organs. Lynching also represented a monstrous fulfillment of the sympathy crisis: a frenzied unification of White sentiment, a segregated, incestuous sympathy gone wild. The lynch mob was the logical culmination of sympathy's rewriting as a circumscribed intragroup exchange. Here group identity was founded in the ritual sacrifice of social strangers. This aspect of sympathetic identification was especially apparent to James Elbert Cutler, a disciple of William Graham Sumner and author of the social scientific study *Lynch-Law* (1905). As a stage for the problems of mob behavior, intolerance, and social disintegration, and a litmus test for the shortcomings of liberalism, it is easy to see why lynching caught the attention of contemporary social scientists. In this light, Du Bois's disclaimer, that lynching made him doubt the value of rational analysis, seems more a matter of personal experience than professional judgment. Still, Cutler's obvious sympathies for lynching, and the fact that his effort to explain lynching scientifically often amounted to explaining it away, serve to substantiate Du Bois's charge. There is no doubt that the resemblances between American lynchings and the violent, cannibalistic rites of uncivilized peoples were deeply disconcerting to the liberal practitioners of social science.[103] But Cutler views lynching as both an expression of social instability and a critical means for managing social difference. Lynch law could not have escalated, he points out, were the majority of citizens "not in of sympathy with the mob." Nor would lynching subside until the American legal system was relieved of its commitment to "abstract principles concerning the rights of all men" and brought into conformity with the "ethnic and 'societal' factors involved in the 'race question'" (279). Cutler's claim is fully consistent with the conclusions on sympathy reached by Nathaniel Shaler and F. H. Giddings. Political ideals were one thing, social facts another. Until they were reconciled, there would be collective effusions such as lynchings.

Undoubtedly, the most striking passage in *Lynch-Law* is Abraham Lincoln's account of those "sacrificed" in an exemplary rash of violence: "First ... gamblers—a set of men certainly not following for a livelihood a very useful or very honest occupation. ... Next, negroes suspected of conspiring to rise an insurrection ... then, white men supposed to be leagued with the negroes; and finally, strangers from neighboring States ... till dead men were literally dangling from the boughs of trees by every roadside, and in numbers almost sufficient to rival the native Spanish moss of the country as a drapery of the forest" (111). Lincoln's haunting description transforms lynched strangers, even in death, into "rivals," now of the more "native" moss. Despite differences in content, Lincoln's list anticipates, in its apparent oddity, another assortment of victims, drawn from classical sources by René Girard: "prisoners of war, slaves, small children, unmarried adolescents . . . to the king himself."[104] These analytical attempts to discriminate the identities of typical victims can be seen as fragile borders, in their own right, against the chaos that is supposedly foreclosed by ritual violence. But they help to pinpoint just what is at stake in sacrificial designs. Sacrifice is always, at least in part, motivated by a threatened erasure of social distinctions. The victims are considered expendable because they are casteless or have somehow abandoned the bounds of caste. As social strangers, or neighbors without strong allies, their deaths do not entail acts of vengeance.

Cutler's book manages to foreground the elements in lynching that matter most to this analysis. Significantly, sexual explanations are downplayed. In Cutler's view, the lynch mob is spurred on, above all, by uncertainty over kinship bonds. It is a pathological outgrowth of social sympathy. He acknowledges lynching's sacrificial pattern. These various emphases inform his apocryphal account of the term's origins. Lynch law, he believes, originated in sixteenth-century Ireland, when James Lynch, then mayor of Galway, "hanged his own son out of the window for defrauding and killing strangers without martial or common law to show a good example to posterity." While Cutler's case fits the prescriptions of sacrifice, as we have come to understand them, it ultimately violates every one. The familiar elements include the invocation of "retributive justice" (an aura of intertribal hostility overshadows all the events); the hint of sexual transgression (involving stolen "money" or "affections"); the highlighting of "public sympathy" (is it with lyncher or lynched?); and finally, the familial paradigm (this is a father who condemns his son "to die as a sacrifice to public justice"). Cutler himself catalogs the divergences. Among the most prominent: this lynching, executed by a "constituted authority," is atypical in its legality; law is exerted on behalf of an alien; and public sentiment sides with the victim. The lyncher must stand alone, *High Noon*–style, in defense of justice. Why offer this "romantic" version as his original case? (14–15). Cutler's choice is revealing of his own unscientific aims. Cutler wants to protect lynching. The sign of this is his habit of projecting that purpose onto most of his examples. His original example is especially illuminating in this regard: a father offering the son he is obliged to protect instinctively, on behalf of a public welfare he is obliged to protect professionally.

This theme extends to Cutler's account of the first lynchings in the United States: it was a method of punishment "employed by the early settlers for protection against Indian depradators" (45). Lynch law, he suggests, protects against social instability. It prevails, he says, at social pressure points, when society requires "a stable equilibrium under new and changed conditions" (107). It is never clear, however, why that instability intensifies in any given circumstance, nor how lynch law affects it. For lynch law is repeatedly dramatized as a reflexive response to extremism or crime. The truth is that Cutler admires those who are sufficiently simple (as opposed to modern and scientific) and sufficiently self-righteous (as opposed to skeptical) to take the law into their own hands. Cutler ends the book with a highly compromised view of what he calls the "peculiar" American attitude toward "law." His entangled study confirms how much safer it was for sociologists to avoid the whole matter of lynching and sacrifice. And in fact, few sociologists at the time were willing to confront the subject head-on. But most seem to have entertained some glimmer of Orlando Patterson's subsequent insight: that White Americans were the last ritual sacrificers in the West.

The novelty of their own situation may explain why so many turn-of-the-century sociologists were engaged in the comparative analysis of sacrificial rites. Walter Willcox, for example, in discussing the Sam Hose lynching (*Negro Criminality*), likens it to the actions of the *juramentado* in the Phillipines. Both examples highlight the absolute divide between White and "Colored" judgments of crime and innocence. To Phillipine natives, the *juramentado*, who shaves his eyebrows, arrays himself in white, and vows to "die killing Christians," is "an innocent man and a martyr." To Whites, he is "a peculiarly fiendish criminal." But what does this "peculiar" blend of racial and religious hatred have to do with the "terrible events" that "have occurred sporadically at the South of recent years"? Like many sociologists, Willcox intuits beneath the animosities driving both sides in the American race wars a menacing reserve of spiritual passion. He quotes a commentary from the *Atlanta Constitution*, following the Hose lynching, on the behavior of Black criminals: they conduct themselves like "candidates for a martyr's crown; they murder, ravish and rob with all the zeal and fervor of religious fanatics." This only confirms for Willcox the inefficacy of "lynch law as a deterrent." Martrydom and lynchdom are complementary. Willcox's analogies, to medieval Christians as well as to Mohammedan Malays, suggest their range (19–21). Lynching, in Willcox's book, and this is consistent with the conclusions of Page and Cutler, has more to do with the spirit than with the law. Other sociologists found less disturbing, because of its remoteness, evidence of the same ritual acts in contemporary ethnography.

In the classic sociology of Emile Durkheim and Robert Hertz, based on studies of the Australian aborigines, sacrifice concludes mourning. More precisely, sacrifice is the key that unlocks the prison of mourning. According to Hertz (*The Collective Representation of Death* [1907]), death threatens social *and* physical existence. Formally, death is a split narrative about the material individual (details of burial methods) and the spiritual collectivity (beliefs about the state of the soul). Thematically, death is a story of blame and revenge. Society (and he always intends modern civilization as a realization of primitive) "cannot normally believe that its members, above all those in whom it incarnates itself and with whom it identifies itself, should be fated to die. Their destruction can only be the consequence of a sinister plot." The ultimate sacrifice of a group enemy is precipitated by collective forms of the rite. "Men and women throw themselves pell-mell on the dying person, in a compact mass, screaming and mutilating themselves atrociously" (77–78). Hertz's theories are incomplete without the elaborations of his teacher, Durkheim, who gives much thought to the mysterious rage expended at mourning ceremonies, a rage that, in his view, has little to do with any real sense of obligation to the dead. Durkheim's conviction is the source of his famous postulate: "Men do not weep for the dead because they fear them; they fear them because they weep for them." His interpretation emphasizes the intensity of collective experience itself. As he describes it, the group bands together in response to the perceived assault upon its identity; "leaping from mind to mind . . . a veritable panic of sorrow" ensues.[105] Bodily mortification at once enhances and contains this panic. There seems no way around the fact that the fervor of primitive mourning expresses the ecstasy of survival. People mutilate themselves because they believe it minimizes their own vulnerability. Mutilation is humble speech, addressed to gods with presumably limitless appetites for sacrifice. Self-mortification is the price for sparing a particular body; the identification of a scapegoat is the price for the preservation of society itself.

Emotions are high at funerals because people fear death's contagion. Death is "catching": the closer we feel to the corpse, the more we feel for ourselves. Mourning is a form of possession, even disease. Hertz writes that, an "'impure cloud' . . . surrounds the deceased, pollutes everything it touches." This includes the deceased's relatives; "a ban separates them from the rest of the community" (38). Sacrifice breaks the ban: sometimes hens are sufficient (40). The Dayaks of Indonesia supply Hertz's example of the times when they are not: a day-long mourning ceremony called *Tivah*.

The prisoners or slaves, who have previously been deprived of their souls by a magical intervention, are chained to the sacrificial post; the male relatives [of the deceased] act collectively as sacrificers, dancing and leaping around the victim and striking him at random with their spears. The screams of pain are greeted with joyful shouts, because the more cruel the torture the happier the souls are in heaven. At last, when the victim falls to the ground he is solemnly decapitated in the midst of an intense joy; his blood is collected by a priestess who sprinkles it on the living 'to reconcile them with their deceased relative'; the head is either deposited with the bones of the deceased or attached to the top of a post. . . . The liberation of the mourners is only the most obvious among the changes brought about simultaneously by virtue of the sacrifice. (63)

Hertz emphasizes "change" as an end of sacrifice. The purpose of the rite here is no different from sacrifices offered upon a marriage or the "inauguration of a new house." Sacrifice transforms "persons or things in order to permit them to enter a new phase of their lives" (141). Like any new phase, death is "initiation into an infinite civilization." Sacrifice is a companion event; it assists the "passage from the world of men to the world of gods" (149). It is a transformation performed in the name of an initiation, enabling a new beginning for the deceased and his collectivity. The collectivity bathes in blood to liberate and renew itself. The pain and blood generated by the victim's body are objectified as ritual materials. Hence the theatrical quality of sacrifice: a macabre dance of torture where "screams of pain" inspire "joyful shouts."

Hertz's account of sacrifice among the Dayaks fits the pattern of contemporaneous lynchings in the American South. The extreme cruelty of these rites, which, Walter White notes, "were seldom practised until the new century had begun," confirm typical associations of these barbarisms with "advanced" cultures.[106] Probably the most gruesome lynching described by White is that of Mary Turner. For vowing vengeance against the mob that had murdered her innocent husband, Turner, eight months pregnant, was hung by the heels and burned alive. "Mocking, ribald laughter," eyewitnesses report, greeted her "screams of pain and terror." As life "lingered," her abdomen was "ripped open . . . in a crude Caeserian operation." Mother and infant were deposited in a shallow hole: "an empty whisky-bottle," with a smoking cigar stuffed down its neck, served for a "headstone." The Turner murder features the same celebrational atmosphere and stunning disregard for the victim's humanity captured in Hertz. It is also consistent with sacrifices performed in fulfillment of ancient kinship laws, as defined by Robertson Smith. The key to the Turner murders is the way in which guilt is transmitted along the series of Black victims. Hayes Turner is killed because he happened to know an "alleged slayer"; his wife is killed, supposedly for her rage, but more importantly, because she is kin to Hayes. Her infant (barely alive at "birth") is killed as her issue. Guilt is a contagion that runs along lines of kinship. Robertson Smith writes, "the members of one kindred looked on themselves as one living whole, a single animated mass of blood, flesh and bones, of which no member could be touched without all the members suffering."[107] In biblical Hebrew, he adds, "flesh" and "clan" are synonymous terms (274). Smith's gloss seems almost literalized in the Turner episode. One Black man has "allegedly" murdered a White, and there is no limit to the Black lives that must serve as recompense. Like a brush fire, mob vengeance follows a train of guilt by identification, until spent, reduced to the phallic smoldering of a cigar in a whiskey bottle. Liable kin also reduce to the smallest possible form: premature infancy.

Du Bois regularly condemned lynching in writings from this period, most often from the standpoint of the practical economics underwritten by these inflammatory acts. In Du Bois's view, dominant cultures everywhere benefited from residual barbarisms of this kind. The lynch mob was "given its glut of blood," in part because it distracted from more civil forms of oppression. But it also helped to rationalize these forms as the inevitable lot of a wretched group. The paradox, as James Weldon Johnson articulated it, was that it took "such tremendous effort on the part of the white man" to keep Blacks in the place where "inferior men naturally fall." [108] At the same time, Johnson acknowledged, in a visceral portrait of one response to a lynching (*The Autobiography of an Ex-Colored Man*), how this inhuman rite pulled everyone down in its wake. With "the smell of burnt flesh" still "in [his] nostrils," Johnson's narrator, and ironically conceived antiself, is overcome by a "great wave of humiliation and shame . . . shame that I belonged to a race that could be so dealt with; and shame for my country . . . the only state on earth, where a human being would be burned alive."[109] There is nothing this immediate in Du Bois, though *The Souls of Black Folk* has its personal and national moments of mourning. One of the most important forums for Du Bois's confrontation with these issues was *The Philadelphia Negro*. Du Bois's first sociological study can be read as a careful critique of the sacrificial basis of capitalism and the functional sociology that supports it.

DU BOIS'S SOCIOLOGICAL APPRENTICESHIP

The Philadelphia Negro elaborates, as an exercise in social theory, a central recognition of *Souls*: the compatibility between the folk elements it catalogs and the social scientific assumptions it uses and critiques. This compatibility is founded on a shared preoccupation with how protections are apportioned in a society that locates an inherent racial basis for inequality. Whether the method is a social scientific type, like Black morbidity, or a folk symbol, like graveyard dirt, it can be seen as ritual confirmation of the idea that denigration enables transcendence, and darkness (somehow) produces light. A modern rational society, Du Bois believes, needs martyrs and scapegoats. That necessity helps to explain the curious persistence of a certain postemancipation stereotype. S. C. Armstrong, in his commentary on Nathaniel Shaler's *Atlantic Monthly* piece "The Negro Problem," pictures Black populations, "who cling to the skirts of our civilization; there is a black fringe on the edge of most towns in this country" (707).

This is echoed in Walter Willcox's characterization of migratory Blacks as "negro driftwood" (14). Both authors envision Blacks in permanent suspension, somewhere between holy land and wasteland (a symbology of Sermons on Mounts and inflamed martyrs informs both analyses). Toni Morrison confirms the reach of this metaphor when she appropriates it for Black consciousness in *The Bluest Eye*. "We moved about," her child narrator observes, "on the hem of life, struggling to consolidate our weaknesses and hang on, or to creep singly up into the the major folds of the garment." Pecola, the novel's scapegoat, caught between "the tire rims and the sunflowers," comes to embody this margin.[110] Assumptions of this kind, Du Bois reveals in detailing the origins of *The Philadelphia Negro* are also fundamental to sociology.

The Philadelphia Negro was commissioned by White leaders convinced that the morbid condition of the city's Black community was responsible for a more general municipal malaise. Their conviction reflected the organicism that dominated urban studies at this time: the presence of one diseased part was bound to infect the social whole. Du Bois's assignment was to codify this urban eyesore on behalf of its eventual removal. But Du Bois's revisionary sociology ended up challenging the functionalist theory it was supposed to sustain. In Du Bois's ironic retrospect, sociology was christened "the mud-sill theory of society that civilization not only permitted but must have the poor, the diseased, the wretched, the criminal upon which to build its temples of light."[111] A sacrificial heart, Du Bois implied, beat at the center of this "City of Brotherly Love" (397), which needed the myth of Black morbidity to fortify the doctrine of White superiority. It's worth recalling Simon Patten's elaboration of this principle as a national agenda. "Each class or section of the nation is becoming conscious of an opposition between its standards and the activities and tendencies of some less developed class. . . . Every one is beginning to differentiate those with proper qualifications for citizenship from some class or classes which he wishes to restrain or exclude from society."[112] Patten's catalog of exclusions begs the same question raised by Du Bois's speculations on racism's practicality. Why would White Philadelphians in particular and Americans in general *need* a degraded social element? Du Bois's one-word answer is capitalism.

Racism, he argues, is a function of context. In a developing capitalist economy, racism amplifies "Negro" pauperdom and criminality and erases the Negro middle class. In Du Bois's reading, the degradation of Black labor is circular and systematic: any occupation identified with Blacks lacks or loses prestige. Take barbering, merely a form of Black servitude until it is overtaken by immigrants and turned into a profession. Most turn-of-the-century social science, as we have seen, attributed such developments to group traits and tendencies.[113] Du Bois counters such claims with a record of acts deliberately designed to undermine Black labor. "Most people were willing and many eager that Negroes should be kept as menial servants rather than develop into industrial factors," he observes at one point (126). "Special effort was made not to train Negroes for industry," he adds at another (128). Owners and managers encourage prejudice, because it ensures surplus labor. Du Bois cites one notorious case where Blacks are employed simply for the sake of unifying a crew split by ethnic tensions (130).

As I have suggested, the argument for the interdependence of racism and capitalism is a staple of Du Bois's early career. This is why the commercial ambition of his contemporaneous Atlanta Studies seems so dissonant. *The Philadelphia Negro*, however, does not reflect nostalgically on some primordial alternative to capitalism. In every era, Du Bois suggests, prejudice displays a new shape and energy, conforming like an ideal parasite to dominant social forces. In the age of *The Philadelphia Negro*, Du Bois believes, motivations are plain. He cites population statistics on the vitality of Black Philadelphia (the largest Negro constituency in any American city by 1890), which help to explain the durability of racism. Du Bois dismisses the 1870 census—the basis for Hoffman's work—and notes that the Negro population has not only grown but "spread." He also disputes Spencerian correlations of high status and low birthrate—at least among Blacks (319).

Du Bois's emphasis on the economic threat posed by Blacks in this era is supported by recent research, which likewise treats race as a secondary cause. "The racial emphasis resulted from the use of the most obvious features of the group," argues Stanley Lieberson, "to support the intergroup conflict generated by a fear of blacks based on their threat as economic competitors."[114] Higher rates of Black migration (beyond those of other "immigrants") throughout the twentieth century not only threatened Whites but also impeded Black efforts to locate occupational niches. Du Bois implies as much in noting how each new wave of Black "barbarians" ushers in a "dark age" for the established Black community (11). Du Bois and Lieberson agree that Black progress (rather than alleged morbidity) complicates their social success, in part by motivating attempts to limit it.[115] But these successful elements, Du Bois insists, must be the standard for all social scientific judgment. Du Bois's purpose, then, is the application of sociological method to the circumstances of a stratified and self-actuated Black community. *The Philadelphia Negro* is structured in terms of an immigrant thematics: Philadelphia is a Negro Ellis Island, a racial gateway between feudal South and modern North. The book also represents Du Bois's quest for professional legitimacy, his immigration ticket, as it were, into the newfound land of sociology.

But if Du Bois is the starting point of the "good immigrant" analogy, he is also its end. For the contentious footnote on the book's first page is at odds with any helpless desire to be "accepted." Du Bois's decision to capitalize "Negro . . . because I believe that eight million Americans are entitled to a capital letter" contains at least three pointed references (1). The note contradicts Samuel Lindsay's prefatory wisdom concerning Du Bois's avoidance of "personal judgment" (xvi). It challenges prevailing extinction arguments by offering a national population count, and it embraces a foreign (as opposed to homegrown) sociology: the gesture, in Weberian fashion, controls Du Bois's bias by foregrounding it.[116] In the strictest empirical sense, however, the note serves as much to displace his Blackness as to own up to it. DuBois invests a social scientific convention with racial (and political) meaning. To inhabit and then not to inhabit your "personal" point of view, to become an invisible mediator of social knowledge—this is the Black definition of success. Du Bois's opening embrace and erasure of his own social position enacts in small his presentation of life as a middle-class Black in turn-of-the-century Philadelphia. First he will make them appear, in opposition to claims for the uniform pathology of "Negroes"; then he will make them disappear, in keeping with their own aspirations. Du Bois recognizes invisibility as an index of achievement among Blacks themselves.

I want to stress the importance of this poetics of visibility for Du Bois's book as a whole. Black problems are characterized early on as "conspicuous," as exceptionally "patent to the eye" (5). Black crime has much to do with the peculiar exposure of the poor, whose lack of "privacy," even walls, make their homes "public resorts for pedestrians and loafers" (294). It seems inevitable, given this focus, that the topics of intermarriage and amalgamation would enter in. Du Bois announces meaningfully at the start of this section that he had no "intention" of discussing them, but their high incidence made it imperative (358–61). Little is known in the way of hard fact about "the mingling of white and black blood" under the institution of slavery. Less is known about such mixing today (360). As for intermarriage, in a single ward of the city, thirty-three mixed marriages were verified, and more are likely (361). While "the sacrifice in such marriages" is great, they can be found among all classes of society (367). The rush to demarcate Black Philadelphia, he goes on to argue, signals the increasing imprecision of racial boundaries. White demands for a delimitable Black are satisfied by one type alone: the criminal-pauper whose attributes justify his marginalization and censure.

The helpless visibility of Philadelphia's Negro underclass anticipates the particular shape that social subversion takes in Ralph Ellison's *Invisible Man* (1952). The novel begins (and ends) with its hero's sabotage of the

"Monopolated Light and Power company."[117] He lines his basement hole (a section of a Whites-only building closed off during the nineteenth century—imagine Harriet Jacobs's elevated crawl space underground) with 1,369 of the costliest lights, for which he pays nothing. Ellison's hero drops out of an American society that refuses to see him, with a luminous embrace of invisibility. His physical assault upon the first White who sees him ("because of the near darkness") suggests that he can only exist as a stereotype of Black violence. "Despite the bland assertions of sociologists," Ellison writes, Black "'high visibility' actually rendered one un-visible." The high point of invisibility is the moment when he is most "illuminated by flaming torches and flashbulbs while undergoing the ritual sacrifice that was dedicated to the ideal of white supremacy" (xv). According to Ellison, the Black man is only visible to Whites when he has become a nullity to himself as an object of sacrifice.

Like Ellison's hero, who buries himself alive in a crypt of light, the Black middle classes of Philadelphia are caught in a dialectic of their own unmaking. Both Ellison and Du Bois offer significant qualifications of this dialectic. Ellison qualifies it with an aggressive staging of sacrifice. There is the Battle Royal, where adolescent Black boys are arrayed in ritual costume and then submitted to a series of American initiations:—gawking at a "magnificent blonde," beating each other bloody, scraping for electrified gold (18–29). There is the Black brotherhood of the Communist Party, "sacrificed to [the interests] of the whole" (502). Finally, there is the Invisible Man at the novel's end, still struggling to interpret his grandfather's message. Had he intended "to affirm the principle [America?], the plan in whose name we had been brutalized and sacrificed" (574)? In this context, it's hard to know what to make of "the favorite dessert" of the Invisible Man in his hole: "vanilla ice cream and sloe gin . . . the red liquid over the white mound" (8). Is this "colored" blood spilling over the white mound of America? Does Ellison's protagonist consume sacrifice as a daily treat so as to avoid enacting it? Or is he normalizing sacrifice, by ingesting it in this bittersweet form? *The Philadelphia Negro* includes more explicit qualifications of the rite. Take, for instance, Du Bois's account of Catto, the Black schoolteacher, martyred at the hands of a mob for exercising his right to vote. Du Bois details "the scenes of carnage" that answer this murder, a sign that Blacks will have "an eye for an eye and a tooth for a tooth" (41). Catto's burial is a scene of civic and military splendor. "Not since the funeral cortege of President Lincoln had there been one as large or as imposing in Philadelphia" (42). Du Bois concludes his book with a plea and a warning, addressed in turn to each side of the color line. The Black elite, he declares, must realize its responsibility to the masses. But White America has a larger obligation: to recognize its fate as tied to that of Black

America. While enslavement did not prove its end, "economic and social exclusion" might. If Blacks are given up, Du Bois writes, "the republic is a mockery" (388).

Du Bois's attitude toward the discipline of sociology, as I have suggested, grew increasingly ambivalent over the course of his career. *The Philadelphia Negro* represents an early account of the grounds for this ambivalence, which may explain why most members of the profession chose to ignore it. Well beyond the era of his own firsthand contributions, Du Bois remained one of sociology's most profound "inside" critics. His responses could be shrill, as in, notably, his 1928 *Crisis* review of Melville Herskovits's *The American Negro*. "Social science in America has so long been the football of 'nigger'-hating propaganda that we Negroes fail to get excited when a new scientist comes into the field."[118] Du Bois's specificity here—he refers exclusively to the field's American branch—may appear to leave its European variants untouched. Yet Du Bois's relationship to sociology was defined by his Blackness in Germany as well as in the United States, and he had few illusions about the discipline's overall disposition toward Blacks, or his own vulnerability to it. The best example of Du Bois's enduring commitment to sociology, despite all this, is the 1942 review he coauthored, with Rushton Coulbourn (an Atlanta colleague), on the work of Ptirim Sorokin. The review need not be taken as a definitive account of Sorokin in particular or of the discipline in general, but I consider it a valuable testimony to Du Bois's engagement with American sociology, forty-three years after *The Philadelphia Negro*.

The review is dense, even technical, from a methodological perspective. The basis of the authors' complaint, however, is clear, as is its consistency with Du Bois's previous sociological outlook. Du Bois and Coulbourn object in particular to Sorokin's hedging on the matter of "integration." Implied in Sorokin's analysis of systems and agents, they point out, is the potential for some absolute secession from society. "Both hermit and monks [Sorokin's examples] become examples to other persons: they exhibit—many of them with positive purpose—a new system of life . . . the true significance of eremitic and monastic life is the looseness of their integration with the surrounding life in a period characterized by loose integration, and by contrast, the closeness of their internal integration as an example to promote regrowth of the society."[119] Agents and systems, Du Bois and Coulbourn insist, are mutually defining, always reciprocal. Without reference to each other they have no meaning, no reality. There is continuity from this claim to Du Bois's conception of the reciprocity between race and class analysis in the American context. In Sorokin, the reviewers imply, the recognition of man as a creature of system minimizes human control and responsibility for change. Sorokin is mistaken in taking "his 'dominant culture' and painting the mighty and serene countenance of a deity on its backside" (192). In theories like Sorokin's, sociology becomes another religion, with society in its dominant cultural form, "the god actuating all the lesser systems and the men enmeshed in those systems" (195). The reviewers' hostility to this spiritual slant is patent in the observation that one "dare not be too clear that it is man who causes movement and change; that would so terribly constrict the validity of sociology. The sociologist should keep quiet about this." Their charge is Sorokin's overidentification with the "dominant culture." They write, "According to Sorokin, then, man becomes imperfect when he does not obey the dominant culture (which really means, obey Sorokin!)" (194–95). One suspects that their deepest reservations remain unspoken. For instance, their disdain for Sorokin's indulgence in foregrounding a concept like "fluctuation." If only Blacks could rely on independent variables of this sort for improving their social prospects. Still, energy and resolve are on the side of Du Bois and Coulbourn. Sociology, meanwhile, comes off as a tired enterprise, old before its time. "It is men who create systems, operate them, and change them. . . . men do 'act in system,' for that is the very essence of the social, as distinct from the solitary, way of life. And, acting in system, men eventually create the dominant culture and cause the movement of the culture" (195). The review testifies to Du Bois's ongoing awareness of sociology's implicit determinism: its sanctioning, through its forms of "rationality," of a malevolent social order.

Blood, war, and sacrifice, Du Bois suggests in "The Souls of White Folk," are the interdependent parts of the American, and Western, "soul." The piece appeared in 1920, after the war, and after Du Bois had withdrawn conclusively from practical sociology, in part for its underwriting of scenes like the following. "We saw the dead dimly through rifts of battlesmoke. . . . this seeming Terrible is the real soul of white culture."[120] The war was fought, he explains, "for the right to bleed and exploit" dark labor across the world. There is no novelty in the approach per se, Du Bois points out, only in the "scale," the "elaborateness of detail" (933, 932). He continues, "it is curious to see America, the United States, looking on herself . . . as a moral protagonist in this terrible time. No nation is less fitted for this role. For two or more centuries America has marched proudly in the van of human hatred—making bonfires of human flesh and laughing at them hideously." This is "more than a matter of dislike," this is "a great religion, a world war-cry" (937). Du Bois's grimness is inspired by an international continuum of violence and his recognition of world war as one more step in an ongoing battle for White supremacy. Du Bois also seems inured to this violence: in his mind no horror abroad can compete with one lynching at home. The key to Du Bois's analysis, in my view, is his closing reference to White supremacy as a "religion." The characterization confirms his awareness of all those ministers parading around (at least at night) in white gowns.

Modern capitalism has perfected sacrifice, he suggests, through an alliance with Christianity. There is nothing new about the oppression of many by a more sophisticated and forceful few. There is nothing new about war. But there is something new about a diabolical racism buttressed by a conjunction of missionary Christianity and colonial capitalism. The modern West, according to Du Bois, has a sacrificial soul. Nowhere did he explore its dimensions with greater nuance (psychological, spiritual, economic) than in *The Souls of Black Folk*.

THE LEGACY OF SACRIFICE

To confront *Souls* in the wake of Du Bois's sociological work is to recognize the book as a stage for the deadly, but potentially redemptive, rituals of sacrifice. At the funeral scene, and at the moment of death that precedes it in the text, nature "mourns with the mourner" in the classic romantic sense, as if to compensate for the violations of the human order.[121] If these Whites are violating a taboo, their actions also, curiously, fulfill certain customs surrounding death and its ritual reception. Perhaps because of the momentous, inappropriate utterance that dominates the scene, Du Bois emphasizes silence: "whispering trees," "hushed faces," "shadow of a song." Speech is troubled from the start of the chapter, where Du Bois describes Atlanta as "the hard-voiced city" (350). He goes on to elaborate various conditions of speech and speechlessness: "the unvoiced terror of my life" (racism) is balanced by "unspoken wisdom" (his son's); the mystical "unknown tongue" (of mother and child [351]) is set against "that Voice at midnight" (death [351]); the silence of the parents at the moment of death ("we spoke no word"), echoed by the winds (which "spoke not" [352]), anticipates the (twice-mentioned) reticence of the White bypassers ("they did not say much" [353]). In keeping with Freud's view in "Our Attitudes toward Death," death in these moments is the unutterable. A failure or inability to speak is a sign of inhumanity. These are the grounds of the hypothetical dialogue that opens *Souls*, where a chatty White interrogates a wary Black. The White's overture fits the programmed style of sociological investigation. Step one, identify the research topic ("the negro problem"); step two, soften the subject ("I know an excellent colored man in my town"); step three, establish a sympathetic exchange ("Do not these Southern outrages make your blood boil?"). Through it all, the Black subject remains tactfully unresponsive (213).

The Black man arouses foreboding, the kind of "hesitancy" one might feel in approaching a corpse. The concerns of this opening are presaged by two epigraphs. In Arthur Symons's lyric apostrophe on the slave trade, the poet's grief is made present by its projection onto a sea, which is itself enlivened through poetic attention. A lyric animation of the object world is compared to a clinical method that freezes human contact. One could argue that an imaginatively permeable man/nature divide is being used to illustrate the comparative impermeability of racial barriers. There is a potential affinity, Du Bois implies, between ethnological description (which objectifies the human) and romantic apostrophe (which humanizes the object).[122] The second epigraph is musical: the opening bars of "Nobody Knows the Troubles I've Seen." The particular argument of "Nobody Knows" establishes the larger purpose of all these spiritual epigraphs: to mark Black separateness and Black presence. The familiar melody affords the possibility of recognition, but it is not identified for nonreaders of music. The lyrics are well known, but they are not reproduced here, in confirmation of the song's status as oral culture. The epigraph confronts the reader with the melody of a song whose lyrics, if comprehended, deny access to Black experience. Yet, as Du Bois puts it at the book's end, White and Black music are so mixed that a listener might "lose himself and never find the real Negro melodies" (382). Du Bois's comment aligns cultural and physical amalgamation and highlights the book's mixed approach to Black representation.

Three aspects of the spirituals are especially illuminating to Du Bois's symbolics of sacrifice: their conflation of sacred and secular time, their dependence on a call-and-response technique between singer and collectivity, and their declining authority as a Black cultural form at the turn of the century. The spirituals served in the slave era to define community: reminding slaves that their sorrows signaled God's interest and confirmed alternative values. The spirituals were central expressive forms in a preliterate slave culture that forged an "intimate relationship between the world of sound and the world of sacred time and space." The advent of literacy necessarily diminished the centrality of this oral tradition. The juxtaposition of literary, musical, and social scientific dialogues at the beginning of *Souls* captures this process of change. Du Bois's epigraphs reproduce the "denatured" spirituals sung by the Fisk Jubilee and Hampton Institute singers. As one former slave commented after a Hampton performance, "Dose are de same ole tunes, but some way dey don' sound right."[123] Nor was it likely that these songs would sound quite "right" in the ears of the broad audience Du Bois imagined for his "singing book."[124] Du Bois's musical epigraphs challenge White readers (who are expected to retreat in mystification from this fragment of Black culture) and embody a tension between the spiritual unity of an enslaved collectivity and the fragmentation of a modernized Black community.[125]

Amiri Baraka classifies the spirituals as communal songs about gods and labor, featuring a slave view of freedom as a state "that could only be reached through death." The blues, in contrast, detail "the life of the individual and his individual trials and successes on the earth." They express the decentralization of Black life after emancipation—"*solo*" singing possessed in turn by every singer (the Peatie Wheatstraw blues, the Blind Lemon blues). Educated, upwardly mobile Blacks preferred blues, while "the masses" favored a gradual blending of spirituals with "modern" hymns and secular songs drawn from Black and White traditions alike.[126] Du Bois's revival of the spirituals was commonplace among Black intellectuals, who sought to recover different indigenous forms of what Alain Locke calls "Negro genius." It also reflects his ongoing interest in the question of survival. As performative expression (hence unwritten and unrecorded), the spirituals appear to resist the modes of transmission and preservation necessary to the extolling of a culture. Du Bois seems aware that the vitality he claims by the placement of his musical epigraphs between "dead" scripts threatens to justify racist clichés about the primitiveness of Black culture. Because these bars of song presuppose a Black singer, they invest Black cultural representation with a distinct corporeality. Questions about Black cultural "survivals" are tied, inevitably, to the question of group survival. These become especially pressing in the chapter on Du Bois's son.

Du Bois's elegiac reflections in "Of the Passing of the First-Born" provide the book's symbolic center. Here, personal loss is deflected and sustained by an apprehension of its collective ramifications. Grief in *The Souls of Black Folk* takes on a monumental quality, because individual death among certain groups can never be separated from the dilemma of group survival. Du Bois's account of the dread aroused by the infant's mulatto features is a way of acknowledging that all young Black lives are marked from the beginning by uncertainties about the larger group's perpetuation (350). In this sense, Du Bois's treatise on mourning offers a significant contrast to its Emersonian analog, "Experience." For Du Bois, it is not the elusiveness of death that appalls but the ease with which it envelops Black life, destroying an already provisional domesticity. The "fetid Gulf" wind that carries the son's illness, devastating the parental "dreams" and "plans," recalls passages from Du Bois's sociological works describing the perilous exposure of Black homes. Emerson's complaint is that we can never be sufficiently exposed to feel the effects of our exposure. Du Bois complains that there is no way for Blacks to avoid feeling the damage of their experience. Du Bois struggles to reconcile private grief and collective identification, to join Black elite and Black masses. This purpose is complicated by a demographic plot that implies disproportionately lower reproductive rates among the Black elite and distinguishes the relative values of different Black lives.

Constructed with a magisterial formality, in keeping with the conventions of mourning, the chapter is bound from beginning (where giving birth is sleeping "with Death" [349]) to end (where the son is "so coldly wed with death" [354]) by mortuary ritual. The effect of this framework is less to create a sense of narrative immobility than to invest death with a proper motionality. The chapter is filled with images of journeys: Du Bois's trip from Georgia to the Berkshires to retrieve his wife and newborn son and their return south (350); the journey of the corpse from south to north for burial (353); and the journey of the son's soul "far beyond this narrow Now" (353). The son's journey down south fulfills the superstitious warning that the first trip of an infant should be upward to ensure his growth to maturity.[127] These secular travels are portrayed as a series of crisscrossings: south-north, north-south, south-north. They are echoed in Du Bois's reading of his son's crossed features ("dark gold ringlets, his eyes of mingled blue and brown") as an "evil omen" (350). "The junction of the road does not dread sacrifices," says an African proverb, to explain that sacrificial offerings are placed at crossroads in order to reach the extraordinarily mobile spirit world.[128] The trees that enshroud the moment of death ("the trees, the great green trees that he loved, stood motionless") have special sacrificial significance. Recall Robertson Smith's observation that the oldest altars stood under trees.[129]

The Atlanta funeral may even fulfill the custom of "mock-burial," a provisional ceremony for one who has died away from home.[130] Such distinctions—"real" versus "mock," "primary" versus "secondary"—highlight a basic divide in all burials: between the physical remains and the state of the soul. The journey north represents a desire to assist the soul's transcendent progress. The devalued corpse, emblem of individuality and decomposition, almost universally presided over by women, is set against the immortal spirit, which expresses collective endurance. These divisions in burial rites, anthropologists have noted, help to resolve the contradictions of death, to reconcile the necessary continuity of the social system with the obvious impermanence of its members. Belief in an afterlife mediates the opposition between the mortal body and the immortal body politic.[131] The value of this formulation is the way it recognizes individual death as a problem of social and political representation. Confidence in the immortal body politic is less assured when the mortal being in question is a member of a Black community in this context. As suggested by Du Bois's flag image, a permanent body politic inclusive of Blacks is a remote hope at best. Du Bois's politics of death is also framed by the problem of solidarity within: caught by the closing contrast between "the wretched of my race that line the alleys . . . fatherless and unmothered" and the lost son with "Love . . . beside his cradle" (354).

Souls opens with Du Bois's declaration of affinity with his people ("I am bone of the bone . . . flesh of the flesh" [209]); the chapter on his son dramatizes his deepest resistance to it. The most poignant registration of Du Bois's ambivalence is the refusal to bury his son in the mass grave of the South. The body of this small Black hope is separated from the doomed collectivity, just as his life is memorialized. The "pollution and . . . sorrow" of the anonymous multitudes enable the ascension of Burghardt Du Bois, whose "little soul leapt like a star" (352).[132] Their destiny is a contagion, borne on the wind. It can't be escaped, only written. Hence Du Bois's functional grief: "I shirk not. I long for work." Through Du Bois's writing, death and grief are raised to the symbolic level of sacrifice. *The Souls of Black Folk* includes conceptualizations of sacrifice as well as stagings of sacrificial action. These rites frame the narrative, from the Hebrew vow of kinship in the "Forethought" (cited above), an allusion to the sacrificial meal where human and god become one, to the "After-Thought," where Du Bois declares the book an offering in the "wilderness" (389).[133] The chapter on his son recalls two biblical moments of sacrifical substitution. In one, blood drops are substituted for human bodies; in the other, God's body is sacrificed for the sins of humanity. The chapter's title, "Of the Passing of the First-Born," recalls the plot of Passover, where the Hebrews are commanded to mark their doorposts with blood, a sacrificial sign to ensure that the angel of death will "pass over" their homes and spare their firstborn sons. Belief in the protective powers of the color red (persisting to this day in Jewish and Black, among other, folk traditions) can be traced back directly to this passage in Exodus.[134] At the same time, characterizations of the son as a "revelation of the divine . . . his baby voice the voice of the Prophet that was to rise within the Veil" (351) associate his birth and death with the story of Christ.

The echoing lines near the chapter's beginning—"I saw, as it fell *across* my baby, the shadow of the Veil. . . . I saw the shadow of the Veil as it *passed over* my baby" (350, my emphasis)—seem to equalize the sacrificial symbols of the Crucifixion and Passover. But of course they are not equivalent. The obstructed first sentence, where the infant's body, enclosed in commas, appears caught by the shadowy Veil (though perhaps also draped, as in royal robes), recalls a New Testament sacrifice that was.[135] The second sentence, a single breath suggesting immunity through unimpeded movement, highlights a Hebrew sacrifice that was not. These two biblical alternatives provide insight into Du Bois's view of Black American experience at this time: as a sacrificial possibility fulfilled or averted. The collective symbolic status glimmering through the death of this young Black hope (recall Du Bois's image of the entire race as "sacrificed in its swaddling clothes on the altar of national integrity" [238]) is at once the work of an uncommon fate and an all-too-common agency. His uncommon fate is that of a Christian God whose suffering served to justify ever after, as Albert Camus observed, "the endless and universal torture of innocence."[136] The common agency, to recall Du Bois's phrase from *The Philadelphia Negro*, is the economic and social exclusion or slow "murder" of

DU BOIS'S GOSPEL OF SACRIFICE

Blacks "until they disappear from the face of the earth" (388). Its brutal and extravagant extension is lynch law.

The link between his son's death and Christ's sacrifice evidently resonated for Du Bois with lynching, a form of sacrifice that preoccupied him in this period. I have suggested that we are meant to hear the "whistle" in Black John's "ears" before his lynching as the completion of the "shadow of a song" in the "ears" of the mourners at Burghardt Du Bois's funeral (377, 353). "Of the Coming of John" opens upon the "passing forms" of Black students at the Wells Institute, whose ghostly silhouettes provide a kind of macabre theatre for "the white city below" (364). This stark opposition initiates a series of postemancipation sterotypes: from the contending faiths of Black Americans, a homegrown religious fatalism (captured by the superstitious image of thunder curdling ice cream) set against the enlightenment ethos of Black John, to the southern White family's painful drama of succession, featuring the son who bristles at his confinement in a town of "mud and Negroes." Above all there is the lynching drama in revised form, with a White man assaulting a Black woman out of boredom, and all hell breaking loose when she resists. Blacks remain sexually pure, moral defenders of the Protestant ethic, while the White lyncher avenging his licentious son is the "pitied" one.

Perhaps the most striking aspect of this chapter is the way it conforms, in matter and method, with the chapter on the death of Du Bois's son. In fact, the two chapters fulfill the pattern of a call and response. This interdependence, or symbolic coupling, serves in part, as I have suggested, to bring out the violence inherent in the prior drama of mourning. Both chapters picture crosswise journeys from north to south, and back again. In both cases, initial journeys north are followed by returns to a southern scene of violence. Both describe awakenings. In the case of Du Bois's son it is incomplete; he is born to "the Veil" but never knows it. Black John comes slowly to recognize his own place within it. In both chapters, "yellow" signals the world's potential;—the scrap of paper telling Du Bois of his son's birth is echoed by the "yellow world" that confronts Black John as he leaves Georgia. The moment of death in the story of Black John recalls Du Bois's own reaction to his son's death. First Du Bois: "about my head the thundering storm beat like a heartless voice and the crazy forest pulsed with the curses of the weak" (352). Then John, just before his lynching: "Amid the trees in the dim morning twilight he watched their shadows dancing and heard their horses thundering toward him, until at last they came sweeping like a storm . . . the storm burst round him" (377).

In another moment, more biographical then fictional, Du Bois surveys the Atlanta lands of the Cherokees and draws our attention to the spot "where Sam Hose was crucified" (285). The display of Hose's charred knuckles in an Atlanta storefront a month before Burghardt's death (Du Bois heard of it but supposedly avoided the spectacle) turned Atlanta, according to his biographer, into "a poisoned well, polluted with the remains of Sam Hose and reflecting the drawn image of Burghardt from its dark surface."[137] The proximity of these two Black deaths highlights Du Bois's burden throughout the chapter on his son, to accommodate his analytical distance from a Black America stigmatized by high mortality with a first-hand experience that tragically confirms his own implication in it.

In biblical Hebrew, the generic term for sacrifice is *korban*, "to bring near," which implies the effort to bring a god or gods closer to human experience.[138] It is clear from Du Bois's hopeless apostrophes throughout the chapter (alternately to Death, Fate, and God) that he has little faith in the prospects for such intimacy. Du Bois is an unwilling Abraham: he offers up his son with a resentful eye toward all that I have "foregone at thy command, and with small complaint . . . save that fair young form" (354). Du Bois's resentment raises questions about resistance and the place of sacrificial rites within the Black community. In the chapter on teaching in Tennessee, for instance, Du Bois notes how the inhabitants "make the weekly sacrifice with frenzied priest at the altar" (257). These obligations are also met in the elite atmosphere of Atlanta University, where a "morning sacrifice" is routine (266). There is nothing metaphorical about the sacrificial practice of Black folk religion, specifically the Obi worship of slavery days. It's unclear from Du Bois's description who the victims were, or how the particular aims of such "blood-sacrifice" were construed (341–43), but he seems intent on confirming the lingering impact of this vengeful spirituality. In the book's conclusion, likewise, he notes how "fire and blood, prayer and sacrifice, have billowed over this people, and they have found peace only in the altars of the God of Right" (387). American Blacks have been much sacrificed, he suggests, but they are not without their own forms of sacrificial agency. Du Bois's preoccupations with death and sacrifice form a central part of his legacy, to confront them is to recognize how the identification of a negative cultural typology can be a source of creative inspiration, critique, even renewal. There is no stronger evidence of this final possibility than Du Bois's "After-thought," conveyed in the form of a sacrificial offering. "Hear my cry, O God the Reader; vouchsafe that this my book fall not still-born into the world wilderness" (389).

In contrast to Du Bois, who tends to complicate and challenge sacrifice, Charles Chesnutt might be seen as sentimentalizing it. Du Bois and Chesnutt develop similar subjects to ultimately different ends, thus providing separate legacies for imagining Black sacrifice in America. The stigma of Black mortality and its recuperation in popular death rites; passing and its diabolic antithesis, lynching; the symbolic sacrifice of firstborn sons—these are the main themes of Chesnutt's *The Marrow of Tradition*

(1901), a novel based on the riot of 1898 in Wilmington, North Carolina. As veterans of the Civil War, the novel's White characters practice a volatile religion based on a sense of "common ruin." The racist Major Cateret smolders in memory of the family "sacrificed on the bloody altar of the lost cause."[139] Sacrifice in *The Marrow of Tradition* has little to do with redemption or renewal; it is part of an endless cycle of violence. This may explain why the birth that opens the novel "suggested death and funeral wreaths" (1). The narrative as a whole is haunted by death, especially by its folk mediation. In the last scene of chapter 1, "a certain wise old Black woman" performs a mysterious rite on behalf of Cateret's firstborn son, which culminates in the burial of a bottle under a full moon (10–11). These rites, as the novel portrays them, are peculiar atavisms, equally essential to both cultures. They represent, in Newbell Puckett's terms, a shared subculture of belief, or mental underground common to Black and White. Assimilation rituals, by contrast, are divisive and mutually diminishing. The hair straighteners and skin bleachers of the Black servant, Sandy, for instance, support White supremacist doctrine. As Cateret comments they were "an acknowledgment, on their own part, that the negro was doomed. . . . there was no permanent place for the negro in the United States, if indeed anywhere in the world, except under the ground" (244–45). Yet Chesnutt presents the myth of Black "doom" as a White projection, an attempt to master southern decline. Black morbidity mirrors southern degeneracy.

This is the plot of reverse passing, where the dissolute aristocrat, Tom Delamere, who specializes in "'coon' impersonations," assumes blackface in order to rob and murder his aged aunt. The obvious point here is familiar from *The Philadelphia Negro*: Black is the color of crime. "To have a black face at such a time was to challenge suspicion," the narrator comments, "those thus marked . . . [sought] immunity in a temporary disappearance" (179). The crime and the question of its retribution give rise to extensive discussions of lynching among Whites and Blacks. Both sides reflect on the purpose of sacrificial substitution: the deliberate indifference to identifying the true culprit. From the White perspective, the object is to "burn *a* nigger." regardless of guilt. This fulfills an ancient Roman principle that applied to slaves: "the whole race [is] responsible for the misdeeds of each individual." The Roman allusion confirms what is already clear: lynch law is designed to perpetuate slavery. This is all read accurately within the Black community: "De w'ite folks don' want too good an opinion er de niggers,—if dey had a good opinion of 'em, dey wouldn' have no excuse fer 'busin' an' hangin' an' burnin' 'em." Lynch law is blind because White Civilization depends on it. Without a degraded, because constantly menaced, Black community, how could Whites build their temples of light?

In *The Marrow of Tradition*, where the proverb "As he had sown, so must he reap" dominates, Blacks and Whites are steeped in a logic of sacrifice (321). The Black housekeeper sets the stage in the opening, by volunteering to "sac'ifice my own comfo't . . . fer my dear sister's sake" (5). The impoverished journalist Ellis imagines his marriage to the wealthy Clara as "a sacrifice" for her (19). And Jerry, the novel's "Uncle Tom," envisions the impending flood, which he plans to withstand "in de ark wid de w'ite folks" (39). Near the end, Dr. Miller, the heroic Black doctor, "would cheerfully have sacrificed [his life] for those whom he loved" (294), while Mrs. Careret "would shrink at no sacrifice" to save her child (327). These terms are most pronounced in the concluding chapters, where the prospect of a double sacrifice—the loss of two firstborn sons, one White, one Black—is imminent. While Dr. Miller's son is sacrificed (gunned down in a riot initiated by Careret's inflammatory editorial), the novel closes on the likely salvation of Careret's son through Dr. Miller's intervention. Sacrifice here is not equalized, but particularized as the Black man's burden. The doctrine of White supremacy is reinscribed in familiar sacrificial form: Blacks sow, Whites reap. Nevertheless, Chesnutt sees through to an ideal beyond sacrifice. He asks his readers to believe that Miller nullifies sacrifice by refusing to avenge "his own wrongs" (321). For Chesnutt, there may be too much to avenge; the only option is to accept and endure.

There is no twentieth-century novelist who captures the sociological dimensions of African-American life with more depth than Toni Morrison, whose works also evoke a Black symbolic, centered in the possibilities of folk belief. *Song of Solomon*, for example, opens with the suicide of a life insurance agent and centers on the devitalized experience of a Black middle-class family called "the Deads." The Deads' son, Milkman, who "flies" at the novel's end, is identified with an "African" folk tradition in which flight is meant to function reparatively (326, 341). In *The Bluest Eye*, the metaphor for the peripheral existence of Blacks is "the concept of death" (18). The domestic correlative to this conceptual death is a permanently empty kitchen. For Morrison's Black psyche, no experience of possession, no amount of objects, no stocked and swollen cupboards and jars can compensate for the foundational experience and ever-present threat of dispossession. The novel's main character, a small, dark Hester Prynne, ends her days in a "little brown house . . . on the edge of town." Now a compulsive trash picker, in fulfillment of her life as a repository for the waste of the town ("which we dumped on her and which she absorbed"), she is, for Morrison at least, one significant emblem of Black status in America (159).

The Bluest Eye portrays the act of sacrifice as a Black ethnic code. Mrs. Breedlove, the novel's maternal center, cultivates it. A domestic and surrogate mother devoted to order, Mrs. Breedlove finds various routes to the sacred, from communion with film idols, to worship of Christ, to reveling in the material splendor of her White "family." Her husband, Cholly, transcends sacrifice, self-destructively. "He was free to live his fantasies, and free even to die. . . . Abandoned in a junk heap by his mother, rejected for a crap game by his father, there was nothing more to lose. . . . It was in this godlike state that he met [his wife]" (126). Like a god, Cholly can only gain. And he does gain, both within the world of Morrison's novel (where he "loves" both wife and daughter) and within its terms of justice, for Morrison "preserves," by refusing to censor, his incestuous transgressions, which she calls "a gift of love" (160). The narrative opens with a sacrificial ceremony and ends with the admission that it has failed. A baby (the product of Cholly's incestuous act) is given to save a town. The first audible tones of the child narrator, Claudia, convey urgency. Part innocent, part conspirator, she says, "if we planted the seeds, and said the right words over them, they would blossom, and everything would be all right" (9). Perform the proper rite, make the requisite offering, and God will provide. By the end, however, there has been no provision, and Claudia struggles for a rationale: "I did *not* plant the seeds too deeply. . . . it was the fault of the earth, the land, of our town. . . . This soil is bad for certain kinds of flowers" (160). The novel is a search for an explanation, doomed to failure. It can't say *why*, so it says *how*. To ask why is hubris: no one knows the ways of God. To ask how is human.

The Bluest Eye is filled with characters trying to shrink the space between the divine and the human. The most professionalized of these is Soaphead Church, "the supernatural rather than natural" child molester, who passes himself off as a spiritual therapist. Like Cholly, Soaphead violates conventional belief: he is God's rival, not his servant. "God had done a poor job, and Soaphead suspected that he himself could have done better" (136). The realization of this claim is the sacrifice he makes through Pecola, one old dog for a coveted pair of blue eyes. "We must make, ah, some offering, that is, some contact with nature," Soaphead tells her, "some simple creature might be the vehicle through which He will speak" (138). Soaphead's rite is self-serving, of course: fastidious himself, he hates the filthy dog (Bob) he proposes as victim and even imagines its resemblances to the sacrificer (Pecola). Through Soaphead's auspices, their fates are conjoined. Bob consumes a slab of poisoned meat, to become the "simple . . . vehicle" of holiness. The "ugly little black girl" (as Soaphead characterizes Pecola in his subsequent epistolary appeal to God) consumes the myth itself. The dog dies, and Pecola becomes schizophrenic. Her mind cannot contain the split between her degraded being and her precious blue eyes. At the novel's end, she realizes the role of town goat, rummaging among "the tire rims and the sunflowers" (159). This is destiny, the fulfillment of a parental legacy: the father abandoned by his mother, an infant "in the rim of a tire under a soft black Georgia sky" (105); the mother who prefers the sun and flowers of the Fisher home to her own "ugly" apartment and family.

There is simply no way, in the world of *The Bluest Eye*, to "change the course of events and alter a human life" (149). Morrison stages Black self-hatred—Blackness as affliction. Pecola Breedlove is set apart, the ultimate sacrificial victim, who arouses awe and contempt, pity and terror. But her condition is shared by every character, in some way or other. The scenes flash by in succession: Claudia in her sickbed, rubbed raw with Vick's salve, part protectively, part punitively; Cholly's self-evacuation after being rejected by his father; Mrs. Breedlove losing a front tooth while "trying to look like Jean Harlow" (98). The image of Christ as the Man of Sorrows floats through the novel like a curse (73, 76, 100, 112, etc.), defining and masking Black life. But there are characters who come close to fulfilling the redemptive possibilities of sacrifice, possibly closer than any other characters in modern American fiction. The old women who gossip into the night beside the ailing Aunt Jimmy possess the art of sacrificial transformation, which distinguishes them from the novel's troubled cast of dispossessed. They have mastered sacrifice as the ultimate mutable rite. It is basic, first of all, to their existence, their transformation of biological decline into liberation. Here they are young: "Edging into life from the back door. Becoming. Everybody in the world was in a position to give them orders." Old age is pure gain: "They alone could walk the roads of Mississippi, the lanes of Georgia, the fields of Alabama unmolested . . . tired enough to look forward to death, disinterested enough to accept the idea of pain, while ignoring the presence of pain. They were, in fact and at last, free." Throughout life they have perfected the skill of mutability: "the hands that wrung the necks of chickens and butchered hogs also nudged African violets into bloom." They triumph in old age by applying these skills on their own behalf (109–10).

While Morrison denies (in a new introduction to *The Bluest Eye*) the representativeness of Pecola and the Breedloves, it's difficult to overlook the continuities between her portrait and Du Bois's turn-of-the-century work on American constructions of Blacks. From this perspective, the Breedloves are far from uniquely unfortunate. They embody the Black hole upon which the larger national identity rests. It's possible to read Morrison's portrait of the Breedloves as a poeticizing of the Black hole in Du Bois's funeral flag. Consider the sofa, bought new and delivered split, that Morrison invokes as the emblem of their experience. The split soon becomes "a gash," and finally, "a gaping chasm" (32). Unlike Du Bois's color line, which confines Blacks but also potentially empowers them, the losses in this exchange are Black alone. This "hated piece of furniture" figures the Breedloves' social fate: their vulnerability as consumers, the way they are denied any pride of ownership, the thin line between oppression and self-contempt. Is it mere chance that Suzan-Lori Parks, the African-American playwright, whose first work was produced in 1990, is also preoccupied with gashes? Her 1993 drama, *The America Play*, she says, originated with the impulse "to write about a hole."[140] In the play itself, the hole is a mutable symbol, ranging from the protagonist's profession (gravedigging) to the sacrificial wound in his head (when he impersonates the assassinated Abraham Lincoln).

In Parks, holes can also stand for completeness, as suggested by another play, *The Death of the Last Black Man in the Whole Entire World*. In this work, the subjects of death and sacrifice are confronted in the most self-conscious terms, from the perspective of dominant cultural rites as well as Black folkways. Parks is equally drawn to clichés and to classics. She specializes in cataloging stereotypes, parading to deflate. The cast of *Last Black Man* includes Black Man with Watermelon, Black Woman with Fried Drumstick, Lots of Grease and Lots of Pork, and Yes and Greens Black-Eyed Peas Cornbread.[141] Every myth about Black America, it seems, is here, from the absentee father—"Saint mines" is an eternal refrain of the Black Man (84)—to lynching. "Can only eliminate one at uh time," the Black Man says matter of factly. "Folks come tuh watch with picnic baskets" (85). The Black Man swings "from front tuh back uhgain . . . Crossed eyin. . . . Toes uncrossin then crossin for luck . . . It had begun tuh rain. . . . They some of em pointed they summoned uh laughed they some looked quick in an then they looked uhway. . . . They tired of me" (89). The scene is full of ritual detail: the folk superstition associating sacrifice with crossed lines; the rain, spiritual signifier of redemption; and the usual ambivalence on the part of White lynchers and spectators, a mingling of sadism, callousness, brutality, and fear (for themselves and for their imaginary antagonists). So prominent is the role of this spectacle in the play that Parks's privileged category, history, is rewritten as "Histree" (90). The Black American past is littered with trees bearing "strange fruit."[142] But race hatred is not an American exclusive. Parks's lynchers are cheered on by a global community. The contempt for Blackness, in her view, is worldwide and epidemic. When "Voice On Thuh Tee V" announces "the absolutely last living negro man in the whole entire known world—is dead," there are "controlled displays of jubilation in all corners" of it (85–86).

The America Play is more specifically focused on questions of nationality, recognizing Blacks as the center of American culture: burying the dead, professionalizing sympathy, bearing the brunt of the nation's sacrificial violence. Set in the postemancipation era, this stunning drama immortalizes the historic moment when Black America is reborn as a sacrificial culture. It tells the story of a Black gravedigger who resembles Abraham Lincoln and spends his life impersonating "the Great Man" in a variety of commercial ventures, from staged assassinations ("pay a penny . . . and 'shoot Mr. Lincoln'") to recitations of presidential addresses. The enormous ambition of Parks's design is evident from a brief summary of her subjects: the collective struggle to master a national history of violence through the ritualization of violent acts (as in the portrayal of the Lincoln assassination caught in the perverse repetition compulsion of marketplace histrionics); the disappearance of the American past and its reinscription as a leisure industry ("theme parks" and tawdry museums filled with summer tourism's souvenirs); the cliché of Black culture's arrested development, its needing somehow to "catch up" to the dominant culture, offset by the revisionary hint that history might soon be reconceived from the perspective of "the lesser knowns" with the "Great Men" playing "catch up" to them. The play portrays a Black American culture steeped in the rituals of death and mourning. When the Black mother hands her son his father's spade in the scene in act 2 entitled, "Spadework," the ironic doubling of tool and appellation (the handing of a spade to a spade) confirms a legacy (36). In the isolated, surrealist world of *The America Play*, gravedigging, mourning, and confidence keeping (secreting the final words of the dead) are the sole occupations. Perhaps most striking for my concerns is the portrayal of sympathy as a stage effect, devoid of instinctive content. Sympathy, like any other human artifact, needs to be invented. The son recalls the day when his father first showed him "'the Weep' 'the Sob' and 'the Moan.' How to stand just so what to do with the hands and feet (to capitalize on what we in the business call 'the Mourning Moment')." Like any commodity, it can be bought and sold: "There's money in it," the son is told (33).

To identify with Lincoln is to identify with sacrifice. Parks claims that Black America's embrace of Lincoln follows inevitably from a reading of its own destiny. This is plain in the pivotal moment, when the protagonist decides to capitalize on the assassination. "When someone remarked that he played Lincoln so well that he ought to be shot, it was as if the Great Mans footsteps had been suddenly revealed. . . . The Lesser Known became famous overnight. . . . What interested the Lesser Known most about the Great Mans murder was the 20 feet which separated the presidents box from the stage" (28–29). Parks believes that Americans (African Americans in particular) have a compulsion to repeat sacrifice; her protaganist's genius is to bank on it. Lincoln's life represents an ideal staging of sacrifice. The particulars of his murder, according to Parks, reveal how sacrifice inevitably fits the pattern of theatre.

One argument of this chapter, and *The Science of Sacrifice* as a whole, is that turn-of-the-century American literature stages the rite as part of a more general, interdisciplinary preoccupation. The main object of Parks's play becomes the staging of an extraordinarily "stagy" historical sacrifice.

In her account, the staging of the Lincoln assassination becomes a national pastime, an idea that is fully consistent with my claims. As important, she recognizes the connection between sacrificial rituals and questions of kinship. If sacrifice is an affirmation of intratribal ties; if its purpose is to strengthen, clarify the borders between "us" and "them," then what is Parks suggesting through her Black protagonist, consumed by his possible "kin" resemblances to Lincoln and eager to assume Lincoln's martyrdom (especially for the right price)? Are Blacks customary victims of American sacrifice because they are too close or too far? Is postemancipation America struggling to rid itself of Blacks because they complicate kinship bonds from within (they are "brothers" who look strange), or from without (they are "others" who look familiar)? Parks doesn't settle these questions; she presents them as the most pressing problems confronting the nation. *The America Play*, like *Last Black Man*, sees the Black susceptibility to sacrifice as more or less confined to a postemancipation context. For she poses this status as a legacy, with symbolic and practical import for the postmodern era. Parks reinforces her sombre conviction of the Black penchant for sacrifice with her "House of Wonders," a hall of medals awarded to Blacks over time. Most of the medals glorify servile functions: "for trustworthiness and for standing straight; for standing tall; For standing still; For advancing and retreating. For makin do. . . . For cookin and for cleanin. For bowin and scrapin" (34). It all comes down to "the great Black hole" in the head of Lincoln, the gaping sacrificial wound, that eventually encompasses every other hole in the play. The mother and son turn the "Great Hole of History" into a giant grave, in which they rummage for the body of husband and father (the natural gravedigger who knows death). In the play's final moments, they gape together at the gaping wound, the hole to end all holes, "in thuh great head" (39). And the play closes on a note of wonder— "how thuh nation mourns"—in recognition of the Lincoln assassination as one of *the* "mourning moments" in history.

In *The Unwritten War* (1973), Daniel Aaron reproduces a typical retrospect on Lincoln's death. "How closely Nemesis pursues the murderer! The spirit he sought to slay arrests him and brings him down. The genius of America uses her symbols to ensnare him. The national flag catches his heel, breaks his leg, and makes his escape impossible." Aaron comments, "Given the mood of the times, the analogy of Lincoln and Christ proved irresistibly apt. Poets played upon the association of the 'cruelest month' with the Jewish Passover, the Crucifixion day and Resurrection."[143] It's not clear whether we can trust O. B. Frothingham's image of John Wilkes Booth caught (on the boot heel) by the American flag. But the idea turns up again, over a century later, in Gore Vidal's *Lincoln* (1984), which describes, more reservedly, the spur of Booth's boot entangled in the "silken bunting that decorated" the presidential box. Vidal doesn't specify this silk as the flag, and it's hard to believe that he would have passed up such a histrionic image.[144] Still, it's tempting to imagine, with Frothingham, the national symbol itself taking vengeance on an errant citizen. It's even more tempting to imagine the American flag as including, within the bounds of its own symbolism, a commentary on the likely transgression of national ideals. Du Bois's funeral "flag" encourages such a reading. The drama of sacrifice is written in the "Stars and Stripes": a gaping Black wound bleeds red stripes onto the White landscape of America.[145] This seems less far-fetched when we recall the frequency with which Du Bois, throughout this period, drew on the foiled symbolism of the American flag to image Black exclusion. Elsewhere in *Souls*, for example, he observes, "to lay any class of weak and despised people, be they white, black, or blue, at the political mercy of their stronger, richer, and more resourceful fellows, is a temptation which human nature seldom has withstood" (329). In his 1911 "report" on America to the Universal Races Congress, he notes that "Negro blood has furnished thousands of soldiers to defend the flag in every war in which the United States has been engaged,"[146] and in *The Philadelphia Negro*, while discussing its "mixed" forms, Du Bois declares marriage "a private contract. . . . it does not concern anyone but themselves as to whether one of them be white, black, or red" (358).

Parks's play understands how Lincoln's image, and everything connected with it, still inspires amplification. Lincoln assisted mythology not only by chance (by being martyred on Good Friday) but by design (as implied by Aaron's image of "the complicated self behind the melancholy and genial masks of Uncle Abe"). Everyone knows that Lincoln anticipated his assassination in a dream.[147] "Lincoln awakened in his own bed, face covered with sweat," writes Vidal. "Is it I or another? Are dreams the opposite of the future, or the same?" Lincoln's legendary foresight, which establishes his status as a willing victim (Vidal makes much of the fact that he refused extra security even after this dream), heightened the sacrifical connotations of his death. There was no writer who did more to embellish them than Whitman, who called the assassination a "tableau, stranger than fiction." To be sure, Whitman had trouble telling himself and Lincoln apart. In his own mind, Whitman was "sacrificed" to the war. Lincoln, whose martyrdom "enriched the soul of art," represented a different type of offering, as Whitman saw it, to aesthetic practice itself.[148] Lincoln needed neither the Civil War nor poetic assistance to realize the possibilities of sacrifice. Speeches, long before his presidency, reveal the subject as an ongoing interest. The most resounding of these was his 1837 Lyceum Address, which included the memorable image of "strange fruit" . . . rivaling . . . native moss." This was not, as some might have wished, a defense of lynching-victims but a defense of law. "The Constitution and Laws," Lincoln declared, were "sacred" writ: "Let reverence for the laws be breathed by every American mother, to the lisping babe. . . . let it be taught in schools, in seminaries, and in colleges." He christened his policy statement a *"political religion,"* founded on sacrifice. "Let the old and the young, the rich and the poor, the grave and the gay, of all sexes and tongues, and colors and conditions, sacrifice unceasingly upon its altars."[149]

Lincoln's aim, it seems, was the replacement of sacrifice as mob violence with a more orderly form of sacrifice as public duty. To this end, he condemned an anarchic, unlawful sacrifice "revolting to humanity." The lynch mob was unnatural, epidemic. "They have pervaded the country," he writes. "Alike, they spring up among the pleasure hunting masters of Southern slaves, and the order loving citizens of the land of steady habits" (19). Sacrifice is not at issue; it is a question of care and culpability. No one is safe in the mad rush for vengeance—guilty or innocent, kin or stranger. In a subtle reinstatement of a peaceful Hebraism, Lincoln proclaims it the purpose of law to ensure an orderly distribution of sacrifice. Let all who live among us, he implies, within the bounds of our nation, practice this law-abiding art. "Men who love tranquility, who desire to abide by the laws, and enjoy their benefits . . . would gladly spill their blood in the defence of their country" (21). For one who could write this in 1837, the obligation to preside over an internal bloodbath widely classified as "national atonement" must have seemed a prophetic fulfillment. Lincoln was unquestionably in his element, consecrating the cemetery at Gettysburg with the blood of "those who here gave their lives that that nation might live," and accepting his second term in mind of a possible divine compensation—was "every drop of blood drawn with the lash . . . [to] be paid by another drawn with the sword"? (295, 321).

Lincoln was the ultimate politician of sacrifice, as Parks, and Du Bois before her, recognized. In a controversial portrait of Lincoln in 1922, Du Bois captures this dimension of the great man's life and work. As Du Bois tells it, Lincoln's story is the *Life of Jesus*. "I love him not because he was perfect but because he was not and yet triumphed. . . . He was one of you and yet he became Abraham Lincoln. . . . I glory in that crucified humanity that can push itself up out of the mud of a miserable, dirty ancestry; who despite the clinging smirch of low tastes and shifty political methods, rose to be a great and good man and the noblest friend of the slave."[150] "Illegitimate," of "low tastes" and "ancestry," Du Bois's Lincoln is destined for vindictiveness, but becomes more. His greatness lies in what is gotten by to get there: "the scars and foibles and contradictions." Du Bois concludes, "it was the bloody sweat that proved the human Christ divine . . . that proved Abraham Lincoln a Prince of Men." It's hard to tell how far Du Bois means to take this rhetoric, nor how much of his own animosity toward the creed of American individualism had to be swallowed in the process. But Du Bois is often unpredictable around the issue of "greatness." It seemed to complicate his usually staunch resistance to the American "religion" of sacrifice. I have described the Black identification with Lincoln in *The America Play* as consistent with Lincoln's own sacrificial rhetoric. Du Bois's treatment of Lincoln supports these conventional associations. Lincoln is Christ, and Blacks, by implication, the collectivity identified with his glorified sufferings.[151] To say that Parks and Du Bois suggest this is far from saying that they endorse it. For both, representation is the only route to criticism and challenge.

One could argue that Du Bois admires sacrifice as self-actuated mission, whether his model is Lincoln or "The Talented Tenth," but resists its application to collectivities. Du Bois's adaptation of sacrifice as an ideal for a Black elite must be seen as a response to larger attempts to circumscribe it within the domain of Black culture. Still, his articulation of "the Gospel of Sacrifice" remains one of the most curious passages in *The Souls of Black Folk*. "Not at Oxford or at Leipsig, not at Yale or Columbia, is there an air of higher resolve or more unfettered striving; the determination to realize for men, both black and white, the broadest possibilities of life, to seek the better and the best, to spread with their own hands the Gospel of Sacrifice,—all this is the burden of their talk and dream" (267). This message of elite distinction and obligation has alienated many of Du Bois's recent critics.[152] It was repeated elsewhere. In "College-Bred Negroes," an 1898 Fisk University Address, Du Bois defended a naturalized "law of sacrifice [which] we see . . . everywhere: in the fruit we save to ripen, in the fields that lie fallow, in the years given to training and education, and in the self-sacrifice of a Socrates, a Darwin, or a David Livingstone."[153] We find it where we expect to, but it is not always what we expect to find. It *is* predictable, for instance, to find a rhetoric of sacrifice being invoked as the medium for Du Bois's qualification of women's rights. In "The Damnation of Women," Du Bois defined his titular phrase as female fate: that women mother "only at the sacrifice of intelligence and the chance to do their best work." His closing designation of "sympathy and sacrifice as characteristic of Negro womanhood" comes as a barely disguised defense of group survival.[154]

Du Bois's quiescence on issues of gender, it seems to me, only reinforces the intensity with which he disavowed sacrifice as a collective Black "destiny." This chapter has demonstrated the variability and refinement of sacrificial modes in Du Bois's work. He recognizes sacrifice as a persistent religious practice, gruesomely evident in the barbaric yet Christian rite of lynching. (He compared it to "cannibalism" in a 1919 *Crisis* review, but declared it, typologically, Christian in "The Talented Tenth.")[155] He recognizes Darwinian accounts, where Blacks are an excrescent social skin, a debilitated part shed for the good of the whole. Most prominent among Du Bois's formulations of sacrifice, as I have suggested, is as heroic creed.

Du Bois constructs a morality of self-sacrifice for a Black leadership, as a willed version of a more collective, helpless surrender. The sacrifices of a Black intelligentsia are inseparable from these other sacrifices, because, according to Du Bois, Black existence is always collectively defined. He often denounced "a color-prejudice that classe[s] Phyllis Wheatley and Sam Hose in the same despised class." The substance of his protest tended to be sociological: "Few modern groups show a greater internal differentiation of social conditions than the Negro American and the failure to realize this is the cause of much confusion."[156] Still, Du Bois's repetition of the word "class" tells much of the story. There is unbreakable continuity among different statuses and experiences, because Blacks are a class unto themselves in turn-of-the-century America. While this was not practically true, it had enough imaginary weight, as we saw in Philadelphia and Atlanta, to carry the day, so far as dominant constructions were concerned. This is why Du Bois viewed the confrontation and redirection of a collective sacrificial identity as a particularly viable strategy for a Black elite.

Du Bois's "Gospel of Sacrifice" redefines the rite as possession rather than dispossession. As such, it becomes the basis of a social mission. Sacrifice is monumentalized, writ large, to remember collective sufferings. It's routinized as a means to different ends. Du Bois has not absorbed sacrifice. He's making it pay, in the classic sacrificial sense. I want to clarify this point with the help of an image from a later work, beyond the turn-of-the-century context that has largely confined this analysis. The book is *Dusk of Dawn: An Essay toward an Autobiograhy of a Race Concept* (1940), the personal chronicle billed as "An Autobiography of a Race," in confirmation of the reciprocity I have named. Black American existence here is a fulfillment of Du Bois's turn-of-the-century legacy. Du Bois ends the chapter on race with a dramatic characterization of his people: they are "entombed souls," enclosed within "invisible but horribly tangible plate glass." The brittleness of their humanity is implied, and consequently overlooked by White passersby, who are pictured here as acutely insensible. Thus far, the passage reads as a sequel to the scene with which we began, the child's burial that occasions race hatred. By 1940, Du Bois is prepared to take things further. Frustrated to the point of madness, the entombed sometimes "hurl themselves against the barriers. . . . They may even, here and there, break through in blood and disfigurement," only to confront a "horrified, implacable . . . people frightened for their very own existence." Whites contrive Blackness as monstrosity, Du Bois suggests, then run in terror from the success of their own designs. There is little potential for redress from the outside. Outsiders, Du Bois notes, "will continually misinterpret and compromise and complicate matters, even with the best of will." The only workable advocacy is that which renders the "submerged caste" itself "articulate." The futility of external aid leads to an inevitably "provincial" mentality within. Loyalty to the group "tends to be almost unending and balks at almost no sacrifice." Attitudes "toward the environing race congeals into a matter of unreasoning resentment and even hatred," a "refusal to conceive honesty and rational thought on their part."[157] This is how things look from inside, thirty-seven years later.

The legacy of sacrifice persists variously. "Blood and disfigurement" suggests the ongoing threat of the lynch mob, the lot of those ("here and there") who defy their entombment. The ceremonial stillness reveals Black-White relations as still enclosed within a sacred-profane divide. Finally, there is sacrifice as the internal gospel—a gospel possessed, so that there might be no further dispossession. As portrayed here, and throughout Du Bois's early writings, the concepts of race and sacrifice are one. Don't look to Whites, Du Bois warns, for a "rational" apprehension of these dilemmas. For it is Blacks who are gifted with double consciousness, an intense dialectical condition of self and social awareness—call it a rationalized sixth sense. Those who are most debilitated by an American legacy are the most likely to find a way out of it. Blacks don't internalize sacrifice; they rationalize it. And for the first time in the modern era, sacrifice is recognized as the ancient barbaric rule that it always was.

Afterword

THE commentary on the Akeda in Genesis tells us that "Abraham seems to move like a sleepwalker." That is what ritual is from a certain perspective, the things we do in our sleep. By this I mean that ritual, while usually a matter of consent and deliberation, may at times, and even gradually over time, lose its consensual and deliberate character. Deeds are performed with a sense of spiritual purpose that is profound, but not necessarily apparent to the actor. I began by saying that this book is about reading. But I see now that it is also about ritual—the rituals that fortify kinship and those that stage its absence. *The Science of Sacrifice* is about the ritual assumptions—good or (more often) bad, but never indifferent—that structure human exchanges in this society. I have been concerned with ritual acts and with those who try to understand them, usually from a great distance. My book stands in relation to its late-nineteenth-century objects of analysis very much as their authors stood in relation to their ancient sources. After all, this is a recovery of a recovery of sacrifice. It is marked, like every other interpretation featured here, by the rituals I have sought to bring to light. The reason is not that sacrifice is so dazzling but that we are still doing it in our sleep. Yet implicit in every line of this book is the hope that historical representation can have recuperative effects. Perhaps it can't make us know what we do while we sleep, but it can help us to understand actions committed by others in similar states of unconsciousness. History itself may be empty; its symbolic recovery is full.

This book came to life in an interdisciplinary region between literature, theology, and the social sciences. Indeed, this book can be thought of as an interdisciplinary exercise whose governing premise is that this type of exercise has been far more a thing of the past than of the present. It highlights an historical moment when the sorts of divisions that define our intellectual world were more than less inchoate. It captures a point in American cultural history when the interdisciplinary insight we now seek remained a practical as well as a conceptual possibility. This was a moment when disciplinary boundaries were understood as the condition of knowledge, not as the impediment to it. There was greater interest in what these boundaries might reveal than in how they might be transgressed. My intention has been to recognize the histories of disciplines as properly heterogeneous. For "our familiar disciplines have secret histories, their apparently monolithic integrity sometimes obscuring a radically disparate and interdisciplinary core."[1] Contemporary critics, in other words, strive for intellectual crossings that were taken for granted by many of the artists and thinkers they study. My own further point is that our presumption that the past is as limited as the present (it just has other limitations) may have blinded us to what we can find there and learn by way of it.

Staging a confrontation between the languages of transcendence and particularity, sacredness and secularism, aesthetics and science, revealed a common story about sacrifice. The writers who speak here were participants in a conversation about the ends of modern social life, and the conversation kept gravitating toward an ancient subject. What explains the attraction of sacrifice for Anglo-Americans in the late nineteenth century? First, there is the rite's early and ongoing identification with spiritual uncertainty. Sacrifice was uniquely suited to a late-nineteenth-century scene where religious doubt seemed both epidemic and incurable. Second is the rite's status as a type of spiritual economics. Sacrifice was in part a prosperity ethic, a means of equalizing wealth so as to preserve it. The rich might express thanks to God by sacrificing a portion of their bounty (a portion that could then be distributed as alms to the poor), but the poor themselves, in seasons of calamity, might be defined as expendable and persuaded or forced to give their own lives. Thus sacrifice sustained divisions between haves (ritual donors or beneficiaries) and have nots (ritual victims or inadvertent recipients). And these divisions made sense to an expanding industrial capitalist democracy regularly confronting extreme differences of poverty and wealth.

The third and most important tie was the significance of sacrifice for modern reconceptualizations of kinship. What had been common knowledge since the time of the "early Semites" was discovered anew: the recognition that absolute sanctions for defining communal and national boundaries were untenable. That recognition was growing in the late nineteenth century, throughout the human sciences, as well as in religion and literature. Writers like Du Bois and Durkheim, Henry James, F. H. Giddings, and Robertson Smith distinguished the assurances of traditional kinship, where membership has a primal force issuing in a "common life . . . common religion . . . common social duties," from a modern situation, where kinship has no absolute value, but is measured by degrees and means "much or little, or nothing at all."[2] Sacrifice is the practice that formalizes the fury occasioned by that gap. Through sacrifice, this gap is both expressed and suppressed. For sacrifice in this period was also a fervent staging of blood kinship, a melodramatic, even violent theatre of common bonds.

Sacrifice here is defined as an interdisciplinary enterprise and located as an historic event. It is given a street address or rather, many street addresses, in a variety of adjacent neighborhoods.[3] Sacrifice appears, for instance, as a staple of theological debates on the higher criticism (the antiquarian source of the notorious split Christ—beneficent and benighted, twisted and sweet—immortalized by Melville and later analyzed by Max Scheler). Sacrifice figures in a theoretical history on the social function of sympathy that eventually reaches institutional form in the life insurance industry. Sacrifice proves central as well to more familiar late-nineteenth-century social scientific discussions (both popular and classic) on the fate of social Darwinism. And sacrifice is tragically realized in contemporary lynchings, as ritually precise as they were brutal.

Sacrifice endures; it remains a fixture of our national scene. The violence of urban youth gangs and the revenge plot that culminated in the catastrophic bombing of the Oklahoma City federal building can be seen as different eruptions from a single postmodern crisis of kinship. Sacrificial principles continue to polarize intellectuals (Richard Dawkins versus Stephen J. Gould on fitness and survival) and to inspire popular artists (the "eat or be eaten" mentality that governs the world of *Pulp Fiction*). The concept of sacrifice informs every forum on welfare where people speculate on whether poverty can ever be fully eliminated, every attempt to rationalize economic inequality on essential grounds, every conviction that AIDS is a retribution for sexual excess or transgression.

Sacrifice is deep with us, a foundational script of our multicultural becoming. That is why it has taken a special history to bring it out. Ideas appear as cultural pressure points; they lie at the center of professional discussions; they are the source of public institutions. Elite and more popular discourses converge and blur. History is relentlessly bookbound. But books are only the most articulate form of sacrificial acts and events; books direct us to the encoded meanings in other cultural forms. Cultural interpretation is a continuum: past and present actors, whether ordinary or extravagant, look familiar. This is not because we are remote and confined to seeing our own reflections in what they do. It is because they are closer than we think, prodding us to interpret them, and demanding, above all, that we use their symbolic gifts to replenish ourselves.

Notes

❧

Introduction

1. One of the most striking features of Girard's analysis is his embrace of a scientific terminology of "evidence" and "empirical" validity. He admits that his "literary background. . .[is] the worst possible recommendation for the type of research that interests me," while advancing a revisionary postmodern conception of scientific significance. "When the failure of all dogmatic methodologies is fully acknowledged, the scientific threshold is close. . . . The sciences of man have been dogmatic and philosophical for so long that they have lost sight of what scientific knowledge is really about." Girard predicts optimistically that "the type of coherence I am trying to establish will come more and more within our reach as the sacrificial resources of our culture become exhausted and the mythical compartments of Western knowledge further disintegrate." His own ethical research "represents a higher stage in a process" begun by Freud and other practitioners of what was still in Freud's time a comparatively new "science of man." See "Interview" in *Diacritics: Special Issue on the Work of René Girard* (Baltimore: Johns Hopkins University Press, 1978), 32, 43–45. Sacrifice is central to Kenneth Burke's reading of Genesis in *The Rhetoric of Religion: Studies in Logology* (Berekeley: University of California Press, 1970), and one could argue that it has a critical significance throughout his work. "The sacrificial principle," he writes, "is intrinsic to the idea of Order." Burke describes a Judaeo-Christian legacy whereby a "purely worldly order of motives" spawns "a correspondingly worldly kind of 'defilement,' with its call for a correspondingly worldly need of cleansing by sacrifice." He finds in Nazism "the most dramatically obvious" case—"a 'perfect' victim in the guise of a 'total' enemy" (4,224). Burke's insight resonates in a key paradox of Nazi terminology: that the German word for vermin, *Ungeziefer*, which was regularly applied to the Jews, translates as "creature unfit for sacrifice." This is from the word *zebar*, meaning "sacrificial beast," a derivation from the biblical Hebrew term *Zébah*, "slaughtered victim." M.O.C. Walsh, *A Concise German Etymological Dictionary* (London: Routledge and Kegan Paul, 1951), 233.

2. My point is not that all sociology (nor for that matter, all religion or all literature) originating at this time was sacrificial in form or concept. My point rather is that sacrifice was a particular interdisciplinary preoccupation of a particular social scene. When the specific group of literary writers, social scientists, and theologians I treat talked about the meaning of social life, their conversation tended to gravitate to the subject of sacrifice. Sacrifice provided a certain way of representing society in religious terms at this time.

3. Alvin Gouldner, *The Coming Crisis of Western Sociology* (New York: Basic Books, 1970), 254–66. A fuller discussion of functionalism can be found in chapter 1 below.

4. Shortly before this, the man, who was Jewish, had renewed his religious observances; indeed, had become obsessed with them. Was this eerie murder of his non-Jewish wife, with its clear sacrificial overtones, an attempt to avenge a firstborn infant son who had died the year before, presumably, from a weak heart and lungs? Was it an extravagant display of tribal loyalty, an attempt to atone for a regretted marriage to an outsider? See the series of articles on the case in the *Boston Globe*, August 30, September 1, and September 10, 1995. The *Globe* coverage of the 1996 trial in Cambridge, Massachusetts, has supplied increasingly bizarre details. According to the defense (which filed an insanity plea), the husband returned home after temple services, and he and his wife argued about their burned supper. During the argument she took on (in his mind) the appearance of an "alien" (presumably the space-age kind?), and he killed her. Alison Fife, a psychiatrist testifying for the prosecution, argued that "Richard Rosenthal's belief that his wife was an alien as he beat her in their Framingham backyard does not fit the defense assessment that he was delusional during the killing." She concludes instead that he was "a perfectionist" and "narcissistic." Testimony has thus centered on the extent of Rosenthal's "control" over his actions. The defense characterizes the murder as "primitive," highlighting a moment on the Massachusetts Avenue Bridge when Rosenthal believed God spoke to him directly, explaining that "his son had died because Rosenthal was not strictly observant." Dr. Fife dismisses these claims: "a heightened interest in one's religion" is not "a sign of mental illness." The murder scene, she contends, was "staged by a man who knew what he was doing." Yet read in terms of sacrificial ritual, each of these characterizations is accurate: Rosenthal's violence looks both horribly extreme and cold-bloodedly rational. See the *Boston Globe*, October 26, 31, November 1, 1996.

5. This study might be conceived as an attempt to alleviate what Giles Gunn has described as a "crippling polarization . . . between the literary and cultural on the one side and the religious and theological on the other," by extending the field of inquiry to social science. Gunn refers to a "common ground" between literature and religion that is to be found in a recognition of their "derivation from the same common substance . . . culture itself." Alert to social scientific sources throughout, Gunn ends his study with an appeal, by way of Clifford Geertz, to understand religion in terms of questions and problems rather than "fixities and definites." *The Interpretation of Otherness: Literature, Religion and the American Imagination* (New York: Oxford University Press, 1979), 6ff., 226. The work of Jonathan Z. Smith might be understood as an answer to this appeal. See, for instance, his essay "The Devil in Mr. Jones," which considers the Jonestown massacre in terms of an institutional history of religious studies. Smith notes that the Jonestown case has been ignored by academicians in his field, a field built on "the amalgamation between religion and liberalism . . . a major argument for the presence of religious studies in the state and secular universities." Smith concludes "If the events of Jonestown are a behavioral *skandalon* to the Enlightenment faith, then the refusal of the academy to interpret Jonestown is, at least, an equivalent *skandalon* to the same faith." Smith's own methods represent an exemplary blend of anthropological, literary, and historical interpretation. See Jonathan Z. Smith, *Imagining Religion: From Babylon to Jonestown* (Chicago: University of Chicago Press, 1982), 102–20. The quotations above are from 110–11.

6. Emile Durkheim, *Sociology and Philosophy*, trans. D. F. Pocock (New York: Free Press, 1974). These quotations from Durkheim's writings are cited in the introduction by J. G. Peristiany xxi, xvii–xviii. They are drawn, respectively, from *Division of Labor* and Durkheim's 1892 thesis, an early version of *Division*, entitled *Quid Secundatus politicae scientiae instituendae contulerit*.

7. The phrase, a self-characterization of Max Weber's, is cited in Fredric Jameson's "The Vanishing Mediator: Narrative Structure in Max Weber," *New German Critique* 1 (Winter 1973): 86. Floyd House describes "the ecclesiastical bias" that prevailed on the American scene in particular, where courses in "'Biblical sociology'... were fairly common." Floyd Nelson House, *The Development of Sociology* (New York: McGraw-Hill, 1936), 294.

8. The resemblances between Durkheim's occasional remarks on Jewish practices and Bourdieu's arguments, in "Belief and the Body" especially, are quite marked. For the biographical details on Durkheim, see Stephen Lukes, *Emile Durkheim His Life and Work: A Historical And Critical Study* (New York: Penguin, 1977), 39–44; and Dominick LaCapra, *Emile Durkheim: Sociologist and Philosopher* (Ithaca, N.Y.: Cornell University Press, 1972), 28–29ff. And see Pierre Bourdieu, "Belief and the Body," in *The Logic of Practice*, trans. Richard Nice (Palo Alto, Calif.: Stanford University Press, 1990), 66–79ff.

9. Quoted in Harry Elmer Barnes, *Introduction to the History of Sociology* (Chicago: University of Chicago Press, 1948), 787.

10. My use of the term "universal" here should not be confused with the distinction that developed later in sociology and was associated, for example, with the work of Talcott Parsons, between "universalistic" and "particularistic" standards, the former implying "role-expectation," the latter, "appreciative values." See Don Martindale, *The Nature and Types of Sociological Theory* (Boston: Houghton Mifflin, 1981), 475–76.

11. John Guillory, *Cultural Capital: The Problem of Literary Canon Formation* (Chicago: Chicago University Press, 1993), 273.

12. Some of the works in this study are more readily classified as "realist," others as "naturalist." I use both terms throughout and distinguish them where appropriate. The borders between these two American literary genres were often indistinct, from the perspectives of both authors and readers.

13. Max Weber, "The Nature of Social Action," in *Weber: Selections in Translation*, ed. W. G. Runciman, trans. Eric Matthews (Cambridge: Cambridge University Press, 1978), 9.

14. Franklin Henry Giddings, *The Principles of Sociology: An Analysis of the Phenomena of Association and of Social Organization* (New York: Macmillan, 1896), 61.

15. Of the many accounts of the origin of social science, including perspectives on sociology in particular, I have benefited most from the following: Albion Small, *The Origins of Sociology* (Chicago: University of Chicago Press, 1924); Harry Elmer Barnes, *An Introduction to the History of Sociology* (Chicago: University of Chicago Press, 1948); Anthony Giddens, "Classical Social Theory and the Origins of Modern Sociology," *American Journal of Sociology* 81, no. 4 (1974): 703–29; Stefan Collini, "Sociology and Idealism in Britain 1880–1920," *Archive Européennes de Sociologie* 19 (1978): 3–50; Thomas Haskell, *The Emergence of Professional Social Science: The American Social Science Association and the Nineteenth-Century Crisis of*

Authority: (Urbana: University of Illinois Press, 1977); David Hollinger, "The Knower and the Artificer," *American Quarterly* 39 (Spring 1987): 37–55; and Dorothy Ross, *The Origins of American Social Science* (New York: Cambridge University Press, 1991).

16. For an account of nineteenth- and twentieth-century America along these lines, see Lawrence Levine, *Highbrow/Lowbrow: The Emergence of Cultural Hierarchy in America* (Cambridge: Harvard University Press, 1988).

17. Albion Small, "The Era of Sociology," *American Journal of Sociology* 2 (July 1895): 3.

18. A blurb from the *New York Times* on the cover of a recent border text, Richard Dawkins's *The Selfish Gene* (1989 edition) gives some idea of these aspirations: "the sort of popular science writing that makes the reader feel like a genius." See also Glenn Loury's indictment of what he calls the "false, immoral intellectuality" of Herrnstein and Murray, who fashion themselves as "technicians reporting to the public on what the experts already know." *On the Role of Black Intellectuals, Center for Humanistic Studies Monograph Series, no. 8* (Claremont, Calif.: Claremont McKenna College, 1996), 7.

19. Edward A. Ross, *Sin and Society: An Analysis of Latter-Day Iniquity* (Boston: Houghton and Mifflin, 1907), vii.

20. For Roosevelt quote, see ibid., xi. For second quote, from Albion Small, see Edward A. Ross, *Social Control: A Survey of the Foundations of Order* (1901; reprint, Cleveland: Case Western Reserve University Press, 1969), xxxv. For Ross's litany of readers, see *Seventy Years of It* (New York: Appleton-Century, 1936), 110–11.

21. On the gains of women in this period, see, for example, Rosalind Rosenberg, *Beyond Separate Spheres: Intellectual Roots of Modern Feminism* (New Haven: Yale University Press, 1982); Nancy Cott, *The Grounding of Modern Feminism* (New Haven: Yale University Press, 1987); Ellen Fitzpatrick, *Endless Crusade: Women Social Scientists and Progressive Reform* (New York: Oxford University Press, 1990); and Theda Skocpol, *Protecting Soliders and Mothers: The Political Origins of Social Policy in the United States* (Cambridge: Harvard University Press, 1992). On Black achievements, see, for example, Sterling Stuckey, *Slave Culture: Nationalist Theory and the Foundations of Black America* (New York: Oxford University Press, 1987); Henry Louis Gates, "The Trope for a New Negro and the Reconstruction of the Image of the Black," *Representations* 24 (1988): 129–55; Wilson Moses, *The Golden Age of Black Nationalism, 1820–1925* (New York: Oxford University Press, 1988); and Eric Sundquist, *To Wake the Nations: Race in the Making of American Literature* (Cambridge: Harvard University Press, 1993). On the working classes, see, for example, Herbert Gutman, *Work, Culture, and Society in Industrializing America* (New York: Vintage, 1977); Alan Trachtenberg, *The Incorporation of America* (New York: Hill and Wang, 1982); David Montgomery, *The Fall of the House of Labor: The Workplace, the State, and American Labor Activism, 1865–1925* (Cambridge: Cambridge University Press, 1987); and Wai Chee Dimock and Michael T. Gilmore, eds., *Rethinking Class: Literary Studies and Social Formations* (New York: Columbia University Press, 1994).

22. I have in mind here, especially, Stefan Collini's account of the emergence of British sociology from the shards of British idealism, Anthony Giddens's tracing of sociological origins to the Enlightenment philosophers, and Harry Elmer Barnes's

treatment of the elaborate social planning of the Greeks. Barnes's own analyses are as detailed and comprehensive as any that come after them. See Collini, "Idealism," 9–10, 25, 48; Giddens, "Origins," 722–23, 726–27; and Barnes, *Introduction*, 1–78.

23. This is a paraphrase by Weber's editors in *From Max Weber*, ed. and trans. H. H. Gerth and C. Wright Mills (New York: Oxford University Press, 1946), 17.

24. This point is also brought home to us by René Girard, *Violence and the Sacred*, trans. Patrick Gregory (Baltimore: Johns Hopkins University Press, 1977).

Chapter One
Sacrificial Arts and Sciences

1. For more on this lineage, see Anthony Giddens, *Central Problems in Social Theory: Action, Structure and Contradiction in Social Analysis* (Berkeley: University of California Press, 1986), 240ff., and "Classical Social Theory and the Origins of Modern Sociology," *American Journal of Sociology* 81, no. 4 (1974): 703–29.

2. Peter Berger, *The Sacred Canopy: Elements of a Sociological Theory of Religion* (New York: Anchor, 1969), 116–17.

3. The gravity of the dangers these social scientists imagined issuing from modern interdependence is exemplified by the worry of one of F. H. Giddings's students that producers can fill their milk cartons or egg crates with anything and escape detection, since no one in an impersonal marketplace knows the ultimate source of consumable goods. See James Williams, *An American Town* (New York: James Kempster, 1906), 191–93. One wonders what Williams would have made of the postmodern letter bomb.

4. Thomas Haskell, *The Emergence of Professional Social Science: The American Social Science Association and the Nineteenth-Century Crisis of Authority* (Urbana: University of Illinois Press, 1977), 29; Max Weber, "Science as Vocation," in *From Max Weber*, ed. and trans. H. H. Gerth and C. Wright Mills (New York: Oxford University Press, 1946), 155; and Georg Simmel, *On Individuality and Social Forms*, ed. and trans. Donald Levine (Chicago: University of Chicago Press, 1971), 13. See also James Beniger, *The Control Revolution: Technological and Economic Origins of the Information Society* (Cambridge: Harvard University Press, 1986), 1–6.

5. Haskell, *Emergence*, 40.

6. Fredric Jameson, "The Vanishing Mediator: Narrative Structure in Max Weber," in *New German Critique* 1 (Winter 1973): 61.

7. I am reminded here of Frank Manuel's observation: "Theorizing about the nature of the gods, even other people's gods, has rarely if ever been an indifferent subject pursued out of pure scientific curiosity." *The Eighteenth Century Confronts the Gods* (Cambridge: Harvard University Press, 1959), 21. He goes on to describe the struggle of Protestant Deists "to invent a commonsense rationale for the growth of the multifarious burdensome superstitious ceremonials of all organized priesthoods, among the heathen, savage and civil, in Judaism, and in Christianity . . . to explain the pollution of what was originally the adoration of a benign God with bloody sacrifices of animals, and fellow men" (62). One such explanation was Pierre Bayle's revision of ancient sacrifice, which serves as Manuel's epigraph to chapter 1. "I have often said that Paganism was nothing but a traffic or a banking

operation between the gods and men. People attached themselves to the ceremonies of this religion in the hope of acquiring temporal goods and of turning away evils which might hurt either their persons or their harvest. . . . It was as if they were making loans at a high interest rate" (13).

8. William James, *The Varieties of Religious Experience: A Study in Human Nature* (New York: Longmans, Green, 1902), 462, 501–3. James's view of religion as an individual and "personal" phenomenon, largely explains my decision to focus on other writers.

9. Victor Turner continues, "I am trying to make sense of the customs, values, norms, concepts, forms of social organization, and other institutions in forming the behavior from which arises the sacrificial process." Turner's formulation, based partly on a study by Allan Hanson, is set forth in the wonderful essay "Sacrifice as Quintessential Process: Prophylaxis or Abandonment," *History of Religions* 16 (February 1977): 190 and passim.

10. Georg Simmel, "Exchange," in *Georg Simmel on Individuality and Social Forms*, ed. and trans. Donald Levine (1900, in German; reprint, Chicago: University of Chicago Press, 1971), 53. Simmel's theories on exchange appeared in the *American Journal of Sociology* from the late 1890s. The March 1900 issue (5, no. 5, 577–603), for instance, featured another version of Simmel on exchange, translated by Albion Small. Entitled "A Chapter in the Philosophy of Value," the article opens with Simmel's characterization of value as accruing "only at the price of a sacrifice; while from the opposite point of view this sacrifice appears as a good to be enjoyed, and the object in question, on the contrary, as a sacrifice" (577).

11. Review of William Benjamin Smith's *The Color Line: A Brief in Behalf of the Unborn, American Journal of Sociology* 11 (November 1905): 574.

12. See Nathaniel S. Shaler, *The Neighbor: The Natural History of Human Contacts* (Boston: Houghton Mifflin, 1904); Edward A. Ross, *Social Control: A Survey of the Foundations of Order* (New York: Macmillan, 1901); and Simon N. Patten, *The Theory of Social Forces* (Philadelphia: American Academy of Political and Social Science, 1895), 143. Not coincidentally, Patten introduces his concept of "pain" versus "pleasure" economies in this book.

13. René Girard, *Violence and the Sacred*, trans. Patrick Gregory (Baltimore: Johns Hopkins University Press, 1977), 4, 30, 318.

14. Arnold Van Gennep, *The Rites of Passage*, trans. Monika B. Vizedom and Gabrielle L. Caffee (1909; reprint, Chicago: University of Chicago Press, 1960).

15. Williams, *An American Town*, 11. And see the chapter entitled "Religious Activity," 227–40.

16. Giddens, *Central Problems in Social Theory*, 7, 111–15. See also Jeffrey Alexander's *Neo-Functionalism* (Beverly Hills: Sage, 1985), for a valuable account of the history and resurgence of functionalist ideas in social scientific theory.

17. As one sociologist notes in a survey of functionalist approaches in the field, "there is substantial basis to the charge that functional theories tend to be conservative in their implications. . . . questioning the contribution made by elements for the maintenance of a system is not likely to generate much appreciation for radical or revolutionary forces in a society." Mark Abrahamson, *Functionalism* (New Jersey: Prentice-Hall, 1978), 49. Abrahamson emphasizes the historic centrality of functionalism in sociology. Kingsley Davis's 1959 presidential address at the

American Sociological Association, according to Abrahamson, claimed "that whatever types of analyses were non-functional were also non-sociological" (50). Abrahamson goes on to highlight the varieties of functionalist thought, citing examples from classical works (Comte, Marx, Durkheim), anthropology (Malinowski, Evans-Pritchard, Radcliffe-Brown), and modern theory (Parsons, Merton). He characterizes functionalism as a Kuhnian "paradigm" that dominated sociology up to the mid-twentieth century and concludes that the profession has since become "a multi-paradigm discipline" (52–3). The work of Jeffrey C. Alexander testifies to the ongoing vitality of functionalist thought. See his edited collection *Neo-Functionalism*, which opens with a later ASA talk (1975) that proclaims, "There are no functionalists under thirty years old!"—a testimonial the volume is designed to disprove (7). For more on the specific anthropological history of these issues, see George W. Stocking, ed., *Functionalism Historicized: Essays on British Social Anthropology* (Madison: University of Wisconsin Press, 1984), particularly Stocking's introduction, 3–9. See also, Stocking's essay "Radcliffe-Brown and British Social Anthropology," 131–91, where he comments, "Malinowski cast himself as the 'humble craftsman' of functionalism, against Radcliffe-Brown's black-caped 'High Priest' exorcising demons with black magic formuli. In truth, both of them were functionalists with minor divergencies." He goes on to categorize functional analysis by way of four prominent concepts in their work: "use and utility, mutual dependence," the "satisfaction" of "biological needs," and "cultural imperatives" (174).

18. Jameson, "Vanishing Mediator," 62, 61.

19. Fredric Jameson, *Postmodernism: or, The Cultural Logic of Late Capitalism* (Durham, N.C.: Duke University Press, 1991), 210, 188.

20. The same can be said for Bourdieu's "Belief and the Body," which recalls Durkheim's descriptions of the elaborate circumscription of appetite in a Jewish orthodox home. See Lukes, *Emile Durkheim, His Life and Work: A Historical and Critical Study* (New York: Penguin, 1977), 39–44. And see Lukes's valuable guide to Durkheim's influence in his time, chapter 20, 392–409.

21. Jameson, *Postmodernism*, 199, 190; "Vanishing Mediator," 71.

22. For recent critiques of New Historicism that follow turn-of-the-century interpretations, see H. Avram Veeser, ed., *The New Historicism* (New York: Routledge, 1989). I view the various representations of sacricial ideology in my study as implicit critiques of the consumer idealism articulated by Williams and Patten, among others.

23. *Postmodernism*, 356; and "Vanishing Mediator," 76.

24. Simmel, "Exchange," 44.

25. Georg Simmel, "The Poor" (1908), reprinted in *On Individuality and Social Forms*, 154–55.

26. Georg Simmel, "Fashion" (1904), reprinted in *On Individuality and Social Forms*, 310.

27. Georg Simmel, "The Miser and the Spendthrift" (1907), reprinted in *On Individuality and Social Forms*, 180.

28. Georg Simmel, "Prostitution" (1907), reprinted in *On Individuality and Social Forms*, 122.

29. Emile Durkheim, *Suicide: A Study in Sociology*, trans. John A. Spaulding and George Simpson (1897; reprint, New York: Free Press, 1966), 251.

30. William Robertson Smith, *Lectures on the Religion of the Semites: The Fundamental Institutions* (1889; reprint, New York: Ktav, 1969), 435–6.

31. Quoted in Dominick LaCapra, *Emile Durkheim: Sociologist and Philosopher* (Ithaca, N.Y.: Cornell University Press, 1972), 28–29. Also relevant is Durkheim's account of the relative Jewish immunity to suicide in chapter 2 of *Suicide*. "Primitive in certain respects," Durkheim writes, "in others he is an intellectual and man of culture. He thus combines the advantage of the severe discipline characteristic of small and ancient groups with the benefits of the intense culture enjoyed by our great societies. He has all the intelligence of modern man without sharing his despair" (168).

32. Franklin Henry Giddings, *The Principles of Sociology: An Analysis of the Phenomena of Association and of Social Organization* (New York: Macmillan, 1896), 347.

33. John Franklin Crowell, *The Logical Process of Social Development* (New York: Henry Holt, 1898), 6, 10.

34. W.E.B. Du Bois, *The Dusk of Dawn*, in *Du Bois: Writings*, ed. Nathan Huggins (New York: Library of America, 1986), 678.

35. The "counterfeit" offering of Baudelaire's protagonist can be understood as a direct offshoot of the deceptive sacrificial practices described by Robertson Smith and others (discussed below). These ancient worshipers offer fraudulent substitutes in the hope that the gods won't notice, and sometimes (like the Carthaginians) suffer the consequences. Derrida's account of Baudelaire's story, which includes a reading of Mauss on the gift, appears in *Given Time: I. Counterfeit Money*, trans. Peggy Kamuf (Chicago: University of Chicago Press, 1992). My quotations are from 142, 134–35, 121–23, 125. Derrida's notion of "pure gift" recalls the theory advanced by Lewis Hyde in *The Gift: Imagination and the Erotic Life of Property* (New York: Random House, 1979). Hyde also implies that sacrifice is a form of social regulation, a containing function that he contrasts with the magical properties of gift. Hyde's ideal is artistic creativity, which he portrays as a "protected gift-sphere." Art is an "un-reckoned, positive reciprocity," more or less opposed to a "reckoned, negative reciprocity" identified with the marketplace (274–75). Among the many inspired passages in Hyde's book is the ending, which reproduces part of Pablo Neruda's essay "Childhood and Poetry." Neruda describes a boyhood exchange, "a marvellous white toy sheep" for "a pine cone opened full of odor and resin." Neruda comments, "this small and mysterious exchange of gifts remained inside me also, deep and indestructible, giving my poetry light" (281–82). Is it accidental or functional that Neruda's exchange leaves him with a sheep, an object that carries the sacramental, historical, and magical residue of sacrificial convention?

36. Friedrich Nietzsche, *On the Genealogy of Morals*, ed. and trans. Walter Kaufmann and R. J. Hollingdale (New York: Vintage, 1969), 61.

37. Hermann L. Strack, *The Jew and Human Sacrifice. Human Blood and Jewish Ritual: An Historical and Sociological Inquiry*, trans. Henry Blanchamp (first pub. in German, 1891, London: Cope and Fenwick, 1909), x, ix. Strack's book had a very wide readership: following its first printing in 1891, it went through eight editions before 1909.

38. Strack's book is complemented by a less merciful example from contemporary French scholarship, Leon Bloy's *Le Salut par les juifs* (Paris: Mercure de France, 1905–6), cited by Derrida in *Given Time: I. Counterfeit Money*. Jews, in

Bloy's analysis, are perpetrators of an "algebra of turpitude called *Credit* [which] has definitively replaced the old *Honor*, which was all chivalrous souls needed to accomplish everything." Bloy continues, "the living and merciful WORD of the Christians, that used to suffice for fair transactions, was once again *sacrificed*, in all the commerce of injustice, to rigid WRITING that is incapable of forgiveness" (101).

39. See Georges Bataille, "Sacrificial Mutililation and the Severed Ear of Vincent Van Gogh," in *Visions of Excess: Selected Writings, 1927–1939* (Minneapolis: University of Minnesota Press, 1985), 61–72 especially. This particular essay was written between 1927 and 1930.

40. Quoted in Theodore Porter, "The Death of the Object," in *Modernist Impulses in the Human Sciences 1870–1930*, ed. Dorothy Ross (Baltimore: Johns Hopkins University Press, 1994), 144–45.

41. Max Weber, *The Protestant Ethic and the Spirit of Capitalism*, trans. Talcott Parsons (1904–5; reprint, New York: Scribners, 1930), 51.

42. Quoted in Jeffrey Alexander, *Structure and Meaning: Relinking Classical Sociology* (New York: Columbia University Press, 1989), 107. As a major contemporary theorist interested in the relationship between classical sociological theory and religion, Alexander is rather unique. Recall that Alexander has also written on functionalism, both in its turn-of-the-century form and in its later variants.

43. Weber was alluding to a known source (possibly Durkheim?), because he enclosed the phrase in quotes without a precise reference.

44. In his introduction to the 1922 edition of Weber's *Sociology of Religion*, trans. Ephraim Fischoff (New York: Free Press), xxvii, Talcott Parsons doubts that Weber ever read Durkheim's *Elementary Forms* (or anything else of Durkheim's). In *The Stucture of Social Action: A Study in Social Theory with Reference to a Group of Recent European Writers* (New York: McGraw-Hill, 1937), 669–77, Parsons concludes that there was "no trace whatever of mutual influence," but affirms striking correspondences between their respective accounts of religion.

45. Edward A. Ross, *Sin and Society: An Analysis of Latter-Day Iniquity* (Boston: Houghton Mifflin, 1907), 6, 33.

46. Simon N. Patten, *The New Basis of Civilization* (New York: Macmillan, 1907), 150, 153, 155.

47. Nearly every sociologist writing at this time, from Franklin Giddings to Max Weber, makes reference to Robertson Smith and/or to Mauss and Hubert. Simmel is an exception to this rule, but then, his writings contain few references whatsoever. As far as my literary authors are concerned, Melville, James, Norris, and possibly Stein are most likely to have been familiar with the contemporary literature on sacrifice, and all were sufficiently steeped in the biblical tradition upon which it was based. Du Bois, of course, also knew the classic sociology.

48. Emile Durkheim, *The Elementary Forms of the Religious Life*, trans. Joseph Ward Swain (1915; reprint, New York: Free Press, 1965), 380–83.

49. This could be seen from the psychoanalytic point of view as the human attempt to "keep" God. God is dead, *"save in me,"* a regular instance in the larger procedure of mourning—a ritual whose great significance for Durkheim is obvious, and possibly more layered than has heretofore been recognized. Properly conceived from Durkheim's perspective, the psychoanalytic "me" would require re-

conceptualization as the sociological "we." See Nicolas Abraham and Maria Torok, *The Wolf Man's Magic Word*, trans. Barbara Johnson (Minneapolis: University of Minnesota Press, 1986), 16–17. This passage is cited by Derrida in *Given Time*, 129.

50. Quoted in LaCapra, *Durkheim*, 287–88.

51. Lukes quotes from letters in which Durkheim describes the importance of Smith's work. See *Durkheim*, 450–51ff.

52. Max Horkheimer and Theodor W. Adorno, *Dialectic of Enlightenment*, trans. John Cumming (New York: Continuum, 1987; orig. English trans. 1944), 43–80. Quotation is from 50.

53. Smith is credited with having modernized and improved the *Encyclopedia*, by enlisting authors whose reputations were based on their progressive and scholarly views. At the same time, Smith worked to expand the *Encyclopedia*'s readership by encouraging its mass, international distribution (extending to America) and lowering its price. For more on Smith's work with the *Encyclopedia*, see T. O. Beidelman, *W. Robertson Smith and the Sociological Study of Religion* (Chicago: University of Chicago Press, 1974), 23–26. Smith's renown as a Bible scholar is confirmed by the fact that he was twice (in 1879 and in 1880) offered a chair of Hebrew at Harvard during the course of his Aberdeen heresy trial.

54. Smith is quoted in Robert Alun Jones, "Robertson Smith and James Frazer on Religion," in *Functionalism Historicized*, 31–58. This particular quotation is from 37–38. See also in this volume, George Stocking's "Dr. Durkheim and Mr. Brown," 106–30; for an account of Durkheim's impact on comparative sociology at Cambridge.

55. Quoted in Beidelman, *W. Robertson Smith*, 33.

56. See the essay by J.H.M. Beattie in M.F.C. Bourdillon and Meyer Fortes, eds., *Sacrifice* (New York: Academic Press, 1980), 39

57. In addition to Durkheim's *Elementary Forms*, cited above, see also the discussion of E. E. Evans-Pritchard in *Nuer Religion* (Oxford: Oxford University Press, 1956), 272–86.

58. William Robertson Smith, "Sacrifice," in *Encyclopedia Britannica*, 9th ed. (1875–80), 21: 133.

59. Shaler, *The Neighbor*, 435–36. Shaler's book, and this scene in particular, will be considered in detail in chapter 4 below.

60. Léon Bing, *Do or Die* (New York: HarperCollins, 1992), 24–25.

61. See the dazzling speech on "the things worth dying for" in *Do or Die*, 120–27.

62. *The Usual Suspects*, an extraordinary postmodern detective drama directed by Bryan Singer (1995), provides another striking formulation of these concerns. A variation on the classic film-noir genre, *The Usual Suspects* blurs the line between reality and fiction. One might read the film's aim as the deliberate heightening of a detective film convention. For film noir takes an ironic approach to the usual detective morality play, where a readily distinguishable good always triumphs over evil. The characteristic gloom of its scenes complicates this normative divide. Film noir insists that good and evil are inseparable, though it offers stable characters and plot lines sufficiently clear to resolve most of the moral ambiguity it arouses. *The Usual Suspects* offers little in the way of stability or clarity. One sign that moral

absolutes have been further complicated is the film's technical innovations in perspective. While some scenes are bathed in light, the film affords little faith in what's visible. Often the viewer is wrenched around by a camera that offers so many angles that it's impossible to tell what has been revealed. In the bungled parking garage robbery, for instance, McManus's gun is the pivot for the viewer's darting glances. We shift from one crook to another, as uncertain about what the gang is after as we are about where the greatest danger lies. And there is the scene where Keaton returns, in the company of Kint/Soyzay, to the apartment (or law office?) of his girlfriend just before "the big heist." He looks down from a balcony to see her engrossed in paperwork with an older (wiser?) version of herself. The girlfriend doesn't look up, and Keaton leaves without establishing eye contact. A minute later, the girlfriend stares up at the empty balcony. Are we to read this as an implicit exchange, her retrospective acknowledgment of his presence? Are we to read these communications to blind profiles and empty spaces as confirmations of the ephemerality of human connection in this world? Or is the scene meant to highlight a bond so deep that she can't bear to see him go and prefers to confront his having been. For the scene may be tapping into the same nostalgia for lost connection that drives the dominant obsession with Kayser Soyzay.

Like the works that I analyze in this book, *The Usual Suspects* is a narrative about a narrative. It is told by a physically crippled, rhetorical wizard, aptly named Verbal Kint. Kint, it turns out, is not only eloquent but remarkably inventive (and this includes his cripple impersonation). At the film's end, we learn that his story has been woven from whatever happened to have caught his eye in the police interrogation office: a Kobayashi coffee mug supplied the name of the story's hit man; a bulletin board made in Quartet, Illinois, spurred the "reminiscence" on time spent in a barbershop quartet (in Illinois, of course), and so on. This plot of a plot of a plot leaves the viewer with a heap of questionable fragments. Only one thing is certain, that the soft-spoken charmer Kint (the lyrical, criminal-innocent with an incredible eye for detail, who even resembles Huckleberry Finn in certain respects) is in all likelihood the story's demonic mastermind, Kayser Soyzay. Kint has already foreclosed potential skepticism on this point. As he warns in the film's most menacing line, "The greatest trick the devil ever pulled was convincing the world he didn't exist." In the last scene, Kint lurches down the street, dragging his shriveled foot, his clawlike hand held at its usual gut level, as if to emphasize what it can't protect. The camera pans to the sidewalk sea of legs, striding forward: the cripple shuffles, now one among many. "Why are we down here?" we ask, and in the second that it takes to ask the question, we know the answer. Suddenly, magically, the crippled foot straightens, the claw becomes a hand. "Kobayashi" pulls up in an expensive car, sporting a slightly servile grin, and we recognize the man who steps into it as Kint/Soyzay.

This is not the "usual" suspense and intrigue of detective films. *The Usual Suspects* betrays the larger sense of mysterious social interconnectedness that is common to all the thinkers in this book. And it is also consistent with the social scientific ideas about God that we have been analyzing, particularly those that stress his danger—because he is near, and because he is not; because we think we understand him, and because we know we do not. Kint makes the connection between God and Soyzay explicit, in quoting his fellow criminal Keaton: "I don't believe in God but I'm afraid of him." "Well I believe in God," Kint adds, "and the only thing that scares me is Kayser Soyzay." Whether he is the Devil or God, Kayser Soyzay represents a lost principle of kinship. He is identified throughout with essentialism. As Verbal Kint declares early on, "A man can't change what he is; he can convince anyone he's someone else except for himself." Kint/Soyzay takes everything personally. His criminal kingdom runs on a principle of guilt by (blood) association. According to the film's legend, Soyzay's career begins when a mob breaks into his home and threatens his family. Soyzay retaliates with a killing spree. "He kills their parents' family and their parents' friends, he burns their houses, their stores, and everyone knows. He becomes a myth, a spook story that criminals tell their kids." Soyzay's genius and fiendishness is to "know everything" about the people he deals with. At the same time, he remains, like a mystifying sacrificial deity, completely unknown, except to those he kills. To know him is a death sentence. Soyzay's criminal sidekick reminds the assembled criminal crew he wants to dominate, "Mr. Soyzay is very real and very determined," and then proceeds to highlight what might be done to this one's "uncle" or that one's "nephew." The principle of Soyzay's power is to have no kin: "One cannot be betrayed if he has no people." This seems the clear motivation behind Soyzay's most terrible act: before turning on the mob that has seized his wife and children, Soyzay wipes them out himself. Kint's comment: "You have to have the will to do what the other guy won't. He showed those men of will what will really was." Kayser Soyzay kills his whole family, not only to display his determination, but to make himself invulnerable. Without kin or friends, his line is pure credit.

Kayser Soyzay is necessary: to the postmodern film audience as well as to the characters in the film. Like a God, Kayser Soyzay is revered in part for his mythic violence. The final frame, which pictures him chauffeured away by his devilish assistant, is supposed to be satisfying. He may be cruel, but meaning is all on his side. Kint/Soyzay lives in a layered, intentionalist world, where every act is traceable to a culpable human being. The world of the film's police, in contrast, is reductive and commonsensical. Theirs is a society of modern interdependence, of accidental connections without larger significance. As Verbal says, "To a cop things are simple. There's no mystery, no arch criminal behind it all." The detectives are not interested in generating meaning; their concern is the explanation of a limited series of events. *The Usual Suspects* is not simply another romantic celebration of criminality as a richer approach to experience. But there *is* a powerfully simple message at the film's center: the dangers hidden in an exaggerated nostalgia for meaningful social ties.

63. Smith, "Sacrifice," 134.

64. Edward B. Tylor, *Primitive Culture*, 7th ed., 2 vols. in one (1871; reprint, New York: Brentano's, 1924), 375.

65. Henri Hubert and Marcel Mauss, *Sacrifice: Its Nature and Functions*, trans. W. D. Halls (1898; reprint, Chicago: University of Chicago Press, 1964), 8.

66. Smith, "Sacrifice," 135.

67. For more on Tylor's profile among anthropologists, contemporary and subsequent, see Michael Izard and Pierre Smith, *Between Belief and Transgression: Structuralist Essays in Religion, History, and Myth*, trans. John Leavitt (Chicago: University of Chicago Press, 1982), 11, 17, 45–46.

68. These quotations, from Hyman and Frazer, respectively, can be found in Jones's "Robertson Smith and James Frazer," 38–39.

69. Sir James Frazer, *The Dying God*, vol. 3 of *The Golden Bough: A Study in Magic and Religion* (1890; reprint, London-MacMillan, 1911), 21–23.

70. Frazer, *The Scapegoat*, vol. 9 of *The Golden Bough*, 407.

71. I find it revealing that late-twentieth-century America, which has experienced a rash of sacrificial actions, underwritten by a reinvigoration of sacrificial-type thinking, has also seen a renewal of debates over capital punishment.

72. I want to emphasize the historical significance of Mauss and Hubert's *Sacrifice*, its saturation with the preoccupations of a late-nineteenth-century intellectual agenda. "Essay on the Nature and Function of Sacrifice" was first published in the "Année Sociologique" in 1899, while the more renowned "Essay on the Gift" (by Mauss alone) did not appear until over twenty-five years later (first published in 1925 in the same journal). While Mauss's later theory of gift exchange took priority among subsequent social scientific analysts, the earlier theory had a special prominence during the formative period of sociological development.

73. For more on historicist thought, see R. G. Collingwood, *The Idea of History* (Oxford: Oxford University Press, 1946), and for more recent treatments, on turn-of-the-century America, see my *The Power of Historical Knowledge: Narrating the Past in Hawthorne, James, and Dreiser* (Princeton: Princeton University Press, 1988), esp. chapters 2 and 6; and Brook Thomas, *The New Historicism and Other Old-Fashioned Topics* (Princeton: Princeton University Press, 1991).

74. W.E.B. Du Bois, *The Souls of Black Folk*, in *Three Negro Classics*, ed. John Hope Franklin (1903; reprint, New York: Avon, 1965), 238.

75. Gertrude Stein, *3-Lives* (New York: Vintage, 1909), 13, 15.

76. Smith, *Religion of the Semites*, 195.

77. Stein appears to have been more of a reader than is usually acknowledged by her critics. Otto Weininger's *Sex and Character*, an anti-Semitic and homophobic social scientific study by a Jewish homosexual, was a special favorite. Stein called it her "bible." This makes the recent discovery that Stein nominated Adolf Hitler for a Nobel Prize legible from a less than ironic angle (see the *Jewish Daily Forward*, April 1996). Stein could also have come across Mauss and Hubert, or Hermann Strack's *The Jews and Human Sacrifice*. Both were widely known among European intellectuals and very much in line with her interests.

78. In *The Dark End of the Street* (Minneapolis: University of Minnesota Press, 1993), Maria Damon analyzes Stein's relationship to Yiddish language and culture.

79. The term sacrifice was naturally a rallying cry of the American Civil War on both sides. For two especially vivid treatments, one from the southern, the other from the northern point of view, see Augusta Evans, *Macaria or, Altars of Sacrifice* (New York: J. Bradburn, 1864); and Jeremiah Taylor, *The Sacrifice Consumed: Life of Edward Hamilton Brewer* (Boston: Henry Hoyt, 1863).

80. Stephen Crane, *The Red Badge of Courage* (Indianapolis: Bobbs-Merrill, 1964), 1.

81. Terry Mulcaire elaborates the relationship between Crane's war novel and modern industrial development in "Progressive Visions of War in *The Red Badge of Courage* and *Principles of Scientific Management*," *American Quarterly* 43, no. 1 (1991): 46–72.

82. Smith, *Religion of the Semites*, 344. Hubert and Mauss, *Sacrifice*, 43; Durkheim, *Elementary Forms*, 383.

83. We can recognize something about the contemporary politics revealed by editorial decisions by noting that the second Doubleday and McClure edition of the novel omits this scene but preserves the offensive color coding of McTeague's kitchen ("nigger's hide"). In contrast, the more recent Norton edition restores the humiliation scene but revises (partly; see below) the racial slur.

84. Frank Norris, *McTeague* (1899; reprint, New York: Norton, 1977), 146.

85. See Walter Michaels's reading of *McTeague* in *The Gold Standard and the Logic of Naturalism* (Berkeley: University of California Press, 1987), chapter 4.

86. Smith, "Sacrifice," 138.

87. *McTeague*, in my opinion, provides a near perfect fictional elaboration of Catherine MacKinnon's brilliant theories on female sexuality and commodification. See *Toward a Feminist Theory of the State* (Cambridge: Harvard University Press, 1989).

88. Gilbert Herdt's account of nose-bleeding ceremonies in homoerotic rites of passage among Sambian males in New Guinea provides a valuable register for Norris's portrait of male identity and friendship in *McTeague*. Like Herdt, Norris understands masculinity as earned rather than given. It is not only provisional, in the sense that it is never entirely separated from the pollution of femininity, but is also never fully achieved on its own terms. Norris is well aware of the symbolic importance of orality to masculine rites of passage. It's no accident that Norris's protagonist is a dentist and gains his "one intimate friend," Marcus Schouler, after refusing payment for treating Schouler's ulcerated tooth (6). See *Guardians of the Flutes: Idioms of Masculinity* (New York: McGraw-Hill, 1981), particularly, 203–55. The parallels between Herdt's study and Norris's novel are much richer than this brief exposition can suggest.

89. Bourdieu, *The Logic of Practice*, 69. Bourdieu's phrase is adapted from Proust.

Chapter Two
The Return to Sacrifice in Melville and Others

1. The original manuscript of *Billy Budd* (Houghton Library, Harvard University) contains hints that these images were superimposed in Melville's own mind. Initially, the handsome sailor was identified as "the *white* handsome sailor," but Melville crossed out "white." Apparently, Melville feared that the two figures were so blurred that readers would assume that Billy was Black; he felt the need to specify Billy's racial identity. In the end he seems to have decided he was being heavy-handed. Another emendation on the same page registers a similar concern and outcome: Melville's excision of the word "innate" from the phrase "natural innate regality." Here too, Melville's stress on "inherence" apparently seemed, on second thought, too great. (*Billy Budd, Sailor: An Inside Narrative*, in *Great Short Works of Herman Melville*, ed. Warner Berthoff (New York: Harper and Row, 1969), 430. In this same vein, it is worth noting that among Melville's papers is a letter from Havelock Ellis, dated July 1890, in which Ellis asks Melville "to what races you trace yourself back on father's and on mother's side, and what (if any) *recent strains of foreign blood* you lay claim to?" (my emphasis). Ellis requests the

information, he says, for a book he is writing on "the ancestry of distinguished English and American poets and imaginative writers, with reference to questions of race."

2. As Marcus Rediker points out, eighteenth-century Liverpool "profited . . . handsomely from the sailor's labor that carried commodities to the 'coast of Guinea' to be exchanged for human cargoes." The slave trade proved equally deadly to White sailors and Black captives. *Between the Devil and the Deep Blue Sea: Merchant Seamen, Pirates, and The Anglo-American Maritime World 1700–1750* (Cambridge: Cambridge University Press, 1987), 43–47.

3. Not all of this is hard fact. Merton Sealts notes that Melville's library "included many theological works that were scrapped after his death as unsuitable for resale." The sacrificial accompaniment to that bibliographic bonfire has been a certain critical intelligence. Without unconditional knowledge about the nature of Melville's extraliterary interests, we have tended to disregard the deeper texture of his extraordinarily allusive fiction. See *Clarel*, vol. 12 of *The Writings of Herman Melville* (Evanston, Ill. and Chicago: Northwestern University Press, and Newberry Library, 1991), 611, 721. See also Merton Sealts, *Melville's Reading* (Columbia: University of South Carolina Press, 1988), 87–90, 122. In *Social Darwinism in American Thought* (Boston: Beacon, 1955), Richard Hofstader details the extent to which popularized versions of Darwinian and Spencerian ideas appeared in journals where Melville published his own writings: *Appleton's*, the *Nation*, the *Atlantic Monthly*; see 22–23 ff.

4. Albion Small, *The Origins of Sociology* (New York: Russell and Russell, 1924), 9.

5. Quoted in Barbara Packer, *The Transcendentalists*, in *The Cambridge Literary History of the United States, Prose Writing 1820–1865*, ed. Sacvan Bercovitch (Cambridge: Harvard University Press, 1995), 2:345. Throughout this section: I draw on Packer's fine study, as well as on Daniel Walker Howe's *The Unitarian Conscience* (Cambridge: Harvard University Press, 1979).

6. Henry David Thoreau captures yet another muscular dimension of this vitality by identifying a posture that is peculiarly suited to the apprehension of classics and sacred texts. For this "noble intellectual exercise," which hé calls, "reading in a high sense," "we have to stand on tiptoe." Our minds have to be conditioned to attain the heights of the canon. *Walden and Civil Disobedience* (New York: Penguin Classics, 1983), 149.

7. See John W. Rogerson, *W.M.L. de Wette, Founder of Modern Biblical Criticism: An Intellectual Biography* (Sheffield, England: Sheffield Academic Press, 1992), 109–12 ff.

8. Quoted in Jerry Wayne Brown, *The Rise of Biblical Criticism in America, 1800–1870* (Middletown, Conn.: Wesleyan University Press, 1969), 161.

9. Quoted in Packer, *The Transcendentalists*, 421–22.

10. Quoted in Brown, *Rise of Biblical Criticism*, 159.

11. Sydney E. Ahlstrom, *A Religious History of the American People* (New Haven: Yale University Press, 1972), 602, 599.

12. Much of this discussion is derived from Ahlstrom, *Religious History*, which places Emerson's religious thought in the context of broader changes. See 599–614.

13. Quoted in Lawrence Buell, *New England Literary Culture* (Cambridge: Cambridge University Press, 1986), 167, 177, which provides an illuminating discussion of these issues. See also Giles Gunn, ed., *The Bible and American Arts and Letters* (Philadelphia: Fortress, 1983).

14. Herman Melville, *Typee: A Peep at Polynesian Life* (1846; reprint, New York: Signet, 1964), 242. All subsequent quotations from this edition will appear parenthetically.

15. Consider Melville's complaint in his 1856–57 *Journals*, vol. 15 of *The Writings of Herman Melville*, that Strauss and his compatriot Niebuhr, "have robbed us of the bloom" (Evanston, Ill. and Chicago: Northwestern University Press and Newberry Library, 1989), 97.

16. Self-characterization by David Friedrich Strauss, quoted in Peter C. Hodgson, introduction to *The Life of Jesus, Critically Examined*, trans. George Eliot (1846; reprint, Philadelphia: Fortress, 1972), xvi–xvii.

17. For an account of Strauss's late-nineteenth-century discovery of Schopenhauer, see the introduction to David Friedrich Strauss, *The Christ of Faith and the Jesus of History: A Critique of Schleiermacher's The Life of Jesus*, trans. and intro. Leander Keck (Philadelphia: Fortress, 1977, orig. pub. in German, 1865), xlvi–xlvii.

18. Quoted in Hodgson, introduction to Strauss, *Life of Jesus*, trans., Eliot, xvii.

19. Quoted in notes to Herman Melville, *Moby-Dick, or, The Whale* (1851; reprint, New York: Norton Critical Edition, 1967), 560.

20. This formulation of Strauss's "disappearing minimum" is by de Wette, quoted in Hodgson, introduction to *Life of Jesus*, xlii.

21. Melville's copy of the work of this prominent theologian is in the Houghton Library. William Rounseville Alger, *The Solitudes of Nature and of Man: Or, The Loneliness of Human Life* (Boston: Roberts Brothers, 1865), 381.

22. Daniel Dorchester, *Christianity in the United States: From the First Settlement Down to the Present Time* (New York: Hunt and Eaton, 1889), 660.

23. Max Scheler, *Ressentiment*, trans. William W. Holdheim (New York: Free Press, 1961), 74, 83.

24. Arthur Penrhyn Stanley, *Sinai and Palestine: In Connection with Their History* (New York: W. J. Widdleton, 1865), vii, x. Melville owned a copy of this version of Stanley's book.

25. This is all highly suggestive for Melville's *Pierre* (1852), which might be said to have anticipated Stanley's theories on sacred geography.

26. Arthur Penrhyn Stanley, *The History of the Jewish Church*, 2 vols. (New York: Scribner's, 1862), 1: xvi, 129–31.

27. Quoted in the notes to *Clarel*, 511.

28. In *Social Darwinism in American Thought*, Richard Hofstader observes that "the rise of Bible criticism and comparative religion . . . prepared many Americans for the acceptance of Darwinism" (14). "James Freeman Clarke's *Ten Great Religions*," Hofstader writes, "a liberal study of world creeds, ran through twenty-two editions in the fifteen years after its first appearance in 1871," 14–15.

29. James Freeman Clarke, *Ten Great Religions: An Essay in Comparative Theology* (Boston: James Osgood, 1871), 489–90.

30. For the range of sacrificial practices in *Ten Great Religions*, see 91, 134–35, 175, 217–18, 252–53, 297, 334–35.

31. Berdmore Compton, *Sermons on The Catholic Sacrifice and Subjects Connected with It* (London: Rivingtons, 1875), 11.

32. Matthew Arnold, *Literature And Dogma: An Essay towards a Better Apprehension of the Bible* (New York: Macmillan, 1881), 60, 46. Melville's annotated copy of this edition is in the Houghton Library, Harvard University.

33. H. Clay Trumbull, *The Blood Covenant: A Primitive Rite and Its Bearings on Scripture* (New York: Scribners, 1885), 3–4, 5.

34. George Fitzhugh, *Sociology for the South, or, The Failure of Free Society* (1854), reprinted in *Antebellum*, ed. Harvey Wish (New York: Putnam's 1960), 83, 90.

35. George Fitzhugh, *Cannibals All, or, Slaves without Masters* (1857), reprinted in *Antebellum*, 120, 129.

36. Annual Report of the Board of State Charities of Massachusetts (Boston: Wright and Potter, 1867), 3: xxi. For more on the origins of American sociology, see L. L. and Jessie Bernard, *Origins of American Sociology* (New York: Thomas Crowell, 1943); Floyd House, *The Development of Sociology* (New York: McGraw-Hill, 1936); Herman Schwendinger and Julia Schwendinger, *The Sociologists of the Chair* (New York: Basic, 1974); Thomas Haskell, *The Emergence of Professional Social Science: The American Social Science Association and the Nineteenth-Century Crisis of Authority* (Urbana: University of Illinois Press, 1977); Henrika Kucklick, "Restructuring the Past: Toward an Appreciation of the Social Context of Social Science," *Sociological Quarterly* 21 (Winter 1980): 5–21; and "The Organization of Social Science in the United States," *American Quarterly* 28 (1976): 124–41; and Dorothy Ross, *The Origins of American Social Science* (New York: Cambridge University Press, 1991).

37. *Journal of Social Science* (Boston: Damrell and Upham), nos. 3–27.

38. Quoted in Dwight Bozeman, "Joseph Le Conte: Organic Science and a 'Sociology for the South,'" *Journal of Southern History* 39, no. 4 (1973): 579. My analysis here is indebted to Bozeman's essay. See also Hofstader on Le Conte in *Social Darwinism in American Thought*, 28–29.

39. Harriet Beecher Stowe, *Uncle Tom's Cabin* (1852; reprint, New York: Pocket, 1963), xix. Subsequent references are to the Penguin edition (New York, 1981).

40. See Philip Fisher's account of the different realms of the novel in *Hard Facts: Setting and Form in the American Novel* (New York: Oxford University Press, 1985), 87–127.

41. See Booker T. Washington's *Up from Slavery*, in *Three Negro Classics* (New York: Avon, 1965), especially chapter 3, "The Struggle for an Education"; and Du Bois's parable "A Mild Suggestion," in *Du Bois's Writings*, ed. Nathan Huggins (New York: Library of America, 1986), 1138–41.

42. It's telling that Henry James's reformist zealot in *The Bostonians*, Miss Birdseye, has trouble telling them apart. "When causes were embodied in foreigners (what else were the Africans?), they were certainly more appealing" (1886; reprint, New York: Penguin 1978), 26. For some suggestive psychological and political analysis, in historical perspective, of slave consciousness among the American lower classes, see Richard Sennett and Jonathan Cobb, *The Hidden Injuries of Class*

(New York: Vintage, 1972). In a chapter called "Freedom," the authors ask, "What does it mean to be free, in a class society? To be unfree . . . has two meanings: the simpler one is that men cannot do what they want because class circumstances pen them in; the more complicated one involves the idea of compulsion . . . where the responsibility of self-validation then channels consciousness into the path of sacrifice and betrayal" (220). It is the latter form that is especially relevant to *Billy Budd*.

43. See my earlier analysis of Melville's story, part of which appears here in revised form, "Cataloging the Creatures of the Deep: *Billy Budd, Sailor* and the Rise of Sociology," in *Boundary* 2 17 (Spring 1990): 272–304, reprinted in *Revisionary Interventions into the Americanist Canon*, ed. Donald Pease (Durham, N.C.: Duke University Press, 1994), 272–304.

44. For more on capital-labor conflict and radical activism in this era, see Bruce Nelson's study of Chicago anarchism, *Beyond the Martyrs: a Social History of Chicago's Anarchists, 1870–1900* (New Brunswick: Rutgers University Press, 1988), especially part 3, 175–242. On working-class culture, see Herbert Gutman, *Work, Culture, and Society in Industrializing America: Essays in American Working-Class and Social History* (New York: Vintage, 1974); Alan Trachtenberg, *The Incorporation of America: Culture and Society in the Gilded Age* (New York: Hill and Wang, 1982), chapter 3; David Montgomery, *The Fall of the House of Labor: The Workplace, the State, and American Labor Activism* (Cambridge: Cambridge University Press, 1987); and Alan Dawley, *Struggles for Justice: Social Responsibility and the Liberal State* (Cambridge: Harvard University Press, 1991). See also Carlos Schwantes's study of vagabonds and other social marginals, *Coxey's Army: An American Odyssey* (Lincoln: Nebraska University Press, 1985); and Leah Hannah Fedler, *Unemployed Relief in Periods of Depression: A Study of Measures Adopted in Certain American Cities, 1857 through 1922* (New York: Russell Sage Foundation, 1936). Edward Saveth, in *American Historians and European Immigrants 1875–1925* (New York: Russell and Russell, 1965), analyzes the means by which one prominent intellectual group displaced threats of internal turmoil onto foreign immigrants. Finally, see the following works by historians on the late-nineteenth-century: Philip S. Foner, *History of the Labor Movement in the United States*, vol. 3 (New York: International Publishers, 1972–75); William Appleman Williams, *The Contours of American History* (Cleveland: World, 1961); Thomas C. Cochran and William Miller, *The Age of Enterprise* (New York: Harper Torchbook, 1961); James Weinstein, *The Corporate Ideal in the Liberal State: 1900–1918* (Boston: Beacon, 1968); and Alfred D. Chandler, Jr., *The Visible Hand: The Managerial Revolution in American Business* (Cambridge: Harvard University Press, 1977).

45. Quoted in notes to Herman Melville, *Billy Budd, Sailor: An Inside Narrative, Reading Text and Genetic Text*, ed. Harrison Hayford and Merton Sealts (Chicago: University of Chicago Press, 1962), 196.

46. *Christ of Faith*, Strauss, quoted in introduction, lxxix.

47. Herbert Spencer, *The Study of Sociology* (New York: Appleton, 1873), 15–16.

48. Albion Small, "The Era of Sociology," *American Journal of Sociology* 1 (July 1895): 3, 6, 8. See also F. H. Giddings, "The Relation of Sociology to Other Scientific Studies," *Journal of Social Science* 32 (November 1894): 144–50.

49. Albion Small, quoted in Haskell, *Emergence of Professional Social Science*, 203.

50. Weber was less convinced of the prospects for a "neutral" social science than

has usually been assumed. Indeed, his use of ideal types was an attempt to develop a system of categories that could account for the subjective factor. Weber's "objective" set of ideal concepts were designed to sustain some reflexive recognition of their cultural specificity. See *From Max Weber*, ed. and trans. H. H. Gerth and C. Wright Mills (Oxford: Oxford University Press, 1946), Introduction, "Politics as a Vocation," and "Science as a Vocation." See also, "The Methodology of the Social Sciences," in *Weber: Selections in Translation*, ed. W. G. Runciman, trans. Eric Matthews (Cambridge: Cambridge University Press, 1978). For more analysis of Weber along these lines, see chapter 1 above. As one of the "princes of reason," a key articulator of a social scientific defense for corporate liberalism, Durkheim serves for Herman and Julia Schwendinger as an important European analog for the rise of American social science. See *Sociologists of the Chair*, 70–71, 254–273. Georg Simmel had the most direct impact on American sociology. Albion Small was already translating his essays for *American Journal of Sociology* in the 1890s. See *Georg Simmel: On Individuality and Social Forms*, ed. Donald Levine (Chicago: University of Chicago Press, 1971), Introduction, and chapter 1 above.

51. Beecher, quoted in Haskell, *Emergence of Professional Social Science*, 83. See also Beecher's book on science and religion, *Evolution and Religion* (New York: Fords, Howard and Hulbert, 1885).

52. Paul Starr, *The Social Transformation of American Medicine: The Rise of a Sovereign Profession and the Making of a Vast Industry* (New York: Basic, 1982), 19.

53. Spencer, *Study of Sociology*, 270–71.

54. This is the phrase given to characterize the mind of William Graham Sumner by his first biographer, Harrison E. Starr; (1925) quoted in *Social Darwinism in American Thought*, 54.

55. Miller's description appears in *American Thought: Civil War to World War I* (New York: Holt, Rinehart, and Winston, 1954), xxvi. For more on these other crises, see chapter 1 above.

56. See Harry Elmer Barnes, ed., An Introduction to the History of Sociology (Chicago: University of Chicago Press, 1948), 767ff.

57. Barnes, *History of Sociology*, 787.

58. Albion Small, "The Scope of Sociology," *American Journal of Sociology* 6, no. 3 (1900): 348–49.

59. Horace Bushnell, *Vicarious Sacrifice: Grounded in Principles of Universal Obligation* (1866; reprint, Hicksville, N.Y.: Regina, 1975), 4d.

60. The grounds for this debate were laid in the now classic contest between Ann Douglas's account of sentimental fiction in *The Feminization of American Culture* (New York: Avon, 1977) and Jane Tompkins's competing interpretation in *Sensational Designs: The Cultural Work of American Fiction, 1790–1860* (New York: Oxford University Press, 1985). It has been elaborated in a series of essays collected by Shirley Samuels in *The Culture of Sentiment: Race, Gender, and Sentimentality in Nineteenth-Century America* (New York: Oxford University Press, 1992). See also Richard Brodhead's treatment of Warner in *Cultures of Letters: Scenes of Reading and Writing in Nineteenth-Century America* (New York: Oxford University Press, 1993) and John Guillory's critique of the terms of the debate in *Cultural Capital: The Problem of Literary Canon Formation* (Chicago: University of Chicago Press, 1994), chapter 1.

61. These observations by Victor Branford were made at a professional forum in England, and were later published in "The Founders of Sociology," *American Journal of Sociology* 9/10 (1904–5): 94, 123.

62. Small, "Era of Sociology," 6, 12. Small is quoting Huxley from an essay by Benjamin Kidd published in *Nineteenth Century* (February 1895). Huxley's lectures were being published in American newspapers like the *New York Tribune* during his visit to the United States in 1876. See, Hofstader, *Social Darwinism in American Thought*, 24.

63. Ross draws on the work of Sacvan Bercovitch, whose anthropological account of Puritanism lends itself especially well to her adaptation, and to my own. See, especially, *The American Jeremiad* (Madison: University of Wisconsin Press, 1978) and *The Rites of Assent: Transformations in the Symbolic Construction of America* (New York: Routledge, 1993).

64. Edward A. Ross, *Social Control: A Survey of the Foundations of Order* (New York: Macmillan, 1901), 441, 207.

65. Each volume was dedicated to a certain stage in Ward's career, collecting every essay published within a frame of years. Volume 1 covers 1858–71, that is, from Ward's sixteenth to his thirtieth year. Conceived as part professional history, part autobiography, *Cosmos* testifies most of all to the immensity of Ward's ego. It's hard to imagine a place for God in Ward's crowded "cosmos." Lester Ward, *Glimpses of the Cosmos*, vol. 1 (New York: Putnam's, 1913).

66. Herbert Spencer, *The Principles of Sociology*, 3 vols. (1876–96; reprint, New York: Greenwood, 1975), 3: 173.

67. Spencer, *Study of Sociology*, 312.

68. J. B. Bury, *The Idea of Progress: An Inquiry into Its Growth and Origin* (New York: Macmillan, 1932), 343. Possible avenues for Melville's own acquaintance with Reade's book are 1872 reviews in the *Saturday Review* (October 12) and the *Atheneum* (May 11), both magazines where Melville published, and which he also evidently read with some regularity. See also *Social Darwinism in American Thought* on the extent of Spencer's popularity in the United States among all classes (34–35).

69. Winwood Reade, *The Martyrdom of Man* (1872; reprint, London: Jonathan Cape, 1927), 181.

70. Ralph Waldo Emerson, "Self-Reliance," in *Selections from Ralph Waldo Emerson: An Organic Anthology*, ed. Stephen Whicher (1839–40; reprint, Boston: Houghton Mifflin, 1957), 150.

71. Emerson, "Experience" (1844–45), reprinted in, *Selections from Emerson*, 269.

72. Nathaniel Hawthorne, *The Scarlet Letter* (1850; reprint, New York: Penguin, 1983), 147, 165. Jenny Franchot has done much to illuminate the Catholic implications of that worship in *Roads to Rome: The Antebellum Protestant Encounter with Catholicism* (Berkeley: University of California Press, 1994), 260–69.

73. Harriet Jacobs, *Incidents in the Life of a Slave Girl: Written by Herself* (1861; reprint, Cambridge: Harvard University Press, 1987), 87.

74. See, for example, Michael T. Gilmore on *Moby-Dick* in *American Romanticism and the Marketplace* (Chicago: University of Chicago Press, 1982), 113–

31; Carolyn Porter, "Call Me Ishmael, or How to Make Double-Talk Speak," in *New Essays on Moby-Dick, or, The Whale*, ed. Richard Brodhead (Cambridge: Cambridge University Press, 1986), 73–108; and Jonathan Arac on *Moby-Dick* in *Narrative Forms*, in *The Cambridge History of American Literature, Prose Writing 1820–1865*, ed. Sacvan Bercovitch (New York: Cambridge University Press, 1995), 2: 725–34.

75. Lord Byron, *Hebrew Melodies*, vol. 4 of *The Poetical Works of Lord Byron* (Boston: Little Brown, 1853), 81–82. Melville's copy of this book is in Houghton Library.

76. As I have pointed out, the significance of this rite in *Billy Budd* has not been overlooked by Melville critics. H. Bruce Franklin was among the most persuasive analysts of the sacrifice theme. "After a lifetime of comparing religions," Franklin writes, "Melville sees Calvinism as only an extreme development of Persian sacrifice. He distinguishes neither religion from a sorcerous opiate." *The Wake of the Gods: Melville's Mythology* (Stanford, Calif.: Stanford University Press, 1963), 13. Franklin's is a learned book, which lends credence to the seriousness and breadth of Melville's religious ideas. He was joined by a range of critics, some of them preceding him, such as, William Braswell, Nathalia Wright, Charles Anderson—all of whom offered valuable discussions of Melville's religious and specifically sacrificial designs. None of these readings, however, seeks to elaborate the profound range, whether cultural or interdisciplinary, of those designs. One final critical work deserves mention, Lawrance Thompson's powerful *Melville's Quarrel with God* (Princeton: Princeton University Press, 1952). In Thompson's reading, Melville dedicates his life and work to an impossibility: securing the attention of a God who is "above quarreling with a human being" (6). At a certain midcentury point, according to Thompson, Melville recognizes the absurdity of his aim and turns on God in an impotent rage. He spends the remainder of his career "making a scapegoat of God" (52; see also 5, 12, 124, 423 for the repetition of this claim).

77. The story's narration is an historical pastiche drawn by an inhabitant of late-nineteenth-century America. See the numerous allusions that range throughout the nineteenth century in the notes to the Hayford and Sealts edition. This edition also provides a helpful review of the story's complicated writing and editing history.

78. Stanley, *History of the Jewish Church*, 1:518.

79. Charles Zeublin, "The World's First Sociological Laboratory," *American Journal of Sociology* 4, no. 5 (1899): 585, 586–88.

80. Frank Manuel, *The Prophets of Paris: Turgot, Condorcet, Saint-Simon, Fourier, and Comte* (New York: Harper and Row, 1962), 1, 302.

81. See Geroges LeFébvre, *The French Revolution: From 1793 to 1799*, vol. 2 (New York: Columbia University Press 1964), 347–48.

82. Herman Melville, "The House-Top," in *Selected Poems of Herman Melville*, ed. Robert Penn Warren (1863, reprint, New York: Random House, 1967), 127.

83. Michael Rogin departs from this critical consensus by introducing his chapter on *Billy Budd* with an account of Melville's customhouse experience. See *Subversive Genealogy: The Politics and Art of Herman Melville* (New York: Knopf,

1983), 288–94. Information on what Melville was actually doing during his long tenure at the customhouse remains scant. *Billy Budd* testifies to Melville's deep engagement with the growing diversity of American society and the variety of responses to it, a fascination for cultural difference that is evident throughout his career, from the early anthropological investigations of *Typee*, to the anatomy of forms—philological, religious, philosophical, biological—in *Moby-Dick*. For another view of Melville in the customhouse, see Stanton Garner's "Surviving the Gilded Age: Herman Melville in the Customs Service," *Essays in Arts and Sciences* 15 (June 1986): 1–13.

84. R. Wheatly, "The New York Custom-House," *Harpers Magazine* 69 (June 1884): 47, 49–51, 53, 61.

85. By indicating the significance of this late-nineteenth-century historical and biographical context, I do not mean to argue that Melville set out in *Billy Budd* to write an allegory of contemporary American social change. But Melville knew the impact of the present on any apprehension of the past, a preoccupation that had informed another story published nearly forty years before. In "Benito Cereno" (1854), a narrative set in the eighteenth-century era of slavery, written in a nineteenth-century era split by controversy over slavery, as well as in *Billy Budd*, set in a turbulent late-eighteenth-century context, and written in a time rife with its own class and racial conflict, Melville was obliged to "hold the Present at its worth without being inappreciative of the Past" (*Billy Budd*, 441). Thus, Melville selected an historical-fictional setting for its strong affinities to his present, a distant yet compatible ship society that offered a realm for contemplating freely the exigencies of the late nineteenth century. For Melville, to reconstruct the past was to confront his own era in its full historicity, not as something personal that one "experiences," but as part of previous, and perhaps future, eras. In his overview of *Billy Budd* criticism, Robert Milder cites Melville's "response to contemporary social and political developments" as "among the most promising [avenues] for future investigation." The story, he suggests, illuminates "how social thought is a function of history," revealing "the consciousness of a late-nineteenth-century writer brooding on experience through the ideological cul-de-sacs of his age." *Critical Essays on Melville's Billy Budd, Sailor* ed. Robert Milder (New York: G. K. Hall, 1989), 14–15.

86. Ross, *Social Control*, 244.

87. This is the starting point of Barbara Johnson's essay, "Melville's Fist: The Execution of *Billy Budd*," in *The Critical Difference: Essays in the Contemporary Rhetoric of Reading* (Baltimore: Johns Hopkins University Press, 1980), 79–109.

88. Edward A. Westermarck, *The Origin and Development of the Moral Ideas* (London: Macmillan, 1908), 1:495.

89. Melville owned Lavater's *Essays on Physiognomy*, but his edition has not been identified. This quotation is from *Essays on Physiognomy*, trans. Thomas Holcroft (London: W. Tegg, 1869), 248.

90. Theodore Porter, *The Rise of Statistical Thinking 1820–1900* (Princeton: Princeton University Press, 1986), 37.

91. As Theodore Porter observes, statistical method was "seen as especially valuable for uncovering causal relationships where the individual events are either concealed from view or are highly variable." Statistics became the sphere of liberals

who favored a limited definition of government action at the same time that they advocated intervention to defend selected interests. *Rise of Statistical Thinking,* 3. Francis A. Walker contemplates "Some Results of the Census," in the *Journal of Social Science* 5 (1874): 71–97, and L. L. Bernard and Jessie Bernard describe how sociologists interested in shaping human behavior "into conformity with the best standards and patterns of social organization that they knew . . . developed as methods to this end various types of analysis and measurement." *Origins of Sociology,* 843. See also the section entitled "Early Conception and Promotion of Statistics in the United States" (783–96). For another literary analysis of these issues from a different perspective, see Mark Seltzer, "Statistical Persons," *Diacritics* 17 (Fall 1987): 82–98.

92. John Highman, *Strangers in the Land: Patterns of American Nativism 1860–1925* (New York: Atheneum, 1966), 55.

93. All these quotations from *Public Opinion* between 1886 and 1887 are cited in *Strangers,* 55. Herbert Gutman also notes how "class and ethnic fears and biases combined together to worry elite observers about the diverse worlds below them and to distort gravely their perceptions of these worlds." Gutman quotes John L. Hart, a professor of English at the College of New Jersey, describing the "brute-like" immigrants, who obliged the "more intelligent classes . . . to guard them with police and standing armies, and to cover the land with prisons [and] cages." *In the School-Room* (1879). See Gutman, *Work, Culture and Society,* 72–73.

94. See Hayford and Sealts, *Billy Budd,* 163.

95. Milton Stern, *The Fine Hammered Steel of Herman Melville* (Urbana: University of Illinois Press, 1968), 211.

96. Henry James, *Hawthorne* (1879; reprint, New York: Collier, 1966), 125.

97. Thus, theories of "the end of American innocence" are presented as objective rather than ideological. See, for example, Henry May, *The End of American Innocence: A Study of the First Years of Our Own Time, 1912–1917* (Chicago: Quadrangle, 1964); R. Jackson Wilson, *In Quest of Community: Social Philosophy in the United States, 1860–1920* (New York: Wiley, 1968); and Hofstader, *Social Darwinism.* For an important counterperspective see David F. Noble, *America by Design: Science, Technology, and the Rise of Corporate Capitalism* (New York: Knopf Press, 1977).

98. See, Johnson, *Melville's Fist,* 87.

99. My point here raises the much considered question of Melville's modernity. As Charles Feidelson, for example, has suggested, in *Symbolism in American Literature* (Chicago: University of Chicago Press, 1953), American novelists, and Melville perhaps most of all, are generically closer to twentieth-century modernist writers than to nineteenth-century realists. In my view, the significant task is not to specify the story's generic affinities, but to elaborate the ways in which it destabilizes generic norms. Thus, *Billy Budd* invokes the concrete typologies of realist fiction, as well as the abstract typologies of modernist allegory, on behalf of its interest in the political uses of such categories.

100. Albion Small, *Adam Smith and Modern Sociology: A Study in the Methodology of the Social Sciences* (Chicago: University of Chicago Press, 1907), 80, 125, 83, 187.

101. Small, "Scope of Sociology," 368.

102. The debate over the "sacrificial" claims of Darwinian theory has been revisited powerfully in recent years by the work of Richard Dawkins, who defends a social Darwinist reading of Darwinism, and Stephen J. Gould, who argues, convincingly, against it. See Dawkins's *The Selfish Gene* (Oxford: Oxford University Press, 1976); and Gould's *Ever since Darwin: Reflections in Natural History* (New York: Norton, 1979). Both of these books, in addition to others by Gould that explore these themes, have secured a wide readership. For more on the Darwin/Spencer divide, see chapter 4 below.

103. See Ahlstrom, *Religious History*, 769–72.

104. See chapter 1, especially 18–19ff.

105. Lester Ward, *Dynamic Sociology* (New York: Appleton, 1883), 2: 292–93. Sealts, in *Melville's Reading*, describes Melville's newspaper-reading habits (127–28), which included routine reading of the *Tribune*.

106. Trumbull notes that the sacred importance of the color red extends to other traditions, including Chinese, Native American, and Indian.

107. Melville owned all of these works by Schopenhauer. His annotated editions are in the Houghton Library at Harvard. See, Arthur Schopenhauer, *The World as Will and Idea*, trans. R. B. Haldane and Kemp, 3 vols. (London: Kegan Paul, Trench, Trubner, 1888), 3:491; *Counsels and Maxims*, trans. T. Bailey Saunders (London: Sonnenschein, 1890), 118; *Studies in Pessimism: A Series of Essays*, trans. T. Bailey Saunders (London: Sonnenschein, 1891), 118.

108. Schopenhauer, *The World as Will and Idea*, 1:502, 3:106, 114; *Studies in Pessimism*, 24–25.

109. See Melville's copy of *The Wisdom of Life*, xxii, at Houghton Library.

110. The passage can be found in Melville's copy of *The World as Will and Idea*, 3: 112–13.

111. Hayford and Sealts, *Billy Budd*, 165.

112. Bushnell, *Vicarious Sacrifice*, 452.

113. Byron, *Hebrew Melodies*, 77.

114. Henri Hubert and Marcel Mauss, *Sacrifice: Its Nature and Functions*, trans. W. D. Halls (1898; reprint, Chicago: University of Chicago Press, 1964), 33, 109.

115. William Robertson Smith, *Lectures on the Religion of the Semites: The Fundamental Institutions* (1889; reprint, New York: Ktav, 1969), 418–19, 421–22, 424.

116. Mark Twain, *Huckleberry Finn* (1884; reprint, New York: Penguin, 1986), 154, 129.

117. I can write "of course" here because of Eve Kosofsky Sedgwick's reading of these issues in *Billy Budd*. See *The Epistemology of the Closet* (Berkeley: University of California Press, 1990), 91–130.

118. Robert Holloway, *The Phoenix of Sodom; or, The Vere Street Coterie* (London: Holloway Printer, 1813), 64, 12, 13, 17. See also, Arthur N. Gilbert, "Sexual Deviance and Disaster during the Napoleonic Wars," *Albion* 9 (Spring 1977): 98–113, which I drew upon in this section.

119. See on this point, Robert Southey, *The Life of Nelson* (New York: Harper's, 1855), chapter 1, and Melville's annotated copy, Houghton Library.

120. These quotes are from Scheler, *Ressentiment*, 45, 50, 53, 52.

Chapter Three
Rites of Passage in an "Awkward Age"

1. Henry James, *A Small Boy and Others* (New York: Scribner's, 1913), 315–16.

2. James is quoted by Martin Meisel in "Seeing It Feelingly: Victorian Symbolism and Narrative Art," *Huntington Library Quarterly* 49, no. 1 (1986): 67–92. I am indebted to Meisel's essay for highlighting James's adolescent memory of the Hunt painting and for its discussion of Hunt in the context of the exhibition. Hunt, a founding member of the Pre-Raphaelite Brotherhood, was known for the strong moral vision of his works and for his use of natural light and settings. True to form, he traveled to the Dead Sea in Palestine in 1854 to paint this scene of sacrifice. See William Holman Hunt, *Pre-Raphaelitism and the Pre-Raphaelite Brotherhood*, 2 vols. (London: Macmillan, 1905). Like Meisel, I am impressed by the painting's restraint: "Hunt takes great care not to subvert or sentimentalize the reality, the *goatness* of the goat." Ford Maddox Ford appears to have agreed, marveling that "out of an old goat and some saline encrustations, can be made one of the most tragic and impressive works in the annals of art" (83, 88).

3. This passage from the exhibition catalogue is quoted in Meisel, "Seeing It Feelingly," 82.

4. Quoted in Meisel, "Seeing It Feelingly," 84, from an anonymous review in the *Leader*, May 1865.

5. Henry James, *The Awkward Age: With the Author's Preface* (1908; reprint, New York: Penguin, 1981), 36–37. Meisel cites reviews that note "the red reflections" on the goat's fur. See "Seeing It Feelingly," 84.

6. Leviticus 16:21, in *The Five Books of Moses*, ed. Dr. M. Stern (New York: Star Hebrew Book, n.d.), 191.

7. James was exactly fifty-six himself at the time of the novel's writing. His biographer Leon Edel notes James's preoccupation with the perspectives of adolescent girls during this period in general. Edel describes James's graduation from explorations of "growing up" (largely from the feminine point of view) to a deeper engagement with his own artistic "religion of doing." *The Treacherous Years: 1895–1901* (New York: Avon, 1969), 261–67.

8. *The Compact Edition of the Oxford English Dictionary*, 1: 1770.

9. The following works provide anthropological discussions of these issues, contemporary with or subsequent to James's era: Walter E. Roth, *Ethnological Studies among the North-West-Central Queensland Aborigines* (Brisbane: E. Gregory, 1897); Arnold Van Gennep, *The Rites of Passage*; trans. Monika B. Vizedom and Gabrielle L. Caffee (1909; reprint, Chicago: University of Chicago Press, 1960); and Jack Goody's edition of Meyer Fortes, *Religion, Morality, and the Person: Essays on Tallensi Religion* (Cambridge: Cambridge University Press 1987). Fortes, whose insights are anticipated by Roth and Van Gennep, was an anthropologist who studied and later taught at the London School of Economics in the 1920s. Fortes writes that a woman giving birth for the first time is given a "perineal belt" by "a proxy for [her] mother," which "reflects a notion of competition for limited reproductive resources between successive generations of the same sex." Fortes concludes that such assumptions are continuous with "beliefs and practices in our own society that

are attributed to individual experience but reflect the same underlying forces in family relationships" (228–29).

10. Edel, *Treacherous Years*, 258, 88.

11. Every significant contemporary study of morals and ritual I have consulted discusses purification rituals associated with rain. I refer to Sir James Frazer, *Golden Bough: A Study in Magic and Religion* (1890; reprint, London: Macmillan 1911); Jane Ellen Harrison, *Prolegomena to the Study of Greek Religion* (Cambridge: Cambridge University Press, 1903); W. Robertson Smith, *Lectures on the Religion of the Semites: The Fundamental Institutions* (1889; reprint, New York: Ktav, 1969); Henri Hubert and Marcel Mauss, *Sacrifice, Its Nature and Functions*, trans. W. D. Halls (1898; reprint, Chicago: University of Chicago Press, 1964); and Emile Durkheim, *The Elementary Forms of the Religious Life*, trans. Joseph Ward Swain (1915; reprint, New York: Free Press, 1965). For a valuable summary of these issues, see Mircea Eliade, *The Myth of the Eternal Return; or, Cosmos and History*, trans. Willard Trask (Princeton: Princeton University Press, 1954), especially chapter 2, "The Regeneration of Time," 49–92.

12. Edward A. Westermarck, *The Origin and Development of the Moral Ideas*, 2 vols. (London: Macmillan, 1906), 1: 552.

13. In general, I believe, literary and cultural historians have been insufficiently attentive to the convergences among literary, theological, and social scientific ideas in this period. The following studies are somewhat exceptional in their cross-disciplinary perspectives: James T. Kloppenberg's *Uncertain Victory: Social Democracy and Progressinism in European and American Thought, 1870–1920* (New York: Oxford University Press, 1986); Wolf Lepenies's *Between Literature and Science: The Rise of Sociology*, trans. R. J. Hollingdale (Cambridge: Cambridge University Press, 1988); and Jeffrey Alexander's *Structure and Meaning: Relinking Classical Sociology* (New York: Columbia University Press, 1989). But none of these works brings together all three areas of inquiry.

14. The most recent example is Alfred Habegger's biography of Henry James Sr., *The Father: A Life of Henry James, Sr.* (New York: Farrar, Strauss, Giroux, 1994). For an earlier example, see Frederic Harold Young, *The Philosophy of Henry James Sr.* (New York: Bookman, 1951). The only serious attempt to relate their concerns is Quentin Anderson's *The American Henry James* (New Brunswick, N.J.: Rutgers University Press 1957), which clearly warrants reconsideration in light of new critical developments and historical information.

15. F. O. Matthiessen, in *The James Family* (1947; reprint, New York: Vintage 1980), supplies a rich fund of information on William and Henry reading each other's work. Especially suggestive is Matthiessen's evidence that they kept abreast of each other's reviews (a kind of running scorecard, as it were) in contemporary periodicals. Sometimes the cross-fertilization was even more direct. For instance, Henry edited William's essay "The Progress of Anthropology," *Nation*, February 6, 1868. See Matthiessen on this editorial transaction 316. Richard Hocks's *Henry James and Pragmatist Thought* (1971) is one of the first works to explore how the relation informed Henry's fiction. For two more recent and sophisticated explorations, see Sharon Cameron, *Thinking in Henry James* (Chicago: University of Chicago Press, 1989); and Ross Posnock, *The Trial of Curiosity: Henry James, William James and the Challenge of Modernity* (Oxford: Oxford University Press, 1991).

16. Leon Edel makes much of this in the first volume of his biography, *The Untried Years: 1843–1870* (New York: Avon, 1953), 33, 63–66; 132. Ross Posnock has advanced thinking on these relations, that of the brothers especially, in promising ways. Posnock notes, for instance, that "in his memoirs Henry not only flaunts his abjectness and celebrates William's prowess but also carefully conceals his elder brother's floundering, and his own near effortless achievement of professional and social success." *The Trial of Curiosity*, 17–18. By highlighting the function of abjection as a family style, Posnock helps us to see it as a deliberate affect of Henry's. Posnock qualifies the fraternal rivalry immortalized by Edel, but he does imply some absolute divide, with his image of "Henry's diffuse, feminized identity, [which] mimics his mother's relational self" and "provides an alternative to his father's insulated autonomy" (203). See also Kim Townsend's admirably balanced account of the James family in *Manhood at Harvard: William James and Others* (New York: Norton, 1996), especially chapter 1.

17. One might read into this scene a triangulation whereby William's blankness stands for Henry's homoerotic leanings, which found expression early on through his relationship with his handsome, and alternately aggressive and incapacitated, older brother. On the historical status of homosexuality at this time see Havelock Ellis, *Sexual Inversion* (London: Macmillan, 1896); Jeffrey Weeks, *Sex, Politics, and Society: The Regulation of Sexuality since 1800* (London: Longman, 1981); Eve Kosofsky Sedgwick, *The Epistemology of the Closet* (Berkeley: University of California Press, 1990); and David Halperin, *One Hundred Years of Homosexuality* (New York: Routledge, 1989). On the Henry-William relation in these terms, see Edel, *Untried Years*.

18. Posnock, *Trial of Curiosity*, 203.

19. Henry was plagued throughout life by a pain that Edel traces most credibly to a back injury, though the innuendos of sexual trauma of some kind remain relevant. See *Untried Years*, 167–83, and Posnock, *Trial of Curiosity*, 182–85.

20. Laurence Holland, *The Expense of Vision: Essays on the Craft of Henry James* (Baltimore: Johns Hopkins University Press, 1964), provides an early sustained treatment of the sacrifice theme in James. But his formal emphasis minimizes its historical, political, and even moral content. Peter Brooks's characterization of James's "melodramatic imagination" is more compatible with my own approach. With reference to *The Awkward Age*, Brooks emphasizes the "depths of violence, hostility, and conflict" implied in the most mannered scenes (164) and notes in general that "the ritual of melodrama . . . can offer no terminal reconciliation, for there is no longer a clear transcendent value to be reconciled to. There is, rather, a social order to be purged, a set of ethical imperatives to be made clear" *The Melodramatic Imagination: Balzac, Henry James, Melodrama and the Mode of Excess* (New York: Columbia University Press, 1984), 17.

21. This chapter centers on a single James novel. My purpose is to explore the extraordinary detail of Jamesian sacrifice, which takes a subtler and more obsessive form in his writings than in the authors I consider elsewhere, Melville and Du Bois. Yet, this method risks obscuring the remarkable scope of James's achievement in this respect. Let me point out, therefore, that there are few works by James where sacrifice is not evoked, whether as promise or as fulfillment. In "The Jolly Corner," a story about regret, sacrifice is a psychic wound transferred to a "black stranger."

"The Jolly Corner" (1908), reprinted in *The Beast in the Jungle and Other Stories* (New York: Dover, 1993), 100. The ghost hunted in that narrative is the alternative self, whose lost and alienated condition is figured in the mutilated hand he holds up for inspection when he is finally spotted by the protagonist. The self who might have been becomes the cultural other, whose difference is symbolized by the physical evidence of lingering sacrificial rites. To read the mangled hand of Spencer Brydon's alter ego as an image of sacrificial mutilation is to recognize a potential symbiosis between an unrequited (because unselected) life and supposedly obsolete cultural practice. A similar atmosphere of confusion issuing from the clash of cultures and selves prevails in *The Sacred Fount* (1901). But here sacrifice is particular to the matrimonial relation. Sacrifice, in the surreal and malevolent world of this novel, is a facet of human interdependence, typified by marriage. Like the nervous alter ego of Melville's *Typee*, the narrator of *The Sacred Fount* struggles to find coherence in a scene that seems as monstrous as it is mystifying, and his dominant ordering principle is sacrifice. All of this is caught by the novel's dominant symbol, the Fount itself, the flow, whether evolutionary or periodic, that stands for social process. The Sacred Fount is a scarce resource, and this scarcity is understood as a social inevitability. There is, in one character's words, "not enough to go round." The narrator pieces it together: " 'One of the pair,' I said, 'has to pay for the other.' " One partner in the marriage is an unconscious beneficiary, while the other, conscious partner is "the author of the sacrifice" *The Sacred Fount* (1901; reprint, New York: Grove, 1979), 29–30. What remains unclear, through the end, is the riddle of the narrator's part. For at times he appears as the sacrificial beneficiary, accepting the gift of characters who are "bound hand and foot," and "made . . . in that sorry state" to pull him through (222). Sacrifice, in other words, is a necessity of plot; his narrative requires it. As with the narrator of *Typee*, we can never be sure that he has not "made it up," for the sake of an audience. By giving us a first-person narrator struggling to decipher a sacrificial procedure that might be all in his head, James, like Melville, portrays sacrifice as a nineteenth-century intellectual dilemma. In the realist world of *The Bostonians* (1886), as orthodox as it is limited, sacrifice has a specific political import. To begin with, it is an American cultural habit, an offshoot of the long-standing American ideal of innocence, an ideal tragically compromised by Civil War. It is also a necessity of the feminist revolution projected by the novel's female protagonist. Olive Chancellor's Comtean "religion of humanity," like any spiritual program, requires martyrs. *The Bostonians* (1886; reprint, New York: Penguin, 1978), 18. This is the history of women from Olive's "Birdseye" view: "uncounted millions had lived only to be tortured, to be crucified. . . . the day of their delivery had dawned. . . . it must exact from the other, the brutal, bloodstained, ravening race, the last particle of expiation!" (34). These feminist grievances are shadowed, and from the unsympathetic perspective of Basil Ransom, trivialized by a greater martyrdom, celebrated in the Civil War tableau at Memorial Hall, which tells of "sacrifice," "manhood," and "generosity" (210). According to the novel's deepest lights, however, collective sacrifice inevitably reduces to self-serving ends. Whether the actor is Basil Ransom as John Wilkes Booth, "a young man . . . [who] had made up his mind, for reasons of his own, to discharge a pistol at the king or the president" (371) or Olive Chancellor, political objectives are driven by sexual desire. This reduction has as much to do with the notorious Jamesian resistance to politics as with the Durkheimian premise that sacrificial cravings are most intense when revolutionary ideals have worn down or worn thin. Craving is a particularly apt term in *The Bostonians*, given the graphic consumptive metaphors used to describe the different designs on Verena Tarrant. To Basil Ransom, who tracks her like a famished beast, she is sacrificial food of the most literal kind. But Olive's intentions are no less predatory, for all her tragic guilt. In *The Bostonians*, sacrifice is cheap melodrama, the second-rate theatre of a misguided radicalism ("left" and "right"). Indeed, one could argue that it is when James's interests are *most* overtly political that his fiction is the *least* responsive to the politics of sacrifice. The difference of *The Bostonians*, as critics have often pointed out, is that James has little respect for its characters. As a result, he does not respect their sacrificial obligations. "The Altar of the Dead," a reverential account of lives sacrificed to the dead, has an altogether different tone. Death hangs heavy here, suffocating all other prospects. Published two years before Grant Allen's book on ancestor worship, "The Altar of the Dead," seems to actualize certain primitive notions about ancestral expectations. The need to be worshiped in the afterlife by offspring or lovers is the dominant human instinct. This peculiar trait makes for an astonishing willingness to defer experience. Mourning ritual, or as the story's protagonist puts it, "numbering his Dead," dwarfs all live engagements, most obviously because dead people, though entirely beyond the control of those who survive them, afford the illusion of complete control. "The Altar of the Dead" (1895), reprinted in *The Beast in the Jungle and Other Stories*, 2. Death, as James's protagonist recognizes, is cleansing, allowing "everything that was ugly in him to be washed out in a torrent" (23). George Stransom, who dies in a typically lavish display of self-sacrifice, is revived in Merton Densher of *The Wings of the Dove*. Thus it is not the sacrifice of Milly Theale that preoccupies Densher but the sacrifice of her construction of it. "The part of it missed forever was the turn she would have given her act. . . . it was like the sacrifice of something sentient and throbbing, something that, for the spiritual ear, might have been audible as a faint far wail." Whenever he is home, "he took it out of its sacred corner and its soft wrappings." *The Wings of the Dove* (1903; reprint, New York: Norton, 1978), 398. Notice the conjunction of sentience and spirituality, which are both in doubt. The object of ritual attention is emotion itself, the melodramatic affect that is enshrined in part to contain (it might overpower) and in part to keep (it might disappear). Densher, observing Milly at a typical gathering, "looked very much as some spectator in an old-time circus might have watched the oddity of a Christian maiden, in the arena, mildly, caressingly, martyred" (209). Sacrifice is like this in *The Wings of the Dove*, and it happens again and again as a symbolic reenactment and compensation for a fundamental loss of faithful feeling. This is why it has the appearance of a social fate or contagion. The key to Milly's sacrifice is that it is so widely shared. Kate Croy's history is littered with losses, of her brothers, of her mother, and colored by the "submersion" and "discomfort" of her father and sister. Kate's "state of abasement" is an accident of birth (she is "the second-born"). She is all her shrunken family has to give, and she imagines herself "a trembling kid, kept apart a day or two till her turn should come" (37). Misfortune is generalized to include Densher, who ends in presumably heroic resignation to loss on all sides—of Kate, Milly, a fortune. However melodramatically conceived, sacrifice is serious business in *The Wings of the Dove*. Still, it doesn't approximate its status in *The Awkward Age*, where it is the very ground of culture, essential to collective life, the means by which the young are socialized, initiated into group mores. My point, in highlighting these examples, is twofold. In all climes and on all occasions, James specializes in sacrificial acts, but in *The Awkward Age* this pattern assumes the form of a deep structure.

22. I borrow the terms "cosmic paranoia" and "upside down" world from Jonathan Z. Smith's "Birth Upside Down or Right Side Up," in *Map Is Not Territory: Studies in the History of Religions* (Leiden, The Netherlands: E. J. Brill, 1978), 156, 161. The significance of Smith's work for my analysis will become apparent later in this chapter.

23. Marcel Mauss clarifies the function of alms, drawing upon the theories of Robertson Smith and Edward Westermarck. "Alms are the fruits of a moral notion of the gift and of fortune on the one hand, and of a notion of sacrifice on the other. Generosity is an obligation because Nemesis avenges the poor and the gods for the superabundance of happiness and wealth of certain people who should rid themselves of it. . . . The gods and the spirits accept that the share of wealth and happiness that has been offered to them and had been hitherto destroyed in useless sacrifices should serve the poor and children." *The Gift: The Form and Reason for Exchange in Archaic Societies*, trans. W.D. Halls (1923–24; reprint, New York: Norton, 1990), 17–18.

24. It seems a marvelous coincidence, another remarkable example of art "making" life, that the 1899 *Lamb* House fire that traumatized James occurred while he was engaged in reading proof for *The Awkward Age*. See *Treacherous Years*, 268–70. See also *Untried Years*, 180–81, on the special significance of fire for the James family as a whole (from the fire that resulted in the amputation of Henry Sr.'s leg as a child to the fire associated with the "obscure hurt" of Henry Jr.).

25. See Hubert and Mauss, *Essay on Sacrifice*, 26; and Smith, *Religion of the Semites*, 236–38, 632, and 647, where he describes the use of fire as a purifying agent.

26. Frazer, *Dying God*, vol. 3, 191.

27. Victor Turner, "Sacrifice as Quintessential Process: Prophylaxis or Abandonment?" *History of Religions* 16 (February 1977): 189–215.

28. For more on these concerns in James, see Nancy Bentley's superb analysis of *The Spoils of Poynton*, in *The Ethnography of Manners: Hawthorne, James, Wharton* (Cambridge: Cambridge University Press, 1995), 114–59.

29. This is consistent with numerous contemporary social scientific treatments on the metonymies of dress and possessions, from W. I. Thomas (on prejudice) and Georg Simmel (on fashion) to Arnold Van Gennep (on rites of passage) and W. E. Roth (on ceremonial self-adornment among the Australian aborigines).

30. Gilbert Murray, *The Four Stages of Greek Religion* (New York: Columbia University Press, 1912), 48–49. James owned Murray's book.

31. Frazer, *Corn God*, quoted in Grant Allen, *The Evolution of the Idea of God: An Inquiry into the Origins of Religion* (New York: Henry Holt, 1897), 283. Allen notes, in the same chapter, "The Corn-Field Victim," that "All the world over, savages and semi-civilised people are in the habit of sacrificing human victims, whose bodies are buried in the field" (283ff.). James was familiar with Grant Allen, an intellectual antagonist of William James's.

32. Turner, "Sacrifice as Quintessential Rite," 208; Mary Douglas, *Purity and Danger*, quoted by Smith in *Map Is Not Territory*, 137.

33. Smith, *Map Is Not Territory*, 165–67.

34. Murray, *Four Stages*, 112–13. Compare this to Jonathan Smith's sense that "cosmic disorder" can also be taken as "a positive sign . . . that the rulers of the world have been overthrown." *Map Is Not Territory*, 165.

35. This state of affairs may be consistent with Jane Harrison's characterization of the primary sacrificial oath of the Hellenistic era, where "do ut abeas" ("I give so that you may go, and keep away") replaces "do ut des." ("I give, that you may give"). *Study of Greek Religion*, 7.

36. "Sacrifice as Quintessential Rite," 203. Robertson Smith, however, locates this injunction in the earliest sources. In ancient Palestine, for instance, "a flock of sheep [would] be driven past the shrine, and the one that enters has chosen it." *Religion of the Semites*, 602; see also 309–10.

37. Theodore Porter, *The Rise of Statistical Thinking, 1820–1900* (Princeton: Princeton University Press, 1986), 270–314.

38. In Max Nordau's *Degeneration* (1893), scientific positivism, together with bourgeois morality, are presented as class correctives to prevailing tendencies, from above (the aristocracy) and below (the lower classes), toward degeneracy and atavism. See also Havelock Ellis, *The Criminal* (1895), as well as the theories of S. R. Steinmetz, which were translated and adapted by Albion Small in "The Scope of Sociology," his series of essays for the *American Journal of Sociology*.

39. G. Stanley Hall, *Adolescence: Its Psychology and Its Relations to Physiology, Anthropology, Sociology, Sex, Crime, Religion, and Education* (New York: Appleton, 1904), cited by Dorothy Ross in *G. Stanley Hall: The Psychologist as Prophet* (Chicago: University of Chicago Press, 1972), 339, 413. Hall was a student of William James's. See also Hall's essay on female adolescence, "The Awkward Age," *Appleton's Magazine* 12 (1908): 149–56.

40. In "Animal Sociology and a Natural Economy of the Body Politic, Part I: A Political Physiology of Dominance," in *The Signs Reader: Women, Gender, and Scholarship*, ed. Elizabeth Abel and Emily K. Abel (Chicago: University of Chicago Press, 1983), 123–38, Donna Haraway complains that "[we women] have challenged our traditional assignment to the status of natural objects by becoming antinatural in our ideology." Women have worked against themselves "by agreeing that 'nature' is our enemy and that we must control our 'natural' bodies . . . at all costs to enter the hallowed kingdom of the cultural body politic as defined by liberal (and radical) theorists of political economy" (125). Implicit in Haraway's remarks is the claim that an intellectually self-aware, revitalized essentialism might be the basis for a new feminist politics. A number of the essays collected by Cass Sunstein in *Feminism and Political Theory* (Chicago: University of Chicago Press, 1990) offer additional perspectives on these issues.

41. Pearson's essay is included in *The Chances of Death and Other Studies in Evolution* (London: Edward Arnold, 1897), 1: 103–39. Quotations are from 110 and 117. Part of Pearson's essay is devoted to a review of Benjamin Kidd's *Social Evolution*, which he criticizes for its view of religion as "ultra-rational." Pearson endorses Robertson Smith's emphasis on the rational function of religion, whose purpose is "strengthening the social feeling at the expense of the individualistic." As Pearson

goes on to comment, "that the killing of a cow, for example, was not to be undertaken without tribal sanction of the most solemn kind, can be easily recognised as of social utility" (118).

42. Guy de Maupassant's "The Mother of Monsters" was published in a volume of his stories entitled *Toine* (Paris: C. Marpon and E. Flammarion, 1885).

43. Quoted in Leon Edel, *The Master: 1901–1916* (New York: Avon 1972), 87–88.

44. James's encounter is described in Edel, *The Master*, 35. For contemporary views on maternity and conscription, see Weeks, *Sex, Politics, and Society*, 125–26ff.

45. Havelock Ellis, quoted in Weeks, *Sex, Politics, and Society*, 126.

46. See Henry James's review of the collection *Modern Women and What Is Said of Them* (New York: Redfield, 1868). James's review was originally published in the *Nation* and can be found in *Essays on Literature: American Writers, English Writers* (New York: Library of America, 1984), 19–25.

47. Adrienne Rich, *Of Woman Born: Motherhood as Experience and Institution* (New York: Norton, 1976), 163–64. After twenty years of feminist (and nonfeminist) reflections on maternity, Rich's book remains, in my view, among the most eloquent works ever written on the subject.

48. Van Gennep analyzes these customs in *Rites*, 50–59. For more recent treatments see Meyer Fortes on Tallensi religion, and Victor Turner's classic work on Ndembu ritual, *Forest of Symbols* (Ithaca, N.Y.: Cornell University Press, 1967).

49. Georges Bataille, *Visions of Excess: Selected Writings, 1927–1939* (1936; reprint, Minneapolis: University of Minnesota Press, 1986), 94.

50. See Frazer, *Dying God*, 187–88, 253–56.

51. "Eugenics: Its Definition, Scope, and Aims," *Sociological Papers* (London: Macmillan, 1905): 1: 78, 76.

52. Westermarck points out that the words for sin, guilt, and punishment in the Hebrew and in the Vedic languages are "interchangeable." *Origin of Moral Ideas*, 1: 52, 55.

53. The scholarly analogy for James's portrayal of reading in *The Awkward Age* is Andreas Huyssen's "Mass Culture as Woman," in *After the Great Divide: Modernism, Mass Culture, Postmodernism* (Bloomington: Indiana University Press, 1986), though I believe that James stops short of feminizing mass taste. The more popular analogy is Quentin Tarantino's postmodern film *Pulp Fiction* (1994). *The Awkward Age* might be seen as supplying the metaphysic for Tarantino's dead-end world of greed and violence—that is, if we can take seriously for a moment James's references to the murderous effects of books. At the same time, Tarantino's postmodern scene feels curiously anachronistic, Spencerian. It is a realm of killers and corpses, eaters and eaten. Though the film is so graphic that it's difficult to see beyond all the torture and suffering, it's impossible to miss how much feeding there is and how much food (of a "fast" variety) is emphasized. Killing and eating are interdependent. Nearly every act of murder requires a preliminary act of consumption. In what appears a peculiar reversal of the sacrificial rite, men must eat before they kill, whether the fare is Hawaiian-style hamburgers or basic steak. It is as if the act of snuffing out a life demands the initial fortification of another. The obvious moral here is, "Eat or be eaten." But there may be another suggested by the film's title and realized in the

scene where a protagonist is blown away while sitting on the toilet reading "pulp fiction." Far from a transcendence of danger, reading is dangerous. Books don't take you away from dirt and waste; they keep you there, perhaps permanently (as in the case of the John Travolta character, whose predicament would have been appreciated by Joyce). If books are the source of life, there is no doubt they are also its end.

54. For a recent anthropological treatment of reproduction, which discusses the status of the menopausal woman, see Emily Martin, *The Woman in the Body: A Cultural Analysis of Reproduction* (New York: Beacon, 1992), 174–75 and passim.

55. This quotation is from Simone de Beauvoir, *The Second Sex*, trans. H. M. Parshley (New York: Knopf, 1953).

56. Gayle Rubin, "The Traffic in Women: Notes on the 'Political Economy' of Sex," in *Toward an Anthropology of Women*, ed. Rayna Reiter (New York: Oxford University Press, 1975), 157–211. See 205.

57. Richard H. Brown, in "Dialectical Irony: Literary Form and Sociological Theory," *Poetics Today* 4 (1983): 543–64, uses this term to characterize a variety of modern social thinkers.

58. Frazer, *Dying God*, 189–90.

59. Andrew Lang offers an extensive discussion of this rite in *The Making of Religion* (London: Longmans, Green, 1898), chapter 9.

60. In *Origin of the Idea of God*, Grant Allen traces the conception of God "from the earliest practices of Ancestor worship." According to Allen, religion is not "Faith or Creed" but "Ceremony" or "Practice." He continues, "Its core is worship. Its centre is the God—that is to say, the Dead Ancestor or Relative" (32). Allen sometimes engaged in debate with William James in journalistic forums. In a response (in the early 1880s) to William's essay, "Great Men, Great Thoughts, and Their Environment," Henry commented, "I shall read what Grant Allen and John Fiske reply to you in *The Atlantic*, but I shall be sure not to enter into what they say as I did into your article, which I greatly appreciated." Matthiessen, *James Family*, 325.

61. Fortes, "The First Born," in *Religion, Morality, and the Person*, 228–34.

62. Frazer, *Golden Bough*, quoted in Jonathan Z. Smith, "When the Bough Breaks," in *Map Is Not Territory*, 213. My discussion is indebted to this analysis by Smith, who traces Frazer's changing treatment of the priest at Nemi through various editions of *The Golden Bough* (208–39). This scenario was popularized in James's time in Renan's play *Le Pêtre de Nemi*. As paraphrased by Andrew Lang, Renan's message was, "the sequence of seasons . . . depends upon the due performance of immemorial religious acts." Lang concludes with an admirably succinct distillation: "Ritual . . . preserves *luck*." *Myth, Ritual, and Religion* (London: Longmans, Green, 1899), 1:251.

63. "When the Bough Breaks," in *Map Is Not Territory*, 211. Smith, throughout his book, emphasizes the variation and dissemination of religious practices and values, which might be simultaneously "diasporic" and "nationalistic," and the "conscious archaicization" of religion in late antiquity. He prefers to see any faith, "Gnosticism, Judaism, or Apocalpticism," as "a shifting cluster of attributes, which, for a particular purpose and in terms of a given document, makes one or another of these labels appropriate" (x, xiii).

64. Virgil, *Aeneid* 6: 136, quoted in Smith, *Map Is Not Territory*, 215.

65. James's Roman affinities are discussed in Elizabeth Block, "The Rome of Henry James," in *Roman Images*, ed. Annabel Patterson (Baltimore: Johns Hopkins University Press, 1984), 141–62; and William L. Vance, "The Colosseum: American Uses of an Imperial Image," in *Roman Images*, 105–41, and *America's Rome*, vols. 1 and 2 (New Haven: Yale University Press, 1989).

66. James was a reader of contemporary journals and books where Frazer's work (first series, published in 1890) was discussed and reviewed. James's friendship with Andrew Lang alone, and knowledge of his work, would have provided at least one obvious avenue.

67. James's edition of Plato's *Republic* would have been the Benjamin Jowett translation (he owned the Jowett translation of the *Dialogues*); see the recent Vintage edition (New York, 1991), 232–36.

68. "Like everyone else, he will suffer from detraction." Plato, *Republic*, 237.

69. Linda Dowling, *Hellenism and Homosexuality in Victorian Oxford* (Ithaca, N.Y.: Cornell University Press, 1994), 35, 28. For more on the history of homosexuality in this period, see Eve Kosofsky Sedgwick, *Between Men: English Literature and Male Homosocial Desire* (New York: Columbia University Press, 1985) and *Epistemology of the Closet*. For more on the Wilde case in particular, see Richard Ellmann, *Oscar Wilde* (New York: Knopf, 1987), 178–79, 367, 493.

70. Dowling defines "paiderastia" as "Greek love . . . a higher male eroticism that is more spiritual precisely as it has been freed from the baser imperatives of merely instinctual or animal reproductivity." *Hellenism and Homosexuality*, 28–29. I draw throughout my discussion of Hellenism on Dowling's elegant book.

71. Dowling, *Hellenism and Homosexuality*, 72.

72. This image comes from a letter by Symonds, whose correspondence James borrowed from Edmund Gosse and scrutinized during the Wilde case. James first encountered Symonds in 1877 through their mutual friend Andrew Lang. Subsequently, in 1891, James read Symonds's privately printed *A Problem in Modern Ethics* on the subject of male love. Dowling discusses Symonds's letters in *Hellenism and Homosexuality*, 76, and Edel treats the James connection in *Treacherous Years*, 128. In *The Awkward Age*, the Duchess notes how "the young men hang about Mrs. Brook," especially "the clever ones" (192). Cleverness is the most prized attribute of her many pupils.

73. Dowling calls it a "cruel pedagogical contradiction" (129).

74. John Addington Symonds, *Letters*, quoted in *Hellenism and Homosexuality*, 129.

75. Edel, *Treacherous Years*, 127–28.

76. See Edel, *Treacherous Years*, 129–30, on James's refusal to sign a clemency appeal on Wilde's behalf. See also Ellmann's *Wilde*, 178–79, 364, 493, for more on James's refusal and on his overall aversion to Wilde.

77. Throughout *Epistemology*, Sedgwick analyses the coupling of homosexuality and blankness. Leland Monk explores James's aestheticism in the context of these issues. Monk's description of James's own renunciation is especially compelling: "He would escape with his fiction into the temple of art, the sanctuary of culture, a safe and sacred place where beauty is neither mortal nor fatal. But these solicitations continue beyond that threshold, tugging at his sleeve, hissing in his ear." "A

Terrible Beauty Is Born: Henry James, Aestheticism, and Homosexual Panic," in *Bodies of Writing, Bodies in Performance*, ed. Thomas Foster, Carol Siegel, and Ellen Berry (New York: New York University Press, 1996), 261.

78. Dowling, *Hellenism and Homosexuality*, 88.

79. Plato, *Phaedrus*, quoted in Dowling, *Hellenism and Homosexuality*, 143. For more on the pederastic implications of Apollo, see, 138–39.

80. Arthur N. Gilbert, "Sexual Deviance and Disaster during the Napoleonic Wars," *Albion* 9 (Spring 1977): pp. 98–113.

81. Jacques Derrida, *Given Time: I. Counterfeit Money*, trans. Peggy Kamuf (Chicago: University of Chicago Press, 1992), 112.

82. Edward A. Ross, for example, charges that cigarette smoking causes "nerve fatigue and brain blight . . . sacrificing the future to the present." *Social Control: A Survey of the Foundations of Order* (New York: Macmillan, 1901), 294.

83. Ellman, *Wilde*, 436.

84. *The Letters of Oscar Wilde*, ed. Rupert Hart-Davis (London: Rupert Hart-Davis, 1962), 449.

85. Hart-Davis, *Wilde's Letters*, 468.

86. Important accounts of the history of such discriminations include Havelock Ellis and John Addington Symonds, *Sexual Inversion* (London: Wilson and Macmillan, 1897), and then the revisionary discussions of David Halperin, Linda Dowling, and Jeffrey Weeks. See also Ian Hacking, "Making Up People," in *Forms of Desire: Sexual Orientation and the Social Constructionist Controversy*, ed. Edward Stein (New York: Garland, 1990).

87. Eve Sedgwick draws out these connections in her reading of the late nineteenth century through the AIDS epidemic, in *Epistemology of the Closet*, 91–130.

88. Bennett Simon describes how a cultural mind (and matter) was transmitted to the young Greek through the semen of his older lover and teacher. This form of " 'Educational' homosexuality" was based on the belief that "the *arete* of the man was in the semen." *Mind and Madness in Ancient Greece: The Classical Roots of Modern Psychiatry* (Ithaca, N.Y.: Cornell University Press, 1978), 248–50.

89. Anxieties about female independence and power were often couched during this era in accounts of society's "primitiveness." John Ferguson McLennan, for example, describes "the licentious wantonness of the women of Patan, against which the men had to adopt measures of self-protection." McLennan sees the subsequent "system of confining women" and the enforcement of exogamy and wife capture as signs of progress. The practice of exogamy and capture and the introduction of taboos on marriage reverse a previous barbarism by transforming women from promiscuous subjects to passive objects of male lust. As McLennan's alarmist tone suggests, the idea of feminine independence from social institutions was a commonplace of late-nineteenth-century social science. *Studies in Ancient History Comprising a Reprint of Primitive Marriage: An Inquiry into the Origin of the Form of Capture in Marriage Ceremonies* (London: Macmillan, 1886), 95–96. In a review of Emile Durkheim's *Suicide* (1897), Havelock Ellis highlights Durkheim's conclusion that women are less dependent on marriage than men. Contrary to conventional wisdom, Durkheim finds, as we have seen, the widower not the widow, the divorced man rather than the divorced woman, more prone to suicide. A social institution designed to protect women from male caprice acquired, in

effect, an opposite purpose. Havelock Ellis, review of *Suicide*, by Emile Durkheim, *Mind* 7 (1898): 249–53.

90. Thorstein Veblen, "The Barbarian Status of Women," *American Journal of Sociology* 4 (1898): 503–14.

91. Stephen Greenblatt, *Renaissance Self-Fashioning: From More to Shakespeare* (Chicago: University of Chicago Press, 1980), and Stephen Toulmin, *Cosmopolis: The Hidden Agenda of Modernity* (Chicago: University of Chicago Press, 1990), describe the "modernity" of the Renaissance era; and Robert Nisbet and Tom Bottomore, *A History of Sociological Analysis* (New York: Basic, 1978), discuss the overall difficulties of periodization.

92. As I have argued in chapter 1, these developments were most pronounced in the United States, but lectures such as Edward Westermarck's "Sociology as a University Study" confirm a comparable "vogue" of sociology in Britain. Sociology, from the perspective of assorted British thinkers, offered a means for informed intervention into social processes, for understanding, in the words of Henry Drummond, "the rationale of social progress." *Lowell Lectures on the Ascent of Man* (New York: James Pott, 1894), 3. Westermarck was more practical in his conception of the field's uses. Noting the new union of imperialist, humanitarian, and capitalist values, he remarked, "I am convinced that in our dealings with non-European races, some sociological knowledge, well-applied, would generally be a more satisfactory weapon than gunpowder. It would be more humane and cheaper too." "Sociology as a University Study" (University of London, 1908), quoted in Gretta Jones, *Social Darwinism and English Thought: The Interaction between Biological and Social Theory* (Sussex, England: Harvester, 1980), 149.

93. Aaron Friedberg analyzes the climate of economic and political decline in England at this time in *The Weary Titan: Britain and the Experience of Relative Decline, 1895–1905* (Princeton: Princeton University Press, 1988), especially chapters 2 and 3. For accounts of the institutionalization of social science in the British context, see Stefan Collini, *Liberalism and Sociology: L. T. Hobhouse and Political Argument in England, 1880–1914* (Cambridge: Cambridge University Press, 1979) and "Sociology and Idealism in Britain, 1880–1920," *Archives Européennes Sociologie* 19 (1978): 3–50; and Philip Abrams, *The Origins of British Sociology, 1834–1914* (Chicago: University of Chicago Press, 1968). Harry Elmer Barnes gives detailed treatments of some major theorists, Hobhouse among them, in his *An Introduction to the History of Sociology* (Chicago: University of Chicago Press, 1948). A number of social scientific journals had their origins in this period: *Mind* and *Sociological Papers* (subsequently, the *Sociological Review*). Magali Sarfatti Larson traces the emergence of an English professional class that internalized traditional forms of status stratification and legitimation in *The Rise of Professionalism: A Sociological Analysis* (Berkeley: University of California Press, 1977), especially 80–103. Perry Anderson, *New Left Review*, July–August 1968, 12–15, and Alvin Gouldner, *The Coming Crisis of Western Sociology* (New York: Basic, 1970), trace the particular fate of the sociological profession in England. Anderson's point is that the English middle class, "traumatized by the French Revolution and fearful of the nascent working-class movement" fused with the aristocracy to form a "composite 'ruling class'"—an "aristocratic combination of 'traditionalism' and 'empiricism.'" Gould-

ner elaborates this idea into an explanation for the absence of a fully formulated "functional sociology" in modern Britain. Gouldner sees functionalism as "consistent with the middle class's need for an ideological justification of its own social legitimacy." Since justification of this sort was not sought by a British middle class fully identified with the aristocracy, sociological development in England was limited (125–26).

94. Leonard T. Hobhouse, *Mind in Evolution* (London: Macmillan, 1901), 318.

95. Quoted in Samuel Hynes, *The Edwardian Turn of Mind* (Princeton: Princeton University Press, 1968), 308–9. Chapters 6, 7, and 8 provide detailed exploration of these developments.

96. Friedberg explores the problem of English efficiency in this era in *Weary Titan*, 21–88.

97. Jones, *Social Darwinism and English Thought*, 102. Galton's eugenics was termed a religion by the *New York Nation*, quoted in "Press Comments," *Sociological Papers* 1 (1905): 81.

98. Francis Galton, "The Possible Improvement of the Human Breed under the Existing Conditions of Law and Sentiment," lecture first published in *Man* (1901), reprinted in Abrams, *Origins*, 260–64. George Bernard Shaw also endorsed a eugenicist breeding program in a 1904 letter to the English Sociological Society. *Sociological Papers* 1 (1905): 74–75. Karl Pearson joined the chorus of socialists endorsing Galton. In "Woman and Labour," he warned that "the limitation of population has indeed begun where it was socially undesirable," and presents it as "one of the chief difficulties of our present transitional social state, and one which will have to be directly faced by the socialism of the future." *Chances of Death*, 1: 246–47.

99. Thomas H. Huxley, *Method and Results: Essays* (London: Appleton, 1893), 428–29. See also Huxley's *Science and Hebrew Tradition: Essays* (London: Appleton, 1896).

100. Sidney Webb, quoted in Weeks, *Sex, Politics, and Society*, 133; Hall, quoted in Ross, *Stanley Hall*, 413.

101. Benjamin Kidd, *Social Evolution* (London: Macmillan, 1894), 331–48; Huxley, *Method*, 380–82; L. T. Hobhouse, *Mind in Evolution* (1901; reprint, London: Macmillan, 1926), 385–86.

102. Thorstein Veblen, *The Theory of the Leisure Class: An Economic Study of Institutions* (New York: Macmillan, 1899), 86–87.

103. F. H. Giddings, review of *Chances of Death and Other Studies in Evolution* (1897), *Political Science Quarterly* 13 (March 1898): 158–61.

104. This is a quote from John Stuart Mill. Habermas continues, "Against a public opinion that, as it seemed, had been perverted from an instrument of liberation into an agent of repression, liberalism, faithful to its own *ratio*, could only summon public opinion once again. Yet what was needed now was a restricted arrangement to secure for a public opinion finding itself in the minority an influence against the prevailing opinions that *per se* it was incapable of developing." Jürgen Habermas, *The Structural Transformation of the Public Sphere: An Inquiry into a Category of Bourgeois Society*, trans. Thomas Burger (Cambridge: MIT Press, 1989), 136–37ff.

105. Leonard T. Hobhouse refers to the "sacred" character of maternity in *Morals in Evolution: A Study in Comparative Ethics* (London: Macmillan, 1906), 146. Spencer more often implies it: see *Principles of Sociology*, 1: 745–61. Rubin's "The Traffic in Women" is also relevant here, as is Thomas Laqueur, "Orgasm, Generation, and the Politics of Reproductive Biology," *Representations* 14 (1986): 1–41.

106. Hobhouse, *Mind in Evolution* (1926 reprint), 473.

107. The work of Carol Gilligan (*In a Different Voice: Psychological Theory and Women's Development* [Cambridge: Harvard University Press, 1982]), as well as the various essays collected by Cass Sunstein in *Feminism and Political Theory*, some of them direct responses to Gilligan, represent latter-day explorations, in a more appreciative vein, of women's values applied to a public sphere.

108. Though the novel's English setting would seem to warrant an exclusively English focus, American social developments were always on James's mind. As he wrote in a letter to his brother William, "I can't look at the English-American world, or feel about them, any more, save as a big Anglo-Saxon total, destined to such an amount of melting together that an insistence on their differences becomes more and more idle and pedantic." Quoted in *Theory of Fiction: Henry James*, ed. James E. Miller (Lincoln: University of Nebraska Press, 1962), 52. Likewise, while there are major differences between the shape of English and American social science and the contexts in which they developed, these should not blind us to the continuities, ensured in part by the consistent interaction of English and American social scientists.

109. Seth Koven and Sonya Michel, "Womanly Duties: Maternalist Politics and the Origins of Welfare States in France, Germany, Great Britain, and the United States, 1880–1920," *American Historical Review* 95 (1990): 1076–1108, describes the fortunes of "maternalist politics" in four major Western states. "In all four countries," they observe, "factors such as the 'anomie' of modernity, the social consequences of rapid industrial and urban growth, and the growing power of class-based movements threatened the foundations of bourgeois civil societies and created political climates that were receptive to social welfare initiatives." Yet maternalist programs, "were more likely to be effective when their causes were taken up by male political actors pursuing other goals, such as pronatalism or control of the labor force. The decades before World War I were supercharged with nationalist agendas and anxieties concerning depopulation, degeneration, and efficiency, as states vied for military and imperial preeminence" (1079–81). James's special alertness to international issues is signaled not only by his dependence on Gyp, whose Durkheimian "social studies" so often concerned the subject of women and marriage, but also by his career-long preoccupation with the writings of French "social botanists" like Balzac and Zola. In 1899, Zola published a novel called *Fecundity* (which James reviewed), whose trinity of themes—female socialization, maternity, and race suicide—overlap with those of *The Awkward Age*. Consider also the significance of James's early transatlantic attentions to questions of maternity and demographic politics. His early short story "The Madonna of the Future," for example, published in *Atlantic Monthly* (March 1873) and in *Revue des deux mondes* (April 1875), portrays a painter whose ambition to create a modern Madonna results in artistic paralysis. This is until he finds his "subject marvelously realized" in a beggar woman with her lost illegitimate child. Two comparable anal-

yses of the prominent ideology of decline in fin-de-siècle France are Robert A. Nye, *Crime, Madness, and Politics in Modern France* (Princeton: Princeton University Press, 1984); and Karen Offen, "Depopulation, Nationalism, and Feminism in Fin-de-Siècle France," *American Historical Review* 89 (June 1984): 648–76.

110. Theda Skocpol, *Protecting Soldiers and Mothers: The Political Origins of Social Policy in the United States* (Cambridge: Harvard University Press, 1992), 34–38.

111. Rich, *Of Woman Born*, especially chapters 6 and 7; Constance Nathanson's *Dangerous Passage: The Social Control of Sexuality in Women's Adolescence* (Philadelphia: Temple University Press, 1991; Margaret Atwood's *The Handmaid's Tale* (1985), one of many feminist science fictions to experiment with utopian and dis-topian reproductive models; and Michelle Stanworth's "Birth Pangs: Conceptive Technologies and the Threat to Motherhood," in *Conflicts in Feminism*, ed. Marianne Hirsch and Evelyn Fox Keller (New York: Routledge, 1990), 288–304, all reveal the striking contemporaneity, or rather, alarming persistence, of questions about who controls female sexuality and reproduction.

112. Quote from Kidd, *Social Evolution*, 109–10.

113. James's definition appears in an 1863 letter to Thomas Sargent Perry. It is quoted and discussed in Christopher Ricks, *T. S. Eliot and Prejudice* (London: Faber and Faber, 1988), 101–3.

114. James's signed copy of *Primitive Marriage* is in the Barret Collection at the University of Virginia.

115. Most of the surnames in the novel's circle are of Scottish derivation, e.g., Brook, Cash, More, Grendon, Long, Don, and Van. See George F. Black, *The Surnames of Scotland: Their Origin, Meaning, and History* (New York: New York Public Library, 1946). Place names are also of Scottish origin, e.g., Brander (where Mrs. Brook sends Harold early in the novel), Buckham (the novel's "Buckingham Crescent"), and Becc (the novel's "Beccles"). In *Sketches of the Character, Institutions, and Customs of the Highlanders of Scotland* (Inverness: Mackenzie, 1885), 380, David Stewart describes "public opinion operating as a punishment, to the extent of forcing individuals into exile."

116. Pearson, "Socialism and Natural Selection," in *Chances*, 1: 111, 113.

117. Eric Hobsbawm and Terence Ranger analyze the role of folk traditions in nationalist agendas throughout the nineteenth century in *The Invention of Tradition* (Cambridge: Cambridge University Press, 1983).

118. Pearson, *Chances*, 1:103.

119. Pearson points out that Kidd would not have made this egregious error had he been familiar with the theories of Robertson Smith. See *Chances*, 1:118.

120. It's worth emphasizing that Kidd considered his own work "sociological." The fact that he was selected to write the *Encyclopedia Britannica* entry on the field confirms that some authorities agreed. Moreover, Kidd's work was at the center of early debates on the purpose of sociology in the United States as well as in England. Richard Hofstadter describes the American reception of *Social Evolution* in *Social Darwinism in American Thought*, 99–102.

121. There is no evidence that James knew Kidd's book, but there are some notable continuities in their respective reading interests. Both were familiar, for example, with J. P. Mahaffy's "Social Life in Greece." Kidd paraphrases Mahaffy's description of the decline of Athens—"social morality grew exceedingly

lax; marriage became unfashionable. . . . ambitious and accomplished women were avowed courtesans, and consequently infertile"—which might serve as a précis of *The Awkward Age. Social Evolution,* 294. James owned a number of signed books by Mahaffy, including this work on Greece. James was acquainted with Balfour and owned his book.

122. Quoted in Dowling, *Hellenism and Homosexuality,* 64–65.

123. Arthur Balfour, *The Foundations of Belief* (London: Longmans, Green, 1895), 219.

124. Pearson, "Reaction! A Criticism of Mr. Balfour's Attack on Rationalism," in *Chances,* 1: 195–96.

125. Collini, *Liberalism and Sociology,* 211.

126. James's reviews of French writers, which provide many insights on literary versus social theory, have been collected in *Henry James: Literary Criticism: French Writers, Other European Writers, the Prefaces to the New York Edition,* ed. Leon Edel (New York: Library of America, 1984).

127. I mention here only the works directly pertinent to my analysis. I could not begin to list all of his social theory. Most of the works I do list were signed by James; some include marginal markings. Twenty-five books by Andrew Lang, including *Custom and Myth* (London: Longmans, Green,1884), *Myth, Ritual, and Religion* (1887; reprint, London: Longmans, Green, 1899); George S. Robertson, *The Kafirs of the Hindu-Kush* (London: Lawrence and Bullen, 1896); Herbert Spencer, *Education: Intellectual, Moral, and Physical* (New York: Appleton, 1870), *Illustrations of Universal Progress* (New York: Appleton, 1864), *Essays: Moral, Political, and Aesthetic* (New York: Appleton, 1871), *An Autobiography* (London: Williams and Norgate, 1904); T. H. Huxley, *Man's Place in Nature* (London: Macmillan, 1894), *Method and Results* (1894); J. F. McLennan, *Primitive Marriage* (1886); Arthur Balfour, *Foundations of Belief* (1895); Leslie Stephen, *Social Rights and Duties* (London: Sonnenschein, 1896); Walter Bagehot, *Biographical Studies* (London: Longmans, Green, 1889), *Economic Studies* (London: Longmans, Green, 1888), and *Literary Studies* (London: Longmans, Green, 1891); J. P. Mahaffy, *Greek Life and Thought: From the Age of Alexander to the Roman Conquest* (London: Macmillan, 1887), *The Greek World under Roman Sway: From Polybius to Plutarch* (London: Macmillan, 1890), and *Social Life in Greece: From Homer to Menander* (London: Macillan, 1874); William Morton Fullerton, *Patriotism and Science* (1893); John Fiske, *American Political Ideas Viewed from the Standpoint of Universal History* (New York: Harper's, 1885), and *The Idea of God as Affected by Modern Knowledge* (Boston: Houghton Mifflin, 1890); twenty books by John Addington Symonds, in addition to Horatio F. Brown, *John Addington Symonds: A Biography* (London: Nimmo, 1895); Gilbert Murray, *Four Stages of Greek Religion* (1912), *A History of Ancient Greek Literature* (New York: Appleton, 1897); and twelve books by Ernest Renan, including, *L'Antechrist* (Paris: Levy, 1873), *Etudes d'histoire religieuse* (Paris: Levy, 1857), *Histoire du peuple d'Israël* (Paris: Levy, 1887). As for James's awareness of Frazer and Robertson Smith, many of the above works discuss their ideas. James had access to a library through his club, and we know that he read there. There are also the many debates conducted in contemporary periodicals like the *Fortnightly Review,* which regularly published Frazer and Pearson, in addition to James himself. For more on James's library, see *The Library of Henry James,* comp.

and ed. Adeline Tintner and Leon Edel (Ann Arbor: University of Michigan Research, 1987).

128. Young, *The Philosophy of Henry James Sr.*, 76.

129. Quentin Anderson discusses these dimensions of Henry Sr.'s work and their impact on the writings of Henry Jr. in *American Henry James*, chapter 1 especially. See also Giles Gunn's introduction to his collection of Henry James Sr.'s work, *Henry James Senior: A Selection of His Writings* (Chicago: American Library Association, 1974).

130. Henry James Sr., *The Secret of Swedenborg: Being an Elucidation of His Doctrine of the Divine Natural Humanity* (Boston: Fields, Osgood, 1869), 102, 105–6, 109.

131. Henry James Sr., *The Nature of Evil* (New York: Appleton, 1855), 339. See also 333ff.

132. Henry James Sr., *Moralism and Christianity: Or Man's Experience and Destiny* (New York: Redfield, 1850), 139, 160ff.

133. James, *Nature of Evil*, 335.

134. James, *Secret of Swedenborg*, 101; Henry James, *Hawthorne* (1879; reprint, New York: Macmillan, 1966), 48.

135. Nathaniel Hawthorne, *The Marble Faun*, in *Nathaniel Hawthorne: Novels*, ed. Millicent Bell (1860; reprint, New York: Library of America, 1983), 854.

136. James, *Nature of Evil*, 336–38.

137. William James, in *The Principles of Psychology* (1890; reprint, Cambridge: Harvard University Press, 1983), 1055–56, endorsed the idea of the "maternal instinct," as did W. I. Thomas in "The Psychology of Race-Prejudice," *American Journal of Sociology* 9 (March 1904): 593–611.

138. *Henry James and H. G. Wells*, ed. Leon Edel and Gordon N. Ray (Urbana: University of Illinois Press, 1958), 134–35. See also Wells's characterization of social science in "The So-Called Science of Sociology," *Sociological Papers* 3 (1907): 357–77, which closely parallels his remarks on James.

139. F. O. Matthiessen, *The James Family*, 323. William's comments may suggest, beyond the question of taste, some rivalry. Insecurity in this highly ambitious fraternal pair ran in both directions. For William had his own unfulfilled painterly and even literary ambitions.

140. On the institutionalization of literary studies, see, for example, Terry Eagleton, *Literary Theory: An Introduction* (Minneapolis: University of Minnesota Press, 1983); Francis Mulhern, *The Moment of 'Scrutiny'* (London: New Left Books, 1979); and Gerald Graff, *Professing Literature: An Institutional History* (Chicago: University of Chicago Press, 1987), which focuses more on the American context. For the institutionalization of social science, see the scholarship of Collini and Abrams, cited above.

141. Quoted in Jonathan Z. Smith, "When the Bough Breaks," 210–11.

142. Sir James Frazer, *Psyche's Task: A Discourse Concerning the Influence of Superstition on the Growth of Institutions* (London: Macmillan, 1909), 82–83.

143. *Elementary Forms*, 18ff. For more on the era's fascination with the primitive, based on an analysis of the general interest in Frazer, see John Vickery, *The Literary Impact of the Golden Bough* (Princeton: Princeton University Press, 1973).

144. Sigmund Freud, *Totem and Taboo: Some Points of Agreement between the Mental Lives of Savages and Neurotics*, trans. James Strachey (London: Macmillan 1950) 11: 11, vii. For a fascinating account of changing anthropological perspectives on the rule-bound nature of primitive society, see Christopher Herbert, *Culture and Anomie: Ethnographic Imagination in the Nineteenth Century* (Chicago: University of Chicago Press, 1991), especially 60–73.

145. Hubert and Mauss, 13; Smith, *Religion of the Semites*, pp. 361–66ff. Lang, *Myth, Ritual, and Religion*, 1:264.

146. Simon N. Patten, *The Social Basis of Religion* (New York: Macmillan, 1911), 187–190.

147. See Nathaniel S. Shaler, *The Neighbor: A Natural History of Human Contacts* (Boston: Houghton Mifflin, 1904), especially, 103–25, for a contemporary American version of this stereotype. See also Sander Gilman, *Jewish Self-Hatred: Anti-Semitism and the Hidden Language of the Jews* (Baltimore: Johns Hopkins University Press, 1986) for a more general European and Continental history of it.

148. Fredric Jameson, "The Vanishing Mediator: Narrative Structure in Max Weber," *New German Critique* 1 (Winter 1973): 68.

149. William Robertson Smith, *Lectures on the Religion of the Semites*, 2d and 3d ser., ed. John Day (Sheffield, England: Academic Press, 1995), 44.

150. Frazer, *Scapegoat*, 410–11.

151. Westermarck, *Origin of Moral Ideas*, 1: 462–465; *Essay on Sacrifice*, 65, 78, 102, 146.

152. Mauss highlights the complexity of potlatch, and the diversity of its cultural expressions, though he privileges what he calls "*total service of an agonistic type,*" stressing the hostility and rivalry latent in the custom. *The Gift*, 6–7, 39–46.

153. William Robertson Smith, "Sacrifice," *Encyclopedia Britannica*, 9th ed., (1875–80), 21: 138.

154. Hobhouse cites instances in which even the poor are enjoined to "give alms." *Morals in Evolution*, 345.

155. Sidney Webb and Beatrice Webb, *English Poor Law History*, part 1 (London: Longmans, 1897), 2: 551. They are quoted in Lynn Hollen Lees "The Survival of the Unfit: Welfare Politics and Family Maintenance in Nineteenth-Century London," in *The Uses of Charity: The Poor on Relief in the Nineteenth-Century Metropolis*, ed. Peter Mandler (Philadelphia: University of Pennsylvania Press, 1990), 81.

156. W.E.B. Du Bois, *The Souls of Black Folk*, in *Three Negro Classics*, ed. John Hope Franklin (1903; reprint, New York: Avon, 1965), 335. Georg Simmel, "The Poor," in *Georg Simmel on Individuality and Social Forms*, ed. Donald Levine (1908; reprint, Chicago: University of Chicago Press, 1971), 178.

157. Quoted in Friedberg, *Weary Titan*, 97.

158. Quoted in Derek Fraser, *The Evolution of the British Welfare State: A History of Social Policy since the Industrial Revolution* (London: Macmillan, 1973), 128. See also Skocpol, *Protecting Soldiers*, 251.

159. D. G. Ritchie, *Darwinism and Politics* (London: S. Sonnenschein, 1891), 70–71.

160. Sybella Graham, "Civic Reconstruction and the Garden City Movement," *Sociological Review* 3 (1910): 35.

161. Francis Walker, quoted in Dorothy Ross, *The Origins of American Social Science* (New York: Cambridge University Press, 1991), 59, 394.

162. Ross, *G. Stanley Hall*, 98, 256–60.

163. Henry Adams quoted in T. J. Jackson Lears, *No Place of Grace: Antimodernism and the Transformation of American Culture 1880–1920* (New York: Pantheon, 1981), 267. See also 266–69.

164. Martha Vicinus, *Independent Women: Work and Community for Single Women, 1850–1920* (Chicago: University of Chicago Press, 1985). Vicinus's valuable institutional approach looks at church communities, hospital associations, women's colleges, and settlement houses, in addition to other public forums for women's work.

165. Koven and Michel, "Womanly Duties," 1095.

166. This is not to overlook the fact that the process of rationalization I am describing was developing over the course of the nineteenth century. Nevertheless, the century's end saw the expansion and institutionalization of reform efforts, most of it social scientifically informed, designed to "publicize" social duties that had formerly been privatized. As Jürgen Habermas observes, the family in this era "increasingly lost . . . the functions of upbringing and education, protection, care, and guidance. . . . [It] lost power as an agent of personal internalization." *Structural Transformation*, 155–56. Or consider Edward Westermarck, "When national life grew more intense, when members of separate families drew nearer to one another in pursuit of a common goal, the family again lost in importance. It has been observed that in England and America, where political life is most highly developed, children's respect for their parents is at a particularly low ebb. Other factors also, inherent in progressive civilisation, contributed to the downfall of the paternal power—the extinction of ancestor-worship, the decay of certain superstitious beliefs, the declining influence of religion, and last, but not least, the spread of a keener mutual sympathy throughout the State, which could not tolerate that the liberty of children should be sacrificed to the despotic rule of their fathers." (*Origin of Moral Ideas*, 1: 628.

167. Hubert and Mauss, *Sacrifice*, 22, 114; and Smith, *Religion of the Semites*, 278–79, 297–99, 379.

Chapter Four
Du Bois's Gospel of Sacrifice

1. W.E.B. Du Bois, *The Souls of Black Folk*, in *Three Negro Classics*, ed. John Hope Franklin (New York: Avon, 1965), 352–53.

2. W. I. Thomas, "The Psychology of Race Prejudice," *American Journal of Sociology* 9 (March 1904): 599.

3. These are drawn from Victor Turner's work on color symbolism in Ndembu ritual. *Sacrifice*, ed. M.F.C. Bourdillon and Meyer Fortes (London and New York: Academic, 1980), 21–22.

4. See Samuel Preston and Michael Haines, *Fatal Years; Child Mortality in Late Nineteenth-Century America* (Princeton: Princeton University Press, 1991), which points out that the key variable in child mortality statistics was rural versus urban life and cites Du Bois (*The Philadelphia Negro*) in support of their claim for the

negative effects of Black "progress" (from farm to city) in the early modern period. Blacks in urban areas, they contend, "were subjected to many of the same mortality hazards as foreign immigrants to cities. But . . . [they] were essentially beyond the pale of the social programs and settlement houses that were designed to ease the transition for immigrants to a new land" (95). They attribute the notably high rates of child mortality among Blacks to their isolation within populated areas: "Race was a caste-like status in 1900, and the degraded social and economic circumstances of blacks, who had virtually no chance of entering the mainstream of American life, is undoubtedly reflected in their exceptionally high mortality." In general, "people furthest from the reach of the modern state—and furthest from one another—enjoyed the best health conditions." The modern state at this point in its history knew how to bring people together but had yet to achieve "the technical and social triumphs" that would reduce the risks of that association (210).

5. From the *Dial*, May 1, 1905, collected in *Book Reviews by W.E.B. Du Bois*, comp. and ed. Herbert Aptheker (New York: Kraus-Thomson, 1977), 12–13.

6. This is the term used to characterize this postemancipation period by Pierre L. van den Berghe, quoted in George Frederickson, *The Black Image in the White Mind: The Debate on Afro-American Character and Destiny, 1817–1914* (Middletown, N.Y.: Harper and Row, 1971), 255.

7. Ralph Ellison, "*An American Dilemma*: A Review in *The Death of White Sociology*," ed. Joyce Ladner (New York: Vintage, 1971), 86.

8. Orlando Patterson, "The Feast of Blood," in *Rituals of Blood; God, Sex, and Violence in Ethnic America* (Washington, D.C.: Counterpoint, forthcoming).

9. W.E.B. Du Bois quoted in "Discussion of the Paper by Alfred Holt Stone, 'Is Race Friction between Blacks and Whites in the United States Growing and Inevitable?'" *American Journal of Sociology* 13 (May 1908): 835.

10. Ellison, "*Dilemma* Review," 82.

11. George R. Stetson, *The Southern Negro as He Is* (Boston: G. H. Ellis, 1877), 20; and Ellwood, review of Smith's *The Color Line*, *American Journal of Sociology* 11 (November 1905): 574.

12. William Benjamin Smith, *The Color Line: A Brief in Behalf of the Unborn* (New York: McClure, Phillips, 1905), x.

13. Thomas Nelson Page, *The Negro: The Southerner's Problem* (New York: Charles Scribner's, 1904), 299, 250.

14. Philip Bruce, *The Plantation Negro as a Freeman: Observations on His Character, Condition, and Prospects in Virginia* (New York: Putnam's 1889), 96.

15. Robert Hertz, *A Contribution to the Study of the Collective Representation of Death*, trans. Rodney and Claudia Needham (1907 in French reprint; Aberdeen: University Press of Aberdeen), 76, 85.

16. Thomas, "Psychology of Race Prejudice," 600–604.

17. See, for instance, William Tegg, *The Last Act: Being the Funeral Rites of Nations and Individuals* (London: W. Tegg, 1876); Frank D. Rogers, *Confessions of an Undertaker* (Chicago: Trade Periodical, 1900); and the journal begun in Rochester, New York, during this time, *The Casket*.

18. H. C. Yarrow, *Introduction to the Study of Mortuary Customs among the North American Indians*, in *First Annual Report of the Bureau of Ethnology* (Washington: Government Printing Office, 1881), 87–203. Cyrus Thomas, *Report on the Mound*

Explorations of the Bureau of Ethnology, in *Twelfth Annual Report of the Bureau of Ethnology* (Washington: Government Printing Office, 1894), 27–742; Baldwin, Spencer, and F. J. Gillen, *The Northern Tribes of Central Australia* (London and New York: Macmillan, 1904); Walter E. Roth, *Ethnological Studies among the North-West-Central Queensland Aborigines* (Brisbane: E. Gregory, 1897), and *Burial Ceremonies and Disposal of the Dead*, North Queensland Ethnography Bulletin 9 (1907); Joseph Tillinghast, *The Negro in Africa and America* (New York: American Economic Association, 1902); Bruce, *Plantation Negro*.

19. See "Fate of Indian Burial Research Hangs by a Hair," *Los Angeles Times*, December 6, 1994, A5, which reported that efforts to apply recent DNA techniques to studies of human hair located at these mounds were being impeded by the objections of Indian descendants protesting the desecration of their sacred sites.

20. Kelly Miller, "A Review of Hoffman's Race Traits and Tendencies of the American Negro," American Negro Academy Occasional Papers, no. 1 (Washington: ANA, 1897), 35–36.

21. Fredrick L. Hoffman, *History of the Prudential Life Insurance Company of America 1875–1900* (Newark, N.J.: Prudential Press, 1900), and *Pauper Burials and the Interment of the Dead in Large Cities* (Newark, N.J.: Prudential Press, 1917).

22. Fredrick L. Hoffman, *Race Traits and Tendencies of the American Negro* (New York: Macmillan, for the American Economic Association, 1896), 246–47.

23. Du Bois might also have had in mind Charles Chesnutt's striking short story "The Bouquet," which portrays a Black girl's efforts to honor her former (White) teacher with a funeral bouquet during burial rites divided by the color line. From *The Wife of His Youth, and Other Stories of the Color Line* (Boston: Houghton Mifflin, 1899).

24. Edward A. Ross, "Western Civilization and the Birth-Rate," *American Journal of Sociology* 12, no. 5 (1906–7): 612, 607, 619.

25. Newbell Niles Puckett, *Folk Beliefs of the Southern Negro* (1926; reprint, Montclair, N.J.: Patterson Smith, 1968), vii 1–2. See Eric J. Sundquist, *To Wake the Nations: Race in the Making of American Literature*, for a full elaboration of these racial paradoxes as dramatized in nineteenth- and twentieth-century American fiction.

26. Thomas Wentworth Higginson, *Army Life in a Black Regiment* (1869; reprint, New York: Norton, 1984), 188; quoted in Sterling Stuckey, *Slave Culture: Nationalist Theory and the Foundations of Black America* (New York: Oxford University Press, 1987), 27–28.

27. Lester Ward, "Social Differentiation and Social Integration," *American Journal of Sociology* 8 (May 1903): 733. Ward's "great united world-race" of the future, with non-Aryan features reduced to a feminized "softening influence" seems eerily fulfilled ninety years later by a special issue of *Time* magazine (142, no. 21 [Fall 1993], "The New Face of America: How Immigrants Are Shaping the World's First Multicultural Society," which features a computer-generated composite of "the kind of offspring that might result from seven men and seven women of various ethnic and racial backgrounds." Presented, according to its editors, "in the spirit of fun and experiment," the image, like Ward's, seems miraculously "White."

28. Paul Reinsch, "The Negro Race and European Civilization," *American Journal of Sociology* 11 (September 1905): 145; and H. E. Belin, "A Southern View

of Slavery," *American Journal of Sociology* 13 (November 1907): 519. These views are consistent with Nathaniel Shaler's assertion that the Negro has no "power of continuous will," is "incapable of firm resolve," and lacks the "monogamic instinct." A similar view is implied in F. H. Giddings's claim that the Negro is "plastic" and "readily takes the external impress of civilization." See Nathaniel S. Shaler, "The Negro Problem," *Atlantic Monthly* 54 (November 1884): 701–2; and Franklin H. Giddings, *The Principles of Sociology: An Analysis of the Phenomena of Association and of Social Organization* (New York: Macmillan, 1896), 328–9.

29. This position was described and refuted in Hoffman, *Race Traits*, 178.

30. Walter F. Willcox, *Negro Criminality* (Boston: George Ellis, 1899), 8, 11–14.

31. Nathaniel S. Shaler, "Science and the African Problem," *Atlantic Monthly* 66 (July 1990): 43

32. Nathaniel S. Shaler, *The Neighbor: A Natural History of Human Contacts* (Boston: Houghton Mifflin, 1904), vii. Shaler's references to the status of the modern Negro regularly combine an assurance of intimacy with a deeper conviction of decreased access. This is perhaps why his dealings with the race invariably refer to the "precious memories of simple, faithful men" harbored by "those of us who knew the Negroes when they were much more knowable than they now are" (142).

33. Alfred Holt Stone, "Is Race Friction between Blacks and Whites in the United States Growing and Inevitable?" *American Journal of Sociology* 13 (March 1908): 676. See also "Discussion of the Paper by Alfred Holt Stone," *American Journal of Sociology* 13 (May 1908): 820–40.

34. Walter L. Fleming, "'Pap' Singelton, The Moses of the Colored Exodus," *American Journal of Sociology* 15 (July 1909): 78, 75, 66.

35. Quoted in Walter White, *Rope and Faggot: A Biography of Judge Lynch* (1929; reprint, New York: Arno, 1969), 27.

36. Quoted in *The Health and Physique of the American Negro*, vol. 11 of Atlanta University Publications (1906; reprint, New York: Arno, 1968), 111–12.

37. *The Negro in Business*, vol. 4 of Atlanta University Publications (1899; reprint, New York: Arno, 1968), 4.

38. President Bumstead of Atlanta University makes this case. The report following his remarks includes statistics on Atlanta that show the increase (72 percent) of the Black population there to be over three times greater than the increase for the nation as a whole (20 percent), as one indication of the dependence of cities on Black populations. His remarks establish the inseparability of urban growth, Black mortality, and the rise of urban sociology as a field of study. *Mortality among Negroes in Cities*, vol. 1 of Atlanta University Publications (1896; reprint, New York: Arno, 1968), 5–7.

39. *Social and Physical Conditions of Negroes in Cities*, vol. 2 of Atlanta University Publications (1897; reprint, New York: Arno, 1968), 26.

40. See the essays by L. M. Hershaw, and Professor Harris in *Social and Physical Conditions*, 10–19, 20–28.

41. *Social and Physical Conditions*, 44–45. Proctor's use of the term "mudsills of society" anticipates Du Bois's "mud-sill theory of society," which he coins years later in *Dusk of Dawn; An Essay toward an Autobiography of a Race Concept, in W.E.B.*

Du Bois: Writings, ed. Nathan Huggins (1940; reprint, New York: Library of America, 1986), 678.

42. Du Bois's editorship began with volume 3, *Some Efforts of Negro Americans for Their Own Social Betterment* (1898), which was subsumed by volume 4, *The Negro in Business.*

43. Local tables on Black businesses with the largest capital investments consistently show undertakers among the top five (ahead of barbers, druggists, publishers, and building and loan associations, and behind grocers, bankers, insurance salesmen, and merchandisers). In national tables on Black businesses, undertakers take a marked share of overall profits. In Norfolk, Virginia, for example, of twelve businesses listed, the total investments in undertaking exceed those of the other business investments combined. Likewise, in Washington, D.C., which Du Bois considers "typical" of Negro business development, there are four undertakers, with a combined capital of $25,500. These examples can be multiplied: in Portsmouth, Virginia, the investment in undertaking ($6,500) is second only to real estate; Charleston, South Carolina, has no fewer than seven undertakers, etc. *Negro in Business*, 7–39.

44. In their 1945 study *Black Metropolis: A Study of Negro Life in a Northern City*, St. Clair Drake and Horace Cayton quote a Chicago undertaker, who observes that while Black burials represent a "closed market," there are "few [White] families that will not have a Negro undertaker" (New York: Harcourt, Brace), 456–57.

45. Du Bois describes the incident and quotes from Allen in *The Philadelphia Negro* (New Jersey: Kraus Thomson, 1899), 18–24; and *The Negro Church*, vol. 8 of Atlanta University Publications (1903; reprint, New York: Arno, 1969), 123–25. For a later view of Blacks as undertakers during the Harlem Renaissance, see James Vanderzee's *Harlem Book of the Dead* (Dobbs Ferry, N.Y.: Morgan and Morgan, 1978), a photographic essay, which depicts from various perspectives, including the centrality of the Black funeral industry, group rituals for dealing with death.

46. Nathaniel Hawthorne's classic fiction "Roger Malvin's Burial" can be read as an early glimmer of Du Bois's insight. One could argue that the story's plot turns on the idea that a proper burial is a human right. At the same time, the story's setting, in Indian territory, and its references to distinctive Indian burial practices suggest an awareness of the significance of variable cultural customs and beliefs. The added point may be that this variation determines Roger Malvin's ability to receive a proper burial (most literally, in the fact that the war issuing from this clash of cultures impedes Reuben Bourne's fulfillment of his obligation).

47. See, for example, John Hope's observations in *Negro in Business*, 56–60.

48. Douglas Massey, *American Apartheid: Segregation and the Making of the Underclass* (Cambridge: Harvard University Press, 1993), 40.

49. Characterizing ethnology as "a science for American culture," J. R. Nott and G. R. Gliddon observe that "here three of the five races [of] mankind, are brought together to determine the problem of their destiny. . . . the proposed importation of Coolie laborers threaten to bring us into equally intimate contact with a fourth. It is manifest that our relation to and management of these people must depend, in a great measure, upon their intrinsic race-character." The point here is clear; the science of ethnology and capitalist-industrial expansion emerge in tandem. Part of ethnology's raison d'être is to balance the need for cheap alien labor against the

ideal of racial purity it had helped to create. *Types of Mankind: or, Ethnological Researches* (Philadelphia: Lippincott, Grambo, 1854), xxxii–xxxiii.

50. For more on the subject of "passing" in American culture, see Werner Sollors's "Passing; or Sacrificing a *Parvenu*," a chapter in his important new study *neither black nor white yet both: Thematic Explorations of Interracial Literature* (New York: Oxford University Press, 1997), 246–84.

51. *Health and Physique* concludes with a series of propositions coauthored by Du Bois, Franz Boas, and R. R. Wright. First, the Negro death rate is on the decline; second, high mortality is a product of social conditions; third, there is pressing need for more Negro doctors and health facilities; fourth, the health and endurance of the nation as a whole is dependent on the fate of Negro Americans; and finally, there must be greater "sympathy" for Negro problems throughout America, 110.

52. *Efforts for Social Betterment among Negro Americans*, vol. 14 of Atlanta University Publications (1909; reprint, New York: Arno, 1968), 132.

53. *The Compact Edition of the Oxford English Dictionary*, 2:3051.

54. See the letters at the end of *Health and Physique*, 111–12.

55. See his 1911 retrospective for a British audience, "The Economics of Negro Emancipation in the United States" *Sociological Review* 4 (1911): 313.

56. Pierre Bourdieu, "What Makes a Social Class?" *Berkeley Journal of Sociology* 32 (1987): 13.

57. Ellison, "*Dilemma* Review," *The Death of White Sociology*, 83.

58. E. Franklin Frazier, "The Failure of the Negro Intellectual" (1962), reprinted in *Death of White Sociology*, 66.

59. Quoted in Léon Bing, *Do or Die* (New York: HarperCollins, 1991), 44.

60. See Stanley Lieberson, *A Piece of the Pie: Blacks and White Immigrants since 1880* (Berkeley: University of California Press, 1980), 365. "American Apartheid" is the title of Douglas Massey's sociological account of segregation, as implemented from the turn of the century (see note 52, above). My use of the term "social death" is indebted to Orlando Patterson's *Slavery and Social Death: A Comparative Study* (Cambridge: Harvard University Press, 1982). Patterson's term finds a literary register in Jean Amery's definition of the Jew "in German hands" as "a dead man on vacation." Quoted in Primo Levi, *The Drowned and the Saved*, trans. Raymond Rosenthal (New York: Vintage, 1989), 128.

61. Elizur Wright, "Life Insurance for the Poor," *Journal of Social Science* 8 (May 1876): 147.

62. Nathaniel S. Shaler, *The Individual: A Study of Life and Death* (New York: Appleton and Company, 1900), 219.

63. It's worth noting (a reference I owe to Werner Sollors) that the Nazis, at a certain point, made Jews uninsurable. This might be taken as further evidence for the far ranging implications of empathy's removal. The creation of a separation in insurability, that is, the refusal to share a joint fate, may eventuate in genocidal acts.

64. Du Bois, *Philadelphia Negro*, 186–92, 225; Booker T. Washington, *The Future of the Negro* (Boston: Small, Maynard, 1899), 167.

65. Sheppard Homans, "Life Insurance," *Journal of Social Science* 2 (June 1869): 159.

66. Featuring "fine military bands" and an "ox-roast," the gathering culminates with an address by "the patriarchal President Dryden" (192).

67. See, for instance, the advertisment opposite the first page of the *American Journal of Sociology* 11, no. 2 (September 1905). The Prudential ad on p. 144 faces the start of Paul Reinsch's "Negro Race and European Civilization," 145.

68. Thomas Haskell, "Capitalism and the Origins of the Humanitarian Sensibility, Part 1," *American Historical Review* 90, no. 3 (1985): 339–61; and "Capitalism and the Origins of the Humanitarian Sensibility, Part 2," *American Historical Review* 90, no. 3 (1985): 547–66. This quotation is from part 2, 566.

69. Haskell, "Humanitarian Sensibility, Part 1," 340. While some historical accounts of these developments have ranged broadly, their narratives pitched on a high intellectual (and theoretical) plane, others have been more local and detailed, focused on mediating structures—Unitarianism, revivalism—in specific contexts. Elizabeth B. Clark, for example, in " 'The Sacred Rights of the Weak': Pain, Sympathy, and the Culture of Individual Rights," *Journal of American History* 82, no. 2 (1995), understands an abolitionism centered in "the story of the suffering slave" as expressive of a shift in moral convention made possible by "changing notions about pain," in liberal Protestantism and "new imperatives for sympathy" popularized by evangelicalism (464). Clark sees these developments as relatively confined; they do not, in her view, represent some definitive shift in moral sensibilities. As she observes in her conclusion, the particular form of abolitionist argument—its graphic focus on the slave's brutalization—"may have worked to set them apart as a class." More importantly, their emphasis on the slave's " 'right' to physical autonomy proved a poor stand-in for a more comprehensive vision of social and economic justice" (493). Clark recognizes effusions of social sympathy of the kind displayed in abolitionism as "limited" (492). Thomas Haskell's analysis, as I have suggested, proposes a fundamental progress in Anglo-American conceptions of moral responsibility from the eighteenth century on. Its flowering is abolitionism, but its impact is ongoing. According to Haskell, the capitalist marketplace was not merely an economic mechanism but a new mode of "social discipline," especially conducive to humanitarianism. This "social discipline" taught two lessons: "Keep [your] promises," and "Attend to the remote consequences of action." While any morality "entails selectivity," everyone enjoys the "ethical shelter afforded [by] conventions of moral responsibility." "Humanitarian Sensibility, Part II," 550, 551; "Humanitarian Sensibility, Part I," 352. This is consistent with Du Bois's own ritualized sense of morality.

70. In responding to a later sociological mystification of sentiment (Daniel Lerner's work on modernization in the Middle East), Stephen Greenblatt observes that "there are periods and cultures in which the ability to insert oneself into the consciousness of another is of relatively slight importance . . . others in which it is a major preoccupation. . . . Professor Lerner is right to insist that this ability is a characteristically (though not exclusively) Western mode, present to varying degrees in the classical and medieval world and greatly strengthened from the Renaissance onward, he misleads only in insisting further that it is an act of imaginative generosity." Greenblatt concludes that "when he speaks confidently of the 'spread of empathy around the world,' we must understand that he is speaking of the exercise of Western power, power that is creative as well as

destructive, but that is scarcely ever wholly disinterested or benign." *Renaissance Self-Fashioning: From More to Shakespeare* (Chicago: University of Chicago Press, 1980), 227–28.

71. Bruce, *Plantation Negro*, 81; Reinsch, "Negro and European Civilization," 150.

72. *Proceedings Of The National Negro Conference: 1909* (1909; reprint, New York: Arno, 1969), 149.

73. Charles Darwin, *The Expression of the Emotions in Man and Animals* (1872; reprint, Chicago: University of Chicago Press, 1965), xiii.

74. See *Du Bois: Writings*, ed. Nathan Huggins (New York: Library of America, 1986), 816.

75. Herbert Spencer, "Bain on the Emotions and the Will," in *Illustrations of Universal Progress: A Series of Discussions* (New York: Appleton, 1864), 310.

76. Albion Small, *Adam Smith and Modern Socioloy: A Study in the Methodology of the Social Sciences* (Chicago: University of Chicago Press, 1907), 21–22.

77. David Marshall provides a valuable account of an eighteenth-century preoccupation with sympathy, especially as it pertains to prevailing notions of "theatricality," in *The Surprising Effects of Sympathy: Marivaux, Diderot, Rousseau, and Mary Shelley* (Chicago: University of Chicago Press, 1988).

78. Robert E. Park, *The Crowd and the Public and Other Essays*, ed. Henry Elsner, trans. Charlotte Elsner (1904; reprint, Chicago: University of Chicago Press 1972), 31.

79. Max Scheler, *The Nature of Sympathy*, trans. Peter Health (1913; reprint, Hamden, Conn.: Archon 1970), 263.

80. Giddings cites "race hatreds and class prejudices," which he sees typified by the taboo among White men against Black wives. See preface added to the reprint of *The Principles of Sociology: An Analysis of the Phenomena of Association and of Social Organization* (New York: Macmillan, 1926), xiii–xiv.

81. Lester Ward, *Dynamic Sociology, or Applied Social Science* (New York: Appleton, 1883), 2: 369.

82. Edward A. Ross, *Social Control: A Survey of the Foundations of Order* (New York: Macmillan, 1901), 8–9.

83. One of Cooley's respondents uses the example of New Jersey State Senator Dryden's Prudential insurance fraud, to highlight the far-reaching consequences of immoral acts. By convincing "a compliant" legislature to give him "the accumulated surplus of his insurance company," Dryden, effectively, robbed the national treasury. *American Journal of Sociology* 12, no. 5 (1906–7): 693. Cooley's is the lead essay; the quotation is from 687.

84. Charles Horton Cooley, *Human Nature and the Social Order* (New York: Scribner's, 1902), 152–55.

85. Shaler, *Neighbor*, 213. Among the questions raised by the writings of Nathaniel Shaler, one of the most important (for this study), is how to explain the consistent affinity between Du Bois's interests and those of this Kentucky-born southern sympathizer who taught him geology at Harvard. What explains the shared preoccupations, images, ideas: the problem of Black survival in particular and cultural survival in general, the social reception of death, the recognition of "sympathy" and "neighborliness" as prominently troubled categories, even the be-

lief in the idea of essential and distinctive Black cultural modes? *The Neighbor* appeared a year after *The Souls of Black Folk* and seems to be filled with echoes from Du Bois's work. Likewise, when Du Bois declares in the 1908 debate on race friction, that "the world is shrinking together, it is finding itself neighbor to itself in strange, almost magic degree," it is hard to avoid hearing the title of his teacher's 1904 book. By the time he taught Du Bois, Shaler's reputation as a writer on the topic of race was well established. They published in many of the same journals (*Atlantic Monthly* and the *Independent*, for example). *The Neighbor* appears in the bibliography of Du Bois's edited volume *The Negro American Artisan*, vol. 17 of Atlanta University Publications (1912; reprint, New York: Arno, 1968), 14.

86. W. I. Thomas makes a similar point in "The Mind of Woman and the Lower Races," *American Journal of Sociology* 12 (January 1907): 469 "the participation of women and the lower races will contribute new elements" and aid "in the reconstruction of our habits on more sympathetic and equitable principles."

87. See Reinsch, "Negro and European Civilization," 148; Proctor, in *Social and Physical Conditions*, 44–45; Hope, in *Negro Business*, 56; Bruce, *Plantation Negro*, 242; Hoffman, *Race Traits*, 1.

88. For W. I. Thomas, sympathy had its physical correlative in the maternal womb. The faculty evolved in correspondence with the "structural modification" of female reproduction, which culminated in a self-enclosed intrauterine system. This was complemented by the intense claustrophobia of maternal affection. Operating "to the exclusion or disparagement of contrasted aspects," a monstrous maternal devotion represents "an important condition in the psychology of race-prejudice." "Race-Prejudice," 595–96. For Nathaniel Shaler, sympathy was "a great ... combination of ganglia and nerves," distinguishable in turn from the brain (rational organ) and the spinal cord (reflex organ). His chapter title, "The Growth of Sympathy," conveys much about his sense of the faculty's organic dimensions. See *Individual*, 117.

89. William Robertson Smith, *Lectures on the Religion of the Semites: The Fundamental Institutions* (1889; reprint, New York: Ktav 1969), 437–38ff. Smith notes that belief in the "sacred purposes" of the sacrificial skin predominated "at the stage of religious development in which the god, his worshippers, and the victim were all members of one kindred" (435–36).

90. Patterson, *Slavery and Social Death*, 46–47.

91. Quoted in Daniel Aaron, *The Unwritten War: American Writers and the Civil War* (New York: Oxford University Press, 1973), 156.

92. Max Scheler, quoted in Lewis Coser, introduction to Scheler's *Ressentiment*, trans. William W. Holdheim (New York: Free Press, 1961), 5.

93. Werner Stark, quoted in introduction to *Ressentiment*, 11.

94. Herbert Spiegelberg, *The Phenomenological Movement: A Historical Introduction* (Hague, Netherlands: Nijhoff, 1960), 259.

95. Paul Barringer, "The American Negro: His Past and Future," address at Charleston, South Carolina, 1900 (Raleigh, N.C., Edwards and Broughton, 1900), 3.

96. Paul Barringer, "The Sacrifice of a Race," address delivered at the Race Conference, Montgomery, Alabama, May 10, 1900 (Raleigh, N.C.: Edwards and Broughton, 1900), 11.

97. Newbell Niles Puckett's account of the enormous war drums used "to make a horrific din" at the "human sacrifices" of the Ashantees, now reduced to folk music curiosities—the "patting" and "rattling" of banjo music betrays a similar note of evolutionary diminishment. *Folk Beliefs*, 58.

98. Johnson and Sumner are quoted in White, *Rope and Faggot*, 33 and 7, respectively.

99. Reade's book is quoted in White, *Rope and Faggot*, 14.

100. Browne is quoted in White, *Rope and Faggot*, 42. White's own comments appear on 40, 47–48.

101. See Charles R. Wilson, *Baptized in Blood: The Religion of the Lost Cause, 1865–1920* (Athens: University of Georgia Press, 1980), 116.

102. James Elbert Cutler, *Lynch-Law: An Investigation into the History of Lynching in the United States* (New York: Longmans, Green, 1905), 141, 145–46.

103. Orlando Patterson has noted in this regard, that American lynchings occurring around the turn of the century sometimes had cannibalistic overtones. "Feast of Blood," in *Rituals of Blood*, forthcoming.

104. Girard goes on to note how the second ritual slaughter of the scapegoat often included the flagellation of its genitals, the sign that some sexual transgression, threatening "the violent abolition of distinctions," was being avenged. René Girard, *Violence and the Sacred*, trans. Patrick Gregory (Baltimore: Johns Hopkins University Press, 1977), 12, 98.

105. Emile Durkheim, *The Elementary Forms of the Religious Life*, trans. Joseph Ward Swain (1915; reprint, New York: Free Press, 1965), 446–47.

106. White, *Rope and Faggot*, 20. For Hertz on barbarism among the comparatively "advanced" cultures, see *Death*, 65.

107. White, *Rope and Faggot*, 28–29; Smith, *Religion of the Semites*, 274.

108. Quoted in White, *Rope and Faggot*, 155.

109. James Weldon Johnson, *Autobiography of an Ex-Colored Man*, in *Three Negro Classics*, 497.

110. Toni Morrison, *The Bluest Eye* (New York: Pocket Books, 1970), 18, 159.

111. See, Du Bois, *Souls*, 267; and *Dusk of Dawn*, in *Du Bois: Writings*, 678.

112. Simon N. Patten, *The Theory of Social Forces* (Philadelphia: American Academy of Political and Social Science, 1895), 143.

113. Frederick Hoffman believed that Blacks naturally gravitated toward work unlikely to result in "permanency of income and development of local attachments." Nathaniel Shaler highlighted a desire to "shape himself on the masterful race" that made the Negro "most domesticable," and suited to forms of labor "which do not tempt White people." Walter Willcox listed poor nutrition and weak generational ties (impeding the transmission of skills from father to son) among the factors that impaired Black survival in a modern labor market. See *Race Traits*, 286; *Neighbor*, 323–24, 336; and *Negro Criminality*, 11–12.

114. Lieberson, *A Piece of the Pie*, 382–83.

115. Du Bois observes "that a discrimination which was originally based on certain social conditions is rapidly becoming a persecution based simply on race prejudice." W.E.B. Du Bois, "The Negro Race in the United States of America," in *Papers on Inter-Racial Problems, from the First Universal Races Congress,*

University of London, July 26–29, 1911, ed. G. Spiller (London: P. S. King, 1911), 363.

116. Du Bois's reappraisals of sociological ideas in this period were enriched by contact with the German sociologist Max Weber. Among his many correspondences, there was none that he valued more than the five letters he exchanged from 1904 to 1905 with Weber. (So seriously did Du Bois take this exchange that he transcribed Weber's crabbed scrawl into his own more legible hand.) Weber's letters show him to have been an avid student of what he called "The Race Problem in America": he consulted Du Bois on what to read and seems to have felt that he could learn much from Du Bois, especially given Weber's preoccupation with nationalist and ethnic polarities in his native Germany. Weber met Du Bois during a 1904 visit to the United States and participated in the 1904 Atlanta University annual conference, on race presided over by Du Bois. Upon his return to Germany, Weber published Du Bois's essay "The Negro Question in the United States," in his *Archiv für Sozialwissenschaft und Sozialpolitik* 22 (1906): 31–79, and began efforts to have *The Souls of Black Folk* published in Germany. By 1905, Weber had located a translator as well as a publisher, but for some reason these plans for a German edition fell through. See Herbert Aptheker, *The Literary Legacy of W.E.B. Du Bois* (White Plains, N.Y.: Kraus International Publications, 1989), 75.

117. Ralph Ellison, *Invisible Man* (1952; reprint, New York: Vintage, 1989), 4.

118. *Reviews by Du Bois*, 114.

119. Rushton Coulborn and W.E.B. Du Bois, "Mr. Sorokin's Systems," in *Reviews by Du Bois*, 186.

120. W.E.B. Du Bois, "The Souls of White Folk," first published in its entirety in *Darkwater: Voices from within the Veil* (1920), is collected in *Du Bois: Writings*, 929.

121. Quoted in Melanie Klein, *Love, Guilt, and Reparation and Other Works, 1921–1945* (New York: Delacorte, 1975), 359. Klein calls this "Nature . . . the internal good mother." See "Mourning and its Relation to Manic-Depressive States," 344–69.

122. For more on the question of lyric animation, see Barbara Johnson's analysis of lyric apostrophe as a convention central to recent abortion debates. "Apostrophe, Animation, and Abortion," in *A World of Difference* (Baltimore: Johns Hopkins University Press, 1987), 184–99.

123. Quoted in Lawrence Levine's *Black Culture and Black Consciousness: Afro-American Thought from Slavery to Freedom* (New York: Oxford University Press, 1977), 166, 158. According to Levine, slave songs expressed the spiritualization of ordinary life, the slave tendency to look upon man, God, and nature as a unity. In Levine's words, "they extended the boundaries of their restrictive universe backward until it fused with the world of the Old Testament, and upward until it became one with the world beyond" (32–33). The songs were published in *Hampton and Its Students, With Fifty Cabin and Plantation Songs*, ed. M. F. Armstrong and Helen Ludlow, arr. Thomas Fenner (New York: Putnam's, 1874); and J.B.T. Marsh, *The Story of the Jubilee Singers with Their Songs* (Boston: Houghton Mifflin, 1880).

124. This is Houston Baker's characterization of Alain Locke's work, a term which, Baker suggests, also befits *Souls*. See his account in *Modernism and the Harlem Renaissance* (Chicago: University of Chicago Press, 1987), 58–68. Readers will recognize my debt throughout this section to Eric Sundquist's *To Wake the Nations*, especially 490–539.

125. Frederick Douglass's haunting analysis of the spirituals in his *Narrative* confirms on the part of this "representative" colored man an ambivalence that anticipates the skepticism of the educated Black at the turn of the century. See *Narrative of the Life of Frederick Douglass, an American Slave* (1845; reprint, New York: Penguin, 1986), 57–58.

126. Amiri Baraka [LeRoi Jones], *Blues People* (New York: William Morrow, 1963), 40, 66–67.

127. See Puckett, *Folk Beliefs*, 343–44. I don't mean to suggest that superstitions are confined to Du Bois's elegy chapter. In his chapter on the Black Belt, for example, where he describes the meagre interiors of rural cabins, the image of newspapers used as "decorations for the walls" is revealing in these terms. Puckett cites a common folk superstition that newspapers on walls protected against malevolent spirits, since the spirits were obliged to "count every letter before working harm" (142). This superstition may be inspired by the politics of Black literacy—a perverse reproduction of literacy requirements on prospective Black voters, now imposed on ghosts.

128. Puckett, *Folk Beliefs*, 320.

129. Smith, *Religion of the Semites*, 188. See also Henri Hubert and Marcel Mauss, *Sacrifice: Its Nature and Functions* (1898; reprint, Chicago: University of Chicago Press, 1964), 27–28.

130. Puckett, *Folk Beliefs*, 91ff.

131. See Jack Goody, *Death, Property, and the Ancestors: A Study of the Mortuary Customs of the LoDaaga of West Africa* (Stanford: Stanford University Press, 1962), especially 13–46. Maurice Bloch and Jonathan Parry, *Death and the Regeneration of Life* (Cambridge: Cambridge University Press, 1982), especially 223–25ff.; and Richard Huntington and Peter Metcalf, *Celebrations of Death: The Anthropology of Mortuary Ritual* (Cambridge: Cambridge University Press, 1979), especially part 2.

132. Bloch and Parry, *Death and the Regeneration of Life*, 224.

133. Smith, *Religion of the Semites*, 313ff.; and Freud, *Totem and Taboo*, 135.

134. See Elaine Scarry's reading of the Passover mark's significance throughout the Hebrew Bible. She notes, for example, how it is "elaborated into an intricate blueprint of rescue" through God's instructions on the fine points of ark building in the story of Noah, and how it embodies a "rhythm of substitution and sparing" in the book of Malachi. *The Body in Pain: The Making and Unmaking of the World* (New York: Oxford University Press, 1984), 238–39.

135. Scarry cites the work of the art historian Kenneth Clark on "draped" and "undraped" portraits of Christ on the cross. *Body in Pain*, 360.

136. Quoted in Peter Berger, *The Sacred Canopy: Elements of a Sociological Theory of Religion* (New York: Anchor, 1969), 76–77.

137. David Levering Lewis, *W.E.B. Du Bois: The Biography of a Race* (New York: Holt, 1993), 228.

138. Bourdillon and Fortes, *Sacrifice*, xv.

139. Charles Chesnutt, *The Marrow of Tradition* (1901; reprint, New York: Arno, 1969), 1–2.

140. Suzan-Lori Parks is quoted in an interview published with "The America Play," *American Theatre*, March 1994, 25–39. The quote appears on 26.

141. Suzan-Lori Parks, "The Death of the Last Black Man in the Whole Entire World," *Theatre* (1990), 82. It's hard to imagine Parks, for instance, responding to the work of Crumb, the comic strip artist, with charges of racism. One point of controversy is his parodic stereotype: "canned" "Nigger Hearts." Crumb's figure, which combines aspects of Livingstone's tobacco-shop African with those of the Black in minstrel shows, is highly suggestive for my analysis of race and sympathy at the turn of the century. Like Parks, Crumb denies the complexity of his design, insisting that he intended nothing in particular. This has the obvious effect of motivating the search for deeper cultural content, by implying that the meaning of the image extends beyond the range of his own limited consciousness. Does Crumb's invention of Black feeling as an alluring commodity suggest that Blacks have it and Whites don't? Is he attributing a physical exclusiveness (the kind we've been tracing) to sympathy—We have to eat [like] them to feel for them? Is he implying that Blacks represent "the heart" of American culture? Crumb's image invites all these interpretations, and more. See Terry Zwigoff's 1994 film *Crumb*, a powerful documentary biography, which explores the artist's life and work and various political reactions to it.

142. These horrific burdens are memorialized in a line that runs from Langston Hughes's poem "The Haunted Oak" to Billie Holiday's song "Strange Fruit."

143. Aaron, *Unwritten War*, 352.

144. Gore Vidal, *Lincoln: A Novel* (New York: Random House, 1984), 648.

145. See Martin Delaney's *Blake: or, The Huts of America* (1859–61; reprint, Boston: Beacon 1970) for an earlier use of this image.

146. Du Bois, "Negro Race in the United States," 362.

147. See Aaron, *Unwritten War*, 351; and Ward Hill Lamon, *Recollections of Abraham Lincoln* (Washington, D.C.: Government Printing Office, 1911), on Lincoln's dream.

148. See Vidal, *Lincoln*, 640; and Aaron, *Unwritten War*, 71, 73–4, 70, respectively, for Whitman quotes.

149. *The Portable Lincoln*, ed. Andrew Delbanco (New York: Viking, 1992), 22.

150. W.E.B. Du Bois, "Again, Lincoln," (1992), reprinted in *Du Bois: Writings*, 1198.

151. See Eric Sundquist on "The Black Christ," especially as a "figure ... of resistance" and as "the incarnation of the diasporic nation," in *To Wake the Nations*, 592–625. These quotations are from 600 and 592, respectively.

152. Cornell West offers one of the most powerful of these critiques in "Black Strivings in a Twilight Civilization," in Cornell West and Henry Louis Gates, Jr., *The Future of the Race* (New York: Knopf, 1996), 53–111.

153. W.E.B. Du Bois, "College-Bred Negros," Commencement Address, Fisk University, June 1898, collected in *Du Bois: Writings*, quotation from 830.

154. W.E.B. Du Bois, "The Damnation of Women," in *Darkwater*, in *Du Bois: Writings*, 953, 962.

155. *Du Bois: Writings*, 1178 and 846–47.

156. For quotations, see *Souls*, 336; and *The Negro American Family*, vol. 13 of *Atlanta University Publications* (1908; reprint, New York: Arno 1968), 127–28.

157. Du Bois, *Dusk of Dawn*, in *Du Bois: Writings*, 650–51.

Afterword

1. Michael McKeon, "The Origins Of Interdisciplinary Studies," *Eighteenth-Century Studies* 28, no. 1 (1994): 25.

2. See William Robertson Smith's distinction between ancient and modern kinship in *Lectures on the Religion of the Semites: The Fundamental Institutions* (1889; reprint, New York: Ktav, 1969), 274–75.

3. This metaphor comes from Hayden White's essay "Getting Out of History," *Diacritics* 12, no. 3 (Fall 1982), 11.

Index

segregation (*cont.*)
415n.23, 417n.44; color line, 278–280,
290–293, 297, 300–301, 341, 349; as euthanasia, 285–286; and mortality, 273,
290, 295–296
Sennett, Richard, 387–388n.42
Shaler, Nathaniel, 31, 326, 420–421n.85;
The Individual, 274, 303, 310, 317, 322–
323, 330, 421n.88; "The Negro Problem,"
341; *The Neighbor*, 3, 15–16, 60, 277, 291,
295, 321–326, 330, 336, 416n.32, 420–
421n.85, 422n.113; "Science and the African Problem," 291
Simmel, Georg, 5, 9, 18, 28, 37–38, 41, 44,
389n.50; "Exchange," 30–31, 36–37, 70,
376n.10; "Fashion," 36–37, 400n.29; "The
Miser and the Spendthrift," 37, 85; "The
Poor," 36, 42, 259–260; "Prostitution," 37
Simon, Bennett, 405n.88
Singer, Bryan: *The Usual Suspects*, 380–
382n.62
Singleton, Pap, 293–294
Skocpol, Theda, 238–239
Small, Albion: on religion, 9, 126; seminary
training of, 126; as translator, 18, 376n.1,
389n.50, 401n.38. WORKS: *Adam Smith
and Modern Sociology*, 157, 274, 315, 330;
"The Era of Sociology," 15, 124, 129–130,
141; *The Origins of American Sociology*, 17,
95, 128–129; "The Scope of Sociology,"
126–128, 157
Smith, Adam, 157, 273, 315–318, 330
Smith, Jonathan Z., 223, 372n.5, 400n.22,
403nn.62 and 63
Smith, William Benjamin: *The Color Line*, 3,
272, 274, 276–280, 282, 290, 293, 302,
334
Smith, William Robertson, 35, 44, 50, 82,
84, 87, 91; and Durkheim, 38–40, 57–58;
as editor of *Encyclopedia Britannica*, 56;
heresy trial of, 380n.53; influence of, 56–
57, 65, 67, 130, 160, 379n.47, 380n.53; on
religion as practice, 57, 72, 401–402n.41;
sacrifice, definition of, 28, 53, 57–58, 69,
72; on sacrifice, evolution of, 59–61, 72,
250, 421n.89; on sacrifice as mechanism of
kinship, 58–60, 65, 340, 368. WORKS: *Lectures on the Religion of the Semites*, 3, 5–6,
25, 38, 52–53, 56–61, 79, 93, 183–184,
253, 266–267, 324, 340, 368, 380n.53,
401n.36, 421n.89; "Sacrifice," 58, 65–66,
71–72, 256–257

smoke: as food for the Gods, 79, 111; as purifying agent, 400n.25; in ritual, 179, 229–
230, 268; smoking, 198–199, 201, 229–
230, 405n.82
social Darwinism: bestiality, 77, 83–84, 86;
competition, 158–160, 174; decline, 83,
206, 234–235, 401n.38; emotional selection, 308–315, 317–318, 325–326; explanatory power of, 214; and social progress,
241–242, 322, 326; survival, 212, 271, 333
social death: of African-Americans, 294,
302–303, 324–325, 356–359, 365–366; of
Jews, 324, 371n.1, 418nn.60 and 63. *See
also* Patterson, Orlando
social science: and class, 19, 130; and death
rites, 281–282; as elitist, 143; history of,
13–18, 25–27, 93, 120–124, 143, 148,
193–194, 205, 214–215, 233–234, 243–
244, 374–375n.22, 383n.72, 386n.28,
392–393n.91; liberal vs. Marxist versions
of, 9–10, 33; and literature, 4–27, 87–88,
246–247, 371n.1; vs. popular social theory, 13, 129–130, 241, 276, 282–284, 315,
322, 332, 409n.120; and primitive culture,
220, 233, 237, 239, 246, 248; and race,
272–276, 286–299, 301–302, 312, 316,
322, 331, 336–338, 341–348; and rationalism, 6–12, 20, 74, 128–133, 233–239, 246–
248, 272, 275, 288, 336, 341, 347, 366,
413n.166; and religion, 9, 33, 48–49, 54–
55, 92–95, 120, 126–133, 143, 154, 157,
194, 241–244, 373n.7, 379n.47; sociology
defined, 8–16, 74, 234; as value-free, 124,
286, 389n.50; women and, 214–215, 236,
246, 261–264
social types, 5, 10–12, 20–21, 146–151, 155–
156, 207
Sollors, Werner, 418n.63
Sorokin, Ptirim, 346–347
Spencer, Herbert, 133, 196, 390n.68; *Illustrations of Human Progress*, 274, 312–315,
318, 330; *The Principles of Sociology*, 25,
125, 158–160, 236–237; *The Study of Sociology*, 124–126, 132–133, 157–158
Stanley, Arthur Penryhn: *History of the Jewish
Church*, 13, 112–114, 142–143, 161–166;
Sinai and Palestine, 109–113
Stark, Werner, 326, 421n.93
Starr, Paul, 124–125
Stein, Gertrude, 3, 12, 25, 44–45, 383n.77;
3-Lives, 17, 76–80
Stern, Milton, 154

ABOUT THE AUTHOR

Susan L. Mizruchi is Associate Professor of English and American Studies
at Boston University. She is the author of *The Power of Historical Knowledge:
Narrating the Past in Hawthorne, James, and Dreiser* (Princeton).